Sexual Assault in Canada

LAW, LEGAL PRACTICE AND WOMEN'S ACTIVISM

Sexual Assault in Canada

LAW, LEGAL PRACTICE AND WOMEN'S ACTIVISM

Elizabeth A Sheehy, editor

UNIVERSITY OF OTTAWA PRESS
OTTAWA

UOP

The University of Ottawa Press acknowledges with gratitude the support extended to its publishing list by Heritage Canada through the Canada Book Fund, by the Canada Council for the Arts, by the Federation for the Humanities and Social Sciences through the Awards to Scholarly Publications Program, by the Social Sciences and Humanities Research Council, and by the University of Ottawa.

We also gratefully acknowledge the Shirley E. Greenberg Chair for Women and the Legal Profession and the Faculty of Law at the University of Ottawa, whose financial support has contributed to the publication of this book.

Library and Archives Canada Cataloguing in Publication Data

Sexual assault in Canada : law, legal practice, and women's activism / Elizabeth A. Sheehy, editor.

Includes bibliographical references and index.
Issued also in electronic format.
ISBN 978-0-7766-3044-1

1. Sexual abuse victims—Legal status, laws, etc.—Canada. 2. Criminal justice, Administration of—Canada. 3. Women--Crimes against—Canada. 4. Sex crimes—Canada. 5. Rape—Canada. 6. Sex crimes—Investigation—Canada. 7. Feminism—Canada. 8. Doe, Jane. I. Sheehy, Elizabeth A.

HV6569.C3S48 2012 364.15'30971 C2012-901633-0

Printed and Bound in Canada
Design by Sandra Friesen

Part I

Part II

This book is dedicated to all the Jane Does and the feminists who advocate for and with them: may you find validation, strength and inspiration among these pages to continue the struggle to end sexual assault.

Part 1

FOREWORD

Still Punished for Being Female

The Honourable Claire L'Heureux-Dubé

International Women's Day is a time to remember past struggles, contemplate present realizations, and envision a path to a better future. I could not imagine a better day than March 9th, International Women's Day, to hold the "Sexual Assault Law: Practice and Activism in a Post-*Jane Doe* Era" conference at the University of Ottawa in 2009. I was very grateful to participate in this conference, graciously organized by Elizabeth Sheehy, a professor in the Faculty of Law at the University of Ottawa and a dedicated, long-time advocate for women's rights. The conference was exceptional: I had previously never seen so many people gathered together in one place to work for change around the law and practice of sexual assault. The conference presented me with an unprecedented opportunity to share with a great pool of minds and hearts our thoughts on a topic that is and always will be very close to my heart.

On the occasion of this conference, I was reminded of past struggles. I was not legally a person when I was born. I was born in 1927, two years before the "Persons Case."[1] Women in Canada then were not allowed to participate in politics; we were not permitted to be members of the Senate or Parliament. It was then commonly understood that higher education and the professions were places for men, not women. We were left penniless on divorce.[2]

Yes, there has been progress towards equality in many respects. On International Women's Day, we should and do celebrate our successes. However, while progress has been made, our struggles continue. Our struggles will not cease until women are treated with dignity, until we are treated with the same respect and consideration as any other member of society. Respect, consideration, and dignity are fundamental to the attainment of equality. Equality is a fundamental human right guaranteed to every human being internationally as well as by the *Canadian*

1 *Edwards v Canada (Attorney General)*, [1930] AC 124 (PC).

2 See *Murdoch v Murdoch*, [1975] 1 SCR 723.

Charter of Rights and Freedoms [*Charter*].[3] The right to equality is an entitlement of everyone based on the sole fact that he or she was born.

Since being declared persons under the law by the Privy Council, women in Canada have undertaken important struggles. We have successfully fought, and continue to agitate for, equal pay for work of equal value. We continue to fight for inclusion in the workplace. Although men continue to sexually harass, we have avenues of legal recourse when we face sexual harassment at work.

However, one aspect of women's inequality where little progress has been made in Canada is violence against women. Violence against women, including sexual violence, remains commonplace and condoned here and around the world. The title of this foreword, "Still Punished for Being Female," is a phrase I have borrowed from the Op-Ed columnist of the *New York Times*, Bob Herbert,[4] who wrote about "bride burnings, honour killings, female infanticide, sex trafficking, mass rape as a weapon of war and many other forms of hideous violence against women," as documented in a report released in 2007 by the United Nations.[5] He states:

> We can start by recognizing the systemic subordination and brutalization of women and girls around the world is in fact occurring. What we are talking about here is the war against women all over the planet. In many parts of the world, men beat, torture, rape, and kill women with impunity.

Mr. Herbert concludes that we need to do something about the systemic, worldwide subjugation of women that takes place through deployment of violence against us. His imperative for action is precisely the reflection I want to engage, with particular emphasis on the role of the judicial system in dealing with violence against women in our society.

In Canada we do not commonly burn brides or generally practice genital mutilation (although there have been recent instances of both). However, cases of trafficking in women, juvenile prostitution, sexual assault and even murder of women in prostitution, spouses, ex-spouses,

3 *Constitution Act, 1982*, being Schedule B to the *Canada Act 1982* (UK), 1982, c 11.

4 Bob Herbert, "Punished for Being Female" *New York Times* (2 November 2006) online: <http://www.mijd.org/pn/modules.php?op=modload&name=News&file=article&sid=120> (retrieved May 24, 2010).

5 For the full report, see General Assembly of the United Nations, Secretary General's *Study on Violence Against Women* (2007), online: <http://www.un.org/womenwatch/daw/vaw/violenceagainstwomenstudydoc.pdf>.

and girlfriends, as well as domestic violence, are the everyday menu of our criminal courts.

It is progress that our laws were rid of their most blatant gender bias at the time that equality provisions of our *Charter* came into force. Requirements that women complainants in sexual assault prosecutions obtain corroborating evidence as well as the doctrine of recent complaint have been removed from the *Criminal Code.*[6] Past sexual conduct of women who have been raped has been ruled generally irrelevant in law.[7] The forced production of complainants' medical records is generally not permitted.[8] The consent and the mistaken belief in consent defences have been clarified and narrowed in the *Criminal Code.*[9]

However, more remains to be done to remove the myths and stereotypes about women that still impregnate the minds as well as the practices of lawyers and judges and other members of Canadian society. Women's struggle to attain equality through autonomy and bodily integrity continues. The concept of "NO means NO" is still a problem even after the *Ewanchuk* decision.[10] Speculative myths, stereotypes, and sexist assumptions about women who have been sexually assaulted have too often hindered the search for truth and imposed harsh and unnecessary burdens on complainants in prosecutions of sexual offences.[11]

The most injurious myth is that women and children are not credible in this area of criminal law.[12] Women may be generally viewed as credible, but they are still not seen as credible in cases of sexual assault. Recent examples abound. Notoriously, in the 2003 Kobe Bryant trial in the US, rape shield laws were completely disregarded in order to discredit the complainant's credibility.

We have to recognize that there are no quick solutions for elimination of violence against women. Because the problem defies easy solutions, we need sustained efforts by civil society, governments, and dedi-

6 RSC 1985, c 46 [hereafter *Code*].

7 *R v Seaboyer*, [1991] 2 SCR 577.

8 *R v O'Connor*, [1995] 4 SCR 411.

9 *Code* ss 273.1, 273.2.

10 [1999] 1 SCR 330.

11 See, eg, *R v Mills*, [1999] 3 SCR 668 at 741: "Speculative myths, stereotypes and generalized assumptions about sexual assault victims ... have too often in the past hindered the search for the truth and imposed harsh and irrelevant burdens on complainants in prosecutions of sexual offences."

12 The same perception does not apply in other criminal activities such as theft, burglary, and even murder.

cated men and women to pursue gender equality and to eradicate gendered violence, including sexual violence against women. Although much has been done, and important progress has been achieved in the past century, there is still a need for the judicial system to examine the way it deals with crimes of violence against women. All these myths and stereotypes and more were the basis of the majority judgment in the court of appeal in *Ewanchuk* in Alberta in 1998. That was 1998, not 1798 or 1898. We still have a long way to go.

Change is crucial in order to ensure that such crimes will be reported, that the system is fair for both accused and complainant, that complainants are treated with respect at all stages of the process, and that the psychological trauma suffered by victims of male violence is recognized and taken into account by our legal responses to sexual assault.

The system must recognize that victims of violence against women fear that they will not be believed. They often blame themselves and suffer a sense of defilement, depression, anxiety, and split personality, as well as problems with physical and emotional intimacy. While physical injuries will often heal, psychological scars may last forever. Only when all actors in the judicial process recognize the need to revamp attitudes and practices will legislative reform efforts produce the kind of justice for victims of violence against women that international convention and national legislation have mandated.

On International Women's Day, at the Jane Doe conference, I asked attendees, how do we go about envisioning and implementing the full equality of women in Canada? I turned my mind to education, which is one of the main elements in the pursuit of that objective. At all levels, in schools, even in kindergarten, respect for the dignity of women as human beings should be taught; it cannot start too soon. Colleges, professional colleges, universities, and law schools in particular, as well as all the actors in the judicial system, such as police, prosecutors, and judges, should all have gender sensitivity training.

Justice system actors need to be able to recognize the hidden gender of laws, and to understand the reality of women's lives. Officials need to comprehend women's reluctance to report sexual assault and domestic violence. System actors need to forge a clearer role for the judicial system to help reduce women's fear that they will suffer further at the hands of the criminal law. Defence counsel and Crown prosecutors should object to the tendering of irrelevant evidence in sexual assault prosecutions, such as evidence of what the complainant was wearing or how she habitually dressed. Sentencing judges need to consider whether women and children are protected or endangered as a consequence of their dispositions. People who make decisions in the justice process should hear women's stories and visit sexual assault centres, women's shelters, and jails. It is crucial to realize the consequences of violence on society as a whole in terms of human suffering, physical and mental ill health, and the lost opportunities for women's talent to enrich society.

In sum, International Women's Day is a yearly occasion on which we can recall women's social, economic, and legal successes and struggles in the last century. We have come to be recognized as persons entitled to the same respect and to be treated with the same dignity as any other member of society under the law. This day also provides a pause to take stock of the present as well as an opportunity to look at the road to the future necessary to ensure that women enjoy the full protection of the law in all aspects of their lives.

To tread a path to a better future, all actors in the judicial system must be able to walk in the shoes of women, must come to understand the real lives of women. Officials must not fantasize that women dream of being raped, that they are in a constant state of consent,[13] or that they are not credible. The activism behind the litigation effort and the court's judgment in *Jane Doe v Metropolitan Toronto (Municipality) of Police*[14] have done a great deal to achieve this goal of showing police, lawyers, judges, and other players women's lived realities. This collection of essays, in its diversity, proposes a substantive reflection on the issues that sexual assault law, practice, and activism raise, as well as strategies for change on the road to the future. I welcome this publication and salute the incredible work of Elizabeth Sheehy in convening the conference and ensuring that the revised and edited contributions of the presenters will have a lasting influence in pursuing the goal of full equality for women, so that one day we will no longer be punished or punishable for simply being female.

13 Chief Justice Fraser of the Alberta Court of Appeal in her dissent in *R v Ewanchuk*, 1998 ABCA 52

14 (1998), 39 OR (3d) 487 (Ont Ct (Gen Div)).

Introduction

Elizabeth A Sheehy

This edited collection assesses sexual assault law, legal practice, and activism in Canada as of 2009. It represents both a celebration and a review of where Jane Doe's brave advocacy has taken us in the more than ten years that have passed since she won her case against the Toronto Police in 1998 in her litigation, *Jane Doe v Metropolitan Toronto (Municipality) Commissioners of Police.*[1]

Jane Doe initiated her legal action after the first wave of feminist-inspired reform to the law of rape, which took place in 1981-82-83.[2] Before her case went to trial, Canadian criminal law governing sexual assault underwent another wholesale reform in 1992,[3] again led by women's activism and informed by feminist thought.[4] Additional, narrower reforms were enacted in 1995[5] in response to public outcry about the "extreme intoxication" defence used to exculpate a man who brutally raped a woman in a wheelchair,[6] and in 1997[7] as a result of the widespread disclosure of women's personal records to defence lawyers in rape trials. While Jane Doe's legal arguments and the judgments rendered in her case show the impact of feminist intervention in the law governing sexual assault, they also reveal starkly that the law in practice — as implemented by police, prosecutors, and defence counsel — has quite successfully resisted women's just demands for equal protection of the law.

1 *Jane Doe v Metropolitan Toronto (Municipality) Commissioners of Police* (1998), 39 OR (3d) 487 (Ont Ct (Gen Div)) [*Jane Doe*].
2 *An Act to Amend the Criminal Code (sexual offences),* SC 1980-81-82-83 C 125, s 6.
3 *An Act to Amend the Criminal Code (sexual assault)*, SC 1992 C 38, s 2.
4 Sheila McIntyre, "Redefining Reformism: The Consultations That Shaped Bill C-49" in Julian M Roberts & Renate V Mohr, eds, *Confronting Sexual Assault: A Decade of Legal and Social Change* (Toronto: University of Toronto Press, 1994) 293 [Roberts & Mohr].
5 *An Act to Amend the Criminal Code (self-induced intoxication)*, SC 1995, C 32, s 1.
6 *R v Daviault*, [1994] 3 SCR 63.
7 *An Act to Amend the Criminal Code (production and disclosure of personal records),* SC 1997, C 30, s 1.

As the first English-language book since 1994 to assess the current state of rape law and practice in Canada,[8] this collection aspires to present a picture of the many difficult issues that continue to plague Canadian women who attempt to report and prosecute sexual violence committed against them, even after successive waves of law reform and the ground-breaking victory achieved by *Jane Doe*.[9] The chapters in this book emerged from a major conference at the University of Ottawa, Faculty of Law, where I have taught law since 1984 and where Jane Doe has lectured regularly to law students since 1988. Together we convened, raised funds, and organized a highly successful event to celebrate International Women's Day, on March 6th and 7th 2009, titled "Sexual Assault Law, Practice and Activism in a Post *Jane Doe* Era." To do so, we established an Organizing Committee composed of ourselves and Professors Beverly Bain, Natasha Bakht, Pascale Fournier, Tracey Lindberg, and Rakhi Ruparelia. The committee reviewed proposals submitted in response to our call for papers and invited seventy speakers to present their work over the two-day event.

The presenters themselves were LLB and Masters candidates from many disciplines; researchers and professors from Law, Women's Studies, Criminology, Legal and Justice Studies, Counselling Psychology, World Indigenous Knowledge and Research, Sociology, Political Studies, Politics, and Political Science; and community-based activists from the Violence Against Women sector. These activists, students, and academics were joined by an internationally acclaimed young artist, a celebrated author, a national journalist, and two lawyers — one who represents the Native Women's Association of Canada, and another who was one of Jane Doe's lawyers. The Canadian focus of the conference was exemplified by speakers from Alberta, British Columbia, Manitoba, New Brunswick, Nova Scotia, Ontario, Saskatchewan, and Quebec, and by attendance from all these provinces as well as Newfoundland and Nunavut. This national concentration was expanded by speakers from South Africa, Israel, the United States, New Zealand, and Ghana.

These seventy presenters — sixty-six women and four men — delivered papers to a standing-room only audience of over 350 students, community activists, researchers, lawyers, and academics. The con-

8 Roberts & Mohr, *supra* note 4. See Constance Backhouse's book on the legal history of sexual assault in Canada, *Carnal Crimes: Sexual Assault Law in Canada, 1900–1975* (Toronto: The Osgoode Society for Canadian Legal History, 2008); and Julie Desrosiers, *L'aggression sexuelle en droit canadien* (Cowansville, Qué: Éditions Yvon Blais, 2009).

9 *Jane Doe*, *supra* note 1.

ference was opened by the inspiring words of The Honourable Claire L'Heureux-Dubé, whose contributions to the development of sexual assault jurisprudence consistent with women's equality rights have been widely acknowledged and justly celebrated.[10] Conference speakers received at least five standing ovations and the organizers were overwhelmed by repeated calls for a biannual conference on sexual assault.

Many organizations were represented, including Springtide Resources (Women with Disabilities and Deaf Women's Program), Parkdale Community Legal Services, Kenora Sexual Assault Centre, University of Saskatchewan Students' Union (Victim Advocate), Native Youth Sexual Health Network, Mouvement Contre le Viol et l'Inceste (Montreal), Sexual Assault Support Centre of Ottawa, Assaulted Women's and Children's Counsellor Advocate Program (George Brown College), Vancouver Rape Relief and Women's Shelter, African and Canadian Women's Human Rights Project, Women's Sexual Assault Centre of Renfrew County, Canadian HIV/AIDS Legal Network, and the Ontario Coalition of Rape Crisis Centres.

The event was funded by the Law Foundation of Ontario, the Ontario Women's Directorate, the Social Sciences and Humanities Research Council, the Department of Justice Victims' Fund, the Shirley Greenberg Chair for Women and the Legal Profession, the University of Ottawa (including the Common Law and Droit civil sections), the National Association of Women and the Law, Sack, Goldblatt, and the Social Justice Fund (University of Ottawa). A number of law student volunteers, including Kerry McVey and Miriam Yosovic, among others, worked tirelessly with us to guarantee a successful and celebratory event but also to welcome law students from other law schools and create space for their contributions. Not all of the excellent essays that resulted could be squeezed into this collection; special issues of Canadian Woman Studies[11] and the Canadian Journal of Women and the Law[12] take over where this collection signs off.

10 See, for example, Elizabeth Sheehy & Christine Boyle, "Justice Claire L'Heureux-Dubé and Canadian Sexual Assault Law: Resisting the Privatization of Rape" in Elizabeth Sheehy, ed, *Adding Feminism to Law: The Contributions of Justice Claire L'Heureux-Dubé* (Toronto: Irwin Law, 2004) 247.

11 See Special Issue, *Women Resisting Rape: Feminist Law, Practice, Activism* (2009–2010) 28:1 Can Woman Stud (Guest Editors Jane Doe, Carol Latchford, Rakhi Ruparelia & Elizabeth Sheehy).

12 See Special Issue, *The State of Rape: Ten Years After Jane Doe* (2010) 22:2 CJWL (Guest Editor Elizabeth Sheehy).

PART I

The scope of this book is wide. Part I ranges from an examination of sexual assault committed by coaches and players in the context of the "total institution" of hockey; to police practices of unfounding women's rape reports; to the role of racism and colonization in the perpetuation of crimes against Aboriginal women and girls; to the part played by "social handicapping" in our abandonment of disabled women who experience sexual assault; to the state-initiated pressures on women's grassroots rape crisis and sexual assault centres to eschew feminist politics; to a reinvigorated feminist response to rape as realized by the Garneau Sisterhood; and finally to forward-looking practices of feminist art and narrative that enable us to move past the stalemates so often presented by law.

The first section of Part I attempts to capture both the enormous potential of law to respond to sexual assault when feminists shape the arguments, as well as the heavy burden placed on the individual women whose rapes are the subject of litigation. This section opens with my chapter, "The Victories of Jane Doe." I provide an account of three legal landmarks achieved by Jane Doe's engagement with the Canadian legal system, but more importantly, I suggest that the value of Jane Doe's work extends beyond these precedents that open up new legal avenues for women, to include her insistence on feminist practice, language, and accountability as part of any legal strategy.

Reflections by Sean Dewart, Jane Doe's lead counsel for her lawsuit against the police, constitute the next paper in this section. Sean's expertise was in negligence law, one aspect of Jane Doe's case that secured her legal win. Sean also brought to the trial his manifest enthusiasm for suing major institutions, especially the police. His chapter describes what the case has meant to law by opening up a new cause of action in tort law that speaks to police accountability for how they do their job. While both of these chapters are celebratory of all that the case accomplished, Jane Doe the woman paid a heavy price for her bravery, including disclosure of her personal health and counselling records to the police, the court, and the public.[13]

"New Zealand's Jane Doe," by Julia Tolmie, tells a far less celebratory tale in terms of the perils of turning to law. She recounts the story of Louise Nicholas, a courageous woman who, like our Jane Doe, took on the powerful institution of police, this time by prosecuting sever-

13 See Jane Doe, *The Story of Jane Doe: A Book About Rape* (Toronto: Random House, 2003) at 257.

al NZ police and alleging that they repeatedly raped her when she was a young woman. Julia describes the resilience of Louise Nicholas, who went through three criminal trials, none of which resulted in a conviction. Julia uses her three trials to show the resistance of NZ lawyers, judges, and media to women's accounts of rape, but also to acknowledge the positive outcomes from Louise Nicholas's bravery, which included several public inquiries and research projects aimed at reforming NZ law and practice around the response to sexual violence.

Our national sport is indicted by Laura Robinson's paper in this section, in her chapter "Hockey Night in Canada." Hockey is a "total institution," as captured in the concept used by Erving Goffman, in which coaches and their players enact their masculinity through sexual assault and abuse of young female girlfriends and fans. Laura's chapter focuses on the trial of former coach and NHL agent David Frost for sexual assault, wherein all charges involving his assaults against two young women were abandoned by the prosecutor and the remaining charge of sexual assault against a male player was dismissed by the court. She paints a picture of a hyper-masculine courtroom atmosphere that mirrors the sexist world of junior hockey, and shows how the young women who testified against David Frost were discarded by the legal system.

The second section of Part I addresses the sexual assault of Aboriginal women and children as an extension of colonization. In this section, the authors describe a legal response to the catastrophic rate of male violence against Aboriginal women and children that is, at best, indifferent and, at worst, complicit. First in this section is a collaborative piece by Tracey Lindberg, Priscilla Campeau and Maria Campbell, "Indigenous Women and Sexual Assault in Canada." Their work tells the story of Aboriginal women's lives through the seasons of Spring — the girl, Summer — the young woman, Fall — the mature woman, and Winter — the older woman. For every season, each author speaks in a different voice, describing sexual attacks on Aboriginal women and girls from a different perspective. Priscilla outlines the facts and outcomes of these crimes from her position as an Indigenous woman; Tracey speaks to the legal processing of these crimes, separating the "relevant" information from that which is "not relevant," and providing a critical Indigenous analysis of each; and Elder Campbell completes each telling by addressing the stories in terms of Cree laws as they protect and honour Indigenous women and girls. Their work reveals the terrible gap between law's treatment of these crimes against women and girls and how they affect and are understood by Indigenous women and Indigenous laws.

Lucinda Vandervort's contribution to this section is a detailed analysis of a disastrously failed prosecution of three non-Aboriginal men charged with the sexual assault of a twelve-year-old Aboriginal girl in Saskatchewan. In "Legal Subversion of the Criminal Justice Process? Judicial, Prosecutorial, and Police Discretion in *R v Edmondson, Kindrat and Brown*," the author recounts legal and procedural errors committed by police, prosecutors, and judges that infected the investigation, two trials, appeals, and two retrials, all of which inured to the benefit of the accused men. Lucinda makes the compelling argument for adherence to national legal standards for the prosecution of sexual assault, identifying confusion about the relevant law, failure to apply criminal law principles designed to eschew sex discriminatory beliefs, and erroneous reliance on law rejected or reformed by Parliament, as instrumental in the botched prosecution. She highlights the role played by racism and sexism in this case, using this analysis to generate three significant recommendations for federal reform, including a proposal to ensure legal representation for all sexual assault complainants.

The last chapter in this section is Sheila McIntyre's piece, "The Supreme Court of Canada's Betrayal of Residential School Survivors: Ignorance is No Excuse," a searing indictment of the Supreme Court's response to compensation claims by Aboriginal men and women who were sexually abused as children. Using as backdrop nine civil suits decided by the court from 1999 to 2005, she focuses on the last decision, *EB v Oblates of Mary Immaculate in the Province of BC*,[14] to illustrate the central failure of the Court in all of these decisions — the refusal to address what she describes as the "obvious, compound, structural and situational inequalities" that produced the harms to these survivors: "racism, colonialism, poverty, misogyny, and cultural supremacism." Sheila shows how the Court has overwhelmingly ignored the extensive research on residential school abuse in its decisions and rejected the opportunity to develop a new jurisprudence equal to the task of responding to such large-scale neglect and violence. It has instead decided these cases using narrow and formalistic reasoning that obliterates the social, political, and historical context of these claims, treating these survivors the way they were treated as children — as invisible and irrelevant.

The third section of Part I examines women's credibility problems with the police, our knowledge gap around women's experiences of sexual assault and the services women need, as well as strategies and mech-

14 [2005] 3 SCR 45.

anisms of accountability. It starts with Fran Odette's paper, "Sexual Assault and Disabled Women Ten Years after *Jane Doe*." Fran focuses on the invisibility of disabled women in the research, policy-making, and service delivery around sexual assault. In spite of the fact that disabled women experience the highest rate of sexual assault among women, research tends to exclude their specific experience of sexual assault, which often involves, for example, caregivers as opposed to strangers or intimate partners. Fran delineates the many barriers presented to disabled women who wish to use the legal system, as well as those who attempt to engage the support of women's centres. She calls for meaningful dialogue among women in the Violence Against Women movement around these issues.

This section then turns to Teresa DuBois's chapter, which demonstrates that the wrongful unfounding of women's reports of rape is a widespread, systemic, and harmful practice of police in many countries. Moreover, Canadian cities experience some of the highest rates among the countries surveyed, with a range of up to 28 percent of women's rape reports being dismissed by police. These rates can be attributed to police adherence to rape myths as well as police reliance on simplistic and unverifiable "investigative" techniques such as "statement analysis" and "behavioural analysis," as set out in investigatory handbooks. Particularly troubling is the fact that police continue, even after successful lawsuits like *Jane Doe* and after decades of reforms, to start from the assumption that women are lying about rape. The collection of national data on police unfounding and the development of uniform practices for recording police decisions is a necessary first step in stemming these discriminatory practices.

Blair Crew's contribution to this section, "Striking Back: The Viability of a Civil Action Against the Police for the 'Wrongful Unfounding' of Reported Rapes," surveys the legal remedies for women whose rapes have been "unfounded" by police. He examines the availability of a newly recognized wrong in Canadian negligence law — that of "negligent investigation" — as delineated by the Supreme Court of Canada in *R v Hill*.[15] Blair reviews the data on police unfounding of rape reports, noting that while the practice is widespread and discriminatory, with serious effects for women, there is no strong demand for law reform, leaving litigation as the only option to provoke change in the police. After looking at the proof requirements for "negligent investigation" and identifying the serious hurdles for women, he concludes that

15 [2007] 3 SCR 129.

the legal theories pursued by Jane Doe, those of unconstitutional sex discrimination and negligence for failure to warn, remain more fruitful avenues for redress. Blair shows, in a step by step analysis, how a s 15 *Charter* claim for wrongful unfounding or a negligent failure to warn case could be constructed on behalf of a woman whose rape report has been rejected by police.

The fourth section of Part I speaks to the contributions and challenges faced by activist women who work with and for women who have been raped. Lise Gotell interrogates the police response to a series of rapes committed in Edmonton, in the Garneau neighbourhood in 2008. She offers a critique of a policing style she describes as "risk management," aimed at making women responsible for their own safety. In "Third-Wave Anti-rape Activism on Neoliberal Terrain: The Garneau Sisterhood," Lise exposes the gendered regime of "risk management" through police warnings and media coverage of the Garneau rapes. Against this regime she counter-poses the strategy of postering the neighbourhood with feminist messages, an action engaged in by anonymous members of the Garneau Sisterhood. She applauds their subversive messages that challenged woman-blaming, condemned rape culture, and allocated responsibility to men, individually and collectively, to prevent rape, arguing that direct action may be a most significant tactic in our arsenal.

Meagan Johnston's paper also celebrates women's activism by demonstrating how much more powerful and radical the alternative analysis of the Garneau Sisterhood is compared to the "solutions" offered by the criminal justice system. In her chapter, "Sisterhood Will Get Ya: Anti-Rape Activism and the Criminal Justice System," she contrasts the legal order offered by the criminal law versus that of the Sisterhood. On every front examined, from the substantive and procedural rules for defining rape and determining when rape has occurred, through to the fundamental principles that underpin these two orders, she demonstrates how little the law can offer women and how much more vibrant and empowering is the model the Sisterhood imagined for the community affected by rape.

In "Where Has All the Anger Gone?" Diana Yaros reviews thirty-five years of grassroots work in the Violence Against Women movement, describing the shifts towards government funding and government "partnership," and the ensuing de-politicization of the women's movement. She laments our loss of vision, courage, and anger occasioned through this process of collaboration, but secures hope in her centre's work to include and serve the needs of racialized and immigrant women, and to return the focus of their work from service provision to advocacy.

In the final section of Part I, the authors explore other strategies to pursue social change, using art and narrative forms to communicate and educate. Shary Boyle, in "Vitreous Fragility: Re-imagining Women through Art," traces her path as a feminist artist, including her work as illustrator for Jane Doe's book, *The Story of Jane Doe*.[16] She describes her work re-interpreting Greek myths in porcelain as feminist tales where women are active, as opposed to acted upon. Shary's photographs of her work enrich our understanding of her vision and of art's possibilities for forging new understandings of women's agency and resistance.

Gillian Calder and Rebecca Johnson's final chapter in Part I is an unabashed tribute to the book, *The Story of Jane Doe*. The title of their paper, "The Jane Doe Coffee Table Book about Rape: Reflections on Rebellious Writing and Teaching," refers to Jane Doe's original title for her manuscript, which was rejected by her publishers. The subversive intent behind Jane Doe's preferred title remains evident, however, throughout her book, as she uses unconventional means — art, doodles, journaling, fictionalization — to tell the story of her fight to hold police accountable for sex discrimination in the investigation of sexual assault. Gillian and Rebecca's paper is sprinkled with photographs of the book, lovingly captured by the conference participants, in many hands and in many places. Their message, backed by their dialogue, is that this book is a powerful piece of feminist law-making.

The papers in Part I both describe our current realities and offer feminist visions of new social and legal orders. Without the experiences of all women assembled in Part I — Aboriginal, racialized, young, disabled, artist, activist, and academic — we cannot find a common ground from which to advocate together or separately for change. These papers are intended to comfort and inform, agitate and inspire the next generation of feminists determined to challenge male violence against women.

PART II

Part II of this book has a decidedly more legal focus than Part I. The themes here explored move from issues in the prosecution of sexual assault, such as the challenges posed for niqab-wearing women who testify as complainants; to problems in the adjudication of rape, where the

16 *The Story of Jane Doe*, *supra* note 13.

linguistic practices of rape trials encode rape myths; to the sentencing of men convicted of rape; and to questions surrounding compensation for women.

The first section of Part II investigates the role of social workers, health care providers, police, prosecutors, defence lawyers, and judges in creating a hostile environment for women and girls who must testify in rape trials. Jane Doe's paper, "Who Benefits From the Sexual Assault Evidence Kit?" is based on interviews with women who have undergone the Sexual Assault Evidence Kit [SAEK], as well as with feminists who work in community-based rape and sexual assault crisis centres, nurses who administer the SAEK, and hospital-based counsellors. She shows that the relocation of feminist-based services for raped women to hospitals has shored up the medicalization of rape as "illness" and increased medical authority such that women's "consent" to the SAEK is more illusory than real. The lack of consistent practices for its collection and its dubious legal utility mean that the SAEK's terrorizing effects on women are not outweighed by any concrete gains for women. Jane Doe's paper concludes with women's understandings of the benefits that accrue to players in the medical-legal system who derive authority and control through the SAEK.

Susan Ehrlich uses linguistic analysis to demonstrate the distorting effects of trial discourse premised upon rape myths. Her paper, "Perpetuating — and Resisting — Rape Myths in Trial Discourse," sets out to expose one reason why progressive law reforms have failed to achieve significant change in sexual assault prosecutions. She illustrates how different forms of questioning devices — those that demand a yes/no answer, and those premised upon presuppositions that the witness cannot refute if she answers the question — allow lawyers to control the information that emanates from the complainant and to subtly exploit prevailing cultural myths about women and rape. At the same time as she traces these devices through trial transcripts, Susan also takes care to point the way to outcomes that do justice to women's experiences of rape, by showing how prosecutors can anticipate and pre-empt defence lawyers' invocations of rape myths, and how some complainants assert their agency by resisting victim-blaming presuppositions.

Sunny Marriner's paper, "Questioning 'Expert' Knowledges," takes up a related theme — that of the credentializing of expertise around male violence against women and its impact on grassroots women who work to support women who have been raped and to challenge the legal system. She recounts how expertise is assessed in courtrooms, the male biases that permeate psychiatry and psychology, and the implications in terms of the distortion of women's experiences through the psy-disciplines. Identifying the junctures in the criminal process at which the "experts" enter, Sunny demonstrates the ways in which the legal and psy-disciplines reinforce each other's power over women. Grassroots women have been co-opted in this process, she argues, vying for authority and playing a role in referrals. She calls for activist women to challenge psy-expertise and to instead defend the expert knowledge of feminist political practice.

Another way of thinking about the prosecution and proof of rape is presented in Sanda Rodger's contribution to this section, "Zero Tolerance Some of the Time? Doctors and Sexual Abuse in Ontario." Her paper looks at the implementation of the *Regulated Health Professions Act*,[17] ratified in response to *The Final Report of the Task Force on Sexual Abuse of Patients*.[18] While this legislation was intended to enact a zero tolerance approach to sexual assault committed by doctors, with mandatory license revocation as the most serious penalty, Sanda's research shows that a small percentage — 5.53 percent of women's allegations — ever reach the stage of adjudication and that the same doctrines that make criminal prosecution so problematic also infect the disciplinary policing of doctors. These features include the doctrine of corroboration, reliance upon discriminatory myths about confused and vindictive women, invocation of a quasi-criminal burden of proof, and the use of women's confidential records to discourage and discredit them. She urges the College of Physicians and Surgeons to address these barriers to "zero tolerance," in keeping with its original mandate.

In the second section of Part II, the authors unpack specific legal doctrines that obscure or excuse male violence. They also advance recommendations that would ameliorate the gap between the promise of criminal law and its adjudicated reality. In my paper, "Judges and the Reasonable Steps Requirement: The Judicial Stance on Perpetration Against Unconscious Women," I review decisions from the appellate and superior courts to evaluate how judges are interpreting the reformed "mistake of fact" defence available to men who have proceeded to have sexual intercourse with sleeping or passed-out women. While the criminal law now requires that men take "reasonable steps to ascertain consent" before they are entitled to the defence that they mistakenly believed the woman consented, some judges simply fail to apply the proviso, or they interpret "reasonable steps" to extend to touching —

17 SO 1991, C 18, as am by SO 1993, C 37.
18 (Toronto: College of Physicians and Surgeons, 1991).

even sexual touching. In many cases, defence lawyers are able to raise doubts before the judges who hear these cases — doubts about whether the women really were asleep, doubts about whether men believed the complainants were conscious, and doubts about whether the men were mislead by the bodily movements of sleeping women. I outline the principles that judges ought to respect as they assess men's culpability, wherein serious attention to women's entitlement to dignity, equality, and security of the person should easily outweigh men's interest in sexual contact with women who neither know nor desire them.

David Tanovich critiques the evidentiary rule that works to bar evidence of an accused's prior sexual misconduct from sexual assault trials in his paper, "An Equality-Oriented Approach to the Admissibility of Similar Fact Evidence in Sexual Assault Prosecutions." He uses the Supreme Court's decision in *R v Handy*[19] to make the compelling argument that this form of "similar fact" evidence should be presumptively admissible in sexual assault prosecutions because it shows a specific form of propensity to engage in non-consensual sexual contact. David demonstrates the pervasive influence of gender bias in rulings that have excluded sexual misconduct from rape trials, even where there is corroborative evidence shoring up the reliability of the evidence. He also exposes the language of these judgments, which conveys deep suspicion of the motives and reliability of complainants. Highlighting the unique nature of sexual assault prosecutions, where identity of the perpetrator is seldom an issue and where the credibility of the complainant becomes the central focus of the defence attack, David argues that fairness, truth-seeking, and equality would all be advanced were his proposed rule of presumptive admissibility to be adopted by either legislation or common law.

Julie Desrosier's paper, "Raising the Age of Sexual Consent: The Renewing of Legalistic Moralism?" analyzes the 2008 reforms that raised the age of consent for sexual contact from fourteen to sixteen years of age. Julie situates this reform in its historical context as well as in liberal, conservative, and feminist political theory in order to argue that the real impetus behind this reform is not the protection of young women from sexual aggression, but rather the perpetuation of legal moralism aimed at curtailing adolescent sexuality. She cautions that these reforms were never intended to protect young women against sexual aggression, which has always been criminalized, and that they have been

19 [2002] 2 SCR 908.

enacted without any consultation with young women as experts in their own lives, a foundational principle of feminist practice.

In "What's in a Face? Demeanour Evidence in the Sexual Assault Context," Muslim women who wear the niqab are centred in the analysis. Acknowledging that this group of women is small numerically, Natasha Bakht argues that the convergence of racism and misogyny that occurs when rights to religion and culture are claimed by women imperils the equality rights of all. Natasha situates the case of *R v NS*,[20] wherein the complainant fought to wear her niqab while testifying, in the context of the jurisprudence that questions the utility of "demeanour" evidence to the assessment of credibility and the other cases where women's rights to wear the niqab have been challenged. She lays out the legal arguments in support of Muslim women's claims, relying on an intersectional analysis that exposes the demand for Muslim women to undress in order to testify as yet another defence strategy aimed at obscuring, not pursuing, truth.

Section three of Part II opens with Holly Johnson's chapter, "Limits of a Criminal Justice Response: Trends in Police and Court Processing of Sexual Assault." She presents an overview of official knowledge about sexual assault in Canada and demonstrates how very marginal the criminal law response to sexual assault really is. Her chapter draws upon statistics from victimization surveys, police recording practices, studies of public attitudes towards sexual assault, and data regarding attrition of rape cases as they proceed through the criminal justice system. Holly concludes that law reforms cannot stem the effect that rape myths held by criminal justice personnel have on the discounting of women's experiences of sexual violence.

In "HIV Exposure as Assault: Progressive Development or Misplaced Focus?" Alison Symington reflects on the implications of the Supreme Court's 1998 decision in *R v Cuerrier*[21] for the criminalization of persons living with HIV/AIDS. She argues that the increased rate at which police are laying charges of aggravated and sexual assault against persons with HIV/AIDS demonstrates problems in terms of assessing culpable knowledge on the part of the accused regarding their health status, and exposes legal uncertainty as to whether use of a condom will suffice to avoid criminal liability. Both problems, she argues, suggest that the criminalization strategy is fraught with unfairness. She ques-

20 [2009] OJ No 1766 (Ct J).
21 [1998] 2 SCR 371.

tions whether women's health and autonomy can truly be advanced by the *Cuerrier* decision, and argues that disclosure of HIV/AIDS by sexual partners is unlikely to be the outcome of a one-sided obligation with criminal implications.

Rakhi Ruparelia's contribution, "All That Glitters Is Not Gold: The False Promise of Victim Impact Statements" uses a feminist and critical race theory lens to examine the use of "victim impact statements" as a means for victims of crime to communicate to the sentencing court the impact of the offence upon their lives. She argues that only a narrow category of "ideal victims" can possibly gain from the opportunity to submit a statement, and further that racialized and Aboriginal women actually have much to lose should they participate in this process: they can easily be discounted as non-ideal victims, and negative stereotypes of racialized women can be thereby reinforced. Rakhi uses Canadian cases and data from the US and Canada that show how racism shapes our understanding of who is a "victim." She concludes that the greatest beneficiary of victim impact statements is the criminal justice system itself, which gains the co-operation of women by appearing to address the harms caused by sexual assault and by the sexual assault trial.

In "Confronting Restorative Justice in Neo-Liberal Times: Legal and Rape Narratives in Conditional Sentencing," Gillian Balfour and Janice Du Mont study the use of conditional imprisonment—"house arrest"—a restorative justice sentencing option, for sexual assault offenders. Starting from the Statistics Canada report in 2006 that this sentence is more likely to be imposed for sexual assault than for any other crime, Gillian and Janice analyze thirteen such sentences imposed between 1993 and 2001 for rapes with serious aggravating factors. They examine the legal and rape narratives in these decisions, focusing on the invisibility of the woman in the judgments, the ways in which responsibility is assigned to her for her own rape, the minimization of the harm caused by the perpetrator, and the exaggeration of the effects of "embarrassment" on the offender, obviating the need for more denunciatory punishment. While lauding house arrest as a progressive sentencing option, the authors urge feminist engagement with conditional sentencing in light of its enmeshment with rape mythologies.

Finally, Constance Backhouse explores avenues other than criminal law for redressing the harm of sexual assault. In "A Feminist Remedy for Sexual Assault: A Quest for Answers" she revisits a decision from 1974, *R v Angione*,[22] in which the sentencing judge accepted a guilty

22 (1976), 26 CCC (2d) 474 (Ont H Ct).

plea from the accused for indecently assaulting a female employee and ordered him to forfeit $1,000 payable as compensation to the complainant. She commends the judge in *Angione* for his recognition that jail is inappropriate — often counter-productive to the goal of eliminating sexual violence — and she uses the case as a discussion point for thinking, from a feminist perspective, about what remedy is appropriate for sexually violent men. Constance considers the various goals of sentencing, the real need for financial support for women who have been raped, and the eradication of the stigma of rape, all in the service of asking, if not answering, questions feminists would pose in the search for remedies.

The collected works in this book, while often providing negative assessments of the progress of feminist reforms to the law and practice surrounding sexual assault, are nonetheless full of new ideas, proposed changes to law, and concrete and practical strategies for women, activists, legislators, lawyers, and judges. This book also identifies numerous gaps in research that await the next generation of feminist activists, and posits some of the questions we need to begin to ask. I hope that this book will be followed by many more on the law and practice around the crime of sexual assault, for Canadian women deserve no less in our ongoing struggle to realize women's just demands for equality.

1.
The Victories of Jane Doe

Elizabeth A Sheehy

In the chapter that follows, Elizabeth A Sheehy sets the stage for this book. She describes three legal landmarks that Jane Doe's engagement with the Canadian legal system achieved, but her real point is that Jane Doe waged and won her legal battles on her own terms. These terms included her insistence on being present in the courtroom when her rapist was on trial, which was contrary to "business as usual"; her active participation in the development of the legal arguments and evidence for her case, which again disrupted the ordinary practice of the law; and her questioning of sexist language and concepts such as the "gentleman rapist," which helped to win the lawsuit.

In 1986, an audacious woman known only as "Jane Doe" initiated a chain of radical actions against the Toronto Police on both political and legal fronts. In August of 1986 she had been raped in her bed in the middle of the night by a man armed with a knife. When she reported the crime to Toronto Police, they informed her that his modus operandi fit the pattern of a man they had dubbed the "Balcony Rapist" for his use of apartment balconies as his entry point to women's homes. Outraged that her rapist was familiar to police, Jane Doe demanded to know why she had not been warned. She told police that if they did not, she would warn other women in the area about this rapist.

Defying Toronto Police threats to prosecute her for "interfering with an investigation," Jane Doe and other feminists postered her neighbourhood. Feminist grassroots knowledge tells us that rapists are ordinary men who operate within their comfort zones, often their own neighbourhoods. It was therefore no surprise, least of all to Jane Doe, when the rapist was turned in by his parole officer (he was up on wife assault charges at the time) within twenty-four hours of the appearance of the posters. He was prosecuted and pled guilty to raping five Toronto women, including Jane Doe. The police explanation for their failure to warn Jane Doe, "women would become hysterical and the rapist would flee the area," became the match to the fire. Jane Doe spent a year working together with Women Against Violence Against Women [WAVAW] agitating for police accountability on how they investigate rape. But after watching police stonewall women's legitimate demands for change in rape investigations, Jane Doe announced her intention to sue. She initiated a ground-breaking lawsuit in 1987 against the police for sex discrimination in the policing of rape and for failing to warn her of the danger she unwittingly faced alone. By a wonderful stroke of luck, the Women's Legal Education and Action Fund [LEAF], a feminist legal fund dedicated to advancing women's equality through law, had opened its doors only two years earlier, in 1985. Jane Doe's case was taken on *pro bono* by some of the leading feminist lawyers in the country. Eleven years later, Jane Doe was vindicated by a $220,000 damage award against the police and a judicial declaration that stated that police had violated her right to equality and had been negligent in failing to warn her.

THE STORY OF JANE DOE[1]

Jane Doe tells her own story in her book of the same name. Of course her battle with the criminal justice system and the Toronto Police is neither the beginning nor the end of her story. This chapter focuses on Jane Doe's tenacity and strategic brilliance over her twelve years of litigating to hold the criminal justice system accountable. It also highlights her ongoing contributions as an educator, activist, and researcher in the struggle to make rape law and legal practice live up to its constitutional obligation of equal protection and equal benefit of the law for women who have been raped.

In the course of Jane Doe's protracted legal fight, she met many obstacles, not the least of which was that she was forced to change counsel when LEAF could no longer act for her as the trial date approached. She found lawyer Sean Dewart, an accomplished civil litigator who delights in suing police — a perfect match. But it soon became clear to him that he needed a lawyer with expertise in equality law, and so another search ensued until Cynthia Petersen stepped in to develop the sex discrimination argument. Along the way, as Jane Doe approached many lawyers as possible counsel or for advice, she was told that her case "didn't have a chance in hell." She persevered, and painstakingly put together the witnesses whose testimony her lawyers would use to educate the judge about rape, from a feminist standpoint.

1 Jane Doe, *The Story of Jane Doe: A Book About Rape* (Toronto: Random House, 2003) [*The Story of Jane Doe*].

Jane Doe's legal saga ended in a stunning victory against the police in July of 1998. Justice Jean MacFarland delivered a judgment that damned the police and ordered them to pay Jane Doe damages for breaching her right to equal treatment under the law, guaranteed by the *Charter of Rights and Freedoms*; for her right to security of the person, also guaranteed by the *Charter*; and for carelessly failing to warn her that she fit this rapist's pattern of targets. Between the criminal trial of her rapist and her lawsuit against the police, Jane Doe made legal history at least three times.

FIRST LEGAL LANDMARK

Jane Doe fought for and won the unprecedented right to stay in the courtroom throughout her rapist's preliminary inquiry in 1987 for his five charges of rape. She had been told by the Crown attorney that she would be excluded from the courtroom during this legal process so that her trial testimony would not be "tainted" by hearing the other witnesses. This is standard practice in criminal trials; it is followed unquestioningly by lawyers. Defence lawyers will suggest that if a witness has heard other witnesses for the prosecution, they may change or at least shade their testimony to render it consistent with that of others. Alternatively, defence lawyers will claim disadvantage because they have been precluded from surprising the witness by confronting her with contradictory evidence given by others. From the Crown's point of view, they worry about the defence ability to destroy their case in just those ways described above. Knowing the odds against successful prosecution of rape in this country, Crowns may be extremely risk-averse.

Complainants — those "primary witnesses"[2] who testify as to criminal wrongs committed against them — and other witnesses have no "legal standing" to object on their own to matters that arise during a criminal trial. They are considered to have no personal stake in the trial. Instead, the trial is framed as a contest between the state, represented by the Crown attorney, and the accused individual, represented by a defence lawyer. Crown attorneys do not represent the interests of any witness, even the complainant. Rather, they represent the "public interest," and thus cannot be counted upon to defend the individual interests of their own witnesses, such as Jane Doe.

2 For discussion of the term "primary witness" see T Brettel Dawson, "Sexual Assault Law and Past Sexual Conduct of the Primary Witness: The Construction of Relevance"(1987–1988) 2 CJWL 310.

What this means is that a woman who wishes to challenge "the way things are done" in the trial of her rapist must first find a lawyer to argue for her right to "standing" to address the court on the issue. If the lawyer wins standing, he or she will then be given the opportunity to make the substantive argument to the court. However, most provincial legal aid societies will not provide funding for a complainant or witness to hire a lawyer to speak on their behalf. One relatively recent exception is that complainants whose private health and counselling records are sought by defence lawyers to discredit them are entitled to standing[3] and to legal aid, at least in some provinces, so that they can defend their privacy and equality rights.[4] But this is a very narrow exception that did not exist when Jane Doe wanted to stay in court during her rapist's preliminary inquiry.

As Jane Doe describes in her book, her search for a lawyer to advance her right to stay in the courtroom to hear the prosecution's case against her rapist was arduous. Many lawyers are so embedded in the legal system that to challenge some of its ways of doing business is heresy. She needed a *pro bono* lawyer to advance her claim to "standing" — one willing to make a significant court appearance without necessarily being paid for the preparation or the court time. Then she needed that lawyer to turn the legal system on its head.

Jane Doe's persistence paid off, finally, when lawyer Rebecca Shamai accepted the challenge. To the displeasure of defence lawyers and prosecutors alike, Shamai waded into the fray to make this very unpopular argument for her client. The victory was sweet, for the judge accepted the argument that justice must not only be done; it must be seen to be done by those who have been subjected to criminal violence.[5] The victory was sweeter still for Jane Doe when her lawyer was appointed as a justice of the Ontario criminal courts a few years later.

3 *R v Beharriel*, [1995] 4 SCR 536.

4 Legal Aid Ontario has developed a program whereby complainants in sexual assault cases whose records are sought are entitled to advice and assistance from a panel of specially trained lawyers. For discussion, see Saadia Dirie, *O'Connor/Mills Survey Report: Draft Client Satisfaction Evaluation* (Legal Aid Ontario, 2002) at 5, as cited in Lisa Addario, *Six Degrees from Liberation: Legal Needs of Women in Criminal and Other Matters* (Ottawa: Department of Justice, 2002) at Chapter Three; and "Women as Witnesses, Complainants and Third Parties in Cases of Intimate Violence and Sexual Assault," online: <http://www.justice.gc.ca/eng/pi/rs/rep-rap/2003/rr03_la20-rr03_aj20/p16.html>.

5 *R v Callow* (Ont Prov Ct Crim Div) (unreported judgment of Justice Kerr, 5 February 1987) [on file with the author].

Still, this important legal decision remains obscure, since it was never "published" by any legal reporter. The only known copy of it was obtained from Justice Shamai, who had stored it in a box in her basement. Legal reporters make determinations every day as to which legal decisions should be published. Sometimes they are published on the basis of their value as a "precedent," meaning that a case might bind lower courts, and other times even lowly decisions, such as that rendered by Justice Kerr in February 1987, might be published on the basis of their interest to other practising lawyers. Herein lies the rub: while this decision was noteworthy in that it was novel, neither defence lawyers nor Crown attorneys would have been likely to use it in their pleadings. Both camps see damaging consequences for their own cases if raped women are to stay in the courtroom while others testify. And, unfortunately, standing for those who would see value in this precedent — witnesses and complainants who wish to insert themselves into the criminal trial process — is rarely and begrudgingly granted.[6] In other words, apart from feminist activists and lawyers working to change the legal system, there was no one to whom this legal advance would have been "of interest."

SECOND LEGAL LANDMARK

Jane Doe made legal history a second time when her novel legal claim against the Toronto Police survived a motion to dismiss. Her successful fight to remain in the courtroom during her rapist's preliminary inquiry provided her with critical information and the impetus to launch her civil suit one year later. During the course of the preliminary inquiry, she heard that she bore over one hundred similarities to the other women attacked by this rapist. She also learned about the role played by misogyny in the police failure to believe the first three women and to connect their rapes. As Jane Doe describes in her book, her overwhelming impression was that she had been used as bait by police, and that her rape was preventable.[7]

Once her statement of claim was filed, alleging *Charter* breaches and negligence by police, counsel for the police made a motion to dismiss. They asked the judge to throw Jane Doe's case out of court before it was

6 For example, victims of crime do not have standing in an offender's sentencing hearing to address the court, as was made clear by McLachlin J (as she then was) in *R v Antler* (1982), 69 CCC (2d) 480 (BCSC), except for the narrow opportunity now available under s 722 of the *Criminal Code* to read a Victim Impact Statement.

7 *The Story of Jane Doe*, *supra* note 1 at 80.

even to be heard on the merits. They argued that her claim failed to state a previously recognized legal theory of responsibility. Therefore, even if she could prove the facts she alleged, the law would afford her no remedy. Not only did Jane Doe win this motion but, like her first victory in the courtroom, she won this battle on her own terms — feminist terms. As she describes in her book, she insisted that LEAF prepare a statement of claim, here reproduced as Appendix A, written in ordinary language that she and other non-lawyers could understand, drawing upon feminist analyses of rape.[8] For example, her claim did not use technical legal language, which in turn prompted the police to argue that "the plaintiff has failed to allege explicitly that the circumstances created a relationship of proximity between the police and the plaintiff so as to create a private law duty of care towards her."[9] This argument was ultimately rejected by the judge who, on hearing the motion, said, "[t]he pleading does not fail merely because the 'traditional' words are omitted."[10]

This statement of claim advanced an early articulation of the "wrong" of the sexual assault evidence kit, a reform advocated by feminists seeking to strengthen the prosecution's case. Paragraph eight reads: "The Plaintiff was required to submit to necessary invasive examinations to obtain evidence and to take potent medication to prevent pregnancy and infection."[11] The claim articulated a feminist understanding of rape: "The Plaintiff states that the targets of sexual assault are overwhelmingly women while the perpetrators of the crime are overwhelmingly men."[12] In paragraph seventeen, the claim asserted women's agency, arguing that had police provided women with the relevant information, Jane Doe and other women would have been more vigilant than usual and therefore would have had the information necessary to ensure their safety. In addition, she would have known that the rapist had not murdered any of the women he had sexually assaulted. This information would have somewhat ameliorated the intense fear for her life that Jane Doe endured during the time that the rapist was in her apartment.[13]

8 *Ibid.*

9 *Jane Doe v Toronto (Metropolitan) Commissioners of Police* (1989), 58 DLR (4th) 396 (Ont HC) at para 116 [*Jane Doe No 1*].

10 *Ibid.*

11 *Ibid*, appendix at para 8.

12 *Ibid* at para 12.

13 *Ibid* at para 17(c).

The claim also described police failures in systemic terms: failure to direct adequate resources to investigating and apprehending rapists because the targets are women; pursuing a policy that favoured apprehension of rape suspects over protecting likely targets because the targets are women; and discriminatory impact upon women of the policies and practices of police regarding sexual assault investigations. Finally, in paragraph twenty-five, the claim articulated the harm of discrimination and negligence by the police as well as the rape as requiring legal recognition and redress: "The Plaintiff endures continuing emotional upset as a result of this crime, including fear and insecurity about her safety, recurring violent nightmares, a sense of powerlessness and vulnerability, recurring and intrusive conscious memories of the event and the ensuing ordeal with the Police and the Courts...."[14] This statement of claim laid out two different theories of responsibility for the police. It proposed that the police owed a "duty of care" to warn those women who were identifiable potential victims of the rapist. Knowing the pattern of his attacks, the area in which he was perpetrating, and the common features of his targets, police were in a position to seek out and warn women like Jane Doe. Instead, they "intentionally failed to notify her of the risk she faced."[15]

The claim also proposed that the police relied on sex discrimination regarding women and rape in sexual assault investigations, including the investigation of the "Balcony Rapist." Jane Doe was denied equal protection of the criminal law in violation of her s 15 right to equality under the *Charter*. Had the police not been handicapped by their tragically sexist beliefs, they would have been able to resolve the investigation far earlier, preventing the rapist's attack on Jane Doe. Because her bodily security was put in jeopardy by the police decisions, she also argued that her s 7 right to security of the person was violated by their actions: police effectively used her as "bait" to catch the rapist.[16]

Lawyers for the Toronto Police urged the court to strike out her statement of claim for failure to state a legitimate "cause of action." This was an interesting strategy, suggestive of some anxiety on the part of police that Jane Doe's claim could open them wide up to legal liability for failure to do their job. In fact, one of their arguments was that if the City of Toronto, as employer of police, owed Jane Doe a private "duty

14 *Ibid* at para 25.

15 *Ibid* at para 20(c).

16 *Ibid* at para 24(c).

of care," it "would encourage members of the public to bring actions against the police for every perceived failure to protect them against harm from criminal activity."[17]

The motion to dismiss was argued in the Supreme Court of Ontario, High Court of Justice over five days at the end of January and the beginning of February in 1989. Judgment was rendered February 22nd that same year, when, in a carefully reasoned 101 page decision, Mr Justice Henry gave Jane Doe the green light to proceed to trial. He found that Jane Doe's proposed "duty to warn" theory could, if the underlying facts were proven, show that the police knew enough about the specific danger in which Jane Doe stood, as a member of a "very limited group of foreseeable victims," to place upon them a legal obligation to warn her or protect her.

Justice Henry also found that Jane Doe's proposed *Charter* claims were valid legal theories of liability if the facts alleged could be proven at trial. While police are protected by common law from legal responsibility for harms caused by the lawful exercise of their discretion in carrying out their jobs, sex discrimination — for example, Jane Doe's claim that police decided not to warn her and other women because they would become hysterical, "a judgment formed on the basis of women as perceived stereotypes," and the deliberate use of another as "bait" — falls well outside this legitimate zone of immunity as either an abdication or abuse of police discretion.[18] Justice Henry observed several times in his judgment that "the plaintiff will face an uphill battle in proving these assertions."[19] Jane Doe recalls that while affirming her right to proceed with her lawsuit, he kindly said to her, "Good luck, you're going to need it."[20]

Unhappy with this result, Toronto Police appealed the judge's decision to the High Court of Justice, Divisional Court of Ontario. Ironically, it was Justice MacFarland, who later presided over the trial itself, who granted leave to the police to appeal. The appeal was argued before a panel of three justices in 1990. This court agreed unanimously with Justice Henry and dismissed the appeal on 30 August 1990.[21]

The judges found that if Jane Doe could prove the facts alleged, the police would have been responsible in negligence law for either warn-

17 *Ibid* at para 69.

18 *Ibid* at para 177.

19 *Ibid* at para 121.

20 *The Story of Jane Doe*, *supra* note 1 at 144.

21 *Jane Doe v Metropolitan Toronto (Municipality) Commissioners of Police* (1990), 74 OR (2d) 225 (H Ct Just Div Ct) [*Jane Doe No 2*].

ing or protecting those women identifiable as foreseeable targets of the serial rapist. While police claimed that a decision not to warn in these circumstances was immune from liability as an exercise of discretion in the legitimate fulfillment of their policy function, Jane Doe's argument posited that the decision was motivated by discriminatory beliefs, rendering it arbitrary and irresponsible. The court accepted this argument in favour of the validity of the legal theory and went further. For the court Justice Moldaver said, "I would go further and suggest that even if the decision not to warn was one of policy and was responsibly made, it may have carried with it an enhanced duty to provide the necessary resources and personnel to protect the plaintiff and others like her."[22]

The court also upheld the validity of the *Charter* theories of liability using sections 7 and 15. The police attempted to persuade the court that there was no evidence of sex discrimination against women because Jane Doe could not easily compare how men were treated in similar investigations: "men are generally not subject to this kind of offence." The court rejected this argument, noting that while it was "superficially attractive," it was not determinative. The court rejected this formalistic approach to discrimination, and instead asked whether police ever would have failed to warn an identifiable group of men stalked by a serial killer for fear they would become hysterical? It was apparent to them that Jane Doe's discrimination theory presented a triable case, and they dismissed the appeal. Doggedly, Toronto Police attempted a further appeal to the Ontario Court of Appeal. This time their appeal was dismissed out of hand, without reasons, in February of 1991.[23]

THIRD LEGAL LANDMARK

Having survived the persistent attempt to dismiss the claim, Jane Doe's case then languished in the lengthy civil litigation process for six years. During this time, her lawyers battled in the "discovery" process to secure documents and evidence from the police, in order to put flesh on the bones of the two claimed legal theories of police responsibility.

As I have argued elsewhere,[24] Jane Doe and her original lawyers, Mary Cornish and Susan Ursel, took a leap of faith — faith in feminist grassroots knowledge about how police process women's reports of

22 *Ibid* at para 33.

23 *Jane Doe v Metropolitan Toronto (Municipality) Commissioners of Police* (1991), 74 OR (2d) 225 (Ont CA) (leave to appeal denied with costs) [*Jane Doe No 3*].

24 Elizabeth Sheehy, "Causation, Common Sense, and the Common Law: Replacing Unexamined Assumptions with What We Know About Male Violence Against Women, or, From *Jane Doe* to *Bonnie Mooney*" (2005) 17 CJWL 97.

rape — when they boldly claimed they would prove systemic sex discrimination by the police in the Balcony Rapist investigation. At the time of filing the claim, Jane Doe had some documents secured through WAVAW's engagement with Toronto Police in 1986–87. But the discovery process secured for her the "smoking gun": internal reviews and memoranda that demonstrated that senior officials were well aware of the systemic problems raped women faced when dealing with Toronto Police, as well as the individual notes taken by police with respect to the reports made by the first four women attacked in their beds by the Balcony Rapist.

Jane Doe worked tirelessly to find feminist experts to testify for her, who would educate the judge and the public following her case about rape, systemic sex discrimination, and women's equality. As she put it:

> I wanted to call … some expert witnesses of my own who could smash through police lines and provide the court with a definition of the crime of sexual assault, its inherent harm and the mythology that prevents us from understanding it. I wanted experts who could describe the sexist, discriminatory practices in policing and present me on the stand as an adult woman with some intelligence who reacted to her rape in ways that were "normal."[25]

The trial was lengthy: over eight weeks, presiding Justice Jean MacFarland heard some thirty witnesses and read "voluminous documentary evidence." At the close of the trial, Justice MacFarland reserved judgment for seven months, and so the waiting began. Jane Doe describes that period of her life: "For seven months I just held on, waiting, unsleeping, barely able to work."[26]

Jane Doe and her lawyers claimed victory because they had managed to get this ground-breaking claim to a full trial on the merits. In her book, where she includes her daily trial journal and cartoons of the witnesses, Jane Doe describes the trial as "magnificent in its horror and glory both. Grand theatre. Theatre of the absurd."[27] It was a landmark simply to have a case of this magnitude and nature publicly aired. Most lawsuits against police are either shut out of the legal system or settled

25 *The Story of Jane Doe*, *supra* note 1 at 172.

26 *Ibid* at 275.

27 *Ibid* at 273.

out of court,[28] which means that the evidence is kept from the public and no admission of wrong-doing is conceded.

On 3 July 1998, Jane Doe made legal history a third time when Justice MacFarland released her one-hundred page judgment finding the police responsible in law for violating Jane Doe's sections 7 and 15 *Charter* rights and for negligence.[29] This judgment represented the first time in Canadian law that police were found liable for failing to warn a potential victim of a crime. It was also the first time that they were held accountable for systemic sex discrimination in their enforcement of the criminal law. Toronto Police combed the decision looking for appealable errors, but the decision was carefully supported by the evidence and the law. Further, city council, the employers of the Toronto Police, refused to fund the appeal.[30]

Beyond generating new law, Justice MacFarland's judgment is significant as a feminist primer on rape, as a record of police discrimination, and as a manual for lawyers showing how to prepare a systemic discrimination case. It represents the first time that a Canadian court has conceptualized rape in a feminist manner, "as an act of power and control rather than a sexual act. It has to do with the perpetrators' desire to terrorize, to dominate, to control, to humiliate; it is an act of hostility and aggression."[31] Justice MacFarland described the effect of rape and the fear of rape on women's lives: "male sexual violence operates as a method of social control over women."[32]

The judgment painstakingly reviewed the internal police reports that showed long-standing patterns of sex discrimination in the police processing of rape reports, official awareness of these reports, and persistent failure by police to remedy the deficiencies. For example, officers were responsible for unprofessional, incomplete rape investigations; women were "brushed off" by police when they tried to follow up on their reports and some were threatened with criminal charges if

28 For example, after the family of Albert Johnson, an unarmed African-Canadian man shot and killed by Toronto Police, managed to win against a police attempt to have the case dismissed for failure to state a legitimate legal theory (*Johnson et al v Adamson et al* (1982), 34 OR (2d) 236 (CA)), they settled with police out of court, on conditions that included no acknowledgement of liability and non-disclosure of the terms of settlement.

29 *Jane Doe v Metropolitan (Municipality) Toronto Commissioners of Police* (1998), 39 OR (3d) 487 (Ont Ct Gen Div) [*Jane Doe No 4*].

30 Discussed in more detail in *The Story of Jane Doe*, *supra* note 1 at 285–89.

31 *Jane Doe No 4*, *supra* note 28 at para 8.

32 *Ibid* at para 9.

they persisted; women were disbelieved, often without explanation or further investigation; and women were described in occurrence reports as liars and as fantasizers by misogynist officers.[33] Justice MacFarland commented: "I find it unsettling that in at least half of this random selection [of police occurrence reports] the 'motive' ascribed to the offence is that of 'sexual gratification' which to me belies a very basic misunderstanding of this crime."[34] This evidence of widespread and systemic discrimination, "in every station in every division in the force,"[35] was particularized in the details of the investigations of the rapist's first two rapes reported to police. Toronto Police occurrence reports for these rapes demonstrated disbelief of the complainants, overt sexism that interfered with their ability to reason, failure to investigate, and in one case, threats to the woman that she would be charged with mischief for falsely reporting rape, in addition to other serious defects.

The police inability to see rape as inherently and highly violent was also manifest in the specific investigation that Jane Doe challenged. Even when the police began to link the rapes after the third and fourth women reported being attacked, their response continued to be hampered by harmful sexist beliefs. Justice MacFarland concluded that police failed to devote sufficient resources to the investigation, failed to either warn or protect identifiable targets, and failed to release details to the public that could have sped up the investigation. She compared this "low key" investigation with another high profile investigation, and concluded that: "because [the rapist's] victims were 'merely raped' by a 'gentleman rapist' — according to the Oliver Zink Rape Cookbook definition [a police text that categorizes different types of offenders] — this case did not have the urgency of the other."[36]

Their method of investigation was to identify likely targets and watch and wait for the next attack: "the women were being used — without their knowledge or consent — as 'bait' to catch a predator whose specific identity then was unknown but whose general and characteristic identity most certainly was."[37] A warning was not issued to the women because police operated on the basis of a sexist stereotype,

33 *Ibid* at para 45, where Justice MacFarland reproduced the opinion of one officer, who said, "it would appear to me from talking to her, this young man is only fulfilling a fantasy of hers."

34 *Ibid* at para 43.

35 *Ibid* at para 153.

36 *Ibid* at para 128.

37 *Ibid* at para 112.

believing women would become hysterical and the investigation would be jeopardized.

The judge rejected the police claim that they took sexual assault to be "a serious crime, second only to homicide": "do they really believe that especially when one reviews their record in this area?" "I must conclude, on the evidence, they did not."[38]

The *Jane Doe* case as a legal precedent has been cited in over forty Canadian legal decisions, but because settled lawsuits do not receive wide publicity, we will probably never know the extent of the pressure that this case has exerted upon police to settle lawsuits against them. The decision has been analyzed in case comments and articles,[39] is taught as part of criminal law, tort law, and sexual assault law courses in Canadian law schools, and has served to inspire and galvanize feminist activists and university students across the country.

AFTER LEGAL VICTORY ...

Jane Doe continued and continues to work to implement her legal victories on the ground. The *Jane Doe* case found constitutional violations of women's rights occasioned by police practices and awarded damages, but did not order police to actually change how they investigate rape. However, the Auditor General for the City of Toronto was tasked by city council with reviewing Toronto Police practices regarding sexual assault investigations in the wake of the *Jane Doe* decision. Jane Doe and other feminists formed the Audit Reference Group (popularly known as the Jane Doe Social Audit) in order to provide input and expertise to the audit process.

The Auditor General, Jeffrey Griffith, released his report in 1999. The *Review of the Investigation of Sexual Assaults — Toronto Police Services*[40] found that, contrary to the claims of the lawyers who defended the police against Jane Doe's suit, many of the problems identified by Justice MacFarland continued to plague women who reported sexual assault to Toronto's police. Among many other problems, for example, police

38 *Ibid* at para 125.

39 See, for example, Melanie Randall, "Sex Discrimination, Accountability of Public Authorities and the Public/Private Divide in Tort Law: An Analysis of *Doe v Metropolitan Toronto (Municipality) Commissioners of Police*" (2001) 26 Queen's LJ 451 and Scott Childs & Paul Ceyssens, "*Doe v Metropolitan Toronto Board of Commissioners of Police* and the Status of Public Oversight of the Police in Canada" (1998) 36 Alta L Rev 1000.

40 Jeffrey Griffiths, *Review of the Investigation of Sexual Assaults — Toronto Police Service* (Toronto: Toronto Audit Services, 1999).

continued to deploy myths of so-called "false allegations" to unfound women's rape reports; to allow untrained, first response officers, rather than members of the sexual assault unit, to erroneously make the determination of unfounded sexual assaults; to fail to maintain contact with the women who reported rapes; and to insist on lengthy and repetitive statements/interviews with women who reported rape. In consequence, Griffiths issued fifty-seven recommendations for change. He also urged police to work with community-based women's groups to implement his recommendations.

In response, a group of feminist activists, led by Jane Doe, lobbied city counsel to support a proposal for a Sexual Assault Audit Steering Committee, composed equally of community-based women from the Violence Against Women sector and senior police, charged with the task of bringing the audit's recommendations to fruition. Council passed the motion in early 2000, but the steering committee was not formally struck until 2003. In 2004, the Auditor General released a follow-up report[41] that refuted the claim made 13 November 2003 by Julian Fantino, then chief of police, to the Police Services Board that all of the 1999 recommendations had been implemented. This second report found, among other problems, that there was little if any change regarding police follow-up with women who had reported sexual assaults; that police failed to engage in meaningful consultation with community-based experts in the area of sexual assault; that no progress had been made toward the implementation of a civilian complaints system specific to Aboriginal and racialized women who are raped; and that multiple shortcomings continued to undercut police training and the investigation of sexual assault.

The steering committee only began its work in 2005, when the Toronto Police Service finally gave its official approval for the participation of police. In an article devoted to analyzing the work of the steering committee,[42] Beverly Bain, Amanda Dale, and Jane Doe explain that the committee's Terms of Reference and Mandate required the members to address police training for sexual assault investigations, to examine police practices regarding the issuance of warnings regarding serial rapists, to deal with the use of technology in investigations, and to

41 Jeffrey Griffiths, *Auditor General's Follow-Up Review on the October 1999 Report Entitled: "Review of the Investigation of Sexual Assaults — Toronto Police Service"* (Toronto: Toronto Audit Services, 2004).

42 Beverly Bain, Amanda Dale & Jane Doe, "A New Chapter in Feminist Organizing: The Sexual Assault Audit Steering Committee" (2009–2010) 28 Can Woman Stud 6.

develop a civilian complaints system focused on the needs of racialized and Aboriginal women. While Jane Doe's work with the steering committee produced recommendations for change on all of these fronts, the work was abruptly terminated in 2007 when the chair of the Toronto Police Services Board unilaterally dissolved the committee and cut the community-based women out of any further role in monitoring or facilitating implementation of the recommendations.[43]

Sadly, Jane Doe's assessment is that many of the Auditor General's recommendations remain dormant to this day. She continues, however, to engage in research, activism, and public speaking aimed at exposing and challenging police and lawyers with respect to how they deal with women who have been raped and the crime itself. She published her book, *The Story of Jane Doe*, in 2003, to great acclaim. The book was nominated for several awards;[44] was reviewed in glowing terms;[45] and is required reading in several law school courses.[46] Jane Doe has also developed an original research agenda that includes interviewing women about their experiences regarding the publication ban,[47] the sexual assault evidence kit,[48] and police warnings.[49] She continues to lecture at conferences and on university campuses, to advocate for so-

43 *Ibid* at 10.

44 The book was nominated for the Writers Trust Prize for Political Writing, the Arthur Ellis Award for Crime Writing (non-fiction), and the Bouchercon Award for Crime Writing (non-fiction), all in 2004. It was re-issued in paperback in 2004 by Vintage Canada.

45 See, for example, Janine Benedet, "A Book Review About Rape — *The Story of Jane Doe: A Book About Rape*" (2003) 15 CJWL 215; Drew Mildon, "Book Review: *The Story of Jane Doe: A Book About Rape*" (2005) 14 Dal J Leg Stud 221; Marion M Lynn, "*The Story of Jane Doe: A Book About Rape*: Book Review" (2005) 25 Can Woman Stud 204; Lynn Crosbie, "A story of rape: One woman's fight against the system produces a vital document; Jane Doe rejects the kind of linear narrative memoirs demand" *The Toronto Star* (20 April 2003) D12; and, most importantly, see the tribute to Jane Doe's book by Gillian Calder & Rebecca Johnson, "The Jane Doe Coffee Table Book About Rape: Reflections on Rebellious Writing and Teaching," Chapter 15 in this book.

46 CML 4111: Sexual Assault Law, University of Ottawa, Faculty of Law, as well as law courses at the University of Victoria and the University of Western Ontario.

47 Jane Doe, "What's in a Name? Who Benefits From the Publication Ban in Sexual Assault Trials?" in Ian Kerr, ed, *Lessons from the Identity Trail: Anonymity, Privacy and Identity in a Networked Society* (New York: Oxford University Press, 2009) 265.

48 Jane Doe, "Who Benefits From the Sexual Assault Evidence Kit?" Chapter 16 in this book.

49 Jane Doe, "A Warning About Warnings: Who Benefits From Rape Warnings?" Plenary Address, "Sexual Assault Law, Practice and Activism in a Post-*Jane Doe* Era," University of Ottawa, Faculty of Law, 6–7 March 2009.

cial and legal change around sexual assault, and to provide countless hours of support and strategizing to women who have been raped. Jane Doe has been recognized with numerous awards for her courageous activism,[50] but perhaps her greatest victory lies in the fact that more than twenty years after she started her legal challenge against the police, and ten years after she won it, she, with all her brilliance, glamour, and humour, inspires feminists young and old to keep on keeping on.

50 Constance E Hamilton Human Rights Award, City of Toronto (2004); Women Who Have Made a Difference Award, The Linden School for Girls (2001); Rebel With a Cause Award, Canadian Association of Elizabeth Fry Societies (2000); Woman of the Year Award, Chatelaine Magazine (2000); Woman of Distinction, YWCA (2000); and Woman of Courage, National Action Committee on the Status of Women (1998).

APPENDIX A

Jane Doe v Board of Commissioners of Police

Court File No 21670/87

SUPREME COURT OF ONTARIO
BETWEEN
JANE DOE

Plaintiff

— and —

BOARD OF COMMISSIONERS OF POLICE FOR THE
MUNICIPALITY OF METROPOLITAN TORONTO,
JACK MARKS, KIM DERRY and WILLIAM CAMERON

Defendants

AMENDED STATEMENT OF CLAIM
(NOTICE OF ACTION ISSUED AUGUST 10, 1987)

1. THE PLAINTIFF'S CLAIM IS FOR:
   (a) general damages in the amount of $500,000.00;
   (b) special damages in the amount of $100,000.00;
   (c) pre-judgment interest pursuant to section 138 of the *Courts of Justice Act*;
   (d) a declaration that the Plaintiff's constitutional rights as provided for in the *Canadian Charter of Rights and Freedoms* and, in particular, by virtue of sections 7, 15 and 28 thereof, have been violated by the Defendants;
   (e) damages resulting from the violation described in paragraph (d) hereof in the amount of $600,000.00;
   (f) costs on a solicitor and client basis;
   (g) such further and other relief as to this Honorable Court may deem just.

2. The Plaintiff is a thirty-five year old woman who is employed as a free-lance worker in the film industry in the City of Toronto in the Province of Ontario.

3. The Defendant Board of Commissioners of Police for the Municipality of Metropolitan Toronto, (hereinafter referred to as the "Commissioners") have the statutory author-

ity and responsibility under the *Police Act*, RSO 1980 c 381 and in particular sections 14, 16 and 17 with respect to policing in the Municipality of Metropolitan Toronto.

4. The Defendant Jack Marks (hereinafter referred to as "Chief Marks") was at all material times the Chief of Police, responsible to the Defendant Commissioners. Chief Marks has authority and responsibility under the *Police Act*, and in particular section 57 thereof, as the Chief Police Constable, and under the regulations passed by the Defendant Commissioners for the governance of Metropolitan Toronto Police Force to direct the activities of all police officers and employees under the jurisdiction of the Defendant Commissioners. Chief Marks is liable in respect of torts committed by members of the police force under his direction and control in the performance or purported performance of their duties under the *Police Act*, s 24. Police Constables under the direction of Chief Marks whose names are unknown to the Plaintiff are hereinafter referred to as "Police Constables."

5. The Defendant Kim Derry is a police officer and was one of the investigating officers responsible for the investigation of the Plaintiff's rape and sexual assault. At all material times he was responsible to the Defendant Commissioners, and the Defendant Chief Marks.

6. The Defendant William Cameron is a police officer and was one of the investigating officers responsible for the investigation of the Plaintiff's rape and sexual assault. At all material times he was responsible to the Defendant Commissioners, and the Defendant Chief Marks.

7. On August 24, 1986, the Plaintiff was sexually assaulted and raped in her own apartment, located on the second floor of an apartment building in the neighbourhood of Church and Wellesley Streets in Toronto. The rapist had gained access to the Plaintiff's apartment by climbing up the outside of the building, and by forcibly entering through a locked balcony door. The rapist wore a mask, held a knife to the Plaintiff's throat and threatened to kill her. He covered her head, and sexually assaulted and raped her. He then escaped through the front door which he had unlocked upon entering the apartment.

8. Immediately following these events, the Plaintiff reported the sexual assault and rape to Police Constables. Several Police Constables attended at the Plaintiff's apartment to question her. She subsequently was taken to the Women's College Hospital where she was examined in the Sexual Assault Centre of that Hospital. The Plaintiff was required to submit to necessary invasive examinations to obtain evidence and to take potent medication to prevent pregnancy and infection.

9. On October 3, 1986, Paul Douglas Callow was arrested by the Police and charged with the sexual assault of the Plaintiff, along with several other counts of sexual assault and other charges pursuant to the Criminal Code of Canada relating to similar attacks against other women in the same neighbourhood as the Plaintiff over the prior year.

10. A preliminary inquiry into the charges commenced in Toronto on February 2, 1987 before His Honour Judge Kerr. The Plaintiff was required to give evidence at the preliminary inquiry.

11. Following the preliminary inquiry, Paul Douglas Callow pleaded guilty to all charges against him. On February 20, 1987, he was sentenced to twenty years in prison and is now incarcerated in a penal institution.

12. The Plaintiff states that the targets of sexual assault and rape are overwhelmingly women while the perpetrators of the crime are overwhelmingly men.

13. The Plaintiff states that the Defendants knew or ought to have known that during the months prior to the assault on the Plaintiff several other women residing in the general vicinity of the Plaintiff's apartment had been sexually assaulted in a very similar manner indicating that the rapes were the work of a serial rapist.

14. The Plaintiff further states that the Defendants Derry and Cameron and Police Constables undertook an investigation in or about August, 1986 prior to the Plaintiff's sexual assault and rape which resulted in the identification of the likely apartments which would be the target of the said serial rapist, namely second and third floor apartments with balcony access occupied by single women in the Church-Wellesley area.

15. The Plaintiff asserts that she was readily identifiable by the Defendants as a likely target of the serial rapist by virtue of her distinguishing characteristics which included the fact that she was a white, single woman who resided on a second or third floor apartment with a balcony in the Church-Wellesley area.

16. The Plaintiff states that, although the Defendants identified the Plaintiff as a likely target, they specifically decided not to warn her or other women similarly situated to her for reasons which included the belief that such warning would cause hysteria on the part of the women and would alert the suspect to flee and not engage in further criminal activity.

17. The Plaintiff states that prior to her sexual assault and rape on August 24th, 1986 no steps had been taken by the Defendants to warn her or other women living in her

neighbourhood of the fact that other sexual assaults and rapes had occurred recently, nor to alert her as to the circumstances in which the sexual assaults and rapes had taken place. If she had been warned of this potential danger, the Plaintiff states that she and other women in the area would have been more vigilant than usual and that she therefore would have had the information necessary to have chosen to take steps to ensure her safety. In addition, the Plaintiff would have known that the rapist had not murdered any of the women he had sexually assaulted. This information would have somewhat ameliorated the intense fear for her life that the Plaintiff endured during the time that the rapist was in her apartment.

18. The Plaintiff further asserts that the Police Constables knew the ethnicity and certain physically distinguishing characteristics of the serial rapist from an early date and in any event prior to August 24, 1986.

18a. The Plaintiff relies on the fact that the Defendants or persons acting on their behalf have admitted that they should have issued a warning in the circumstances of this case.

19. The Plaintiff further asserts that an investigation of this serial rapist conducted without the negligence of the Defendants would have led to an arrest at a much earlier stage and that as a consequence the Plaintiff would not have been raped or sexually assaulted.

20. The Plaintiff states that the Defendants Derry and Cameron were under a duty to take all reasonable steps to prevent the occurrence of the sexual assault and rape of the Plaintiff and women similarly situated to herself as identifiable victims. The Plaintiff alleges that the actions of the Defendants Derry and Cameron constitute negligence. The particulars of the alleged negligence are that they:

(a) failed to advise the Plaintiff, or other potential victims or to cause to be advised in a timely fashion of the nature of danger to which they were exposed and failed to alert them to steps that could be taken by them to protect themselves from the rapist;
(b) failed to warn the Plaintiff or other potential victims, or cause them to be warned, of the information that had been compiled on the rapist and, in particular, failed to warn the Plaintiff that she was a vulnerable and likely victim;
(c) knew or ought to have known that the Plaintiff was a member of a very narrow group of women who were likely victims of Paul Douglas Callow and intentionally failed to notify her of the grave risk she faced.
(d) failed to identify, or cause to be identified Paul Douglas Callow as a suspect notwithstanding they ought to have been aware of his prior criminal record for sexual assault and his residence in the area;

(e) failed to investigate Paul Douglas Callow adequately or at all and failed to take steps to permit victims and members of the community to identify and locate him;
(f) within the limits of their responsibilities, failed to devote adequate resources and personnel to the protection of the Plaintiff and other women similarly situated to her;
(g) breached their statutory duty as provided in the *Police Act*, and in particular section 57 thereof;

21. The Plaintiff alleges that the actions of the Defendant Commissioners constituted negligence. The particulars of the alleged negligence are that they:

(a) authorized, allowed, or failed to correct, a policy, regulation or practice carried out by persons under their direction which favoured apprehension of rape suspects over the protection of likely victims;
(b) failed to direct adequate resources to the investigation and apprehension of rapists, and this serial rapist in particular, when they knew or ought to have known that he would strike again against the Plaintiff or other women like her.
(c) breached their statutory duty as provided in the *Police Act* and in particular their responsibility under s 17 for policing and maintenance of law and order; under s 14 for ensuring the police force has adequate resources to fulfill that mandate; and under s 16 for enacting appropriate regulations to govern the force so as to prevent neglect or abuse and to render it efficient in the discharge of its duties.

22. The Plaintiff alleges that the actions of the Defendant Chief Marks constituted negligence. The particulars of the alleged negligence are that he:

(a) directed or permitted those persons under his command to follow a policy of preferring apprehension of rape suspects over the protection of the Plaintiff and other women in a similar situation;
(b) failed to direct and organize those persons under his command for an efficient and effective effort to identify, investigate and arrest Paul Douglas Callow prior to his attack on the Plaintiff.
(c) failed to direct and organize those persons under his command to devote sufficient resources to the investigation of violence against women and in particular the activities of this serial rapist;
(d) breached his statutory duty as provided in the *Police Act*, and in particular section 57 thereof, and failed to exercise the responsibility put on him by virtue of the regulations passed by the Defendant Commissioners.

23. The Plaintiff states that the actions of the Defendants referred to in paragraph 24 below constitute actions which are subject to the application of the *Charter*.

24. The Plaintiff states that the Defendants violated the Plaintiff's right to security of the person provided under section 7 of the *Charter* and her right to equality both before and under the law and her right to equal protection and equal benefit of the law without discrimination and more particularly on the basis of sex all of which are provided under sections 15 and 28 of the *Charter*, the particulars of which are as follows:

(a) the Plaintiff repeats the allegations contained in paragraphs 12–22 hereof;
(b) the Defendant Commissioners and Chief Marks authorized or allowed and the Defendants Derry and Cameron carried out a policy, regulation or practice which placed the value of the criminal investigation above their duty to protect the Plaintiff by using women such as the Plaintiff as bait. They did this by choosing not to warn potential targets like her by going into the community to release detailed information, especially to those at highest risk (i.e. single women in second and third floor apartments with balconies), but rather continuing to collect evidence for prosecution at the expense of ensuring women's safety;
(c) the Defendants failed to assign to the apprehension of the rapist an appropriate or adequate degree of energy and resources because the victims of such potential crimes were women;
(d) in the alternative, because the victims of sexual assault and rape are overwhelmingly women, the Defendants' policies and investigative practices in dealing with sexual assault and rape had the effect of discriminating against the Plaintiff on the basis of her sex.

25. As a result of the negligence, breach of duty and breach of the Plaintiff's constitutional rights by the above named Defendants, the Plaintiff has suffered and continues to suffer pain, inconvenience and loss of enjoyment of life. The Plaintiff endures continuing emotional upset as a result of this crime, including intense fear and insecurity about her safety, recurring violent nightmares, a sense of powerlessness and vulnerability, recurring and intrusive conscious memories of the event and the ensuing ordeal with the Police and the Courts, prolonged bouts of depression and anxiety and a generalized sense of uncertainty and distrust. She has been required to undergo psychiatric counselling and therapy. Her normal habits of daily life have been adversely and permanently affected, and she has incurred expenses and lost income.

The Plaintiff proposes that this action be tried in Toronto.
October 14, 1988.

CORNISH & ASSOCIATES
Barristers & Solicitors
210 Dundas Street West
Suite 500
Toronto, Ontario
M5G 2Z8
(416) 971-5011

MARY CORNISH Solicitors for the Plaintiff

2.

Jane Doe v Toronto Commissioners of Police: A View from the Bar

Sean Dewart

Sean Dewart, Jane Doe's legal counsel, contributes to our understanding of the promise of law for sexually assaulted women by discussing the strategic considerations at play in the Jane Doe *litigation, taking the position that it was a victory to even get the case to court so that previously unheard voices could be articulated in a legal forum. Beyond the legal victories chronicled by Elizabeth A Sheehy in the previous chapter, Sean notes that the possibility of holding police accountable in law for their conduct of investigations created by the* Jane Doe *case represents a public service for others wronged by police, a point picked up later in this volume by Blair Crew when he considers the possibility of a suit for wrongful unfounding by police of women's reports of sexual assault.*

"Did *Jane Doe* (the case, not the person) make any difference?"

"Was it worth it?"

"Did it achieve anything?"

To answer these questions, one must reflect on the context in which the *Jane Doe* trial was conducted.

I kept a scrapbook during the trial and dusted it off to prepare this paper. The *Jane Doe* trial lasted eight or nine weeks in the fall of 1997 and received saturation coverage, largely due to Jane Doe's media savvy. The *Toronto Star*, which at the time was the largest circulation paper in Canada, had a reporter there and ran stories every day of the trial. The coverage in the other newspapers was only slightly less extensive. The electronic media obviously have a different attention span. However, their treatment of the matter was, by their standards, comparable.

The headlines just kept coming: "Failure to warn women morally indefensible"; "Ex-cop blasts sex-crime unit"; "Police buried damaging report"; "Rape cases given low priority trial told"; "Police too busy to focus on rapes, court told." And on and on it went for weeks and weeks. My scrapbook, which is undoubtedly incomplete, has more than seventy newspaper articles that appeared in the three major Toronto papers between mid-September and mid-November 1997.

This seemed completely natural at the time, because we were at the centre of the vortex, but when I looked back at the clippings ten years later, it amazed me. Because of Jane Doe's courage, and the skill of Mary Cornish and the lawyers who worked on the file in the ten years before I became involved, the police were being questioned in a highly public forum they could neither dodge nor control. During the trial, we obviously had no idea how things would turn out. Most lawyers were persuaded that the case was unwinnable. Therefore, our official position was that simply getting to trial and airing the issues in this public forum was a victory.

Speaking for myself, I thought this was hogwash at the time. To my way of thinking, a victory would be a victory. Telling people that merely getting to trial was a victory was a defence mechanism, or as people say today, "managing expectations." We probably wouldn't win, so we declared victory where none existed.

I see now that I was wrong. The simple fact of a public trial was a victory for a voice and for voices that had previously been silenced. As the saying went at the time, Jane Doe was "speaking truth to power," and people were paying a great deal of attention. I am not oblivious to the fact that the "speaking" was being done in a legal process in which Jane Doe herself was muzzled. My point is that, however imperfect the process, her story was being told and her message was getting out.

The trial ended on 1 December 1997, and the police enjoyed a respite for six months. However, the verdict came down in July of 1998 and, to put it mildly, things picked up. Banner headlines appeared on all the front pages: "Judge blasts sexist police"; "Police failed"; "Police found grossly negligent"; "Police must act on Jane Doe ruling." I discovered a phenomenon about the media at the time, which has been proven true ten times in the ensuing ten years: whatever story is in the media at the beginning of July in Canada, as reporters and politicians begin to head out on vacation, will run for weeks, regardless of its intrinsic news value. In this case, the story was dead simple: Jane Doe won. And the news value was high.

Nevertheless, my scrapbook has another seventy-five clippings of stories that appeared between the date of the judgment, 3 July 1998, and the date when the police announced they were not appealing, 5 August 1998. Again, the electronic media and, in particular, radio stations, provided comparable coverage. The national and international press picked it up, and all three Toronto papers ran lead editorials.

There was a frenzied debate about whether or not, and in what way, the police should apologize to Jane Doe. Ultimately, Jane Doe got her apology and, according to the front page of the *Toronto Star* on 10 July 1998, "City also says sorry to all Toronto women." The police, however, could not do anything right. According to the next wave of headlines, "Apology just doesn't cut it" and in the *Ottawa Sun*, "Apology not enough." City council began to debate an audit of the Toronto Police Service; thus on and on it went, until 31 July 1998, when the head of the police union spoke out. The front page story in the *Toronto Sun* says it all: "We've had it Toronto cops say"; "Embittered by Jane Doe case and car-chase ruling, police threaten to turn blind eye on some crime." That, of course, had been precisely our point, but the irony was lost on the police! It was truly a media frenzy for thirty days, until a decision was made that there would be no appeal, and life carried on.

My interest in the Toronto Police began when I was a teenager and just beginning to read the newspaper. I remember a week when the *Globe and Mail* ran a series of five or six stories about the Toronto Police hold-up squad. The series documented the use of torture (plumber's claws) to extract confessions from accused men and various other corrupt practices. What I remember even more vividly than the stories, however, is the backlash. There was public fury that the *Globe and Mail* would attack the hard-working men — no mention of any hard-working women as I recall — who put their lives on the line every day to keep us safe. There were seething letters to the editor about the *Globe's* "yellow journalism." City councillors were up in arms and, smelling blood, the other newspapers piled on. Becker's, a chain with hundreds of convenience stores, handed out free buttons for all right-thinking people to pin on their coats, claiming that "Our Cops Are Tops." The *Globe* and the one or two councillors who foolishly thought the allegations might warrant further investigation slinked away with their tails between their legs.

It is fair to say that the image of the Toronto Police has taken a bit of a beating since then. While most community members are respectful of the difficult work that is honestly carried out by many police personnel, most people at least recognize that there are massive problems with the manner in which we are policed. There is little or no political will to fix things, as far as I can discern, but at least we have stopped collectively pretending that no problems exist.

I posit that the *Jane Doe* case was a pivotal factor in the continuum of events that has brought about this change in public attitudes. And this change is not confined to Toronto. It is safe to say that police services across Canada are viewed today with a healthy degree of skepticism that would have been unthinkable twenty-five years ago. The RCMP in particular has finally lost its mythic status, and while I do not pretend that meaningful reform is under way, I suggest that Canadians are finally asking the right questions, or at least are asking questions. I go so far as to say that reform is now possible, where this was not true previously. I also say that the *Jane Doe* case is one cause, and not an effect, of this change in attitudes.

The point can be seen most easily by tracing the development of the law in the United Kingdom, where courts and politicians continue to fawn over police. *Jane Doe* has been repeatedly cited in the UK by plaintiffs seeking redress for various types of police misconduct, and has been repeatedly shot down by trial and appeal courts. The House of Lords, in particular, is very sniffy about *Jane Doe*.

Anyone who has paid attention to the experience in Britain in the wake of 9/11 has seen that British authorities are as eager as those in the United States to gut basic civil liberties in the name of fighting terrorism. The rise in police power in the UK in the last ten years is dramatic, and largely unchallenged. Whatever the realities on the ground, there is no doubt that public discourse in Canada concerning police powers and responsibilities is different than in most places in the world.

Even if I am wrong about public discourse, our legal discourse on these topics is unquestionably unique. This can be seen in both the growing number of trial level decisions where police are held liable for various types of wrong-doing, and in the Supreme Court of Canada's 2007 decision in *Hill v Hamilton-Wentworth Regional Police Services Board*.[1] As a result of this case, people who have been wrongly convicted or wrongly charged can sue police investigators, if the detectives' negligence caused the wrongful prosecution. There is no doubt that this is a uniquely Canadian case. Lawsuits of this type have been theoretically possible, although very rare, in Quebec for a number of years, but were absolutely unheard of anywhere else in the world.

Let me digress to tell a story that illustrates my point. When *Hill* was being argued in the Supreme Court, the lawyer for the police sensed, I think, that things were not going well. Towards the end of his argument,

1 [2007] 3 SCR 109.

his voice had a somewhat desperate tone, and he implored the judges not to make Canada the laughingstock of the common law world. "Imaginez-vous," il disait, "que le droit commun au Canada serait différent que le droit aux États Unis, au Royaume Uni, en Australie, en Nouvelle Zélande et en Afrique du Sud. Il n'y pas un seul pays au monde où on peut réclamer des dommages en telles circonstances," il disait. "Nous serons seul au monde," a-t-il répété. Le Juge LeBel l'a arrêté. "Ce n'est pas grave," il disait. "Vous serez avec le Québec."[2]

To be clear, although I maintain that we in Canada discuss police accountability issues differently than elsewhere, I am not an utter idiot. Our enlightened public attitudes didn't do Robert Dziekanski[3] any good, and his is only one of countless stories about the problem with the way we are policed. I have already said several times that I do not see any signs of systemic reform.

In the absence of any political will, I think we have to be realistic about what we can demand from the legal system. If the legal system can play a meaningful role in creating an environment where reform is possible, it will have served us well. Remember, after all, what a lawsuit is, or at least what the model lawsuit is. A single person with an individual problem comes to the law for a solution, or at least a way out of the problem, tailored to his or her circumstances.

Jane Doe was an individual who challenged the legal system to respond to a massive, intractable, and deeply entrenched social and political problem. In the euphoria after she won, some of us believed that the court's judgment would be enough to effect real change by itself. This, of course, was naïve and wrong.

The truth, however, is that more and more people who have been wronged by the police in Canada are obtaining redress in individual lawsuits. I believe there is some merit to the conventional theory of tort law. As the number of individual suits increases, municipal accountants and insurance underwriters will demand that their clients, the police,

2 "Imagine," he said, "if the common law in Canada was different from the law in the United States, in Great Britain, in Australia, in New Zealand, and in South Africa. There isn't a single country in the world where one can claim damages in such circumstances," he said. "We would be alone in the world," he repeated. Judge LeBel stopped him. "That isn't important, he said. "You would be with Quebec." Remarks from the bench during oral argument before the Supreme Court of Canada on November 10, 2006 in *Hill, ibid.*

3 For more information on Robert Dziekanski, see <http://www.cbc.ca/news/background/tasers/video.html>.

change. This, together with the advances in public dialogue I have alluded to, will create circumstances in which real, broadly-based change is possible. The political will to do anything will have to come from somewhere other than the legal system, but that does not mean that the legal system has failed. *Jane Doe*, the case, accomplished as much as one could reasonably expect. For that reason, Jane Doe, the person, is a Canadian hero.

3. New Zealand's Jane Doe

Julia Tolmie

Julia Tolmie argues that Louise Nicholas' monumental effort to prosecute three police officers for sexual assaults committed against her, commencing when she was a girl, also achieved what Sean Dewart suggests Jane Doe's case did, by exposing abuse of power by police and generating a public demand for accountability. In contrast, however, Louise Nicholas' case was not informed by feminist analysis and she was not vindicated personally by the trial outcomes. Like Lucinda Vandervort who, later in this volume, explores the multiplicity of legal errors in another disastrous sexual assault prosecution involving a gang assault on an Aboriginal girl, Julia chronicles how police and prosecutorial errors played a significant role in the multiple retrials that the complainant endured and that finally produced the officers' acquittals. Louise Nicholas' bravery did, however, result in more women coming forward to identify these officers as perpetrators, and several related convictions ensued. Julia's discussion of the public inquiries and law reform proposals that the Louise Nicholas case prompted reminds us that legal wins and losses are only a starting point for feminist activism.

Jane Doe's protracted legal battle took place in Toronto, Canada, in the late 1980s to the late 1990s. On the other side of the world in the 2000s, New Zealand had its own Jane Doe. By briefly describing her journey and some of its outcomes, I also take the opportunity to honour those women whose costly stands for justice with respect to sexual violence make the law more habitable for all women. The woman I have dubbed "New Zealand's Jane Doe" is called Louise Nicholas[1] and her cases were not tort cases but criminal prosecutions against the police who were, *themselves*, her rapists.

I am, of course, drawing the connection between Jane Doe and Louise Nicholas very loosely. What was extraordinary about what Jane Doe

1 For a full account of her experience, see Louise Nicholas & Philip Kitchin, *Louise Nicholas: My Story* (Auckland: Random House, 2007).

did is that she succeeded in holding the police accountable with respect to what was standard policing, exposing it as illegally rooted in sexist assumptions and sloppiness. There is plenty of evidence that the New Zealand police force has an overly masculine culture, which operates in a sexist and frequently sloppy fashion when it comes to dealing with rape complaints. Jan Jordan ably exposes the degree to which sexist myths and assumptions are the norm amongst the New Zealand Police (even amongst those elite officers who are highly experienced in the area of sexual violence[2]). For example, the pervasive and inaccurate belief is that high proportions of sexual violence complaints are false; there are misinterpretations of victim behaviour because of stereotypes about how genuine victims act; and stereotypical definitions of rape prevail (for example, the drawing of a distinction between "real rapes" and cases that are not rape even though they might fit within the legal definition of rape, such cases being more in the nature of "non-consensual sex"[3]). Nonetheless, no one has taken the kind of litigation in New Zealand that Jane Doe took in Canada even though there have been obvious situations that have warranted such action. For example, Malcolm Rewa went on to rape twenty-six known women after the police chose to believe him instead of a young Maori female complainant who named him as her attacker in 1987.[4]

What Louise Nicholas did, by way of contrast, was to go after behaviour that no one would view as *standard* policing[5] — police officers having sex, often in uniform, with women who were extremely vulnerable because of their age and, sometimes, past histories of abuse, and who were physically "compliant" but verbally expressing their unwillingness to participate. It is indicative perhaps of the difficulty in securing convictions in sexual violence cases that the prosecution failed to secure convictions in two of the three criminal trials in which Louise was the complainant,[6] and in one of the two cases brought by other complainants against the same group of men for similar violations.

2 Jan Jordan, *The Word of a Woman? Police, Rape and Belief* (Hampshire: Palgrave MacMillan, 2004).

3 *Ibid* at 141.

4 *Ibid* at 192.

5 Having said this, one of the officers in question, Clint Rickards, had been promoted to a very senior level within the police force despite the fact that his employment records noted some aspects of this behaviour.

6 Ultimately there were no convictions with respect to the actual sexual assaults she had experienced. Instead, police officer John Dewar was convicted for his actions, which prevented the successful prosecution of those Nicholas had accused of sexually assaulting her.

Another point of difference between the trials involving Louise Nicholas as a complainant and Jane Doe's litigation is that the legal battle involved in the latter, but not in the former, was self-consciously shaped by a sophisticated feminist political framework. This reflects differences between the two women involved.[7] It may also reflect subtle jurisprudential and political differences between the two jurisdictions in which these legal battles were played out. New Zealand does not have organisations like the Women's Legal Education and Action Fund [LEAF] and lacks a positive statement of equality for women in its constitution.[8] Instead, there is simply a right to be free from discrimination on the grounds of sex.[9] Early indications are that the New Zealand provision may have been used more often by men to challenge affirmative action measures for women on the basis that they do not treat men and women in exactly the same fashion, than to advance women's equality,[10] although this has also arguably been a feature of the Canadian experience as well.[11] Nonetheless, it is possible to assert that New Zealand has yet to develop a sophisticated jurisprudence around gender equity issues, and that it lacks both the legal framework that might facilitate the development of such a jurisprudence, as well as resourced legal actors who might educate lawmakers and force their engagement with such issues.

What both Jane Doe and Louise Nicholas have in common, however, is their remarkable courage and tenacity in using the legal system

7 Compare the accounts in *Louise Nicholas: My Story*, *supra* note 1 and Jane Doe, *The Story of Jane Doe* (Toronto: Random House, 2003).

8 This difference may not be as significant as it first appears. Article 15(1) commences with a positive statement of equality — "Every individual is equal before and under the law" — before going on to define equality in terms of non-discrimination: "… and has the right to the equal protection and equal benefit of the law without discrimination and, in particular, discrimination based … on sex"). See Paul Rishworth *et al*, *The New Zealand Bill of Rights* (Melbourne, Australia: Oxford University Press, 2003) at 366–67.

9 Section 19(1) of the *Bill of Rights Act 1990* (NZ) does not contain an affirmative statement of equality. It simply says, "Everyone has the right to freedom from discrimination on the grounds of discrimination in the Human Rights Act 1993" (which includes sex). *The New Zealand Bill of Rights*, *ibid* at 375–93. See the discussion in Regina Graycar & Jenny Morgan, *The Hidden Gender of Law*, 2d ed (Sydney: The Federation Press, 2002) at 28–55.

10 Caroline Morris, "Remember the Ladies: A Feminist Perspective on Bills of Rights" (2002) 33/34 VUWLR 451.

11 See, for example, *The Hidden Gender of Law*, *supra* note 9 at 35–36. See also Gwen Brodsky & Shelagh Day, *Canadian Charter of Rights and Freedoms: One Step Forward or Two Steps Back?* (Ottawa: Canadian Advisory Council on the Status of Women, 1989).

to demand justice and accountability from the police force/officers for the role that it/they played in their violent victimizations. In addition, the public fallout from both these cases has been a demand for accountability on the part of the police force and an attempted overhaul of police behaviour afterwards.

AN ACCOUNT OF WHAT HAPPENED IN NEW ZEALAND

Louise Nicholas' trauma began when she was thirteen in the 1980s. She claims that she was regularly raped by a police officer, Sam Brown,[12] stationed in her rural town. She complained to the other officer stationed there (Trevor Clayton), who was a family friend, and says that she was also subsequently raped once by him. In addition, she was indecently assaulted several times by Bob Schollum, another officer. The school guidance counsellor, in whom Louise Nicholas confided, told her mother who, in turn, complained to Trevor Clayton. Her mother discovered that everyone involved denied that anything had happened and that no one would believe her or her daughter instead of a police officer.

The family moved to Rotorua and, five years later, when Nicholas was eighteen, she began to be visited regularly alone at home by Brad Shipton and Clint Rickards, in their police uniforms, for sex. She had only briefly met them once before they first showed up at her house. She would tell them that she did not want to have sex with them, but they would go ahead anyway. On one occasion, she claims that she was offered a lift when she was walking home from work by Bob Schollum and was then taken to a house where she was raped by Schollum, Shipton, Rickards, and a fourth man. On this occasion, she was also raped using a police baton. When Shipton's journals were seized by Operation Austin[13] years later, it became apparent that Shipton had information about her and where she was living before she had even met him. It was obvious from this that her details had been passed on to these officers from someone else as a person whom they could sexually abuse.

In 1992, Nicholas laid a formal complaint. Chief Detective Inspector John Dewar was assigned to her case and arrested and charged Brown, who by that stage had left the police. Dewar did nothing about her allegations against Schollum, Shipton, and Rickards and, in fact, advised

12 Not his real name because of a suppression order.

13 This was the name given to the police team responsible for investigating and prosecuting the recent historic sexual assault complaints made against the police, beginning with those made by Louise Nicholas.

her against making a statement about those officers and did not inform their superiors about her complaint. It later transpired that Dewar had taken over the handling of Nicholas' complaint at the request of Shipton. Dewar acted as a close friend and confidante to Nicholas throughout his dealings with her, while at the same time, it appeared, managing the case so that Brown would be acquitted and the other officers would not be charged.

A depositions hearing[14] took place. At the time, rape victims were not obliged to give oral evidence at depositions, but Dewar told Nicholas that she was so obliged. The result was that she was grilled by an experienced QC about information that no one except her family, Dewar, and the original officer she had been interviewed by, knew about.[15] This included information about the baton rape and some false allegations that she had made to the guidance counsellor years before (she had made these allegations at the time because they seemed more believable to her than the truth of what was happening to her). The result of Dewar's advice at this point is that allegations of other incidents that had not been prosecuted, and the earlier lies that she had told, were put on public record and were therefore available to be brought up in the subsequent trial. She had also been through her first gruelling court experience.

The case then went to trial *three* times. The first two times the trial was aborted because Dewar, spontaneously and without any prompting, gave hearsay evidence. This was a "remarkable" mistake for a senior and experienced police officer to make once, let alone twice.[16] By the the third trial, all the advantages that Nicholas had had in the first two rounds had dissipated. At the first trial, the judge had ruled that evidence of the other unprosecuted rape allegations that Nicholas had made were not allowed in evidence, but that was not the ruling in the two subsequent trials, with the result that these allegations were used to diminish her credibility. By the third trial, Nicholas was also heavily pregnant and her testimony, which had been given before two times in trial and once in deposition, was flat and unemotional. In the third trial also, to her surprise, Rickards, Schollum, and Shipton were called

14 A depositions hearing is a preliminary hearing in which the court decides whether or not there is enough of a case to go to trial.

15 It later transpired that the notebook from the first police officer, whom she had spoken to when she first complained, had gone missing and had fallen into the hands of the defence.

16 *Louise Nicholas: My Story*, *supra* note 1 at 91.

to testify. They testified that they had had sex with her, but there was no baton and the sex was consensual. This evidence, which undermined Nicholas completely, was called by the Crown on Dewar's advice. The result of the third trial, at which Dewar testified without giving hearsay evidence, was that Brown was acquitted. He received name suppression, more than $20,000 in costs against the police, and the benefit of double jeopardy, meaning that he could never be tried for these crimes again.

The judge awarding costs to Brown said that it was astonishing that Schollum, Shipton, and Rickards had not been investigated or prosecuted, given the serious allegations against them:

> Such disclosures should have triggered alarm bells that would have permanently silenced Big Ben. Even more surprising than the failure to record is the officer's deliberate advice to the complainant not to make a statement about her allegations against these officers. That a then non-serving officer is pursued with vigour and the allegations against currently serving police officers are not recorded and the complainant advised not to make a statement ... supported an argument that Brown "was a sacrificial offering."[17]

The police investigated Dewar, who got Nicholas to sign a statement that he had drafted saying that she was pleased with how he had investigated and responded to her complaints.[18] Dewar was subject to some minor disciplinary action and transferred.

There things remained until 1998, when a journalist started putting together a story about these events. This story broke in January of 2004. Once the story became public, other women came forward with accounts of their experiences at the hands of these three men, and other police officers, when they were young and/or otherwise vulnerable.[19]

17 *Ibid* at 93.

18 "As a senior policeman with 21 years experience, he knew he shouldn't be talking to a key internal inquiry witness, let alone taking a statement from her" (*ibid* at 112).

19 For example, one woman claimed to have had a relationship with Shipton, and eventually an abortion as a result of this relationship. On the day of her termination, she said that Rickards showed up in uniform, knowing that she had just had an abortion, demanding sex. She gave him oral sex and he left. Another woman said she was fifteen and on a work experience program at the police station when Schollum seduced her. She was alarmed when, while having sex with Schollum, Shipton entered the room and she was told he was going to join in. She said no and asked him to leave, but Shipton watched while Schollum continued to have sex with her. Another woman said that she had had consensual sex with the men in question with a baton. She said that, although at the time she thought it was consensual, she later realized that she

Some of the women had been bullied and intimidated into dropping their complaints.[20] Criminal charges were pursued by some of the women who came forward. For example, Waikato Police Commander Kelvin Powell was charged with the rape of another police officer in the 1980s. The alleged offence took place after the complainant's twenty-first birthday celebrations. She said she had not complained at the time because she knew what happened to rape complainants in the witness stand, "especially ones who had been drinking." She also thought a complaint would end her career, which had only just begun. The defendant in this case was acquitted.

In late 2005, investigators conducted an audit of police computer systems as part of a probe into police culture sparked by a string of damaging controversies around the police in 2004, including the historical rape charges being laid against longstanding and senior current and former officers.[21] The result of the audit was that 327 staff members were found to have around five thousand pornographic images stored on their computers, taking up to 20 percent of the police computer storage capacity. As a consequence of this audit, disciplinary and criminal investigations were conducted against individual officers.

Ultimately, there were three criminal trials involving Shipton and Schollum (now ex-police officers), and in two of these cases Rickards was also charged. The first involved a woman who had been living in Australia and read about Louise Nicholas while she was back in New

had been manipulated. She said that one of her reasons for coming forward publicly with her story was that people did not believe Nicholas' baton allegations. She requested anonymity, but was named in the media and three months later committed suicide.

20 One woman, for example, whom Shipton knew had been sexually abused as a child, said she received frequent visits from him demanding sex. She went to the police station to complain and was in the waiting room alone when another officer came and told her that he knew why she was there and to get out. She fled the station and changed addresses several times afterwards.

21 See Julia Tolmie, "Police Negligence in Domestic Violence Cases and the Canadian Case of Mooney: What Should Have Happened, and Could it Happen in New Zealand?" [2006] NZ Rev 243 at 249–51. For example, other scandals included the negligent handling of a 111 call by a young woman, Iraena Asher, who has not been seen since the night she called the police asking for help. The number of cases in which the police did not log, did not record accurately, or did not respond promptly or efficiently to emergency calls resulted in an independent review of the police call centre and sixty-one recommendations for improvement. See Michael Corboy *et al*, *Communications Centres Service Centre Independent External Review: final report* (New Zealand Police, 11 May 2005).

Zealand for a holiday.[22] Two of the men involved — Shipton and Schollum — had been party to her rape by a group of men in Mount Maunganui in 1989, which also involved violating her with a police baton. She contacted the police and supplied the names of four of the five men who she said had assaulted her. The four conceded that sex had taken place,[23] but said that it was consensual. They were found guilty of rape, but were acquitted on the charges involving the violation with a baton. Subsequently, one of these men was then able to successfully appeal the rape charges and plead guilty instead to abduction.[24]

In March of 2006, Louise Nicholas was the complainant in a trial that involved Rickards, Schollum, and Shipton.[25] The public was not permitted to know that Shipton and Schollum were already serving sentences for the rape of another woman. The three men admitted sex (although not with a police baton), but said that it was consensual. They were acquitted of all twenty charges against them.

In February of 2007, there was a third trial involving another woman with respect to the same three men.[26] The prosecution had tried to have this complainant's case heard with Louise Nicholas' case, because of the factual similarities between the two, but had been unsuccessful.[27] The complainant had had a sexual relationship with Shipton in the mid 1980s. She said that, during this time, Schollum, Shipton, and Rickards once took her to a house, handcuffed her, and violated her with a bottle. She did not contact the police about this incident. Instead, the police found her while investigating Nicholas' complaint when they called her number in Shipton's phone book. Next to her name and number Shipton had written the words "milk bottle." In a devastating pretrial ruling, the judge held that the note of her name and number with the words

22 See the account in *Louise Nicholas: My Story*, *supra* note 1 at 155–57.

23 There were tapes recording the men's conversation about the day in question, which were damaging for the defence although not completely incriminating. The Crown offered the defendants the choice that, either they conceded that group sex had taken place, or the tapes would be admitted.

24 He was able to appeal and to obtain a retrial on the basis of the testimony of two witnesses, who were subsequently charged with perverting the course of justice because of allegations that they had fabricated their testimony in this case. He was not re-tried; he pleaded guilty to abduction in exchange for having the rape charges dropped.

25 *Louise Nicholas: My Story*, *supra* note 1 at 197–202.

26 *Ibid* at 214–17.

27 The New Zealand Court of Appeal overturned the trial judge's decision to hear the cases together on the basis that this created a risk of prejudice to the accused (*ibid* at 177).

"milk bottle" written next to it was not admissible in evidence because the violation took place in 1984 and the notebook was dated 1986. This meant that any link was "'speculative' and would seriously prejudice Shipton's right to a fair trial."[28] Moreover, recent complainant evidence was not admitted on the basis that the then sixteen-year-old had had a chance to tell her mother before speaking to her best friend.[29] She had therefore not complained of the assault at the first reasonably available opportunity.[30] The result of this case was that all three men were found not guilty of all charges.

There was public outrage after the three verdicts were delivered and all of the information about the cases came to light. Effectively, three women had independently made similar allegations of pre-planned group rape, including violation with objects, by serving police officers, largely the same men, while they were teenagers in the same geographical location during the same period of time. Only two of the men had been convicted, and only with respect to one complainant. None of the men had been held accountable for a single object violation.

In May of 2007, Dewar was tried with respect to four charges of "attempting to obstruct, prevent, pervert or defeat the course of justice" related to his behaviour in suppressing Nicholas' sexual assault complaints, manipulating her during the police review, and giving inadmissible hearsay evidence at the Brown trials. He was found guilty.

Media attention in New Zealand focussed again on the issue of sexual violence when, in January of 2008, another high profile New Zealander — Tea Ropati (a former rugby league star) — was acquitted of six offences, including rape and unlawful sexual connection. On this occasion, the media was less sympathetic to the complainant. Much was made of her alcohol and drug use and the police came under some public criticism for even prosecuting Mr Ropati. The day after his acquittal, Ropati's lawyer, Gary Gottlieb QC, was reported as suggesting that the prosecution was irresponsible and that the trial process is "bloody PC" and "so anti-male it's not funny."[31]

28 *Ibid* at 215.

29 "I wondered just how many 16 year olds would really want to tell their mother that they have been violated by a bottle by serving police officers" (*ibid* at 215).

30 Ted Thomas, "Was Eve Merely Framed; Or Was She Forsaken?" [1994] NZLJ 368; *R v H*, [1997] 1 NZLR 673, per Thomas J. But see section 35 of the *Evidence Act 2006* (NZ). Julia Tolmie, "Women and the Criminal Justice System" in Julia Tolmie & Warren Brookbanks, eds, *Criminal Justice in New Zealand* (LexisNexis, 2007) 295 at 316–17.

31 Andrew Koubardis & Alanah Eriksen, "Ropati Lawyer Hits at Police" *New Zealand Herald* (1 February 2008) A1. Mr Gotlieb also made the implausible suggestion that

In spite of these remarks, Mr Ropati's acquittal was yet another illustration of how difficult it is to achieve convictions in New Zealand cases involving sexual violence. The evidence in the case seemed particularly solid. The complainant was so drunk that she was unconscious at the time that the offence took place — which means that, by definition, she was not consenting to sexual activity — and it seems implausible that the defendant did not know this to be the case.[32] Certainly, even if he was so obtuse that he did not notice that she was unconscious at the time and believed she was consenting, it is difficult to see how he had reasonable grounds for his belief, which must be demonstrated in New Zealand if the *mens rea* for sexual violation is to be negated.[33] The defendant's intoxication has never been accepted in criminal law as an excuse for failing to meet a negligence standard.[34] The victim had physical trauma to her genital and anal area and there was actual security video footage of Mr Ropati being sexual with her at some point earlier in the evening while she was clearly fading in and out of consciousness.[35]

Interestingly, Mr Ropati was permitted during the course of the trial to introduce testimony from high-profile, long-standing *male* friends to the effect that he was always respectful of women in his social dealings with them and this testimony was uncritically covered by the media. Aside from being irrelevant to what took place on the night in question, this testimony was incredible. Even in Mr Ropati's version of events, an argument four months into his marriage resulted in his departure from the matrimonial home to be sexual with a stranger whom he had picked up in a bar. It is impossible to tell how influential this testimony was in the minds of the jurors, although it is clear that Ropati's acquittal was not straightforward, as it took twelve hours in deliberation.

the complainant alleged rape because she was embarrassed by what had happened. Subjecting herself to the humiliating public scrutiny and speculation that accompanied the trial hardly seems like something that someone who was "embarrassed" would put themselves through. Andrew Koubardis, "Case 'absolute rubbish' say supporters, as Ropati freed" *New Zealand Herald* (31 January 2008); TV3 News Story, "Police defend decision to prosecute Ropati," online: www.nzherald.co.nz.

32 Sections 128, 128A(3) and (4) of the *Crimes Act 1961* (NZ).

33 In other words, New Zealand effectively has a negligence standard of *mens rea* for sexual violation (rape or unlawful sexual connection). Sections 128(2) and (3) of the *Crimes Act 1961* (NZ) define the *mens rea* for sexual violation as being "without believing on reasonable grounds that person B [the complainant] consents to the connection."

34 See *R v Clarke*, [1992] 1 NZLR 147.

35 Catherine Masters, Joanna Hunkin & David Eames, "Dicing with Drink" *New Zealand Herald* (2 February 2008) B1.

THE FALL OUT

Aside from the cases that were actually won and lost, what were the consequences of Louise Nicholas' courageous actions? One could look at the media coverage of and the jury decision in the *Ropati* case and conclude that not much progress had been made in educating the public, the legal profession, or the judiciary about the gendered realities of sexual violence or the difficulty of prosecuting sexual offences, in spite of the public anger that followed the acquittals in her case. And I think that is a fair comment. However, the consequences of her public stand are still unfolding.

Clint Rickards will never be the New Zealand Police Commissioner.[36] He was stood down on full pay when the story first broke and resigned years later once the criminal trials were complete, but before his police disciplinary hearing was held.[37] Although he has been acquitted of all criminal charges, it is clear that public opinion has condemned his actions.[38]

Furthermore, as a direct consequence of Louise Nicholas' stand, there have been a significant number of public inquiries and research projects covering a wide range of issues surrounding sexual violence. The first was a Commission of Inquiry into Police Conduct, headed by

36 He was, at the time the scandal erupted, the Auckland Central Police Commander. He was also Assistant Police Commissioner and considered next in line for the penultimate job of Police Commissioner.

37 Patrick Glover, "$19M bill to taxpayer for police sex scandal" *New Zealand Herald* (27 November 2008) online: www.nzherald.co.nz. Rickards engaged in an angry outburst outside the court after the last verdict was handed down in which he attacked the Operation Austin investigation as a "shambles" and said that Shipton and Schollum were good friends of his who should not be in prison for rape. Had he kept quiet at this point, the police would have been in an embarrassing position regarding his employment status because Rickards had been repeatedly promoted in spite of his employment record that stated he had had sex with teenagers as an acting officer. The police were therefore unable to use this behaviour as grounds for terminating his employment. Once he had been acquitted of rape charges, there may have been no grounds for terminating his employment or demoting him.

38 While he was suspended on full pay, he completed a law degree and applied to the Auckland District Law Society to become a practising lawyer. They passed his application on to the New Zealand Law Society who eventually held that he was a "fit and proper person" to practice law. During the public debate surrounding this decision, the *New Zealand Herald* polled its readers to find that 89 percent felt that he should not be admitted. See Craig Borley, "Rickards Faces Hurdle to Become Lawyer" *New Zealand Herald* (2 September 2008) online: www.nzherald.co.nz.

Dame Margaret Bazley,[39] which released its report in April of 2007.[40] The commission found 313 complaints of sexual assault made against 222 police officers from 1979 to 2005. It made sixty wide-reaching recommendations for the reform of police practises and processes around the sexual conduct of individual officers, as well as their handling of sexual violence cases.[41]

The report has a number of strengths. One of these is the recognition that the problems experienced by women such as Louise Nicholas go beyond the issue of individual "bad apples" in the police force and involve the culture of the force itself.[42] Implicitly, it is recognized in the report that phenomena like the amount of pornography passing through police computers during work time cannot be severed from the

39 Information about the links to the "Mr. Asia" drug syndicate that Dame Bazley's husband, Steve Bazley, had during the 1970s and 1980s was released to the media during the Commission of Inquiry. Dame Bazley's lawyer alleged that Clint Rickards, Brad Shipton, and Bob Schollum had hired a private investigator to attempt to discredit her role as head of the Commission of Inquiry. The claim was denied by Rickards' lawyer, Arnold Karen. See "Police Conduct Inquiry into Bazleys Haunted by Past" *Sunday Star Times* (15 April 2009) online: www.sundaystartimes.co.nz.

40 Honourable James Robertson & Dame Margaret Bazley, *Report of the Commission of Inquiry into Police Conduct* (3 April 2007).

41 Including rationalizing police policies, developing a code of conduct for sworn officers, developing guidelines on inappropriate sexual conduct towards members of the public (which include a prohibition on police entering into sexual relationships with a person over whom they are in a position of authority or where there is a power differential), developing police email and computer use policies, improving staff training, making complaint processes more transparent, improving practises for ensuring investigations are independent, management assurance, setting up early warning systems and data bases for staff engaging in inappropriate behaviour, improving community feedback and initiatives through groups of community leaders, and improving the practises of the police complaints authority by, for example, making its processes more accessible and transparent, seeking regular feedback, and reducing backlog.

42 *Report of the Commission of Inquiry into Police Conduct, supra* note 40 at 283–99. Features of police culture generally included a strong bonding among colleagues, a male orientated culture, certain attitudes towards the use of alcohol, and dual standards with respect to on-duty and off-duty behaviour. Inappropriate attitudes that were part of police culture were identified as attitudes that reflected stereotyped views of complainants of sexual assault and raised general doubts about whether police officers may have been prejudiced in their approach to complaints; evidence of a culture of skepticism in dealing with the complainants of sexual assault; evidence of other officers condoning or turning a blind eye to sexual activity of an inappropriate nature by police officers and their associates; evidence that when senior police officers came to investigate complaints they were confronted with a wall of silence from the colleagues of the officers against whom complaints had been made.

attitudes of the police to cases involving sexual violence, for example.[43] The report recommends, amongst other things, that the police:

> increase the numbers of women and those from ethnic minority groups in the police force in order to promote a diverse organizational culture that reflects the community it serves and to enhance the effective and impartial investigation of complaints alleging sexual assault by members of the police.[44]

It suggests that the States Services Commissioner carry out an independent annual "health of the organization" audit of police culture for at least the next ten years, particularly looking at whether the organization provides a safe work environment for female staff and staff from minority groups.[45] In addition, the report recommends that the police seek to strengthen community groups that support sexual assault complainants by actively seeking consistent government funding for these groups.[46] This will have the dual effect of strengthening women's groups working in the field of sexual violence (which currently are hampered in their efforts by the precarious nature of their funding and therefore the amount of effort needed to continuously apply for funding so that they can stay afloat), as well as the police force's relationship with such groups.

In spite of the strengths of the report, it could be said that one of its major weaknesses is that responsibility is placed on the police force *itself* to implement the majority of the changes.[47] Given that the police commissioner, in his apology to the New Zealand public after the re-

43 The connection is implicit rather than explicit. See *Report of the Commission of Inquiry into Police Conduct*, *supra* note 40 at 11, 21, 256–58.

44 *Ibid* at 22.

45 *Ibid.*

46 *Ibid* at 17: "The New Zealand Police should initiate co-operative action with the relevant Government agencies to seek more consistent Government funding for the support groups involved in assisting the investigation of sexual assault complaints by assisting and supporting complainants."

47 The Commissioner of Police is currently working through the recommendations of the Commission of Inquiry into Police Conduct and making quarterly reports on the implementation of these recommendations. So far, the police have taken measures like introducing a new New Zealand Police Code of Conduct and forming the New Zealand Police Adult Sexual Assault — Core Reference Group, a body of subject matter experts who will focus on the police role in responding to sexual assault. See *Fourth Quarterly Report on the Implementation of Recommendations by the Ministry of Justice and the Independent Police Conduct Authority as of 31 March 2008.*

lease of the report, implied that the issue was one of renegade officers,[48] it is questionable whether there will be the necessary institutional commitment by the police to the scale of the changes identified as needed. It therefore remains to be seen if the response of the police will be one of "impression management" — a phrase coined by the judge who decided Jane Doe's claim of sex discrimination — as opposed to a serious commitment to a change in police culture around the issue of sexual violence.[49]

In May of 2008, the Law Commission released its review of the law concerning the extent to which a jury in a criminal trial is made aware of the prior convictions of an accused person and allegations of similar offending on their part.[50] The commission received this reference as a result of public anger about the fact that the jury had not been permitted to know that Schollum and Shipton had been convicted of similar offences with respect to another complainant when they were tried for sexual offences with respect to Nicholas and the third complainant. Significantly, although the commission's response to its particular terms of reference was disappointingly conservative,[51] it expressed strong dis-

48 After the report was released, the Commissioner of Police at the time, Howard Broad, said, "I find it difficult to express in words my feelings about these people for they have caused immeasurable damage to a number of New Zealanders that they had sworn to protect. I unreservedly and unequivocally apologise to the women who were caught up in the actions of *those few officers* [emphasis mine]. I acknowledge the hurt and harm that's been done and the grief that's been caused to you, your families and supporters. To the women of New Zealand I say: I have been disgusted and sickened, as you will be, by the behaviour put before the Commission of Inquiry in many of the files that covered some 25 years of our recent history" (3 April 2007) online <http://www.police.govt.nz> (last accessed 27 July 2009).

49 See *The Story of Jane Doe, supra* note 7 at Chapter 30 at 301.

50 *Disclosure to Court of Defendants Previous Convictions, Similar Offending and Bad Character* (NZLC R103), Wellington, New Zealand.

51 The commission recommended no legal changes on the basis that, although the law on the admissibility of previous convictions that applied prior to 1 August 2007 was unduly restrictive, the *Evidence Act 2006* possibly changed the law. It was proposed that the commission should monitor the case law implementing the new provisions in order to assess whether further legal reform was needed, and report back to the government by the end of February 2010. The Right Honourable EW Thomas argued in his submission to the commission ("Submissions to the Law Commission in Response to the Issues Paper: 'Disclosure to Court of Defendants Previous Convictions, Similar Offending and Bad Character'" 11 February 2008) that there are compelling reasons to treat sexual offences differently and to inform the jury of the defendant's convictions for similar offending in such cases. These reasons include the facts that the credibility of the complainant is a central issue in such cases, that the evidence often comes down to the complainant's word against the defendant's because such of-

quiet about the role of the adversarial process in sexual violence cases even though this issue did not form part of its original terms of reference. It noted the low reporting[52] and conviction rates[53] for sexual offences, as well as the brutalizing nature of the trial process as experienced by sexual assault victims, and expressed the opinion that there could be value in investigating whether the adversarial system should be modified or replaced with some alternative model for sex offences.[54]

Perhaps the most important work, however, is being currently undertaken by a Taskforce for Action on Sexual Violence[55] set up in July of 2007 to lead and coordinate multi-agency action on sexual violence. The taskforce brings together a number of government agencies and community groups to address both problematic *societal beliefs and attitudes* about sexual violence, as well as *legislative and procedural* barriers to the reporting, prosecution, and conviction respecting crimes of sexual violence.[56] Te Ohaakii a Hine-National Network Ending Sexual Violence Together is a taskforce member and represents seventy to eighty of the organizations, individuals, and academic experts working in the sexual violence sector, including, pleasingly, Jan Jordan whose work I referred to earlier.

A number of organizations affiliated with the taskforce have begun the process of public consultation with respect to various briefs around issues of sexual violence. In August of 2008, the Ministry of Justice released a discussion document, *Improvements to Sexual Violence Legislation in New Zealand*, seeking public submissions on possible changes to

fending generally occurs in private, and the need for fairness to the complainant as well as to the accused, particularly when considering the severe impact of the offence on the complainant, the impact of the trial itself on the complainant, and the impact of an acquittal on the complainant, coupled with the difficulty in getting complainants to report such crimes and in successfully prosecuting such cases.

52 In New Zealand the rate is as low as 12 percent. See A Morris & J Reilly, in collaboration with S Berry & R Ransom, *New Zealand National Survey of Crime Victims 2001* (Wellington: Ministry of Justice, 2003) at 99.

53 See Tolmie, "Women and the Criminal Justice System" *supra* note 30 at 295, 314–15.

54 *Disclosure to Court of Defendants Previous Convictions, Similar Offending and Bad Character*, *supra* note 50 at v-vi.

55 The taskforce will support the Sexual Violence Ministerial Group. The ministerial group consists of the Minister of Justice; Minister of Women's Affairs; Minister of Police; Minister for ACC; and Minister for Maori Affairs. Representatives from these ministries and other key groups have membership on the taskforce.

56 The six key priority areas of the taskforce are prevention, early intervention, recovery and support services, treatment and management of offenders, system responses to sexual offending, and system responses to victims.

improve the way in which the criminal justice system deals with sexual violence. Public opinion is invited on three possible revisions of the law. First, it is proposed to include a positive definition of what amounts to consent to sexual activity, as well as requiring that, when determining whether the accused had reasonable grounds to believe that the complainant consented to sexual activity, the court must have regard to any steps the accused may have taken to ascertain whether the complainant was consenting.[57] Second, it is proposed to extend the "rape shield laws" to cover evidence about previous sexual experience between the complainant and the accused.[58] Third, opinion is sought on whether the adversarial system of justice is the best system for sexual assault cases, and whether prosecutors and judges should handle sexual assault cases differently from other cases.[59]

In 2008, the Ministry for Women's Affairs, in partnership with the Ministry of Justice and the New Zealand Police, commenced a two-year research project aimed at improving support services for survivors of sexual abuse.[60]

It is a little too soon to comment on the effects of all of the work undertaken in response to Louise Nicholas' public stand. Although some of this work has been completed, most of it is still in progress and it remains to be seen what the outcome of the different research and

57 In New Zealand, for sexual connection to constitute sexual assault, it must have taken place without the complainant's consent and it must be established that the accused "did not believe on reasonable grounds that the complainant consented to the sexual connection" (Section 128 of the *Crimes Act 1961*, (NZ)). Complainants say that the focus on the reasonableness of the defendant's belief in their consent puts intense inquiry on their behaviour rather than keeping the focus on the defendant's behaviour. The proposed law changes are to remind the jury that consent is not a default option and to shift the jury focus back to the accused.

58 In New Zealand, the law currently is that no evidence can be given, or question asked, relating to the complainant's sexual experience with any person other than the defendant, except with the permission of the judge. No evidence can be given, or question asked, on the reputation of the complainant in sexual matters (Section 44 of the *Evidence Act 2006*, (NZ)).

59 Alternative options include inquisitorial justice, restorative justice (where appropriate), specialist support people, coordinated and tailored multi-agency responses, specialized police responses, specialist courts, and specialized Crown prosecution units.

60 Ministry of Women's Affairs, *Restoring Soul: Effective Contraventions for Adult Victim/Survivors of Sexual Violence* (Wellington: Ministry of Women's Affairs, 2009). The project has four work streams: a literature review on best practises for agencies that respond to survivors of sexual abuse; a study of sexual violence attrition in New Zealand; an environmental scan of systems and agencies available to survivors; and interviews with survivors to determine how they seek help and cope with their experiences.

consultation processes will be. Since this work began, there has also been a change of government in New Zealand and it is not yet clear whether the new conservative government will have the same commitment as the previous government to addressing the chronically low levels of reporting, prosecution, and conviction in New Zealand cases of sexual violence.[61]

CONCLUSION

As I noted in the introduction to this chapter, Jane Doe's litigation was more radical than anything that occurred in New Zealand in Louise Nicholas' trials and those of associated complainants. The immediate outcomes of the various legal actions taken in New Zealand have been a great deal less positive than those in Canada. The best that can be hoped for now is that the less immediate outcomes — the results of the various investigations that have taken place in response to Louise Nicholas' public stand — will make a real and lasting difference to the experience of complainants of sexual assault in the New Zealand criminal justice system, as well as the prosecution's success in securing convictions in deserving cases.

My own view is that many of the proposed reforms may make some difference to the experience of complainants in sexual violence cases traversing the justice system (which is a very good thing), but are unlikely to make an enormous difference to the difficulties experienced in securing convictions in these types of cases. This is because the most significant reforms needed are not so much legal reforms but reforms in the attitudes and perceptions of society, as manifested in the decisions of the New Zealand police, lawyers, judges, and juries in these types of cases.

61 Note that the new Minister of Justice has referred the issue of whether or not an inquisitorial model should be adopted for sexual violence cases to the New Zealand Law Commission and has indicated that he is considering making the other changes based on the Ministry of Justice's original Discussion Paper as part of a tougher stance on law and order. See Simon Power, "The Criminal Justice System: Reform is Coming," online: <http://www.behive.govt.nz> (last accessed 27 July 2009). What is problematic is that it is not clear from his speech whether the current minister actually has a grasp of what the current law is, or what the original proposals for reform were. For example, the speech proposes to make "evidence about previous sexual relationships between the complainant and any person inadmissible without prior agreement of the judge." The original proposal that this suggestion is borrowed from is, as noted above, a proposal to extend the existing ban on evidence of the complainant's previous sexual relationships to the relationship between the complainant and the defendant.

First, there appears to be a perception that certain sexual violations, because of the manner and context in which they take place, are not really rapes, *even when they fit within the legal definition of rape or sexual assault.* Even if the victim is believed (and victims may struggle with credibility in such cases, particularly where they are intoxicated or have had a prior relationship with the defendant), it is perceived that she may have felt violated and she may *even* have failed to consent, but what occurred was more in the nature of "non-consensual sex" or "consensual but unwanted sex" than rape. It was a travesty of justice in my opinion, for example, that Tea Ropati was not convicted on the evidence that was apparently available in that case and the clear wording of section 128 of the *Crimes Act 1961* (NZ). What this means is that there are types of male sexual behaviour and male obtuseness to which we do not want, as a community, to apply the label "criminal," even though such behaviours appear to fall within the definitions of criminal law. The result of protecting male obtuseness in certain social situations as "normal" or non-deviant or understandable, particularly when the victim was vulnerable because of her level of intoxication, is to put the burden and cost of managing predatory male sexuality on the women exposed to it, rather than on the men who engage in it. This is a more pressing issue than further reforms to the current criminal laws.[62] Another more pressing issue is the kinds of credibility issues[63] that women struggle with in cases of sexual assault, particularly because these cases hinge on the credibility of the complainant.

Second, an attitude change is also needed in the New Zealand judiciary (with some notable exceptions). The strong emphasis given to the due process rights of the defendant in sexual violence cases places many unreal and overzealous obstacles in the way of the jury fully and fairly appraising the facts when determining the verdict, as demonstrated by the Louise Nicholas and companion trials. A move towards

62 Although the introduction of a positive definition of consent, and a mandated inquiry into what the defendant did to actually secure the consent of the victim, might shift more of the jury focus onto the defendant's responsibility for ensuring that he actually has his partner's consent before proceeding with sex, it is unlikely to change fundamental community attitudes, manifest in jury decisions, which appear to balk at viewing certain forms of predatory male sexual behaviour as criminal.

63 However, it is true that the extension of the rape shield laws to cover evidence of a prior relationship between the complainant and the defendant may be of assistance in bolstering the complainant's credibility in some cases. Note also the criticisms offered by EW Thomas in "Submissions to the Ministry of Justice Taskforce for Action on Sexual Violence" (2007, copy on file with author) at 23–24.

a more flexible and open model of justice might go some way towards preventing the harm that is done when, in the interests of avoiding the conviction of one innocent man, nine guilty men walk free to continue preying on the community.[64]

64 It is often said (usually in the context of discussing the burden and standards of proof in criminal trials) that it is better for nine guilty men to walk free than for one innocent man to be convicted.

4. Hockey Night in Canada

Laura Robinson

While the preceding chapters in this section explore the promise and peril of using law to confront the role of police and policing in sexual assault, Laura Robinson's chapter looks at another institution implicated in sexual assault — Canada's national sport, hockey. Laura's account of the trials of David Frost, a junior hockey coach, for sexual assaults committed against girls — employees, fans, and girlfriends of his players — picks up on Julia Tolmie's point that social definitions of "real rape" often override what are otherwise clear criminal law violations. Laura allocates responsibility for the failure of these prosecutions not to the evidence or to the law, but to police, prosecutors, and judges, as does Julia Tolmie. She also connects the hyper-masculinity of hockey violence to practices of sexual coercion as well as to the way that even prosecutors protected each other and the system, forcing the young women to take the stand as witnesses, not complainants, thereby losing their anonymity, and calling their violations "consensual."

> Last night when I was sleeping, Dave came and woke up me up and said why don't you wanna make Shel happy? Then I'm like whatta mean? Then he goes you can make him happy by letting me fuck you then he will fuck you. Then I said if that is the only way he will not be a prick any more than fuck him. SO Dave left and then they both came back in the room. Then Shel asked me I said no then he kept bugging me finally I said I do not care. So I just laid there. Shel tried to kiss me and stuff but I just kep pushing him away. They both just fucked me then left the room. I started crying my eyes out. How bad was I used last night? Then when Shel came in to go to bed I was still crying so I got up to go downstairs. He asked what was wrong. I said it does not matter how I feel as long as YOUR happy. I said it really smart and walked out. I felt so sick and dirty ya know? Anyways I'll call Stac and tell her.... I just tried to cal Stac but there is no answer. I will try later. Do not write about the sex thing on this email address. I am going to try and get my own email then you can email me there about it ok?[1]

1 Email contained in a statement given to Napanee Ontario Provincial Police by Witness Two, 9 March 2007, p. 6, line 176.

This is an excerpt from an email sent on 12 August 1998 by one of three female witnesses in the trial of former hockey coach and NHL player agent David Frost, who was tried and acquitted on four counts of touching for a sexual purpose. The trial was the latest chapter in a litany of chapters detailing the rape culture of Canadian hockey. The complicated details of this case can be found in the coverage by the *Toronto Sun*'s Steve Simmons, the *Toronto Star*'s Rosie DiMano, and *The Globe and Mail*'s Christie Blatchford, or my coverage at www.playthe game.org.

What was apparent to all the journalists at the trial was how the "justice" system utterly failed the young women. These women endured this rape culture during the 1996–97 season when Frost "coached" the Quinte Hawks, a junior hockey team, in the small town of Deseronto in eastern Ontario. One young woman, who I will refer to as Witness One, endured forced sex with Frost and various hockey players for six years. She witnessed many other girls being forced to do this too. So widespread was the practice of hockey players luring girls to their hotel room and then insisting they have sex with multiple partners, starting with Frost, that after he was charged with the original twelve sex crime charges and one assault charge on 23 August 2006, Frost was forbidden to contact forty women, most of whom had been girls in the time period of the alleged offences.

I am purposely using the word "girl" as opposed to the phrase "young woman" because the dozens of females who found themselves in Room 22 at the Bay View Hotel in Deseronto were between the ages of twelve and sixteen. They lived in a small, conservative town where there was no hockey yet for females — in many respects it could still be the 1950s in terms of what the municipality offered girls and women. Some of the girls may have physically looked like older teenagers, but in this period they were girls. By the time they gave evidence at the trial of David Frost, they were young women.

No charges were laid relating to the alleged sexual assaults that took place outside of Deseronto despite evidence given by a minimum of *two* women witnesses who said they witnessed or were part of sexual acts with Frost and hockey players in other locations until 2001. There appears to have been no investigation of the role the players had as pimps for Frost, luring in girls under the guise of promising to be their hockey player boyfriend, whether the players were in Deseronto or in other locations.

BACKGROUND

Frost came to the team in November of 1996 and brought his four favourite players with him from Brampton, Ontario. By this time, he had been banned from the then Metro Toronto Hockey League (now the Greater Toronto Hockey League) after he was caught committing fraud in hockey-related business. He was also seen as an intimidating, punishing coach of boys between the ages of ten and fifteen. When his favourite boys moved up in age categories, Frost followed them as coach. Despite the ban and his reputation, Frost appeared to be untouchable. This could have been in part because he co-coached his Brampton team with Bob Goodenow, who was at that time executive director of the NHL Players' Association. Goodenow's son John was on the team. Frost's untouchable status was likely a combination of Goodenow's presence behind the bench and because the culture of hockey allows for the public abuse — both emotional and physical — of young males, and allows coaches a high degree of "private" time with their players in locker rooms where the edict "what happens in the locker room stays in the locker room" is law.

In the case of this trial, the locker room moved to Room 22 at the Bay View Hotel in Deseronto where Frost had a suite with three of his players: two sixteen-year-olds and a nineteen-year-old. From there, Frost set up what Erving Goffman calls a "total institution" in that the subculture of the team and of Room 22 had its own set of rules and schedules determined independently from the larger culture surrounding them. Goffman described a total institution in the following way:

> The central feature of total institutions can be described as a breakdown of the kinds of barriers ordinarily separating these three [where we sleep, where we work, and where we play] spheres of life. First, all aspects of life are conducted in the same place and under the same single authority. Second, each phase of the member's daily activity will be carried out in the immediate company of a large batch of others, all of whom are treated alike and required to do the same thing together. Third, all phases of the day's activities are tightly scheduled, with one activity leading at a prearranged time into the next, the whole circle of activities being imposed from above through a system of explicit formal rulings and a body of officials. Finally, the contents of the various enforced activities are brought together as parts of a single overall rational plan purportedly designed to fulfill the official aims of the institution.[2]

2 "On the Characteristics of Total Institutions," in Erving Goffman, *Asylums: Essays on the Social Situation of Mental Patients and Other Inmates* (New York: Random House, 1961) 1 at 6.

In his doctorate at the University of California, Berkeley, sport sociologist Steven Ortiz found that all of the above characteristics described professional male sport teams. He translated these characteristics to male sport teams by factoring in the mobile nature of teams as they travel, calling them mobile total institutions. What matters most to sport teams is not location, but rather the presence of the coach, a team that obeys the "rules" and the psychological and physical power the team and coach command over any space they occupy.[3]

It is difficult to write about hockey as a total institution in Canada because there is such a pro-hockey bias in the media and amongst many Canadians. Organized, elite Canadian hockey, such as the NHL, CHL, junior provincial leagues, and rep leagues have never accepted that these characteristics are fundamental to the team experience, despite significant evidence that in many instances there is a cult-like relationship in hockey circles. For instance, while the events in Deseronto unfolded in the 1996–97 season, the biggest sports story of the year was uncovered in Swift Current, Saskatchewan. Swift Current Broncos' coach Graham James pled guilty to 350 charges of sexual assault after his former player, Sheldon Kennedy, who by then played in the NHL, went to police about the abuse he suffered from age fourteen to eighteen. It was impossible to pick up a newspaper sports section or watch sports TV during that season without knowing about the James/Kennedy case. Soon after, a pedophile ring run out of Maple Leaf Gardens was exposed. This too occupied the media for months. Despite the evidence that hockey can be a dangerous place for boys off the ice as well as on it, no one intervened when, during the same season, Frost moved into Room 22 with his entourage of teenage players. No one intervened when great amounts of alcohol were brought into the room, raucous parties took place, and many local girls ended up there.

While there were officially four inhabitants of the suite, many players stayed there. At the helm of all that happened in Room 22 was David Frost. North Americans know Frost best as the coach and then agent of NHL player Michael Danton, who was Michael Jefferson until, under Frost's coaching, he became estranged from his family and eventually legally changed his name. In 2004, Danton pled guilty to conspiracy to

3 Steve Mortiz, *When Happiness Ends and Coping Begins: The Private Pain of the Professional Athlete's Wife* (Doct Thesis, Department of Sociology, University of California at Berkeley, 1994) [unpublished]; see also Steven Mortiz, "Traveling With the Ball Club: A Code of Conduct for Wives Only"(1997) 20 Symbolic Interaction 225.

murder charges after trying to have Frost killed in the US. Both men to this day deny that Danton was trying to hire someone to murder Frost.[4]

When the news broke about the conspiracy to murder charges against Danton, Witness One and Witness Two from Deseronto contacted police. They said that many things had happened to them and to the players in Room 22 that were illegal: they had been sexually assaulted by Frost and so had the players. Frost refused to allow sex to take place between players and their girlfriends unless he had the girls first. He also participated in sex when the hockey players were with the girls by assisting them to insert their penises into them or by having the players insert his penis into the girls.

Witness One writes in February of 2009:

> After Mike was arrested I was upset and sad and so emotional. My fiancee at the time was worried as to why I was so invested and so upset about what had happened so I told him everything that had happened to me and explained to him why I believed that Mike, in his mind, had no other solution to escape from Dave. I explained the control and the things that Dave would make all of us do and he thought it was best to go and talk to the police about it. We called the Napanee OPP station and spoke to an officer whom, once they heard the name Dave Frost, immediately contacted Chris Nicholas [police officer] and he set up an interview with me.[5]

A two-year investigation took place, and on 23 August 2006, Frost was charged with thirteen charges of sexual exploitation. But on 6 March 2007, Crown Attorney Adam Zegouras dropped seven of these charges, six of which concerned the sexual exploitation of the girls:

> This matter, Your Honour, has been reviewed by a number of senior crown counsel, all of whom have reached a similar conclusion. As Your Honour is aware, this has taken a significant time period to do that. There were thousands of pages worth of documents, and hours and hours worth of video tapes that had video recordings that had to be reviewed. After that review

4 See Frost's website <http:/ www.hockeygodonline.com> for evidence of their ongoing relationship and CBC TV's *The Fifth Estate* website for more documentary evidence. When Danton was released from jail in September of 2009, he stated it was his father, not Frost, he was trying to have killed despite the fact it was Frost who was to have come to the house where he arranged for the murder.

5 18 February 2009 email from Witness Two to the author.

> and lengthy discussions, there has been a conclusion that there's insufficient evidence that Mr Frost was in a position of trust or authority with respect to complainants contained in counts seven through 12. As a result, those charges require in law that there be a position of trust or authority for those charges to be grounded. Given that conclusion by a number of crown attorneys, I would ask that counts seven through 12 be endorsed as withdrawn, as no reasonable prospect of conviction exists on those grounds.[6]

When two of the female complainants (Witness One and Witness Two) were told, prior to the 7 March 2007 hearing that the Crown was planning on dropping all the charges concerning assaults against them, but not those charges on behalf of the players, they were devastated. They say they had received virtually no updates from any of the many Crowns who passed their file from one to another. In February of 2009, Witness One wrote:

> I didn't get a lot of information about how the investigation was going or anything about the charges. I found out the charges were dropped by one of the Crowns on our first and only meeting with him before he dropped the case. He told us that because of the charge 'sexual exploitation' which involves an authority figure committing sexual advances etc. on a child he has authority over and Dave technically did not have authority over us, they had to drop the charges. It was so devastating because I KNOW that I am a victim and for the judges, or the decision makers to dismiss it so callously really irritated and angered me. It was actually pretty hard to continue on with the case knowing that so much of my private life was going to be 'assaulted' — in a way — and I was not considered a victim. It made me sick to my stomach. I wanted to see justice served for Dave and I had to continue on to help get closure.[7]

There are many questions that need to be asked in this case. The first is why the police simply did not charge Frost with sexual assault of the girls, as opposed to sexual exploitation. Clearly Frost was in a position of trust, authority, and power over the players, so sexual exploitation charges were correct in his relationship with them. These cases presented a different difficulty for the prosecutors because the players categorically denied he ever touched them sexually. Frost also ran

6 *R v David Frost*, Proceedings before the Honourable Mr Justice GJ Griffin, 6 March 2007 (Napanee, ON, File #: 2001-998-06-700273).

7 19 February 2009 email from Witness Two to the author.

the hockey school where Witness One worked for an entire summer in Brampton, Ontario, making him her boss. She says the police decided that since someone else owned the hockey school (who Witness One says she saw twice all summer, while she had to work for and report to Frost and live in the same house as him daily), technically he was not in authority over her.

Upon being told that the Crown was going to drop all charges relating to the abuse of females, Witness One and Witness Two went through all their belongings from the 1996–97 season and found evidence, such as the email above and the diary of Witness Two that held very intimate sexual notations, and gave them to the police. Later, the authenticity of this evidence was called into question, not only by the defence, but even by Judge Griffin because it was surmised that the complainants, by the time the trial rolled around in the fall of 2008, were possibly colluding against Frost and that Witness One was the mastermind behind the collusion.

In February of 2009, Witness One wrote:

> I did not give the diary to the police. Kristy called me one night very upset and she told me that she found her diary from when all of that stuff was going on. She was embarrassed by her immaturity and stupidity and asked me if she should hand it in. She was very hesitant because it was so embarrassing for her. I told her that it would be a good idea to hand it in because it may help the case and she asked me to call Chris and let him know that she had found a diary. I did call Chris [OPP officer] and how it got into the OPP's hands I do not know. The email was also submitted by Kristy, she called me and read them to me and forwarded them on to the OPP.[8]

Operative in this prosecution was the assumption that this woman could not possibly have been a victim because she had had sex when she was sixteen, she had had multiple partners, and she was strong enough, at the age of twenty-eight, to speak clearly and without shame in a courtroom about her experiences. At one point, quite unrelated to his train of questions, Crown Attorney Sandy Tse made Witness Two state that the sex she had had was consensual. She had testified that she "felt uncomfortable with it, but ... I felt kind of pressured to do it," with reference to having sex with Frost. She added that she "didn't want to do it again, but finally I got persuaded into it." She testified that she was "placed" on top of Frost by one of his players who stood behind her,

8 20 February 2009 email from Witness Two to the author.

and told to wrap her arms around him as he stood behind her while she was on top of Frost. Both she and Witness One spoke of being afraid and shaking, and wanting it to be over as soon as possible. They each testified that Frost had put a hockey player's penis into her vagina, or a hockey player had put Frost's penis into her vagina. The sexual exploitation charges laid on behalf of the players were based on this evidence from Witness One and Witness Two.

This case went through a total of eight Crown Attorneys before it landed on Tse's desk. His pointed question to Witness Two, to ensure that she said under oath that she had consented, appeared to be a way to protect the collective justice system, starting with the police, who had laid sexual exploitation instead of sexual abuse charges, and then of his colleagues in the Crown's office who, instead of advising the laying of the correct charges, dropped the sexual exploitation charges and turned the girls into witnesses. Once they were witnesses and not complainants, they lost the benefit of the publication ban on their identities. Their names were then attached to their very sexually explicit testimony and to exhibits that chronicled what happened to them during the 1996-97 hockey season in Deseronto.

The legal logic here, in terms of consent, is that there could not be consent when it comes to men and boys (coach and players) who touch one another, but no one, including Crown Attorney Sandy Tse and the seven Crowns before him, questioned the purported "consent" of the girls. It was as if any vagina that found its way into a hotel room was automatically consenting to sex. It did not matter that the men and boys in the hotel room called all the shots, creating a perfect storm for Ortiz's mobile total institution in which the girls were trapped. It did not matter that the hotel room was the home base of Frost and his players and that the girls were only allowed in with their permission, and only if they agreed to do everything they were told to do once in the room. It did not even occur to the Crowns or Judge Griffin that the reason why Frost and his hockey players had to force each other's penises into the girls was because the bodies of both girls rejected being entered. Their bodies had not consented to sex. The closing of a vagina to a penis somehow was not a sign that the owner of the vagina did not want to have sex. This case shows that we need to think about how the legal system understands the female body, the social coercion of the patriarchal nature of sport, and consent.

Witness One wrote in February of 2009:

> To think that the sex was consensual makes me want to throw up! I agreed to it yes, but I was bullied, controlled, manipulated and forced into saying

yes. They did ask me if I said yes and I did say yes.... But they never asked WHY I said yes...[9]

COURTROOM ATMOSPHERE

The assumption that consent was freely given by the girls was part of an atmosphere in the courtroom that was, at best, disturbing. Judge Griffin exhibited a clubby, folksy relationship with male witnesses and professionals. Listen to the tone of the courtroom banter on 6 March 2007 when all charges concerning alleged assaults against the girls were dropped:

> Crown Attorney Adam Zegouras: You Honour, Mr Clifford is here from Mr Edelson's[10] office.
>
> Justice Geoffrey Griffin: Mr Clifford. Oh, long time no see. How are things?
>
> Vincent Clifford: Fine, thank you, your Honour. Good to see you.
>
> Justice Griffin: You look well. You obviously do, very successful. That is no surprise.[11]

This chummy atmosphere continued as Justice Griffin welcomed hockey players as witnesses, asking them about their season, offering his opinions on this year's professional season, etc. One player no longer played, but had become an RCMP officer in Manitoba. For Judge Griffin, this was just as good as he bantered back and forth about that profession. He also singled out *Toronto Sun* journalist Steve Simmons from the large crowd of journalists, mostly women, and asked him about the football game from the day before.

Judge Griffin's conduct changed when three female witnesses were on the stand. There was no banter; the chummy boy's club atmosphere was long gone. Two of these young women were complainants until the Crown dropped the charges. The Crown had asked that their names be kept confidential; Judge Griffin ruled their names could be used in the media. Judge Griffin appeared to have a fatherly troubled look while the young women testified. One said that she had brought a bottle of bubblebath to Room 22 after she had been coerced over the phone to

9 20 February 2009 email from Witness Two to author.

10 Mr Edelson is Michael Edelson, who acted on behalf of David Frost since 2001. Vincent Clifford is his law partner and was representing Frost as his defence lawyer.

11 *R v Frost*, *supra* note 5 at 1.

"try a threesome." As she continued her testimony, Griffin interjected with "I'm still back with the bubblebath."[12]

Judge Griffin did not only rely on sexist assumptions. He also made mistakes in his decision, abetted by the silence of Sandy Tse, the Crown Attorney. In his "Analysis," Judge Griffin started, "One aspect of this case that I found to be of interest is that all of the young people, whether hockey players or girlfriends, from the 1996–97 Quinte Hawks hockey season, have gone on to be productive members of our society. They are leading pro-social and effective lives..."[13] This statement simply was not true. Judge Griffin himself, in his decision, cited "the significant amount of evidence in this case that exposed a dark and very unhealthy side of hockey, where young women are used as sexual playthings. Defence counsel referred to it as the misogyny of the hockey world. Such treatment by men of women is extremely offensive and should be denounced." Yet these young men are pro-social and leading effective lives? Judge Griffin had forgotten that the females in Room 22 were not women, but girls, some as young as thirteen. Describing, for reasons unknown, children who have been sexually objectified as "women" shows perfectly his inability to understand what was at issue from the start.

The mother of Witness Two revealed that her daughter "was not doing well; she's devastated by all of this." A lawyer who accompanied one of the hockey players who testified told journalists privately that his client had a "domestic violence problem." Another player had a temper tantrum in the courtroom as he screamed back at Crown Sandy Tse that there was no one in the courtroom who had more reason to hate David Frost than he did. All of the players spoke of girls and women as objects for group sex. Up to six players having sexual intercourse with one female was not unusual, they stated, in matter-of-fact voices. They used this sex as a bonding experience with one another. Their disdain for any of the females who were lured into Room 22 was clear. They called them sluts, puckbunnies, and gold-diggers.

And what of Witness One and Witness Two? Judge Griffin stated that Witness One had come from a good family. Crown Attorney Sandy Tse did nothing to correct this assumption. While we can only imagine what a "good family" meant to these men, Witness One explained that nothing was further from the truth:

12 Author's notes from trial (27 October 2009).

13 *R v Frost*, *supra* note 5 (Partial Reasons for Judgment) (28 November 2008).

> I am not sure if the Crowns knew about all the circumstances surrounding the male influences I had in my life. I know that the investigators were aware. Just to clarify, my dad passed away when I was 18 and my mother's boyfriend went missing when I was 16. My mother and I went to his house to grab a pair of rubber boots for my brother and when I went into the house it was like a murder scene. His body was not there but there was blood and brain matter everywhere and bullet holes in the walls. It was terrifying and very traumatizing. My mother was in the car with the radio on and I was inside the house with the doors closed and she could hear my screams.[14]

"Do you know how awful it is to have someone die who you have a very unresolved relationship with?" said Witness One in February of 2009, with reference to her father. Both her father and her mother's boyfriend — two father figures — died during the time she was under what she called Frost's "control": "I was so angry at Sandy Tse for letting the judge think I came from a good, healthy family," she said in February of 2009; "I couldn't believe he didn't challenge that. I had, and still have struggles and lots of problems."

PUTTING THE DAVID FROST TRIAL IN PERSPECTIVE

The above abbreviated account of the experience of Witness One and Witness Two reflects other cases I have chronicled as a journalist since 1993 when I started looking at the cyclical nature of sexual violence in hockey. My book,[15] which looked at case studies of alleged gang rapes and sexual abuse committed by junior hockey players, was published in 1998. Thirteen years later, nothing has changed, including the hockey establishment's attitude towards violence against girls and young women. It is equally disappointing to see men who claim to want to find solutions to violence in hockey form "new" old boys clubs. Even this "progressive" turf appears to be well-guarded.

On 24 February 2009, the Middlesex-London Health Unit in London, Ontario, held a "Violence in Hockey" symposium. One panel specifically addressed hockey violence off the ice and how girls and women are affected. All panelists in this discussion were male, which reflected virtually all other panels. Out of sixteen speakers, only one was female — Dr Laura Purcell, who spoke on concussions. When I asked the con-

14 18 February 2009 via email.

15 Laura Robinson, *Crossing the Line: Violence and Sexual Assault in Canada's National Sport* (Toronto: McClelland & Stewart, 1998).

ference organizers why there was only one female panelist, but a number of male media personalities who have no expertise in the sociological and psychological implications of young male violence, they did not respond.[16]

In March of 2009, two weeks after the Violence in Hockey symposium, we observed that very few men chose to attend the "Sexual Assault Law, Practice and Activism in a Post-*Jane Doe* Era," conference in Ottawa. Indeed, just as the London conference heightened a gendered solitude, so did Ottawa's. Women were not given a voice at the former, and men chose not to attend the latter. The Summary of Proceedings from the hockey conference articulates no relationship between male violence in hockey and violence against women. Ironically, one conclusion in the summary was, "women, especially mothers must be encouraged and assisted to realize the power of their voices in bringing about changes to eliminate violence and fighting in hockey."[17]

In the fall of 2010, as I put the finishing touches on this chapter, there is yet more evidence of how the gendered solitude in sport perpetuates the relationship between hockey violence, male privilege, and a culture of sexual violence against women. It is found in the aftermath of the 2010 Vancouver Olympics. In mid-March, two weeks after the Games ended, the Vancouver Police Department [VPD] disseminated information on crime during the Olympics to the media and to "hundreds of Olympic related organizations," according to VPD media relations officer Lindsay Houghton. Recipients included dozens of Vanoc — Vancouver Olympic organizing committee — decision-makers.[18] The VPD reported that, while property crime decreased 6 percent during the Olympics, assaults increased nearly 30 percent, and sexual assaults skyrocketed by 71 percent over the same period in 2009.[19] Vancouver's Battered Women Support Services [BWSS] separately reported a 30 percent increase in domestic violence during the Olympics, not only when compared to February of 2009, but compared to January and March of 2010 — the "before and after" months bookending the Games. The BWSS office was closed on 28 February 2010, the last day of

16 Author's emails to conference organizers in February of 2009 before the conference.

17 "Summary of Proceedings: Violence in Hockey Symposium" Middlesex-London Health Unit (23 April 2009), online: <http:/ www.healthunit.com/article.aspx?ID=14881 >.

18 Emails and telephone interviews conducted by author with Constable Lindsay Houghton, August–September 2010.

19 See online: <http:/www.vancouver.ca/Media_wac/media.exe >.

the Olympics, when Canada's men's team won gold in hockey, yet still saw a 12 percent increase in calls during the two days after the game.[20] But perhaps the most glaring statistic comes from Vancouver's Women Against Violence Against Women [WAVAW] who, on average, accompany five to six women per month to the hospital to have the "rape kit" administered that gathers medical evidence of rape. WAVAW is the first to acknowledge that its numbers reflect a tiny proportion of actual rapes, and that women who were visiting Vancouver during the Olympics probably did not know of its existence. Still, WAVAW reported in February of 2010 that, not only did calls for this service jump to eight, but four calls came in the 24 hours after Canada's men's team won the gold medal in hockey, all from women at hockey "celebrations."[21]

When asked about these statistics at Canada's Hockey Summit in August of 2010, Vanoc CEO John Furlong said it was "the first time" he had heard them,[22] despite the fact that Vanoc received copies of the VPD media release through Public Safety Canada, and the Vancouver and national press carried the stories.[23] Could there be a relationship between the triumph of men in a game that enshrines male aggression and violence and the messages men take from it about their own right to aggression and violence? Furlong ended the interview and went back to his real job at the summit, which was not to examine hockey, but to make sure that Canadian hockey maintains its mythological status.

And how does this myth-making relate to the gendered solitudes of sport that ensure that the voice of women is effectively silenced and disempowered? Don't forget Furlong's job as Vanoc's CEO was also to fight against women athletes who, in the lead-up to the Olympics, argued in court that not allowing them to compete as ski jumpers at the Games contravened their *Charter* right to equality. Vanoc argued back that they should not have to adhere to the *Charter of Rights and Freedoms.*

20 Emails and telephone interviews conducted by the author with BWSS staff, September 2010.

21 Emails and interviews conducted by author with WAVAW executive director Irene Tsepnopoulos-Elhamier, July, August, and September 2010.

22 Author's interview with John Furlong (25 August 2010 immediately after "Vancouver 2010 Evaluation" panel, Sheraton Hotel, Toronto, ON).

23 Jack Keating, "Violent Crime and Assaults Up While Property and Overall Crime Down at Olympics" *The Vancouver Province* (18 March 2010), online: www.theprovince.com/news/violent+crime+assaults+while+overall+crime+down+during+Olympics/2695341/story.html; see also Shadi Elien, "Link Between Hockey–Rape Studied" *The Georgia Straight* (13 May 2010) online: www.straight.com/article-323639/vancouver/link-between-hockey-rape-studied.

Instead of protecting the rights of women, they had a much larger obligation to the International Olympic Committee: to follow the IOC's orders, which was to host an Olympics where women ski jumpers did not participate.[24]

Ask a Canadian what the most memorable legacy of our Olympics was. Will they answer that it was the brave and beautiful way in which women athletes from around the world came together in Vancouver and argued for their fundamental right to be treated equally, or will they speak about the great way in which the Canadian men's hockey team played on the final day of the Games when they won the gold medal? Indeed, the Canadian myth remains intact. Let us hope that the men who say they want to see real changes in hockey violence start to understand women as agents of change. We are, after all, experts when it comes to violence against women. Real change in the sexual violence now found in hockey culture will not come until we cease existing in two gendered solitudes.

24 *Sagen et al v Vancouver Organizing Committee for the 2010 Olympic and Paralympic Winter Games*, Supreme Court of BC (No SO83619, "Defendant's Argument" 20 April 2009), and *Sagen et al v Vancouver Organizing Committee for the 2010 Olympic and Paralympic Winter Games*, BC Court of Appeal (No. CA037306, BC Court of Appeal, "Respondent's Factum" 21 September 2009).

5.
Indigenous Women and Sexual Assault in Canada

Tracey Lindberg, Priscilla Campeau, and Maria Campbell

In this chapter, Tracey Lindberg, Priscilla Campeau, and Maria Campbell make visible the gaping chasm between the criminal law's treatment of sexual assault committed against Indigenous women and girls and how those crimes are understood by Indigenous women and judged by Indigenous laws. Their discussion of four well-known prosecutions of men who preyed upon Indigenous girls and women challenges the law's understanding of what is a "fact" and how we judge which "facts" are "relevant." The authors refuse to look away from both the horror of these crimes and the way that they have in turn been minimized, discounted, and rationalized by actors in the Canadian legal system.

We would like, first, to thank the Algonquin people for allowing us onto their territory. We would also like to thank the Indigenous women who have taken their cases to court, the families who support them, and the communities who continue to build and re-build safe nations and communities so that Indigenous women and children may be provided with the confidence that they are living in communities where their safety and the integrity of the person is valued.

This is a hard thing to talk about. Talking about it, however, provides us with possibility. The possibility of seeing our struggle mirrored in other women. The possibility of violence-free homes, the possibility of acknowledging the seriousness of the nature of sexual violence against Indigenous women and children. There is the possibility of acknowledging the colonial construction of communities, individuals, governments, and citizens that do not value Indigenous women and children. There is the possibility of an open discussion of the particular devaluation of our humanity and the possibility of re-assigning values to the roles, responsibilities, and personhood of Indigenous women and children. There is a possibility of hope.

It is for this reason — the possibility of hope — that we open up our toolkits of experience to build something that we hope facilitates this possibility.

It is for this reason as well that we apologize, in advance, to the women, families, and communities we discuss. We want you to know, relatives, that we do so with good intent and with this hope at the back, front, and centre of our minds and hearts.

Home: Where We Are

When we look in the reflecting mirror that Canadian justice provides in the area of sexual assault, we do not see ourselves "at home." Indeed, when we read case law and news reports and hear people talk about their particular trauma of sexual assault, we see fragments of our colonial selves — our selves away from home. Home has balance, home is safe, and home is where we are spiritually sound. Home is where our laws matter; home is where we are honoured, as women. Home is not a courtroom.

Home: Where We Are Not

In order for this not to be a parenthetical discussion (this happens all the time, when we tell our stories, when we achieve personal bravery), we need to tell you that the experience of sexual assault cannot be broken down on lines related to gender or race. Dehumanization, a particularly colonial breaking down of the understanding, valuing, and recognition of Indigenous peoples as human, has played a part in the construction of our understanding of sexual assault and Canadian law. We possess a shared understanding and one that we fear will be universalized: this is each of us, this is our family, and this is any one of us. To say that we are victimized cleans this colonial mess up. It whitewashes it in a way that does not ascribe responsibility to its rightful place.

Mind you, we are not cleaning up. It is important to note that in our perception we are not perceived as individuals in Canadian justice. We are seen as collectively impacted by the anger, power, and control of individuals. However, in our truth, we see that there are individual perpetrators but also that there is a collective responsibility.

We cannot separate our individual experience of sexual assault from our collective experience of sexual assault, which we know is matricide/genocide. No one needs to name this for us: we have experienced it through our great-grandmothers, our grandmothers, our mothers, and our children. There is little difference, for us, between the colonial assertion of presence and domination in the kidnapping and raping when we first met and in the contemporary domination of flesh and control of space and nationhood through attacks on our women in lands we held before settlement, and which are still being wrested from our hands.

We think of constructions of Canadian law, things like "known danger," "equal benefit and protection of the law." Our known danger is largely unknown to most Canadians. And it comes from and resides alongside most Canadians. Our known danger is not just the men who pick us up in cars, our known danger is not just the person who lures us into his hotel room, and our known danger is not just the person who arrests us or who adjudicates us. Our known danger is the fact that most people do not know about this, do not care about this, and consider Indigenous womanhood a generally cognizable and acceptable risk. Without hyperbole, we assert with some security in the knowledge (and fear of the understanding) that our known danger is that we are Indigenous women.

How do you effectively police this danger? We cannot see, when hundreds of our women are missing or murdered, how Canadian law has been of equal benefit or protection to us. We cannot know, with cousins missing and going missing, granddaughters gone in an instant, sisters lost from cities, towns, and the countryside, how Canadian law is of equal benefit to us. It certainly is not protecting us. So, with this in our minds, we believe we have to tell Indigenous women's stories. In taking away the right not to know about this, and in addressing the danger of being Indigenous women, we, at least, address the known danger of ignorance.

Approach

We have, in this instance, decided to approach this lesson in the way we are most comfortable. As only one of us is a lawyer (although all of us should be), and we started with the presumption that Canadian law does not effectively address the silencing, sexual assault, and murder of Indigenous women, we are addressing this in the way we think the story can best be told.

Priscilla Campeau will first tell the story of the violence against Indigenous women in a way that is intelligible, but which is not profoundly connected to Canadian legal storytelling. As a Cree and Métis woman, and as an Indigenous woman who believes in the elegance, self-determination, and power of women, she will tell you four stories of sexual violence against Indigenous women.

Second, Tracey Lindberg will address the stories as an Indigenous woman, Indigenous scholar, a person schooled to some degree in Cree traditions and laws (although still in training), and as a law professor. Her job is to tell you how these stories resonate and require intellectual and actual activism. Her job is to show you yourself, in these four stories.

Elder Maria Campbell will finally take over, addressing the stories in terms of Cree-Metis (Neheyiwak) laws related to the societal role of protecting and honouring Indigenous women, the laws related to the sacredness of Indigenous women and children, and the laws related to the restoration of wellness and balance.

SPRING

Priscilla Campeau: Spring takes us to Tisdale, Saskatchewan, where a twelve-year-old girl has filed a complaint with the Royal Canadian Mounted Police [RCMP]. She is a small girl, five feet tall, eighty-seven pounds, and Aboriginal. She is in Grade 7 in school. She has made allegations that she has been sexually assaulted by three men on a country road. How did she get there? Like most teenage girls, she has had an argument with her parents. Unlike most girls, she finds herself in the company of three men. She alleges that they plied her with alcohol and assaulted her.

Her first court case takes place when she is fourteen years old. The first alleged assailant is Dean Trevor Edmondson, twenty-four years old at the time of the trial. The girl takes the stand for five hours, thirty minutes. Edmondson is convicted by a jury of being a party to a sexual assault. The two other men she identifies as assailants, Jeffrey Lorne Brown and Jeffrey Chad Kindrat, are then tried in her alleged assault. Brown and Kindrat are acquitted of the sexual assault. In this trial, they state that they believed that she was fifteen years old and that she had consented to have sex with them. The Crown appeals this verdict and a new trial is set.

In January of 2005, Edmondson appeals his conviction of being a party to a sexual assault. The Crown also appeals his sentence of two years less a day, to be served in the community. The appeal from conviction and sentence is dismissed.

Case 1

Tracey Lindberg: A Cree girl reports a sexual assault by three men.[1]

Relevant Facts

She is a child: twelve years old. She is picked up by three adult males. They give her alcohol.

1 *R v Edmondson*, [2005] SJ No 256 (Sask CA) at para 1.

In the courtroom, she is characterized as "Ms" and the accused as "the boys" at trial before the jury by Judge Kovatch.[2]

The Court of Appeal characterizes her as "the girl."[3]

Edmondson is twenty-four years old.[4]

Edmondson states that his friends held her hips while they had sex with her, or tried to have sex with her, since he was too drunk to perform.[5] She was held while an act of violence, any way you look at this, occurred and she then started vomiting.[6] When they dropped her off at a friend's house, she was screaming and hysterical.

Counsel for Edmondson said she was a child whose memory of the events was so uncertain, her credibility so suspect, and her background so clouded, as to have required a "clear and sharp warning to the jury."[7]

Six times she testified. The effect of post-traumatic stress disorder on her memory should be a relevant fact.

That she is a citizen of the Yellowquill First Nation is a relevant fact.

2 Norma Buydens, "Beyond Borders: Ensuring Global Justice for Children." The Winnipeg-based Canadian affiliate of ECPAT, the leading international Non-Governmental Organization against the child sex trade, brought a complaint because Judge Kovatch referred to the defendants, all over age twenty at the time of the trial, as "boys" twenty-eight times, while calling the complainant "Ms" Canadian Centre for Policy Alternatives, *Saskatchewan Notes* (2005) 1:42, online: <http://www.policyalternatives.ca/documents/Saskatchewan_Pubs/2005/ sasknotes 4_1.pdf> (26 Nov. 2009).

3 *Edmondson, supra* note 1 at paras 2, 18, 20, 22, 76.

4 *Ibid* at para 114.

5 *Ibid* at para 22.

6 *Ibid* at para 22.

7 As per the case of *R v McKenzie* (1996), 141 Sask R 221 (CA).

What Is Not Relevant

Whether she went willingly with Edmondson[8] cannot possibly be relevant. What is will to a drunken twelve year old? Surely there cannot be such a thing. Whether she had previous experience with alcohol,[9] and whether she may have been sexually assaulted by her father, and the unpredictable effects this may have had on her behaviour,[10] cannot be regarded as relevant to whether or not she was sexually assaulted by three other men.

There is, in the discussion of the sentence appeal, a paragraph addressing Mr Edmondson as a first-time offender, single, living at home, gainfully employed, with a very supportive family.[11]

The stated judicial understanding that this was an isolated act fuelled by excessive alcohol consumption all around is not a fact and is not rel-

8 Referring to the decision of the trial judge, the Court of Appeal wrote in their decision. Later, in the context of the specific issues to which the case gave rise, the judge reminded the jury that the complainant was twelve years old at the time of the occurrence, though she had told the three men she was fourteen, going on fifteen. He also drew their attention to her testimony that she had deliberately tried to appear older than she actually was. Still later, he referred to the need for the jury to take account of the indications of her attitude or state of mind at the time, drawing their attention to the frailties of her testimony in relation to whether she had willingly engaged in sexual activity with the accused, or had led the accused to believe she was a willing participant. He also reminded the jury that it was up to them to assess her credibility in this connection, having regard for the whole of the evidence. *Edmondson*, *supra* note 1 at para 54.

9 Cameron JA noted that the victim had "consumed alcohol on previous occasions." *Ibid* at para 55.

10 *Ibid* at paras 47, 59. It is important to note that the assault by her father is characterized as "her father had sex with her" and "having sex with her father" by the court (in one instance reporting the statement of her foster mother). The trial judge also reminded the jury that she may have been sexually assaulted. Additionally, the Canadian Press reported that the same information was provided at trial: CP, "Doc Tells Sask Trial Some of Girl's Injuries Could Have Been Caused by Father" (23 May 2003), *Saskatoon Star Phoenix*.

11 The Court of Appeal found that:
As the trial judge pointed out, Mr Edmondson was 24 years old at the time of the occurrence giving rise to his conviction and was a first time offender. He was single, living at home, and gainfully employed, with a very supportive family. What he had done on this occasion appeared to the trial judge to have been an isolated criminal act, fuelled in very significant part by excessive alcohol consumption all round. The trial judge went on to observe that many members of the community had come forward to express their confidence in Mr Edmondson and assure the court he posed no risk of further harm to anyone (*Edmondson*, *ibid* at para 114).

evant. Neither is the shared information that many community members came forward to express their confidence in Edmondson and assure the court he posed no risk of further harm to anyone. We wonder about the contrasting characterizations of the victim and the perpetrator and have to ask: whose community is represented and relevant in this discussion?

Critical Indigenous Analysis

The child in this case[12] was twelve years old. Why we do not label this pedophilia? Legally, we understand the distinction. Perhaps calling it pedophilia allows the rapists to absolve themselves of responsibility. It transmutes into an illness, leaving the power, hatred, and violence outside of the neat word-box. This is someone's daughter and these are someone's sons. We do not apply a label such as this without thinking of grandmothers, mothers, and daughters. But she is a child.

Assaulter. Rapist. Torturer. These are all she has, the only way that she can fight back anymore. Within those words, she gets to house the cruelty externally, keeping the ugliness where it belongs and away from her.

However, this is not sexual assault against a woman; somehow it is worse, in the spring of her existence. What we know about this, what our understanding of relevancy, leads us to say: this is the sexualization of a child and the dehumanization of a person. It strikes us that we are not just talking about the physical acts/assaults. We are also talking about her legal evisceration. A person who testifies about the brutality that was perpetrated on her/him is one of the bravest people we can imagine; sitting there in the courtroom while she is legally constructed as a drunken, potentially willing, and definitively sexual being is unbelievably brutish. Additionally, she is brutally constructed as a sexualized adult woman. Her childhood discarded on the courtroom steps, previous incidents of sexual assault are detailed, shaming her and making her act of bravery an act that must have been diminished by the revelation about previous sexual assault(s). The sexualization and assault by her father, in her home, is a continuum of violence. We wonder if this revelation should have been hers to make as well.

If she is a child for the purposes of her memory assessment, as argued by Edmondson's lawyer,[13] then she is a child when they take her into the truck, she is a child when they give her alcohol, when they hold

12 The defendants in this case were actually tried separately. See *Edmondson*, [2004] SJ No 643 (CA) and *R v Brown*, [2008] SJ No 325 (QB).

13 *Edmondson*, *ibid* at para 46.

her by her child's hips, and she is a child when they perpetrate sexual violence on her.

The relative disempowerment and the racialized nature of the crime is not even addressed. How can that be possible? It is an erasure.

In police questioning,[14] the police officer states that the girl "might have been the aggressor."[15] How do you pursue evidence and address relevance in a way that is meaningful to a child, a child with toxic familial support? How do you address her as doubly victimized? How do you address the colonial settlement: the victim's citizenship in Yellowquill First Nation,[16] her Indigeneity as a Cree child, and the particular vulnerability of Indigenous children to settler violence? There is an amorphous blob of colonization here that is unaddressed, which holds many hips and offers many drinks. There are also power relations here and an intrinsic judicial assessment of what is community, of the worth and imbalance of community support, of which communities have voice, and of which communities have worth.

Finally, we are concerned about the nature of the investigation and the courtroom discussion that does not utter the words "racism," pedophilia, or child sexual assault. Even if these words are found to be inapplicable, someone has to make sure that they are raised in the discussion.

Maria Campbell: *Miwoskumik, the spring. A time of dawn, of new beginnings and new birth. It is the time of the child, a people's future and the inheritor of a nation.*

When a woman became pregnant, the family rejoiced and precautions were put in place to create a safe journey for that little spirit into the world of human kind. The pregnant mother was taught how to care for herself during this time and the foods she should eat to ensure good health. She was not to be in the presence of anything that might negatively influence the new life she carried. She was taught the songs and the stories she must pass on to her unborn child. And medicines were picked and prepared by the old women for her time of birthing.

When the baby was born, the placenta was returned to the earth by the old women to ground this new life in "place" and as a form of respect and

14 *Ibid* at paras 17, 19.

15 *Ibid* at para 18.

16 Buydens, *supra* note 2 at 1.

reciprocity to mother earth. Later a ceremony would be held, thanking the Creator for lending us this new life. A name was given and lullaby songs were sung, stories were told and speeches made about the baby's life journey and who she might become. Perhaps she would be an artist, a healer, a teacher, a mother, maybe an auntie, a hunter, or a leader. Always she was surrounded by the old ones, who were the keepers and teachers of cultural and spiritual knowledge and, whose life experiences would make her road easier.

Stories upon stories upon stories that contained the family and tribal histories, the taboos and the laws of the people. There were naming ceremonies, walking out ceremonies. Ceremonies for a first tooth, for a first meal cooked, a first basket made and finally a ceremony to celebrate her passage into womanhood. The child was given kisaywatisowin, kindness, gentleness, and above all, a safe place to grow up.

SUMMER

Priscilla Campeau: Summer takes us to Northern British Columbia. It is a story of sexual assault, breach of trust, and intimidation. David William Ramsay is a member of the Provincial Court of British Columbia, appointed in 1991 to preside over Prince George and other northern communities. He is charged with ten offences. He pleads guilty to five of ten charges.

On count 2 of the charges, Ramsay picks up a sixteen-year-old Aboriginal/Métis girl in Prince George. He drives her out of town and agrees to pay her $150 for sex. She is naked and takes out a condom for his use. He becomes angry and assaults her, slamming her head into the dashboard and making it bleed. She struggles and makes it out of the truck. He catches her and continues his assault, pinning her to the ground, and penetrating her with his penis as she is crying. He finishes his assault, throws her clothes at her, and leaves her outside of town to find her own way back. No money changes hands. One year later, he is the judge presiding over a custody case involving her son.

On count 3, Ramsay picks up a twelve-year-old girl on the streets of Prince George. He pays her $80 for oral sex and intercourse. When she is thirteen years old, she appears before him in court and he becomes aware of her background and past. He sees her on the street months later and makes reference to her court appearance. He offers her $150 to stimulate aggressive sex. She agrees, but before the transaction can be completed, they become involved in a physical altercation. She escapes the vehicle and he drives away, telling her that no-

body will believe her if she reports him. He is convicted of obtaining sexual services from a person under eighteen. He is sentenced to three years.

On count 7, Ramsay picks up a fourteen-year-old Aboriginal girl ("A"). She agrees to perform oral sex for $80; he takes her out of town to complete the act. She provides sex four-to-six times from the ages of fourteen to seventeen years old; none of these acts involve violence. During this time, she appears before him several times in court. He is aware that she has a troubled background, including low self-esteem, limited education, abusive relationships with adults, and a fragile mental state. He is convicted of obtaining sexual services from a person under eighteen. He is sentenced to five years.

On count 8, Ramsay offers to let "A" off of her sentences if she keeps quiet about their sexual encounters. She appears before him eight times, each time expecting leniency. He is convicted of breach of trust. He is sentenced to five years.

On count 9, a fifteen-year-old Aboriginal girl appears before Ramsay in court. She is made a ward of the state and Ramsay is aware of her troubled life and her age. Months later he sees her on the street in Prince George; he offers her $60 for oral sex. She agrees and he takes her to the same out-of-town place "A" was taken. She performs oral sex on him and while nearing completion, he demands his money back. She struggles with him in the vehicle, and he grabs her hair while attempting to get his money back. She escapes the vehicle, naked. He threatens to have her killed if she reports him and leaves her there without her clothes. She finds her own way back to town. He is convicted of obtaining sexual services from a person under eighteen. He is sentenced to five years.

All sentences are to run concurrently.

Case 2

Tracey Lindberg: Northern circuit court judge David William Ramsay was charged with sexual assault, breach of trust, and obtaining for money the sexual services of a person under eighteen, totaling ten violations.[17] These children and young girls were Indigenous.

17 *R v Ramsay*, [2004] BCJ No 1165 (SC) at para 2 and head note.

Relevant Facts

Ramsay was in a position of trust. He had full knowledge of the children's and youths' circumstances, which included relative economic hardship and some substance use. His abuse of those vulnerabilities is relevant. The fact of the continuing violence in their lives is relevant. His role as a participant in a continuum of violence is relevant.

Ramsay admitted that he had obtained sex for money from minors.[18] He admitted that he had offered one minor lenient treatment in return for sex.[19] It is also relevant that those minors had appeared before him in court in his capacity as a judge.[20]

It is exceptionally relevant that these were Indigenous children, confronted with violence from a circuit court judge in the north. One girl appeared before the accused where, by her "consent", she was made a ward of the state.[21]

Control, authority, and acts of violence take place in a continuum. It may be hard for many Indigenous people to distinguish his acts in a vehicle from his acts on the bench. Neither was to be trusted. These are relevant facts.

That they are Indigenous girls, that they experience a particular imperial, racial, and economic vulnerability, are completely relevant factors. Physical and sexual assault and explicit and implicit threats operate upon a continuum of the abuse of imperial and colonial power. These are relevant facts.

What Is Not Relevant

Ramsay's loss of career and respect as a mitigating factor in his trial was not germane to the proceedings.[22]

The court found that, at the time of these events all four girls were juvenile sex trade workers living on the streets in Prince George.[23] We

18 *Ibid* at para 13.
19 *Ibid* at head note.
20 *Ibid* at para 4.
21 *Ibid* at para 4.
22 *Ibid* at para 26.
23 *Ibid* at para 7.

question the relevancy of this characterization because the acts were exploitative and the victims cannot be dismissed as sex trade workers. The characterization of the acts as "sexual activity," when they were violent acts, and the characterization of the victims as "young women," was not relevant. While the girls were highly vulnerable because of their youth, their disadvantaged backgrounds, and their drug use, the relevance of those factors as anything other than an indication of their compounded vulnerability is suspect.

Critical Indigenous Analysis

Power and loss of power are seen as great shaming factors in this case; it is our opinion that affixing the label of pedophilia to the actions of the perpetrator should be the actual shame. Addressing the power imbalance and racism should constitute the actual shaming here.

In some small sense, Ramsay's punishment can also be read as banishment, but a characterization of him as possessing a "split personality"[24] by the sentencing judge separates the person from the action. He did this. He did this mindfully and he did this by exploiting his access to and knowledge of his victims. He exploited his position and power.

There was a joint submission on sentencing that suggested an appropriate sentence was three-to-five years of imprisonment.[25] There were Eurocentric assumptions made about power and disempowerment in this case that were not analyzed or critiqued. We wonder at what point this will be addressed as collective and systematized violence and when the Canadian courts will discontinue the practice of seeing this systematized violence as one person making multiple mistakes?

That the high regard others held for him, his alleged compassion,[26] and his community contributions as a judge[27] should serve as a comparative point for the characterization of the victims as drug-addicted sex trade workers from disadvantaged backgrounds, is beyond comprehensible. That power differential needs to be taken into account; an accounting needs to be made with respect to that failure.

The racialization of the children also needs to be addressed critically and judicially. Describing these girls as coming from disadvantaged

24 *Ibid* at para 14.

25 *Ibid* at head note.

26 *Ibid* at para 13.

27 *Ibid* at para 12.

backgrounds [28] does not address the racialized and sexualized violence that Ramsay visited on Indigenous girls because they were Indigenous, because they did not have access to the vestiges of power, and because he did (and used it to his advantage). That colonial power imbalance not only lies entrenched in his actions; it is underwritten in the decision. Disadvantaged backgrounds does not excuse parenthetical thinking (they were on drugs, they allowed it, they wanted money, they deserved it) and in some way makes the flaws of the children observable, applicable, and actual when these "flaws" might have in no way been a reflection or component of their actuality.

That Indigenous female children and youth are so particularly vulnerable to systemic and personal violence is part of the amorphous blob of colonization. They almost certainly understood the known danger of being Aboriginal, female, and young. They also most certainly knew that the notions of equal benefit and protection of the law is farcical. Who do we turn to for protection and benefit of the law when the law is the rapist? What faith can we have in law?

It is important to note that these are people and cases that we know. We wonder what we will tell our families when they ask why this is not pedophilia?

Maria Campbell: *Neepin is the summer, a time of growth, beauty and strength. The ceremony of passage has been completed and Iskwew, the woman takes her place in the circle of sisters. This is the time for love, passion, for birthing and parenting, for nurturing, providing, and protecting. It is a time of motherhood. A time when there was equality and balance when Grandmother owned half of the circle and her societies and ceremonies taught women to be fierce and courageous protectors and nurturers.*

AUTUMN

Priscilla Campeau: Autumn sees us back in British Columbia, this time in Vancouver. Gilbert Paul Jordan used alcohol as a weapon in the death of Vanessa Buckner. Jordan met Vanessa Buckner in Vancouver in 1987. He asked her to have a drink with him and obtained a room at the Niagara Hotel that same evening using a fictitious name.

They consumed a large bottle of vodka and almost a full bottle of rum. Jordan's main purpose was to have sex with Vanessa while they were intoxicated. After a night of drinking, he left the Niagara Hotel

28 *Ibid* at para 7.

and returned to his room at the Marble Arch Hotel. Upon his return, he called emergency services to report that there was dead body at the Niagara Hotel; he did not leave his name. Police traced his call back to him at the Marble Arch Hotel.

Police found Vanessa's body at the hotel, her blood alcohol reading was 0.91, and her death was attributed to a massive inhalation of gastric contents due to acute alcohol poisoning. At the trial regarding her death, Jordan claimed that Vanessa was alive when he left. He made conflicting statements regarding her death and stated that he did not expect her to die. Jordan was not arrested for causing Vanessa's death. He was released and police monitored his activities with a surveillance team. Police watched him search out Aboriginal women on skid row in Vancouver; they rescued four women. Jordan preyed on their addictions and their dire financial situations.

Between 1980 and 1987, Jordan was present at six parties involving alcohol, each involving an Aboriginal woman. They all passed away from over-consumption of alcohol. Ultimately, Jordan was convicted of manslaughter in the death of Vanessa Buckner. He received a sentence of fifteen-years imprisonment, which he appealed; his sentence was reduced to nine years. He served six years and was released. He was ordered not to drink with any females and was prohibited from attending a licensed establishment.

Upon his release, he was found with an Aboriginal woman and alcohol. An altercation had ensued in his hotel room and, when the woman tried to leave, he wanted his alcohol back. He was arrested and received a maximum sentence of twelve months and probation of three years.

Case 3

Tracey Lindberg: Gilbert Paul Jordan was convicted of one count of manslaughter in the death of Vanessa Buckner.[29] Vanessa was an Indigenous woman.

Relevant Facts

Vanessa Buckner was a mother.[30]

29 *R v Jordan*, [1988] BCJ No 3011 (SC). Jordan later appealed his sentence of fifteen years and had it reduced to nine years. *R v Jordan*, [1991] BCJ No 3490 (CA).

30 *Jordan* (BCCA), *ibid.*

There were eleven other incidents (admissibility ruled upon) and seven Indigenous women died in a similar manner.[31]

Eight of the incidents involved "sexual activity." Jordan's notes state that he was: "Useing (sic) that woman sexually until I am sexually satisfied. Upon completion of my sexual satisfaction she must leave. (Mostly Can. indian women)".[32]

He was a known danger; he was known to kill women with alcohol. The British Columbia Supreme Court held that, "The evidence clearly proves that alcohol is a poison. Jordan knew its over-consumption could cause her death. He was present on six earlier occasions when women died from drinking too much alcohol which he had provided to them."[33]

Jordan writes in a journal that he does it and must stop it.[34] He is under police surveillance; police monitor him and remove four women from his company.[35]

His crimes are racialized: he devalues Indigenous women's humanity. The Court of Appeal notes that when testifying at the trial, Jordan admitted that "he sought out women so that he could do this 200 times per year" (from 1980 to 1988).[36]

Jordan offered the women money to drink; beyond that, he offered women money to drink themselves into unconsciousness.[37] He knows

31 *Jordan* (BCSC), *supra* note 29.

32 *Ibid.*

33 *Ibid.*

34 *Ibid.*

35 *Ibid.*

36 *Jordan* (BCCA), *supra* note 29.

37 *Jordan* (BCSC) *supra* note 29. Police surveillance revealed the nature of one incident:

> Have a drink, down the hatch baby, 20 bucks if you drink it right down; see if you're a real woman; finish that drink, finish that drink, down the hatch hurry, right down; you need another drink, I'll give you 50 bucks if you can take it; I'll give you 10, 20, 50 dollars, whatever you want, come on I want to see you get it all down; you get it right down, I'll give you the 50 bucks and the 13 bucks; I'll give you 50 bucks. I told you that. If you finish that I'll give you $75; finish your drink, I'll give you $20, etc.

he is harming them and potentially killing them because it has happened frequently.

What Is Not Relevant

What is not relevant is the characterization and sexualization of these as "drinking orgies." [38] As a comparative point, is inviting men to your home and then shooting them a "gun party"? Describing the acts as "orgies" has within it a notion of consent. Jordan is fifty-six years of age.[39] He says he has been an alcoholic since he was sixteen.[40] This is not drunk driving; his pattern of alcohol abuse is of little concern. If he had been a drunk who liked to shoot people when drunk, he would be held accountable for that.

Vanessa Buckner was addicted to drugs and she had just had a baby taken from her by the Social Services Agencies because of her addiction to drugs.[41] There was also evidence that she was very depressed about having her baby taken away.[42] At British Columbia Supreme Court, she was characterized as a "female alcoholic."[43] These are irrelevant issues.

Critical Indigenous Analysis

Addressing this crime as manslaughter, and prosecuting only one incident, is likely attributable (and we don't know if this is the case) to the "problem of proof." Yet there are certain observable and probable assumptions that can be made when you have an understanding of the circumstances, the person, and their nature. In this instance, we would say that the problem of proof is that any assumptions that can be made about the circumstances, persons, and natures of the deceased are external ones.

Additional assumptions, outsider assumptions at best, cannot be made about the willingness of their participation, the particular vulnerability to violence of poor Indigenous women, and their circumstances and lives.

Their lives are unknowable to the judge and therefore no accurate assumptions can be made and no accurate understandings predicated upon those can be arrived at.

38 *Ibid.*

39 *Ibid.*

40 *Ibid.*

41 *Jordan* (BCCA), *supra* note 29.

42 *Ibid.*

43 *Jordan* (BCSC), *supra* note 29.

It seems that the judiciary is more able to recognize Jordan and more easily identify the nature of his lifestyle. His alcoholism and his life seems more accessible than the victims' in this case to the judge. For this reason, it might be said that his experience, life or nature is more legally cognizable to the judiciary than that of the women who died because Jordan paid them to drink themselves, in many instances, to death.

We should be asking, in a critical way, "whose voice is not heard?" There is power to engage with Indigenous women's actualities and the power to ignore them.

The characterization of the acts as "sexual activity" does not address consent, does not address assault, and does not address sexual assault with a weapon.

Fifteen-years imprisonment seems appropriate. This sentence was appealed and decreased. What is not addressed is the fact that he was hunting Indigenous women. The stereotypes of Indigenous women remain unaddressed. Finally, we must note that the inability of Indigenous women to protect themselves and insulate themselves from the hunt and the hunter (he who could afford the room, afford the alcohol, continue to hunt) is situated on a terrain of influence and ownership that the original inhabitants of this country could not afford.

Maria Campbell: *Takwakun, the autumn, a time of strength and authority. A time of leadership and the keeping of justice so that children can grow healthy and the community can be safe to ensure a strong nation. It is the time of kaytayiskwew, older woman, kokomnow, our grandmother. The time of birthing is over; now is the time of mystery, medicine, and teaching.*

WINTER

Priscilla Campeau: Winter takes us to Saskatchewan in 1969 in a northern town called Pelican Narrows. A RCMP officer in uniform appears at the home of a fourteen-year-old Aboriginal girl. She is approximately five feet tall and weighs eighty pounds; she lives with her parents and siblings. The RCMP officer is thirty-two years old.

The police officer is the corporal in charge of the local RCMP detachment. He tells the mother of this young girl that he needs to speak with her daughter at the detachment. The mother agrees that her daughter can go with him. He takes her to the detachment and along the way starts asking questions of a sexual nature. While at the detachment, he asks her if her mother knows that she is not a virgin and asks her if she wants to have sex with him.

In 1998, Fred John (Jack) Ramsay appears in court. He is the former RCMP officer and at the time of the trial is a Member of Parliament. At the trial, the young woman testifies that Ramsay approached her in the detachment with his erect penis and penetrated her while she was standing with her pants around her knees. He states that penetration did not take place as he realized what he was doing and stopped. Ramsay is convicted of attempted rape and receives a sentence of nine-months imprisonment.

In 2001, Ramsay appeals his conviction. He argues that the complainant's evidence that she co-operated or did not resist amounted to consent under the law at that time even though she was induced to do so by his authority as an adult and a police officer. He also argues that attempted rape should not have been presented to the jury as there was no evidence supporting it. He asks for an acquittal.

A new trial ensues and Ramsay pleads guilty to indecent assault. He receives a one-year suspended sentence with probation.

Case 4

Tracey Lindberg: An Indigenous woman in her forties[44] comes forward and tells of a sexual assault by a former police officer, Jack Ramsay, when she was fourteen.[45] Her complaint alleged that Ramsay raped her.[46]

Relevant Facts

Ramsay took a fourteen-year-old girl to his police detachment office.[47] He asked her if she was a virgin.[48] She testified that he approached her with his erect penis and penetrated her while she was standing up with her pants around her knees.[49] He stated that he approached her with his erect penis, put his hands on her, and then realized what he was doing and turned away in disgust.[50]

The Saskatchewan Court of Queen's Bench found that: "His actions were a serious assault on her privacy and an attempt to invade her body.

44 *R v Ramsay*, [1998] SJ No 829 (Sask QB) [*Ramsay* (No 1)].

45 *R v Ramsay*, [2000] SJ No 275 (Sask QB) [*Ramsay* (No 3)].

46 *Ramsay v Saskatchewan*, [2003] SJ No 317 (Sask QB) at para 7 [*Ramsay* (No 5)].

47 *R v Ramsay*, [1999] SJ No 843 (Sask QB) at para 2 [*Ramsay* (No 2)].

48 *Ibid.*

49 *Ramsay* (No 3), *supra* note 45 paras 4, 35, 25.

50 *Ibid* at para 35.

They indicated a contemptuous disregard for her dignity and her feelings." [51]

The nature of the contempt and what it stemmed from are relevant facts. The power and authority of a non-Indigenous representative of a non-Indigenous (in origin) institution is a relevant fact. The power imbalance in this relationship is a relevant fact.

What Is Not Relevant

Ramsay stated that he had since married, he had four children, and he had become a Member of Parliament.[52] In addressing Ramsay's remorse at sentencing, Noble J at the Court of Queen's Bench noted that Ramsay accepted "partial responsibility."[53] His failure to accept full responsibility is of no relevance to the mitigation of his crime; partial remorse is not remorse, we would argue.

The court noted that the victim's impact statement painted a sad picture of her life, including alcoholism, bad marriages and relationships, loneliness, and loss of self-esteem. In her view, it all originated with the encounter with the accused in 1969.[54] The court seemed less than sympathetic and informed, finding at the Queen's Bench that "the incident did have a traumatic effect on her life but one cannot reasonably accept that every negative situation in her life can be traced back to this event."[55] To what degree is a judge's understanding of the effect of a non-Indigenous authority figure's sexual assault of an Indigenous child even relevant to the discussion? What judge has the capacity to determine the effects of colonial post-traumatic stress let alone the traumatic effects from the assault of an empowered individual upon a racialized child? We think that the effect on her is relevant and a judge's uninformed assessment of that effect is not. If the court does not have the capacity to determine the effect, they should bring in someone who does.

The judge stated that a "close examination of her statement indicates she has accomplished several good things since the incident. She has

51 *Ibid.*

52 *Ibid* at para 42, 17.

53 *Ibid* at para 41.

54 *Ibid* at para 19.

55 *Ibid.*

conquered alcoholism." [56] Her personal fortitude and strength has no bearing on Ramsay's sentence. As one who overcame (or not) the violence, that information cannot in any way be utilized to minimize what happened to her.

The court addressed Ramsay's position of influence within Indigenous communities:

> In 1977–1978 he worked as an Ombudsman for the Department of Indian Affairs in Alberta. I note that he has acted as an advisor to aboriginal groups over the years which suggest that he was interested in their welfare. His counsel advised the Court of his efforts to free a native person who he considered had been wrongfully convicted of an offence.[57]

The relevance of this is only clear or meaningful to the legal conversation if you do not perceive this as possibly part of a story related to the potential for abuse of discretion. In fact, it makes his abuses of power all the more real because of his access, and less acceptable because of the information he held about his victim.

Critical Indigenous Analysis

The characterization of Ramsay's action as taking the victim to the RCMP detachment[58] does not specifically address the power differential between an Indigenous citizen in an Indigenous community being taken by a non-Indigenous police officer to a police detachment. There is NO addressing the power imbalance in this case and there is also NO addressing the racialized imbalance.

"The girl's age and Ramsay's position of authority added to the gravity of the crime,"[59] the Court of Queen's Bench held in determining the length of the sentence. We wonder why her colonized existence, a particular racialized vulnerability, and the authority that non-Indigenous authority figures have over Indigenous women and children was not addressed in sentencing. Justice Noble found that:

56 *Ibid.*

57 *Ibid* at para 42.

58 *R v Ramsay*, [2001] SJ No 17 (Sask CA) at para 6 [*Ramsay* (No 4)]. Notably, in the QB decision, the action is described as "escort[ing]" the victim. *Ramsay* (No 3), *supra* note 45 at head note.

59 *Ibid* at para 32.

> A sentence of less than two years was appropriate to reflect the seriousness of the crime and Ramsay's individual circumstances. Ramsay did not represent a risk to the community. He was rehabilitated since the offence. However, a conditional sentence did not meet the principles of denunciation and deterrence to others.[60]

There was an assumption about the risk he posed to the public, and an assumption about rehabilitation. Why is his participation in Canadian government a presumption of upstanding citizenship? We wonder if the assumptions are based upon an understanding of what whiteness and privilege provide.

The assumptions from a victim's perspective are often quite different. An Indigenous victim facing a power differential very often sees police, trial courts, and appeal courts as part of the same systemized violence. She should have the opportunity to see that power and the colonial terror that it evokes addressed in a courtroom.

It is about what the uniform represents, in terms of power, and a justice official having additional knowledge, abusing power and potentially knowing the impact of shame and shaming in the Indigenous community. This is a crime of racism and a crime of power.

He is convicted of attempted rape.[61] His sentence was nine months and a firearms prohibition for ten years.[62] On appeal, his conviction was set aside and a new trial ordered on the charge of attempted rape.[63] Critical analysis leads one to believe that there is no equal benefit and protection of the law for Indigenous women and children. Blameworthiness seems more attributable to the victim and less so to Ramsay.

There is a blaming that she took responsibility for: had she not unbuttoned her clothes as he suggested, it might never have happened.[64]

Maria Campbell: *Pipon, the winter, a time of rest and dreaming, a time of teaching of ahtyokewina, the sacred stories that taught us our creation, the taboos and laws of our people and the consequences when they were broken. Pipon is the first grandmother, Notokewew Ahtyokan, keeper of the stories and the laws. This was the foundation of miyo pimachiowin, our good life. Spirit, ceremony, story, song, and societies all to make this*

60 *Ibid* at para 34.

61 *Ibid* at para 1.

62 *Ibid* at paras 49, 51.

63 *Ramsay* (No 4), *supra* note 58 at para 28.

64 *Ramsay* (No 3), *supra* note 45.

journey on earth a kind and balanced one that celebrated and honoured womankind and through her honoured our people.

CONCLUSION

Relevancy is an area of importance in this discussion. The power to make decisions about what is central to a case and what is not is a power that contains both the potential of recognition and critical inclusion and of stereotyping and erasure. The extent to which Indigeneity and womanhood are excluded from these cases is astonishing. Stunning. It renders us incapable of coherent thought and capable action for a moment.

There is a layering of judicial supremacy and the construction and destruction of Indigenous womanhoods and childhoods in these cases. We note that there is a sense of bewilderment and an *absence of discussion about who we really are.*

Worse is that our spirits, spirituality, language, and cultures are unrecognized or unrecognizable when we read these cases. In assessing relevancy, we find Indigenous women's lives have become irrelevant, once by the people who harmed them, and again through their erasure by the judiciary.

The messages should make us angry. We find they make us fearful and sad:

Our homes, if we have them, can be invaded.

Our bodies, without our consent — if we are even old enough to know what consent is — are not protected by Canadian law.

Our bodies are disposable.

Our bodies are vulnerable.

Our experience with the Canadian justice system represents a layering of violence.

Our experience as colonial oppressed goes unnoticed and unanalyzed.

Our communities and our support seem less important than the perpetrators' communities and their support systems.

These Are Relevant Facts

Colonialism is terrifying, continuing and perpetuated so long as we do not take note of it in our actions, inactions, systems, and analysis.

Many Indigenous peoples see Canadian police officers, judges, and justice officials as enforcement arms of the policies, laws, and legislation that dehumanize us.

Violence exists on a continuum with many layers of overlap; Canadian justice is often viewed as a part of that violence.

Oppression includes ignorance and reconstruction of Indigenous women's actualities in ways that mythologize violence, sexualize non-sexual peoples and events, and erase our humanity.

These Too Are Relevant Facts

We come from communities with ancient traditions of honouring women.

We come from Nations who hold us dear in their hearts.

We come from places where women hold each other in the highest regard.

We love our families.

We love our people.

We are grandmothers, mothers, granddaughters, daughters, aunties, cousins, and sisters.

This is for Vanessa Buckner, Mary Johnson, Barbara Paul, Mary Johns, Patricia Thomas, Patricia Andrew, Vera Harry, Rosemary Wilson, Verna Chartrand, Sheila Joe, Mabel Olson, A, M, the unnamed children, and their families in these cases. We continue to hope to see the possibility of violence-free homes, and the possibility of acknowledging the seriousness of the nature of sexual violence against Indigenous women and children because of you. We mean no harm and write all of this with good intent.

6.

Lawful Subversion of the Criminal Justice Process? Judicial, Prosecutorial, and Police Discretion in *Edmondson, Kindrat,* and *Brown*

*Lucinda Vandervort**

Lucinda Vandervort's chapter takes a detailed look at the Edmondson, Kindrat, *and* Brown *prosecutions, also discussed by Elder Campbell, Priscilla Campeau, and Tracey Lindberg in the previous chapter. These cases involved three non-Aboriginal men accused of sexually assaulting a twelve-year-old Aboriginal girl. This saga, like the Louise Nicholas trials presented earlier by Julia Tolmie, was fraught by many legal errors, resulting in long and complex proceedings, including two jury trials, several appeals, and two retrials. Lucinda argues that the failure to adhere to the applicable law governing the prosecution of sexual assault allows decision-makers to rely on racial and sexual biases, stereotypes, and irrelevant "facts," as also seen in the previous chapter. She highlights the unbearable burden placed on this young witness by a process that failed to adhere to the law of sexual assault and, in turn, reinforced the public impression that the race, sex, and age of complainants and accused can be used to subvert justice. Lucinda advocates a combination of innovative systemic remedies and incremental changes in police, prosecutorial, and judicial policy and practice to secure more effective enforcement of the sexual assault laws.*

* This research was supported in part by a grant from the Social Sciences and Humanities Research Council of Canada. This article is respectfully dedicated to the complainant in the *Edmondson, Kindrat,* and *Brown* cases. I wish to thank Robin Ritter, Senior Crown Prosecutor, and Morris Bodnar, QC for sharing some of their insights and perspectives on this case with me; Hugh Harradence, QC and Mark Brayford, QC for answering my questions; and my Saskatchewan academic colleagues, John Whyte, Mark Carter, Norman Zlotkin, Tim Quigley, Glen Luther, and Michael Plaxton, and many students, for their comments in response to an earlier draft of the article or in discussion of specific issues. Any errors and the views expressed are my own. The article was submitted for publication in May of 2009 and does not refer to legal decisions or changes in law or policy subsequent to that date.

R v Edmondson, *R v Kindrat*, and *R v Brown*[1] (2001–2008) provide disconcerting evidence that patterns of practice in sexual assault cases continue to be largely resistant to meaningful change at the grassroots level, at least in the province of Saskatchewan. Misunderstanding and confusion about the applicable substantive law appear to have shaped crucial decisions in handling these cases at key points throughout the proceedings, in both the trial and pretrial phases, and in the Court of Appeal. Police failed to use the tools available to record and preserve testimonial evidence by children and other fragile witnesses for subsequent use at trial. Some relevant evidence was not preserved, while effort appears to have been expended in investigating issues that had no bearing on the case. Preparation of the case may have been shaped by misunderstanding about which facts were material for proof of the essential elements of sexual assault and consent as defined in law. That may also explain why evidence of matters that had no bearing on the case and violated rules prohibiting the introduction of evidence of personal and sexual history was subsequently raised by counsel at trial, admitted into evidence, and referred to by the judge in summing up the case for the jury in 2003. Indeed, many aspects of the case show that some key participants lacked familiarity with sexual assault law and current legal standards for the conduct of sexual assault cases. Overall, the handling of the case stands as a stark indictment of the operation of the criminal justice system in sexual assault cases in Saskatchewan.

Current legal standards are based on the Supreme Court of Canada's interpretation of legal principles and rules within a human rights framework. Those standards require that all legal professionals working in the courts and other branches of the criminal justice system strive to avoid blinding themselves to the influence of racism, misogyny, and

1 *R v Edmondson*, [2005] SJ No 256; 2005 Sask CA 51; [2006] 6 WWR 74; 257 Sask R 270; 196 CCC (3d) 164; 65 WCB (2d) 178, Docket 673 and Docket 703 on appeal from QBC 1358/02 JC of Melfort. (The Crown's application to the Supreme Court of Canada for leave to appeal the Court of Appeal's decision to uphold Edmondson's sentence was filed on 6 June 2005 and dismissed without reasons on 20 October 2005: *R v Edmondson*, [2005] SCCA No 273). See *R v Brown*, [2005] SJ No 43; 2005 Sask CA 7, Docket 687 on appeal from QBC No 1357/02 JC of Melfort for the judgment on the appeal of Kindrat and Brown's acquittal. Dean Edmondson was tried by a jury in 2003 and convicted. Jeffery Lorne Brown and Jeffery Kindrat were tried together in 2003 and acquitted by the jury; a retrial was ordered in 2005. Those cases were severed in 2007. The *Kindrat* retrial by jury proceeded in 2007, leading to an acquittal that was not appealed. Brown's retrial was adjourned until May of 2008. The jury failed to reach a verdict and the matter was stayed by the Crown in early July of 2008: "Balancing justice in a difficult case", Editorial, *The [Regina] Leader-Post* (9 July 2008) B8.

outmoded cultural attitudes and norms on their own perceptions and conduct and those of everyone else who participates in the criminal justice process in any capacity. It is undeniable that these requirements may impose heavy demands on judges and counsel in sexual assault cases, that their performance will not always be perfect, and that when it falls short, they may often be unaware of this fact.

But it is also well recognized that interpretation and enforcement of the sexual assault laws is very easily confounded by error due to the strong influence of invalid generalizations about male and female gender roles and sexuality — myths and stereotypes, generalizations about the links between sexual activity, gender, race, consent, and a wide range of personal and social factors and characteristics. Legal deliberation about sexual assault is known to be easily distorted by attitudes that reflect gender and racial bias and prejudice. Some of that prejudice and attitudinal bias is conscious, but much of it is often outside ordinary conscious awareness. In an attempt to protect "truth-finding" in the legal process against distortion by unsound generalizations and assumptions, Canadian law has developed rules of evidence and procedure specifically designed to restrict the admission of extraneous evidence (not material in law to the issues to be determined), and to protect legal deliberation from the influence of invalid assumptions and generalizations. Adherence to these rules of law and related standards of judicial practice and rules of professional conduct is essential in sexual assault cases. When these rules are not assiduously followed at trial and are not strictly enforced by the appellate courts, the result can easily be an unsound verdict based on fallacious reasoning using invalid premises and evidence of facts not legally material to the issues to be determined.

These considerations may explain much of what went wrong—and was widely seen by the public to go wrong—in the cases of *Edmondson, Kindrat,* and *Brown.* When the practices used in these cases are measured against current legal standards, we certainly do see significant gaps between what was done and what those standards require. It is always the case that jurists who engage in an undisciplined use of discretion, and who rely on personal views and opinions, do justice no service. This is true whether they act in the belief that what they are doing must be "right" because they "mean well" or, in the case of counsel, because they believe, erroneously, that their duty to protect the client's interests requires them to do so.[2] When discretion, unconstrained by law,

2 See, for example, *R v Murray* (2000), 186 DLR (4th) 125 (Ont Sup Ct J).

governs the conduct of a sexual assault case, the proceedings are vulnerable to capture by the very ideologies of prejudice and social ignorance that the law of sexual assault, and the rules of evidence and procedure, are designed to exclude. This is why the choice not to adhere strictly to legal standards in the prosecution and trial of a sexual assault case is so detrimental. The evidence of failure to adhere to current legal standards seen in the record in the *Edmondson, Kindrat,* and *Brown* cases suggests there are serious problems with aspects of the operation of the criminal justice system in sexual assault cases in Saskatchewan. Whatever the root causes of these deficiencies may be, they pose a challenge to the administration of justice in Saskatchewan and call for decisive action.[3]

The proceedings in this case extended over a period of almost seven years through two preliminary hearings, appeals, motions, two trials, and two retrials. The objective of this case study is to examine the evidence and extract and record deficiencies and other problems documented by that evidence. This preliminary report highlights selected issues and begins the process of reflecting on their significance and impact on the criminal justice process as it unfolded in the context of the social realities of Saskatchewan in the period 2001–2008. It is useful to begin with an overview of the facts of the assault and the subsequent legal proceedings.

THE ESSENTIAL FACTS OF THE CASE

On 30 September 2001, Edmondson, Kindrat, and Brown, all non-Aboriginal men in their twenties from the town of Tisdale, were on a Sunday afternoon "booze-cruise" in a pick-up truck, drinking beer and driving from small town to small town in the Saskatchewan countryside two hours northeast of Saskatoon. As the accused left the hotel bar in one of the small towns, after drinking alcohol and playing on the video machines, they saw the complainant sitting on the hotel steps. The complainant remembers that one of them immediately said, "I thought Pocahontas was a movie." Quickly conferring with each other as they got back in the truck, they offered her a ride. She accepted. "You

3 This discussion refers to selected examples of procedural deficiencies and substantive legal errors. The conduct of the trials in 2003 has been aptly critiqued by others, including the Native Women's Association of Canada; see Factum of the Intervener in the appeals in the Saskatchewan Court of Appeal in 2005, *supra* note 1. See also the factums filed by the Crown, *ibid.* Whether the criminal justice process in other provinces and territories is subject to similar deficiencies and legal errors in sexual assault cases is an obvious question but not one this chapter purports to answer.

can trust us," said Edmondson, the driver, as Kindrat, who was sitting with her in the back seat, urged her to accept the first beer. The accused drove, drank, and talked. Under the influence of Kindrat's persistent urging, the complainant finally drank one beer, and then three more within the first half hour. They stopped at a bar in yet another town, ate, drank, and bought more beer to go, bringing the total consumed in the truck that afternoon to about fifty-eight bottles. The accused also consumed alcohol in each bar they visited.[4]

As they approached the Tisdale area in the early evening, travelling on the back roads, the complainant, now quite drunk, was in the front seat kissing Edmondson, the driver, and pulling her pants up as Brown pulled them down. Edmondson stopped the vehicle and lifted the complainant out of the truck. The men took turns holding her down and having sex with her on the ground by the side of the road. Edmondson then carried the complainant to the front of the truck where, leaning back against the hood of the truck, he tried to have sexual intercourse with the complainant who was now naked from the waist down. He held her up with her arms and legs straddled around him. Soon the other two men each in turn came up behind her and attempted to have sexual intercourse with her from the rear as Edmondson continued to hold her. Afterwards none of the accused appeared completely sure whether they had or had not penetrated her, how (penis or finger), or whether it was anally or vaginally, but they all told the police they had tried. When the accused were finished with their sexual activity, the complainant was falling down, passing out, and helpless. They dressed her and put her back in the truck. She asked to be taken to a friend's home in Tisdale. On arrival there, she could not walk unassisted and was screaming and crying about having been raped. The accused left her with the family and drove off.

The friend and his father promptly took her to the local hospital. She was seen in emergency and admitted. Rape kit tests were partially completed by a local doctor who was summoned to the hospital for that purpose. A blood sample was drawn from the complainant while the RCMP were in attendance at the Tisdale hospital, but it was not seized as evidence at that time and was never analyzed for its alcohol content.

4 This initial account of the facts is based primarily on the evidence as presented at the *Kindrat* retrial in 2007. Unsurprisingly, some evidence adduced in the other proceedings was not identical in matters of detail; the rulings on admissibility of the evidence were not identical; and the approaches taken by counsel differed somewhat. Some key differences are noted below.

(When the RCMP investigating officer attempted to obtain that blood sample in 2003 he was advised that it had been destroyed.) Two days later, the complainant was taken to the university hospital in Saskatoon for examination by a specialist. Diagrams were made of the location and size of the lacerations, bruises, and swollen areas on the complainant's body, but no photographs were taken. The complainant's evidence was never videotaped or audio taped for subsequent use in court.

The three men were arrested the day after the assault. Each of them, having first been warned, gave an incriminating statement to the investigating RCMP officers in Tisdale. Their statements included open admissions that they did not know how old she was, that they had given her alcohol in the form of a number of bottles of beer, and that they had engaged in sexual activity with her.

THE LEGAL PROCEEDINGS

Charges by indictment were laid against the three men under s 272(1)(d) of the *Criminal Code*, which provides that, "Every person commits an offence who, in committing a sexual assault, is a party to the offence with any other person." The maximum punishment following conviction under s 272(1)(d) is a sentence of fourteen years pursuant to s 272(2).[5] The Crown prosecutor charged Edmondson separately so that he could be called as a Crown witness in the trial of the other two accused, and they could serve as witnesses in his trial. Preliminary inquiries were held. The two trials, presided over by Mr Justice Kovach, a Queen's Bench judge sitting with a jury, were held in Melfort, Saskatchewan, in the late spring and early summer of 2003. First the trial of Edmondson was held and then the trial of Kindrat and Brown.

The conduct of the trials in 2003 failed to observe the letter and the spirit of s 276 and s 278. These provisions were enacted to protect complainants' privacy and curtail the admission of irrelevant evidence by restricting reference to evidence of a complainant's sexual history and personal records. The evidentiary rules that curtail the admission of evidence of collateral facts were also often disregarded. The trial judge repeatedly allowed questions and answers that put evidence before the jury that directly or indirectly invited speculation and made insinuations or offered conclusions about the significance of the personal and sexual history of the complainant for the matters in issue. The effect was to ignore the restrictions imposed by s 276 and s 278 and to permit the judge, the counsel, and the jury to distract themselves with issues

5 In the text and notes below, section numbers refer to the *Criminal Code*, RSC 1985, c C-46.

that were "red-herrings," not material in law for the matters to be determined in the proceedings. Interest in irrelevant issues was further fuelled by obvious confusion on the part of the judge and counsel about the law of consent and its significance for proof of the elements of the offence of sexual assault in the specific circumstances of this case.

Edmondson was convicted by the jury and, on 4 September 2003, was sentenced to a conditional sentence of two years less a day to be served in the community. Kindrat and Brown were acquitted by their jury. On 19 January 2005, the Saskatchewan Court of Appeal heard and dismissed Edmondson's appeals against conviction[6] and sentence and, in a brief oral judgment, allowed the Crown's appeal from the verdicts of acquittal for Kindrat and Brown on the ground of multiple errors of law in the trial proceedings.[7]

Cameron JA did not provide a detailed account of those errors, but did direct that on the retrial the instructions to the jury were to include reference to s 273.2. That *Code* provision specifies circumstances in which the defence of belief in consent is not available as a matter of law. In this latter matter the court may have seen itself to be adopting the position of the Crown on the appeal. The factum filed in the appeal on behalf of the Attorney General of Saskatchewan, appellant in the appeal from the acquittal of Kindrat and Brown, stated:

> The court did not instruct the jury in accordance with s 273.2. To be fair none of the lawyers, including the prosecutor, thought there was a need to refer to the section. With respect there was no choice in the matter. The court was under a duty to instruct the jury in accordance with s 273.2 and the failure to do so was a fatal one.[8]

The authority given for this proposition was *R v Ewanchuk*[9] per Major J. However, in *Ewanchuk*, Mr Justice Major observed that s 273.2(b) of the *Criminal Code* only applies to cases in which there is an "air of reality" to the defence of mistaken belief in consent.[10] The same comment applies to s 273.2 as a whole. In the absence of evidence on the basis

6 The Court of Appeal substituted a conviction under s 271(a) for the conviction entered at trial under s 272(1)(d).

7 *Supra* note 1.

8 *R v Brown*, [2005] S J No 43, 2005 Sask CA 7, Docket 687 (Factum of the Appellant at para 50).

9 *R v Ewanchuk*, [1999] 1 SCR 330 at paras 50, 65.

10 *Ibid* at para 60; see also paras 58, 64. The comment was made in response to the assertion by L'Heureux-Dubé, J at para 98 that the trial judge in *Ewanchuk* erred in law by not applying s 273.2(b).

of which a reasonable jury deliberating in a judicial manner *could* acquit on the ground that the accused may have believed the complainant consented, the defence is not available. The defence cannot be left with the jury because, as a matter of law, it cannot result in an acquittal.[11]

To ask a jury to consider the defence in those circumstances would be to invite them to arrive at an unsound verdict based on speculation. By ordering that the jury at the *retrial* be instructed on the defence of mistaken belief in consent, Justice Cameron was prejudging the availability of the defence. This was improper and an error of law. The availability of the defence in law could only be determined on the basis of the evidence presented on the retrial. Only if the defence of mistaken belief in consent was available in law based on the evidence adduced at the retrial would it be proper to instruct the jury to consider the defence. The Crown did not seek variation or review of Mr Justice Cameron's order. The Crown may have believed the order to be proper.

The retrial of Kindrat in 2007 showed less flagrant disregard for the *Code* provisions that restrict the admission of evidence of the complainant's sexual and personal history. However, despite submissions to the contrary by the prosecutor on the *Kindrat* retrial, the judge regarded herself as bound by Mr Justice Cameron's direction that the jury was to be instructed on the provisions of s 273.2. The judge who presided over Brown's retrial in 2008 also took this view. Accordingly, in each retrial, the jury was instructed to consider the defence of mistaken belief in consent even though, in each case, as I explain below, this was arguably an error of law. The defence was not available to either Kindrat or Brown on the evidence as a matter of law and should not have been left with the jury.

As noted above, no attempt was made by the chief crown prosecutor to have those directions amended or struck by the Court of Appeal when the order for the retrial was issued in January of 2005. It appears that the chief crown prosecutor, who worked closely with the office of the provincial deputy director of prosecutions [DDP] and argued the appeals before the Court of Appeal, assumed the defence would be available. This likely explains why the deputy director concluded that there were no grounds for appeal from the acquittal rendered by the

11 This is an application of the common law test for availability of defences based on sufficiency of evidence. Applicable to all statutory and common law defences, the test was codified in 1983 in the first branch of s 265(4) of the *Criminal Code* with respect to the defence of belief in consent. In *R v Osolin*, [1993] 4 SCR 595, s 265(4) was held to impose only an evidentiary burden on the accused and not to violate either s 11(c) or (d) of the *Charter*.

jury at the *Kindrat* retrial in 2007, and explains why the charges against Brown were stayed by the Crown in 2008 following Brown's retrial. In my opinion, the deputy director's position on this issue was not defensible. In both cases, the decision to leave the defence of belief in consent to the jury was an error of law. Therefore, there actually were grounds for appeal from the verdict of acquittal rendered by the jury in the *Kindrat* retrial.

Following Kindrat's acquittal by two juries, a further retrial likely would have been condemned by some as an "oppressive" use of prosecutorial authority rather than viewed as necessary duc to legal errors in both the trial and the retrial. However, an appeal of the acquittal on the ground of misdirection of the jury at the retrial was needed to clarify interpretation and operation of the law on the availability of the defence of belief in consent and interpretation and application of s 150.1(4) of the *Criminal Code*.[12] If an appeal from the acquittal had been granted on the ground of error of law and an order for a retrial issued, the Crown would then have had an opportunity to decide whether to prosecute. The chief crown prosecutor's decision not to appeal the verdict denied the court the opportunity to rule on any issue. The decision not to appeal also precluded any possibility of a further appeal to the Supreme Court of Canada.

The approach the DDP took in this case suggests that exercise by the Attorney General of Saskatchewan of prosecutorial discretion in relation to the appeal function does not always reflect current legal standards. The decisions taken by the Attorney General in this case may be indicative of an overall pattern of conduct that has significant long-term implications for judicial practice in sexual assault cases in the province and warrants close scrutiny. Over time and in the aggregate, failure to appeal what are arguably erroneous and regressive interpretations of the sexual assault laws allows those laws to operate differently in the province of Saskatchewan than current legal standards prescribe. This is a grave problem. Consider the following:

An accused may appeal from a verdict of conviction as of right. Only the provincial Attorney General is authorized to appeal acquittals in proceedings initiated by the provincial Attorney General. If prosecu-

12 Section 150.1(4) of the *Criminal Code* provides that the defence of belief in consent is not available where an accused failed to take "all reasonable steps" to ascertain the age of a complainant who is less than fourteen years of age. The provision preserves a mistake of fact defence while, at the same time, requiring a high standard of care to protect underage persons. The section imposes a tactical evidentiary burden on the accused. See *infra* at notes 18 and 19.

torial discretion is not exercised to appeal: (1) acquittals that are unreasonable verdicts or are based on misdirection, and (2) decisions and orders of the Court of Appeal that are arguably incorrect in law, sexual assault jurisprudence and the conduct of many sexual assault trials in the province of Saskatchewan will be inconsistent with current law as interpreted by the Supreme Court of Canada. This is not the first time the Attorney General of Saskatchewan has elected not to appeal a decision by the Court of Appeal in which the court arguably erred in law when interpreting the sexual assault laws. The decisions by the court in *R v Ecker*[13] — impliedly authorizing the admission of evidence other-

13 *R v Ecker* (1995), 96 CCC (3d) 161, 128 Sask R 161, 37 CR (4th) 51, 85 WAC 161 (Sask CA) per Cameron JA, Vancise JA concurring; Lane JA dissenting. This was an appeal by the accused from conviction in a trial in which the judge ruled sexual history evidence inadmissible under s 276. The Court of Appeal granted the appeal and ordered a new trial on the ground that the trial judge should have held a *voir dire* under s 276.2. In dissent, Lane JA observed that the order granting a new trial, so that the *voir dire* could be held, implied that the evidence was admissible under s 276(2) on the ground that it could support a defence of belief in consent. Lane notes that the original application (dismissed at trial) actually sought admission of the evidence for a prohibited purpose, ie to attack the credibility of the complainant. As such the application was properly rejected. Lane observes that even if the reason for seeking admission of the evidence had instead been to provide evidence of probative value on the issue of belief in consent, it was difficult to see how the alleged sexual touching of the accused by the complainant some weeks before the offence had any probative value for belief in consent in relation to the offence with which the accused was charged. I suggest that the error underlying Cameron's judgment is best viewed as an error about the definition of consent, ie an error of law. *Ecker*'s purported reliance on belief in consent on the basis contemplated here by Cameron J would be a mistake of law, exactly like those so squarely rejected by Major J in *Ewanchuk*, *supra* note 9 at para 51. The decision rendered by Cameron JA for the Court of Appeal in *Ecker* should have been appealed. It was not, and the decision continues to be the leading authority under Saskatchewan law on interpretation of s 276.1 and, indirectly, as Lane JA recognized, on the admissibility of sexual history evidence under s 276(2) of the *Criminal Code*. In ruling on the latter issue, other provincial appeal courts generally omit any reference to *Ecker* or distinguish it — as in *R v CEN*, [1998] AJ No 1001 (Alta CA). Post-*Ewanchuk*, it should be apparent that, on the facts in *Ecker*, an accused could only be acquitted on the ground that the disputed evidence may have led him to mistakenly believe the complainant consented if he were permitted to use a mistake about the law of consent as an excuse. But *Ewanchuk* precludes that; the reasons for judgment by Justice Major invoke established common law principles, long codified in s 19 of the *Code*, to hold that a belief in consent that relies on a mistake of law does not excuse an accused. Reliance on the defence of belief in consent that is based on ignorance of the law or a mistake about the legal definition of consent is barred as a matter of law. The disputed evidence therefore has no probative value and therefore no legal relevance in relation to a material fact in issue and is not admissible. This illustrates the value of *legal* relevance as a tool in assessing the admissibility of evidence under s 276. See also Hamish Stewart, *Sexual Offences in Canadian Law*,

wise excluded under the rape shield provisions, and more recently in the instant case in its decision in *R v Brown*[14] — directing that the jury be instructed on the defence of belief in consent before it could be known whether the defence would be available on the evidence at the retrial, seriously impede effective enforcement of the sexual assault laws in Saskatchewan. The effect is that of balkanization: the creation of an island within Canada where key aspects of the sexual laws as amended in 1992 are not correctly interpreted and applied by judges and regressive interpretations of the sexual assault laws go unchallenged by the provincial Attorney General. This pattern of inaction by the provincial Attorney General is an issue of leading importance. Further evidence of such a pattern is seen in the Crown's decision to stay the charges against Brown following the jury's failure to agree on a verdict at his retrial in 2008. The Attorney General may have failed to appreciate that the jury's difficulty was most likely a direct consequence of misdirection, not weakness in the case for the prosecution.

At the *Brown* retrial, the evidence adduced by the Crown and ruled admissible by the judge provided a slightly different portrait of the facts of the case than had been presented to the juries in the earlier proceedings. Neither Kindrat nor Edmondson were called as witnesses for the Crown or for the defence. They were therefore not available for cross-examination. No sexual history evidence was admitted. *Voir dires* were held to screen the witnesses' testimony for hearsay statements before they testified in the presence of the jury. Brown's warned statement, ruled admissible as a voluntary statement at the *voir dire* in March of 2009, was read into the record. In that statement, Brown admitted all elements of the offence; he stated that it happened because they had had "too much booze" and the complainant had "come onto them" by kissing them. Mr Brown did not testify in his own defence. In fact, the defence called no evidence.

Defence counsel (who had not represented any of the accused at the previous trials), tried to establish through cross-examination of the Crown witnesses that the complainant had appeared to be two or three years older than she actually was, was "strong-willed," and perhaps had

loose-leaf (consulted on 1 May 2009) (Aurora, ON: Canada Law Book, 2005). Stewart observes that *Ecker* "may come perilously close to permitting an accused … to engage one of the 'twin myths' in order to assert a mistaken belief in consent" (8:200.20). In truth, this is precisely what it does.

14 *Supra* note 1.

not been as intoxicated as she now claimed. Under cross-examination by defence counsel, the complainant agreed that because she had "blacked-out" from time to time and could only remember portions of the trip from Chelan to Tisdale, she could not deny that she might have used words and engaged in conduct that the three men might have interpreted as communication of consent. This, which was not evidence but rather *speculation* about what she *might have said and done* that *might have been perceived* as communication of voluntary agreement or consent to the sexual activity that occurred, was then used by the defence to support the spurious argument that there was an *evidentiary* basis for the defence of belief in consent.

By contrast, the Crown pointed to the complete absence of evidence of words and conduct that constituted what the law would define as communication of consent by the twelve-year-old complainant to "group sex with three adult men in a ditch." Similarly, the Crown found no basis in the evidence for the proposition that the accused actually believed she was at least fourteen years old and that they had taken reasonable steps to ascertain her age.

Availability of the defence of belief in consent as a matter of law was thus the crucial issue in the *Brown* retrial. The trial judge and counsel engaged in extended discussions about how the jury should be instructed. Defence counsel argued that the jury should be permitted to consider the possibility that the accused were mistaken about the child's age and believed she consented. The Crown took the position that, on the evidence, there was no air of reality to these possibilities; the evidence did not provide a foundation for reasonable doubt on these issues and therefore the defence of belief in consent could not go to the jury. The defence objected that that approach would be tantamount to a directed verdict of guilty given that there was no basis for doubt about the identity of the parties, the complainant's age, or the sexual nature of the physical touching. The options discussed ranged from the simple instructions required to put the elements of the offence to the jury to the complex and lengthy instructions the judge believed would be required to instruct the jury on the defence of belief in consent.

The trial judge expressed dismay and discomfort at the direction issued by the Saskatchewan Court of Appeal in 2005 and made it clear on the record that, although she would prefer to take the approach advocated by the Crown, she would not.[15] She clearly saw herself to be

15 *R v Jeffrey Lorne Brown*, QBC 1 357/2002, JC of Melfort (Criminal jury); re-trial, Transcript of Proceedings, held: March 4, 2008, May 20, 21, 22, 23, 26, 27, 28, and 29. Volume IV, pp 594–767 at 692, 727, 735.

required to instruct the jury on s 273.2 as directed. So she did, stating, despite the Crown's objection that there was no evidence of consent as defined in law, that the jury would decide whether there was a basis for belief in consent.[16] Closing addresses by counsel were brief; the jury instructions were long. The transcript shows, 120 pages later, that the jury was unable to arrive at a unanimous verdict. The trial was adjourned and the charges against Jeffery Lorne Brown were subsequently stayed by the Crown.[17]

The Crown was undoubtedly correct. It was an error of law to put the defence of belief in consent to the jury at the *Brown* retrial without a sufficient evidentiary foundation. In addition, the charge was arguably longer and more complex than was necessary and it is likely the jury was confused by the instructions. The charge included instructions on consent and belief in consent, and thus invited the jury to determine whether the complainant consented even though they were also told that she lacked legal capacity to consent because of her age. The question put to them should have been limited to whether the evidence showed that the accused could have believed the complainant communicated consent or voluntary agreement to the sexual activity that occurred and, if so, whether any of the grounds set out in s 150.1 or s 273.2 to preclude the accused from relying on a belief in consent as an excuse were proven. The phrase "honest belief" easily misleads even experienced jurists and should have been avoided in instructing the jury. The charge by the judge should have omitted the term "honest" and used only the statutory terms — "belief," "intoxication," "recklessness," and "wilful blindness" — in relation to s 150.1 and s 273.2. After *Esau* and *Ewanchuk*, there can be no question but that mistakes about consent that are reckless, wilfully blind, or due to intoxication, do not exculpate. Deliberate physical contact of a sexual nature entails culpability if the accused acts with awareness or suspicion that consent to that contact is absent, or relies on a mistake about the legal definition of consent. The instructions failed to make it clear that if the jury was

16 When the trial judge asked defence counsel to point to specific facts in evidence that showed communication of consent, he asserted that it was the "context" overall, not specific facts in evidence, that he relied on to provide the foundation for the defence. That is not what the law requires. In the end, the trial judge concluded (transcript, p 733) that the jury would decide whether the *evidence* that was available about the complainant's specific words and conduct supported the conclusion that the accused might have believed that she communicated consent to the sexual activity. Here we see a judge complying with an order that requires her to abdicate her role as arbiter of the law to the jury.

17 *Supra* note 1.

satisfied that the evidence as a whole proved beyond a reasonable doubt that the accused had been callously indifferent to the issues of age and consent, or had pursued his sexual activity with awareness that the complainant either was or might be younger than fourteen years of age, he was barred from using the possibility that he was mistaken about her age as an excuse, and could not rely on the defence of belief in consent.

UNREASONABLE VERDICT ON THE EVIDENCE?

The complainant was only twelve years of age at the end of September of 2001; therefore, as a matter of law, consent was not available as a defence.[18] Testimony about her condition prior to and following the assault was available from numerous witnesses — the police officers, the physician who attended her at the Tisdale hospital, the specialist who documented her lacerations and bruises in Saskatoon, the Pierces who took her to the Tisdale hospital, and the bar-keeper in Mistatim. Other witnesses who saw her with the accused prior to the assault and in Tisdale following the assault undoubtedly could also have been subpoenaed. Evidence was adduced to prove that when she arrived in Tisdale shortly after the assault she was not only grossly intoxicated, but her clothes were covered with dirt and mud, and she was extremely distraught. Evidence from witnesses confirmed that it was impossible to communicate with her at the hospital, that she could not stand up, and that she was unable to co-operate or assist with any procedures. There were also incriminating statements from the three accused, obtained by the RCMP on 1 October 2001. Those statements, held to be admissible at trial, showed: (1) that each of them had engaged in sexual activity with the complainant, and (2) that they did not know how old she was. The evidence from these sources, all independent of the complainant, sufficed to show the nature and severity of the assault and, combined with a copy of the complainant's birth certificate to prove her age, provided admissible evidence of all the essential elements of the offence.

Evidence in the record shows the accused alleged that the complainant told them both that she was fifteen years of age and that she was almost fifteen years of age, and that the accused took no other steps to ascertain her age. One or more of the accused could have testified at trial in an attempt to show that he believed the complainant consented and that he should be allowed to rely on the defence of belief in consent

18 In 2001, the *Code* specified that valid consent to sexual activity could not be obtained from a person under the age of fourteen years. See s 150.1(1).

because he took steps to ascertain her age and believed her to be fifteen years old.[19] But no accused testified in any of the proceedings other

19 In 2001, s 150.1 of the *Criminal Code* provided that where the complainant was under the statutory age of consent (fourteen years of age in 2001), no accused who was more than two years older than the complainant could rely on the defence of belief in consent *unless* the accused took "all reasonable steps to ascertain the complainant's age." Evidence of the steps taken is required to raise this issue. Ordinarily it will be necessary for the accused to testify to provide that evidence, but the accused may rely on any evidence before the court. For a few years the leading case on s 150.1(4) was *R v Osborne* (1992), 17 CR (4th) 350, a decision of Goodridge, CJN in the Appeal Division of the Newfoundland Supreme Court. Justice Goodridge stated: "It is more than a casual requirement. There must be an earnest inquiry or some other compelling factor that obviates the need for an inquiry. An accused person can only discharge the requirement by showing what steps he took and that these steps were all that could be reasonably required of him in the circumstances." In *R v RAK*, [1996] NBJ No 104, [1996] ANB No 104, 175 NBR (2d) 225, 106 CCC (3d) 93, 30 WCB (2d) 213, No 293/95/CA (NBCA) per Hoyt CJNB, (Ryan and Turnbull JJA concurring), the court observed: "Almost without exception, the greater the disparity in ages, the more inquiry will be required."

Since the mid-1990s, however, some provincial courts have moved beyond working with the provision as if it were a free-standing defence that merely requires a demonstration of "objective reasonableness" and instead now explicitly view it as a means of asking whether there is reasonable doubt about culpable awareness in relation to the age of the complainant. Thus *R v Westman*, [1995] BCJ No 2124, 65 BCAC 285, 28 WCB (2d) 440 (BCCA) per Southin, JA (Legg and Hinds, JJA concurring) construes s 150.1(4) as follows: "For the purposes of this section, a person who believes the complainant not to be under the age of fourteen years but who has failed to take all reasonable steps to ascertain the age of the complainant is recklessly indifferent." In *R v P (LT)* (1997), 113 CCC (3d) 42 (BCCA) the court reviewed the authorities including Westman and concluded at para 19: "[W]here the defence of honest but mistaken belief in the complainant's age arises in circumstances where s 150.1(4) applies, the Crown must prove beyond a reasonable doubt that the accused did not take all reasonable steps to ascertain the complainant's age, or that he did not have an honest belief that her age was fourteen years or more. For the defence to succeed, it must point to evidence which gives rise to a reasonable doubt that the accused held the requisite belief, and in addition, evidence which gives rise to a reasonable doubt that the accused took all reasonable steps to ascertain the complainant's age." This approach, in which all reasonable steps are used to test the honesty of the belief, is explicitly approved in *R v Slater*, [2005] SJ No 412, 2005 Sask CA 87, [2006] 5 WWR 233, 269 Sask R 42, 201 CCC (3d) 85, 31 CR (6th) 112, 66 WCB (2d) 35 per Jackson JA, (Sherstobitoff and Lane JJA, concuring). The case law has, in effect, reaffirmed that at its root the issue is one of mistake of fact (in this case a mistake about age). Mistake of fact is a defence that operates by negativing *mens rea* and therefore the ultimate issue has commonly been articulated as whether the accused "honestly" believed that the complainant was of the age of consent. Thus at paragraph 23 in *Slater*, discussing the companion provision, s 150.1(5), which is the same as s 150.1(4) in all material aspects, Jackson JA observes: "Section 150.1(5) was added so as to test the foundation of an honest belief, not to impose an additional burden on the Crown. The purpose of s 212(4) and s 150.1(5) is to protect minors from becoming involved in the sex trade by than as a witness for the prosecution. Any accused who testified in his own defence would have been subject to cross-examination[20] by the prosecutor. The statements the accused gave to the RCMP on 1 October 2001 showed that the accused did not actually *know* her age and provided ample grounds to infer that their sexual conduct demonstrated callous indifference to her age, to her capacity to consent, and to the issue of consent.[21] Had the accused testified, these issues might have been canvassed, along with the question of just how her words and conduct (allegedly kissing Edmondson, putting her arms around their necks) communicated agreement to the specific and highly invasive sexual assaults they performed on her body. But no such evidence was offered by the defence. Even when the evidence on the record is viewed in the light most favourable to the accused, there was no evidence to support the defence. On the evidence, any belief the accused may have had that the complainant consented to have sex with them could only have been based on a mistake about the law and, as the decision by the Supreme Court of Canada in *Ewanchuk*[22] affirmed, that is not a lawful excuse.

discouraging those who would, but for the provision, choose to exploit them." These developments are consistent with the jurisprudence in *R v Esau*, [1997] 2 SCR 777 and *Ewanchuk*, *supra* note 9, in which the Supreme Court of Canada held that an "honest" belief is never reckless or wilfully blind. As a consequence, whenever the availability of the defence of belief in consent depends on whether the accused took "all reasonable steps" to ascertain the complainant's age, the trial judge must also determine whether there is sufficient evidence to raise a reasonable doubt that any belief about the complainant's age was reckless or wilfully blind. If not, there is no "air of reality" to the accused's claim to have believed that the complainant was old enough to give valid consent and the defence of belief in consent is therefore unavailable to the accused as a matter of law. In a jury trial, the trial judge must make this determination before instructing the jury. It is my contention that in the *Kindrat* and *Brown* retrials, there was insufficient evidence of steps taken to ascertain the complainant's age to raise a reasonable doubt about either accused's culpable awareness (recklessness, wilful blindness) with respect to the complainant's age. Their statements contained open admissions that they did not know how old she was. Clearly they were aware that they did not *know* her age. The defence of belief in consent was not available in law in those circumstances and should not have left with the jury.

20 Because none of the accused testified in their own defence, but only as Crown witnesses, the Crown prosecutor had no opportunity to cross-examine any of them.

21 Compare *R v Whitely and Mowers*, [1992] OJ No 3076 (Ont Ct J Gen Div) (reasons for sentence per Locke J); [1993] OJ No 2970 (Ont CA); and [1994] 3 SCR 830. The case concerned the sexual assault of a mildly intoxicated young female university student by three young men indicted as principals under s 271(a), tried as co-accused in a jury trial, and convicted. Availability of the defence of belief in consent and alleged misdirection of the jury were the grounds relied on in the appeal from conviction (unsuccessful on both grounds) and sentence (reduced in part).

22 *Supra* note 9 at para 51. See also *supra* note 13 for discussion of the bar against reliance on mistakes of law.

A judge, sitting alone and properly interpreting and applying the law to the evidence, would have concluded without difficulty that the Crown had proven the essential elements of the offences beyond a reasonable doubt with respect to all three accused and that the defence of belief in consent was unavailable. The evidence was insufficient to provide an evidentiary foundation for the defence of belief in consent as defined in law and, in addition, not only showed that the accused failed to take "all reasonable steps" to ascertain the complainant's age as required by s 150.1 but, more to the point, showed that they *knew* that they did not know how old she was. All three accused would therefore have been liable to be convicted under s 271(1).

Further findings of fact by the judge based on the evidence in the record might have included: (1) that the complainant was in a relationship of dependency on the accused at the time of the offences; (2) that the complainant was incapable of consenting to sexual activity due to gross intoxication at the time of the offences; and (3) that the accused were all aware of, recklessly indifferent, or wilfully blind with respect to the complainant's age and her dependency and incapacity. They had, after all, supplied and encouraged her to drink multiple bottles of beer and had witnessed its impact on her. If the trial judge were alleged to have erred in law, an appeal on a question of law would have been available. The appeal judge or court would have been in a position to uphold the conviction of each accused as a principal to the offence of sexual assault by affirming that, on the facts as found at trial, any belief in consent could have only been a mistake about the law of consent and the defence was therefore unavailable. The conviction of each accused as a party to the offences committed by the other two would also have been possible as long as the trial judge made and recorded the findings of fact necessary to support convictions on these other counts.

TWO THEORIES AND ONE CONCLUSION

There are at least two theories to account for the handling of the *Edmondson, Kindrat,* and *Brown* cases. Both are generally consistent with the publicly known facts. One theory is that the case reflects the firm commitment of the provincial Attorney General to persevere with enforcement of the sexual assault laws without regard for the race and cultural backgrounds of the complainant or the accused, despite delays caused by multiple errors of law, retrials, and complexities arising from the fact that there were three rather than only one accused. Another theory is that the prosecution was undertaken reluctantly and was pursued only due to significant political pressure. But it is immaterial for my purposes which theory is preferred because my focus is on consequences, not on motive. Motive, good or bad, does not change effects; and it is effects, results, consequences that matter in this context. The evidence suggests that the prosecution of this case was hindered from the beginning by strategic misjudgments, and by the loss and neglect of key evidence, and was ultimately undermined by serious legal errors in the conduct of the trials and the retrials. The effects of those errors include the ineffective prosecution of the criminal laws prohibiting sexual violence against a twelve-year-old Aboriginal girl, a complainant who is a member of at least three historically disadvantaged groups — females, Aboriginals, and children, and the creation of a bad precedent for the instruction of Saskatchewan juries in sexual assault cases. The effects remain the same whatever the motives may have been. In the end, one conclusion emerges: changes are required in the conduct of prosecutions of sexual offences against women and children in the province of Saskatchewan. Effective remedies must be found; there is no excuse for the flawed approach to enforcement of the sexual assault laws this case reveals.

INEQUALITIES BASED ON RACE, GENDER, AND AGE

Race, gender, and age, as well as the interlocking inequalities with which these factors are associated, were all significant in this case. At each stage of the proceedings, the judge and counsel should have been fully alert to the possible influence of these factors on the manner in which the accused and the complainant interacted. Failure to squarely name and acknowledge inequalities linked to race, gender, and age as potent factors in the social reality that formed the context for this case only made it more, not less, likely that those same factors would also distort the legal proceedings. When one of the accused first saw the complainant, he immediately referred to her as "Pocahontas," invoking a well-recognized, sexualized, and racialized stereotype and script.[23] It was downhill from there. This small child's considerable vulnerability to abuse by the three older, much larger, accused[24] appears to have been significantly amplified by their distorted and self-serving perceptions of the social significance of her age-race-gender, the very characteris-

23 See discussion of the history of the common stereotypes of "princess" and "squaw" and their relationship to the indifference in the dominant culture to violence against Native women in *Principles of Advocacy: A Guide for Sexual Assault Advocates* (Duluth, MN: Mending the Sacred Hoop Technical Assistance Project, 2004) at 6–9.

24 She weighed about eighty-seven pounds and was less than five feet tall; the combined weight of the three accused was well over five hundred pounds. The clothing she was wearing at the time of the assault shows how very tiny she was.

tics they associated with the name "Pocahontas."[25] These same factors appear to have affected the choices made by some participants in the subsequent investigation and legal proceedings as well.

Treatment of the issues of age, race, and gender in the proceedings involved deficiencies of omission and commission. On the one hand, in instructing jurors, the presiding judges failed to draw attention to the differences in race, gender, and age between the complainant and the accused for the purpose of suggesting that the jurors needed to avoid being inappropriately influenced by stock stereotypes associated with those factors when assessing the evidence and deliberating on the issues. On the other hand, the record contains numerous examples of comments about the evidence by some counsel and at least one of the judges that invite inferences based on common racist and sexist stereotypes. Repeated questions and comments suggesting that irrelevant and collateral facts are relevant necessarily undermine any attempt to curtail the impact of prejudicial myths and stereotypes on a jury's deliberation process.

In cases that appear to include racist elements, as this case undeniably does, it is not appropriate for judges to invite jurors to blind themselves and assume that the significance of the facts is invariably race-neutral, gender-neutral, and age-neutral, devoid of social context. To do so is to deny social reality and distort the truth-seeking process. It is likewise inappropriate for judges to permit and even encourage discourse in the courtroom that invokes discriminatory stereotypes and suggests that invalid inferences may be drawn from the evidence. Counsel, as officers of the court, need to examine their personal perceptions of the facts of cases for the influence of assumptions and stereotypes. Questions and comments that incorporate those assumptions and stereotypes should not be used; to use them is to imply that they are based on valid generalizations. Both judges and counsel need to re-examine how discourse and conduct in the courtroom detracts from conditions conducive to non-biased perception of the evidence and non-discriminatory deliberation that nonetheless remains alert to the realities of the social context within which the case arose. These issues are challenging and need to be examined and widely discussed by members of the judiciary, counsel, and by legal educators.

25 Similarly, in a written statement to the police the following day, Brown referred to the complainant they saw sitting on the hotel steps as "a native girl."

REMEDIAL ACTION ON MULTIPLE LEVELS

The problems highlighted by the handling of this case require remedial action on a number of levels, from the practical to the political and back again. On the practical front, a few obvious steps can be taken. Better training and resources could improve the collection and preservation of evidence and ensure that prompt and appropriate health care is available to complainants. Prosecutorial and judicial discretion, exercised within the framework of current rules of practice and procedure, can be used to reduce delay and the number of times complainants and Crown witnesses are required to testify. Ideally, the decision in a sexual assault case should explain the law, develop the jurisprudence as necessary to arrive at a decision, and provide the accused and other members of the community with notice of what the law requires of them. Well-drafted and accessible decisions can serve all of these essential socio-legal functions.

However, this case also involved social ignorance and racial and gender inequality as factors in the offence itself, in the conduct of the legal proceedings, and in the "social meaning" and impact of this case on the parties, the community, and social relationships between individuals and groups in the community. In fact, most sexual assault cases incorporate one or more of these elements, and the eradication of the effects of racist and misogynist bias in social interactions related to sexual assault remains far more of a challenge than the practical issues mentioned above will ever be.

On all these levels, we can identify specific and general objectives for the handling of sexual assault cases by the criminal justice system that were not well-served in this case, and were instead frustrated or subverted. The nature of the socio-legal phenomena the sexual assault laws address and the magnitude of the attitudinal changes in the community and the legal profession that appear to be required to secure broad compliance with, and accurate interpretation and application of those laws, are unique. We need a set of remedies designed to ensure that the functioning of criminal legal process itself, as it is organized and operated, does not frustrate and ultimately subvert the objectives of the sexual assault laws as enacted by Parliament. Some may argue that further modifications in legal procedures, policies, practices, and institutions are necessary to prevent the very same beliefs and attitudinal factors that are implicated in the commission of the offence of sexual assault from the subverting of proper interpretation and application of the sexual assault laws. Such factors certainly had a significant role in both the offence and the legal process in the *Edmondson, Kindrat,* and

Brown cases. Others may assert that adequate legal tools are available, and the problem is simply failure to use them due to the lack of specialized training or lack of commitment to the rule of law.

No one, in any event, should underestimate the significance of practical issues for both *outcomes* and *attitudes*. The effort and commitment required from investigators, health care providers, and legal professionals first to imagine and then to make the choices required to address practical matters — delays, multiple proceedings imposing a burden on complainants, acquittals attributable to poor investigation and file preparation, questions about legally extraneous issues used in defiance of the rape shield and personal records provisions, errors due to lack of a sound working knowledge of the sexual laws, etc. — will undoubtedly produce changes that affect outcomes. That same personal effort and commitment will, I predict, support gradual changes in the attitudes of these professionals towards sexual assault complainants and the legal process in sexual assault cases. At the same time, the overall improvement in the handling of the practical aspects of sexual assault cases will, in turn, have a positive impact on the self-esteem and social profile of complainants, individually and as a group. The combination of these effects, working in tandem, will contribute to re-shaping widely held beliefs and attitudes that presently marginalize complainants in society and in the legal process. However, the process of designing incremental and systemic remedies to address the weaknesses in police, prosecutorial, and judicial policy and practice of the types highlighted by the handling of this case needs to be open-ended and subject to ongoing review and modification based on experience within specific social and practice contexts. All participants need to remain alert to the diverse and ever-emerging new ways in which the principle of equal protection of the law can be hijacked in a sexual assault case.

COLLECT AND PRESERVE EVIDENCE

Proper investigation and timely collection and preservation of evidence are essential for the effective prosecution of sexual assault cases. In *Edmondson, Kindrat,* and *Brown,* police did not formally interview the complainant until October of 2002, more than twelve months after the assault. Even then the interview was in connection with another file, not this case. An officer from the local RCMP post attended at the Tisdale Hospital emergency department on 30 September 2001, but the complainant was not capable of being interviewed at that time. A videotaped statement by the complainant, made as soon as reasonably possible after the assault, would not only have preserved her evidence at a time close to the events in question, but would also have preserved a record of her image and demeanour as the twelve-year-old child she then was. The complainant would have been spared the trauma of testifying in court again and again. Sensitive judicial practice encourages the use of videotaped statements by children.[26] This omission, like the failure to seize the complainant's blood sample at the hospital for testing, remains unexplained. The accused were all residents of Tisdale. The investigating officers knew them and may have believed that the case against the "boys," as one officer described them in evidence at the *Brown* retrial in 2008, would not proceed.

On the other hand, the RCMP did take steps to obtain evidence that, in law, had no bearing on the case. Better police training might have not only ensured the preservation of relevant evidence, but also prevented the investigation in this case from being polluted and tainted with irrelevant information from other open files. There clearly are questions about the approach taken to investigation of the case by the police. Was the investigation and decision-making in this case shaped by police preoccupation with one or more *other* cases? Police obtained DNA evidence from persons other than the accused for comparison with a stain on the complainant's underwear. That evidence was immaterial to this case because the identity of the accused and the sexual nature of the assault were not in question. To bring that evidence into the public forum for consideration at trial, as was done in this case, constituted a clear invasion of the complainant's privacy rights and an overt attack on her dignity. The evidence was subject to the restrictions under s 276 of the *Criminal Code* and should have been excluded at the trials as it later was at the retrials.[27] Instead, it was seized on by defence counsel and the media in 2003 and made the focus of widespread comment and discussion in the community. The members of the media and the community appeared not to understand that whether there was or was not a DNA match between the stain and persons *other than* the accused had no bearing on the case.

When the complainant arrived at the Tisdale hospital, no one on duty had the specialized skills and experience required to care for her

26 *R v F (CC)* (1997), 120 CCC(3d) 225 at 243–44 (SCC) per Justice Cory. See also *supra* notes 34, 35, and the accompanying text. It is surprising that none was prepared for use in this case.

27 The trial judge failed to appreciate this issue; the judges who presided over the retrials were alert to it. No application was ever actually brought under s 276 by defence counsel in either trial or retrial. Both trials were presided over by the same judge; the retrials had different judges. One prosecutor represented the Crown at both trials; a second Crown prosecutor handled the case at the two retrials.

and collect the standard forensic evidence. Even the physician called to the hospital to attend to her lacked the training and experience required to complete all aspects of the rape kit, especially with a patient who could not stand up or otherwise co-operate due to her gross intoxication and distress. The next day, arrangements were made for the complainant to be seen by a child abuse specialist in Saskatoon.

In this case, current standards for the provision of health services following sexual assault were not met. The physical and psychological healthcare needs of complainants are best assessed and addressed without delay by providers who have specialized training and experience. A Sexual Assault Nurse Examiner [SANE] trained and certified in accord with current protocols, and supplied with all necessary equipment, should be available in a hospital or clinic in every community. Forensic evidence that is not collected and preserved in accordance with strict protocols is not admissible in subsequent legal proceedings, civil or criminal. Potential complainants should have the opportunity to secure and preserve forensic evidence without being required to make an immediate decision about criminal or civil action.

AVOID DELAY, STREAMLINE PROCESS

This case extended over almost seven years, involved appeals and retrials, and led to largely inconclusive results. The one accused who was convicted received a sentence of two years less a day, only marginally longer than the maximum sentence of eighteen months available on conviction in summary conviction proceedings. There is no one — the accused, the complainant, their families, and the affected communities — who would not have benefited from a prompt disposition of the case. The delays and indecision experienced in the case, as prosecuted, only exacerbated social strain and conflict between the Aboriginal and non-Aboriginal communities, heightened public exasperation with the criminal justice process, and further eroded general public trust in the justice process in the province. All these effects were socially divisive and harmful. In addition, awareness of the course of these legal proceedings will inevitably deter many individuals who are sexually assaulted in Saskatchewan from filing complaints with the police. Given a choice, no complainant would wish to be required to participate in legal proceedings even half as long, personally intrusive, and frustrating as the proceedings were in this case. Cases like this are one of the reasons such a small proportion of sexual assaults are reported to the police.

Courts and counsel can work together to expedite or "fast-track" the trial process in sexual assault cases. Courts can give priority to these cases when allocating use of resources such as courtrooms and judges. When proceeding by indictment, prosecutors can ask the provincial Attorney General to issue a direct indictment and proceed to trial without a preliminary hearing. Prior to the ruling in the *Stinchcombe* case,[28] which requires the Crown to provide the defence with full disclosure of the case for the prosecution, the preliminary inquiry served a disclosure function. Post-*Stinchcombe*, disclosure is available by other means. In addition, insofar as the purpose of the preliminary inquiry is to prevent weak cases from going to trial, this function is served within the trial itself in that the judge may withdraw the case from the jury and issue a directed verdict of acquittal in those cases in which a properly instructed jury could not convict on the admissible evidence in the case.[29] The use of direct indictments in sexual assault cases therefore appears highly desirable. It is not inconsistent with maintaining procedural protections for the accused and would both alleviate some stress for complainants and other Crown witnesses and expedite the legal process by eliminating the need to schedule both a preliminary hearing and a trial when proceeding by indictment.

When a direct indictment is not issued and a preliminary inquiry is held, the burden imposed on the complainant and other Crown witnesses can be reduced by submitting evidence at the preliminary inquiry by means of a written statement under the authority of s 540(7) or, in some cases, in the form of a videotaped statement. At the conclusion of the preliminary inquiry, the judge either discharges or commits the accused to trial. The decision to commit to trial or discharge is reviewable. The standard for committal to trial is the same as that applied to directed verdicts of acquittal.[30]

In cases with more than one accused, the prosecutor must also decide whether to charge the accused jointly or separately. Separate charges require separate preliminary hearings and separate trials and thus multiply the number of times Crown witnesses will be required to testify. By charging Edmondson separately from Kindrat and Brown, the Crown was able to call Edmondson as a witness at the others' trial and vice versa. This appears to have been the Crown's reason for wanting to sever Edmondson's case. But the rules governing joinder and severance of the trials of co-accused favour the joint trial of co-accused even where there are mutually incriminating statements by the co-accused, as was the case here. This is in accord with the general rule that

28 *R v Stinchcombe*, [1991] 3 SCR 326.

29 *R v Rowbotham*, [1994] 2 SCR 463; *R v Charmenski*, [1998] 1 SCR 679.

30 *Criminal Code*, s 548(1); *R v Arcuri*, [2001] 2 SCR 828; *R v Fontaine*, [2004] 1 SCR 702.

those charged with offences based on an enterprise or transaction, in which each is alleged to have played a part, ought to be tried together. The statement of each is only evidence against the party who made the statement and is not to be used as evidence against any co-accused implicated in the statement. The jury is to be carefully instructed on the use they may and may not make of the evidence with respect to each accused. Defence counsel for each co-accused has full rights to cross-examine other co-accused.[31] In this case, it would appear that under the rules there should have been only one trial and, at most, one preliminary inquiry.

But the complainant had some difficulty talking about the assault, especially in a formal interrogation setting. Therefore, even though all the key elements of the offence were contained in the incriminating statements the accused gave to the RCMP in 2001, the Crown prosecutor may have believed the case could not be presented at trial without a narrative account of the offence by one or more of the accused. The Crown's dilemma over how to present the case to a jury in these circumstances underscores the importance of obtaining a videotaped statement from the complainant as soon after the offence as is reasonably possible. In *Edmondson, Kindrat,* and *Brown*, the time and equipment required to record that one videotaped statement could have resulted in the saving of significant public and private legal resources — courtrooms, judges, court-reporters, counsel fees, lives on hold, etc. In addition, by eliminating most of the uncertainty about what the complainant would say in evidence at trial, the existence of a videotaped statement by the complainant might well have had the effect of changing the advice defence counsel gave their clients, leading to guilty pleas.

The case is striking in another respect as well. It dramatically illustrates the link, common to all cases tried by jury, between: (1) trial by a jury, (2) the fact that juries render verdicts but do not issue reasons for their decisions or otherwise record their findings of fact, and (3) the re-

31 *Criminal Code*, RS, c C-34, s 591(3)(b); *R v McLeod* (1983), 6 CCC (3d) 29, per Zuber, Goodman, Grange JJA (Ont CA); affirmed [1986] 1 SCR 703, (sub nom *Farquharson v R*) 27 CCC (3d) 383, per Beetz, McIntyre, Chouinard, Lamer, Wilson, Le Dain, La Forest JJ; *R v Lapointe* (1981), 64 CCC (2d) 562, Graburn Co Ct J (Ont Gen Sess Peace); reversed on other grounds (1983), 9 CCC (3d) 366, Lacourcière, Cory, Tarnopolsky JJA (Ont CA); affirmed [1987] 1 SCR 1253, 35 CCC (3d) 287, Dickson CJC, Beetz, Lamer, Wilson, Le Dain, La Forest, L'Heureux-Dubé JJ; and *R v Quiring* (1974), 27 CRNS 367, 19 CCC (2d) 337, Culliton CJS, Woods, Brownridge, Maguire, Hall JJA (Sask CA); leave to appeal to SCC refused (1974), 28 CRNS 128n, Judson, Ritchie, de Grandpré JJ (SCC) — Approving the trial judge's refusal to try two jointly indicted parties separately.

quirement that there be a retrial following a successful Crown appeal from an acquittal by jury.

All judges who try cases *without* a jury are now required, pursuant to a series of decisions by the Supreme Court of Canada, to provide reasons that record their findings of fact, the basis for those findings of fact, and the rationale for their decision in the case. The reasons must be sufficiently detailed and complete to permit meaningful review by an appellate court, which must be able to determine whether the decision is reasonable and sustainable in law on the evidence in the record.[32] When an appeal court overturns a verdict of acquittal or conviction rendered by a judge alone on the ground that the trial judge misdirected herself on the law, the appeal court is often able to correct the error and substitute the proper verdict by applying the law to the findings of fact recorded in the reasons for decision by the trial judge. Only when the trial process itself was conducted in an unlawful manner is it generally necessary to order a retrial.

When a jury arrives at a verdict because they have misunderstood or misapplied the law to the facts, no remedy is available unless the verdict is unreasonable or the record shows that the trial judge misdirected the jury on the law. In the latter circumstances, the appeal court may order a retrial, but cannot substitute a conviction for a verdict of acquittal rendered by the jury even in those cases in which the evidence in the record cannot reasonably support any verdict but conviction. In such cases, a retrial is ordered.[33]

These differences between proceedings by a judge alone and proceedings by a judge and jury suggest that prosecutors would be well advised to use summary conviction proceedings, whenever it is feasible to do so, rather than proceeding by indictment, unless they are confident that the accused will elect trial by judge alone. The decision to lay summary conviction charges ensures that there is no preliminary inquiry,

32 *R v Sheppard*, [2002] 1 SCR 869, 2002 SCC 26; *R v Gagnon*, [2006] 1 SCR 621, 2006 SCC 17.

33 When an accused is charged by indictment under s 271(a), he or she may elect to be tried by a jury or by a judge sitting alone without a jury. The same range of dispositions available on appeal from summary conviction proceedings are also available on an appeal from a verdict of acquittal by a judge sitting without a jury on an indictable offence: see *Criminal Code*, ss 686 and 822(1). On an appeal from a verdict of acquittal by a jury, appellate courts do not have the power to substitute a conviction: see *Criminal Code*, s 686(4)(b)(ii). An order for a jury retrial may be issued on the ground that, but for errors of law, the verdict might have been different: see *Criminal Code*, s 686(4)(b)(i).

any trial will be by a judge sitting alone without a jury and, as a direct consequence, as long as the verdict is reasonable and the legal process is conducted in a lawful manner, there will be no retrial. When an appeal is granted on the ground that the trial judge erred in instructing herself on the law, the appeal court will often be able to substitute a verdict based on the findings of fact at trial. A retrial will not be necessary and, absent a further appeal, the decision of the appeal court will conclude the proceedings in the case.

Had the accused in this case been jointly charged and tried in summary conviction proceedings, the verdict and reasons for the decision could have been reviewed on appeal by a superior court judge (in Saskatchewan, a Queen's Bench Judge) on the basis of the record, including oral or written reasons, to determine whether errors of law were made by the trial judge or whether the verdict was unreasonable given the evidence adduced at trial. In limited circumstances, such as a deficiency in the transcript of the trial, the appeal would have proceeded as a trial *de novo*, a new trial. Two further levels of appeal, to the provincial Court of Appeal and to the Supreme Court of Canada, would have been possible on those grounds. At each level of appeal, the judge or appellate court would have had the power to substitute a conviction or acquittal for the trial verdict, based on the findings of fact at trial, or order a new trial if necessary. In proceedings by indictment tried by a judge sitting without a jury, the appeal court also has those powers.

In this case, the use of either summary conviction proceedings or direct indictment followed by trial by a judge sitting alone without a jury would have reduced the number of proceedings in which the complainant was required to appear as a witness from *six* to *one* (assuming her testimony was indeed *required* — as, strictly speaking, it actually may not have been in the circumstances of this case).[34] If a videotaped statement of her evidence had been prepared in advance of trial, and the Crown chose to call her as a Crown witness, her testimony at trial would have been brief; she would have been asked whether she adopt-

34 *R v Cook*, [1997] 1 SCR 1113. There is no need for testimony from the victim of an offence where it is not required to prove the Crown's case. The defence or even the judge may call a witness who the Crown does not call. In some circumstances (eg, the complainant who is unconscious when the offence takes place as in *R v Ashlee*, [2006] ABCA 244, [2006] AWLD 2841, [2006] AWLD 2851, 61 Alta LR (4th) 226, [2006] 10 WWR 193, 40 CR (6th) 125, 212 CCC (3d) 477, 391 AR 62, 377 WAC 62) the complainant may simply have no evidence of any probative value in relation to the legal issues before the court. If so, nothing they could say would be admissible and there is no reason to call on them to testify.

ed the videotaped statement as her evidence and she would have been subject to cross-examination by defence counsel on the content of her videotaped statement and any additional evidence she might have provided for the Crown at trial.[35] The trauma the proceedings caused the complainant could have been significantly reduced as a direct consequence of eliminating both preliminary inquiries and holding one trial instead of two trials and two retrials.

Further support for an expedited process is found in studies of deterrence that show that the comparative efficacy of any penalty or punishment is greatest where it is swift and certain. A grave punishment that is unlikely to be imposed is a far less effective deterrent than a lesser punishment that is almost certain to be swiftly imposed.[36] The observation that a swift response is more efficacious applies with equal force to the denunciation component of conviction. Swift discharge or conviction on grounds that are clearly articulated in the reasons for judgment educates the parties, the public, and the legal profession about the law. Jury trials produce verdicts, but not reasons for decision. All of these considerations suggest that in sexual assault cases prosecutors should prefer trial by judge alone, not trial by a judge sitting with a jury; to that end, they should be prepared to use summary conviction proceedings whenever it is feasible to do so rather than proceeding by indictment.

SUBVERSIVE IMPACT OF THE CASE

Established patterns of racist and misogynist conflict are reinforced by trials in which counsel and judges invoke racist and sexist stereotypes. Such spectacles lead members of the community to interpret the

35 This procedure is authorized by s 715.1 of the *Criminal Code* and was upheld as constitutional in *R v L(D)* (1993), 25 CR (4th) 285 (SCC). The use of video statements by children is not new, nor was it new in 2001.

36 Had each accused been charged as a principal with one count of the summary conviction offence under s 271(b) and with two summary convictions counts as a party under s 271(b) and s 21, convicted on all three, and given consecutive sentences, the aggregate sentences could have been as long as fifty-four months, rather than the two years less a day imposed on Edmondson, the only accused actually convicted of the indictable offence under s 271(a) as prosecuted. Of course, Parliament could also increase the maximum sentence, now eighteen months, for conviction of the summary conviction offence under s 271(b) without triggering the right to trial by jury. Under section 11(f) of the *Charter*, the right to trial by jury is only protected where the maximum sentence is five years or more. It is arguable, however, that the present maximum sentence of eighteen months is fully adequate, on the assumption that only the truly incorrigible will reoffend and tools (long-term and dangerous offender designations) are already available to deal with such cases as they arise.

proceedings as evidence of ongoing racial and cultural conflict and the continuing persistence of systemic and historic racism and misogyny.

The conduct of the case of *Edmondson, Kindrat,* and *Brown* must be seen as "subversive" for these reasons and on other grounds. The overall effect of the case was to undermine or subvert the policy objectives set out in the preambles to the 1992 and 1997 bills amending the sexual assault provisions of the *Criminal Code*.[37] The handling and disposition of the trials and retrials of these accused suggest that legal consciousness in Saskatchewan continues to function in accord with pre-1992 norms in the area of sexual assault, as if the legislative and judicial developments of the last two of decades had not taken place.[38] Certainly, complainants in Saskatchewan are on notice that the criminal justice process may not protect their privacy rights and that the disposition of any sexual assault complaint might take many years. The inevitable effect will be to silence many complainants who may legitimately fear being made the subject of an extended public spectacle. The implications of the case for the conduct of legal professionals in sexual assault cases are equally regressive.

This case may, for example, leave Saskatchewan judges, prosecutors, and defence counsel with the understanding that instructions to the jury in sexual assault cases must always include reference to s 273.2 of the *Criminal Code*, even when the trial judge finds the defence is unavailable as a matter of law. The *Criminal Code* bars the defence of belief in consent under two circumstances: (1) when there is insufficient evidence that the accused had a "belief in consent" to make the defence available under s 273.2; and (2) when the accused's "mistake" is based on ignorance of the law or a mistake about the law and is therefore barred by s 19. In either case, pursuant to s 265(4), the jury is not to be instructed with respect to the defence of "mistaken belief in consent" because, as a matter of law, the defence could not result in a valid verdict of acquittal. The decision taken by the provincial director of public prosecutions not to appeal the acquittal in the *Kindrat* retrial on the ground of errors of law in the instructions to the jury does leave trial judges in Saskatchewan in a quandary. Judges may either apply current

37 *An Act to Amend the Criminal Code (sexual assault)*, SC 1992, c 38; *An Act to Amend the Criminal Code (production of records in sexual offence proceedings)*, SC 1997, c 30.

38 Many counsel may be unfamiliar with the preambles to the 1992 and 1997 bills because the preambles do not form part of the *Code* itself and are not routinely published along with it for easy reference.

legal standards on the availability of the defence of belief in consent as legislated in the *Criminal Code* and construed in a series of decisions by the Supreme Court of Canada, and risk appeal by the accused, or follow the precedent set by the direction issued by Cameron J in 2005 and instruct the jury on the defence in all sexual assault cases, even those in which the defence is unavailable in law.

Mr. Justice Cameron appeared to believe that in Saskatchewan triers of fact, whether a judge sitting alone or a jury, have unique talents and, in a sexual assault case, are able to deliberate about a defence that is not available in law, without there being any risk that a perverse verdict may be the result. Such confidence in the trier of fact echoes Dickson J's observation in *Pappajohn* that the common sense of the jury can be relied on to detect and reject a "cock-and-bull" story told by an accused who claims "mistaken belief in consent."[39] But since that case was decided in 1979, legal standards have been more fully articulated and codified in an effort to remind trial judges that the trier of fact may only consider defences *that are actually available in law*.[40] The Crown should have challenged Mr Justice Cameron's order when it was issued in 2005 or appealed the acquittal in the *Kindrat* retrial on the ground of misdirection of the jury on this very point.

The assumption that the defence of mistaken belief in consent was available affected not only the terms of the order for the retrial, but also appears to have influenced other aspects of the case from the very beginning. This is a flagrant example of the preference for, and the tendency to revert to, "local common sense" and "local social norms" in legal interpretation, in defiance of decades-long efforts by the Supreme Court of Canada to clarify the law on the point at issue. It is not the first example of the phenomenon of amnesia among jurists about decisions at the Supreme Court of Canada, nor is it likely to be the last, but it is profoundly troubling. A decision not to limit the defences that the trier of fact is asked to consider to those actually available in law, is a recipe for suspension or subversion of the rule of law.

ACCESSIBLE REASONS FOR DECISION

Reasons for decision that provide a reviewable record of the deliberation process are essential if the law is to provide guidance for the choices individuals make. Reasons are also essential to ensure that the legal process can be subjected to scrutiny. A bare decision does not clarify the law, lacks any educational value for the affected community,

39 *Pappajohn v R*, [1980] 2 SCR 120, 155–56.

40 See *supra* note 11.

and frustrates any attempt by the public, social critics, and academics to assess the quality of the decision-making process. Judges, counsel, affected parties, and members of the community do not obtain direction from it. A bare decision issued following trial by a judge sitting alone without a jury, can be set aside on the ground that it fails to disclose the reasoning process on which it is based. But many decisions issued by judges are accompanied by oral reasons recorded on audio tape and never transcribed or published. For most practical purposes, these decisions are indistinguishable from "bare" decisions because they are not generally accessible; few members of the community actually know the reasons for any specific decision and can only speculate. In speculating, members of the public and the legal professions fill in the blanks with what they assume were the most likely reasons for the decision. These are some of the ways in which the failure to issue and publish written reasons for decision undermines the social utility of a legal system governed by the rule of law.

In sexual assault cases, prosecutors should therefore routinely request that judges sitting alone without a jury issue reasons for decision in written form. Oral reasons should be transcribed and in either case the reasons should be reported. The public has a right to know the basis for the decisions judges make in the public's name. Without disclosure of that information, the criminal justice process escapes public scrutiny and accountability. The absence of mechanisms to ensure accountability is anomalous in a system of self-government based on the rule of law. Everyone vulnerable to being sexually assaulted has an interest in the public disclosure of information about the actual interpretation and application of the sexual assault laws. In addition, the lack of ready access to that same information makes it more difficult for the federal government to fulfill the responsibilities with respect to criminal law assigned to the federal government under s 91(27) of the *Constitution Act* or to fulfill its obligations under international law.[41]

41 See, for example, the *Convention on the Elimination of All Forms of Discrimination Against Women,* Can TS 1982 No 31, (entered into force 3 September 1981), to which Canada is a party, and the *Concluding Observations of the Committee on the Elimination of All Forms of Discrimination Against Women: Canada*, 42nd Sess, (20 October–7 November 2008). In its answers to questions from the committee, Canada has repeatedly excused its non-compliance with the convention by asserting that the provinces, rather than the federal government, have jurisdiction over a number of areas that affect the equality rights of women and children, including enforcement of the criminal laws prohibiting violence, and the development of programs and policies to address the social causes of violence.

JURY TRIALS AND PUBLIC LEGAL EDUCATION

Unlike trial judges, juries do not prepare and release reasons for their verdicts. Nonetheless the manner in which jury trials are conducted inevitably serves as an exercise in public and professional legal education. The lessons about the law which the public and the legal profession derive from any individual trial may be either accurate or misleading. This is certainly true in the case of sexual assault trials.

For example, consider the following extremely basic issue. For some time, it has been recognized that the legal and social definitions of sexual assault in Canada are often not identical.[42] Widespread compliance with the law is unlikely to come about until the social and legal definitions converge in public and professional legal consciousness. The fact that the reasons for decision produced in the vast majority of sexual assault cases are oral reasons by judges and not generally available for public scrutiny or academic critique, only increases the probability that in an indeterminate number of cases the judge's decision will be based on a non-legal or social definition of sexual assault, entangled as it has long been with an array of myths and stereotypes, not on the legal definition.[43] The record from the jury trials in *Edmondson, Kindrat,* and *Brown* shows that the judge and counsel, all experienced legal professionals, relied heavily on non-legal social conceptions about consent and sexual assault, not the legal definitions, and they all invited the jury to do likewise. In the retrials, the defence counsel did the same thing. The use of outmoded social definitions by these legal professionals in these proceedings undoubtedly undermined achievement of the objectives set out in the preamble to the 1992 amendments to the sexual assault provisions of the *Criminal Code.*

Whether a trial is by judge alone or by judge and jury, the judge and counsel perform their professional roles on the basis of their understanding of the law. That appears to be what occurred in these cases. But at the same time, members of the public and other lawyers and judges were aware of media reports about the questions and arguments by counsel during the trials. Based on the premise that what law is, is to be seen in its application, some of these observers likely concluded that there really have not been any significant changes in the sexual assault laws in Canada. Members of the community can only speculate about

42 Lucinda Vandervort, "Enforcing the Sexual Assault Laws: An Agenda for Action" (1985) 13 RFR 44; Vandervort, "Mistake of Law and Sexual Assault: Consent and *Mens Rea*" (1987–88) 2 CJWL 233.

43 The legal definition of consent to sexual activity was codified in 1992. See s 273.1 of the *Criminal Code.*

a jury's reasons for its verdict on the basis of what is publicly known about the conduct of the proceedings, just as they must speculate in cases where a judge, sitting alone, issues oral reasons that are unreported or not easily accessible. But the words and conduct of the presiding judge and counsel in open court are public and are the subject of media reports. The combined net effect of the conduct of the judge and counsel in the trial proceedings in the *Edmondson, Kindrat,* and *Brown* cases on community beliefs and assumptions about the legal definition of sexual consent, sexual assault, and the operation and effect of the sexual assault laws was racist and misogynist. The trial proceedings did not provide accurate lessons about current legal standards for the handling of sexual assault cases. The conduct of sexual assault cases, from beginning to end, should be recognized as an exercise in public legal education and handled in a manner that provides the public and professionals who work in the criminal justice system with reliable information about current law and legal standards, not misinformation.

SYSTEMIC REMEDIES

Sexual violence violates the human rights of the persons it targets and has a significant negative impact on their health status and well-being. In turn, such violence has multiple serious secondary impacts on Canadian society and the social fabric, on families, on relationships, and on communities, including how they do or do not function and how their resources are and can be used. The federal government has constitutional responsibility for criminal law in Canada under s 91(27) of the *Constitution Act* and has assumed obligations under international law to promote and advance the equality rights of women in Canada and to protect them against violence. Those responsibilities and obligations have not been fulfilled. If anything, in recent years, there has been a retrenchment in support and funding for women's equality. What is required is a fundamental change, a sea-change in perspective, not simply a few more workshops for legal counsel and police supported by limited federal and provincial grants. The new approach must be multi-pronged and designed to provide expertise, organized, resourced, and allocated in a manner that makes effective enforcement of the laws prohibiting violence against women and other vulnerable people a realistic objective. The familiar excuses for the *status quo* are old and stale.

In this discussion, I proposed a series of remedial steps to improve adherence to the rule of law in the handling of sexual assault cases by the criminal justice system, and to make its operation more transparent and open to public scrutiny. These are modest steps that can be taken by the police, prosecutors, and the judiciary acting within their respective spheres of authority, using legal powers that each already possesses. In addition, below I propose three initiatives that require Parliamentary action. These recommendations flow from my reflections to date on issues seen in the *Edmondson, Kindrat,* and *Brown* cases as discussed above. Further research and consultation may show that some of the objectives of these proposals can be achieved or supported by means other than, or in addition to, those proposed here.

Recommendation 1

Parliament should amend the Criminal Code to provide concurrent federal-provincial jurisdiction over the initiation and conduct of legal proceedings in sexual assault cases and all other Criminal Code offences involving violence against women and children, including the conduct of appeals and all motions and applications related to the proceedings.

Parliament should grant the Attorney General of Canada concurrent jurisdiction over the prosecution of all sexual offences and all other *Criminal Code* offences involving violence and other forms of coercion against women and children. There is no constitutional impediment to the assertion of federal jurisdiction in this area. In 1983, in reasons by Chief Justice Laskin, the Supreme Court of Canada affirmed that the Attorney General of Canada has exclusive jurisdiction under s 91(27) of the *Constitution Act* to prosecute all federal offences.[44] The Court observed that provision for prosecution of *Criminal Code* offences by the provincial Attorneys General was statutory, not constitutional, and, as such, subject to amendment by Parliament. In recent years, s 2 of the *Criminal Code* has been amended to provide for concurrent federal–provincial jurisdiction in the prosecution of terrorist offences.[45] Clearly, Parliament is not reluctant to use the federal criminal law power under s 91(27) of the *Constitutional Act* to assert a role for the federal government in selected circumstances.

Recently, others have argued that the merely statutory basis for the prosecutorial authority of the provincial Attorneys General permits the latter to operate in relation to the criminal laws of Canada only as a matter of grace, not "right," pursuant to agreements that have evolved over more than 140 years. Some argue that under these arrangements the provincial Attorneys General may not be "obliged" to prosecute

44 *AG Canada v CN Transportation*, [1983] 2 SCR 206, and *R v Wetmore*, [1983] 2 SCR 284.

45 See also *Criminal Code*, ss 696 and 830(4) dealing with authority in relation to the conduct of appeals.

Code offences; that as a matter of law, they remain free to determine when and how prosecutorial resources shall be deployed.[46] Others may hold contrary views.[47] It is well-known, however, that regardless of which view is preferred from a strictly legal perspective, the general experience of women and children in Canada under the current arrangement is one of violation of their rights to security of the person and equal protection, benefit, and enjoyment of the law under ss 7, 15, and 28 of the *Charter of Rights and Freedoms*, as well as a violation of their human rights under international law, contrary to the obligations the government of Canada has assumed under international covenants and conventions.[48] In these circumstances, it is incumbent on the federal government to take concrete steps to assume its responsibilities for enforcement of the criminal laws prohibiting all forms of criminal violence, exploitation, and coercion against women and children.[49]

46 For a recent discussion of the constitutional issues, see Mark Carter, "Recognizing Original (Non-Delegated) Provincial Jurisdiction to Prosecute Criminal Offences" (2007) 38 Ottawa L Rev 163. As an example of a province's assertion of a non-enforcement option, Carter discusses the announcement by the Attorney General of Saskatchewan that the province would not enforce fire-arms legislation (at 165–68, 180–82). Carter examines the tension between the expectation that prosecutorial authority will be exercised in a quasi-judicial and hence apolitical manner and "indications from the provinces that prosecutorial resources will not be invested in certain federal criminal law initiatives which are 'politically' unpopular" (at 168).

47 See, for example, *R v Catagas* (1978), 38 CCC (2d) 296 (Man CA), concluding that an explicit policy of non-prosecution of Aboriginals hunting on Crown land in violation of the federal *Migratory Birds Convention Act*, RSC 1970, c M 12 was "a clear case of the exercise of a purported dispensing power by executive action in favour of a particular group" and, as such, was null and void on the ground that "the Crown may not by executive action dispense with the laws" (at 301). By contrast, decisions to stay and withdraw charges in *individual* cases, absent abuse of power or clear impropriety, are presumed to be within the scope of prosecutorial discretion because they do not purport to suspend a law enacted by Parliament. This distinction merits critical examination.

48 See *supra* note 43, for example.

49 Given that the Supreme Court has held that the provincial Attorneys General exercise a statutory authority granted to them by the federal Parliament, the courts (federal and provincial) may be persuaded that judicial review of the reasonableness and propriety of the exercise of that statutory authority is available and appropriate in cases where the issues include failure to act. In the past, the courts have declined to supervise the exercise of prosecutorial discretion unless abuse of prosecutorial power threatened to oppress individual rights. Hence most of the limited case law related to review of prosecutorial discretion concerns itself with staying prosecutions. Traditionally, the Courts have been loath to curtail prosecutorial discretion in the absence of "flagrant impropriety." See Philip Stenning, *Appearing for the Crown: A Legal and Historical Review of Criminal Prosecutorial Authority in Canada* (Cowansville, Quebec: Brown Legal Publications, 1986) at 197–281. See also *R v Power*, [1994] 1 SCR 601, for discussion of the rationale for judicial reticence. David Layton, "The Prosecutor-

The federal Attorney General, acting through the office of the director of public prosecutions,[50] is already responsible for the prosecution of *Criminal Code* offences in the territories. Initially, the proposed concurrent federal statutory powers under s 2 of the *Criminal Code* should be primarily exercised to consult with the provincial Attorneys General about the functioning of the sexual assault laws in the various provinces rather than to prosecute individual cases. The provincial Attorneys General would continue to carry responsibility for the ordinary operation of provincial prosecutions, just as the federal Attorney General, acting through the federal director of public prosecutions, does with respect to prosecutions in the territories. The federal Attorney General would direct its resources primarily towards monitoring performance and evaluating policy. Only when there was evidence of prosecutorial nonfeasance or malfeasance that was not addressed and appropriately resolved as a result of discussions with the provincial Attorney General or the director of public prosecutions, or that involved criminal activity with inter-provincial or international elements, such as trafficking persons across borders, would federal prosecutors initiate or assert authority to take responsibility for individual prosecutions in the provinces pursuant to federal statutory powers under section 2 of the *Criminal Code*. Under this concurrency model, consultation with provincial and territorial prosecutors should, in due course, result in the development of policies, training programs, and reference manuals that would

ial Charging Decision" (2002) 46 Crim LQ 447 at 457, reports that a faulty or suspect decision *not* to prosecute will almost never be challenged and when it will be subject to a strict abuse of process standard (at 457). *Kostuch v Alta A G*, [1995] AJ No 866 Alta CA provides an example of a case in which the Crown's decision to stay a private prosecution was upheld.

A quite different analytic approach may be available if the Attorney General of Canada, as the applicant, seeks review of the exercise of what are now understood to be *statutory powers* granted by the federal Parliament to the Attorney General of Saskatchewan, for example. This is an especially promising approach in relation to sexual violence against women and children because deference to regional differences (and to local conceptions of the "public interest" as referenced in the *Public Prosecutions Policy Manual*, Department of Justice, Saskatchewan, 1 June 1998, for example), commonly raised in discussions about federal and provincial jurisdiction in defence of the *status quo*, is overtly offensive when the human rights of women and children in the various provinces and territories are at stake. It should be noted in connection with sensitivities related to "regional values," that action to enforce and clarify interpretation and application of the substantive and procedural criminal laws does not affect the sentencing process or impinge upon provincial jurisdiction over corrections in cases in which the sentence is less than two years.

50 *Director of Public Prosecutions Act*, Part 3 of the *Federal Accountability Act, Statutes of Canada 2006*, c 9. In force 12 December 2006.

facilitate bringing the rule of law to the handling of sexual assault cases throughout the criminal justice system.

Recommendation 2

Parliament should create a federal Office of the Sexual Exploitation Auditor to monitor the operation and efficacy of programs and actions taken in relation to sexual assault and exploitation pursuant to the federal government's constitutional responsibilities for criminal law under s 91(27) of the *Constitution* Act. The auditor would exercise powers analogous to those of the Auditor General, function at arms length from the Attorney General of Canada, and report directly to Parliament and the public.

Systematic review of how federal and provincial prosecutors and judges handle individual cases and categories of cases is needed to ensure that necessary legislative reforms or policy changes can be made in a timely way by Parliament or the appropriate authority. This model contemplates the creation of a system of ongoing review and the issuance of regular reports to Parliament and the public, on the operation and efficacy of federal and provincial prosecution of sexual assault offences under the *Criminal Code* and offences involving sexual exploit ation under federal legislation other than the *Criminal Code*, such as legislation dealing with human trafficking and criminal organizations, by a federal officer exercising powers analogous to those of the federal Auditor General and operating at arms length from the office of the Attorney General of Canada. This modification to the design of the institutions by which Canada secures the benefits of responsible government for its citizens is overdue.

Recommendation 3

Parliament should create a federal Office of the Sexual Assault Legal Representative [SALR] to provide legal representation to women and children who are complainants in sexual assault cases in any of the provinces and territories of Canada, from the time of the initial contact between the complainant and health care providers or criminal justice system personnel until final disposition of the case.

Empirical research on service and treatment delivery options shows that the well-being of complainants is enhanced when rape crisis advocates participate in intake service delivery.[51] Such services need to

51 For example, Rebecca Campbell, "Rape Survivors' Experiences with the Legal and Medical Systems" (2006) 12 Violence Against Women 30; Lee D Preston, "The Sexual Assault Nurse Examiner and the Rape Crisis Center Advocate" (2003) 25 Top Emerg

be far more generally available to complainants in urban, rural, and under-serviced areas than they are at present. In addition, specialized legal counsel — autonomous and fully independent from police, victim services, and the Crown — should be available to complainants at point of first intake, whether that is a police station or a health-care setting, with ample arrangements for follow-up. A number of objectives would be served by this arrangement: timely protection of complainant rights, preservation of evidence, and timely identification of sources of evidence, amongst others. Legal services should continue until such time as the case is closed or disposed of in legal proceedings and should encompass representation of the complainant throughout both the pretrial and trial proceedings. In the investigative stage and at trial, a SALR would be in a position to advise the complainant about how to respond to questions that explore issues that: (1) are not relevant because they have no legally probative value in relation to the material facts at issue, or (2) disregard the complainant's privacy.

A SALR could also take steps, as appropriate, to obtain standing and make submissions in relation to specific issues before the court. The case law suggests, as seen in *Edmondson, Kindrat,* and *Brown*, that the rape shield and personal records provisions in the *Code* are easily circumvented by counsel's choice of witnesses and use of questions that refer to aspects of a complainant's personal history or invite responses that may refer to aspects of the complainant's personal history. A SALR, based in a properly funded and resourced federal Office of the Sexual Assault Legal Representative, could take steps to secure greater compliance with the rule of law in the investigation and trial proceedings. Complainants should not be placed in the position of needing to vet the legal relevance and propriety of the questions they are asked when giving testimony in court or in the course of a police interview. In both contexts, the SALR could provide the justice process with a much-needed prophylactic against distortion of the truth-seeking process by the time-consuming, distracting, and potentially prejudicial exploration of irrelevant or personally invasive matters.[52] In time, judges and

Med 242. There are now a significant number of empirical studies and a growing body of literature dealing with these issues.

52 When an application is made under either the rape shield or personal records provisions of the *Criminal Code*, the trial judge should order that legal representation be provided for the complainant on the ground that disposition of the application will affect the complainant's rights. Section 278.4 provides that the complainant, the record holder, and "any other person to whom the record relates," have standing to make submissions at the hearing of an application for production. In Manitoba, those

prosecutors alike will come to view this development in the criminal justice process as long overdue.[53]

rights, in the case of a "victim," are supplemented by s 4(2) of *The Victims' Rights Act*, SM 1998, c V55, which provides: "Victims are entitled to be given access to free, independent counsel when access to personal information about them is sought under section 278.3 of the *Criminal Code* (Canada)." Some but not all other provinces have made equivalent provision for representation of the complainant by independent, funded counsel in connection with personal records applications.
But even that is arguably too little, too late. Widespread use of informal means to circumvent the procedures in the *Criminal Code* that govern production of records and admission of sexual history shows that legal representation is required from the point of initial contact with health and criminal justice personnel. At minimum, the *Criminal Code* should be amended to provide standing for the complainant in relation to any application or appeal brought under s 276.1–276.6 on the grounds that the complainant's dignity and privacy and security rights are affected by all attempts to introduce sexual history in any legal proceedings related to a sexual assault charge. In the absence of such an amendment to the *Criminal Code*, standing can be sought on a case-by-case basis on grounds of the *Charter* and the common law.
In *R v Morgentaler*, [1988] 1 SCR 30 Dickson CJC held that "state interference with bodily integrity and serious state-imposed psychological stress, at least in the criminal law context, constitutes a breach of security of the person" (at 56), thereby triggering the protections available under section 7 of the *Charter*. Similarly, Claire L'Heureux-Dubé, Justice of the Supreme Court of Canada, 1987–2002, addressing Ontario prosecutors in 2003, urged them to assume the challenge of developing the equality rights jurisprudence under s 15 of the *Charter* in relation to the privacy and security interest of complainants and other witnesses. However, noting that both prosecutors and judges, hoping to avoid appeals, may be tempted to defer to the defence on issues affecting the complainant's privacy and security interests, she opined that it "will take some time before all levels of court give ... [the personal records and sexual history] ... provisions their full effect," in "The *Charter* and the Administration of Criminal Justice in Canada — Where Have We Been and Where Shall We Go?" (2006) 3 Ohio St J Crim L 487. These observations, coming as they do from someone who has had ample opportunity to observe jurists in action, provide significant support for the conclusion that complainants, whose interests and knowledge of the matters at issue are unique, require independent counsel. Ironically, although fuller protection for the unique interests of complainants arguably is required under the *Charter* and at common law, legal argument to that effect will rarely be heard in court unless complainants are represented by independent publicly-funded legal counsel.

53 Others recognize the need for legal representation of sexual assault complainants, eg, Wendy J Murphy, "The Victim Advocacy and Research Group: Serving a Growing Need to Provide Rape Victims with Personal Legal Representation to Protect Privacy Rights and to Fight Gender Bias in the Criminal Justice System" (2001) 10:1 Journal of Social Distress & the Homeless 123. A few jurisdictions have experience with legal services models that provide some protection for complainants' rights in the legal process. See the multi-national survey information in Jennifer Temkin, *Rape and the Legal Process*, 2d ed (New York: Oxford University Press, 2002). In due course, expansion of the jurisdiction of the Office of the SALR to encompass representation of women and children who are subjected to criminal violence, coercion, and exploitation that is not specifically sexual, should be considered.

In addition, the Office of the SALR, as a fully autonomous institution, federally funded, and at arms length from the federal Department of Justice, would be well-positioned to observe and report directly to Parliament, from time to time, on the overall functioning of the criminal process in relation to enforcement of the federal laws prohibiting sexual assault and sexual exploitation, from the unique perspective of complainants.[54] This arrangement would complement but not replace the functions to be undertaken, as proposed above, by the Office of the Sexual Exploitation Auditor and the Attorney General of Canada.

CONCLUSION

The cases of *Edmondson, Kindrat,* and *Brown* provide compelling evidence that reliance by the federal government on the provincial Attorney General to prosecute offences of sexual and non-sexual violence against women and children in the province of Saskatchewan is not justified. Failure by the federal government to take steps to fulfill its constitutional responsibilities for the proper interpretation, application, and enforcement of laws prohibiting violence against women and children in Saskatchewan, in the face of evidence of nonfeasance and serious errors by provincial actors in the criminal process, is a betrayal of the trust of some of the most vulnerable members of Canadian society.[55] History shows that the negative spiritual and social effects of betrayals of trust are corrosive, and may often do as much damage to individuals and the threads and texture of the social fabric as the underlying acts of violence.

54 This, like the two other systemic recommendations, can be seen as an application of the principle of "functional effectiveness" to the profound challenges encountered in implementation of the sexual assault laws within the context of Canadian federalism. For discussion of "functional effectiveness" as a rationale for the assertion of federal paramountcy, see John Leclair, "The Supreme Court of Canada Understanding of Federalism: Efficiency at the Expense of Diversity" (2003) 28 Queen's LJ 411. See also Carter *supra* note 43 at 186–89, discussing Leclair's article.

55 Consider the situation of Aboriginal women in Canada as documented in *Stolen Sisters: A Human Rights Response to Violence Against Indigenous Women in Canada* (Ottawa: Amnesty International, 2004).

7.

The Supreme Court of Canada's Betrayal of Residential School Survivors: Ignorance is No Excuse

Sheila McIntyre

Moving away from the criminal law focus of the prior two chapters and examining tort law, Sheila McIntyre's chapter exposes the heavy costs of seeking legal redress for Aboriginal survivors of sexual abuse committed in the context of the enterprise of residential schools. She argues that the Supreme Court of Canada abuses Aboriginal survivors in the same manner as did the institutions themselves, by discounting the corporeal, sexual, psychological, and spiritual harms the children experienced, and subjugating their interests to those of "innocent" taxpayers and institutions. Erving Goffman's concept of a "total institution," used in an earlier chapter by Laura Robinson to describe hockey culture, is powerfully invoked by Sheila in condemning the racism of the entire enterprise of residential schools. Given that the Supreme Court was free to develop the legal principles to govern the liability of residential schools, and that it maintained "studied ignorance" about the real context in which the claims arose, despite mountains of available social science evidence, it is impossible to remain optimistic about the potential of law to recognize and compensate these deeply racialized and gendered harms.

Between 1999 and 2005, the Supreme Court of Canada decided nine civil lawsuits brought by adult survivors of child sexual abuse against those who created and operated institutions in which such abuse was enabled, licensed, ignored, and covered up.[1] Elsewhere I have analyzed in detail the court's deeply disappointing record in adjudicating four distinct areas of tort law engaged by those nine claims.[2] In this chapter,

1 See *Bazley v Curry*, [1999] 2 SCR 534 [*Bazley*], *Jacobi v Griffiths*, [1999] 2 SCR 570 [*Jacobi*], *KLB v British Columbia*, [2003] 2 SCR 403 [*KLB*], *EDG v Hammer*, [2003] 2 SCR 459 [*EDG*], *MB v British Columbia*, [2003] 2 SCR 477 [*MB*], *John Doe v Bennett*, [2004] 1 SCR 436 [*Bennett*], *HL v Canada (AG)*, [2005] 1 SCR 401 [*HL*], *Blackwater v Plint*, [2005] 3 SCR 3 [*Plint*], *EB v Oblates of Mary Immaculate in the Province of British Columbia*, [2005] 3 SCR 45 [*Oblates*], and *Jesuit Fathers of Upper Canada v Guardian Insurance Co of Canada*, [2006] 1 SCR 744 [*Guardian*].

2 This paper is adapted from a far longer analysis of the Supreme Court of Canada's de-

I focus on the last of the nine decisions, *EB v Oblates of Mary Immaculate in the Province of BC* [*Oblates*][3] as an illustration of the court's refusal to engage the realities of systemic inequality in institutional child abuse decisions. I argue that this refusal amounts to a stark indictment of the limits of our current Supreme Court and, thus, of current Canadian civil law, in holding our governments and public institutions accountable for abuses of children forced or entrusted into their care.

There is much to lament and deplore in the terrible history exposed in these cases. The court, however, appears mostly unmoved and remote. It reasons as if policing its out-of-date, highly formalistic versions of tort doctrine is more important than framing current doctrine to remedy and deter the individual and collective harms done by public institutions that failed profoundly in their responsibilities to the vulnerable children involuntarily subjected to their care. It analyzes the facts and law hermetically, each case in isolation, even as thousands of claims from numerous institutions were flooding the court system,[4] and even if the abuser had already been convicted of multiple abuses.[5] In short, the court's reasoning is abstract and utterly decontextualized when it looks backward in time. However, when it looks forward to the policy

cisions in institutional abuse cases entitled, "Guardians of Privilege: The Resistance of the Supreme Court of Canada to Institutional Liability for Child Sexual Abuse," that was published simultaneously in (2009) 44 SCLR (2d) 1 ["Guardians of Privilege"], and in Sanda Rodgers, Rakhi Ruparelia & Louise Bélanger-Hardy, eds, *Critical Torts* (Markham: LexisNexis Canada, 2009) 1.

3 *Oblates*, *supra* note 1.

4 An estimated 10,000 lawsuits arising from Aboriginal residential school abuses were being processed in 2002. See JR Miller, "Troubled Legacy: A History of Native Residential Schools" (2003) 66 Sask L Rev 357 at 381.

5 Prior to the launching of the civil institutional abuse suits that ultimately went to the Supreme Court of Canada, the assailant had already been found to have committed the assaults either in criminal proceedings or civil suits by others of his victims. Curry had been criminally convicted on nineteen counts of sexual assault, two of them concerning Bazley (see *Bazley*, *supra* note 1, at para 4). Griffiths had been criminally convicted of fourteen sexual assaults against the Jacobi children and other members of the Boys and Girls Club (see *Jacobi*, *supra* note 1, at para 3). The club was not found vicariously liable for the assaults on the Jacobis. Thirty-six plaintiffs sought damages from the church for Bennett's abuse (Bennett, *supra* note 1, at para 1). Canada had settled civil suits with sixteen of Plint's victims prior to the Blackwater proceedings launched by seven additional plaintiffs, one of whom was found not to have been abused, see Susan Vella & Elizabeth Grace, "Pathways to Justice for Residential School Claimants: Is the Civil Justice System Working?" in Joseph E Magnet & Chief Dwight A Dorey, eds, *Aboriginal Rights Litigation* (Toronto: Butterworths, 2003) 195 at 218. Canada had settled nearly two hundred claims against Starr before HL launched his suit (Vella & Grace, *ibid* at 221).

implications of imposing liability on institutions, its sympathy is awakened. It becomes preoccupied with an array of benignly imagined dominant interests whose routines and expectations would be unacceptably burdened if institutions were to be found liable for harms committed on their watch. Seemingly disinterestedly, the court explicitly asks itself which of two "innocents" — public institutions judicially deemed unaware of abusers in their midst or children — should, in the broader "public interest," bear the cost of institutional abuse. In most cases, the court sides with the institutions and against the children. It invokes floodgates[6] or utilitarian calculations[7] and fatuous imaginings about the unfairness to taxpayers,[8] or the undue burden on charitable enterprises[9] and religious institutions,[10] or the unfair stigmatization as inherently risky of all mentoring relationships,[11] or the harms to family spontaneity of child welfare monitoring of foster placements,[12] as self-evidently undesirable consequences of awarding damages to the individual victims of institutional failures.

The failing that lies at the heart of these decisions is the court's absolute refusal to engage the multiple relations of inequality that generated and rationalized children's institutionalization and that empowered abusers, facilitated serial abuse, inhibited or discredited reporting, excused institutional inaction, and compromised resort to law as a vehicle of redress. None of the obvious, compound, structural, and situational inequalities that permeate these cases is acknowledged or addressed by the court. Racism, colonialism, poverty, misogyny, and cultural supremacism are never adverted to in the majority judgments. Nor are hunger, social isolation, confinement, harsh discipline, loneliness, or terror. The cases are surreal and frightening narratives of studied ignorance and privileged innocence in the country's top court.[13] The Supreme Court of Canada abuses survivors in the same ways and from the same supremacist presumptions as did institutional defendants. Plaintiffs are never truly seen or truly heard. Their evidence and experi-

6 See *EDG*, *supra* note 1, at para 54, KLB, *ibid* at para 26.

7 See majority opinion in *Jacobi*, *supra* note 1 at para 76.

8 See *MB*, *supra* note 1 at para 34.

9 See *Jacobi*, *supra* note 1 at para 78.

10 See *Oblates*, *supra* note 1 at para 48.

11 See *Jacobi*, *supra* note 1 at para 83.

12 See *KLB*, *supra* note 1 at para 54.

13 For an extended elaboration of these habits of the dominant, see Sheila McIntyre, "Studied Ignorance and Privileged Innocence: Keeping Equity Academic" (2000) 12 CJWL 147.

ence are diminished from the lofty and detached heights of privileged insularity and imaginings. Their humanity and its injury are persistently discounted as their claims are reflexively subordinated to the material interests and policy preferences of the dominant.

Pivotal to the court's privileged logic is resort to rape myths and stereotypes long debunked by thirty years of data from rape crisis centres, by thirty years of feminist legal and social science scholarship, and by facta and judicial dicta in not a few Supreme Court of Canada cases.[14] Long after feminist scholarship had unpacked sexual violence as an abuse of power enabled and rationalized by systemic sexual, racial, class, and other inequalities, the court continues to cling to rape myth. Where the court refuses to hold institutions liable, the individual abuser is an isolated, sexual deviant who just happens to work in the institution and to whom the institution provides no more than "mere opportunity" to prey sexually on institutionalized children. He is unforeseeable, undetectable with ordinary screening and oversight, and undeterrable. So it would be unfair and serve no policy goal to saddle institutions with damages for his deviant misconduct.[15] Only if the abuser has so much institutional power that he IS the institution,[16] or if his

14 For arguments derived from rape crisis workers' records and from feminist scholarship, see, eg, intervenor facta filed by the Women's Legal Education and Action Fund [LEAF] in *Seaboyer and Gayme v R*, [1991] 3 SCR 577; *R v MLM*, [1994] 2 SCR 3; and *R v O'Connor*, [1995] 4 SCR 411, in LEAF, *Equality and the Charter: Ten Years of Feminist Advocacy Before the Supreme Court of Canada* (Toronto: Emond Montgomery, 1996) at 173, 271, 427 respectively. For Supreme Court dicta acknowledging and rejecting some rape myths and stereotypes, see *Seaboyer*, *ibid*, per McLachlin J at 604, 630, and per L'Heureux-Dubé J at 647–95; *Osolin v The Queen*, [1993] 4 SCR 595 per Cory J at paras 162, 168, and per L'Heureux-Dubé J at paras 48–52, 55; *R v W(R)*, [1992] 2 SCR 122 per McLachlin J at 136; and *R v Ewanchuk*, [1999] 1 SCR 330 per L'Heureux-Dubé J at paras 82–101. It should be noted, however, that the Court has sometimes invoked rape myths even within decisions purporting to reject them. See, eg, hypothetical scenarios cited in *Seaboyer* by the majority that they claimed warrant admission of sexual history evidence (at 613–17). See also the majority's embrace, without hearing any evidence, of defence counsels' invocation of the risks of so-called "false memory syndrome" and the corollary spectre of ill-motivated therapists who implant false memories in clients and then urge them to report imagined violations, in *R v O'Connor* (*ibid* at para 29).

15 For the most distilled versions of this insistence on the absence of linkage between the institution and abuses that occurred within its walls, see *Jacobi* and *Oblates*, *supra* note 1.

16 Hence, the Court was able to see a link between the spiritual and social power and trust invested in a rural Catholic parish priest and his unchecked sexual exploitation of altar boys and other parish youth. See *Bennett*, *supra* note 1. Likewise, an on-reserve residential school administrator who organized community sports open

residential duties routinely include intimate or bedtime access,[17] will the court see a sufficient link between the abuser and the institution to be comfortable imposing liability on the employer. For the court, institutional liability turns on the abuser's formal job description, independent of institutional mission, operating culture, and relations of power and powerlessness, and on whether the court itself, rather than institutionalized children, ascribes power to holders of such jobs.[18]

Save for one solo dissent by Justice Abella in the last of the nine institutional abuse cases decided between 1999 and 2005,[19] the court completely ignored the extensive scholarship on institutional abuse in Canada, particularly the 1996 *Report of the Royal Commission on Aboriginal People* [*RCAP Report*],[20] and the 2000 Report of the Law Commission of Canada [LCC] entitled *Restoring Dignity: Responding to Child Abuse*

to non-resident youth was found to be empowered sufficiently by the institution to hold the institution vicariously liable for his assaults. See *HL*, *supra* note 1. It may be that the liability decision was influenced by the fact that Starr the administrator had abused hundreds of children during his tenure.

17 For instance, in *Bazley*, *supra* note 1, the employer was found vicariously liable for abuses of boys in a group home by Curry who was a resident staff member. Likewise, in *Plint*, *supra* note 1, the church and federal government that ran an Aboriginal residential school were found jointly vicariously liable for abuses of resident students by the dormitory supervisor. However, in *KLB* and *MB*, *supra* note 1, child welfare officials were found to be neither vicariously liable nor liable for breach of non-delegable duty or of fiduciary duty in respect of Crown wards they had negligently placed with foster parents whom they also failed to monitor adequately. Although intimate access to foster children is as inherently a part of foster parenting as it is of being overnight staff in a residential school setting, the court found narrow doctrinal grounds for delinking provincial officials from abuses of children they had entrusted to abusive foster parents.

18 Hence the majority refused to find a non-profit organization vicariously liable for sexual assaults on children who attended its after-school activities program by Griffiths, the program director. The majority was skeptical of the children's claim that they considered Griffiths to be "God-like," a claim accepted by the trial judge. In any event, the majority reasoned that enjoying God-like influence over the children he mentored was neither part of the program director's job description nor a risk inherent to adult–child mentoring relationships (*Jacobi*, *supra* note 1 at paras 39, 85). A majority of the Court likewise found that neither a public school janitor nor a residential school "odd job" man enjoyed institutional power that enhanced their ability to abuse Aboriginal children at their schools. See *EDG* and *Oblates*, *supra* note 1. The reasoning in both cases shows no awareness of the multiple inequalities that gave abusers power over the children they abused. In my view, the inability to imagine that janitors might have power in such settings and the failure to engage inequalities of race, gender, and class in these cases smacks of privileged ignorance.

19 See her dissent in *Oblates*, *supra* note 1.

20 (Ottawa: Minister of Supply and Services, 1996) [*RCAP Report*].

in Canadian Institutions [*Restoring Dignity*].[21] Both reports decisively refute the isolated "bad apple" characterization of abusers for whom institutions provide no more than "mere opportunity" to prey on children. The *RCAP Report* documents the supremacist genesis of the Aboriginal residential schools, their culturally genocidal function, and the financial and other governmental and church interests they served. It methodically links physical and sexual abuse to other injuries endemic to the persistent underfunding and understaffing of the schools: overcrowding, systemic malnutrition, inadequate shelter, poor or no medical care, including for lethal infectious diseases, and the substitution of harsh subsistence labour for "school" work. The *RCAP Report* exposes how the schools' lab experiment in cultural erasure and reprogramming was executed by means of deliberate familial and social isolation, programmatic humiliation and degradation, regimentation, authoritarian structures, and a harsh regimen of corporal discipline administered by poorly trained and supervised religious and lay staff committed to the premise of Aboriginal children's lesser humanity.[22] The *RCAP Report* leaves no doubt that state and church officials knew throughout the one-hundred-year tenure of the schools about the severe neglect, epidemic abuse, and high mortality of resident children.[23]

The LCC's study, *Restoring Dignity*, unpacked these same basic operational dynamics in a wide variety of other residential institutions in which institutional staff and children were systematically schooled in the children's lesser humanity. Its introduction rejects any illusion that the physical and sexual abuse pervasive across a significant number and range of institutions can be characterized as the unforeseeable and unpreventable misconduct of isolated, deviant, individuals. The introduction to *Restoring Dignity* underlines three "clear" lessons. First, most institutionalized children come from society's most marginalized and powerless groups, and lack the financial and political leverage to make themselves heard or taken seriously.[24] The structural inequalities

21 (Ottawa: Minister of Public Works, 2000) [*Restoring Dignity*].

22 See Chapter 10 of Volume 1, *Looking Forward, Looking Back*, *RCAP Report*, *supra* note 20.

23 *Ibid* at 353–74. See also Roland Chrisjohn & Sherri Young, *The Circle Game: Shadows and Substance in the Indian Residential School Experience in Canada* (Penticton: Theytus Books, 1997); John Milloy, *A National Crime: The Canadian Government and the Residential Schools System, 1879 to 1986* (Winnipeg: University of Manitoba Press, 1999); and JR Miller, "Troubled Legacy: A History of Native Residential Schools" (2003) 66 Sask L Rev 357.

24 "Issues of race, class, ability and gender were never far from the surface in decisions

that allowed dominant society to regularize such children's institutionalization also made it easier to discount their disclosures of abuse and to discount its harms.[25] Second, there was an "enormous" imbalance of power, status, and authority between the children and the governments, churches, and social agencies that ran the institutions. Institutional power and status facilitated the disbelief or discreditation of disclosures.[26] Lastly, *Restoring Dignity* noted the invisibility of the children once institutionalized. Although vigilance in ensuring the welfare of children entrusted to institutional care was essential, very little oversight of any kind was exercised by those ultimately in charge of the institutions. The result was "a recipe for abuse of power."[27]

The LCC study emphasizes the particular abuse-enabling dynamics of residential institutions such as those involved in the litigation in the *Bazley*, *HL*, *Plint*, and *Oblates* cases.[28] Such "total institutions" in different degrees aimed to fundamentally re-socialize residents to habits and values deemed superior to those the residents had internalized during their upbringings.[29] Re-socialization typically was pursued by isolating children from all external community supports and all familial connections, subjecting them to daily routines modelling dominant norms that were enforced by rigid institutional hierarchies, authoritarian formal and informal instruction, harsh and frequently arbitrary

about which children would wind up in institutions" (*Restoring Dignity*, *supra* note 21 at 21).

25 *Ibid* at 4–5. The *RCAP Report* contains many instances of officially documented reports of physical and sexual abuse, as well as of unsafe residential conditions over the century that residential schools operated (*supra* note 20). "Head office, regional, school and church files are replete, from early in the system's history, with incidents that violated the norms of the day" (*Looking Forward*, *supra* note 22 at 367). A persistent pattern of inaction and cover-up was also a well-documented response of many other institutions to reported abuses. See, eg, Goldie Shea, "Redress Programs Relating to Institutional Child Abuse in Canada" (paper prepared for Law Commission of Canada, 1999, on file with author).

26 *Restoring Dignity*, *supra* note 21 at 5.

27 *Ibid* at 5, 6. Note these three lessons would apply to current institutions as well.

28 *Supra* note 1.

29 Aboriginal residential schools were explicitly designed to eliminate Aboriginal culture, as well as the fiscal obligations of the federal government associated with treaty obligations, reserves, and forcible relocations. Schools for the deaf had assimilative purposes designed to discourage deaf culture and deaf sign languages in favour of communication methods accessible to the hearing population. Reform and training schools were intended to discipline young women and men considered socially, sexually, or criminally delinquent and to convert them to middle-class values and norms.

discipline,[30] and individual humiliation and degradation. The resulting message to those in power and to the children alike was of the children's lesser humanity.[31] Throughout, *Restoring Dignity* stresses the importance of contextualizing abuse within the systemic relations of inequality — racism, classism, sexism, ablism — that rationalized children's institutionalization and then compounded their powerlessness and perceived worthlessness within the institutions, thereby virtually ensuring little or no political or legal accountability or redress for the wholesale abuses incubated in so corrupted an environment. *Restoring Dignity* contains a twenty-eight page bibliography of studies on sexual abuse generally and on Canadian institutional abuse in particular. None of these specialized studies, far less the *LCC Report* itself, is referred to in any of the Supreme Court majority decisions.

In deciding these cases, the court had considerable scope to develop jurisprudence adequate to the widespread and devastating harms of institutional abuse. In six of the cases there was no binding precedent concerning similar legal claims on similar facts. In aggregate, it was appeal courts that defeated claimants. Plaintiffs were successful at trial more often, and under more causes of action, than on appeal, perhaps because trial judges were able to observe plaintiffs and saw in their deportment and testimony the harms done to them. Well-resourced defendants, by contrast, benefited from the abstractions that structure the appeal process and its focus on doctrine and the policy implications of liability findings.[32] All nine plaintiffs won at least one of their institu-

30 A "reign of disciplinary terror punctuated by incidents of stark abuse" was "the ordinary tenor of many [residential] schools throughout the system" over their one hundred years of existence: see *Looking Forward*, *supra* note 22 at 373. For an indicator of the severity of abuses recognized as sufficiently standard to be itemized in benchmarks for compensation under the Indian Residential Schools Agreement, see The Independent Assessment Process Guide, online: <http://www.irsrrqpi.gc.ca/ english/ index.html> at 13.

31 *Restoring Dignity*, *supra* note 21 at 22–28. For a compelling synthesis of this inequality analysis of abuse as applied to *Plint*, *supra* note 1, see factum of the interveners LEAF, Native Women's Association of Canada and DisAbled Women's Network of Canada in *Barney v Canada* at the Supreme Court of Canada, online: <www.leaf.ca/legal/ briefs/barney-2005.html>.

32 Defendant institutions can well afford to appeal. Given the volume of cases coming forward, defendants also have much to gain from using the appeal process not only to limit or reduce liability and damage awards, but to induce discount settlements and discourage under-resourced potential claimants from even launching civil actions. Where institutions have faced multiple civil suits from adult survivors, they have often established claims resolution vehicles that process individual claims according to standardized compensation schedules and without any adversarial structure. De-

tional liability claims at trial, and a total of sixteen claims succeeded at trial against ten of the thirteen institutional defendants.[33] However, only seven of the sixteen wins survived final appeal. In particular, only five defendant institutions were ultimately found vicariously liable, two of them jointly in the *Plint* case.

Regardless of the cause of action, plaintiffs mostly lost. In my view, they lost because the court refused to inform itself about abuse when developing four separate new lines of doctrine for the adjudication of the wave of abuse claims that hit the courts in the 1990s. Beyond ignoring the vast array of authoritative research on the history and power dynamics of institutional abuse, the court also consulted little jurisprudential theory and comparative law even though it was creating landmark precedents in what was new legal territory. The very few references by the court to tort scholarship were to traditional tort textbooks and to very dated doctrinal commentary.[34] This disinterest in relevant historical, social science, and legal scholarship strikes me as shockingly anti-intellectual in a final appeal court that effectively shapes both social and legal policy. Rather than learning about and engaging the social, political, and legal factors underpinning institutionalization and enabling abuse, the court narrowed its inquiry to the search for direct causal links between an individual perpetrator's official duties and his institutional employers or principals. This search was conducted in relation to narrow and literal-minded readings of job descriptions, institutional contracts, and statutory powers and duties — all abstracted from socio-historic context and the lived realities of institutional players. When the court referred to inequalities of power at all, its analysis was cursory and superficial: the abuser had parent-like power, or children were from "troubled" homes. Racism, poverty, disability, and sex-

fendant institutions have considerable incentive to contest early lawsuits very aggressively in order to establish lowered compensation benchmarks in advance of group settlement negotiations. For examples, see Shea, *supra* note 25.

33 None of the reported decisions in the *Bazley* litigation explains why there were no findings against two named provincial ministries.

34 *Bazley*, eg, cites nine secondary sources: five of them are doctrinal textbooks, one article is from 1916, and one text is from 1967. Fully six of the authorities cited pre-date 1990. *KLB*, which revisited four distinct bodies of tort doctrine, cites only two torts textbooks (including the 1967 text cited in *Bazley*), and a 1987 article (also cited in *Jacobi*). See *Bazley*, *Jacobi*, and *KLB*, *supra* note 1. Notwithstanding a joint intervention from three feminist organizations citing thirty-seven books or articles that offered egalitarian, feminist, and anti-racist analysis of the legal issues in play, *Plint* cites only the 1967 text plus one 1995 article on strict liability, *supra* note 1. See factum of LEAF *et al* in *Plint*, *supra* note 31.

ism were, by omission, adjudged irrelevant to the institution's purposes, its typical residents or service population, the abusers' power vis-à-vis their victims and, thus, the inherent risks of the institutional enterprise. In sum, the decisions lack any meaningful attempt to grapple with the multiple inequalities that generated and rationalized both institutionalization and institutional abuse, inhibited or discredited reporting, excused institutional inaction, compromised resort to law as a vehicle of redress, and accounted for the unconscionable defence tactics[35] deployed by defendant institutions to continue to evade responsibility for abuses of children in their care. I count this as an egregious instance of privileged ignorance in operation.

The first of the court's nine decisions appeared to lay the foundations for an approach to institutional liability that does take into account the systemic relations of inequality that permeate the history and abusive dynamics of institutions like residential schools, orphanages, adolescent reform schools, schools for the deaf, child welfare placement facilities, and the like. In *Bazley v Curry*,[36] a unanimous Supreme Court rejected a century-old doctrinal formula for determining an employer's liability for injuries caused by an employee in the course of employment.[37] That formulaic framework required convoluted reasoning and led to inconsistent results where the employee engaged in intentional criminal misconduct, such as theft or violence at work. The *Bazley* court proposed a substantive test for vicarious employer liability where there were no unambiguous precedents applicable to the case being litigated. As the court found no unambiguous precedent applicable to the *Bazley* facts — sexual abuse of boys in a group home by a resident staffer — it appeared that the new test would apply to all cases of institutional abuse committed by institutional employees.

The new test implicitly rejected the decontextualized conception of abuse as the misconduct of an isolated, deviant perpetrator. Instead of

35 For three compelling critiques of routine resort to hyper-aggressive defence tactics even after the defendant institutions have globally apologized for such abuses, see Elizabeth Adjin-Tettey, "Righting Past Wrongs Through Contextualization: Assessing Claims of Aboriginal Survivors of Historical and Institutional Abuses" (2007) 25 Windsor YB Access Just 95; Bruce Feldthusen, "Civil Liability for Sexual Assault in Aboriginal Schools: The Baker Did It" (2007) 22 Can JL & Soc 61; and Vella & Grace, *supra* note 5 at 249–58.

36 *Supra* at note 1. Prior to 1999, the Supreme Court had heard a criminal appeal by an Indian residential school principal and priest accused of raping four Aboriginal women at the school: *R v O'Connor*, [1995] 4 SCR 411.

37 See John Salmond, *The Law of Torts* (London: Steven and Haynes, 1907) at 83.

focusing solely on the abuser's formal job duties and looking for a link — however contrived — between authorized duties and the misconduct, it focused on the nature of the enterprise that employed the abuser and on whether that enterprise carried inherent risks of abuse. The court reasoned that, as a matter of fairness, an enterprise that introduces risk into a community to advance its own interests should be responsible for damages that occur in the course of operating that enterprise. Practically, the court held, such a policy will promote effective compensation by improving the likelihood that those injured will recover damages from a solvent defendant and by ensuring that the party best able to spread the costs of inherent enterprise risks bears the losses of those risks that materialize.[38] As well, such a policy should deter the risk of future harm by encouraging the enterprise to take imaginative administrative and supervisory steps beyond those required in negligence law to reduce those risks that are inherent to the enterprise.[39]

In determining whether the enterprise enhanced the risk of employee misconduct which, in fact, materialized, the court proposed consideration of five contextual factors:

(a) the opportunity the enterprise afforded employees to abuse their power;
(b) the extent to which the tort may have furthered the employer's aims;
(c) the extent to which the tort was related to conflict, confrontation, or intimacy inherent in the enterprise;
(d) the extent of power conferred on the employee in relation to his victim;
(e) the vulnerability of potential victims to wrongful exercises of employee power.[40]

In cases of sexual abuse, the court offered that such contextual analysis might address the frequency and duration of employee contacts with children, especially intimate contacts; the frequency of opportunities to be alone with children; the degree and nature of employees' employment-related power and authority over children and the children's

38 *Bazley, supra* note 1 at paras 30, 31.

39 *Ibid* at para 34. This distinction between owing a duty of care to take steps to prevent foreseeable risks caused by specific employees (negligence) and having a policy-based, legal incentive (vicarious liability) to take steps to prevent risks inherent to the enterprise generally is reiterated (paras 39, 42). It is this distinction that should have eliminated resort to the deviant perpetrator or "one bad apple" view of institutional abuse.

40 *Ibid* at para 41.

dependency on or trust of the employee; and the spatial and temporal proximity of wrongful conduct to authorized work functions. It should be noted that these illustrations relate to job duties rather than to systemic enterprise risks, and do little to illuminate factors (a), (d), and (e). Applying the five factors to the *Bazley* facts, the court also emphasized that the group home was a "total intervention" institution that "created the environment that nurtured and brought to fruition" Curry's sexual abuses of resident youth. He enjoyed full-time parent-like power over all aspects of the child residents' lives. His duties of tucking children into bed or overseeing their personal hygiene afforded him "special opportunities for exploitation" of the proximity and routine intimacy expected of his job. Concluding that "it is difficult to imagine a job with a greater risk of child abuse," McLachlin, CJC, underlined that future cases need not rise to the same level to impose vicarious liability.[41]

Although the *Bazley* decision was well received in the torts bar,[42] its substantive import was eroded almost immediately in a companion case released the same day, *Jacobi v Griffiths*.[43] In subsequent cases, the majority reverted to a decontextualized formalism focused on narrowly defined job descriptions of isolated abusers deemed unforeseeable or undeterrable. Its focus dimmed on risks inherent to the enterprise and the power hierarchies it created or enhanced, and its attention shifted to risks to defendant enterprises of vicarious liability findings. The case law quickly became inconsistent as the original rationales for enterprise risk liability were abandoned.

Perhaps the most shocking instance of the post-*Bazley* jurisprudence is the last of the court's decisions on the vicarious liability of the enterprises that managed Aboriginal residential schools, *EB v Order of the Oblates of Mary Immaculate in BC*.[44] The trial began in 2001, ten years after the Order of the Oblates issued an apology for their role in

41 *Ibid* at para 58.

42 Jason Neyers and David Stevens offer a comprehensive list of explicitly and implicitly positive comments in "Vicarious Liability in the Charity Sector: An Examination of *Bazley v Curry* and *Re Christian Brothers of Ireland in Canada*" (2005) 42 Bus LJ 371.

43 *Supra* note 1. In that case, the program director at an after-school club for young girls and boys molested several children. His employer, the club, was found by a narrow majority of the court not to be vicariously liable for his misconduct on a variety of policy grounds that contradict the *Bazley* reasoning. For a more detailed analysis of the contradictions between *Bazley* and *Jacobi*, see McIntyre, *supra* note 2 at 15–18, and Vaughan Black & Sheila Wildeman, "Parsing the Supreme Court's New Pronouncements on Vicarious Liability for Sexual Battery" (1999) 46 CCLT (2d) 126 at 127.

44 *Supra* note 1.

"the cultural, ethnic, linguistic and religious imperialism" that animated their treatment of Aboriginal people and for the harms it caused.[45] The Supreme Court's decision was released in 2005, nine years after the *RCAP Report*, five years after the *LCC Report*, and seven years after the federal government's "Statement of Reconciliation" that acknowledged its role in the "culture of abuse" within Aboriginal residential schools and that established a $350 million healing fund to help alleviate the individual and collective harms done.[46]

Despite the general apology issued by the Oblates for its role in the harms caused by residential schooling, the Order adopted an aggressive, three-part defence against EB's claims of abuse by Saxey, an employee at the Christie Indian Residential School operated by the Oblates at the relevant time.[47] First, it denied any abuse had occurred, rigorously challenging the credibility of EB on numerous testimonial details concerning whether and how Saxey secured his acquiescence and silence, the sexual specifics of what occurred, and the time and place it occurred.[48] Secondly, and in the alternative, it argued that Saxey alone was responsible and that imposition of vicarious liability was inappropriate because there was no link between Saxey's job duties and his power or opportunities to abuse.[49] Saxey, it claimed, lacked routine proximity to children in the school, and had no authority or responsibility over the children. Finally, it sought to minimize the quantum of damages by attributing EB's numerous psychological problems to causes that pre-dated and post-dated the abuse.

The facts found by the trial judge were as follows: EB was sexually abused by Saxey on a weekly basis for five years beginning when EB

45 See *Restoring Dignity*, *supra* note 21 at 82.

46 For the text of the Statement of Reconciliation, see online: <http://www.ainc-inac.gc.ca/ai/rqpi/apo/js_spea-eng.asp> (accessed 31 July 2009). For the terms of the healing fund, see George Erasmus, "Reparations: Theory, Practice and Education" (2003) 22 Windsor YB Access Just 189.

47 *EB v Order of the Oblates of Mary Immaculate in the Province of BC*, [2001] BCJ No 2700 (BCSC). The decision is 335 paragraphs long and contains lengthy, painful excerpts from cross-examination of the plaintiff about minute details of the sexual assaults he endured. The Oblates' efforts to discredit experts for the plaintiff also consume several pages of the trial decision.

48 Defence witnesses testified that the children were supervised at all times and could never have been alone with Saxey in the bakery, on the school grounds, or in his residence. The trial judge rejected this evidence, effectively finding school religious staff to be lying.

49 Defence witnesses denied Saxey assigned children chores in the bakery and played with them during their free time. The trial judge also rejected this evidence.

was around six years old. Saxey was employed by the Christie residential school on Meares Island very shortly after his release from prison for manslaughter. He was primarily employed as a baker. However, due to the severe understaffing chronic in Aboriginal residential schools,[50] he also worked as a general maintenance man at the school and operated the tractor and the boat linking Meares Island to the Tofino area. The trial judge quoted a letter from the school principal describing Saxey as the "main cog" at the institution.[51] He lived on the school property near the playground in an apartment separate from the student residence. All resident children were required to obey all staff, whether religious or lay members, on pain of physical punishment. The frequency of harsh discipline created a climate of fear and intimidation for students. A defence witness had testified that both religious and lay staff subjected resident children to "physical and emotional violence, deprivation, belittling and intimidation." He described the disciplinary regime as "very threatening" and "very stern."[52] All lay staff, including Saxey, had and exercised authority to assign children chores related to the operation of the school. Saxey sometimes gave children chores in the bakery and oversaw their performance.

The trial judge rejected the defendant's reliance on precedents that found no link between the abuser's misconduct and the institution. He also specifically rejected the defendant's claim that to find the church vicariously liable would be to rest liability solely on the fact that both students and Saxey resided at the school.[53] Instead, he adopted the plaintiff's analysis, emphasizing features of the school that materially enhanced the risk of abuse: the removal and isolation of children from all external familial supports, their separation from siblings within the school, being held "in custody" in overcrowded and understaffed surroundings that facilitated school employees' unrestricted and unsupervised access to them, and a regime that compelled compliance with all lay and religious staff demands by constant threat of physical discipline.[54] He also cited passages from expert testimony linking the environment and operating norms of the school to an enhanced likelihood of abuse.[55] He concluded that the witness and expert evidence

50 See text at *supra* notes 22 and 23.

51 See *supra* note 47 at para 93.

52 *Ibid* at para 80.

53 *Ibid* at para 121.

54 *Ibid* at para 122.

55 *Ibid* at paras 123–30.

established "a significant connection between the creation or enhancement of a risk and the wrong that accrues therefrom,"[56] and held the Oblates vicariously liable for Saxey's assaults on EB

The BC Court of Appeal reversed the imposition of vicarious liability on the basis of a lack of nexus between Saxey's official duties "on the fringes of school life" and the assaults.[57] The Supreme Court of Canada affirmed that conclusion, purportedly on the basis of precedent and policy. For the eight judge majority, Binnie, J characterized the trial judge's ruling to be that liability flowed directly from risks created by the school's operational characteristics without demonstrating a strong connection between the assaults and Saxey's job-created power and authority. The flaw, held Binnie, J, was the trial judge's placing of all school employees on the same footing and his failure

> to put adequate weight on the school-created features of the relationship between *this* claimant and *this* wrongdoing employee, and the contribution of the ... enterprise to enabling the wrongdoer Saxey to do what he did in *this* case.[58]

This failure, he reasoned, led to an unacceptable result: the school would be liable for all tortious acts of its employees, "no matter how remote the wrongdoing from job-created power or status."[59] This floodgates argument overstates the case: on the trial judge's reasoning, the church would have been liable for all abuse of residents by employees of the school because the church created and oversaw an environment that normalized routine abuse of students. Why such an outcome is problematic as a matter of justice is not explained by the majority. If an enterprise creates a climate conducive to abuse, enterprise risk principles indicate it should be held responsible for damages when such risks materialize. This is the basic *Bazley* premise. Nor is the policy argument against institutional liability self-evident, particularly considering that abuse was endemic to the schools for decades to the knowledge of school administrators and sponsors, and was an outgrowth of the school's basic culture, as well as the subject of a pending mass settle-

56 *Ibid* at para 131, quoting Bazley, *supra* note 1 at para 4.

57 *EB v Order of the Oblates of Mary Immaculate in the Province of British Columbia*, (2003) 14 BCLR (4th) 99 (BCCA). The quotation is the Binnie J's in his description of the Court of Appeal decision. See *Oblates, supra* note 1 at para 2.

58 *Oblates, ibid* at paras 3 and 4 [emphasis in original].

59 *Ibid.*

ment by the federal government that funded all former residents for the harm inherent in forced school attendance and supplied a grid for damages for all proved abuse no matter the job status or title of the abuser.[60]

However, for the majority, Saxey's mechanical job functions "on the fringes of the school" — baking, driving, doing equipment repairs — provided the only measure of his job-related power in relation to resident children. It concluded that such tasks, in themselves, reflected little institutional power. This reasoning depends on dissociating the job from the larger enterprise of the schools. For the majority, the job did not enhance Saxey's power over the children; it merely provided an opportunity for a pedophile. Even this narrow definition of Saxey's role at the school is factually questionable given that feeding the school, operating the boat that connected the school to the mainland, and keeping equipment functioning were probably vital to the enterprise. Hence, one principal considered Saxey "the main cog" in running the school's functional operation.[61] As well, the trial judge had emphasized that children were required to obey all staff — lay and religious — equally.

But Saxey's power and the children's comparative powerlessness were not just a question of job duties, or even of brutally enforced institutional rules requiring strict obedience of all staff, even mere "odd job" men. The majority could only de-link Saxey's abuse from the residential school enterprise by studiously ignoring the historical, social, racial, and physical context of Saxey's functions in a culturally genocidal project serving the fiscal interests of the federal government and the fiscal and spiritual interests of the Catholic Church. For the majority, there was no *enterprise* behind Saxey, nor any of the "cultural, ethnic, linguistic and religious imperialism" that the Oblates acknowledged and apologized for in 1991.[62] Because the majority seems to look

60 *Oblates* was issued by the Supreme Court in late October of 2005. The Agreement in Principle for settlement of residential school claims was signed in November of 2005 and approved by the federal government in May of 2006. For details of the settlement agreement, see online: < http://www.residentialschool settlement.ca >. For an indicator of the severity of abuses recognized as sufficiently standard to be itemized in benchmarks for compensation under the Indian Residential Schools Agreement, see the Independent Assessment Process Guide, online: <http://www.irsr-rqpi.gc.ca/english/index.html> at 13.

61 *Supra* note 51.

62 See text at *supra* note 45. I should note that, as defendants, the Oblates also disregarded their earlier apology. Before the Supreme Court of Canada, they raised "their good intentions towards the students in their care … and the fact that the Oblates attempted on a not-for-profit basis to meet a need for education of First Nations' children that otherwise perhaps would have gone unmet" as policy arguments against

down on Saxey as a menial labourer, they discounted his institutional and institutionalized leverage as a staffer-who-must-be-obeyed by an isolated, frightened six year old in a systemically hostile and alien environment. They specifically rejected expert evidence accepted by the trial judge that children were unlikely to distinguish among school staff given the pervasive reliance of all staff on fear, intimidation, and harsh discipline.

The majority decision is almost surreal in its non-advertence to race and racism in applying doctrine to facts. Had it actually respected *Bazley* principles, it would have had to engage the hard truth that the residential school enterprise was racist. The enterprise was a classic "total institution,"[63] a violent social experiment to eradicate an entire culture by destroying its families and reprogramming children through a variety of abuses and humiliations to become assimilated into the dominant society as self-supporting individuals of little or no cost to the federal purse. Even the educational mission of the schools was racist. Students were not educated for middle-class jobs, but for employment as labourers in disrespected jobs just like the job held by Saxey.[64] Because the enterprise pursued its explicitly imperialist agenda on the cheap, it knowingly risked resident children's physical and mental health and their lives over a period of a century.

In a paradigmatic illustration of white privilege, the only reference to race in the majority judgment was notice in the first paragraph of the judgment of the fact that Saxey was Aboriginal,[65] which fact was pressed by the church to diminish the evidence of EB's isolation and absence of support within the school.[66] The majority viewed Saxey as an isolated perpetrator whose assaults were "abhorrent," but "in direct opposition" to the church's aims.[67] Not surprisingly, the church's "aims,"

imposition of vicarious liability (*Oblates*, *supra* note 1 at para 56). Binnie, J rejected such policy arguments — but note the rosy picture of residential schools offered by the Oblates.

63 See text at *supra* notes 28–31.

64 See *Restoring Dignity*, *supra* note 21 at 52–54, and George Erasmus, *supra* note 46 at 189–92.

65 *Oblates*, *supra* note 1 at para 1.

66 See trial decision, *supra* note 47 at paras 129–30.

67 *Oblates*, *supra* note 1 at para 48. Sexual abuse by an institutional employee will always be contrary to an institution's aims. *Bazley* recognized this fact, *supra* note 1. In *Bennett*, the Court unanimously held the church liable for serial sexual abuses of young parishioners by a priest (*ibid*). Such abuse was even more in opposition to the defendant church's aims than Saxey's misconduct. The contradiction between abuse and church mission was no obstacle to liability.

since discredited by the church itself, were not discussed by the majority. Binnie, J decreed that Saxey's formal job as baker and handyman conferred on him no power beyond being an adult among children who were no more vulnerable than in "any" residential setting: "it is the nature of a residential institution rather than the power conferred by the [Oblates] on Saxey that fed [EB's] vulnerability."[68] In short, in the view of eight judges of the court, the trial judge had pushed the boundaries of vicarious liability "too far":

> global inclusion of all employees, including odd-job men, in the "enterprise risk" paints with too broad a brush. It goes against the policy of ensuring that compensation is both effective and *fair*.[69]

For the majority, Saxey was just any baker, any odd-job man in any residential context, save for his unaccountable, unforeseeable, undeterrable sexual proclivities that just happened to be directed at this child who was no more vulnerable than any child in any residential setting. Only in this judicially constructed socio-economic, cultural, racial moonscape, would it be "unfair" to legally link a child abuser to the "operational dynamics" of the enterprise.

The majority concocted this raceless, classless, innocent version of the Christie school and of Saxey's role within it in the face of powerful challenges to such perversely benign abstractions. Interveners supported arguments in favour of employer liability for Saxey's sexual violence by reference to considerable scholarship on the Aboriginal residential schools as well as scholarship illuminating the risks of abuse under conditions of systemic inequality. They also relied on modern tort theory. The majority judgment referred to none of this material in its reasoning. In fact, the majority judgment referred to no secondary sources of any kind.

As problematic, every falsely benign premise underpinning the majority's reasoning was explicitly confronted and refuted in the compelling solo dissent by Justice Abella. Abella, J returned to *Bazley* and its call for a contextualized, substantive approach to determining whether the relationship between the residential school enterprise and the abuser's employment enhanced his power and opportunity to abuse. Her

68 *Oblates*, *ibid* at para 48. This is an odd assertion if any shred of the enterprise risk underpinnings of *Bazley* still exists in Canadian tort doctrine. If the residential setting did confer power on Saxey in relation to child residents, and such power enhanced the risk of the abuse that, in fact, materialized, vicarious liability should follow.

69 *Ibid* at para 30 [emphasis in original].

analysis methodically exposed and contradicted significant misrepresentations both by the Court of Appeal and by the Binnie majority of the trial judge's findings of fact and of law. She also directly challenged the majority's abstractions about Saxey's job-related power and about EB's vulnerability to Saxey within the residential school context. The second paragraph of her analysis emphasized these power dynamics as follows:[70]

> These events occurred in the context of a residential school, where children were forcibly removed and segregated from their families to facilitate the obliteration of their Aboriginal identity. Few environments could be more conducive to enhancing the vulnerability of children.[71]

She endorsed the trial judge's emphasis on the complete obedience to all staff required of the children, and linked it to the "power structure" of the enterprise where discipline was "strict and harsh," order was maintained "largely through fear and the threat of punishment," and students' daily experience included "physical and emotional violence, deprivation, belittling, and intimidation."[72] She affirmed the trial judge's understanding of the operational characteristics of the school in giving all employees, including a mere "odd-job" man, power over young children whom the school also disempowered and rendered vulnerable through isolation and intimidation designed to condition them to obey all staff members. In short, even if members of the majority of the final appellate court in the country were uninterested in informing themselves of what is well-documented and relevant to determining links between institutions and abuse, it had squarely before it a trial judgment and a dissent insisting on these links and pointing to legal and social science authorities to substantiate the trial and dissenting rulings. Yet the majority preferred to pronounce on tort policy generally and on the "fairness" of the trial outcome specifically swaddled in privileged ignorance and innocence.

In *Oblates*, as in the other eight institutional abuse cases decided since 1999, the majority devoted little or no attention to the history, nature, and dynamics of the institutional enterprises where children

70 Part I of Abella J's opinion, entitled "Background," begins with a ten-paragraph review of the *Bazley* framework and of the trial judge's core reasoning. Part II, entitled "Analysis," commences at para 71. The quoted passage is at para 72.

71 *Ibid* at para 72, citing three authorities on institutional abuse, including the *RCAP Report* and *Restoring Dignity*, *supra* note 20.

72 *Oblates*, *ibid* at para 81.

were abused. The enterprise of the residential schools was thereby judicially rendered innocent. Its defining power inequalities were erased. Its employees' job-related authority and power were utterly dissociated from the cultural supremacism of the enterprise and from the routine physical, psychological, spiritual, and cultural violence intrinsic to implementation of the enterprises' goals. The floodgates argument underlying the refusal to hold a church institution vicariously liable for predation by an odd-job man betrays an unreflective identification with dominant interests. The majority emphatically asserted that it would be going too far to hold the church liable for Saxey's abuse of EB because that would mean residential school operators would be liable for abuses of children by any employee, however lowly in institutional rank. Such an outcome was declared "unfair" without explanation. But from whose point of view and why would that outcome be unfair? The schools were established to destroy Aboriginal identity in order to reduce governments' fiscal obligations to First Nations communities and to facilitate settler expansion. The effective beneficiary was taxpayers. Why should the enormous costs borne by a very small community of a deeply, destructive government-sponsored cultural experiment not be spread among the vastly larger community of taxpayers? Likewise, why should the churches who took public funding to indoctrinate new souls be immunized from the harms they caused on a massive scale? When government and the churches have actually reached settlement agreements entitling every survivor to automatic compensation for the harms done,[73] why is judicially imposed institutional liability "unfair"? Why does the court presume fairness to taxpayers trumps fairness to the lost generations of Aboriginal children?

My answer is that the socially marginalized and racially devalued plaintiffs in these cases were (mis)treated by strong majorities of the Supreme Court of Canada the way they were (mis)treated within institutions dedicated to reprogramming such children. Never truly seen, heard, or credited with their full humanity, their needs and welfare were eclipsed by privileged imaginings and subordinated to dominant material interests and policy goals. Their vulnerability, its exploitation, and the devastating individual and multi-generational damage done counted less than judicial endorsement of the innocence of power holders and their (our) institutional instruments of domination. The court had ample opportunity to develop a modern doctrine to achieve *Baz-*

73 For details of the settlement agreement, see online: <http://www.residentialschool-settlement.ca>.

ley's two goals — effective and just compensation for tens of thousands of victims of institutional and institutionalized inequality and abuse, and deterrence of institutional recurrences through preventive institutional interventions. Instead, the court rationalized a blend of laissez-faire legalism and utilitarianism propped up by myths about isolated deviants operating independently of their social, economic, and racial contexts. Where the damages were greatest and most widespread, the court found policy reasons to immunize individual institutions from liability.

8.
Sexual Assault and Disabled Women Ten Years after *Jane Doe*

Fran Odette

This section deals with institutional and community responses to women's disclosure of sexual assault. Fran Odette writes about the specific experience of disabled women who are sexually assaulted, highlighting the additional consequences they face — such as being institutionalized — if their reports are disbelieved by police or by the courts. Disabled women's vulnerability to assault is increased by the credibility gap they face, but Fran goes further in this chapter, identifying inadequate research and feminist services as implicated in the underdevelopment of disabled women's equality rights in the context of sexual assault. Arguing that disability is a social category that is imposed, she argues that if disabled women are not "othered," it will become obvious that the supports they require when they experience sexual assault are no different than what all women need.

Ten years after the *Jane Doe* legal victory,[1] and decades since the crime of sexual assault was reconceptualized in the *Criminal Code*,[2] the specificity of the sexual assault of disabled women remains largely unaddressed and meaningfully chronicled. The manner in which this ongoing failure plays out in feminist legal and academic research and theory, and in our communities, is the subject of this article.

In Canada, women with physical impairments and differences — similar to Aboriginal, racialized, and other women facing discrimination and oppression — experience the crime of sexual violence at rates of two to three times that of women who do not live with impairment or bodily difference.[3] Disabled women experience and define sexual vio-

1 *Jane Doe v Metropolitan Toronto (Municipality) Commissioners of Police* (1998), 39 OR (3d) 487 (Ont Ct (Gen Div)).

2 *An Act to amend the Criminal Code in relation to sexual offences and other offences against the person and to amend certain other Acts in relation thereto or in consequence thereof*, SC 1980-81-82-83, c 125; *An Act to amend the Criminal Code (sexual assault)*, SC 1992, c 38.

3 DisAbled Women's Network (DAWN), *Women with Disabilities: Physical and Sexual Assault* (Toronto 1994), online: <http://dawn.thot.net/sexual_assault.html>. See also

lence/sexual assault in a particular context, wherein we are devalued, desexualized, and discounted.[4] The experience of disabled women who are also racialized, Aboriginal, poor, or otherwise further marginalized, in terms of male sexual violence is further layered by discrimination.[5]

A prevailing mythology holds that women living with disabilities are not sexual beings and therefore are not sexually active.[6] Rape myths tell us that disabled women are not "real targets" of sexual assault. The lived experience of disabled women who are sexually assaulted is that when such crimes are reported to authorities, our credibility is called into question, particularly those of us who live with the label of intellectual impairment, who have been psychiatrized, or who have learning differences. According to Suellen Murray and Anastasia Powell, writing for Women with Disabilities Australia:

> … how "disability" and "vulnerability" are understood may be reflected in the responses of those to whom the disclosure would be made and may also result in creating barriers to disclosure. For example, a woman with disabilities may be concerned that she will not be believed because of ideas that people with disability are asexual (or promiscuous), that they lie or exaggerate, or would not be sexually assaulted (Chenoweth, 1996; Lievore, 2005; Women with Disabilities Australia, 2007b). In relation to disclosure to police by people with intellectual disabilities, Keilty & Connelly (2001) found that "two myths, in particular, emerged consistently: women with intellectual disability are promiscuous and the complainant's story is not a credible account" (280). Police, in particular, may appear dismissive of allegations of sexual assault as the victim may be perceived as someone who could be too readily influenced and hence make a poor witness (Phillips, 1996; Victorian Law Reform Commission, 2003; Victorian Law Reform Commission, 2004).
>
> These negative responses may be expressed as disbelief, ridicule, blame, rejection or persecution (Davidson, 1997). Due to these responses, she may be concerned that nothing will happen when she does disclose, that some-

Dicky Sobsey, *Sexual Abuse and Exploitation of People with Disabilities* (Edmonton: Developmental Disabilities Centre, University of Alberta, 1988).

4 Sandra L Martin, "Physical and Sexual Assault of Women with Disabilities" (1986) 12 Violence Against Women 823.

5 For a general discussion of discrimination encountered by women with disabilities, see Lesley Chenoweth, "Violence and Women with Disabilities: Silence and Paradox" (1996) 2 Violence Against Women 391.

6 For discussion, see eg Rosemary Basson, "Sexual Health of Women With Disabilities" (1998) 159 CMAJ 359.

> thing may happen that she does not want to happen, or indeed, that the situation is made worse or it is taken out of her hands.[7]

Indeed, the situation becomes much worse for disabled women when charges are unfounded by police or unproven in court. These negative consequences can, in turn, result in loss of caregivers, institutionalization, forced sterilization, unwanted pregnancy, racism, sexism, deportation, further sexual assaults, and even death. The case of a Toronto woman named Cinderella Allalouf, referred to later in this paper, is one such example of such dire consequences for the woman.

My work in this area and my passion stem from my location as a feminist, queer-identified, white woman with disabilities who uses a wheelchair. I became politicized regarding the realities facing disabled women and the critical intersections of gender, race, and socio-economic status as a result of the work of the Disabled Women's Network [DAWN] and the mentorship of two of its founders, Pat Israel and Liz Stimpson. I first immersed myself in the work of violence against women as a result of working on the first Ontario government publication on disabled women.[8] Freedom from violence and the rights to sexual expression and healthy sexuality as human rights led me to co-author the *Ultimate Guide to Sex and Disability* in 2003.[9]

The myths that continue to deny disabled women access to our own identity and sexuality inform my ongoing community-based work with Springtide Resources.[10] The prevalence of these myths contributes to the rape and sexual assault of disabled women. And while there is no lack of personal narratives and statistics about our rapes/sexual assaults, there are no role models, little research, and no mainstream media representations to "talk back" to such constructions and falsehoods.

7 Suellen Murray & Anastasia Powell, "Sexual Assault and Adults With a Disability: Enabling Recognition, Disclosure and a Just Response" (2008) 9 Aust Inst Family Stud Issues, online: <http://www.aifs.gov.au/acssa/pubs/issue/i9.html>.

8 *Violence Against Women with Disabilities: A Service Needs Assessment* (Toronto: Ontario Women's Directorate, 2003). This study provides an overview of the service needs of women with disabilities in Ontario who experience violence in community settings. The directorate's website is located online: <http://www.citizenship.gov.on.ca/owd/english/index.shtml>.

9 Miriam Kaufman, Cori Silverberg & Fran Odette, *Ultimate Guide to Sex and Disability* (Berkeley: Cleis Press, 2003).

10 Springtide Resources promotes healthy and equal relationships by engaging diverse communities in educational strategies designed to prevent violence against women and their children, online: <http://www.springtideresources.org>.

This chapter identifies and unpacks barriers — blockades, really — that remain unaddressed in our feminisms and that confront disabled women and women with physical differences who are sexually assaulted. Ten years after Jane Doe successfully addressed sexual assault in the context of women's equality rights, the rights of disabled women remain undeveloped and inaccessible. Decades since we first identified the paucity of research and meaningful data collection to capture the lived experiences of disabled women who are sexually assaulted, our agency continues to be ignored or infantilized. We are further disappeared within rape discourse, social services, government bureaucracies, and legal, medical, and other institutions.

In the first part of this chapter, I discuss questions of terminology and disability, for linguistic constructs in turn shape our thinking and practice around disability. In the second part, I expand upon the current understanding of disability, which is that it is socially constructed and imposed upon disabled persons. This discussion turns the third part into an overview of the specific experience of disabled women who have been sexually assaulted. Finally, in the fourth and fifth parts, I discuss two significant impediments to the promise of equality for disabled women who have been raped: the research gap, which means that we are hindered in our policy and legal responses, and the failure of feminist community-based services to respond to the lived experience of disabled women.

1. A FEW WORDS ABOUT LANGUAGE

I prefer to use the terms "disabled women" and "impairments" rather than "women with disabilities" and "disability," in solidarity with the Disability Rights Movement's [DRM] decision to move away from the medical model of disability towards a social model.

Canadian activists fought long and hard to say that I, for example, am "a woman with a disability." It was critical, especially in our feminisms, to insert gender before disability. That particular naming practice was/is also often preferred by many women who acquire their disability after birth through accident or illness, versus those of us who are born with our impairments, who are in fact a tiny minority of the disability population. Placing the term "disabled" before gender acknowledges that the problem does not lie within the individual, but rather in a social environment that assumes ability. The reality is that any one of us can and will become physically or mentally disabled at any time,[11]

11 See Susan Wendell, *The Rejected Body* (New York: Routledge, 1996).

especially in a time where we (especially women) live longer lives, and, increasingly, with less access to housing, money, and healthcare. And, sadly, often with an increased risk of experiencing violence.

Recently the terminology of "disAbility" has become popular, and while I recognize the intent, it can be seen or understood to prefer ability — with a capital "A."[12] Likewise, the terms "non-disabled" and "able bodied" assume ability or advantage over someone else. People in the deaf community do not identify as disabled — the "dis" is understood to be negative or tragic. They have named their community with pride in a shared identity. Although historically efforts have been made to eradicate deafness, Deaf activists have long held to a social model of disability that sees a world designed to provide access for all forms of communication. For instance, hearing children could go to school to learn sign language rather than forcing deaf kids to find ways to communicate in spoken word, which denies that American Sign Language is their first language as well as their cultural identity and connection to the Deaf community.

The language used to conceptualize violence against women leaves out many disabled women. Terms within the literature include "intimate partner abuse," "wife assault," and the antiquated "domestic" and/or "family violence." Naming practices such as these fail to include disabled women whose experience of violence is at the hands of attendants, health-care providers, and other service providers.[13] Language and linguistic choices then must be understood as barriers in existing discourse about disability that prevent disabled women who are sexually assaulted from realizing agency and action, especially when we speak of so-called "mental disabilities" versus, for example, "mental wellness."

I do not intend to address what "disability" or impairment means in the lives of disabled women or women living with difference. The label in and of itself does not give us information about women's experience, but rather evokes preconceived ideas about what that experience is. It is not my intention to add further to the marginalization of my sisters by framing our experiences within what has been called the tradition-

12 I also use the terms "sexual assault" and "rape" interchangeably to acknowledge the outrageous labelling of those acts as non-violent. While I often use the terminology of "survivor" to describe women who have been sexually assaulted, I do so in celebration and recognize that "survivor" and "victim" are terms that are felt negatively by some women.

13 For discussion, see eg Malcolm Gordon, "Definitional Issues in Violence Against Women" (2000) 6 Violence Against Women 747.

al "personal tragedy theory of disability."[14] What is most important to remember when we speak of disabled women is that they are mothers, sisters, friends, daughters, wives, girlfriends, lovers, nieces, cousins, aunts, neighbours, and co-workers. They are professional and unemployed workers: some women are working, while others cannot find employment. Some women live with observable characteristics and many have disabilities that are invisible. What is important and should be at the forefront always is that we are women.

2. THE SOCIAL MODEL OF DISABILITY

I propose that "disability" be viewed through the social model, which frames an understanding of disability as reflective of barriers, prejudices, and exclusion within society, whether intentional or not, as the determining factors that define who is and who is not "disabled" in a particular cultural context.[15]

Originating in the UK during the 1970s and continuing to develop, this politic frames disablement as stemming from environmental and structural barriers in society rather than from a person's characteristics or physical attributes. Michael Oliver and others have written regarding this framework of the experience of disability/impairment.[16] Social theories of disability turn the traditional medical and conceptual models inside out. No longer is a disability the disadvantage caused by a medical impairment, such as blindness or deafness. Instead, disability is disadvantage caused by the way society is organized, the way the environment is built, and the attitudes of others. The blame has been shifted away from disabled people and their impairments and onto society. If, for example, my impairment is my lack of sight, I am disabled by a society that is structured in such a way that I cannot read most written materials, know what bus is coming, or read the contents of a food package. I am disabled by a society that patronizes me, pats me on the head, and thinks "oh dear how brave" when I walk past. I am disabled by a society that believes that I should go to a special school, not have sex, and certainly not have another baby who might be blind or who might suffer because of my "disabled" parenting skills.

14 For a recent discussion of this theory, see Michael Oliver, "The Social Model of Disability: An Outdated Ideology?" (2002) 2:9 Research in Soc Sc & Disability 28.

15 Ena Chadha, "The Social Phenomenon of Handicapping" in Elizabeth Sheehy, ed, *Adding Feminism to Law: The Contributions of Justice Claire L'Heureux Dubé* (Toronto: Irwin Law, 2004) 209.

16 Oliver, *supra* note 14.

And, if I am sexually assaulted, the crime is "worse," seen as more violent, or more contemptible, because of my disability. Or it is my fault because I am seen to have no sexuality and will not "mind" the intrusion, or will be grateful for the "interest." Or, I will be blamed for taking my disabled sexuality out in public where it is fair game for rapists/ sexual predators.

According to the *Social Model of Disability Text*:

> The social model of disability is not a traditional diagrammatic model like many psychological and sociological models, but a progressive political concept that opposes the medical model commonly used in the health professions.
>
> The social model of disability makes an important distinction between the terms impairment and disability.
>
> - Impairment — Lacking part or all of a limb or having a defective limb, organ or mechanism of the body (including psychological mechanisms).
> - Disability — The restrictions caused by the organization of society which does not take into account individuals with physical or psychological impairments (UPAIS, 1976).
> - This distinction is embedded in social constructionism (a philosophical foundation of the social model), which states that these terms differ in that impairment exists in the real physical world and disability is a social construct that exists in a realm beyond language within a complex organization of shared meanings, discourses and limitations imposed by the environment at a particular time and place. These barriers can be divided into three categories: environmental, economical and cultural (British Council of Disabled People).[17]

It is fair and critical to say, however, that the social model does not itself differentiate on the basis of gender, much less around sexual assault and other crimes of violence against women. Nor, with some notable exceptions, has race been explored in a feminist context.

3. WHICH WOMEN ARE EQUAL?

A critical piece within the social construct of the experience of oppression based on disability concerns itself with "equality."[18] "Social handi-

17 Best Resources for Achievement and Intervention re: Neurodiversity in Higher Education (BRAINHE), "The Social Model of Disability," online: <http://www.brainhe.com/TheSocialModelofDisabilityText .html>.

18 John Sadler, "Nothing About Us Without Us: Recognizing the Rights of People with Disabilities" (2009) 22 Current Opinion in Psychiatry 607.

capping" means that a person's equality rights are impinged as they are not entitled to the same rights or privileges enjoyed by non-disabled persons. Equal rights are said to provide opportunities for increased empowerment and the "ability" to make decisions and live life to the fullest. This was the basis of Jane Doe's legal argument that sex discrimination by police in their decision not to warn her of a serial rapist deprived her of the opportunity to protect herself from him. The social model of disability acknowledges systemic practices steeped in paternalism and framed as being "in the best interests" of those they are intended to "protect." It acknowledges systemic responses on numerous levels founded on biased perspectives of the potential and value of those of us living with some form of difference, which in this context is called "disability."[19]

We know that remedies offered through the criminal justice system for sexual assault survivors are not in the best interests of the women witnesses. These can result in further subjugating us to the margins of "other" and promoting exclusionary practices that fail to work with survivors with an approach based in human rights and equity.[20] Perhaps the largest barrier for women who have been sexually assaulted is the legal institution's perception of raped women's (lack of) credibility. In consequence, we know that many women do not report sexual assaults.[21]

Yet little substantial research has been undertaken to look at the experiences of disabled women in accessing the legal and justice systems. Much of what we do know is anecdotal. Many disabled women are simply not entering the legal system unless they have accessed supports first. Stereotypes held by police officers impact greatly on whether a woman's report will move beyond the investigating officer.[22] Stereotypes about disabled women's "sexual promiscuity and credibil-

19 Janine Benedet & Isabel Grant, "Hearing the Sexual Assault Complaints of Women with Mental Disabilities" (2007) 52 McGill LJ 515.

20 For a recent discussion of re-victimization effected by complainant testimony in sexual assault trials, see, for example, Lynn Idling, "Crossing the Line: The Case for Limiting Personal Cross-Examination by an Accused in Sexual Assault Trials" (2004) 69 Crim LQ 69.

21 It has been recently estimated that 94 percent of sexual assaults never come to the attention of Canada's criminal justice system. See Margaret J McGregor *et al*, "Why don't more women report sexual assault to the police?" (2000) 5 CMAJ 162. See also Ontario Women's Justice Network, online: <http://www.owjn.org/>.

22 Jennifer Keilty & Georgina Connelly, "Making a Statement: An Exploratory Study of Barriers Facing Women With an Intellectual Disability When Making a Statement About Sexual Assault to Police" (2002) 16 Disability and Society 273.

ity" skew the lens through which individual officers work with women survivors living with disability.[23] Interestingly, in a study conducted by Angela Nannini in 2006, "Women with disabilities tend to disclose to the police or solely the rape crisis centers more often than women without disabilities."[24] In the cases of women with cognitive impairments, women's advocates are often the ones who make the report.[25] Further research in this area is required in order to assess the sample size within which Nannini worked and to uncover the underpinnings of how and why disabled women report sexual assault.

Like other women, if a disabled woman has a report that is acted upon by the police and she then enters the justice system, aspects of her life are put on display as she becomes the focus of the investigation instead of the accused.[26] We also know that the law does not address the similarities of women's experiences by acknowledging existing research and statistics on the high rates at which disabled women are sexually assaulted, nor does it seek meaningful resolutions to the crime outside of a law and order context. As a result, disabled women seeking justice for male violence

> are subject to having the quality of their resistance to unwanted sexual ad vances brought into question, to having their previous sexual experiences used inappropriately to interpret the particular sexual encounter at issue, and to having superficial reference made to sexual autonomy at the expense of the protection of bodily and psychological integrity from exploitation by men in positions of power over them.[27]

Janine Benedet and Isabel Grant have produced an important piece of research that examines the complexities in criminal trial proceedings involving women with cognitive impairments who experience sexual assault. In particular, women with cognitive impairments are viewed as lacking credibility and making poor witnesses because of weaknesses in their narratives, recall, and "suggestibility." Furthermore, disabled women's sexual histories, not unlike non-labelled women's sexual hist-

23 *Ibid* at 280.

24 Angela Nannini, "Sexual Assault Patterns Among Women with and without Disabilities Seeking Survivor Services" (2006) 16 Women's Health Issues 375.

25 *Ibid.*

26 Benedet & Grant, *supra* note 19 at 518.

27 *Ibid.*

ories, become fodder for the defence and even for the Crown,[28] who, in many cases, is also informed by the pervasive mythologies around disabled women's sexuality. In many criminal trials involving women with disabilities as complainants, another binary is imposed: disabled women are either seen as eternal children needing to be protected, or as adult women whose sexuality and behaviour is "deviant" as a result of their disability.

Take the case of Cinderella Allalouf, a Toronto woman who emigrated from Jamaica in 1975 and experienced her first hospitalization for symptoms of schizophrenia shortly thereafter. According to a *National Post* newspaper article, the circumstances of her life and death went like this:

> Ms Allalouf was a profoundly schizophrenic 39-year-old woman with a long criminal history who had been found unfit to stand trial on charges of child abduction, and placed in custody at the Queen Street Mental Health Centre, in the new medium-security forensics ward run by Mr Malcolmson.
>
> She was the only woman among 19 mentally ill male inmates, all there on orders of a criminal court. She became pregnant within a few months of her committal in May 1996.
>
> Her family refused a hospital recommendation of abortion, and she delivered a boy at Mount Sinai Hospital in April 1997. Eight hours later, having received only minimal amounts of pain drugs, she died in a recovery room of a "sudden cardio respiratory arrest." A 1999 coroners' jury would later rule it "a sudden unexpected maternal death following Cesarean section, associated with schizophrenia" by "undetermined" means.
>
> In the malpractice action brought by Ms Allalouf's sister Miriam Eccleston, Mr Malcolmson is named as a defendant along with the province, the Queen Street Mental Health Centre, the Metropolitan Toronto Forensic Service and other medical staff. The claim is that they were negligent in failing to protect Ms Allalouf from harm while she was a patient. The defendants contest the allegations, which have not been tested in court.
>
> According to a 2000 report by Ontario coroner Dr William J Lucas, Ms Allalouf was "sexually aggressive, inappropriate, intrusive, difficult to redirect. Many of her co-patients found her behaviour distracting, unsettling and even repulsive." She was frequently placed in locked seclusion, for up to eight days at a time.

28 *Ibid.*

> A source close to the trial said the parentage of the child is not established. He is now 12 years old, [lives with disabilities] and being raised by his aunt, Ms Eccleston.[29]

Not reported or remarked upon is the fact that Miriam Eccleston reported the rape of Cinderella during her forced confinement at Queen Street — which resulted in her pregnancy — to Toronto police. The charge was not taken seriously and was unfounded due to the circumstances of Cinderella's life.[30] Her crimes, however, appear well chronicled and set the stage for her "deviant"/"disabled" sexuality. We do not read that her agency and autonomy were stripped away, that she was incapable of consenting to sex, or that choices about her reproductive rights were made for her. We are not informed that Mr (formerly Dr) Malcomson was convicted of sexual assault as a result of his relationship with another patient. Likewise, the social and economic impacts of Cinderella Allalouf's race, economic, and immigrant status are unchronicled in the mediated narrative of her life and death.[31]

4. WHAT'S A FEMINIST RESEARCHER TO DO?

It was only in 1985 that the *Canadian Charter of Rights and Freedoms* prohibited discrimination based on disability and in 1986 that the Supreme Court of Canada ruled that persons with mental disabilities cannot be forced to undergo sterilization for non-therapeutic reasons (*Re Eve* case).[32] In theory, the *Charter* ought to ensure that social, government, and legal institutions are held accountable in order to protect the rights and freedoms of citizens. In practice, however, with the exception of the result in *Jane Doe*, we are not examining systemic discrimination within other of our institutions that also impact on survivors of sexual violence. Such intransigence is noted globally, as explained by UNIFEM:

29 Rob Roberts, "The Fall of a Well-Respected Man" *National Post* (12 June 2009), online: <http://network.nationalpost.com/np/blogs/toronto/archive/2009/06/12/the-fall-of-a-well-respected-man.aspx>.

30 See Toronto Office of the Chief Coroner, *Report On the Inquest Into the Death of Cinderella Allalouf* (2000), online: <http://www.ppao.gov.on.ca/pdfs/sys-inq-all.pdf>.

31 *Ibid.*

32 *Re Eve*, [1986] 2 SCR 388, discussed in *Building an Inclusive and Accessible Canada: A National Initiative Support People with Disabilities in Canada*, online: <http://www.endexclusion.ca/archives/2006/english/milestones.asp>.

> Fighting gender-based violence is a major concern for UNIFEM, because violence against women is a universal problem and one of the most widespread violations of human rights. One in three women will suffer some form of violence in her lifetime. Despite some progress on this issue over the past decade, its horrendous scale remains mostly unacknowledged.[33]

In Canada, we know that those most impacted by gender-based violence are Aboriginal women living in cities, and in rural and remote northern communities. We know that disabled women and women with physical differences are members of all of those communities. And we know that many women facing multiple and intersecting forms of discrimination and oppression do not benefit from the social policies designed to respond to violence and abuse.[34]

There is a growing body of research examining the complexities of women's experiences in accessing services.[35] Feminist researchers have challenged the way research and data collection occurred around the issue of violence against women because it was conducted in a vacuum of lived experiences and grounded in methodological approaches that were problematic.

However, with respect to women's experience of sexual violence and disability/impairment, there remain problem areas in our research and theory. They include:

1. A singular focus on specific forms of violence, ie sexual violence, over other forms of violence.
2. A focus on specific "perpetrators," such as intimate partners, to the exclusion of others, such as caregivers (formal and informal). Many disabled women are not in intimate relationships and therefore their experience of sexual assault by those who are not partners is significantly under-explored in the research.[36]
3. The use of "convenience samples," rather than including questions within representative samples where women can self-identify as living with disability or difference, has limited our know-

33 UNIFEM electronic newsletter (2005), online: <http://www.unifem.org/about/fact_sheets.php?StoryID=278>.

34 Stephanie Paterson, "(Re)Constructing Women's Resistance to Woman Abuse: Resources, Strategy, Choice and Implications of and for Public Policy in Canada" (2002) 29 Critical Social Policy 121.

35 See, for example, Patricia Stevens, "Marginalized Women's Access to Health Care: A Feminist Narrative Analysis" (1992) 16:2 Advances in Nursing Science 39.

36 Nannini, *supra* note 24 at 377.

ledge base. As a result, we are only reaching women who come forward versus those in institutional settings and those who are highly isolated because of family and geography, and who do not see their experience as violence that can be reported, but rather as a reality of their lives.

4. The use of narrow definitions of disability that result in the exclusion of some women who live with impairments. The hierarchy of disability experience is replicated in many of these studies depending on how one responds to the questions asked, who is doing the research, and their research objectives.

The first significant contribution on violence against disabled women came from DAWN,[37] which placed the issues of violence against disabled women at the forefront of government and community discussions. In addition, there has been feminist research out of the US[38] and Australia.[39] A noteworthy contribution has been delivered by Dick Sobsey,[40] whose work regarding violence against disabled persons is widely referenced. It lacks, however, a solid, gendered, anti-racist, anti-oppression analysis. While the most recent research on issues related to woman abuse and disability by Douglas Brownridge[41] is more inclusive, the gap in feminist-based research and writing remains.

5. BARRIERS ON OUR FRONT LINES

To recap: we know that disabled women are at a much greater risk of sexual assault than their non-disabled counterparts, and that male violence can be the cause of disability. We are also more at risk for multiple acts of violence by more than one perpetrator, and experience forms of violence that are particular to living with disability,[42] ie in-

37 Jillian Ridington, *Beating the "Odds": Violence Against Women With Disabilities* (Vancouver: DisAbled Women's Network Canada, 1986).

38 See, for example, Wisconsin Coalition for Advocacy, "Cross-Training Handbook: Violence Against Women with Disabilities" (April 2004), online: <http://www.wwda.org.au/wisconsin1.pdf>; Mary Ellen Young *et al*, "Prevalence of Abuse of Women with Physical Disabilities" (1997) 78:12 Archives of Physical Medicine and Rehabilitation Special Issue (Supplement 5) S34.

39 Chenoweth, *supra* note 5.

40 Dicky Sobsey, *Violence and Abuse in the Lives of People with Disabilities: The End of Silent Acceptance* (Baltimore: Paul H Brookes, 2006).

41 Douglas Brownridge, *Violence Against Women: Vulnerable Populations* (New York: Routledge, 2009).

42 Holly Ramsey-Klawsnik, *Widening The Circle: Sexual Assault/Abuse and People with Disabilities and the Elderly* (Madison, WI: Coalition Against Sexual Assault, 1998).

voluntary sterilization, termination of pregnancy, or forced pregnancy. In his comparative study of women living with and without impairment, Douglas Brownridge documents a growing gap between these two groups of women in their vulnerability to violence: in 1993, 19% of women with disabilities experienced violence, rising to 39% in 1999, and to 85% in 2004.[43] Having studied 6,769 women in the 2004 survey, he reports that disabled women experience sexual assault at three times the rate of non-disabled women.[44]

Furthermore, we know that disabled women living with disabilities, including women who are from the Deaf community, have many social locations other than disability or difference.[45] Much of the research tends to identify our experience of disablement or impairment as homogenous, and to collapse our experience of trauma after violence. Nannini suggests that "assault and post assault survivor responses, may influence survivor outcomes."[46] However, few studies have looked at those issues comparatively, and most have focused on one disability experience.[47]

Research that does not examine the complexities and breadth of lived experience, related to trauma and disability, plays into the victimology constructs that even we, as feminists, ascribe to disabled women.[48] Who tells/mediates our stories is also determined by the nature of our disability. Nannini speaks to women with intellectual disabilities who seek support; she argues that we must differentiate between support and "taking over" or "helping." Someone without language, for instance, can trigger our discomfort, pity, and fear and cause us to make arrangements or suggestions that are not in her best interest, but instead assuage our feelings. She states that the stories of "survivors with cognitive disabilities [...] were more often told through another

43 Brownridge, *supra* note 42 at 252.

44 *Ibid* at 240.

45 Keran Howe, "Human Rights of Women with Disabilities" paper presented to 16 Days of Activism Against Violence Against Women Forum (Melbourne, Australia), Women With Disabilities Australia, Conference Papers, Articles and Reports, 2001–2005, online: <http://www.wwda.org.au/confpaps 2001.htm>. See also, online: <http://www.wwda.org.au/confpaps2001.htm>.

46 Nannini, *supra* note 24 at 375.

47 See, for instance, Dicky Sobsey & Tanis Doe, "Patterns of Sexual Abuse and Assault" (1991) 9 J Sexuality & Disability 243. See also Young, *supra* note 39.

48 Jane Doe and others address similar attitudes that position raped women only as victims and deny them sexuality, agency, and choice: Jane Doe, *The Story of Jane Doe* (Toronto: Random House, 2003).

person."[49] Without more research into women's narratives, she suggests that it is possible to attribute the "patterns of disclosure for women with cognitive disabilities [as] influenced by these confidants."[50]

When looking at the hierarchy of disablement and who is credible as the "story-teller," compare a speaking, white woman in a wheelchair who is employed to a young, racialized woman who lives with a cognitive and a communication impairment and who uses a word board. Prejudice, fear, and stigma (conscious or not) associated with each of those locations affects providers' responses to disabled survivors as credible witnesses or victims. Disabled women speak about their experiences with service providers and support workers (feminist and not), who do not "see" her or believe her, which in turn affects her ability to see herself as entitled to services from providers.

Rape mythology lives on, rages on, against women living with and without impairment or difference. Survivors of sexual violence who are not believed or are not seen as "credible" undergo significant levels of isolation, self-doubt, and reluctance to report or seek supports.[51] Providers who fail to recognize that many women who are seeking services, including legal remedies, have a previous history of being undermined and having their potential underestimated, do them a grave disservice. As a result of the limited skills of individual workers and agencies, additional barriers have been created for disabled women.[52]

Few VAW agencies are able to engage in meaningful ways around issues of disability and difference without framing those issues as: "We don't have enough money to build a ramp," or "We've ended up using that accessible room as an office because we don't have enough space, and we can't really 'hold' that room should someone come in that needs it," and so on. I see the rationale behind these statements as simplistic and reflective of a lack of commitment and will on the part of those service providers to engage authentically with the issues around women and disabilities. Many women have been "severed from the

49 Nannini, *supra* note 24 at 378.

50 *Ibid* at 378.

51 Virginia Sexual and Domestic Violence Action Alliance, *Sexual Violence Awareness Fact Sheet — People with Disabilities Overview*, online: <http://www.vsdvalliance.org/secPublications/svapwd.pdf>.

52 Judy Chang *et al*, "Helping Women with Disabilities and Domestic Violence: Strategies, Limitations and Challenges of Domestic Violence Programs and Services" (2003) 12 J Women's Health 699.

sisterhood"[53] because the characteristics of their impairments make others uncomfortable. Their lives and experiences and ways of being in the world counter the images still strongly held by many because they challenge what it means to live in bodies that are impaired, to have ways of learning that are different, and to experience the world through the long-standing effects of discrimination, poverty, and isolation. Thus, disabled women's "impairments run counter to the images of women that feminists promote: strong, smart and powerful."[54] Before we can stop feeling fearful, superior, and uncomfortable, we need to engage in meaningful dialogue — as disabled advocates, as activists, and as academics/researchers who do not live with impairments. Finding excuses as to why it is not possible to be inclusive is just that — an excuse.

At Springtide Resources, while we do not provide direct service such as counselling or legal advice, we often receive calls from VAW agencies saying: "We have a woman here at our facility, and we're not sure what supports we can get for her." After responding, I am left to wonder: "Why do supports for disabled women look radically different than they do for a woman who doesn't currently live with impairment?" How is it that we still continue to "other" women's experiences because of the distancing that occurs when disability or impairment enters the room? How do we apply the social model of disability to and within our feminisms? I wish I could say with confidence that we no longer tolerate indifference, subtle forms of racism, or other forms of oppression against women when they access women's services. While it is true that within the VAW sector we are less likely to tolerate workers' hesitations to engage with women whose race, sexualities, gender identities, or heritage is not the same as their own, we still are not where we should be.

The task before us of eliminating sexual and physical violence against women requires us to create proactive measures and processes in which women are at the core, and to challenge existing myths and stereotypes entrenched in beliefs about all women's deficits and lack of capacity. We know that there are significant gaps in the way that services address intersecting forms of oppression and the impact on violence survivors. We need to be prepared to challenge the work around what constitutes "best practices" and to focus instead on learning from

53 Michelle McCarthy, "Sexuality," in Patricia Noonan Walsh & Tamar Heller, eds, *Health of Women with Intellectual Disabilities* (Oxford: Blackwell, 2002) 90 at 93.

54 Julia Wacker *et al*, "Sexual Assault and Women with Cognitive Disabilities: Codifying Discrimination in the United States" (2008) 19:2 Disability Policy Stud J 93.

women with whom we engage directly as to what does and does not work for them, and then we need to develop new practices. We must acknowledge that in order to move forward in the work, we need to think differently about the work and who it includes. To eliminate all forms of violence against women, we must live up to inherent values that push back against the beliefs that support and promote the privileges of some women over the rights of others. For some of us, this might be the first time we have been "given permission" to make our own decisions. However, for many of us, our lives are considered to be on the fringe of what is known about women's lives and the experience of trauma and violence.

We must ensure that disabled women and our allies ensure that the work we are doing to eliminate sexual violence is inclusive and reflective of the lives of women and children whose voices/perspectives have not been heard. As feminists living with and without impairments, we need to recognize the strength and resilience of women to do the work necessary to change institutional practices and policies that fail to include disabled women as full human beings. We must come out of the silos we have developed in our VAW communities, which replicate the institutional structures we rage against. Above all, we must not make this work the responsibility of disabled women alone.

9. Police Investigation of Sexual Assault Complaints: How Far Have We Come Since *Jane Doe*?

Teresa DuBois

This chapter turns to the "unfounding" problem condemned by Jane Doe's judge in her legal victory in 1998. Teresa DuBois revisits the Jane Doe Social Audit mentioned in the first chapter of this book, "The Victories of Jane Doe." The audit represented an effort by activists to pressure police to respond to the legal judgment against them by reforming their investigatory practices and discarding biased assumptions in their assessments of the credibility of women's reports of sexual assault. Teresa reviews successive audit reports from Toronto and studies beyond that show not only that police continue to unfound sexual assault reports at higher rates than any other crime, but also that "rape myths" seem to be operative in police assessments of whom to believe. Two investigative techniques used by police to assess women's credibility, both premised on women as "hard to be believed," may play a role in sexual assault being "wrongfully" unfounded. Teresa joins Fran Odette in calling for data collection as the basis for policy-making and legal strategy.

Jane Doe's victory against the Toronto Commissioners of Police[1] was expected to mark the beginning of significant reform in police forces across Canada. It was assumed that Jane Doe's exposure and Madam Justice MacFarland's condemnation of reliance on rape myths and stereotypes by the Toronto Police Service would result in a new approach to the investigation of sexual assault. Joan Grant Cummings, then president of the National Action Committee, stated that the decision "propel[ed] us miles in dealing with state accountability where women's security issues and the violation of our human rights [were] concerned."[2] Unfortunately, as this article will demonstrate, over ten years later that vision has yet to be realized.

1 *Jane Doe v Metropolitan Toronto (Municipality) Commissioners of Police* (1998), 39 OR (3d) 487, 160 DLR (4th) 697 (QL) (Ont Ct (Gen Div)) [*Jane Doe* cited to DLR].

2 "(Jane) Doe victory sparks demand for better treatment" (Fall 1998) *Herizons* 8.

In *Jane Doe v Metropolitan Toronto Commissioners of Police*, Madam Justice MacFarland condemned the behaviour and attitudes of the Toronto Police Service, specifically regarding the way that the victims of the so-called "Balcony Rapist" were treated when they reported their sexual assaults to police. She was critical of the incredulity with which the officers handled the women's reports. For example, in the case of BK, the second known victim, the investigating officer went as far as closing the case because he believed that she was lying about having been raped.[3] One of Justice MacFarland's findings was that the police "act as a filtering system for sexual assault cases" by determining that certain complaints are "unfounded."[4] She noted that crimes of sexual assault are "unfounded" at a higher rate than other crimes and she stated that

> One of the reasons suggested for the higher "unfounded" rate in relation to sexual assaults is the widespread adherence among investigating police officers to rape mythology, that is, the belief in certain false assumptions, usually based in sexist stereotyping, about women who report being raped.[5]

The wrongful "unfounding" of sexual assault reports can have a substantial and damaging impact on women. Where a perpetrator of sexual violence is known to his victim, she can be left in a dangerous situation if she is not believed and protected by police. As well, any women whose report of sexual assault has been "unfounded" faces long-term danger, because the police are much less likely to believe her if she reports another sexual assault.[6] Most importantly, wrongful "unfounding" of sexual assault reports reflects a much bigger issue — that of disbelieving attitudes on the part of investigating officers, which are often evident to those making reports.[7] The "unfounding" of women's reports leaves perpetrators free — indeed emboldened — to repeat their crimes, putting the safety of many women at risk.[8]

3 *Supra* note 1 at paras 52–74.

4 *Ibid* at para 11.

5 *Ibid* at para 12.

6 See eg Jan Jordan, *The Word of a Woman: Police, Rape and Belief* (New York: Palgrave MacMillan, 2004) at 151.

7 See eg "'Have you really been raped?': Criminal Justice System Responses" in Jordan, *ibid* at 76; Jennifer Temkin, "Plus ça change: Reporting Rape in the 1990s" (1997) 37 Brit J Crim 507; Jennifer Temkin, "Reporting Rape in London: A Qualitative Study" (1999) 38 How J Crim Justice 17.

8 UK, London Metropolitan Police, *The Attrition of Rape Allegations in London: A Re-*

Negative reactions by service providers — such as blaming, doing nothing to help, doubting their stories, and maintaining a cold and detached demeanour — have been shown to have a harmful impact on women's recovery and general sense of well-being following a sexual assault.[9] As well, women who experience negative reactions after reporting a sexual assault and whose cases are not pursued in the justice system have been found to suffer more severe symptoms of post traumatic stress disorder and depression than do other victims of sexual assault.[10] For these reasons, it was hoped that the unique opportunity for judicial scrutiny of sexual assault investigation presented by the *Jane Doe* case would lead to lasting reform.

Over ten years after *Jane Doe*, there have been some visible changes to the way sexual assault is addressed by police forces.[11] For example, officers in Toronto now receive more training, although it is not clear what is involved in this training.[12] However, victims of sexual assault do not seem to have noticed a difference. The proportion of reported sexual assaults that result in charges being laid has actually decreased, from 44 percent in 1998 to 42 percent in 2006,[13] and the proportion of women willing to report being sexually assaulted has also declined,

view (London: Metropolitan Police, 2007) at 20–22, online: <http://www.met.police.uk/sapphire/documents/ 084796_rr2_final_ rape_allegations_london.pdf>.

9 Courtney E Ahrens *et al*, "Deciding Whom to Tell: Expectations and Outcomes of Rape Survivors' First Disclosures" (2007) 31 Psychology of Women Q 38; see also Judith Lewis Herman, "The Mental Health of Crime Victims: Impact of Legal Intervention" (2003) 16 J Traumatic Stress 159; Rebecca Campbell *et al*, "Community Services for Rape Survivors: Enhancing Psychological Well-Being or Increasing Trauma?" (1999) 67 J Consulting and Clinical Psychology 847.

10 Rebecca Campbell *et al*, "Community Services for Rape Survivors" *ibid*; Rebecca Campbell *et al*, "Preventing the 'Second Rape' With Community Service Providers" (2001) 16 J Interpersonal Violence 1239; Sarah E Ullman & Henrietta H Filipas, "Predictors of PTSD Symptom Severity and Social Reactions in Sexual Assault Victims" (2001) 14 J Traumatic Stress 369; Sarah E Ullman *et al*, "Structural Models of the Relations of Assault Severity, Social Support, Avoidance Coping, Self-Blame, and PTSD Among Sexual Assault Survivors" (2007) 31 Psychology of Women Q 23.

11 See eg Jeffery Griffiths, *The Review of the Investigation of Sexual Assaults — A Decade Later* (Toronto: Toronto Audit Services, 2010), online: <http://www.toronto.ca/audit/reports 2010_ april14.htm> [*A Decade Later*]; *The Ottawa Sexual Assault Protocol*, online: <http://www.sanottawa.com/ index.php?unique=172>.

12 *A Decade Later*, *ibid* at 8.

13 Statistics Canada, *Table 252-0013 Crime Statistics by Detailed Offenses, 1977–2006, Annual* (Ottawa: Statistics Canada, 2007); it should be noted that the proportion of sexual assaults cleared by charge in Toronto has increased by 12 percent.

from 12 percent in 1999 to 8 percent in 2004.[14] Perhaps most troubling is the fact that sexual assault reports continue to be "unfounded" at higher rates than reports of other crimes.

The first part of this article will summarize available evidence with respect to rates of "unfounded" sexual assault reports, as well as indicators that these rates are higher due to wrongful "unfounding" by police. The second part of this article will deal with the question of what these statistics likely indicate — that police investigation of sexual assault reports continues to be based on the false assumption that women who report sexual assault are more likely to be lying than individuals reporting other crimes.

"UNFOUNDED" REPORTS

Crimes reported to the police become the object of a preliminary investigation to determine whether the report is valid. Where the police determine that no crime has actually taken place, the report is classified as "unfounded."[15] An "unfounded" report by an individual claiming to have been victimized presumably involves false allegations.

Studies conducted in the United Kingdom and the United States to address "attrition" of sexual assault cases from the criminal justice system have shown that reports of sexual assault are "unfounded" by police at very high rates. Out of nine studies published between 1996 and 2007,[16] five found that reports of sexual assault were "unfounded" at

14 Canadian Centre for Justice Statistics, *Criminal Victimization in Canada, 1999* by Sandra Besserer & Catherine Trainor (Ottawa: Statistics Canada, 2000) at 11, online: <http://www.statcan.gc.ca/pub/85-002-x/85-002-x2000010-eng.pdf>, (statistic for 1999); Statistics Canada, *Measuring Violence Against Women: Statistical Trends 2006* by Holly Johnson (Ottawa: Statistics Canada, 2006) at 57, online: <http://www.statcan.gc.ca/pub/85-570-x/85-570-x2006001-eng.pdf>, (statistic for 2004).

15 See eg Canadian Centre for Justice Statistics, *Canadian Crime Statistics* (Ottawa: Statistics Canada, 2003) at 78, online: <http://www.statcan.ca/cgi-bin/downpub/listpub.cgi?catno=85-205-XIE2003000>.

16 Jeanne Gregory & Sue Lees, "Attrition in Rape and Sexual Assault Cases" (1996) 36 Brit J Crim 1 at 3; UK, Home Office, *A Question of Evidence? Investigating and Prosecuting Rape in the 1990's* by Jessica Harris & Sharon Grace, (London: Home Office, 1999), online: <http://www.homeoffice. gov.uk/rds/pdfs/hors196.pdf>; Jeffrey A Bouffard, "Predicting Type of Sexual Assault Case Closure from Victim, Suspect and Case Characteristics" (2000) 28 J Crim J 527 at 532; UK, Her Majesty's Crown Prosecution Service Inspectorate, *A Report on the Joint Inspection into the Investigation and Prosecution of Cases involving Allegations of Rape* (London: Her Majesty's Inspectorate of Constabulary, 2002) [HMCPSI]; Susan J Lea, Ursula Lanvers & Steve Shaw, "Attrition in Rape Cases: Developing a Profile and Identifying Relevant Factors" (2004) 43 Brit J Crim 583 at 587; UK, Home Office, *A Gap or a Chasm? Attrition*

rates ranging from 25 to 43 percent,[17] and none found rates below 10 percent. Closer to home, in a study published in 2000, Janice Du Mont and Terri Myhr examined the attrition of sexual assault cases in Ontario. These authors tracked the cases of 284 women who presented at sexual assault care centres and stated that they had been sexually assaulted.[18] Only 187 (66 percent) of those women chose to report to police. Three years later, fifty-one (27 percent) of the reported cases remained unsolved. Of the cases that the police considered "solved," eighty-one (47 percent) resulted in charges being laid, eleven (14 percent) were discontinued by the victim, and fourteen (17 percent) were classified as "unfounded."[19] The authors suggested that the relatively "low" rate of "unfounded" cases and the high number of unsolved cases in this study could be the result of reluctance on the part of the Toronto Police to "unfound" cases, given previous research findings and the high profile *Jane Doe* case.[20]

In a more recent study conducted by Linda Light and Gisela Ruebsaat in British Columbia,[21] the jurisdictions considered were chosen on the basis of "unfounding" rates for sexual assault reports because the authors wanted to examine the reasons for varying rates from one detachment to another. The rates ranged from a low of 7 percent in Van-

in Reported Rape Cases (Research Study 293) by Liz Kelly, Jo Lovett & Linda Regan (London: Home Office, 2005), online: <http://www.homeoffice.gov.uk/rds/pdfs05/hors293.pdf>; London Metropolitan Police, *supra* note 8; UK, Her Majesty's Crown Prosecution Service Inspectorate, *Without Consent: A Report on the Joint Review of the Investigation and Prosecution of Rape Offences* (London: Her Majesty's Inspectorate of Constabulary, 2007), online: <http://inspectorates.homeoffice.gov.uk/hmic/inspections/thematic/wc-thematic/them07-wc.pdf?view=Binary> [HMCPSI follow-up]; UK, Home Office, *Investigating and Detecting Recorded Offences of Rape* by Andy Feist *et al* (London: Home Office, 2007) at 4–5, online: <http://www.home office.gov.uk/rds/pdfs07/rdsolr1807.pdf>.

17 Gregory & Lees, *ibid*; Harris & Grace, *ibid*; Kelly, Lovett & Regan, *ibid*; London Metropolitan Police, *ibid*; Bouffard, *ibid*.

18 Janice Du Mont & Terri L Myhr, "So Few Convictions: The Role of Client-Related Characteristics in the Legal Processing of Sexual Assaults" (2000) 6 Violence Against Women 1109 at 1115–16.

19 *Ibid* at 1121.

20 *Ibid* at 1124.

21 Tina Hattem, "Highlights from a Preliminary Study of Police Classification of Sexual Assault Cases as Unfounded" in Canada, Department of Justice, *Just Research: Issue no. 14* (Ottawa: Department of Justice, 2007), online: <http://www.justice.gc.ca/eng/pi/rs/rep-rap/jr/jr14/jr14.pdf>; citing Justice Institute of British Columbia, *Police Classification of Sexual Assault Cases as Unfounded: An Exploratory Study* by Linda Light & Gisela Ruebsaat [unpublished].

couver to a high of 28 percent in Chilliwack. Other studies that have compared statistics for police stations in more than one jurisdiction[22] have similarly found that "unfounding" rates for sexual assault reports vary greatly. These findings suggest that different, often neighbouring, jurisdictions employ different practices to investigate and/or classify sexual assault reports. As well, the lower rates serve as proof that there is no reason for cases of sexual assault to be "unfounded" at disproportionately higher rates than for other crimes.

Where rates of "unfounded" sexual assault reports are compared with "unfounded" rates for other crimes, sexual assault reports have been shown to be "unfounded" at much higher rates. For example, in 2002, Statistics Canada determined that 16 percent of all sexual offences reported to police were deemed to be "unfounded," while other types of violent offences were "unfounded" at a rate of 7 percent.[23] More recently, however, inconsistent protocol related to the "unfounding" of crime reports has caused Statistics Canada to cease performing any analysis regarding this issue.[24] It is difficult to determine how many crime reports are ultimately deemed by Canadian police to be "unfounded" because police forces do not adhere to uniform methods of classification and Statistics Canada only requires forces to report the number of "crimes" reported and not the number of reports deemed to be "unfounded."[25]

As part of a forthcoming study, this author and Professor Blair Crew of the University of Ottawa Faculty of Law made Freedom of Information requests to selected police forces throughout Ontario, namely the Ontario Provincial Police and police forces in Toronto, Ottawa, Hamilton, Peel Region, Windsor, London, Kingston, and Durham. In addition to requesting the number of sexual assault reports that were "unfounded" each year between 2003 and 2007, we requested the number of "all other crimes" that were "unfounded" during the same period. Many of the forces required a great deal of time and money before responding with the requested information. Kingston and Durham never did provide statistics. While the final analysis of these statistics has not been completed, the table below lists the average rates of "unfound-

22 Light & Ruebsaat, *ibid*; HMCPSI, *supra* note 16; HMCPSI follow-up, *supra* note 16; Feist *et al*, *supra* note 16.

23 Canadian Centre for Justice Statistics, *Sexual Offences in Canada* by Rebecca Kong *et al* (Ottawa: Statistics Canada, 2003) at 9.

24 Hattem, *supra* note 21 at 35; citing Light & Ruebsaat, *supra* note 21 at 80.

25 *Ibid.*

ed" sexual assault reports compared with "unfounded" rates for other crimes during the same period. It is of note that the rates vary greatly from one jurisdiction to another. As well, in every jurisdiction, including Windsor where the "unfounded" rates were comparatively low, the "unfounded" rate for sexual assault reports was higher than the "unfounded" rate for all other crime reports.

Jurisdiction	Sexual Assault			Other Crimes		
London	1,613 541	Total Reports "Unfounded"	33.54%		Statistics not provided	
Ottawa	2,314 720	Total Reports "Unfounded"	31.11%	239,957 6,390	Total Reports "Unfounded"	2.66%
Ontario (OPP)	9,990 3,013	Total Reports "Unfounded"	30.16%	750,800 85,801	Total Reports "Unfounded"	11.43%
Hamilton	2,151 476	Total Reports "Unfounded"	22.13%	175,162 3,054	Total Reports "Unfounded"	1.74%
Peel Region	2,697 541	Total Reports "Unfounded"	20.06%	230,525 4,923	Total Reports "Unfounded"	2.14%
Toronto	12,879 990	Total Reports "Unfounded"	7.69%	999,826 7,331	Total Reports "Unfounded"	0.73%
Windsor	572 11	Total Reports "Unfounded"	1.92%	204,003 648	Total Reports "Unfounded"	0.32%

WRONGFUL "UNFOUNDING" OF SEXUAL ASSAULT REPORTS: REASONS FOR HIGH "UNFOUNDED" RATES

Researchers who have examined police case files have often uncovered instances where sexual assault reports were classified as "unfounded" when they should not have been. For example, in an extensive study published in the United Kingdom in 2005,[26] Liz Kelly, Jo Lovett, and Linda Regan found that between 22 and 26 percent of cases reported to police received a "no crime" designation, meaning that police deemed

26 Kelly, Lovett & Regan, *supra* note 16.

the reports to be "unfounded."[27] The authors concluded that the United Kingdom Home Office's "no crime" category tends to serve as a "dustbin" for sexual assault cases. When they examined the files of rape investigations that had been closed after receiving a "no crime" designation, they found that many reports had been "no crimed" for reasons such as "lack of evidence," "victim withdrawal," "victim being extremely vulnerable," or "suspect not identified."[28] "Unfounding" reports for reasons like this is in clear violation of classification procedures for that jurisdiction. In only 3 percent of cases did the case file actually contain enough evidence to support a conclusion that the woman had "probably" or "possibly" lied about being raped.[29] Other studies of attrition of rape and sexual assault cases from the United Kingdom's criminal justice system have made comparable findings.[30]

Some might suggest that higher rates of "unfounded" sexual assault reports indicate that there are more false allegations of sexual assault than of other crimes. However, the researchers mentioned above have proposed other explanations for the high rates at which sexual assault reports are "unfounded." They are of two general opinions. Researchers connected with police focus a great deal of attention on whether police officers follow proper classification procedures for their jurisdiction.[31] They suggest that the main problem is a lack of understanding or respect for the rules on the part of officers.

While appropriate classification of cases is obviously important, researchers who are independent from police go much further in their assessment of the overall problems surrounding sexual assault investigation.[32] These researchers generally feel that high rates of "unfounding" are indicative of a generalized attitudinal problem within police forces. A New Zealand researcher, Jan Jordan, sums up the immensity of this problem in her conclusion that "the issue of belief is central to investigations" and "issues of belief and credibility will remain vexed and contentious so long as investigative officers approach rape complain-

27 *Ibid* at 36, 38.

28 *Ibid* at 38–39.

29 *Ibid* at 50.

30 Gregory & Lees, *supra* note 16; Harris & Grace, *supra* note 16; HMCPSI, *supra* note 16; Lea, Lanvers & Shaw, *supra* note 16 at 587; UK, HMCPSI follow-up, *supra* note 16; Feist *et al*, *supra* note 16 at 4–5.

31 HMCPSI, *ibid*; HMCPSI follow-up, *ibid*; Feist *et al*, *ibid*.

32 See eg Light & Ruebsaat, *supra* note 21; Harris & Grace, *supra* note 16; Kelly, Lovett & Regan, *supra* note 16; Jordan, *supra* note 6.

ants with a prevailing mindset of suspicion and disbelief."[33] In essence, many of these researchers suggest that high rates of "unfounding" of sexual assault reports are caused by police culture and ways of thinking. Such conclusions are often based on the factors associated with "unfounding" of sexual assault reports. At least six studies[34] have found that sexual assaults perpetrated by someone known to the victim or by an intimate partner are more likely to be "unfounded" by the police. Other factors that make women less likely to be believed include suffering from a mental health problem or a disability,[35] having reported a previous sexual assault,[36] lacking physical injuries,[37] not being hysterical or upset when reporting to police,[38] being young[39] or old,[40] not physically resisting during the attack,[41] or having used alcohol or drugs prior to being assaulted.[42] All of these factors are related to stereotypical beliefs about what constitutes a "real" rape victim.

As well, interviews with police officers have shown examples of how some police officers are inclined to believe that large numbers of women lie about sexual assault.[43] This belief carries over into the way they conduct their investigations. Likewise, in interviews with women who have reported a sexual assault to the police, a major recurring theme is that women are made to feel as though the police do not believe them.[44] Taken together, these findings suggest that police forces

33 Jan Jordan, "Beyond Belief? Police, Rape and Woman's Credibility" (2004) 4 Criminal Justice 29 at 53; also published in *The Word of a Woman: Police, Rape and Belief*, *supra* note 6.

34 Light & Ruebsaat, *supra* note 21; Gregory & Lees, *supra* note 16; Temkin, "Plus ça change," *supra* note 7; Harris & Grace, *supra* note 16; Lea, Lanvers & Shaw, *supra* note 16; Bouffard, *supra* note 16 at 532.

35 Light & Ruebsaat, *ibid*; Kelly, Lovett & Regan, *supra* note 16.

36 *Ibid.*

37 *Ibid.*

38 Light & Ruebsaat, *ibid*; Temkin, "Reporting Rape in London," *supra* note 7.

39 Kelly, Lovett & Regan, *supra* note 16 at 47; UK, London Metropolitan Police, *supra* note 8 at 6.

40 Du Mont & Myhr, *supra* note 18 at 1115–16.

41 Light & Ruebsaat, *supra* at note 21.

42 Kelly, Lovett & Regan, *supra* note 16; London Metropolitan Police, *supra* note 8.

43 Temkin, "Plus ça change," *supra* note 7; Temkin, "Reporting Rape in London," *supra* note 7; Jordan, "Having 'a nose for it': How Investigators Investigate" in Jordan, *supra* note 6 at 139.

44 Temkin, "Plus ça change" *ibid*; Temkin, "Reporting Rape in London," *ibid*; Jordan, "'Have you really been raped?': Criminal Justice System Responses" in Jordan, *supra*

still have work to do in order to eliminate systemic bias against women who report being sexually assaulted.

IMPACT OF THE *JANE DOE* DECISION

A major element of the *Jane Doe* decision was the finding that women were badly treated when they reported being sexually assaulted, along with the suggestion that many sexual assaults were "unfounded" wrongfully by the Toronto police. This did not come as a surprise to those who work directly with sexual assault victims. Anecdotal evidence has long suggested that such treatment is commonplace, but the *Jane Doe* case offered a rare opportunity for judicial scrutiny of investigative techniques and of the way that misogynistic stereotypes affect how police react to women. Of course, the great hope was that Madam Justice MacFarland's decision would lead to lasting change in the way that police investigate sexual assault, including their willingness to believe women who make reports.

The 1999 *Review of the Investigation of Sexual Assaults* conducted in the wake of the *Jane Doe* decision found that a significant number of sexual assaults reported to the Toronto Police Service had been classified as "unfounded," even though the case file did not contain enough information to support this determination. The audit also found that sexual assault reports were being classified as "unfounded" in cases where it was clear that a sexual assault had occurred.[45] The audit report contained the following two recommendations specifically related to the "unfounding" of sexual assault reports:[46]

> 18. Under no circumstances should a first-response officer make a determination as to whether a sexual assault incident is classified as unfounded. The determination of this matter be reviewed and approved by a qualified trained sexual assault investigator. All occurrence reports contain information sufficient to substantiate conclusions.
>
> * * *

note 6 at 76; Kelly, Lovett & Regan, *supra* note 16; Rebecca Campbell, "Rape Survivors' Experiences With the Legal and Medical Systems: Do Rape Victim Advocates Make a Difference?" (2006) 12 Violence Against Women 30 at 34.

45 Jeffrey Griffiths, *Review of the Investigation of Sexual Assault—Toronto Police Service* (Toronto: Toronto Audit Services, 1999) at 53–55, online: <http://www.toronto.ca/audit/1999/102599.pdf> [Jane Doe Audit].

46 *Ibid* at 54–55.

19. The definition of what constitutes an unfounded sexual assault occurrence be reviewed. Incidents in which a woman decides not to proceed with the laying of charges should not be automatically classified as unfounded.

It is not clear whether these recommendations were fully implemented or whether they had any impact on sexual assault investigations. In 2004, *The Auditor General's Follow-up Review* noted that while procedures had been put in place to ensure that incidents of sexual assault are only "unfounded" if a detective sergeant has thoroughly reviewed the case, there was no evidence that these procedures were ever followed.[47] In 2010, *The Review of the Investigation of Sexual Assaults: A Decade Later* made no further mention of recommendations 18 and 19.[48]

WHAT DOES WRONGFUL "UNFOUNDING" INDICATE?: INVESTIGATION OF SEXUAL ASSAULT REPORTS

The preceding section concluded that higher rates of "unfounded" sexual assault reports, compared with reports of other crimes, and varying rates of "unfounding" among neighbouring jurisdictions, are indicators that wrongful "unfounding" of sexual assault reports may be a systemic problem among police forces. However, a review of the academic literature on police investigation suggests that those who train police officers have a different interpretation. Despite findings to the contrary,[49] it is not uncommon for researchers to use the terms "unfounded" and "false allegation" interchangeably in their writing and to indiscriminately refer to the rate of "unfounded" cases as the rate of "false allegations."[50] Researchers who accept the premise that there are more false allegations of sexual assault than of other crimes have promoted investigative techniques that supposedly allow police officers to determine when a woman is lying about being sexually assaulted. It is impossible to confirm whether Canadian police forces have adopted these techniques, as

47 Jeffrey Griffiths, *The Auditor General's Follow-up Review on the October 1999 Report Entitled "Review of the Investigation of Sexual Assaults: Toronto Police Service"* (Toronto: Toronto Audit Services, 2004) at 53–54, online: <http://www.toronto.ca/audit/reports2004_ sub4.htm> [*Follow-up Review*].

48 *A Decade Later*, *supra* note 11.

49 See eg Kelly, Lovett & Regan, *supra* note 16.

50 Philip NS Rumney, "False Allegations of Rape" (2006) 65 Cambridge LJ 128 at 129–31. See eg Andrew D Parker & Jennifer Brown, "Detection of Deception: Statement Validity Analysis as a Means of Determining Truthfulness or Falsity of Rape Allegations" (2000) 5 Legal and Criminological Psychology 237.

they do not share information pertaining to investigations. However, there are indications that these techniques have made their way into the repertoire of Canadian sexual assault investigators.

STATEMENT ANALYSIS

One of these techniques is called Statement Validity Analysis [SVA]. This technique, touted by Andrew Parker and Jennifer Brown, among others,[51] consists of two checklists: the "Criteria-Based Content Analysis" and the "Validity Checklist." Where this technique is employed, a woman who reports a sexual assault will be guided through a semi-structured interview for which the questions are developed based on any other information that the investigator is able to collect about the case. Her statement is then scored on the basis of the two checklists to determine whether it is a "genuine report" or a "possible fabrication." There is disagreement in the literature on SVA as to what score indicates a "false allegation."[52]

SVA was developed in Germany in the 1950s in an effort to evaluate the veracity of children's allegations of sexual abuse.[53] While some authors suggest that this technique has been successfully adapted for use with women,[54] other studies have shown that SVA is probably not even a valid tool for use with children. In a study that examined the accuracy of social workers', students', and police officers' judgments with regards to the veracity of children's statements, the social workers did not improve after training, the students improved slightly, and the police officers became significantly worse.[55] Regardless of their performance, the police officers were significantly more confident in their decision-

51 Parker & Brown, *ibid*; Jennifer Brown, *Statement Validity Analysis*, online: <http://131.227.122.44/cjs/r-statement_validity.htm>. See also Rhona Lucas & Ian K McKenzie, "The Detection of Dissimulation: Lies, Damned Lies and SVA" (1998) 1 Int J Police Science and Management 347; Andreas Kapardis, "Detecting Deception" in Andreas Kapardis, *Psychology and Law: A Critical Introduction*, 2d ed (Cambridge: Cambridge University Press, 2003) 225 at 251–55.

52 *Ibid.*

53 Kapardis, *ibid* at 251–55; Rumney, *supra* note 50.

54 See eg Parker & Brown, *supra* note 50; Lucas & McKenzie, *supra* note 51.

55 Lucy Akehurst *et al*, "The Effects of Training Professional Groups and Lay Persons to use Criteria-Based Content Analysis to Detect Deception" (2004) 18 Applied Cognitive Psychology 877 at 885. It should be noted that it is virtually impossible to provide subjects in studies on SVA with examples of statements that are "true" and "false." Fabricated statements are, by nature, untrue, and real life statements from cases that have been unfounded by police may, in fact, be true.

making than the other two groups.[56] Philip Rumney points out that the use of SVA checklists is open to a great deal of subjectivity on the part of the police officers who apply them, and he questions why it is necessary to develop an investigative technique for the unique purpose of assessing the veracity of women's reports of sexual assault.[57] He suggests: "A sounder approach might be to emphasize the importance of the ongoing education of police officers so that they better understand such things as victim reactions to rape, victim perceptions of their treatment by officers and false allegations."[58]

Another version of statement analysis involves "understanding what is typical of a truthful statement and looking for any deviation from the norm"[59] by evaluating the way that different components of speech are used. In an example given by Special Agent Susan Adams, who teaches courses on statement analyses at the FBI Academy, a rape victim might be lying if she uses the pronoun "we" to describe herself and her alleged attacker, because "normal" rape victims prefer to put distance between themselves and their attackers.[60] This technique does not account for possible language barriers or learning disabilities or for the fact that many victims of rape know the offender before the attack and may be accustomed to using the pronoun "we." According to Adams, the use of past tense in speech is the norm when describing events that have happened, so a victim who refers to events in the present tense may be inventing as she goes along.[61] This technique fails to account for language barriers, for the fact that women may have flashbacks while describing what has happened to them, or for the possibility that questions might be asked in the present tense. Finally, according to this method, an interviewee who "feigns" a memory loss "to avoid giving certain details" might be lying.[62] Interestingly, the SVA checklist described above gives victims credit for admitting when they do not remember certain details.[63] This suggests that different types of statement analysis may attribute varying interpretations to the same behaviours.

56 *Ibid.*

57 Rumney, *supra* note 50 at 150–54.

58 *Ibid* at 154.

59 Susan H Adams, "Statement Analysis: What Do Suspects' Words Really Reveal?" (1996) 65 FBI Law Enforcement Bulletin 12, online: <http://www.crimeandclues.com/oct964.htm>.

60 *Ibid.*

61 *Ibid.*

62 *Ibid.*

63 Brown, *Statement Validity Analysis*, *supra* note 51.

It appears that variations of statement analysis are employed by police forces throughout the world to interview individuals suspected of different types of crimes. One self-proclaimed expert, Avinoam Sapir, claims on his website that he has provided training on the use of "Statement Content Analysis (SCAN)" to over fifty police forces in Canada.[64] While this technique appears to be popular with Canadian police forces, its critics suggest that it has no scientific basis. According to one author: "If the theory underlying statement analysis is based on little more than speculation, the empirical evidence for its claims is no better. Simply put, there is no empirical validation for SCAN … the value of SCAN and statement analysis lies simply in its utility as an interrogation technique."[65]

RAPE INVESTIGATION HANDBOOK

While the different varieties of statement analysis are presented as a supposedly "objective" means for imposing the subjective views of police officers on victims of sexual assault, the methods proposed by other authors are openly hostile towards women who report being sexually assaulted. In a textbook on behavioural evidence analysis,[66] Detective John Baeza and Mr Brent Turvey state that "investigators and criminal profilers are very likely to encounter a false report if they work sex crimes"[67] and comment that "[u]nfortunately, it is common for even seasoned investigators to accept an alleged victim's statement or story without question or suspicion."

Detective Baeza and Mr Turvey base their assertions on a handful of "scientific studies conducted to ascertain false report rates."[68] An example of these studies is that of Eugene Kanin published in 1994. Mr Kanin looked at 109 police files in an attempt to explain the phenomenon of false rape accusations, which he considered to be "a reflection of

64 LSI Laboratory for Scientific Investigation, Inc, *Past Participants of the SCAN Course: Canadian Law Enforcement Agencies*, online: <http://www.lsiscan.com/id65.htm>.

65 Richard A Leo, *Police Interrogation and American Justice* (Cambridge, MA: Harvard University Press, 2008) at 103.

66 John J Baeza & Brent E Turvey, "False Reports" in Brent E Turvey, ed, *Criminal Profiling: An Introduction to Behavioural Evidence Analysis*, 2d ed (San Diego, CA: Academic Press, 2002) 169. The same chapter has been reproduced in John O Savino, Brent E Turvey & John J Baeza, *Rape Investigation Handbook* (Burlington, MA: Academic Press, 2005) 235.

67 Baeza & Turvey, *ibid* at 174–76.

68 *Ibid* at 169.

a unique condition of women, not unlike that of kleptomania."[69] Over a period of nine years, he took the police at their word when they told him that a victim had recanted her story and examined the file to try to determine her motivation for "lying." During this period, the police detachment in question deemed that 41 percent of reported rapes were "false accusations." Kanin concluded that women lie about being raped for three reasons: to create an alibi, to get revenge, and to elicit sympathy or attention.

Both Philip Rumney and Karen Busby have found major flaws in Kanin's work. According to the former, Kanin's finding that all "unfounded" cases in a jurisdiction represented false claims is unique in the academic literature.[70] Most studies have found at least some cases that were "unfounded" in error or "unfounded" for reasons other than the complainant being dishonest. In addition, while Kanin claims that the police in his study acted in a professional manner and did not put undue pressure on victims to recant their stories, he cannot be sure of this, given that he only had access to paper files written by the police officers themselves. He did not have any contact with women who reported being raped in that jurisdiction, and he had no way of assessing their perceptions of how they were treated by the police. Finally, while Kanin claims that the policy of the police department in his study was to "unfound" rape cases only when the victim herself had recanted, it seems naïve on his part to assume that all the officers followed department policy, given that so many studies have shown neglect of official police policy.[71]

Karen Busby points out that Kanin's study does not account for the possibility of one individual making more than one report, which would have a significant effect on such a small sample. Nor does he acknowledge that some of the reports might have been made by a third party.[72] He completely ignores the possibility that the women who supposedly recanted their stories might have been pressured by police or family members. His study does not discuss the possibility that some of the complaints may have been about sexual violations other than "completed forcible rape" and that the laws in that jurisdiction may not have

69 Eugene J Kanin, "False Rape Allegations" (1994) 23 Archives of Sexual Behaviour 81 at 82.

70 Rumney, *supra* note 50 at 139.

71 *Ibid* at 139–40.

72 Karen Busby, "Rape Crisis Backlash and the Spectre of False Rape Allegations" (1995) [unpublished paper on file with the author].

encompassed these crimes during the time of his study.[73] Notwithstanding the fact that Kanin's work is virtually unsupported by recent studies and that there are problems with both his methodology and the stereotypical beliefs upon which his work is based,[74] this study has been cited by defence lawyers and scholars alike to support the idea that women lie about being raped.[75]

Following Mr Kanin's assertions, Detective Baeza and Mr Turvey recommend that investigators use the "Baeza False Report Index" throughout their investigations. They refer to this index as "a list of false report red flags" and suggest that "[o]ne or more of the circumstantial red flags described in this index has surfaced in most, if not all, of the false reports investigated by the authors."[76] According to the list, victims who ask to speak to a female officer, who missed a curfew on the night of the incident, who move to a new home during the course of the investigation, who cry during the interview, or who have a psychiatric history should be investigated more thoroughly because it is possible that they are lying about being raped. The authors suggest that women are motivated to lie for the following reasons: to get revenge; to satisfy a need for attention; to obtain medical treatment; for profit (to file a lawsuit, to obtain better housing, to get custody of a child, etc); if the women is a prostitute, to get back at a customer who did not pay (what they refer to as "theft of services"); to explain a pregnancy, a sexually transmitted disease, infidelity to a partner or drug/alcohol use; or to deal with a change of heart after a consensual sexual encounter.[77]

Baeza and Turvey suggest specific interview techniques to identify women who are supposedly lying. Once a rape victim has given her statement, they suggest using a "frame-by-frame" analysis to scrutinize the story.[78] They compare this technique to watching a movie one frame at a time and paying attention to every detail. They note that it is important to question any and every small inconsistency in the story: "The interviewer should never accept contradictory statements in the victim's statement because the victim was upset or experiencing trauma."[79] Once inconsistencies have been pointed out to the victim, the authors suggest that the interviewer say the following:

73 *Ibid* at 18–27.

74 *Ibid* at 7, 12–18; Rumney, *supra* note 50 at 153–54.

75 See eg Busby, *ibid* at 7; Parker & Brown, *supra* note 50 at 238.

76 Baeza & Turvey, *supra* note 66 at 177.

77 *Ibid* at 178–85.

78 *Ibid* at 174–75.

79 *Ibid* at 175.

> I have been investigating sex crimes for X amount of years and I have interviewed many girls/guys who have for one reason or another not told the whole truth. I know you're not telling me the whole truth but I also know that you seem like a good person. I'm sure there is a perfectly good reason why you are not telling the truth. Without the truth I can't help you with your problem.[80]

They suggest that the interviewer then leave the room to let the woman think about the inconsistencies in her story. According to them: "[q]uite often, upon reentering the room, the interviewer will find the victim crying and the confession will be near."[81] Of course, it is impossible for the public to know whether police in Canada rely on the textbook described above. Even the author of the *Jane Doe* audits made no comment as to specific investigative tools and techniques employed in sexual assault investigations.[82] However, it is of note that the textbook is carried in at least fourteen Ontario university libraries.[83] As well, videotaped interviews obtained by women who reported sexual assaults show that some of these same techniques are employed by the Ottawa Police Service.[84]

The videotaped interviews portray interviews with two women who had been drugged and then sexually assaulted in Ottawa in 2003. The women's interviews with a police investigator follow the pattern described above, with the officer allowing each woman to give her statement and then going over it "frame-by-frame," analyzing minute details and challenging any inconsistencies with what was said before. The officer then suggests to each woman that she remembers more than she is admitting and that she is trying to believe that she was raped in order to justify behaviour that she regrets. The officer tells the women that everyone makes mistakes and that making a mistake does not mean

80 *Ibid* at 176.

81 *Ibid.*

82 *Jane Doe Audit, supra* note 45; *Follow-up Review, supra* note 47; *A Decade Later, supra* note 11.

83 Search of "Racer" Catalogue, Ontario Council of University Libraries, conducted on 31 October 2010.

84 Full videos of these police interviews, conducted by Detective Theresa Kelm of the Ottawa Police Service in 2003, were obtained by the women who reported being sexually assaulted through Freedom of Information requests. Excerpts from those interviews were later aired on CTV News as part of a two-part story by Natalie Pierosara. Both parts of the story have been posted on YouTube, "Cops Ignore Rape Part 1," online: <http://www.youtube.com/watch?v=GhpZjpRd420&feature=related>, and "Cops Ignore Rape Part 2," online: <http://www.youtube.com/watch?v=hO1BiRnnS70&feature=related>.

that she is a bad person. Near the end of the interview, the officer makes the following remarks:

> This is serious, this is a serious police investigation (yeah, I know), and we can't keep tying up resources if it didn't really happen that way… . I think you do remember having had sex with these two guys, and I've been doing this job for a long time, ok, and people make mistakes all the time. I mean, why is there an eraser at the end of a pencil?
>
> * * *
>
> There's no doubt in my mind, that you remember a lot more than what you are admitting to. (No, I do not.) No, listen to me, ok; I've done a very, very thorough investigation here… We've all been in situations in life where we make a mistake, and then, what do we start thinking? (I did not make a mistake.) Ok, well you did make a mistake that night, and now you're regretting it and most people would react that way too.[85]

Eventually, despite the women's continued assertions that they were raped, the officer informs them that their files will be closed. The women are told that their reports will not be classified as sexual assaults because, having been unconscious during intercourse, they cannot remember saying no.

CONCLUSION

The studies examined in this article, the anecdotal evidence from women who have dealt with police, and the police videos described above suggest that the wrongful "unfounding" of sexual assault cases continues to be a systemic problem in Canadian police forces. The most troubling fact uncovered by the studies discussed here is that women who are particularly vulnerable are the least likely to be believed when they report being sexually assaulted. Young women, old women, women who use alcohol or drugs, women who have reported a previous sexual assault, and women who are disabled or suffer from mental health problems are more likely to see their reports of sexual assault "unfounded" by police. Many of these factors are related to stereotypical beliefs about what does or does not constitute a "real" rape victim.

Sadly, it is evident from the research summarized here that some police officers believe that women have a natural inclination to make false allegations of rape. This belief is contrary to what we know about the small number of women who are willing to report to police after being

85 "Cops Ignore Rape Part 1," *ibid.*

sexually assaulted. Nonetheless, the premise that women lie about sexual assault seems to permeate police investigations and has led to the unfortunate development of damaging investigative techniques. The large scale of the problem suggests that it is not individual officers, but rather those who train them and who have the power to frame policies who are responsible for this situation. Individual police officers have a difficult, taxing job, and they require support and training that will enable them to carry out their investigations effectively.

Radical changes are required in order to stop the wrongful "unfounding" of sexual assault reports and ensure that women who are sexually assaulted are not revictimized when they report to police. Police forces will not be held accountable until the problem of wrongful "unfounding" is given more attention. No Canadian police force has been scrutinized in the same way that the Toronto Police Service has since the *Jane Doe* decision. Yet, even in Toronto, reports of sexual assault continue to be classified as "unfounded" at a higher rate than reports of other crimes. It is difficult and expensive to obtain statistics on the rate at which sexual assault reports are "unfounded," and it is even more difficult to access qualitative information that would lend insight to the question of why sexual assault reports are "unfounded" at such high rates. Even where the data is made accessible, it is difficult to compare data across jurisdictions, given that Canadian police forces do not use uniform collection procedures. Therefore, an important first step towards reform would be to institute uniform recording procedures in police forces across the country. It is also imperative that Statistics Canada resume collection of information on the number of crimes "unfounded" by the police and that more research be conducted and published in this area.

10.

Striking Back: The Viability of a Civil Action Against the Police for the "Wrongful Unfounding" of Reported Rapes

A Blair Crew[1]

Building on the evidence that "wrongful unfounding" of sexual assault reports discussed in the last chapter remains a central problem in women's access to justice, Blair Crew insists that we find mechanisms by which to hold police accountable. He explores the potential of the newly recognized wrong of "negligent investigation" made possible, as discussed by Sean Dewart in Chapter Two, by Jane Doe's precedent setting case, to fill this need. However, he notes the many difficulties posed by this avenue, including the need to prove a separate and compensable "harm" caused by the police decision to unfound a woman's report. Blair returns to the legal theories advanced by Jane Doe of failure to warn and of sex discrimination in the enforcement of the law as the most plausible avenues to secure accountability. In so doing, he echoes one of Lucinda Vandervort's urgent recommendations that government enact legislation that would guarantee access to funded legal representation and "standing," as won by Jane Doe in her rapist's criminal trial (see Appendix B at the end of this chapter), for complainants in sexual assault trials.

I came to my pro-feminist views on the investigation of sexual assaults quite by accident. As the only associate working for a lawyer who represented individuals suing the police, I was frequently contacted by women who had been raped who wished to sue, not their attacker, but the local Police Services Board because of their refusal to investigate the complaint. Never mind that there was sometimes proof of a violent assault, or an indication that the woman had been drugged, or a DNA

1 I am very deeply indebted to Sunny Marriner, Young Women At Risk [YWAR] Program Co-ordinator, Sexual Assault Support Centre [SASC] of Ottawa for all aspects of this paper. She cared passionately about the systemic unfounding of sexual assault complaints when I was still completely ignorant of the issue. Many of the thoughts expressed in this paper were worked out in response to her unending cries of "*why not?!!!*" or reflect ideas that were initially hers. In a very real way, Sunny is responsible for my pro-feminist views, and was behind almost all of my advocacy on behalf of sexual assault survivors.

sample that had now been entered into the DNA registry: each woman had been told by the police that she was lying. She would be told that she had consented to forced sex acts. She would be told she simply had a bad "first time." She would be told that the words that she had used to describe the rape had somehow betrayed her because she had not used the words that someone who had "really been raped" would use. Frequently, once the police told the woman involved that she was a liar, the police would persist and insist that, unless the woman recanted, she would be charged with mischief.

Many of these women have related to me that their treatment at the hands of the police was often more distressing than the initial assault. Many continued to bear anger and resentment towards the police long after working through the fact that they were involved in a situation in which they were vulnerable to exploitation by some man or several men. For many of these women, living with the knowledge that, according to society as represented by the police, they were labelled as liars became the most emotionally scarring aspect of their ordeal. The police, after all, are there to protect members of society, not to allow rapists to go about their way.

Although the extent to which sexual assaults are determined by the police to be "unfounded" has begun to be subject of closer academic attention, the many women who contacted me locally led me to question the extent to which local police were clearing reported sexual assaults as being unfounded.[2] A request under the *Freedom of Information and Protection of Privacy Act*[3] filed in 2008 revealed that, in Ottawa, between 2002 and 2007, 914 of the reported 2,817 sexual assaults, or 32.45 per cent, were cleared by the police as being "unfounded."[4] Astound-

2 See, for example, Justice Institute of British Columbia, *Police Classification of Sexual Assault Cases as Unfounded: An Exploratory Study* by Linda Light & Gisela Ruebsaat [unpublished] at 80. According to the Statistics Canada definition, for a sexual assault to be classified as unfounded, the police investigation must establish that a sexual assault did not occur or was not attempted. However, as Light & Ruebsaat point out, there is sometimes confusion with the statistics because of confusion between the "unfounded" category and the "founded but not cleared" category and by the use of an "unsubstantiated" category by the RCMP. In addition, Statistics Canada has discontinued the systematic collection of data on "unfounded" reports. Throughout this paper, the use of the term "unfounded" refers to cases in which a woman has reported a sexual assault, but in which the police concluded that no such assault occurred.

3 RSO 990, F31.

4 This request was filed by Teresa DuBois, when she was an LLB candidate, at the University of Ottawa Faculty of Law, as part of a fall 2007 project that gathered six feminist law students at the University of Ottawa, working under the supervision of the au-

ingly, this represented just more than double the number of cases in which the police actually laid charges. In contrast, only 797 of 23,221, or 3.43 per cent, of non-sexual assaults and 400 of 16,747, or 2.39 per cent, of all property crimes reported in the same period were cleared by the Ottawa police as being unfounded. Overall, women in Ottawa were being told that their report of a sexual assault was fabricated at a rate that was more than ten times greater than for any other crime.[5]

Negligent investigations by police forces that had tunnel vision with regard to a single case theory have lead to a fine Canadian legacy of wrongful convictions. When a person is wrongfully convicted of a high-profile crime, there has often been a public outcry sufficient to merit a judicial inquiry or commission, and compensation follows as a matter of course.[6] Yet there is no public outcry when a woman is wrongfully accused of having falsely reported a rape, even though this may lead to

thor, Professor Elizabeth Sheehy and Professor Daphne Gilbert, to conduct research on the viability of, and in support of, a proposed civil lawsuit on behalf of one woman to hold the police accountable for the wrongful unfounding of her reported rape. One aspect of this research was the gathering of statistical evidence on unfounding rates in Ontario, through filing *Freedom of Information and Protection of Privacy Act* requests. This work, with support of the University of Ottawa Community Legal Clinic, is ongoing. The Ottawa statistics referred to here remain on file with the author.

5 As of the date of writing, responses to the *Freedom of Information and Protection of Privacy Act* requests discussed in note 3 have been received from seven Ontario police jurisdictions: Hamilton, London, Ottawa, Peel Region, Windsor, York Region, and the Ontario Provincial Police. Responses from the Metropolitan Toronto Police Force and Kingston are forthcoming. Requests to the Durham and Halton Regional Police forces were abandoned due to funding restrictions. The statistics from York Region specifically exclude cases where a complainant is not believed. Statistics from London are not available for the entire period of study. Statistics from the reporting jurisdictions that are comparable are included at Appendix "B." These figures confirm that reported sexual assaults are determined by many police departments to be "unfounded" at a rate that is about ten times higher than that reported for any other crime. Two of the reporting police jurisdictions are an exception to this: the Ontario Provincial Police, which has a disproportionately high unfounding rate for all reported crimes, and Windsor, which uniquely reports a very low number of sexual assaults that are determined to be unfounded.

6 *Royal Commission on the Donald Marshall, J, Prosecution*, vol 1, *Findings and Recommendations* (Halifax, 1989); *Report of the Commission on Proceedings Involving Guy Paul Morin*, Kaufman Report (Toronto: Ministry of the Attorney General, 1998), online: <http://www.attorneygeneral.jus.gov.on.ca/English/about/pubs/morin/>; *The Inquiry Regarding Thomas Sophonow: The Investigation, Prosecution and Consideration of Entitlement to Compensation* (Manitoba, 2001), online: <http://www.gov.mb.ca/justice/publications/sophonow/index.html>; *Report of the Commission of Inquiry into the Wrongful Conviction of David Milgaard* (Saskatchewan, 2006), online: <http://www.milgaardinquiry.ca/DMfinal.shtml>. Each of these commissions serves to demonstrate the extent of public outcry for wrongful convictions.

an increased risk to the victim because the perpetrator often has continued access to her. In large measure, this lack of response may be attributed to the fact that many sexual assault survivors begin as the most vulnerable members of society because of their race, economic circumstances, or history of abuse or mental illness. As victims of sexualized violence, these women become even more vulnerable and marginalized. However, in light of the sexist and myth-based reasons that were often provided to women as to why the police were clearing the report, as well as the sheer determination of the women who consulted me, it was clear to me that the police decision to label a complaint as fabricated bore no relationship to reality. Complaints are not only being "unfounded"; they are being "wrongfully unfounded."[7]

Canada's repeated experience with high-profile wrongful convictions has lead to a legacy of reform, including broad Crown disclosure obligations[8] and mandatory jury warnings, for example, about the frailties of eyewitness identifications[9] and the dangers of the evidence of jail-house informants.[10] However, given that the public outcry over wrongful unfounding is non-existent,[11] there has been no public pressure, apart from that of service providers and feminist advocacy groups, for police forces to reform their practices with regard to the investigation of sexual assaults. While the *Jane Doe* case shed light on the practices of Metropolitan Toronto Police Force [MTPF], many of the reforms instituted in Toronto have appeared to be illusory.[12] There is also

7 I used the term "wrongful unfounding" as a focus for the research project discussed in note 3, above. As is discussed in the next section of this paper, Canadians now have a widespread understanding of the notion of "wrongful convictions." I use the term "wrongful unfounding" as a way to reconceptualize the very notion of "unfounded" rape complaints: almost all of the time when the police determine that a rape complaint was "unfounded," they have *wrongfully* arrived at this conclusion, both through the process through which this was determined and in the result.

8 *R v Stinchcombe*, [1991] 3 SCR 326.

9 *R v Trochym*, [2007] 1 SCR 239 at para 46.

10 *R v Khela*, [2009] SCC 4 at para 12.

11 Very recently, there has been just a little public attention beginning to focus on the issue of wrongful unfounding. See, for example, Jennifer O'Connor, "Undone: Hundreds of Sexual Assault Cases Each Year are Labelled 'Unfounded' by Canadian police Departments" (Jan-Feb 2009) *This Magazine*, online: <http://www.thismagazine.ca/issues/2009/01/undone_unfounded.php>.

12 *Jane Doe v Metropolitan Toronto (Municipality) Commissioners of Police* (1998), 39 OR (3d) 487, 160 DLR (4th) 697 (Ont Ct (Gen Div)). The two audits of the practices of the MTPF stemming from the *Jane Doe* case demonstrate that, even in Toronto, progress towards reform has been slow. See Jeffrey Griffiths, *Review of the Investigation of Sex-*

no evidence that any other police force has been particularly concerned about the impugned practices in which the MTPF was engaging.

Given the lack of public outcry or incentive for law reform, it would appear that the only recourse to bring about reform to the practices of police sexual assault squads is through the courts, through judicial scrutiny of the practices of a specific police force, or through monetary damage awards that would attract the attention of many police forces. This paper examines the extent to which the recently confirmed tort of negligent investigation can be used as a means of seeking redress for women who have reported a sexual assault that has been wrongfully cleared by the police, and more generally as a means of addressing the problem of systemic wrongful unfounding of reported sexual assaults. It then compares this strategy to the extent to which the causes of action developed in *Jane Doe* could be again utilized to accomplish these goals.

THE TORT OF NEGLIGENT INVESTIGATION

One intuitive possible cause of action to address the wrongful unfounding of a reported sexual assault is to frame the claim in negligence. Negligence was, after all, one of the bases in which Jane Doe was successful in her claim against the MTPF. In addition, the existence of a tort of negligent investigation has now clearly been recognized by the Supreme Court of Canada.[13] Ultimately, not much turns on the fact that the label of "negligent investigation" has been applied to this tort: given that the court applied a standard negligence analysis to examine the conduct of the police, the term "negligent investigation" is really just a kind of shorthand for "police professional negligence." Ultimately, it would appear that the limited recognition afforded to the victims of crime means that a claim for negligent investigation for wrongful unfounding is likely to face considerable judicial resistance, as I will demonstrate through an examination of the traditional requirements of a negligence claim: the existence of a duty of care, a breach of the stan-

ual Assaults—Toronto Police Service (Toronto: Toronto Audit Services, 1999) at 53–55, online: <http://www.toronto.ca/audit/1999/102599.pdf>; Jeffrey Griffiths, *The Auditor General's Follow-up Review on the October 1999 Report Entitled "Review of the Investigation of Sexual Assaults—Toronto Police Service"* (Toronto: Toronto Audit Services, 2004) at 53–54, online: <http://www.toronto.ca/audit/reports2004_sub4.htm>. There is no evidence that any other police force has in any way examined their own practices in response to *Jane Doe* and the subsequent audits.

13 *Hill v Hamilton-Wentworth Regional Police Services Board*, [2007] 3 SCR 129.

dard of care, compensable damages, and a causal connection between the breach and the damages so caused.[14]

A Duty of Care

In any action for negligence, courts usually still start with an analysis of whether the alleged wrongdoer owed a duty of care to the person who suffered a loss.[15] The test for the existence of duty follows the analysis first introduced in *Anns v Merton London Borough Council*[16] and adopted in Canada as *Kamloops v BC*,[17] as subsequently explained and clarified in a number of cases.[18] As stated in *Hill*, "the test for determining whether a person owes a duty of care involves two questions: (1) Does the relationship between the plaintiff and the defendant disclose sufficient foreseeability and proximity to establish a *prima facie* duty of care, and, if so, (2) are there any residual policy considerations which ought to negate or limit that duty of care."[19]

In *Hill*, the Supreme Court affirmed that the first part of the test requires a finding both that it is "reasonably foreseeable that the actions of the alleged wrongdoer would cause harm to the victim" and that "there must also be a close and direct relationship of proximity or neighbourhood" between the parties.[20] The proximity inquiry asks whether there are additional factors indicating that the relationship between the plaintiff and the defendant was sufficiently close to give rise to a legal duty of care.[21] In *Hill*, a majority of the court clearly pointed out that, in affirming the existence of a duty of care between the police and a suspect, the court was considering only that "very particular" relationship. The majority noted that:

> It might well be that both the considerations informing the analysis of both proximity and policy would be different in the context of other relationships involving the police, for example, the relationship between *the police and a*

14 Lewis Klar, *Tort Law*, 3d ed (Toronto: Thomson Carswell, 2003).

15 *Hill*, *supra* note 13 at para 19.

16 [1978] AC 728 (HL).

17 [1984] 2 SCR 2.

18 See *Cooper v Hobart*, [2001] 3 SCR 537, 2001 SCC 79 at paras 25, 29–39; *Edwards v Law Society of Upper Canada*, [2001] 3 SCR 562, 2001 SCC 80 at para 9; *Odhavji Estate v Woodhouse*, [2003] 3 SCR 263, 2003 SCC 69 at paras 47–50; *Childs v Desormeaux*, [2006] 1 SCR 643, 2006 SCC 18 at para 47.

19 *Hill*, *supra* note 13 at para 20.

20 *Ibid* at paras 22–23.

21 *Ibid* at para 23.

> *victim*, or the relationship between a police chief and the family of a victim. This decision deals only with the relationship between the police and a suspect being investigated. If a new relationship is alleged to attract liability of the police in negligence in a future case, *it will be necessary to engage in a fresh Anns analysis, sensitive to the different considerations which might obtain when police interact with persons other than suspects that they are investigating* [emphasis added].[22]

The court further noted that cases dealing with the relationship between the police and victims of crime were not determinative in this case, even though they might be informative.[23] Finally, the majority noted, distressingly, that the *Jane Doe* decision was "a lower court decision and that debate continues over the content and scope of that case," and specifically left open the question of whether or not there was sufficient proximity between the police and the victim of a crime for another day.[24]

In essence, then, in order to succeed in proving that the police owe a sexual assault survivor a duty of care in conducting a rape investigation, the survivor will need to establish that: (1) it is foreseeable that she will suffer harm if the investigation is not properly conducted; and (2) there is a sufficient relationship of proximity between the police officer and the complainant to give rise to a *prima facie* duty of care; and (3) there are no policy reasons to negate or limit the scope of the duty.

(1) Foreseeability

In *Hill*, the court readily accepted that it was reasonably foreseeable that a negligent investigation could cause harm to a person suspected of committing a crime.[25] At a glance, it would appear that the foreseeable harm caused by wrongful unfounding is obvious: every wrongfully unfounded rape complaint creates an additional risk of physical harm for all women. In specific cases, the conclusion by the police that no rape occurred leads directly to the result that no suspect is sought, and therefore caught, leading directly to a risk that another woman will be raped. This is, of course, exactly what occurred in Jane Doe's circumstances. In these cases, a kind of harm the courts would accept for the foreseeability analysis is abundantly clear. However, since the cause of

22 *Ibid* at para 27.

23 *Ibid.*

24 *Ibid.*

25 *Ibid* at para 33.

action on which I wish to focus is not limited to those circumstances in which a subsequent assault can be proven, it will be necessary to focus the foreseeability analysis on other kinds of harm.

In the case of sexual assault survivors, a court may clearly need to be educated about the kinds of harm a survivor suffers by being called a liar before the court will accept that it is reasonably foreseeable that wrongful unfounding causes harm. There may be a tendency for a court to dismiss a survivor by narrowly focusing on the harm caused by the rape itself, instead of the larger issues of dignity, equality, and emotional and psychological well-being that can flow from having a report of a rape believed and seeing the attacker brought to justice.

(2) Proximity

With regard to proximity, although the court in *Hill* stated that different considerations would apply with regard to victims of crime, instead of suspects,[26] the court did leave tantalizing breadcrumbs that would suggest that the court could be prepared, on a proper foundation, to find that there was a sufficient relationship of proximity between a survivor and the police officer assigned to investigate her complaint. For example, with regard to suspects, the court noted:

> There are particular considerations relevant to proximity and policy applicable to this relationship, including: the reasonable expectations of a party being investigated by the police, the seriousness of the interests at stake for the suspect, the legal duties owed by police to suspects under their governing statutes and the Charter and the importance of balancing the need for police to be able to investigate effectively with the protection of the fundamental rights of a suspect or accused person.[27]

There is no aspect of this discussion that could not be applied to a sexual assault survivor: a rape victim has every reasonable expectation that she will be believed and that the police will investigate a reported crime; the interests of the survivor, including her dignity interests, are very serious interests; the police have a specific duty to investigate crime under various *Police Services Acts*,[28] and important fundamental

26 *Ibid* at para 27.

27 *Ibid.*

28 In *Hill*, writing for a three-member minority, Justice Charron noted that although "investigating crime" is not specifically listed as one of the duties of the police in the Ontario *Police Services Act*, RSO 1990, c p 15, that this duty was implicit within many

Charter rights of a victim, including protection of her safety, privacy, personal autonomy, and dignity are all at stake.

The majority in *Hill* also noted that the proximity analysis should include an analysis of the nature of the plaintiff's interests engaged, and specifically noted that the reputation of the suspect was an important interest.[29] The reputation interests of not being labelled as a liar who "cried rape" is no less engaging than the interest a suspect has in not being labelled as a "criminal."

Furthermore, the court noted that public interests also play a role in the proximity analysis in determining whether a *prima facie* duty of care arises. The court noted that recognizing an action for negligent police investigation may assist in responding to failures of the justice system, such as wrongful convictions or institutional racism.[30] In this regard, the extremely low reporting, charging, and conviction rates for sexual assault can only be regarded as extreme failures of the justice system.[31] Moreover, as it would be argued that the unfounding rates are themselves a result of institutional sexism on the part of the police,[32] the public interest in finding a sufficient relationship of proximity is manifestly clear.

In summary, in light of the statutory duties that the police have to investigate reported crimes, a victim's expectation that her rape will be investigated, and the nature of the personal and public interests in ensuring that such an investigation is handled competently, the proximity analysis should not present a bar to an action for negligent investigation from proceeding.

(3) Policy Reasons to Negate the Duty of Care

Assuming that a court is prepared to recognize both the foreseeabilty of harm and proximity of relationship needed to give rise to a *prima fa-*

of the specific duties listed. Although the *Hill* minority found that the police did not owe a duty of care to suspects of crime, their comments overall are not incompatible with the possibility that the police could owe a duty of care to victims.

29 *Hill*, *supra* note 13 at para 34.

30 *Ibid* at para 36.

31 The most recent statistics confirm that only about 10 percent of sexual assaults are reported to the police, and that conviction rates for sexual assaults are lower than those observed for any other crime. Canadian Centre for Justice Statistics, *Sexual Assault in Canada 2004 and 2007*, Shannon Brennan & Andrea Taylor-Butts (Ottawa: Statistics Canada, 2008) at 6, online: <http://www.statcan.gc.ca/pub/85f0033m/85f0033m2008019-eng.pdf>.

32 See the discussion on this item below.

cie duty of care, the second stage of the *Anns* test asks whether there are broader policy reasons for declining to recognize this duty of care.[33]

In any potential action for negligent investigation by the wrongful unfounding of a rape complaint, the police are likely to immediately respond with at least two alleged policy reasons to negate such a duty: a "floodgates" argument, and the opposing duty, so vehemently denied to exist by counsel for the police in *Hill*, owed to suspects.

The first argument, known as the floodgates argument, would be that, by recognizing a special duty of care owed to rape victims, the police would be exposed to potential liability from the victims of all crime, any time that a perpetrator was not caught and brought to justice. Such arguments are entirely misplaced: in those rare cases of "stranger rapes," I suspect that women will have little problem understanding that, once in a while, no one is brought to justice only because the perpetrator was never caught. Cases that are left as "founded but not cleared" are entirely different than cases that are classified as unfounded. Police need not fear actions being brought by the victims of bicycle thieves unless and until those who report that their bicycles have been stolen are routinely told that they are lying, or that they actually gave their bicycle away.

The second argument, more pernicious than the first, is that there is a policy reason not to recognize a duty of care to women who report a sexual assault because, by doing so, the police will necessarily breach their duty not to subject suspects to the stigma of being publicly labelled as rapists on anything less than a "thorough evaluation of the evidence." A court may find this argument to be tenable as the defendant police force will be likely to cite their own unfounding figures to justify their need to "weed out false complaints." However, if the police were to start from the point of view that a woman who reports a sexual assault should be believed, the police would likely be protected from liability because they would have reasonable and probable grounds to lay charges from the moment a report is received. While the Supreme Court recognized in Hill that the police are properly concerned with evaluating evidence,[34] the court expressly rejected the notion that the

33 *Hill*, *supra* note 13 at para 46.

34 *Hill*, *supra* note 13 at para 49. The police take a fundamentally different approach to "evaluating evidence" in sexual assault complaints than they do for any other crime. For virtually all other crimes, complainants are almost universally believed unless there is an overwhelming reason not to do so. When the methods of "evaluating evidence" are themselves so based in sexist mythology, the "evaluation of evidence" by the police is of no value. See the discussion of this issue below as well as the chapter

police had a "quasi-judicial role" and instead held that it was only prosecutors who must be mainly concerned with whether the evidence will support a conviction.[35] Legislative reform to provide the police with civil immunity for charging a suspect in a sexual assault case, unless done in bad faith, would be beneficial.

The Standard of Care

When evaluating the standard of care of any professional, the central question customarily asked is: "What would the reasonable professional do in like circumstances?" Clearly, the customary practice of others engaged in the same activity plays a central role in this assessment. As stated in Hill:

> The general rule is that the standard of care in negligence is that of the reasonable person in similar circumstances. In cases of professional negligence, this rule is qualified by an additional principle: where the defendant has special skills and experience, the defendant must "live up to the standards possessed by persons of reasonable skill and experience in that calling." These principles suggest the standard of the reasonable officer in like circumstances.[36]

This standard is highly problematic for actions seeking redress for the systematic practices of the police generally. "What a reasonable police officer would do in similar circumstances" is simply an inappropriate yardstick to measure the duty of care when the central allegation is that those customary practices *are themselves* wholly inappropriate and discriminatory.

Teresa DuBois has highlighted evidence that confirms that police officers *are trained* to approach a sexual assault investigation with the suspicion that the complainant is lying.[37] For example, in his text on criminal profiling, Brent Turvey includes an entire chapter entitled "False Reports," which begins with the assertion, utterly unsupported by any scientific analysis, that at least 20 to 30 percent of the sexual assault cases the authors have been involved with were determined to be

by Teresa DuBois, "Police Investigation of Sexual Assault Complaints: How Far Have We Come Since *Jane Doe*?"", Chapter 9 in this book.

35 *Hill*, *supra* note 13 at para 49.

36 *Ibid* at para 69.

37 See DuBois, *supra* note 34.

false reports, and that the authors have observed "many other false reports that were not identified as such by the assigned investigator."[38] John Baeza later provides his own "Baeza False Report Index" that identifies various "red flags" that a report may be false, including that the victim has stated that she wants to speak with a female officer, that the victim has previously reported a "similar crime," or that the "victim has a long psychiatric history."[39] Sexual assault investigators are being trained using materials that begin with misogynistic assumptions and stereotypes.

As long as members of police forces are "trained" using materials like Turvey's text, which promulgates such fundamental rape mythologies, and as long as police continue to be *taught* to believe that women lie about being raped, police will be able to defer to the practices of other police forces to show that they only proceeded in a manner that was "reasonable" and "customary." Clearly, what is required here is feminist advocacy that demonstrates that the standard of "*what would the reasonable sexual assault investigator do in similar circumstances*?" is an entirely inappropriate standard of care. A more appropriate standard by which an investigation ought to be assessed is "*what can women expect of a reasonable sexual assault investigation*?" At a minimum, such an investigation must start from a premise of belief, not disbelief, and must involve an investigation that does not conclude with the taking of the survivor's statement.

Damages: Convincing the Court of Compensable Harm

So far, I have outlined that even if a court were to recognize a *prima facie* duty of care, the policy analysis stage of the *Anns* test might present an obstacle to a viable action for negligent investigation for wrongful unfounding. In addition, even if that hurdle could be cleared, there could also be considerable difficulty with whether the fundamental disbelief of women by the police presented a breach of the duty of care, unless the standard of care by which an investigation is measured can look beyond customary police practices. However, both of these obstacles may be relatively minor when compared to the third element required for a successful action in negligence: the analysis of damages.

38 John J Baeza & Brent E Turvey, "False Reports" in Brent E Turvey, ed, *Criminal Profiling: An Introduction to Behavioural Evidence Analysis*, 2d ed (San Diego, CA: Academic Press, 2002) 169 at 169.

39 *Ibid* at 177.

Leaving aside cases in which a woman is attacked again because she now has a reputation that she should be disbelieved when she reports a rape, and therefore can be raped with impunity, it is clear that any injury a woman suffers as a result of the wrongful unfounding of her rape complaint will be purely psychological injuries. Historically, the common law has had substantial difficulties with claimants' demands for damages for nervous shock and purely economic losses.[40] Even though nervous shock claims are now viewed in much the same way as other claims for damages,[41] occasionally even the Supreme Court still appears to classify claims for psychological harms together with purely economic losses.[42]

Despite this tendency, courts have been prepared to recognize claims for "nervous shock" provided that they are accompanied by a recognizable physical or psychological illness.[43] The courts continue to distinguish between "nervous shock," which is recoverable, and "mere sorrow, grief and emotional upset," which are not.[44] In other words, in order to succeed in an action for negligent investigation for wrongful unfounding, a woman will need to prove that she developed, or at least exacerbated, a mental illness because the police wrongfully refused to investigate her rape. Apart from further pathologizing sexual assault survivors, this requirement creates at least two difficulties: one that applies to all victims of crime, and the other that applies uniquely to victims of sexualized violence.

The first difficulty, which is not unique to sexual assault survivors, is the law's continued reluctance to recognize *any* private interest held by the victim in the outcome of a criminal investigation. The traditional position is that the investigation and prosecution of crime are matters of public law. While the court may acknowledge that a complainant may "derive some personal satisfaction from a conviction," that satisfaction is dismissed as a "purely personal matter" that has "no reality in law."[45]

The second difficulty, more subtle and distressing than the first, is unique to survivors of sexual assault. Any woman who suffers from the wrongful unfounding of a reported sexual assault has, of course,

40 Klar, *supra* note 14 at 426.

41 *Ibid.*

42 *Hill*, *supra* note 13 at para 90.

43 Klar, *supra* note 14 at 427.

44 *Ibid.*

45 *Norris v Gatien* (2001), 56 OR (3d) 441, [2001] OJ No 4415 at para 18 (CA).

been sexually assaulted. Depending on the survivor, this may or may not have led to the development of psychological injuries, including illnesses such as depression or post-traumatic stress disorder. This leaves the plaintiff in the position of needing to prove the extent to which her psychological injuries are a result of the wrongful unfounding of her case, compared to the extent to which her injuries are the result of the initial sexual assault, to a court that may be reluctant to accept that the damages the woman suffered as a result of being labelled a liar could ever be as significant as, or more significant than, the psychological harm caused by the initial rape.[46] Clearly, what is required is significant psychological research that demonstrates the considerable independent psychological harm that is done when women are disbelieved by the very public agency set up to protect them.[47] Of course, it will be helpful, at this stage of any potential case, that the police will be utterly unable to claim in defence that any of the woman's injuries were caused by the initial rape, because, according to the police, this initial rape never occurred at all.

Causation

The final element in a successful action for negligence is proof of the element of causation. Recovery for negligence requires a causal connection between the breach of the standard of care and the compensable damage suffered. As Elizabeth Sheehy has eloquently pointed out, the failure to apply appropriate knowledge and common sense in performing the causation analysis made all the difference between the successful outcome in *Jane Doe* and the unsuccessful outcome in *Mooney v BC (Attorney General).* [48]

46 The difficulty here is that when she is raped, a woman has had the power to control an aspect of her sexual identity taken from her. It may be difficult for a court to accept that any psychological injury could be greater than the injury stemming from the rape itself. Given that many men perceive women primarily as sexual objects, some men will believe that a woman who has been raped has been injured in the one way that is most central to her identity as a sexual object. It is possible that a male-biased court might, therefore, perceive a rape victim *primarily as* a violated sexual object, such that any other subsequent injury would be viewed as being relatively unimportant. Such a court might conclude that any injury to the woman's dignity and psychological integrity by being called a lair *could not possibly be* more significant than the injury caused by the rape itself. The full argument needs to be developed another day.

47 See the discussion of independent psychological harms caused by wrongful unfounding, below.

48 *Mooney v BC (Attorney General)*, 2004 BCCA 402, discussed in Elizabeth Sheehy, "Causation, Common Sense and the Common Law: Replacing Unexamined As-

The starting point for this analysis is the "but for" test — namely, whether, on a balance of probabilities, the compensable damage would not have occurred but for the negligence of the wrongdoer.[49] As such, it would be important for an action for damages for wrongful unfounding to focus carefully on the psychological injuries that occur as a result of this unfounding, and to make it clear that the injuries on which the claimant was relying were as a result of the negligent investigation itself, not the initial sexual assault.

Summary on an Action for Negligence for Wrongful Unfounding

From the foregoing discussion, it would seem that an action for negligence for the wrongful unfounding of a reported sexual assault that was not accompanied by a demonstration of physical injury is likely to face considerable difficulties. Even if the courts were to recognize a *prima facie* duty of care, there is a possibility that the courts might negate the duty at the policy considerations stage of the *Anns* analysis. Furthermore, the analysis of whether there is a breach of the appropriate standard of care will require a paradigm shift in which customary police practice is viewed as the source of the breach of an appropriate standard of care, not the yardstick used to justify incompetent investigations. Significantly, the analysis of forseeability of harm, causation, and compensable damages will need to rely on psychological research able to demonstrate that significant psychological injuries can and do result from telling a trauma survivor that she is lying about the source of her trauma.

Given the difficulties that an action for wrongful unfounding based on the developing concept of negligent investigation would face, it is worthwhile to examine other possible causes of action. In this regard, the twin bases of liability identified in *Jane Doe* present two better avenues for holding the police to account — namely, an action for negligent failure to warn, and an action for damages or other remedies under the *Canadian Charter of Rights and Freedoms*. It is to these possibilities that I now turn.

sumptions with What We Know About Male Violence Against Women, or, From *Jane Doe* to *Bonnie Mooney*" (2005) 17 CJWL 97.

49 *Hill*, *supra* note 13 at para 93.

Characterizing Wrongful Unfounding as a Negligent Failure to Warn

At first glance, an action for a failure to warn a woman seems of little assistance in the search for a solution to the *systemic* problem of wrongful unfounding. However, in a narrow set of circumstances, this action could be used to shed light on inappropriate police practices, including the problem of systemic disbelief, much as it did in the *Jane Doe* case itself.

It is beyond dispute that the wrongful unfounding of reported rapes materially increases the risk of rape. First, once a specific woman has been labelled by the police as someone who has falsely reported a rape, it is almost certain that the police will disregard any further complaint she chooses to make,[50] thereby significantly increasing the risk to that woman of a future attack. Secondly, each time that a reported rape is disbelieved, there are one or more perpetrators who have just gotten away with rape. If the police investigation has gone so far as to at least question a suspect, this may serve *some* deterrent effect, as the police may eventually reconsider their decision to label a complaint as "unfounded" if one man's name were to repeatedly surface during several different rape investigations. In addition, a perpetrator who has been questioned once may be inclined to be more cautious in the future. However, where the investigation never gets to this stage because the complaint has been dismissed as being a fabrication, it seems highly likely that the perpetrator will continue to rape. More generally, the many points of attrition in a rape case, including low reporting rates, high unfounding rates, and low conviction rates, all send a message to men that rape is the most frequently perfected crime.[51] Therefore, each sexual assault that is wrongfully determined by the police to be a false complaint materially increases the risk of sexual assault to all women, at all times.

50 Again, Turvey sees the fact that a woman has previously reported a sexual assault as a reason to be suspicious of any future sexual assault that she reports. See Baeza & Turvey, *supra* note 38 at 177. Anecdotally, I am aware of women for whom the police will take no action, regardless of the nature of a crime she has reported, once she has been labelled as having "credibility problems."

51 UK Home Office, *A Gap or a Chasm? Attrition in Reported Rape Cases* (Research Study 293) by Liz Kelly, Jo Lovett & Linda Regan (London: Home Office, 2005), online: <http://www.homeoffice.gov.uk/rds/pdfs05/hors293.pdf>. This study provides a particularly comprehensive examination not only of the extent of unfounding, but all the points of attrition in reported sexual assaults.

Unfortunately, what will be required in order for an action for the failure to warn, or a similarly framed action to succeed, is, as in the *Jane Doe* case, evidence of police knowledge of a series of similar sexual assaults committed within a narrow geographic range or time frame and this only incidentally and subsequently addresses the problem of wrongful unfounding.

The *Jane Doe* case itself provides an excellent example. It is now well known, of course, that Jane Doe was Paul Callow's fifth known victim.[52] The "investigations" into the first two reported rapes by the same perpetrator and, in particular, the investigation into the second assault, are perfect paradigms of wrongful unfounding. In the first case, that of PA, while the police displayed some tendency to believe she had been attacked, the police wrongfully concluded that the perpetrator was likely her boyfriend and, therefore, did not conduct a further meaningful investigation of her case.[53]

Callow's second reporting victim, BK, represents a classic case of wrongful unfounding. PC Moyer's notes confirmed that, since BK told her story in a calm and relaxed manner, "this shed some doubt on the credibility of her story," [54] thereby invoking sexist and stereotypical myths that a woman who has been raped will be emotional. Moyer used the fact that BK's apartment was "immaculate and undisturbed" to discredit her, evidently believing that this is an indication that no "real rape" could have occurred.[55] Both Cst Moyer and Staff Sgt Duggan disbelieved BK's report based on sexist mythologies, and her report was wrongfully unfounded for what Justice MacFarlane describes as "simplistic, superficial, irrelevant and generally uninformed" reasons.[56] The phenomenon of wrongful unfounding played a crucial role in the decision not to warn Jane Doe.

That said, an action for negligent investigation for wrongful unfounding where a subsequent attack can be proven is unlikely to run into few of the problems of a general action for wrongful unfounding, as discussed above. First, the existence of a duty of care requiring the police to warn women of a danger in certain circumstances has now clearly been recognized in *Jane Doe*: the relationship between the police and potential rape victims now fits a category of recognized rela-

52 *Jane Doe, supra* note 12 at para 1.

53 *Ibid* at paras 56–62.

54 *Ibid* at para 64.

55 *Ibid.*

56 *Ibid* at para 66.

tionships of sufficient proximity. Secondly, here the usual police practices may actually help to impugn a police force that has received repeated reports of similar sexual assaults from within a narrow geographic location or time frame, but the police have chosen to disbelieve the reports. Finally, a woman who is raped after the police have disbelieved, for example, four earlier similar reports will not face problems with the proof of foreseeability, damages, and causation. The difficulty with an action framed in this manner, however, is that it will require the plaintiff to acquire knowledge and proof of a series of similar prior attacks.

EQUALITY CLAIM UNDER THE *CHARTER*

If an action for negligent investigation is likely to face considerable obstacles, and if an action for the "failure to warn" would likely succeed again only in factual circumstances that require evidence that will rarely be available, then it appears that the most promising avenue to address the systemic wrongful unfounding of reported sexual assaults is through an action, as in Jane Doe's case, framed in unequal protection under the Canadian *Charter of Rights and Freedoms.* As Sheehy has noted, the *Jane Doe* case "provides a blueprint for section 15 claims involving systemic discrimination in the enforcement of the criminal law."[57] Conceptually, a *Charter* claim is much better suited than a negligence claim to address systemic unfounding where there has been no subsequent physical attack because the issue of "*who did what?*" becomes somewhat secondary to the central issue in most discrimination claims: "*why did an entity take the actions that it did?*"

The equality-based argument was clearly and concisely laid out by Justice MacFarlane:

> The plaintiff's argument is not simply that she has been discriminated against, because she is a woman, by individual officers in the investigation of her specific complaint — but that systemic discrimination existed within the MTPF in 1986 which impacted adversely on all women and, specifically, those who were survivors of sexual assault who came into contact with the MTPF — a class of persons of which the plaintiff was one. She says, in effect, the sexist stereotypical views held by the MTPF informed the investigation of this serial rapist and caused that investigation to be conducted incompetently and in such a way that the plaintiff has been denied the equal

57 Sheehy, *supra* note 48 at 88.

protection and equal benefit of the law guaranteed to her by s 15(1) of the *Charter*.[58]

Unfortunately, all that Jane Doe and Justice MacFarlane could do in the circumstances of this case was to make a finding of discriminatory beliefs held by one particular police force at one particular time, namely the MTPF in 1985–86. When one police force is found to be engaging in openly sexist behaviour, there is undeniably a public sentiment that is inclined to write this off as one rogue force, instead of a systemic practice common to all, or almost all, police forces. Furthermore, the MTPF could claim that in the twelve years that they vigorously opposed Jane Doe's litigation, they had since moved out of their own dark ages. It will be difficult to bring public attention, and ideally even legislative scrutiny, to the issue of wrongful unfounding unless there are judicial findings that the practices in which the MTPF engaged were not isolated to one police force at one time, but are practices that continue to be very much the norm amongst all police forces.

One risk to future successful *Charter* litigation is that any defendant police force is likely to be much more cautious about their approach than the MTPF was in Jane Doe's case. In *Jane Doe*, counsel for the police directed their efforts towards discrediting the cause of action itself.[59] As such, it is likely that less attention was paid to challenging the actual evidential basis for the case and whether it supported that cause of action. Notwithstanding the broad disclosure obligations in the civil litigation process, any woman, group of women, or organization that brings an application alleging a denial of equality for the wrongful unfounding of reported sexual assaults will face a police force that will be much more cautious about the flow of information and the testimony of witnesses. I now turn to a brief discussion of the elements that would need to be established to succeed in a *Charter* action for wrongful unfounding, and their proof.

(1) Evidence that cases have been "wrongfully unfounded"

The first requirement in order for a Charter action or application to succeed will be to establish that the police are, in fact, wrongfully de-

58 *Jane Doe*, *supra* note 12 at para 152.

59 Of course I am thinking here of the motion to strike the claim and the subsequent appeal of the decision allowing the claim to proceed. See *Jane Doe v Toronto (Metropolitan) Commissioners of Police* (motion to strike) (1989), 58 DLR (4th) 396 (Ont Ct (Gen Div)), and *Doe v Commissioners of Police* (1990), 74 OR (2d) 225 (Div Ct).

termining that reported sexual assaults are unfounded. Public statistics and numerous academic studies readily establish that sexual assault cases are routinely unfounded at a rate much higher than the rate for any other crime.[60] Despite an overwhelming desire to say that the data speaks for itself, this will not be enough, as the police will undeniably assert that the high rate of unfounding only demonstrates that women lie, and lie frequently, about being raped.[61] Accordingly, an application for a remedy for breach of the right to equal treatment will require, at its core, a woman who will be able to establish, on a balance of probabilities, that she was sexually assaulted, despite the fact that the police determined that she was not.[62]

(2) Evidence that "wrongfully unfounding" is widespread and systematic

Once a specific example of wrongful unfounding has been identified, the second requirement is to show that this case was not just one shoddy investigation by one bad police officer. Any potential action is best brought not by one woman alone, but by a group of women, acting together, each of whom can demonstrate that she was subjected to similar treatment. Furthermore, by acting in concert, the women also become less vulnerable to the public character assassinations and sub-

60 See, for example, Home Office Report, *supra* note 51, for a particularly comprehensive study. In the Canadian context, see Tina Hattem, "Highlights from a Preliminary Study of Police Classification of Sexual Assault Cases as Unfounded in Canada" *Just Research: Issue no 14* (Ottawa: Department of Justice, 2007), online: <www.canada.justice.gc.ca/en/ps/rs.> See also the many statistical studies collected in DuBois, *supra* at note 34, as an element of the research project described in notes 3 and 4.

61 In her groundbreaking work on the subject, Jan Jordan found that police detectives in New Zealand had not disagreed with one detective's belief that 80 percent of all reported rapes were false. See Jan Jordan, *The Word of a Woman: Police, Rape and Belief* (New York: Palgrave MacMillian, 2004) at 145. The Home Office Report also contains interviews with UK police officers who expressed views that most reported sexual assaults are fabricated. One officer reported that of the "hundreds and hundreds" of cases that he had dealt with in the past few years, he could "honestly probably count on both hands" the ones he believed were genuine. See Home Office Report, *supra* note 51 at 51. As Teresa DuBois points out, many studies look at the number of sexual assaults determined to be unfounded and immediately conclude that this is evidence that women lie about being raped, without ever asking whether there is any validity to the determination that the cases were unfounded. See DuBois, *supra* note 34. What is needed here is a fundamental shift in society's perception about what the high number of "false allegations" *really* means.

62 The police, of course, will virtually never reopen an investigation into a crime they alleged was never committed. BK, who did not participate in the *Jane Doe* litigation, was ultimately vindicated only because of the subsequent attacks on RP, FD, and Jane Doe.

sequent criminalizations to which the police might resort in an attempt to diminish their credibility.[63] Statistics on the rate of unfounding for the specific police force would be required, and these should be relatively straightforward to obtain, either through Freedom of Information requests or through the discovery process. Academic studies and statistics on the general rate of unfounding would be helpful to demonstrate that not only did this police force disproportionately choose to disbelieve women, but that the practice was very much widespread throughout police culture.

(3) Evidence that the police hold sexist, stereotypical views, and that these beliefs continue to inform investigations

The third link in the chain to the success of an equality-based claim would be to demonstrate that the reason the police were determining that claims are unfounded is that they hold stereotypical beliefs, which continue to inform their approach to the investigation of sexual assaults. Once again, the stories of several women will be required. That said, this task may not prove as difficult as it might appear because many sexual assault investigators have a tendency to voice sexist and stereotypical reasoning behind their decisions to close a case as un founded: Sometimes we do things in our lives that we think is the right thing at the time, and then later on we realize, oops, that was a mistake. Do you think that's what happened here?[64] Sentiments like this and those expressed in the introduction are often voiced by police officers. I am aware of at least one recent case that was cleared as unfounded in which the officer recorded in his notes that the "case may be cleared as unfounded on the basis of implied consent," thereby demonstrating that this particular investigator, a member of a sexual assault squad, did not have even a basic understanding of the law with regard to the most fundamental issue in any sexual assault investigation.[65]

63 I am aware of one rape victim whose name the police "accidentally" released to the media when she acted as a confidential source for a media report about the systemic unfounding of rape complaints. In another case on which I acted, a woman who filed an action against the police for an incident, which also led to criminal charges against a police officer, was picked up on a trumped up charge, released on conditions, and then subsequently arrested on not less than four series of alleged breach charges. By the time of the police officer's criminal trial, the defendant police officer was able to argue that the complainant's criminal history indicated that she was not credible as a witness.

64 O'Connor, *supra* note 11.

65 *R v Ewanchuk*, [1999] 1 SCR 330 at para 31.

More evidence of the sexist beliefs informing sexual assault investigations is likely to be discovered by accessing the very materials used to train sexual assault investigators. For example, sexist stereotypes are rife in Baeza and Turvey's explanation for why women lie about rape.[66] There is also anecdotal evidence that suggests many police forces engage in some form of "Statement Validity Analysis," which is a methodology that has, at its heart, the notion that a woman who has been raped will behave in a certain stereotypical fashion.[67] Additional research that exposes these practices would be of benefit to demonstrate that one of the reasons sexual assault investigators wrongfully unfound reported sexual assaults is that they are trained to do so using materials that start from a sexist vantage point. Additional empirical research that documents the reasons given when the police determine that a case is unfounded would be of great value.[68] The stories of women who do not wish to pursue a claim have a great deal to offer to those women who do.

(4) Resulting investigations are incompetent, or are not conducted at all

The fourth aspect of a *Charter*-based claim would be to prove that the resulting police investigations are conducted in an incompetent fashion. This requirement should be readily satisfied given that once the police have labelled a case as "unfounded," there is often no further investigation whatsoever. It would appear that the police frequently determine that a case is unfounded without interviewing potential wit-

66 Baeza & Turvey, *supra* note 38 at 178–185.

67 Andrew D Parker & Jennifer Brown, "Detection of Deception: Statement Validity Analysis as a Means of Determining Truthfulness or Falsity of Rape Allegations" (2000) 5 Legal and Criminological Psychology 237.

68 While I fully support all available measures to protect the privacy rights of any woman who has been sexually assaulted to the full extent that she desires, there is a manner in which those very protections can serve to protect the interests of the police in hiding police practices. Since the police never lay a charge in a case that they have labelled as unfounded, information on the case does not become a matter of public record now that Statistics Canada does not require the police to report unfounded cases. Rape Crisis Centres and Sexual Assault Support Centres (and even lawyers, for that matter!) must be entitled to hold everything that their clients say in the strictest of confidence. That said, hidden within the knowledge of women who have reported a sexual assault to the police or to a frontline worker is sufficient evidence to overwhelmingly prove, beyond any doubt, that rapes are routinely wrongfully unfounded based on openly stated sexist assumptions.

nesses or picking up the suspect, who is very frequently known to the woman,[69] for questioning.[70]

(5) Disproportionate impacts on women

It is well understood and documented that the victims of sexual assault among adults are overwhelmingly women.[71] As such, the fifth requirement is to demonstrate that women are disproportionately impacted by poor quality or non-existent sexual assault investigations.

(6) Resulting in a denial of equal protection of the law

The final element of a *Charter*-based claim to address wrongful unfounding is proof that the practice of wrongful unfounding results in a denial of equal protection of the law. As the Supreme Court of Canada has stated the test:

> Does the differential treatment discriminate, by imposing a burden upon or withholding a benefit from the claimant in a manner which reflects the stereotypical application of presumed group or personal characteristics, or which otherwise has the effect of perpetuating or promoting the view that the individual is less capable or worthy of recognition or value as a human being or as a member of Canadian society, equally deserving of concern, respect, and consideration?[72]

Providing evidence of the discriminatory impact of the systemic unfounding of sexual assault complaints is likely to be the least problematic aspect of an equality-based claim, as the wrongful unfounding of reported sexual assaults constitutes discrimination in each of the ways discussed by the Supreme Court of Canada in *Law*.

Withholding a benefit

The duties of police officers are defined in the various provincial Police Services Acts. In Ontario, for example, section 42(1) of the *Police Servi-*

69 In 2007, the attacker was known to the victim in 82 percent of the sexual assaults that were reported to the police in Canada (Brennan & Taylor-Butts, *supra* note 31 at 5.

70 Light & Ruebsaat, *supra* note 2.

71 Canadian Centre for Justice Statistics by R Kong *et al*, "Sexual Offences in Canada" (2003) 23:6 Juristat (Ottawa: Statistics Canada), online: <http://www.statcan.gc.ca/pub/85-002-x/85-002-x2003006-eng.pdf>.

72 *Law v Canada (Minister of Employment and Immigration)*, [1999] 1 SCR 497 at para 39.

ces Act[73] specifies that the duties of a police officer include: (a) preserving the peace; (b) preventing crimes and other offences and providing assistance and encouragement to other persons in their prevention; (c) assisting victims of crime; (d) apprehending criminals and other offenders who may lawfully be taken into custody; and (e) laying charges and participating in prosecutions.

As discussed above, in *Hill*, the Supreme Court of Canada interpreted the *Police Services Act* to implicitly include a duty to investigate crime.[74] The police fail to meet any of their legal obligations when they determine that they believe a woman is lying about a sexual assault based on their own discriminatory beliefs. On the most fundamental level, women are denied the equal benefit of the law, or any benefit of the law whatsoever, by police forces that wrongly choose not to investigate sexual assaults. No other class of individuals is routinely denied the protection that is the fundamental function of a police force.

Furthermore, if crimes against women are routinely not investigated because of a systemic belief that women are liars, and charges are therefore not laid on a routine basis, perpetrators are likely to become aware that a complainant is unlikely to be believed, and may thus feel at greater liberty to assault women. A very loud message is being sent by the fact that between 2002 and 2007, the Ottawa Police laid charges in only 453 of 2,817 — just over 16 percent — of all of the sexual assaults that were reported to them. As Sheehy has argued, this message results in an enlargement of power conceded to violent, misogynist men over women.[75]

Imposition of burden

While the denial of a benefit of the law is itself significant discriminatory treatment, the burdens imposed by the manner in which police approach sexual assault investigations run much deeper.

First, the danger to any specific woman once she has reported a sexual assault presented by a specific attacker is significantly increased once her complaint is deemed to be unfounded. In many cases, the perpetrator is someone with continued access to the complainant. By choosing not to believe a woman's complaint, the police have sent the perpetrator the message that they do not believe her, and will not pursue him. He now knows that he is under a significantly decreased risk of arrest when he assaults her again.

73 RSO 1990, c P15.

74 *Supra* note 28.

75 Sheehy, *supra* note 48 at 91.

Second, as discussed above,[76] once a woman has had a reported assault unfounded, the police are considerably less likely to believe any subsequent report she files. This presents an increase in the danger to a specific woman from all potential attackers. A woman who has reported a rape that the police considered to be false has effectively been rendered "rapeable."

Thirdly, there are many anecdotal reports of situations where, once the police have decided that a woman is lying, they then persist and tell the woman, under interrogation-like circumstances, that if she does not recant her story, she will be charged with mischief for filing a false complaint. Recognizing that there is now no chance the police will ever charge the attacker, and under pressure from the police, a woman will often recant in order to extricate herself from the oppressive circumstances that she is now under and to avoid being charged. This practice reinforces the police approach to the investigation because the police now rely on the recantation to "confirm" their suspicions of fabrication, and to affirm that their approach is justified.[77]

Finally, as was discussed above, wrongful unfounding may cause further emotional and psychological harm. While more research is required on this topic, this psychological harm would clearly qualify as another type of burden imposed on women.[78] However, it is also significant that, for the purposes of a *Charter* claim, this is only one additional type of harm that may be caused by discrimination: unlike the potential negligence action, proof of this kind of harm is not a necessary precondition to the success of the action. Given that the causation analysis of a negligence claim is so closely tied to the kind of harm that is cited, it may be that the "best" way to avoid a faulty causation analysis is to sidestep it altogether by proceeding only on equality grounds.

76 *Supra* note 50.

77 Further study on the extent to which threatened counter-charges provokes unreliable recantation is required.

78 Most studies so far have focused on how a determination that a complaint is unfounded has a harmful impact on a woman's recovery following a rape, and the extent to which existing symptoms of depression and post traumatic stress disorder are exacerbated by a negative outcome in the investigation or prosecution of a sexual assault. See, for example, Rebecca Campbell *et al*, "Community Services for Rape Survivors: Enhancing Psychological Well-Being or Increasing Trauma?" (1999) 67 J Consulting and Clinical Psychology 847; Sarah E Ullman & Henrietta H Filipas, "Predictors of PTSD Symptom Severity and Social Reactions in Sexual Assault Victims" (2001) 14 J Traumatic Stress 369; Judith Herman, "The Mental Health of Crime Victims: Impact of Legal Intervention" (2003) 16 J Traumatic Stress 159. I am not aware of any studies that have examined independent psychological harms caused by police disbelief of complaints.

Attitudinal harm

While there are ample ways in which it could be demonstrated that wrongful unfounding both denies women the equal benefit of the law and imposes a burden on women, the most pernicious harm caused by wrongful unfounding is likely in the manner in which reports of unfounded cases cause a shift in general societal attitudes.

Every time that a reported sexual assault is cleared as unfounded, it sends society the fundamental message that, in the eyes of police, all women are liars and, specifically, that women lie about being raped on a frequent basis. To paraphrase the Supreme Court of Canada in Law, this has the effect of promoting the view that women are less capable, less worthy of recognition as human beings, and not equally deserving of concern, respect, and consideration because the fundamental message is that "women lie."

In another way, wrongful unfounding also causes societal harm in that the perception that a woman is going to get hostile treatment at the hands of the police and the justice system is likely a significant reason why women choose not to report sexual assault at all.[79] The practice of wrongful unfounding is fundamentally at odds with a society that claims to have an interest in encouraging the reporting of sexual offences.[80]

Remedies

Once all of the elements of a constitutional tort have been proven, there still remains the question of appropriate remedies. While Jane Doe's *Charter* claim victory is encouraging, it is disappointing that the court determined that she was "not entitled to any additional or 'extra' damages because the police had breached her *Charter* rights" and that a declaration would suffice.[81] To my mind, this judgment failed to separate the specific harms to Jane Doe from the much broader societal harms caused by the general approach to the investigations of sexual assault taken by the MTPF. A strong award of punitive damages in recognition of the breach of Jane Doe's equality rights would not only have provided her with more complete redress, but would have provided a stronger

79 Fear of disbelief is often cited as a reason why women choose not to report sexual assaults. See Home Office Report, *supra* note 51 at 42. Brennan & Taylor-Butts, *supra* note 31 at 8, also found that 41 percent of women who did not report a sexual assault to the police cited "not wanting to get involved with the police" as one of the reasons why.

80 See *Criminal Code of Canada*, RSC 1985, c C-46, s 278.5(2)(f).

81 *Jane Doe*, *supra* note 12 at 194.

incentive for all police forces in Canada to closely examine their own sexual assault investigation practices.

Section 24(1) of the *Charter* allows a court to grant any such remedy as the court considers appropriate and just in the circumstances. While I leave as beyond the scope of this paper a full discussion of the range of creative remedies that might be possible to address proven discriminatory harms caused by wrongful unfounding, it is my hope that further studies might address this issue. Even though many of the women I have spoken with about this issue say that a monetary award is unimportant to them, I believe that significant monetary damages are likely to be the best way to get the attention of Police Services Boards in a meaningful way.

Charter claims and access to justice

Before concluding, it is appropriate to comment on the issue of access to justice. The most significant barrier to any kind of legal action to address wrongful unfounding is access to justice itself: in comparison, finding a pool of potential claimants would not likely be a significant obstacle.

Not only are sexual assaults most frequently committed against society's most vulnerable women, including young women and children, survivors of childhood abuse, women suffering from mental illness, Aboriginal women, women of colour and, overwhelmingly, economically disadvantaged women and women living on the streets, but it is exactly these women whose rape complaints are most likely to be disbelieved.[82] Much deeper than the fact that litigation of the type proposed is beyond the means of these already economically disadvantaged women, the last thing that almost all of these women would ever want to do is deliberately re-engage with a masculine-biased legal system that has already let them down and branded them as liars.

Even for a claimant with modest means and a fervent desire to strike back, protracted *Charter* litigation is far out of reach. As with the *Jane Doe* case, an action of the type proposed would require deeply committed feminist litigators supported by a deep pool of resources and research.

Although it may be a utopian ideal at this stage, there is one potential argument that litigation to address systemic discrimination in sexual assault investigations ought to be publicly funded. The therapeutic value of litigation itself for sexual assault survivors has recently become

82 Home Office Report, *supra* note 51 at 47–48.

the subject of increased attention.[83] If the beneficial effect of litigation on a woman's psychological recovery could be further proven, then this would mean that a claimant could credibly argue that, because the right to security of the person protects the psychological integrity of the individual, she has an entitlement to legal aid funding.[84] Given that non-pecuniary goals appear to drive much sexual battery litigation, it is not an impossible stretch to argue that the more holistic goals of litigation designed to address systemic discrimination in sexual assault investigations ought to be publicly supported, particularly given that it may be in precisely the cases where the police have declined to press charges that further litigation that vindicates the survivor might have the greatest therapeutic effect.[85]

CONCLUSION

Having been privileged to team-teach a law school course in sexual assault law from a feminist and pro-feminist point-of-view, I have often remarked that what is needed to combat the thoroughly sexist manner in which many sexual assault investigations are conducted is more radical action. Although in some ways horrible to contemplate, what if all women in Canada collectively refused to report any sexual assault to any police force, even for just one day? Would this finally bring about the needed legislative scrutiny to the practices of sexual assault squads? What is the sense in women engaging at all with a system that "boomerangs" the focus of a criminal investigation one-third of the time, and only actually lays charges one-sixth of the time? Radical action—striking back in some form—is needed. Resorting to the courts to address the problem of systemic wrongful unfounding is hardly radical, but it would appear to be the only tool we have available.

That said, an action framed in the traditional discourse of professional negligence is unlikely to succeed, particularly in light of the lim-

83 See Bruce Feldthusen, "The Civil Action for Sexual Battery; Therapeutic Jurisprudence?" (1993) 25 Ottawa L Rev 203; and Bruce Feldthusen, Olena Hankivsky & Lorraine Greaves, "Therapeutic Consequences of Civil Actions for Damages and Compensation Claims by Victims of Sexual Abuse" (2000) 12 CJWL 66.

84 See *New Brunswick (Minister of Health and Community Services) v G (J)*, [1999] 3 SCR 46, in which the court held that for a restriction of security of the person to be made out, an impugned state action must have a serious and profound effect on a person's psychological integrity. The effects of the state interference must be assessed objectively, with a view to their impact on the psychological integrity of a person of reasonable sensibility. This need not rise to the level of nervous shock or psychiatric illness, but must be greater than ordinary stress or anxiety.

85 Feldthusen, *supra* note 83 at 211.

ited recognition of a victim's interest in the outcome of a criminal case. There is a greater prospect for a favourable outcome of an action based on the equality provisions of the *Charter*, but only if such an action is properly brought by a sisterhood of survivors, acting in concert, and properly supported by expert testimony and feminist research.[86] Although the institution of policing may not change in response to even many successful legal claims, it may ultimately be only the prospect of being forced to pay potentially considerable financial damages that might prompt changes to police practices that advocacy and discussion alone have been unable to achieve. It is time to build on Jane Doe's remarkable victory and to put the police on notice: *be warned, we are watching*.

86 As Sheehy *supra* note 48 at 115 has noted, wins like Jane Doe's can only be reproduced through comparable investment of resources and ingenuity.

APPENDIX B

Reported Sexual Assaults and Criminal Offences and Unfounding Rates Reported by Ontario Police Forces, 2003–2007

Windsor

Year	Reported Sexual Assaults	Sexual Assaults Classed as "Unfounded"	Percentage	Reported Criminal Offences	Criminal Offences Classed as "Unfounded"	Percentage
2003	117	0	0.00%	41,893	149	0.36%
2004	116	3	2.59%	43,852	138	0.31%
2005	125	3	2.40%	40,186	118	0.29%
2006	101	4	3.96%	40,381	94	0.23%
2007	113	1	0.88%	37,691	149	0.40%
Total	572	11	**1.92%**	204,003	648	0.32%

Peel Region

Year	Reported Sexual Assaults	Sexual Assaults Classed as "Unfounded"	Percentage	Reported Criminal Offences	Criminal Offences Classed as "Unfounded"	Percentage
2003	488	85	17.42%	45,938	714	1.55%
2004	518	84	16.22%	44,864	690	1.54%
2005	534	84	15.73%	43,874	763	1.74%
2006	531	142	26.74%	48,080	1,230	2.56%
2007	626	146	23.32%	47,769	1,526	3.19%
Total	2,697	541	**20.06%**	230,525	4,923	2.14%

Hamilton

Year	Reported Sexual Assaults	Sexual Assaults Classed as "Unfounded"	Percentage	Reported Criminal Offences	Criminal Offences Classed as "Unfounded"	Percentage
2003	545	86	15.78%	40,243	595	1.48%
2004	507	108	21.30%	36,150	581	1.61%
2005	399	103	25.81%	31,773	598	1.88%
2006	371	100	26.95%	32,209	716	2.22%
2007	329	79	24.01%	34,787	564	1.62%
Total	2,151	476	**22.13%**	175,162	3,054	1.74%

Ontario Provincial Police

Year	Reported Sexual Assaults	Sexual Assaults classed as "Unfounded"	Percentage	Reported Criminal Offences	Criminal Offences Classed as "Unfounded"	Percentage
2003	1,989	556	27.95%	154,198	16,471	10.68%
2004	1,922	552	28.72%	151,857	16,484	10.85%
2005	2,065	640	30.99%	147,884	17,270	11.68%
2006	1,978	620	31.34%	149,949	17,766	11.85%
2007	2,036	645	31.68%	146,912	17,810	12.12%
Total	9,990	3,013	**30.16%**	750,800	85,801	11.43%

Ottawa

Year	Reported Sexual Assaults	Sexual Assaults Classed as "Unfounded"	Percentage	Reported Criminal Offences	Criminal Offences Classed as "Unfounded"	Percentage
2003	475	182	38.32%	51,871	1,194	2.30%
2004	419	153	36.52%	46,958	1,222	2.60%
2005	518	137	26.45%	47,947	1,324	2.76%
2006	431	121	28.07%	48,183	1,534	3.18%
2007	471	127	26.96 %	44,998	1,116	2.48 %
Total	2,314	720	**31.11** %	239,957	6,390	2.66 %

11.

Third-Wave Anti-rape Activism on Neoliberal Terrain: The Garneau Sisterhood

Lise Gotell

This section of the book decentres law by exploring the potential for social change in women's community-based activism, which the work of the Garneau Sisterhood exemplifies. Lise Gotell's chapter places the postering campaign of the Sisterhood, consciously modelled on the work of Jane Doe's own posters that defied the Toronto police as described in "The Victories of Jane Doe," in the context of neoliberal erosion of feminist equality gains and the reassignment of the responsibility for managing the risk of rape to individual women. She demonstrates how police warnings to women during the course of the Garneau investigation mirrored many of the same attitudes and assumptions about men, women, and rape that plagued the investigation of the "Balcony Rapist." Lise describes the Sisterhood's campaign as one that successfully inverted the individualizing and woman-blaming that characterizes police and media responses to sexual assault, and argues that its brilliance lay in the fact that it is easily replicable by other communities of women engaging in third-wave feminism.

> Instead of ceding the power to define intervention to administrators caught up in the culture of risk management, feminists might practice publicly perverting and mocking the language in a manner that highlights how nonsensical it is to socialize women to stop rape.[1]

The victory in *Jane Doe v Metropolitan Toronto Police*[2] resulted from the "sustained collaborative work" of "feminist activists, lawyers, experts and judges."[3] Ten years later, however, the basis for such strategic collaborations has been eroded. The possibilities for strategic feminist uses of law have been undermined through the defunding of

1 Rachel Hall, "'It Can Happen to You': Rape Prevention in the Age of Risk Management" (2004) 19 Hypatia 1 at 12.

2 *Jane Doe v Metropolitan Toronto (Municipality) Commissioners of Police* (1998), 39 OR (3d) 487 (Ont Ct (Gen Div)) [*Jane Doe*].

3 Elizabeth Sheehy, "Causation, Common Sense, and the Common Law: Replacing Unexamined Assumptions with What We Know about Male Violence against Women or From *Jane Doe* to Bonnie Mooney" (2005) 17 CJWL 97 at 115.

women's movement organizations, the delegitimization of feminist knowledges, and the political erasure of gender equality.[4] What are the specific implications of neoliberal governance for feminist campaigns against sexual violence? With the decline of national feminist organizing and the removal of state supports that had facilitated political and legal interventions, the possibilities of new policy and law reforms that might address the continued realities of sexual violence may have indeed collapsed. Yet this might also be a time for feminists to explore the creative possibilities of new strategies and tactics that challenge the centrality of law reform and expand the terrain of the extra-legal.

Consciously imitating WAVAW's 1986 poster campaign that led to the arrest of the "Balcony Rapist,"[5] with resistant messages ripped from the pages of *The Story of Jane Doe*,[6] the Garneau Sisterhood's campaign stands as an example of the productive possibilities of contemporary grassroots anti-rape activism.

In 2008, several[7] violent rapes occurred in Garneau, an Edmonton neighbourhood bordering the University of Alberta. It was not until three women living within a one-block radius were attacked that the Edmonton Police Service released a public advisory.[8] After a fourth sexual assault in the suburban neighbourhood of Aspen Gardens, the police warnings intensified and all women "living alone" (in the heat

4 Janine Brodie, "We Are all Equal Now: Contemporary Gender Politics in Canada" (2008) 9 Feminist Theory 145; Lise Gotell, "The Discursive Disappearance of Sexualized Violence: Feminist Law Reform, Judicial Resistance and Neo-liberal Sexual Citizenship" in Dorothy E Chunn, Susan B Boyd & Hester Lessard, eds, *Feminism, Law and Social Change: (Re)action and Resistance* (Vancouver: UBC Press, 2007) 127.

5 Jane Doe, together with Women Against Violence Against Women, postered the downtown Toronto neighbourhood where the rapes were occurring: RAPIST IN THIS AREA. He is medium build, black hair.... The police are not warning women. Why? What can you do? Attend a public meeting at... " The day after the posters went up, the police got a tip that led to the perpetrator's arrest: Jane Doe, *The Story of Jane Doe: A Book About Rape* (Toronto: Random House, 2003) [*The Story of Jane Doe*].

6 *The Story of Jane Doe, ibid.*

7 Four sexual assaults were reported to police. Given that police reporting rates have remained consistently low, never rising above 10 percent since they began to be tracked, it is very likely that this perpetrator attacked more women. It is rumoured that he threatened his victims, vowing to return if they called the police.

8 The first attack occurred in February when a man broke into a house and sexually assaulted a twenty-four-year-old woman. In early May, the man returned, broke into the same house, and sexually assaulted a forty-seven-year-old woman living in a second suite. In late May, a twenty-one-year-old woman who lived in a house across the alley was pepper-sprayed and sexually assaulted by the same perpetrator. "Police warn of Garneau sex assaults" *Edmonton Journal* (28 May 2008), online: <http://www2.canada.com/edmontonjournal/news/cityplus/story.html?id=3549a8d6-63a9-4503-b8ad-ac6c3583d8cd>.

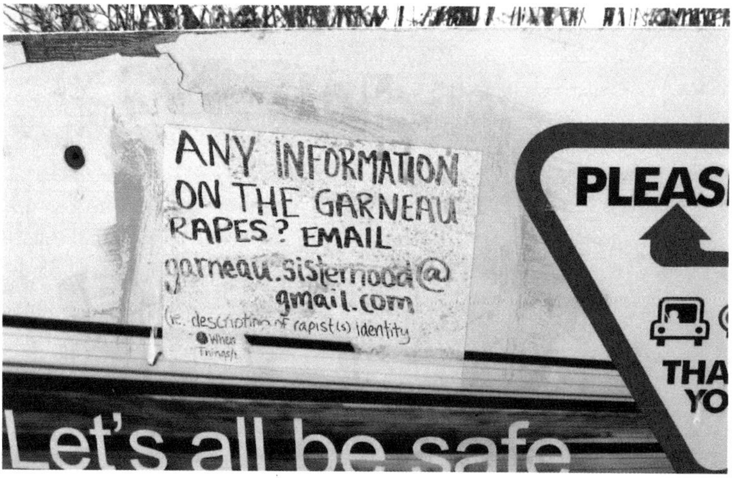

of late summer) were repeatedly advised to be vigilant. In response to these events, a group of neighbourhood women calling themselves the Garneau Sisterhood mounted a poster and media campaign challenging the disciplinary and individualizing thrust of police warnings.

This paper will analyze these events against the backdrop of neoliberalism. As I will argue, practices of risk management and sexual safekeeping have become primary governmental technologies for responding to sexual assault. Police warnings constitute one manifestation of risk management technologies that together have the effect of erasing sexual violence as a systemic problem and transforming it into something that individual women should try to avoid. The Garneau Sisterhood's campaign, conducted anonymously and without links to established organizations, interrupts these neoliberal technologies by calling upon women to actively reject their assigned role as safety-conscious victims-in-waiting. This campaign was marked by great irreverence and a DIY ("do it yourself") style of direct activism characteristic of third-wave feminism. In its creative and edgy challenge to risk management discourses, the Garneau Sisterhood demonstrates the strategic importance of extra-legal feminist struggles within the difficult context of neoliberal governance.

SITUATING MYSELF/LOCATING THE GARNEAU ATTACKS

In an important article on "survivor discourse," Linda Alcoff and Laura Gray[9] interrogate the second-wave feminist strategy of "breaking the

9 "Survivor Discourse: Transgression or Recuperation?" (1993) 18 Signs 260.

silence," arguing that speaking out may not necessarily be liberating. They catalogue the multiple ways that survivor speech can be recuperated, depoliticized, and thus rendered compatible with dominant discourse. Escaping this confessional structure is difficult, though Alcoff and Gray emphasize the resistant potential of survivor discourses that manage to maintain the autonomy of the speaking subject, to disenfranchise outside experts, and to allow survivors themselves to become theorists of experience. *The Story of Jane Doe* exemplifies what Alcoff and Gray refer to as "subversive speaking"[10] — a raped woman chronicling her struggle to effect systematic change, bringing a feminist perspective to the lived experience of rape, and exposing the deep flaws in the criminal justice system.

As for me, I have never had too much confidence that my words could resist recuperation — or perhaps I have just been cowardly, reluctant to surrender the objective voice that has helped to ensure the authority of my own scholarly work on sexual assault. It is hard enough to do feminist work on rape and law, and perhaps harder still when one comes out as a survivor. But I am implicated in what I write here in ways that should not be erased. Like Jane Doe and the women attacked by the Garneau rapist, I was sexually assaulted by a serial rapist who broke into my downtown Toronto house. I was a young graduate student, woken in the night by a man with a knife. Even though the police told me they believed I had been attacked by someone who was responsible for other rapes in the area, there were no warnings. And when, like Jane Doe, I asked why I didn't know that a serial rapist was targeting women in my neighbourhood, I too was told that this just creates hysteria and makes investigations more difficult.

This was now more than twenty years ago, but police unwillingness to provide women with concrete and useful warnings seems to be as much a problem now as it was then, despite the victory in *Jane Doe*.[11] Constructions of women as hysterical and erratic are still used to rationalize police failure to warn women when they become potential targets of serial rapists. Exaggerated beliefs in the prevalence of false reports also appear to have great resilience and longevity. Indeed as Jan Jordan has noted, despite efforts by police departments around the world to improve their investigative procedures and treatment of

10 *Ibid* at 282.

11 In *Jane Doe, supra* note 2, the police were held accountable in law for sex discrimination in violation of s 15 of the *Charter* and for negligence in the investigation of a serial rapist.

complainants (including training and awareness, specialized sex crimes units and greater deployment of women officers), "[a]ttrition rates in rape cases continue to be high, reporting rates remain low and beliefs about false complaints remain high."[12] Teresa DuBois' recent research[13] demonstrates how police officers are explicitly trained to approach sexual assault investigations with the suspicion that complainants are lying. Statistics indicate that police unfounding rates remain high in the Canadian context.[14]

Evidence of systemic sexism in the investigation of sexual assault complaints by the Toronto police that was marshalled at the *Jane Doe* trial[15] could just as easily describe the police response to Edmonton's Garneau rapist. In a depressing repetition of the 1986 response to Toronto's Balcony Rapist, Edmonton police investigators were rumoured to have disbelieved the first survivor's story of having been attacked by a stranger, and to have doubted the second report because of the improbability of a perpetrator returning after three months to attack another woman in the same house.[16] Three and a half months passed and three women (all living within a stone's throw of each other) were assaulted before the police issued any information about these attacks.

Garneau is a hybrid neighbourhood where university professors and doctors live in new infills and renovated historic houses, while students and other young people live in crowded, poorly maintained rental accommodations. But Garneau's proximity to the university and its location close to Edmonton's trendy Whyte Avenue mark it as a middle-class space, rigidly demarcated from the inner city that is across a

12 *The Word of a Woman? Police, Rape and Belief* (New York: Palgrave MacMillan, 2004) at 60.

13 "Police Investigation of Sexual Assault Complaints: How Far Have We Come Since *Jane Doe*?" Chapter 9 in this book.

14 Holly Johnson, "Limits of a Criminal Justice Response: Trends in Police and Court Processing of Sexual Assault," Chapter 24 in this book.

15 For a discussion, see Sheehy, *supra* note 3 at 94–96.

16 Rumours circulated among sexual assault workers and community members that the police disbelieved the first survivor's claim to have been attacked by a stranger, viewing the attack as a probable domestic assault. A second stranger assault in the same house (though occurring in a different suite) was seen as defying probability. As Sheehy, *supra* note 3 at 92–93 recounts, in the 1986 police response to the balcony rapes, "the police simply didn't believe the first two women and apparently remained skeptical even in the face of the third woman's report. The investigative reports were manifestly incomplete, such that a proposed charge of public mischief against the second woman who reported to police may well have succeeded had the police pursued it."

river and to the north. Like the social geography of Regina mapped so carefully by Sherene Razack,[17] Edmonton is a city divided by race and class. Colonization marks the social geography of Western Canadian cities, creating boundaries between the white middle-class spaces, ruled by norms of universal justice, and the racialized spaces of the inner city and reserve, constructed as zones of violence. Edmonton is an epicentre in the national tragedy of missing and murdered Aboriginal women and yet, the routine violence enacted on the bodies of Aboriginal women nearly escapes register.[18] Women engaged in survival sex work in Edmonton are overwhelmingly of Aboriginal descent[19] and the constant violence they experience, documented in the bad date sheets produced monthly by outreach agencies, becomes visible only when it results in death. As Razack[20] has argued, sexual violence against Aboriginal women is an ongoing repetition of the colonial encounter. Violence against Aboriginal women is both sanctioned through law's blindness and contained in spaces like inner-city Edmonton, where this violence it becomes routinized and treated as if it were a naturally occurring phenomenon. By contrast and only in relation, episodic acts of sexual violence in middle-class neighbourhoods like Garneau and suburban Aspen Gardens can be depicted as if sharply separated from the everyday. What connects these sites and rationalizes this dynamic of erasure and (eventual) hypervisibility is the contemporary reconfiguration of sexual violence as a risk to be managed by responsibilized, crime-preventing subjects.

NEOLIBERAL RAPE PREVENTION: MANAGING RISK, MANAGING RAPE

After the Aspen Gardens assault, and in an atmosphere of increasing media scrutiny of the police investigation, a CBC reporter asked me

17 "Gendered Racial Violence and Spatialized Justice: The Murder of Pamela George" (2000) 15 CJLS 91.

18 Safedmonton, Prostitution Working Group, "Working Together to Address Sexual Exploitation in Edmonton" (2007), online: <http://www.edmonton.ca/city_government/city_organization/prostitution-working-group.aspx>; *Stolen Sisters: A Human Rights Response to Discrimination and Violence Against Aboriginal Women in Canada* (Ottawa: Amnesty International, 2004); Sandra Lambertus, *Addressing Violence Perpetrated Against Aboriginal Women in Alberta: Final Report,* Project Lifeline: Study Funded by the Alberta Solicitor General Victims of Crime Fund (2007), online: <http://www.whrn.ca/documents/LifelineEBook.pdf>.

19 Safedmonton Prostitution Working Group, *ibid* at 13.

20 Razack, *supra* note at 17.

to explain how the Edmonton police could be ignoring the lessons of the *Jane Doe* case. The reporter had covered the release of the *Jane Doe* decision in 1998 and was aware of its implications for police investigations. She speculated that the second and third unwarned "victims" of the Garneau rapist had the basis for similar lawsuits. My answer to her could not be contained in a sound-bite. Police response to the Garneau and Aspen Gardens assaults, including the initial failure to warn and the subsequent production and intensification of disciplinary warnings, tells us a great deal about the reconfiguration of sexual violence in and through neoliberalism.

Sexual assault means something different now than it might have once meant. The discovery of a serial rapist brings sexual violence out into public view, making it momentarily visible, ironically revealing a problem that has been erased. We live in a time in which the widespread problem of sexual assault has been dropped from political agendas, contrasting with a brief period when second-wave feminists enjoyed some limited success in gaining legal recognition of sexual violence as an object of state intervention.[21]

In the aftermath of the Montreal Massacre,[22] Canadian feminist anti-violence and anti-rape activists achieved policy advances, particularly on the terrain of criminal law reform, enjoyed discursive successes and participated in innovative consultative forums with federal government actors.[23] The sexual assault law reforms that emerged out of these processes, encoding a legislative definition of consent as voluntary agreement, limiting the defence of mistaken belief, and enacting restrictions on the uses of sexual history evidence and complainants' confidential records in trials, stand as significant feminist achievements in a period otherwise characterized by the increasing marginalization of the women's movement.[24] During government consultations held

21 Gotell, *supra* note 4.

22 On 6 December 1989, Marc Lepine entered an engineering building at l'École Polytechnique de Montréal, ordered the men to leave, shot fourteen young women to death, screaming that they were a "bunch of feminists," and then killed himself. In a note, he described the murders as political and blamed feminism for ruining his life. In 1991, the federal government established December 6th as an annual National Day of Remembrance and Action on Violence Against Women.

23 For analysis of the policy impact of the Montreal Massacre, see Lise Gotell, "A Critical Look at State Discourse on 'Violence Against Women': Some Implications for Feminist Politics and Women's Citizenship" in Manon Tremblay & Caroline Andrew, eds, *Women and Political Representation in Canada* (Ottawa: University of Ottawa Press, 1997) 127.

24 Gotell, *supra* note 4 at 130–31.

during the 1990s, national women's groups and frontline workers laid out an agenda that extended well beyond criminal law reform, framing sexual violence as a systemic problem deeply rooted in gendered and racialized inequalities, and demanding state action on a number of fronts, including social policy, public education and, crucially, the provision of a stable funding base for independent, women-controlled, frontline work and activism.[25] And although state actors successfully channelled this broad agenda into a much narrower emphasis on criminal justice reform, systemic understandings of sexual violence as serious, pervasive, and gendered explicitly framed the legislation enacting the 1990s sexual assault amendments.[26]

The victory in *Jane Doe*, recognizing systemic sexism in police investigations as a violation of *Charter* sexual equality, must be situated in this moment during which feminist claims regarding the structural nature of sexual violence were at least intelligible. This victory, as Elizabeth Sheehy contends,[27] was the result of Jane Doe's intelligence and commitment, and the collaborative work of national women's organizations and feminist lawyers, experts, and judges. But as Sheehy reminds us, legal victories are fragile and must be claimed and reclaimed. And, in the context of the present, the victory of *Jane Doe* must be reclaimed on a new and more difficult terrain where the links that second-wave feminists forged between sexual violence and systemic power relations have been severed.

Feminist analysts have charted the rapid disappearance of gender and the gender equality agenda from public discourse over the past two and a half decades.[28] The ascendance of neoliberalism in Canada has led to erosion of structural factors in the formation of policy and to the delegitimization of feminist actors. Ascendent political rationalities privilege self-sufficiency, stigmatizing public provision and claims-making on the basis of social disadvantage. Canadian feminist organizations have been recast as "special interest groups," antithetical to a public good defined in terms of restraint, privatization, and personal responsibility.[29] The disappearance of sexual violence as an object of

25 Canadian Association of Sexual Assault Centres, *99 Federal Steps to End Violence Against Women* (1993), online: <http://www.casac.ca/english/99steps/99steps.htm>.

26 Gotell, *supra* note 4 at 131.

27 *Supra* note 3.

28 Brodie, *supra* note 4; Jane Jenson, "Citizenship in the Era of 'New Social Risks': What Happened to Gender Inequalities" in Yasmeen Abu-Laban, ed, *Gendering the Nation-State: Canadian and Comparative Perspectives* (Vancouver: UBC Press, 2008) 185.

29 Janine Brodie, "The Great Undoing: State Formation, Gender Politics, and Social

public policy can be linked to these broader transformations in state form and citizenship norms. The policy field once signified by "violence against women" has been evacuated and replaced with degendered and individualized policy frameworks. The recognition of sexual assault as a policy problem, even through the limited and individualized lens of criminal law, has all but disappeared.[30]

With the election of the Harper Conservatives, the defiant erasure of sexual violence as a social problem is evident. While embracing an explicit right-wing law-and-order agenda, the gendered dimensions of "crime" have been deliberately silenced in political rhetoric.[31] One crucial institutional mechanism by which this has occurred is the elaboration of victims' services bureaucracies and the now entrenched policy discourse of "victims' issues." This discourse erases the gendered character of sexual violence, and reconstructs those who experience rape as undifferentiated victims of crime, requiring generic "rights" and assistance. Now preoccupied with the rights and treatment of individualized, degendered, and deraced "victims," new policy frameworks avoid linking "crime" to context.[32]

This clever disappearing act does not signal a victory over sexual violence, but rather its erasure as an object of policy and public discourse. The delegitimization of feminist voices, the intensification of law-and-order policies, and the erosion of the policy field signified by "violence against women" must be viewed within and alongside the ascendance of neoliberal governance. Once constituted a "social problem" and a legitimate object of government intervention, sexual violence has been reprivatized and individualized, contained within discourses of abstract risk and individuated criminal responsibility.

Contemporary technologies for managing sexual assault, dramatically demonstrated in police warnings and disseminated by the media, rely upon the production of self-regulating subjects. As Sally Engle Merry writes, "As states endeavour to govern more by spending less, they have adopted mechanisms that build on individual self-govern-

Policy in Canada" in Catherine Kingfisher, ed, *Western Welfare in Decline: Globalization and Women's Poverty* (Philadelphia: University of Pennsylvania Press, 2002) 90 at 95–96.

30 Gotell, *supra* note 4 at 132–33.

31 Dawn Moore & Erin Donohue, "Harper and Crime: The Great Distraction" in Theresa Healey, ed, *The Harper Record* (Ottawa: Canadian Centre for Policy Alternatives, 2008) 375, online: <http://www.policyalternatives.ca/documents/National_Office_Pubs/2008/HarperRecord/Preface.pdf>.

32 Gotell, *supra* at note 4 at 132–33.

ance and guarded spaces."[33] Critical criminologists identify "self-discipline" as central to neoliberal crime-prevention strategies: the promotion of safe-keeping and private prudentialism are mechanisms for individualizing and privatizing crime control, shifting the problem of crime away from the state and onto would-be victims.[34] Risk management technologies cultivate responsibilized, calculating, crime preventing citizens, who practice and sustain their autonomy by assembling information into personalized strategies that identify and minimize their exposure to harm. As Robert Castel contends, the new preventative politics "deconstruct the concrete subject of intervention, and reconstruct a combination of factors liable to produce risk."[35]

The reconfiguration of sexual assault through risk management technologies relies upon these processes of decontextualization in which the systemic problem of sexual violence, rooted in gendered inequalities, normalizes heterosexuality and, in racialized power, becomes disassembled and reduced to abstract factors that render rape more or less probable. Discourses of risk are circulated in rape prevention programs that instruct women to be tough targets of rape by avoiding behaviours such as drinking, leaving drinks unattended, or leaving parties with new acquaintances, that are "correlated with rape."[36] As I have argued elsewhere, these safety pedagogies also mark judicial decisions that, just as they elaborate and apply stricter legal standards of sexual consent, simultaneously promote new forms of normative sexual subjectivity built upon the anticipation of sexual risk and the necessity of clear sexual communication.[37] Medicalized regimes for "treating victims" psychologize the harms of rape and promote individualized forms of "recovery" intended to restore the capacity for self-management.[38] Risk management discourse frames these various institution-

33 "Spatial Governmentality and the New Urban Social Order: Controlling Gender Violence Through Law" (2001) 103 American Anthropologist, NS 16 at 17.

34 *Ibid*; Pat O'Malley, "Risk, Power and Crime Prevention" (1992) 21 Economy & Society 252; David Garland, "'Governmentality' and the Problem of Crime" (1997) 1 Theoretical Criminology 173.

35 "From Dangerousness to Risk" in Graham Burchell, Colin Gordon & Peter Miller, eds, *The Foucault Effect: Studies in Governmentality* (Chicago: University of Chicago Press, 1991) 281; Hall, *supra* note 1 at 2.

36 Hall, *ibid* at 6.

37 Gotell, *supra* at note 4 at 144–53; Lise Gotell, "Rethinking Affirmative Consent in Canadian Sexual Assault Law: Neoliberal Sexual Subjects and Risky Women" (2008) 41 Akron L Rev 865 at 875–82.

38 Kristin Bumiller, *In an Abusive State: How Neoliberalism Appropriated the Feminist Movement Against Sexual Violence* (Durham: Duke University Press, 2008) at 79–90.

al moments, redefining sexual assault as a problem that responsible individuals must attempt to foresee and prevent. In this way, sexual violence has been rendered virtual, severed from the power relations that constitute its meaning and dynamics.

POLICE WARNINGS AND GENDERED RISK MANAGEMENT

Even as risk management discourses individualize and decontextualize, their materialization relies upon and promotes gender-specific subjectivities and new versions of good and bad victims. As Rachel Hall has argued, in recent years, "the paternalistic myth of women's vulnerability donned the neoliberal cloak of risk management."[39] For women, safekeeping is a "technology of the soul," with the appreciation of risk of male violence long constitutive of feminine identity. While not "new," women's fear of male violence and the accompanying demands of risk avoidance are cultivated in the present and constituted as performative of respectable femininity.[40] The police warnings in response to the Garneau and Aspen Gardens sexual assaults exemplify the manipulation of gender-specific fear through the degendered language of risk management.

In late May of 2008, after a third sexual attack in Garneau, when the existence of a serial rapist could no longer be ignored, the Edmonton Police Service finally issued a concise media release.[41] As a sex crimes detective explained in a media interview: "Because of the similarities of the attacks, we felt it was necessary for the safety of the residents to be notified."[42] No explanation was offered for withholding information about the first two assaults. It is possible that an earlier warning "could have" prevented the pepper-spraying and rape of a young woman living just across the alley from the house where the first two women were assaulted. The May media release provided only the barest details of the three assaults (the ages of the women who were attacked, the general location of the attacks, the approximate time of the attacks), an extremely general description of the suspect ("a man of average build, who was wearing dark clothing"), and an equally vague advisory: "Garneau-ar-

39 *Supra* note 1 at 2.

40 *Ibid* at 10–11; Elizabeth Stanko, "Safety Talk: Conceptualizing Women's Safekeeping as a Technology of Risk" (1997) 1 Theoretical Criminology 479 at 489.

41 Edmonton Police Service, News Release, "Police Looking for Suspect in Sexual Assaults" (27 May 2008).

42 "Police issue warning to women in Garneau" *CBCnews.ca* (27 May 2008), online: <http://www.cbc.ca/canada/edmonton/story/2008/05/27/edm-garneau-attacks.html>.

ea residents" were warned to take "extra safety precautions," "to be on the lookout and report any suspicious activity, and strangers wandering around in the early morning hours."[43] This generic call to genderless "residents" to take "safety precautions" was elaborated by police detectives in media reports, in which "people" were advised to be "diligent in locking doors and windows."[44]

If the third sexual assault displaced the suspicion that was rumoured to have characterized police response to the first two survivors, the sexual assault of an elderly woman living in an affluent and solidly middle-class neighbourhood several blocks south of Garneau led to an escalation of police warnings. The national media attention following this fourth attack and the explicit admission, finally, by the Edmonton Police Service of a suspected "serial offender"[45] must be understood as being related not only to the proliferation of the attacks, but also to the age of the "victim." The intensification of "warnings" after the Aspen Gardens attack was linked to the dominant construction of older women as asexual and, therefore, truly blameless, "innocent" victims. The fact that the women who were attacked by this rapist were young, middle aged, and old, and lived in different neighbourhoods, also momentarily exposed the tensions between the degendered frame of crime prevention/risk management and the gendered realities of sexual violence. As a sex crimes detective explained in a media report, "We have had a large range of victims. There is a male out there who wants to commit sexual assaults and right now, it doesn't matter how old the woman is."[46] The police warnings that followed the Aspen Gardens attack largely repeated the narrative of the earlier police advisory.[47] Yet these advisories now explicitly targeted "women" and, more specifically, "the ones who live alone," as the explicit objects of the warning; women living alone

43 Edmonton Police Service, "Police looking for suspect in sexual assaults," *supra* note 41.

44 *Ibid;* "Police Warn of Garneau Sex Assaults" *Edmonton Journal* (28 May 2008), online: <http://www2.canada.com/edmonton journal/news/cityplus/story.html?id=3549a8d6-63a9-4503-b8ad-ac6c3583d8cd>.

45 Edmonton Police Service, News Release, "Police Meet with Aspen Gardens Residents: Meeting Ends with 450 Residents Cheering, Applauding" (15 August 2008).

46 Ben Gelinas, "Southside Sex Attack Makes Four: Police Link Similarities with Garneau Rape Suspect to Saturday Case 35 Blocks Away" *Edmonton Journal* (12 August 2008), online: <http://www.canada.com/edmontonjournal/news/story.html?id=ca197418-c7e5-4c11-aa53-156588bdbf84>.

47 Edmonton Police Service, "Police Meet with Aspen Gardens residents," *supra* note 45; Edmonton Police Service, News Release. "Police Looking for Suspect in Sexual Assaults" (11 August 2008).

were warned "to be vigilant about locking their doors and windows and securing their homes."[48]

By the time of the fourth attack, critical attention had begun to be focused on the investigation itself.[49] Savvy reporters and commentators drew parallels between these Edmonton sexual assaults and the *Jane Doe* case. Jane Doe herself spoke on CBC Edmonton radio to explain the implications of her legal victory and what it should mean for the conduct of police investigations; and there was growing criticism of the refusal to release detailed information about the attacks.[50] For a few days in mid-August, the local media focused extensively on the existence of a serial rapist and police sex crimes detectives gave interviews and attended a public meeting organized by the local community league. But notably, only the vaguest description of the suspect was made public ("male with a stocky build, approximately 5'8" to 5'10" wearing dark clothing and a disguise on his face"),[51] along with the suggestion that the perpetrator may have stalked his victims. The Edmonton Police Service repeatedly refused to release the kind of meaningful information that might actually have assisted women to make informed decisions about their safety (for example, whether the suspect had tampered with doors or windows, whether he had broken into the women's houses before the attacks, how he had disguised himself). Responding to criticisms about this lack of detail about the rapist's *modus operandi*, senior police officers cited the necessity of maintaining the "integrity of the investigation" and "not compromis[ing] the prosecution of the person responsible."[52] When pressed for concrete advice on just how to avoid being attacked by this rapist, the police provided a generic, if detailed, list of "basic tips" on how to properly secure doors and windows.[53] Police officers rationalized the repetition of disciplinary warnings directed at women, insisting that "[i]t would be extremely

48 Edmonton Police Service, "Police Meet with Aspen Gardens Residents," *supra* note 45.

49 Robin Collum, "Sex Assaults Lead to Criticism of Police" Canwest News Service (15 August 2008), online: <http://www.canada.com/edmontonjournal/news/story.html?id=ca197418-c7e5-4c11-aa53-156588 bdbf84>.

50 "Edmonton police are being criticized for not doing enough to warn women about a series of sexual assaults" *CBCnews.ca.* (15 August 2008), online: <http://www.cbc.ca/canada/edmonton/story/2008/08/14/edm-attacks-thurs.html>.

51 Edmonton Police Service, "Police Meet with Aspen Gardens Residents," *supra* note 45.

52 *Ibid.*

53 *Ibid.*

tragic if we didn't offer suggestions for personal safety and because we didn't, there were additional victims."[54]

Perhaps in an effort to respond to critiques of the sexist victim-blaming of the earlier warnings, a final police advisory, issued six weeks after the Aspen Gardens rape, reverted to the gender-neutral language of crime prevention.[55] This media release offered reassurances that considerable resources were still being devoted to the investigation and urged the "public" to "continue with their increased awareness of personal safety and make sure their homes are secure." The September warning, while articulated in forced degendered terms (public/they/their), continued to mobilize and cultivate women's fear, even after anxieties had begun to dissipate. The advisory raised the possibility that there may have been more attacks that had not been reported to the police given the "well recognized fact that sexual assaults go largely unreported" and encouraged "other victims" to come forward.

What do these warnings tell us about the contemporary construction of sexual assault? What do they tell us about how sexual violence is managed within the context of neoliberal governance? The police warnings hail "woman" as a modern subject into a position of vulnerability. The self-managing subject produced through the warning is, in Hall's words, a "(re)action hero" who exercises agency only through avoidance.[56] Through risk management technologies, the question of how to end rape gets deflected back onto individual women as tough targets. Warnings address the social body of women as a series of individualized bodies each responsible for protecting their own "stuff." A gendered panopticon results, with women's behaviour singled out as the principal governmental object. This focus on women's responsibility for rape prevention means that men's responsibility for sexual violence, including the culpability of the rapist himself, becomes obscured. Likewise, social responsibility for sexual violence evaporates, as the problem of rape is firmly constituted as a personal problem that each woman herself must solve by limiting her own mobility. In the dry

54 "Some Women Disagree Over Rape Warnings: Police Say They Aren't Playing the Victim Game" *Edmonton Journal* (14 August 2008), online: <http://www.canada.com/edmontonjournal/news/cityplus/story.html?id=585274bd-f4b2-4af8-b8ed-85cdbee8b34d>.

55 Edmonton Police Service, News Release, "Police Asking Public to Stay Vigilant with Personal Safety: Detectives Looking for New Information about Linked Sexual Assaults" (25 September 2008).

56 *Supra* note 1 at 6.

heat of a Prairie summer, women are expected to stay "safe," suffocating inside their locked and airless homes.

The rapist himself remains a shadowy figure: disguised, faceless, he becomes an abstract threat. Not only is the rapist rendered virtual, shrouded by police refusals to elaborate his description or *modus operandi*, but the text of the warnings repeatedly constitutes him as an external threat, an outsider. In the words of one of the lead investigators, "*People in the community know who belongs and who doesn't.*"[57] Residents are told to be on the lookout for "any unusual circumstances," "any strangers wandering around," "suspicious activity," a "strange male." This repetition consolidates a false and misleading line between the rapist as stranger/outsider and the everyday, hiding the pervasive realities of sexual violence in everyday heterosexuality. Gesturing to class- and race-based ideologies that provide implicit support for dominant understandings of rape, we are encouraged the view the suspect as the archetypal stranger-rapist, a deviant man lurking in the bushes, *he who does not belong.*[58]

Risk management discourses, as exemplified in these police warnings, also create new versions of good victims and unworthy, unrapable women. As Elizabeth Stanko astutely observes, it is not only women's fear of rape that is mobilized to induce compliance with the warning: "Woman — as subject, multiply positioned and fluid — recognizes that what is at risk is more than just an encounter with men's violence, it is also a risk of self, a fear of being judged imprudent...."[59] Performances of diligent, fearful femininity grant some women access to good citizenship.[60] Within a neoliberal regime of responsibility, populations are divided on the basis of their capacity for self-management; those women who can be represented as failing to adhere to the rules of sexual safekeeping are in turn blamed for the violence they experience. The murders and disappearances of Edmonton Aboriginal women and sex trade workers have been framed in dominant discourse as being an effect of risk-taking, the sad outcome of living a "high-risk lifestyle."[61]

57 Edmonton Police Service, "Police Asking Public to Stay Vigilant with Personal Safety," *supra* note 55.

58 Hall, *supra* note 1 at 13; Stanko, *supra* note 40 at 490.

59 Stanko, *ibid* at 489.

60 *Ibid* at 486.

61 Project KARE, an RCMP task force investigating more than eighty cases of missing and murdered women in Alberta, publishes a list of safety tips for women "at risk." The "most important tip is not to be involved in a high risk profession, lifestyle or ac-

Filtered through norms of risk-management, the gender, race, and class power relations producing extreme vulnerabilities disappear and some women are relegated to a space of risk. The white and middle-class woman is the implicit target of police warnings; she gains access to protection and good citizenship by adhering to the disciplinary norms of rape prevention.

Rape prevention, neoliberal style, relies upon decontextualizaton and self-management and divides women on the basis of adherence to elaborate and constraining safety rules. The warnings in response to the Garneau rapist exemplify the core features of risk management technologies applied to rape. But these warnings stand as more than simply an example; they also demonstrate how the existence of a serial rapist provides a pedagogic moment, an occasion during which the normal silence around rape is briefly shattered, with repeated warnings serving as instruments of normalization.

THE GARNEAU SISTERHOOD

How do we challenge this gendered regime of risk management that privatizes and decontextualizes sexual violence? How do we do this when national feminist organizing is in decline, when gender and the gender-equality agenda have been erased from policy discourse, and when the potential for feminist-inspired policy and law reform seems slim? How do we, in other words, reconstitute a feminist practice of anti-rape resistance within the difficult context of neoliberal governance? The Garneau Sisterhood provides us with one possible strategy — that is, the revival of a grassroots feminism that engages in direct action and decentres the state.

Scholars charting the erosion of feminist organizing under conditions of neoliberalism have inadvertently constructed a depressing narrative of decline.[62] It is critical to dissect the implications of neoliberal governance for feminist politics; at the same time, it is increasingly necessary for us to think beyond this story of despair in which feminist resistance seems impossible. It is most certainly true that what Victoria Bromley and Aalya Ahmad have labelled state-brokered feminism and state-centred forms of feminist activism, including lobbying,

tivity such as prostitution or hitchhiking." "These activities," according to the RCMP, "make you very vulnerable to becoming a victim." RCMP, Project KARE, nd, "Safety Tips," online: <http://www.kare.ca/content/view/14/24/>.

62 See, for example, Brodie, *supra* note 4.

law reform, and litigation, are in decline.[63] The Harper Conservative cuts to Status of Women Canada's funding programs have dealt a near deathblow to many established women's movement organizations.[64] Jane Doe's legal victory was situated within a context of state-brokered feminism and depended upon the legal and political support of established feminist organizations and frontline women's organizations. This legal victory arose when it was still possible to make links between sexual violence, police practices, and gender inequality. Even if the conditions that enabled second-wave anti-rape activism have been eroded, the current context does not mean that feminist resistance to rape culture is impossible; nor should it render us silent and in despair at the repetition of Jane Doe scenarios. Instead, new forms of anti-rape activism are needed that, in Victoria Bromley and Aalya Ahmad's words, are "clearly demarcated from the brokerage and paternalistic oversight of the state."[65]

Young women, loosely identified by the label "third wave," are rising to the challenge of rethinking feminist activism, in part by reviving the grassroots, direct activism of early radical feminists. As R Claire Snyder observes, third wavers tend to take an anarchist approach to politics — calling for immediate direct action and organizing outside of formalized structures.[66] Embracing differential consciousness, third-wave feminists see activism as context-specific and flexible, with tactics shifting depending on the situation.[67] And while this "movement" may seem less visible and more *ad hoc* than second-wave feminism, these characteristics can be reconceived as strengths rather than weaknesses, allowing for flexibility and access to diverse forms of activism. This diversity of tactics approach has the effect of decentring legal strategies.[68] Although the third-wave displacement of law has been critiqued by some as a naïve expression of "pre-legalism,"[69] we might also see this

63 "Wa(i)ving Solidarity: Feminist Activists Confronting Backlash" (2006) 25 Can Woman Stud 61.

64 Brodie, *supra* note 4.

65 Bromley & Ahmad, *supra* note 63 at 67.

66 "What is Third-Wave Feminism? A New Directions Essay" (2008) 34 Signs 175 at 186.

67 Amanda D Lotz, "Communicating Third-Wave Feminism and New Social Movements" (2003) 26 Women and Language 2 at 6.

68 Lara Karaian & Allyson Mitchell, "Third Wave Feminisms" in Nancy Mandell, ed, *Feminist Issues: Race, Class and Sexuality* (Toronto: Pearson Education Canada, 2010) 63 at 67.

69 Bridget J Crawford, "Towards a Third Wave Feminist Legal Theory: Young Women,

extra-legal emphasis as strategic in a context in which spaces for feminist-inspired law reform and litigation have become constrained.

As Lara Karaian and Allyson Mitchell observe, "the third wave places a greater emphasis on activism that works outside of the state and gets into the heart of the communities…."[70] The Garneau Sisterhood campaign exemplifies this movement into the heart of communities, modelling a feminist practice of anti-rape resistance that decentres the state and literally inscribes women's agency onto the familiar features of a neighbourhood streetscape. I noticed immediately when the posters began appearing all over Garneau in May 2008, signed by *the Sisterhood*. Their aesthetic, handwritten in black and white (and sometimes red), was decidedly DIY, in the style of a 'zine. Each day, I climbed on my bicycle and took a different route through the neighbourhood with my camera, desperate to map and to archive this constantly changing and defiant campaign of resistance to rape culture. New posters kept appearing all over the neighbourhood. Many were defaced and ripped down. There were even rumours that the posters were being taken down by the police. In one newspaper report, a police spokeswoman described the Sisterhood's actions as "vigilanteeism" (sic.), characterized the posters as "threatening" and explicitly warned members of the "public" against taking the law into their own hands.[71]

Given this overt hostility, it is easy to understand the Sisterhood's decision to mobilize, to act, and to speak anonymously. The Sisterhood closely guarded the identity of its members, speaking without spokeswomen or leaders, and giving media interviews only on condition of anonymity. But anonymity serves functions extending beyond safety and privacy. Politically influenced by Jane Doe's own embrace of anonymity as a tool for enabling survivor resistance, the Sisterhood used the cloak of anonymity to disseminate a highly radical and edgy anti-rape text that embodies what Alcoff and Grey have labelled "subversive speaking."[72] And because the identity of the sisters is permanently under question, they become anywoman and everywoman. The Garneau Sisterhood represents the promise of a feminist underground and its campaign can be seen as a tactical response to conditions of neoliberalism.

Pornography and the Praxis of Pleasure" (2008–09) 14 Mich J Gender & L 99 at 158–60.

70 Karaian & Mitchell, *supra* note 68 at 67.

71 Gelinas, *supra* note 46.

72 *Supra* note 9 at 282.

In a piece published in an Edmonton weekly, the Sisterhood describes itself in the following way: "*Garneau Sisterhood is a group of feisty concerned citizens in the Garneau area and the larger Edmonton community who are organizing to catch the most recent serial rapist in the neighbourhood, challenge the culture of violence and reclaim safe spaces for women in their communities.*"[73] Reclaiming "safe space," while challenging the disciplinary thrust of safety pedagogies disseminated through police warnings, was the central thrust of the poster campaign. As Hall counsels, feminists should practice mocking and subverting the message of risk management.[74] When read together as a coherent text, the Sisterhood's posters speak back to, undermine, invert, and pervert the framing of sexual violence through risk management discourse. How is this accomplished?

The Sisterhood disrupts the gendered panopticon produced by police warnings, making the rapist (not the potential victim) the subject of scrutiny and the object of fear. By addressing the perpetrator directly, the posters have the effect of unmasking the shrouded rapist, "responsibilizing" him, rather than his potential victims, and situating him in a position of fear:

- ATTENTION RA"PEST". WE ARE WATCHING YOU. WE WIL (sic) FIND YOU.
- ATTENTION RA"PEST." WE ARE ORGANIZING TO FIND YOU AND WE WILL!!
- RAPEST TURN YOURSELF IN NOW 423-4567[75]

The rapist is transformed from a powerful force into a pest, an object of disgust.

If the Sisterhood turns the gaze on the rapist, thereby shifting it away from women, so too is men's responsibility for ending sexual violence highlighted in this campaign. The Sisterhood undermines the exclusive

73 Garneau Sisterhood, "Garneau Sisterhood Organizing in Response to Sexual Assaults" *Vue Weekly* (12 June–18 June 2008), online: <http://www.vueweekly.com/article.php?id=8743>.

74 *Supra* note 1 at 12.

75 Phone number of the Edmonton Police Service.

focus on woman as individualized agent of sexual assault prevention by defiantly and cleverly shifting the site of rape prevention to men.[76] In an allusion to *The Story of Jane Doe*,[77] one poster on blue paper pasted to a red newspaper box, mocks the gendered thrust of the warnings, using irony as a tool for showing how ridiculous it is to tell women that they can stop rape by locking themselves up:

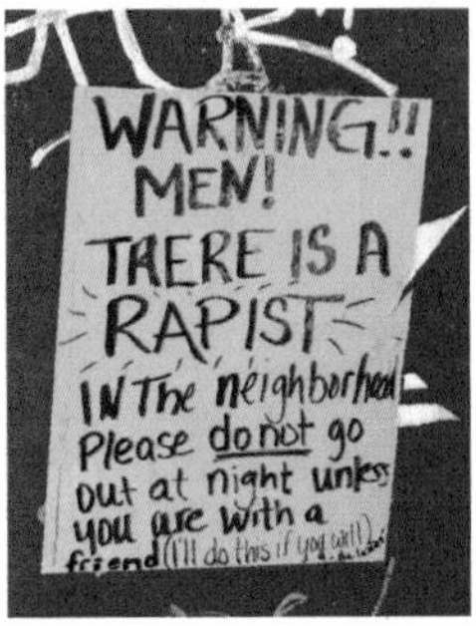

- *WARNING!! MEN! THERE IS A RAPIST IN THE Neighbourhood.* Please **do not** go out at night unless you are with a friend. (I'll do this if you will). *the ladies*

This emphasis on men's complicity in rape culture is complemented by repeated efforts to reinscribe social responsibility and to restate the core message that safety tips directed at women will not end sexual violence:

- It is not because of: — clothing — drinking — locked doors — "assertiveness" ... RAPE HAPPENS BECAUSE OF RAPISTS. *Love the Sisterhood.*
- TELLING ME TO LOCK MY DOOR WILL NOT MAKE ME SAFE. PREVENTING SEXUAL ASSAULT IS EVERYONE'S REPONSBILITY.
- There is something wrong with a society that teaches men to rape women. What are we doing to make men believe that violence against women is okay? What can we do to change that?

The Sisterhood's recontextualization of rape subverts victim-blaming and challenges the neoliberal message that victims are self-made and that sexual victimization is rooted in bad choices and irresponsibility. Instead, and in the admittedly brief form permitted by the DIY poster, the Sisterhood calls attention to the connections between rape and gender disadvantage and to the necessity of social change.

76 Rachel Hall, *supra* note 1, argues that shifting the site of social intervention against rape from women to men is a necessary component of a feminist practice of rape prevention that would reinforce a woman's right to freedom from fear and abuse rather than reinforcing her fear and powerlessness.

77 "MEN: Stay off the buses. One of you is raping women... Stay at home" : *The Story of Jane Doe*, *supra* note 5 at 325.

In an influential feminist re-theorization of sexual violence, Sharon Marcus[78] contends that rape is discursively produced, a scripted event, that depends upon the construction of women as vulnerable. The text of the police warnings and the logic of risk management reproduce this position of feminine vulnerability, constructing women as rape spaces, as objects to be taken. In what could be seen as exemplifying Marcus's call to women to cease being grammatically correct feminine subjects (that is, objects, fearful potential victims hiding away in locked apartments), the Sisterhood declares its defiant refusal to comply with the disciplinary norms of rape prevention:

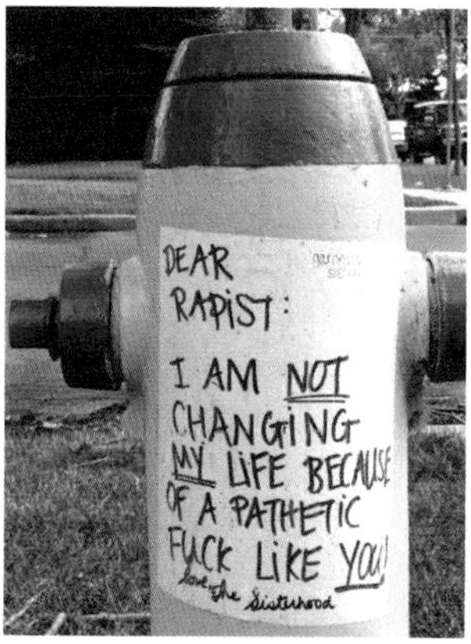

- DEAR RAPIST: I AM NOT CHANGING MY LIFE BECASE OF A PATHETIC FUCK LIKE YOU!
  Love the Sisterhood

The Sisterhood constructs a collectivity based upon this refusal. Blending almost seamlessly into the grey metal window frame of the local grocery, a small poster announces:

- Women of Garneau: You are the Sisterhood.

Intended perhaps as a clever response to the repeated question, "Just who is putting up all these posters?" this brief message is weighted. It situates all women within a space of collective resistance to rape culture and to the specific framing of sexual violence through risk management technologies. Reflecting the third-wave feminist insistence on women's agency, a longer message elaborates the contours of a sisterhood based not upon women's status as potential victims, but instead upon angry resistance:

- IF A WOMAN IS RAPED, **OTHER WOMEN REACT**. THERE IS NO SUCH THING AS AN ISOLATED ATTACK ON AN INDIVIDUAL WOMAN. **ALL WOMEN ARE US!** When a sister

78 "Fighting Bodies, Fighting Words: A Theory and Politics of Rape Prevention" in Judith Butler & Joan Scott, eds, *Feminists Theorize the Political* (New York: Routledge, 1992) 385.

> is raped it is a RAPE OF THE SISTERHOOD and cannot go unpunished! **THE SISTERHOOD is WATCHING!!!!**

This message — that there is no such thing as an isolated rape — disrupts the individualization of sexual violence at the heart of risk management discourse, firmly locating rape within gendered power relations.

In *Grassroots: A Field Guide to Feminism Activism,*[79] third-wave feminists Jennifer Baumgardner and Amy Richards offer several innovative examples of how young feminists are organizing against sexual violence. They describe a German woman's success in getting a bakery to distribute 330,000 bread bags with the logo "Rape is totally unacceptable."[80] This campaign has now been replicated in several communities across Europe and, as Baumgartner and Richards emphasize, has the potential to be adopted almost anywhere. Likewise, the appeal of the Sisterhood's strategy is that it is both accessible and replicable; it is highly adaptable to local context. It is also a strategy that does not depend upon the mediation of law or the receptiveness of the state. The Sisterhood's campaign invites repetition and imitation as it mocks the message of rape management discourses. Over the past year, Sisterhood-like posters have continued to be put up around Edmonton and in other cities. Reclaiming public space for women, this innovative DIY strategy writes and makes visible the power of feminism and repoliticizes rape.

CONCLUSION

I wrote this chapter exactly a year after these events, and the Edmonton summer, though cooler, reminded me of how I felt the summer before. I felt angry, but I also felt increasingly hopeful. The posters responded to a series of brutal attacks on women. In spite of the continued realities of male violence against women, we live in a time when neoliberal political rationalities frame politics as if gender no longer matters. Like so many feminists, I have been decidedly depressed about political possibilities. But because of this campaign, I began to feel optimistic again about the radical potential of feminist anti-rape activism.

Many of the Sisterhood's posters were still there the following summer, ripped, faded, yet visible. The humourous one, the one that made

79 *Grassroots: A Field Guide for Feminist Activism* (New York: Farrar, Straus and Giroux, 2005).

80 *Ibid* at 106–12.

me smile, was still readable: BE A SNITCH. SAVE A SNATCH. STOP GARNEAU RAPES. We have the illusion that when we manage to influence institutional texts (legal decisions and legislation, for example), that the changes we effect will be lasting. But such victories, to be lasting and meaningful, must be reasserted, reclaimed, and brought into the streets.

The Garneau Sisterhood mounted a subversive campaign against the disciplinary norms of rape prevention and it brought its defiant and often irreverent messages to the streets. As with any political action, there is always room for critique and revision. While the Sisterhood disrupted the image of the rapist as a stranger-outsider by insisting on all men's responsibility for ending rape, the implicit whiteness of the privileged and hyper-cautious feminine subject remained uninterrogated in this poster campaign. I wonder what it might have meant to make visible the extreme violence experienced by Aboriginal women by raising critical awareness in the midst of middle-class neighbourhoods like Garneau and Aspen Gardens. Good feminine citizens — cautious, worthy, and blameless — are defined in opposition to their risky sisters who, under the dictates of risk management, are blamed for the violence they experience. Yet taking up and making visible these race- and class-based ideologies that continue to ground dominant constructions of rape within a Sisterhood-like DIY campaign requires little more than a Sharpie, some paper, and some paste.[81]

Clearly, revitalizing feminist anti-rape politics involves much more than this, more than a few posters, more than raising consciousness neighbourhood by neighbourhood, more than localized guerilla feminist actions. But as we examine our arsenal of tactics and strategies, and even as we struggle to restore the power and influence of state-focused organizing, we might do well to keep these forms of defiant, direct action in the mix.

81 The original Garneau Sisterhood posters had an impressive longevity. I've been told that the best method for putting up posters with staying power is simple flour and water.

12.

Sisterhood Will Get Ya: Anti-rape Activism and the Criminal Justice System

Meagan Johnston

Meagan Johnston's paper builds on the work of Lise Gotell by proposing that the activism of the Garneau Sisterhood be read as an alternative legal order to the criminal justice system. She offers a detailed comparison of the premises, principles, and practices of these two legal orders in response to sexual assault. For example, returning to the justice system's skepticism about women's reports and police unfounding discussed by Fran Odette and Teresa DuBois, Meagan contrasts the Sisterhood's "rule" that follows from its understanding that rape is a widespread social phenomenon: women do not need to "prove" they were raped; they are simply believed. She demonstrates that the criminal justice system is woefully inadequate to the task of addressing sexual assault at every turn, from the way that police have narrowly interpreted their legal obligation to warn, established by Jane Doe, through to the systemic devaluation of Aboriginal women's bodies and lives, so eloquently described earlier by Marie Campbell, Priscilla Campeau, and Tracey Lindberg. The Sisterhood's legal order, Meagan argues, offers far more potential for social change.

The spectre of a serial rapist invading homes is terrifying. Women who are conditioned from a young age to monitor their behaviour to protect themselves from rape react strongly when they are faced with the prospect of being attacked in their most vulnerable moments — at home, sleeping, presumptively safe. In the summer of 2008, women in my Edmonton neighbourhood, the Garneau, were being attacked by a serial rapist. Newspaper headlines announced "Southside Sex Attack Makes Four,"[1] "New Crime Target,"[2] and "Neighbours on Alert after Sexual

1 Ben Gelinas, "Southside Sex Attack Makes Four; Police Link Similarities with Garneau Rape Suspect to Saturday Case 35 Blocks Away" *Edmonton Journal* (12 August 2008) online: www.canada.com/edmontonjournal/news/story.html?id=197418-c7e5 B1.

2 Victoria Handysides, "New Crime Target" *Metro Edmonton* (30 September 2008), online: <http://www.metro news.ca/edmonton/Local/article/119359>.

Assault."[3] These messages were manifestations of the fear many women in the largely student neighbourhood felt; friends were walking each other home, creating emergency plans, and making beds on couches so no one would be home alone.

After a few days, however, I began to notice the posters. They were brightly coloured photocopies of originals that had obviously been handwritten in marker. In flagrant disobedience of city bylaws, they were glued to lamp posts, to bus stop benches and shelters, to the sides of buildings, to fire hydrants and power boxes. Instead of fear, they talked about power. They warned, "Attention, rapist. We are watching you. We will find you," and "We are organizing to find you and we will." They announced, "If a woman is raped other women react. There is no such thing as an isolated attack on an individual woman.... When a sister is raped it is a rape of the sisterhood and cannot go unpunished! The sisterhood is watching!" And, triumphantly, one poster proudly stated, "Dear rapist: I am *not* changing *my* life because of a pathetic fuck like *you!*" Many were signed, "Love, the Sisterhood."

The posters were the work of a loose association of neighbourhood women that came to be known as the Garneau Sisterhood. Despite the group's cheesy name — or perhaps because of it — its members, who vehemently remained anonymous, directly challenged and subverted the way the criminal justice system conceptualizes and addresses rape. Through postering, media work, and the operation of an email address to collect tips and provide emotional support to women in the neighbourhood, the Sisterhood's work provides a poignant example of the importance of grassroots feminist responses to a crime that is increasingly being transformed "from an object of political contestation into an issue of criminal law, privatized, individualized, and depoliticized."[4]

The Garneau Sisterhood's work recalls the work of anti-rape activists in the 1970s and 1980s, when feminist responses to rape were based on "women taking action from a position of real or perceived power, either collective or individual."[5] Strategies were developed "by women for women," emphasized "individual or collective resistance," and so represented "unexpected examples of 'acting out' by those meant to

3 Emily Senger, "Neighbours on Alert After Sexual Assault; Nearly 450 Turn Out for Community Meeting Following Another Attack" *Edmonton Journal* (15 August 2008) B1.

4 Lise Gotell, "When Privacy Is Not Enough: Sexual Assault Complainants, Sexual History Evidence and the Disclosure of Personal Records" (2005–06) 43 Alta L Rev 743 at 753.

5 Nora West, "Rape in the Criminal Law and the Victim's Tort Alternative: A Feminist Analysis" (1992) 50 UT Fac L Rev 96 at 98.

have been silenced and made passive by victimization."[6] Feminists argued that rape included much more than isolated incidents of violence — as a manifestation of sexual inequality, rape was a pervasive epidemic.[7] This feminist anti-rape movement gave birth to a wide array of activist work, from Take Back the Night marches to self-defence classes, from sexual assault centres and hotlines to campaigns on rape awareness. Much of this activism took place outside the criminal justice system; indeed, many feminists scorned any engagement with the courts, as it was seen as more important for women to take rape into their own hands.

The criminal justice system and the Garneau Sisterhood can be considered two separate legal orders. Each order purports to have a solution to rape; however, each uses different substantive and procedural rules, and each rests on a distinct set of guiding principles. By juxtaposing the Garneau Sisterhood's proposed legal order with the legal order of the criminal justice system, I expose the criminal law's fundamental inability to deal with rape as a social phenomenon. In this paper, I will explore the ways in which members of the Sisterhood are caught between the two legal orders, and investigate the tension that arises from this relationship. This tension produces a space for sharp critique of the criminal justice system. It is tempting to see the Sisterhood's work as a supplement to the criminal justice system, filling in the gaps where the criminal justice system cannot adequately respond and providing a more "well-rounded" response to rape, one that is more in line with feminist principles. It is also tempting to view the criminal justice system as a small but necessary part of a broad and complex feminist anti-rape strategy. The most radical reading of the Sisterhood's work, and the one that I want to promote here, is a reading that analyzes the way that the criminal justice system is fundamentally at odds with a feminist anti-rape analysis. By considering each response as a legal order unto itself, I can compare them more closely, each on its own terms. Considering the Sisterhood's work as a legal order can also imbue it with a legitimacy that makes its critique of the criminal justice system harder to ignore.

Legal pluralism offers a productive way to map the complex and nuanced relationship between these two orders. Some theorists hold that multiple legal orders always exist in a hierarchy, with state law at the top subsuming all legal orders beneath it. I resist this reading of legal pluralism — arguing instead that different legal orders cannot be conceived

6 *Ibid* at 109.

7 *Ibid* at 97.

of in a neat hierarchy, but instead are tightly interwoven. The relationship between different legal orders is constantly shifting according to the experience of the legal subject who navigates between them. The result is a productive tension between legal orders — a tension here that results in feminist critique of the criminal justice system's approach to rape, while also offering women in the Garneau neighbourhood the opportunity to directly rearticulate anti-rape strategies.

To state that the criminal justice system is a legal order seems embarrassingly obvious. The status of the Garneau Sisterhood as a legal order, however, is more tenuous. Through its work to engage with rape on its own terms, the Garneau Sisterhood can be read as creating its own legal order with its own substantive content, procedural rules, and ideology. To state that the Sisterhood constitutes a legal order may not reflect how group members came to see themselves, or the work of their organization. Indeed, some Sisters could argue that to describe their work as the creation of a new legal order detracts from its grassroots potential. I do not wish to suggest that the Garneau Sisterhood's work *is* a legal order — but rather, I am arguing that it can be *read* as a legal order, and that such a reading permits the most complete articulation of the Garneau Sisterhood's critique of the way the criminal justice system deals with rape, and its efforts to promote a more feminist response to the Garneau rapist.

I will begin my analysis by engaging with models of legal pluralism to highlight the "pervasive plurality" of law, which creates a state of "internormativity," or "interlegality" for the Garneau Sisters. Once the members of the Sisterhood are situated within this theoretical framework, I will describe each legal order on the basis of its substantive rules, procedural rules, and fundamental principles. I will then use this description to evaluate how each order can respond to rape, ultimately concluding that the Garneau Sisterhood's order does much more to address the specificities of rape than the criminal justice system. Finally, I will consider particular examples of the way members of the Sisterhood navigate between the two legal orders. I will consider examples of collaboration between the Sisterhood and the criminal justice system, and then examine the tension and critique that emerges from these relationships.

LEGAL PLURALISM & CREATIVE LEGAL SUBJECTS: FRAMING THE SISTERHOOD

Broadly speaking, legal pluralism describes situations where "two or more legal systems coexist in the same social field."[8] Legal pluralists seek to look beyond the "traditional image of lawyer's law," which limits its recognition of law to "those forms, processes and institutions of normative ordering that find their origins and legitimacy in the political state or its emanations."[9] Legal pluralism challenges conventional accounts of law by maintaining "the existence and circulation in society of different legal systems."[10] In so doing, it illuminates the complexity of the relationship between law and society, "since there is not one single law, but a network of laws."[11]

As a framing device, legal pluralism is particularly well-situated to consider the relationship between the criminal justice system and the Garneau Sisterhood. The idea of legal pluralism emerged from observation of the interaction between indigenous and colonial legal systems in colonial societies.[12] Theorists extended this early analysis to document "forms of local legality in rural areas, [and] in marginalized urban sectors."[13] Legal pluralism came to provide a framework to analyze the "relations between dominant and subordinate groups such as religious, ethnic or cultural minorities, immigrant groups and unofficial forms of ordering located in social networks or institutions."[14] Legal pluralism thus emerged in a context of negotiation between imposed state law and the rules, customs, and norms that mapped more closely onto individuals' and groups' own worldviews.

Over the last twenty years, legal pluralism has expanded significantly beyond its original focus on dual and parallel legal orders. It now signals the "pervasive pluralism in law" — that is, legal pluralism is not a specific feature of particular societies, but a feature of law itself.[15] There is a "diversity of norms, processes and institutions within

8 Sally Engle Merry, "Legal Pluralism" (1988) 22 Law & Soc'y Rev 869 at 870.

9 Martha-Marie Kleinhans & Roderick A Macdonald, "What is a *Critical* Legal Pluralism?" (1997) 14 CJLS 25 at 27.

10 Boaventura De Sousa Santos, "Law: A Map of Misreading. Toward a Postmodern Conception of Law" (1987) 14 JL & Soc'y 280 at 280.

11 *Ibid.*

12 Franz von Benda-Beckmann, "Who's Afraid of Legal Pluralism?" (2002) 47 J Legal Pluralism & Unofficial L 37 at 60.

13 De Sousa Santos, *supra* note 10 at 287.

14 Merry, *supra* note 8 at 872–73.

15 Kleinhans & Macdonald, *supra* note 9 at 31.

any given normative system within any particular legal order."[16] This pervasive plurality recognizes that families, socio-cultural communities, neighbourhoods, and an "almost infinite variety of other sites of human interaction" are experienced as "sites of regulation," and thus all normative interaction between them must be plural as well.[17] De Sousa Santos argues that this plurality represents a "porous legality" as "multiple networks of legal orders [force] us into constant transitions and trespassings."[18] Our "legal life" is one of interlegality, and we constantly experience an "uneven and unstable mixing of legal codes."[19]

I do not wish to locate the Garneau Sisterhood in a particular spot on a hierarchy with regards to the "hard law" of the criminal justice system. I am not referring to a pluralism that conceives different legal orders as "separate entities co-existing in the same political space."[20] The postmodern thread of legal pluralism that most effectively captures the complexities of the Garneau Sisterhood's relationship to the criminal justice system, as it describes a conception of different legal spaces as "superimposed, interpenetrated, and mixed in our minds as much as in our action."[21] Aspects of the Garneau Sisterhood operate as a parallel alternative to the criminal justice system at the same time as aspects of its work operate to critique this system. It is this complexity, this tension, which makes the work of the Garneau Sisterhood so profoundly radical: it is a legal order that empowers women in the neighbourhood by directly addressing rape from a feminist perspective, thus starkly exposing the criminal justice system's failings.

The risk of this new legal pluralism, of course, is that it threatens to subsume all forms of social control under an overly broad definition of what is law.[22] To argue that the Garneau Sisterhood created law, for example, could be to widen the category of "law" so far as to make it meaningless. This argument, however, is based on a rigid understanding of law as a specific domain of social organization.[23] Instead, legal pluralists argue that law is merely a "dimension" of social life, a "system

16 *Ibid* at 32.

17 *Ibid.*

18 De Sousa Santos, *supra* note 10 at 298.

19 *Ibid.*

20 *Ibid* at 297.

21 *Ibid.*

22 Merry, *supra* note 8 at 870.

23 von Benda-Beckmann, *supra* note 12 at 48.

of meanings, a cultural code for interpreting the world."[24] Rather than focusing on what law is, this broad view focuses on the many functions law serves, including "social control, conflict regulation, securing expectations, social regulation, coordination of behaviour, or disciplining bodies and souls."[25] The Garneau Sisterhood provides social control by creating an empowering counterpoint to the police discourse of fear. The Sisterhood rearticulates the conflict between the rapist and the survivors of his attacks, and coordinates the behaviour of women in the neighbourhood who might otherwise have simply reacted with fear. As a cultural code for interpreting the world, the Garneau Sisterhood inserts feminist discourse into public space, providing women with relief from the mainstream chorus of fear and risk management. The Sisterhood literally put its message onto lampposts, mailboxes, bus benches, and fire hydrants, thereby providing an alternative way of interpreting the events surrounding the attacks by the Garneau rapist.

The members of the Garneau Sisterhood play a vital role in maintaining the nuanced relationship between the two legal orders. They epitomized Kleinhans and Macdonald's portrait of the legal subjects of critical legal pluralism, who are "heterogeneous/multiple creatures" with a "transformative capacity that enables them to produce legal knowledge and to fashion the very structures of law that contribute to constituting their legal subjectivity."[26] These legal subjects are "law-inventing, and not merely law-abiding."[27] They possess not only the capacity, but the "responsibility to participate in the multiple normative communities by which they recognize and create their own legal subjectivity."[28] Finally, these (critical) legal pluralist subjects show "an element of construction or creativity ... when they are confronted with internormative conflicts."[29]

The Garneau Sisters fulfill this responsibility by creating and maintaining a legal order that responds to their own feminist vision of what a truly transformative response to rape looks like. They participate in the criminal justice system to a certain extent, critiqued it to a certain extent, and finally provided alternatives to it. They were at once subjects

24 *Ibid* at 48. Merry, *supra* note 8 at 886.

25 Gunther Teubner, "The Two Faces of Janus: Rethinking Legal Pluralism" (1991–92) 13 Cardozo L Rev 1443 at 1451.

26 Kleinhans & Macdonald, *supra* note 9 at 38.

27 *Ibid* at 39.

28 *Ibid* at 38.

29 *Ibid* at 44.

of the criminal justice system, its creators, and its outsiders. The attacks of the Garneau Rapist presented members of the community with a vital internormative conflict between the criminal justice system's response to rape, and feminist analyses as to the nature, cause, and appropriate solution to rape.

Community members responded to this normative conflict by creating their own legal order, one that they saw as more responsive to the conflict in their own neighbourhood. It is this multiplicity, this complexity, and this nuance that is revealed by the legal pluralist framework. It is within this framework that I will examine each of these legal frameworks.

SKETCHING THE LEGAL ORDERS

To explore the relationship between the two legal orders, I will consider the substantive content, procedural rules, and then the ideological foundations of each order in turn. This comparative examination is vital to understanding the way these two orders work together and challenge each other. This examination shows how the neutrality and formal rules of the criminal justice system cannot respond to rape in the same way as the subjective and informal rules of the Garneau Sisterhood's legal order. The Sisterhood's emphasis on the experience of survivors and the widespread gendered impact of rape provides the structure for empowering grassroots anti-rape activism.

1. Substantive Rules

(a) What is rape?

In the criminal justice system, rape refers to a particular category of incidents of individual violence. Canadian jurisprudence defines sexual assault as "an assault committed in circumstances of a sexual nature so as to violate the sexual integrity of the complainant."[30] For a rape to merit the attention of the criminal justice system, however, it must constitute an offence under the *Criminal Code* of Canada. The *Criminal Code* currently recognizes three "levels" of sexual assault: "simple" sexual assault,[31] sexual assault causing bodily harm or accompanied by threats of bodily harm,[32] and aggravated sexual assault.[33] Simple sex-

30 Renu Mandhane, "Efficiency or Autonomy? Economic and Feminist Legal Theory in the Context of Sexual Assault" (2001) 59 UT Fac L Rev 173 at 175.

31 *Criminal Code*, RSC 1985, C-46 at s 271.

32 *Ibid* at s 272.

33 *Ibid* at s 273.

ual assault is a hybrid offence, and can thus be punished either on summary conviction or on indictment, with maximum sentences of eighteen months if pursued on the former, and up to ten years if pursued on the latter.[34] Sexual assault causing bodily harm is an indictable offence with a maximum sentence of fourteen years. Aggravated sexual assault is the most severe offence, referring to sexual assaults where the offender "wounds, maims, disfigures or endangers the life of the complainant" and carries the possibility of life imprisonment.[35] Beyond these provisions, however, the *Criminal Code* does not specifically define sexual assault; jurisprudence has simply referred to the definition of assault in s 265, which states that "a person commits assault when without the consent of another person, he applies force intentionally to that person, directly or indirectly."[36]

As with any other crime, sexual assault has two components: the *actus reus* and the *mens rea*. The *actus reus* of sexual assault is "established by proof of three elements: (i) touching, (ii) sexual nature of the contact, and (iii) the absence of consent."[37] The first two elements are objective; the third is subjective, and is to be determined "by reference to the complainant's subjective internal state of mind towards the touching, at the time that it occurred."[38] The *mens rea* of sexual assault has two elements: (i) the intention to touch and (ii) "knowing of, or being reckless of or willfully blind to, a lack of consent on the part of the person touched."[39]

The defining factor in the criminal justice system's designation of a particular event as a sexual assault is consent. Consent is defined as the "voluntary agreement of the complainant to engage in the sexual activity in question."[40] When first considered as part of the *actus reus* of sexual assault, consent is "subjectively determined from the perspective of the complainant."[41] When considering the *mens rea* of sexual assault, however, courts consider consent from the perspective of the accused — that is, courts ask whether the accused knew of, was reckless

34 *Ibid* at s 271.

35 *Ibid* at s 273.

36 *Ibid* at s 265; *R v Ewanchuk* [1999] 1 SCR 330 at para 24, (1999) 169 DLR (4th) 193. Mandhane, *supra* note 30 at 181.

37 *Ewanchuk, ibid* at para 25.

38 *Ibid* at para 26.

39 *Ibid* at para 41.

40 *Criminal Code, supra* note 31 at s 273.1.

41 Mandhane, *supra* note 30 at 184.

of, or wilfully blind to a lack of consent on the part of the complainant. The *Code* elaborates several circumstances in which no consent can be obtained: these include situations where a person other than the complainant expresses agreement,[42] the complainant is incapable of consenting,[43] the accused has induced agreement through abuse of a position of authority,[44] or when the complainant has expressed her lack of agreement to a particular "activity"[45] or to continuing with activities in progress.[46]

Defences based on consent do, of course, exist. In *Ewanchuk*, the Supreme Court of Canada held that "since sexual assault only becomes a crime in the absence of the complainant's consent, the common law recognizes a defence of mistake of fact which removes culpability for those who honestly but mistakenly believed that they had consent to touch the complainant."[47] Use of this defence, however, is limited. The accused must show that he took "reasonable steps … to ascertain that the complainant was consenting" in the circumstances known to the accused at the time.[48] Currently, "the belief that silence or passivity is indicative of consent is a mistake of law" and the accused must have taken "reasonable steps to ascertain consent — given the circumstances known to him at the time" before he can argue that there was mistaken belief in consent.[49] If the prosecution manages to show that the complainant did not consent, and that the accused did not have an honest but mistaken belief in consent, then the legal system will recognize the event as a sexual assault and find the accused guilty.

For the Garneau Sisterhood, rape is a social phenomenon. It is much more important to identify the systemic problem of rape than to articulate a definition of rape that could help assess whether a particular incident qualifies as rape. The Sisterhood thus use a much looser definition of what rape is. Some posters cite the *Criminal Code* definition of sexual assault as "any form of sexual contact without voluntary consent,"[50] and the Sisterhood's first public statement specifies that sexual assault

42 *Criminal Code*, *supra* note 31 at s 273.1(2)(a).

43 *Ibid* at s 273.1(2)(b).

44 *Ibid* at s 273.1(2)(c).

45 *Ibid* at s 273.1(2)(d).

46 *Ibid* at s 273.1(2)(e).

47 *Ewanchuk*, *supra* note 36 at para 42.

48 *Criminal Code*, *supra* note 31 at s 273.2(b).

49 Mandhane, *supra* note 30 at 184, 188, citing *Ewanchuk*, *supra* note 36.

50 Poster; image on file with author.

included "situations where consent is obtained through pressure, coercion, force, or threats of force."[51] These attempts at definition are much less detailed than those found in the *Criminal Code*. For the Sisterhood, it is much more important to recognize the "astounding prevalence of rape in our culture." Posters and public statements urges people to "truly take a moment to let it sink in that one in four women, and one in eight men, will experience sexual assault in their lifetime."[52] For the Sisterhood, rape is one tool in a "toxic society" where "sex and violence are conflated," and "male violence is accepted, even encouraged."[53]

(b) What is the legal order's threshold for recognizing that a rape has occurred?

For the criminal justice system to recognize that a rape has occurred, the charge must be proved "beyond a reasonable doubt." This is the highest standard of proof in law — higher than either "reasonable probability" or the "balance of probabilities" required in civil law cases. This high standard is deemed necessary by the criminal law because the possibility of imprisonment threatens the liberty interest of the accused. This standard of proof can be very difficult to achieve, as it necessitates significant amounts of evidence and testimony. Due to the nature of the crime, many sexual assaults happen in private, without any witnesses except for the complainant and the accused. As such, many sexual assault trials rely almost entirely on the judge's assessment of the credibility of the complainant.

The Garneau Sisterhood has no corresponding "threshold" for recognizing that a rape has occurred; if someone claims to have been sexually assaulted, the Sisterhood believes her. Individual accounts of rape do not have to be measured against some standard of truth and accountability — they are accepted at face value. The only principle setting out any kind of "threshold" for recognizing rape is the importance of centering the accounts of people who had been sexually assaulted. This low threshold is closely linked to the Sisterhood's definition of rape. If rape is a social phenomenon, then survivors can be easily believed, as there is no need to "prove" the individual instance of rape and establish the guilt of individual rapists.

51 Garneau Sisterhood, "Garneau Sisterhood Organizing in Response to Sexual Assaults" *Vue Weekly* (12 June 2008), online: <http://www.vueweekly.com/article.php?id=8743>.

52 *Ibid.*

53 *Ibid.*

(c) Who can be raped?

The criminal justice system's use of gender-neutral and non-specific terms in the codification of sexual assault offences emphasizes that anyone can be raped. This neutrality has not always been in place — for example, the *Criminal Code*'s definition of rape excluded "forced sexual acts that occurred within the context of marriage" until 1983.[54]

The Garneau Sisterhood also holds that anyone can be a victim of sexual assault. Where the criminal law is gender-neutral, however, the Sisterhood explicitly acknowledged the gendered dimensions of sexual assault. Posters and public statements emphasized the gender disparity between men who will experience sexual assault (1 in 8), and women (1 in 4). Posters also called attention to the fact that "98% of sexual assaults are perpetrated by heterosexual men."[55]

(d) Who does rape affect?

According to the criminal justice system's story of itself, the system recognizes that rape affects the broader "public interest" in addition to the particular individual complainant. At trial, the Crown is charged with serving both of these interests. By vigorously prosecuting criminals, the Crown fulfills the public's interest in deterring future crimes and maintaining confidence in the administration of justice and the rule of law. The Crown represents the complainant's interest by ensuring her rapist is punished and his actions are condemned by the criminal justice system. This conception of the complainant's interests, however, is narrow. Once the trial has begun, the complainant is reduced to one witness among many on the Crown's roster. She may be able to submit a victim impact statement detailing the ways that the accused's attack affected her; however, this right is not guaranteed. If the Crown wins, her rapist will be punished, but the criminal justice system does not provide for an award of damages that could, for example, cover counselling services for a woman who has been raped.

The Garneau Sisterhood, on the other hand, consistently emphasizes how rape affects everyone, not just individual women in isolated incidents. The Sisterhood's first newspaper states that the "trauma" from the Garneau rapes was "psychologically oppressing an entire community of women."[56] A poster in the neighbourhood posited, "if a woman is

54 Janice Du Mont, "Charging and Sentencing in Sexual Assault Cases: An Exploratory Examination" (2003) 15 CJWL 305 at 310.

55 Poster; image on file with author.

56 Sisterhood, "Organizing," *supra* note 51.

raped, other women react. We understand that there is no such thing as an isolated attack on an individual woman. All women are us. When a sister is raped, it is a rape of the sisterhood and cannot go unpunished. The Sisterhood is watching!" For the Sisters, "no one feels 'lucky' that it was 'some other woman' who got raped. There is no such thing as 'some other woman' when you have compassion and love for yourself."[57] This legal order views the question of "who crime affects" more broadly, and focuses on the role of crime in the community instead of the particular relationship between the accused, the complainant, and the public interest in upholding the justice system.

2. Procedural Rules

(a) How does the legal order recognize a rape?

The criminal justice system recognizes rape through the police investigation process and the results of a criminal trial. Rape enters the criminal justice system when a person who has been raped reports the incident to the police. The particulars of the investigation will differ — in some cases, police officers will visit the scene of the crime, a medical report ("rape kit") may be completed, or the complainant may simply recount her story to the police. The police will then evaluate the complainant's credibility. If they believe her story, they will proceed to gather further evidence. If the police have sufficient evidence, they will arrest the accused. Once arrested, the police will lay charges against the accused under the appropriate section of the *Criminal Code*. The case will then proceed to trial, carried by the Crown prosecutor.

At trial, the case is cast as an issue between the state and the accused. Lise Gotell outlines how "constructed as a crime, the 'reality' of rape (that is, whether or not a set of events can properly be called rape) can only be discerned through the rigorous applications of legal method."[58] This involves "careful consideration of all 'relevant evidence' [and] an adversarial confrontation between the defence attorney and the crown prosecutor."[59] This process is necessary for judges to be able to arrive at the "truth of the matter at hand — a determination of the guilt or innocence of the accused beyond a reasonable doubt."[60] It is only once this

57 *Ibid.*

58 Lise Gotell, "The Ideal Victim, The Hysterical Complainant and the Disclosure of Confidential Records: The Implications of the Charter for Sexual Assault Law" (2002) 40 Osgoode Hall LJ 251 at 258.

59 *Ibid.*

60 *Ibid.*

standard of "beyond a reasonable doubt" has been met and the accused declared guilty that the criminal justice system officially recognizes that a rape has occurred.

The Garneau Sisterhood's legal order has no such formal procedure for "recognizing" rape. Indeed, to institute such a set of procedures would be antithetical to the Sisterhood's focus on believing survivors. The Sisterhood's recognition of rape takes place through media reports, and more importantly through messages sent to its email account, where neighbourhood residents sent in accounts of peeping toms, suspicious tenants in their building, and threatening encounters with men in the neighbourhood. The Sisterhood sent a message to each person who sent in a tip or a story reassuring them that the Sisterhood believed them.

(b) Who decides whether or not a rape has occurred?

The criminal justice system restricts the authority to decide whether or not a rape has occurred to particular individuals. Police officers evaluate whether or not they believe the complainant's story and wish to press charges. The Crown will then evaluate whether they have enough evidence to proceed to trial. If the Crown prosecutor does not have enough evidence, or doubts the complainant's credibility, the prosecutor will often attempt to negotiate with the accused for a plea bargain. While this may result in a guilty plea to a lesser charge and subsequent "punishment" for the accused, it also means that the complainant's story will never be heard to the courtroom, and that the legal system will minimize how it has occurred. In rendering their decisions, judges make the penultimate decision as to whether or not a rape has occurred in law.

The Garneau Sisterhood's broad definition of rape and emphasis on believing survivors' accounts of rape means that members of the Sisterhood do not have to decide whether or not a rape has occurred. There was no need to grant particular individuals the power to determine whether or not a particular instance was indeed a rape. Instead, decisions made in this legal order centers on the question of what should be done to prevent future rapes from occurring. In this sense, there are two levels of decision-making: decisions made within the more formal membership of the Sisterhood, and decisions about how to address rape made by members of the community at large. Neither of these types of decisions require the "fact-finding" necessary to support a finding of rape by the criminal justice system. Instead, they either assume the facts or leave the fact-finding to the individual who claims a rape had occurred. This assumption is a logical extension of the Sisterhood's definition of rape as a social phenomenon.

(c) What rules decide whether or not a rape has occurred?

In the criminal justice system, the rules of fundamental justice govern decisions on whether or not a rape has occurred. Many principles of fundamental justice have been codified as part of the *Charter of Rights and Freedoms,* and include the right to remain silent, the right to counsel, and the right to a fair trial within a reasonable delay. The accused also has the right "to be presumed innocent until proven guilty according in a fair and public hearing."[61] This is usually interpreted to mean that the accused has the right to know all the evidence against him and present a full defence. In sexual assault cases, this principle has been used in the past to attack the complainant's credibility by bringing her sexual history as evidence that she consented to the sexual activity in question. More recently, the defence has worked to introduce third-party evidence, such as the complainant's counselling records, into the court to poke holes in the complainant's testimony or impeach her credibility.

While the rules of the criminal justice system are meant to protect the rights of the accused, they give little thought to the larger social context in which rape occurs. The Garneau Sisterhood's analysis gives precedence to this broader social context of rape culture. There are thus no formalized rules for "deciding" whether or not a rape occurred.

3. Fundamental Principles

Having sketched the substantive and procedural workings of each legal system, I now consider the principles that underpin each order. These fundamental principles most clearly illustrate the stark differences between the two legal orders.

(a) Objectivity/subjectivity

Objectivity is a key principle of the criminal justice system. The criminal justice system's role is to arrive at the legal truth of a matter by dispassionately weighing the facts to determine the guilt or innocence of the accused. This need to arrive at an objective perception of "truth" is the reason why the criminal justice system has so many "steps" before arriving at a conviction. A woman's story of sexual assault may be unique, but for it to be recognized by the legal system, it must be meas-

61 *Constitution Act, 1982*, s 11(d).

ured against the objective standards of the *Criminal Code*'s definition of the offence, and then tried by a neutral and impartial judge. As Gotell summarizes, "the rape trial is an abstracted exercise of logic unrelated to the context of sexual interactions and the complainant's own account of her violation. Courtroom scene and [legal] language create an image of law as separating out the "truth" from the hysteria of the victim."[62]

The Garneau Sisterhood, on the other hand, rejects this objectivity in favour of a subjective analysis of rape. This is the natural progression from the Sisterhood's emphasis on believing survivors and empowering community members to take action in whatever way they see fit. To submit incidents of rape to the objective legal framework of sexual assault is to remove experiences of rape from those who are survivors of this crime. This analysis is partially inspired by feminist standpoint theory, which argues that women are the experts of their own experience, and so are best placed to both speak about this experience and create responses to it.

The Garneau Sisterhood emphasizes this "subjective" analysis by encouraging people to respond to the attacks in whatever way they felt was most appropriate. The Sisterhood also nurtures a discourse in which people could create their own definition of rape. In response to an email challenging the group's use of the term "rape," one member wrote, "How do you define rape? Do you strongly differentiate it from sexual assault? Do you feel that we have misrepresented whatever information is currently known about these crimes?"[63] The email emphasized how "the individual crimes that took place may be called sexual assaults by the media ... but [the use of] the term rape on the signs was a sentiment that came from women in the community ... those feelings should not be silenced."[64] Instead of citing an "authoritative" or objective definition of rape, the Sisterhood encourages people to think about what they consider rape, how they name rape, the terms they use — and to think about how the act of defining rape could silence the experience of others. Indeed, these subjective and multiple "tellings" of rape explode the silencing inherent in the criminal justice system's attempts to set out a singular and comprehensive definition of rape.

(b) The appropriate site to address rape

The criminal justice system sees itself as an appropriate mediator between perpetrators and victims. Police protect people by patrolling

62 Gotell, "Ideal Victim," *supra* note 58 at 258.

63 Email correspondence (21 June 2008), on file with author.

64 *Ibid.*

neighbourhoods and catching criminals; those perpetrators caught will then see their fate determined by the objective standards of the criminal trial. The criminal justice system does not see a need for any kind of direct action between complainants and their rapists — indeed, this would be highly undesirable. The rights of the accused can only be infringed if their guilt has been proven beyond a reasonable doubt. As one feminist puts it, "in a traditional patriarchal society such as ours, the first articulated response to fear is to protect the women and children. The good ones anyways. The only way to do that, they say, is to increase police presence, to build more prisons and to enact harsher sentencing."[65] Developments such as the emergent victims' rights movement of recent years fail to modify this principle. Indeed, they strengthen it, by enlisting victims of crimes in the project of legitimizing the criminal justice system as the societal actor best equipped to deal with rape.

The Garneau Sisterhood vehemently disagrees with the criminal justice system's image as the best site to address rape. The Sisterhood continually states that the issue was not just about catching rapists — it was about preventing rape and rearticulating public space. When police and the media accused the group's posters of being "threatening" and warned against "vigilanteeism [*sic*] where the public is going after or targeting or finding their own suspects,"[66] they missed the point entirely. The Garneau rapist put a spotlight on sexual assault in the neighbourhood, but his actions only represented a tiny part of the spectrum of rape in the Garneau. The group did not focus its energies on catching this one perpetrator, but on situating him in a spectrum of perpetrators.

The Sisterhood's posters suggest that women could channel their fear into anger. They could do more than simply lock their doors and their windows. They could assert, in the words of one poster, "I am *not* changing *my* life because of a pathetic fuck like *you*!"[67] They could focus on their own power: "Attention rapist: we are organizing to find you and we will." They could take comfort in the fact that "a lot of brilliant women all thinking about the same thing at the same time is very powerful. We do not have to blame ourselves or quietly accept this violent reality."[68]

65 Jane Doe, *The Story of Jane Doe: A Book About Rape* (Toronto: Random House, 2003) at 324 [*The Story of Jane Doe*].

66 Gelinas, *supra* note 1.

67 Poster; on file with author.

68 Sisterhood, "Organizing," *supra* note 51.

All of these reactions take place outside of the criminal justice system. They can only take place in a legal order that is not governed by the tangle of procedural and substantive rules that must be followed for the criminal justice system to recognize rape. They must take place in a legal order that is focused on preventing rape, not punishing rapists. They grow in a legal order with a broad definition of rape, one that believes survivors and centres their accounts of their experience. They are nurtured by an analysis that sees rape prevention as everyone's responsibility, and that encourages each member of the community to take action as they see fit. The Garneau Sisterhood's legal order permits a much richer and broader understanding set of strategies for rape prevention. This set of strategies makes the suggestion that the criminal justice system is an appropriate site for addressing rape seem farcical.

(c) Justice in the context of rape

The criminal justice system sees two aspects to justice in the context of rape. Firstly, on a micro level, the criminal justice system's goal is to identify and punish individual perpetrators of sexual assault. Sexual assault is treated as any other crime, with a victim and a perpetrator for each incident. There is little recognition of the systemic prevalence of sexual assault or its gendered nature. For victims, justice is served when their rapists are found guilty and punished. Justice is also served for the broader public: as each accused is tried by the same procedural rules and by the same substantive definitions of rape, the public can be confident in the impartial administration of justice. In this sense, then, the public's need for justice is served regardless of the actual substantive outcome of a case.

Second, on a broader level, the criminal justice system sees its task as punishing rapists. According to the criminal law, it is the threat of punishment that prevents people from committing crimes. In this view, crime prevention relies heavily on the justice system's ability to locate criminals, try them, and punish them if they are found guilty. As the criminal justice system's energy is dedicated to the pursuit of individual perpetrators, all other aspects of rape prevention become the responsibility of community members. In the Garneau neighbourhood, police issued warnings but only provided minimal information, citing fears of jeopardizing the investigation by releasing too much. Here, "catching" the rapist in the hopes of punishing him took precedence over any need to provide women with concrete information that could help them protect themselves.

The Garneau Sisterhood's legal order challenges both of these principles. As mentioned above, the Sisterhood's goals are to expose rape culture and reclaim safe spaces for the women in their communities. The Sisterhood uses the Garneau attacks as a point of entry to discuss the larger climate of violence that makes these kinds of incidents possible. The group repeated its message over and over: "rape is not 'something that happens' to women," "it is not because of: clothing, drinking, locked doors, 'assertiveness' — rape happens because of rapists!"[69]

The Sisterhood also uses this argument to challenge the police force's emphasis that women were responsible for protecting themselves from rape. Police attempts at rape prevention were limited to trite warnings for women to lock their doors and windows. The Sisterhood vehemently protested, arguing that "telling me to lock my door does not make me safe" and pointing out that "it's probably safe to say that most women in this city already lock their doors on a regular basis."[70] Instead of providing women with vague warnings that were unlikely to make a significant change, the Sisterhood's legal order rests on the principle that women's behaviour is not a relevant factor when dealing with sexual assault.

4. Evaluating the Legal Orders

By considering the specifics of the different rules and principles underpinning each legal order, we can see how the Garneau Sisterhood challenges virtually every aspect of the criminal justice system's response to rape. Each order recognizes and deals with sexual assault in a particular way based on its goals, features, and function. Mapping the different rules and principles underpinning each order allows us to see how each system achieves the functions of social control, conflict regulation, securing expectations, social regulation, and coordinating behaviour. A closer comparison, however, allows us to see how the Garneau Sisterhood is much more effectively equipped to deal with rape and its consequences in a way that centres the accounts of survivors and empowers a myriad of community responses to rape. This comparison reveals that by using a broad conception of what rape "is," the Garneau Sisterhood sidesteps formal procedural rules and is able to centre the accounts of survivors and focus on grassroots community responses and rape prevention.

(a) Substantive rules

By refusing to set out specific categories of rape, the Garneau Sisterhood permits both a greater variety of survivor discourse and a broad-

69 Posters, images on file with author.

70 Garneau Sisterhood, press release; on file with author.

er public discussion about the nature and prevalence of rape. The lack of categories responds to the feminist argument that "the harm that's done by rape is the same," "whether it's a strange man with a knife, your boss, boyfriend, or doctor."[71] This opens up space for "survivors' discourse [that] exceeds legal discourse in important ways, [thus] reflecting the non-legal conception of rape that describes feelings of violation and is not bound to the nature of the act."[72] By forgoing a systematic definition of what rape is, the Sisterhood challenges the taxonomizing instinct of law, just as "in the early 1970s, feminist activists in the anti-rape movement named the problem of sexual violence in a different way; they claimed that it was not a personal, individual problem, but instead a systemic political problem."[73]

By focusing on the prevalence of rape, the Sisterhood sidesteps the need to "prove" rape. Rape is not episodic, but systematic and engrained in our culture, so it is safe to believe survivors' accounts. The high threshold of "beyond a reasonable doubt" is unnecessary and antithetical to the Sisterhood's objectives. One of these goals is to provoke public discussion about sexual assault. Once we start talking about sexual assault, the Sisters hold, "more people will come forward and feel believed. Through this we will break the silence and stop perpetrators from thinking they can get away with it."[74] Again, because the Sisterhood comes from a place that recognizes the prevalence of rape, it can focus on providing a supportive environment for the vast numbers of sexual assault cases that are unreported. The Sisterhood thus provides a welcome contrast to the criminal justice system's high standard of "beyond a reasonable doubt."

Both the Sisterhood and the criminal law purport to believe that "anyone can be raped." Feminists, however, have long critiqued the criminal law for its use of rape myths — fallacies and misunderstandings about the nature of rape that implicitly shape which sexual assaults will be recognized as crimes in Canadian law. In the words of L'Heureux-Dubé J in *R v Seaboyer*, "sexual assault is not like any other crime. More than any other offence it is informed by mythologies as to who the ideal rape victim and the ideal rape assailant are."[75] Rape myths also "codify what is seen as 'legitimate' or 'real' sexual victimiza-

71 *The Story of Jane Doe*, *supra* note 65 at 114.

72 Gotell, "Ideal Victim," *supra* note 58 at 259.

73 Gotell, "Privacy," *supra* note 4 at 750.

74 Sisterhood, press release, *supra* note 70.

75 *R v Seaboyer; R v Gayme* [1991] 2 SCR 577 at para 84, (1991) 83 DLR (4th) 193.

tion (for example forced intercourse by a stranger resulting in physical injuries)."[76] Rape myths continue to influence all levels of the criminal justice system, from police screening practices, to court processes, to overall rates of conviction.[77] In *Ewanchuk*, L'Heureux-Dubé J cited examples of the way rape myths work:

> Myths of rape include the views that women fantasise about being rape victims; that women mean 'yes' even when they say 'no'; that any woman could successfully resist a rapist if she really wished to; that the sexually experienced do not suffer harms when raped (or at least suffer lesser harms than the sexually 'innocent'); that women often deserve to be raped on account of their conduct, dress, and demeanour; that rape by a stranger is worse than one by an acquaintance.[78]

These words in *Seaboyer* echoed L'Heureux-Dubé J's earlier statements in *R v Osolin*, where she said that rape myths suggest that:

> [w]omen by their behaviour or appearance may be responsible for the occurrence of sexual assault. They suggest that drug use or dependence on social assistance are relevant to the issue of credibility as to consent .... Furthermore, they are built on the suggestion that ... victims in many, if not most sexual assault trials, are inclined to lie about sexual assault.[79]

Through the operation of these rape myths, the law contrasts images of the "good victim — the virtuous, white, middle-class woman assaulted by a stranger in her home" against those of "the 'suspect' victim who is sexually experienced and dares to venture outside after dark."[80]

Despite several high-profile Supreme Court cases, such as *Ewanchuk*, that recognized the existence of rape myths and worked to counteract them, courts still rely on an "ideal victim" when they evaluate the question of whether an individual woman has been raped. Lise Gotell has written extensively about what she terms "neo-liberal sexual citizenship," arguing that "if once the ideal victim was characterized by her chastity and sexual morality, the new ideal victim is consistent,

76 Du Mont, *supra* note 54 at 309.

77 *Ibid* at 311.

78 D Archard, *Sexual Consent* (1998), cited in *R v Ewanchuk*, *supra* note 36 at para 82.

79 *R v Osolin*, [1993] 4 SCR 595.

80 Lynn A Iding, "Crossing the Line: The Case for Limiting Personal Cross-Examination by an Accused in Sexual Assault Trials" (2004–05) 49 Crim LQ 69 at 72.

rational, self-disciplined, and blameless."[81] Women who seek redress for their rapes through the legal system must ensure that their stories are consistent and coherent, and that they did everything they could to prevent their rapes. Gotell documents how the increased use of third-party records, such as counselling notes, has further increased women's vulnerability to "any inconsistency, any undesirable fact, even anything surprised or unexpected about her."[82] While the image of the "ideal victim" has thus changed, it still casts women as "unrapeable," especially "extensively documented women, such as women with mental health histories, Aboriginal women, immigrant women, childhood assault survivors, foster children, and women with disabilities."[83] Rape myths are still alive and well in the criminal justice system, and continue to play a significant, if often unacknowledged, role in the way courts decide who can be raped.

The Garneau Sisterhood, on the other hand, places much less emphasis on the question "who can be raped." The Sisterhood's loose definition of rape and non-existent threshold of proof make the question of "who can be raped" virtually irrelevant. The Sisterhood holds that anyone can be raped, but that it is much more important to ask who *is* raped, and who is a rapist. The Sisters emphasize that consistently and overwhelmingly it is women who are raped. And it is men who rape women. Part of the Sister's response thus called upon men to acknowledge the role they play in perpetuating rape culture. One poster asks if men "watch[ed] women through their windows," or "[made] excuses for other men."[84] Other posters issue warnings to men to avoid circulating alone at night to avoid coming under suspicion. This focus on the gendered nature of rape provides a vital counterpoint to the criminal justice system's insistence on gender neutrality.

The question of "who is raped" also influences the Sisterhood's composition. As women in the neighbourhood experienced a unique vulnerability to sexual assault, members of the Sisterhood were all women-identified persons. While it is unclear whether or not this was a conscious decision at the beginning, as the group mobilized, men were encouraged to form their own solidarity groups. Many Sisters reported that it was vital for them to feel that the women of the neighbourhood were taking action in light of both women's broader systemic vulner-

81 Gotell, "Ideal Victim," *supra* note 58 at 259.

82 *Ibid* at 260.

83 *Ibid* at 262.

84 Poster; image on file with author.

ability as well as in the particular nature of the attacks of summer 2008. This gendered analysis to the question of who can be — and who is — raped is necessary to any political and legal strategy that hopes to address sexual assault substantively.

All of these substantive criteria highlight how the criminal justice system cannot resolve a social problem such as rape. The criminal justice system is designed to address individual instances of sexual assault. It considers each incident in isolation, and operates solely to determine if this particular accused is guilty of sexual assault. As such, the criminal justice system is not equipped to address any vulnerability beyond that of the individual complainant, such as the gendered vulnerability all women experience in the face of sexual assault. It is this very idea of gendered vulnerability upon which the Sisterhood was founded. By centering its work on community responses to widespread vulnerability, the Sisterhood frees itself to take direct action to prevent rape.

(b) Procedural rules

Procedurally, the Sisterhood is better able to address rape because the group eschewed the complicated rules of criminal procedure in favour of the simple principle that survivors will always be believed. This simplicity ensures that the Sisterhood can expose rape as a social phenomenon; it is also necessary in a community where many members do not feel safe sharing their experiences with the police. As one woman wrote, when she told police that a man had attempted to break into her home while she was present, the response she got was that "they couldn't do anything because the perpetrator had not committed a crime."[85]

The criminal justice system's pervasive skepticism of survivors was exemplified in a community newsletter issued some months after the attacks. The newsletter quoted a representative of the Edmonton Police Service who proudly reported that McKernan "is a safe neighbourhood." Although six "sexual offenses" unrelated to the Garneau rapist were reported, "one of these was cancelled, three were unfounded, and the remaining two incidents were of a male subject observed exposing himself."[86] The newsletter does not specify why over half of all reported sexual offenses in the neighbourhood were deemed unfounded, but such a high percentage seems extremely suspicious, especially in the

85 Email to the Garneau Sisterhood (27 June 2008). On file with author.

86 McKernan Community League, "Mckernan Not a Crime Hotspot in Year's Stats" *McKernan Messenger* (October 2008) 1, online: <http://www.mckernancommunity.org/news/messengerOct08p4.pdf>.

context of a police report designed to make people feel safe in the community. The Sisterhood had not, at the time of writing, issued any public statement on the contents of this newsletter, but it is safe to say that the Sisters may call into question how they could feel safe in their community when the police service that purports to protect them is instead likely to find that the "truth" of their story does not match the standard of "truth" required by law and will say that their rapes never happened.

(c) Fundamental principles

My mapping above shows that the two legal orders are based on starkly divergent fundamental principles. The criminal justice system views its objectivity as key to making it an appropriate site for catching and punishing rapists. A hierarchy of police officers, Crown prosecutors, judges, and even juries assess each rape according to the standards outlined in the *Criminal Code* and Canadian jurisprudence. Any allegation of rape must be proven beyond a reasonable doubt before the legal system will attribute criminal liability to the accused. This framework is very limiting when contrasted with the Garneau Sisterhood's grounding in subjective analyses of rape that privilege survivor discourse and promote the responsibility of an entire community to prevent rape by challenging rape culture.

MAPPING THE RELATIONSHIP: COLLABORATION, TENSION, COMPLICITY

The pervasiveness of rape culture often necessitates difficult tactical choices in responding to rape. Many people who have been sexually assaulted still wish to see their attackers caught and punished in the criminal justice system, as it is this system that carries the full weight of moral sanction in our society. Women not "directly" victimized by the crimes also wish to see that perpetrators are punished, as this can help women feel safer. In the Garneau Sisterhood, women experience a state of "internormativity" as they negotiate between the criminal justice system and the Sisterhood's legal order. This makes the relationship between the two orders a complex one, marked by instances of collaboration but also instances of insurmountable tension. This tension, however, is a positive one. It illustrates the shortcomings of the criminal justice system while also giving women the opportunity to take direct action to prevent rape and feel safe in their neighbourhood. As the model of internormativity suggests, subjects do not need to "resolve" the conflicts between the different legal orders they experience. Instead, they can remain in a constant state of flux, experiencing the push and pull of each normative order in different situations.

It is important to note here that I am deliberately resisting the argument that the Garneau Sisterhood simply represents a necessary supplement to the work of the criminal justice system. This argument would locate the Sisterhood's work in the extra-legal world of civil society, and would emphasize the way that it both collaborates with law, but also accomplishes the tasks that the law cannot. This reading of the Sisterhood's work is not altogether false. The Sisterhood *did* collaborate with the criminal justice system in some small ways, and certainly provided space for public discussion and community empowerment in ways that the criminal justice system did not. Indeed, this reading may correspond to the ways some group members conceptualizes the group's work.

What I want to promote, however, is a more radical reading of the Sisterhood's work — a reading that focuses on the fundamental challenge the Sisterhood presents to the criminal justice system. In this more complex account of the dynamics between the two, I first explore examples of collaboration between the Sisterhood and the police. The Sisterhood encouraged people to submit tips on the rapist and his activities, hoping that this would lead to his arrest. The Sisterhood also encouraged police to give women more information on the rapist's *modus operandi*. After considering these two examples, I then explore the way that any collaboration with the criminal justice system threatens to render us complicit in the criminal justice system. To collaborate with or complement the criminal justice system presumes its validity, and indeed further legitimates it. To work with the criminal justice system reinforces the law's power to criminalize people and to issue moral sanctions. By reading the Sisterhood's work from a radical perspective, I will emphasize how the state of internormativity is vital to ensuring that the two legal orders can share an uneasy coexistence; the tension between the two is necessary to ensure that the Sisterhood's legal order is not subsumed by the criminal law.

1. Collaboration

The Sisterhood's direct collaboration with police occurred through messages on posters and attempts to build an information-sharing relationship with police. The Garneau Sisterhood openly acknowledged that the group hoped that the police would arrest the person responsible for the Garneau rapes. The campaign was inspired by the work of Jane Doe, a woman who postered her neighbourhood after she was attacked by a serial rapist in downtown Toronto in 1988. A day after her posters went up, police received a tip from the rapist's girlfriend and he was arrested.[87] In her book, Jane Doe states, "the concept of postering neighbourhoods or workplaces where a rapist is known to be operating was not invented by me. The Toronto Rape Crisis Centre had been promoting and engaging in postering for years."[88] The Sisterhood's posters were part of this tradition, and urged people to send any information they had on the Garneau assaults to the group's email account, or to Crime Stoppers, an anonymous tip line run by the Edmonton Police. Posters also commanded "rapist, turn yourself in now" and warned "attention rapist we are watching *you* we will find *you*."[89]

The posters served part of their purpose, as many community members sent in tips to the Sisterhood. As mentioned above, these included stories of peeping toms, attempted break-ins, suspicious prowlers, and physically violent altercations with men. Furthermore, an individual claiming to be close to one of the victims emailed the group with more details of the attacker's methods. The Sisterhood collected this information in the hopes of passing it along to police; however, the police were reluctant to build a relationship with an anonymous group.[90] Group members were also hesitant to simply hand over the information to the police, as they were unsure how to deal with consent issues on the part of those who had originally sent in the tips. To date, these initial attempts at creating a relationship have not materialized into anything productive.

The Sisterhood also attempted to collaborate with police regarding the issue of warnings. When the police first "broke" the story of the serial rapist, they warned women to lock their doors and windows and "take extra safety precautions."[91] The Sisterhood quickly pointed out that "not only will tips like this not keep us safe, they perpetuate a culture of fear," and that they emerge from dominant narratives that suggest "women should be able to avoid [violent] situations if we follow certain tips: don't walk home alone at night, don't wear 'provocative' clothing, don't put down your drink at the bar, don't engage in 'risky'

87 *The Story of Jane Doe*, *supra* note 65 at 38.

88 *Ibid.*

89 Posters created June 2008; text on file with author.

90 Email received 6 July 2008; on file with author.

91 Patricia Chalpczynska, "Media Release from the Edmonton Police Service" (released 27 May 2008). Gelinas, *supra* note 1.

behaviour."[92] The problem, of course, is that "this lock-your-doors advice puts the onus solely on individual women to protect themselves and leaves them open to blame if they are attacked."[93] This discourse makes women responsible for rape prevention, leaving police free to take on the punishment of rapists. This responsibilization puts women's behaviour under the microscope — a fact that the Sisterhood reiterated on a poster urging people to "start questioning offenders' behaviour and not the survivors.'"[94]

In addition to questioning the warnings' reliance on rape myths, however, the Sisterhood demanded that the police provide women with more information. This is perhaps the most profound moment of interlegality in the experience of the Garneau Sisterhood — to ask for more information for women to protect themselves at the same time as rejecting the idea that women should be responsible for policing their own behaviour. This is a key moment of interlegality and of multiple subjectivities: members of the Garneau Sisterhood were caught between their critique of warnings and their practical urge to have as much information as possible. This contradiction was embodied in a press release that deconstructed the warnings, but then a few paragraphs later admitted:

> we're also questioning the police refusal to release specific information about the attacks. If something is happening to women in this community, why can't we have all the details?...Why not use a strategy that could combat fear, rather than perpetuating it with vague, shadowy details under newspaper headlines that simply run up tallies of attacks as if there's nothing that we can do about it?[95]

Many of the people who corresponded with the Sisterhood over the course of the summer echoed this frustration, seeking information "beyond the police's oh-so-helpful advice to ... beware any average-size male in dark clothes."[96]

Feminist engagement with police warnings is nothing new. Jane Doe, who led the postering campaign in Toronto mentioned earlier,

92 Sisterhood, "Organizing," *supra* note 51.

93 Press release, *supra* note 70.

94 Poster; image on file with author.

95 Somewhat painfully, this rhetorical flourish directly contradicted a poster that announced, "Rape is not 'something that happens' to women."

96 Email received 8 June 2008; on file with author.

successfully sued the Toronto police for failing to warn women of a serial rapist operating in their neighbourhood. McFarland J found that the decision not to warn was made by police who thought "women living in the area would become hysterical and panic and their investigation would thereby be jeopardized."[97] Interestingly, McFarland J then added that police were not motivated by any sense of urgency because they did not see the attacks as violent, another example of the rape myth that there is no violence inherent in the act of rape itself. *Jane Doe* has come to stand for the precedent that "a meaningful warning could and should have been given to the women who were at particular risk ... such warning should have alerted the women at risk, and advised them of suggested precautions they might take to protect themselves."[98] Police cannot cite concerns over their investigation as justification for the refusal to issue a warning.

While *Jane Doe* created a legal duty for police to issue warnings, the way that warnings were handled in the case of the Garneau rapist suggests that police are only taking the bare minimum of this precedent into account. Police refused to release information on the attacker's method of entry into homes or to release details about the facial disguise he wore. After being aggressively taken to task by members of a public meeting in the second neighbourhood where the attacks occurred, police reluctantly revealed that the rapist entered women's homes between midnight and five in the morning. Again and again, they attributed their reticence to concerns over their investigation and claimed that sharing information could harm the criminal trial should the rapist ever be apprehended.[99] Despite Jane Doe's previous efforts to hold the criminal justice system accountable in this way, it remains only minimally responsive.

Although they fought unsuccessfully to get more useful police warnings, the Sisterhood also flipped the commonplace gendered dynamics of warnings. In keeping with their efforts to focus on the perpetrator's behaviour instead of the survivors' and to challenge the culture of fear the warnings perpetuated, the Sisters issued a series of posters pronouncing: "WARNING! MEN! THERE IS A RAPIST in the neigh-

97 *Jane Doe*, *supra* note 65 at 56–57.

98 *Ibid* at 57.

99 Gelinas, "Southside Attack," *supra* note 1. Robin Collum, "Some Women Disagree Over Rape Warnings: Police Say They Aren't Playing the Blame-Victim" *Edmonton Journal* (14 August 2008) B3. I still fail to see how providing women with information about the attacks that target them could jeopardize a criminal trial.

bourhood. Please *do not* go out at night unless you are with a friend." In smaller text at the bottom, the poster read: "I'll do this if you will." This series provides a powerful challenge to the idea that it is women who must be afraid of rapists, women who must police their behaviour, and women who must prevent rape. It refocuses public discourse on the perpetrators of rape, who are overwhelmingly men. These messages were inspired by Jane Doe, who suggests warnings to men could include "one of you is raping women, and we don't know, can't tell which one, so until we find out, stay at home, do not use underground parking or take shortcuts through the park … [unless] you are accompanied by a woman who can vouch for your good male status."[100] Jane Doe shrewdly observes that:

> The warning above and the one we are accustomed to hearing are both stupid and outrageous and call on a large group of people to censor their lives. Our response is to laugh at one and obey the other, when it is the "funny" one that would more effectively address the crime because it puts the onus on the offending group.[101]

Rachel Hall has also written about the subversive potential of warning men, pointing out that this practice "publicly pervert[s] and mock[s] that language in a manner that highlights how nonsensical it is to socialize women to stop rape."[102] By producing posters that focused attention on men's behaviour, the Sisterhood was able to subvert its own engagement with the warnings, producing a sly and provocative message out of this moment of interlegality.

2. (Positive) tension?

This ambivalence about a relationship with police demonstrates the deep ambivalence many community members feel about working with the Edmonton police. By situating the attacks of the Garneau rapist within a spectrum of rape culture, the Garneau Sisterhood called attention to the problem of rape as a whole, not just to these particular incidents. By focusing on rape as a broader social issue, however, the Garneau Sisterhood could not ignore analyses of rape that focused on the race and class differences that shape the ways rape is experienced as

100 *The Story of Jane Doe*, *supra* note 65 at 325.

101 *Ibid.*

102 Rachel Hall, "It Can Happen to You: Rape Prevention in the Age of Risk Management" (2004) 19:3 Hypatia 1 at 12.

much as gender does. With regards to the police, this analysis of race and class imports the question of "who is policed, and how."[103]

Ambivalence towards the Edmonton police service's relationship with Aboriginal people is long-standing. Aboriginal women's groups and, more recently, segments of the White feminist community, have decried police inaction towards the disappearance of thirty-two Aboriginal women from the city's streets since the 1980s. The repeated failure of police to act to investigate these disappearances becomes even more alarming when contrasted with the high-profile police press conferences, public meetings, and investigations regarding the relatively isolated incidents of sexual assault in the middle-class white neighbourhood of the Garneau. This police inaction means that violence against Aboriginal women "becomes routinized and treated as if it were a naturally occurring phenomenon."[104]

A recent series of high-profile incidents further highlights the police force's overt violence towards the city's Aboriginal residents. In the summer of 2005, police detained nine homeless people in a police van on a hot summer afternoon.[105] Their "crime" was to be drunk in public. After holding them in the van for over two hours, the police dropped them off in an isolated neighbourhood in Edmonton's northeast, where they were left to find their own way back into the downtown area.[106]

When the story broke in February of 2007, police tried to argue that this was an isolated incident; however, when a local newspaper conducted interviews with homeless people, outreach workers, and representatives of community associations, all revealed that police had "for years routinely picked up homeless people in various stages of drunkenness from the Whyte Avenue area and released them in inner-city neighbourhoods."[107] Philip Dainard, another Edmontonian, "reported

103 Sherene Razack, "Race, Space and Prostitution: The Making of the Bourgeois Subject" (1998) 10 CJWL 338 at 355.

104 Lise Gotell, "Third-Wave Anti-rape Activism on Neoliberal Terrain: The Garneau Sisterhood," Chapter 11 in this book.

105 John Cotter, "RCMP to Investigate Allegations by Homeless Against Edmonton Police" *Canadian Press* (Factiva) (2 February 2007). I have discussed this incident in another paper: Meagan Johnston, "Hurtin' Albertans: Race, Space and the Law in Edmonton's Housing Crisis." Conference at McGill University (22 April 2008) 13–15 [unpublished paper on file with author].

106 Charles Rusnell & Mike Sadava, "Constitution Violated, Lawyers Say: No Legal Rights to Transport Them Anywhere" *Edmonton Journal* (6 February 2007) A3.

107 *Ibid.* Whyte Avenue is a popular strip of bars, shops, and restaurants in the Old Strathcona neighbourhood, across the river from the inner-city neighbourhoods east of downtown that are home to most of Edmonton's homeless population.

a similar experience of being arrested by three police officers while he was barefoot, drunk, and panhandling on Whyte Avenue. The police drove him to the outskirts of the city, and dropped him off on the side of the road."[108] He walked for hours in the dark before finding a bus stop.[109] In June of 2008, Crown prosecutors announced that while the police conduct was "wrong," they were not criminal, and so no charges would be laid.[110] Police had acted in accordance with their own internal policy, which permits police to pick up intoxicated persons "who are conscious, responsive, and without apparent illness or injury, and able to care for themselves" and transport them to a "residence of friend's place, or a homeless shelter as long as they are left in the care of a responsible person."[111] The investigation further held that the policy was authorized under the *Gaming and Liquor Act*.[112]

These incidents reveal the nature of the criminal justice system's policing of "crime" in Edmonton. Almost all of the detainees were Aboriginal; the policy thus replicates colonial narratives wherein white settlers "claim space as their own, dictate the laws that govern the space, and claims the authority to violently evict Aboriginals when they so choose."[113] This practice has been used many times before. Tragically, in 1990, 17-year-old Neil Stonechild froze to death after police dropped him off on the outskirts of Saskatoon on a bitterly cold prairie night.[114]

By collaborating with the police system, the Garneau Sisterhood is collaborating with a system that claims the power to recognize some violations but not others, all according to its own supposedly objective

108 Johnston, *supra* note 105 at 14.

109 Charles Rusnell, "It Sure as Hell Happened to Me" *Edmonton Journal* (2 February 2007) B1.

110 Ben Gelinas, "Officers Avoid Criminal Charges; Police Dumped Drunken Homeless People on City's North Side" *Edmonton Journal* (12 June 2008) B1.

111 Edmonton Police spokesman Dean Parthenis (as quoted in *ibid*). Many authors have explored how drunkenness has come to be associated with Aboriginality. An Aboriginal person, especially one who is visibly poor and/or homeless, is thus often more vulnerable to being deemed unruly and degenerate and seen as deserving of punishment and violence; see eg Sherene Razack, "Gendered Racial Violence and Spatialized Justice: The Murder of Pamela George," in Sherene Razack, ed, *Race, Space and the Law: Unmapping a White Settler Society* (Toronto: Between the Lines, 2002) 121. Razack outlines in much more nuanced form the complex interactions between gender, race, and class in urban space.

112 RSA 2000, G-1. The investigation results were discussed in Gelinas, *supra* note 110.

113 Johnston, *supra* note 105 at 15.

114 Cotter, *supra* note 105. For an excellent overview of these so-called "starlight tours," see Don Kossick, "Death By Cold: Institutionalized Violence in Saskatoon" (2000) 34:4 *Canadian Dimension* 19.

standards. This collaboration places the Sisters in a profound moment of what De Sousa Santos would term "interlegality" — the moment where subjects find themselves equally subject to different legal orders. The Sisterhood's legal order and the criminal justice system's legal order each has a very different answer to the questions "what constitutes a crime?" and "what factors do we take into consideration in deeming an act criminal?" While the Sisterhood's legal order prioritizes survivors' accounts of violence and locates acts within their broader social and political contexts, the criminal justice system ignores these factors and treats each incident in isolation. The criminal justice system moved to recognize the Garneau rapes as crimes at the same time as it denied the violence and racism of police practices. Collaboration with the police investigation is tantamount to complicity in this dynamic; when members of the Sisterhood assist in police investigations they are acting according to both the norms of the Sisterhood and of the criminal justice system. This is an uncomfortable space, but it is a space that exposes some of the ways that the criminal justice system is at odds with a more radical paradigm.

The Garneau Sisterhood's legal order is also explicitly at odds with the way that rape is treated in Canadian law. Comack and Peter explain how only 6 percent of sexual assaults are reported: "Of those, 40 percent result in charges. Of these, two-thirds result in a conviction." From this data, they estimate a 1.6 percent conviction rate — a rate much lower than most other crimes.[115] Lise Gotell argues that feminists — including feminist judges — have "called attention to how a woman's interaction with the justice system mimics the violation of a sexual assault … the experience of medical evidence gathering, making a police statement and sometimes engaging with Crown prosecutors and enduring a trial leaves a sexual assault complainant with little autonomy, self-determination, or control."[116] The criminal justice system thus only recognizes a farcically tiny proportion of the total instances of rape in society.

The Garneau rapes only represent a tiny fraction of the sexual assaults that occur in the city each year; however, they sparked a media frenzy and public hysteria. The Garneau Sisterhood recognized that

115 Elizabeth Comack & Tracey Peter, "How the Criminal Justice System Responds to Sexual Assault Survivors: The Slippage Between 'Responsibilization' and Blaming the 'Victim'" (2005) 17 CJWL 305.

116 Gotell, "Privacy," *supra* note 4 at 744. See also *Osolin supra* note 79 and *Seaboyer, supra* note 75, both per L'Heureux-Dubé J.

this focus was due to the way the police and the media perceived these rapes as "real." There could be no debate about consent or witness credibility when women were being attacked while sleeping in their homes. The Sisterhood worked to take advantage of this new public focus by pointing out that "only two percent of sexual assaults are assaults by a stranger [and] the overwhelming majority are perpetrated by partners, family members, or co-workers."[117] Indeed, the police's focus on warning women to lock their doors "distracts from our culture of rape ... locked doors do not protect women from their family members, partners and dates."[118] For the Sisterhood, this larger context of rape is the "context of violence that we, the Garneau Sisters are seeking to address. We need to publicly denounce all perpetrators of sexual assault. Each of us in this city needs to ask ourselves what we can do to stop all rape, not just this particular rapist."[119]

The Sisterhood's efforts to locate the Garneau rapes on a broader spectrum of rape culture are particularly necessary given the characteristics of the Garneau neighbourhood. The Garneau is roughly situated between the University of Alberta and Whyte Avenue, a popular strip of bars. Between the fraternity houses, first-time university students living in residence, student parties, and the significant numbers of drunken hooligans patrolling the neighbourhood's streets every weekend, the neighbourhood has many of the perfect conditions for date rape and acquaintance assault. One infamous fraternity house, the "Deke" house, throws a notorious party each Halloween where women have reportedly been sexually assaulted. An organizer of the university's production of *The Vagina Monologues*[120] disclosed to the audience that she had been drugged at a neighbourhood fraternity party and raped on the front lawn. In December of 2005, a good friend of mine was drugged at a popular local pub. Despite these stark examples of "rape culture," the Garneau was never seen as an "unsafe" neighbourhood until the summer of 2008, providing painful proof of the persistence of the idea that stranger rapes are "real" rapes. Everything else presupposes a lesser level of violence and is not worthy of large-scale public concern. This discourse of rape in the criminal justice system and in mainstream society illustrates the many complex dynamics at work for members of the Garneau Sisterhood.

117 Sisterhood, "Organizing," *supra* note 51.

118 Press release, *supra* note 70.

119 *Ibid.*

120 Eve Ensler, *The Vagina Monologues* (New York: Villard, 2001).

CONCLUSION

The summer of 2008 incidents in Garneau provide a potent example of the myriad ways communities can deal with rape. The juxtaposition of the legal orders provided by the activists in the Garneau Sisterhood and the criminal justice system show the systemic inadequacies inherent in the way the criminal law addresses rape. The Garneau Sisterhood posits a vibrant, dynamic, and empowering model of fighting back against rape in which women from the affected community are directly able to reclaim their space in the way they best saw fit. The Sisterhood's work is enabled by a variety of characteristics of their "legal order," including a broad definition of rape and a lack of formal thresholds or rules for determining whether or not a rape has occurred. This loose structure enables the Sisters to centre the stories of survivors to obtain a broad account of how rape affects everyone in the community. Furthermore, as a larger segment of the community is considered "directly affected" in this legal order, a larger segment of the community can invent imaginative strategies that cut to the core of the gendered, racialized, and classed nature of rape as a social phenomenon.

13. Where Has All The Anger Gone?

Diana Yaros

While Lise Gotell and Meagan Johnston explore the anonymous and informal activism of the Garneau Sisterhood, Diana Yaros reconsiders the work of feminist advocates who work in women's shelters, rape crisis centres, and women's centres across the country. She describes the impact that government funding and government "partnership" have had in de-radicalizing women's grassroots organizations, but argues that there is no less need for feminist advocates to challenge police responses to women's disclosures of sexual assault, to accompany women to the criminal trials of their attackers, and to denounce the discriminatory practices of the legal system to the media and the public. Diana highlights her centre's effort to translate feminist theory into action by centring the needs of immigrant and refugee women, including their attempts to seek asylum in Canada, as fundamental to challenging the status quo "banalization" of sexual assault.

Thirty-five years ago, we gathered in kitchens, in living rooms, and in greasy spoons, to connect with other women over our outrage at the appalling injustice following our experiences of rape, incest, and other forms of sexual violence. We began to speak out and to organize ourselves into groups that could take action against the many forms of sexist violence.

We were going to educate, demand law reform, and insist on respectful police response to our complaints. In Montreal we organized the first "Take Back the Night" in August of 1980: hundreds of women came. The next year thousands of women came as we walked through alleyways, parks, and other dark areas, taking strength from our numbers and understanding that because of that solidarity, change just might be possible. We even had our theme songs, our own Ferron with "Testimony," Holly Near with "Fight Back," and Kim Baryluk with "Warrior Song." We would send a call out for a political action and women came! That was how we saw our jobs: using opportunities to bring the injustices facing raped women to public attention and pushing for change.

In the seventies and eighties, we insisted that women were the authority on issues of violence against women. We developed an analysis that was feminist, anti-racist, and anti-oppressive and a language that defined what that meant for Aboriginal and racialized women, women with disabilities, lesbians, and immigrant and refugee women and many others. Our vocabulary reflected our analysis and we insisted that this be the official understanding of rape as a form of social control of men over women. We believed that law reform and public policy were the ways to achieve an end to all the violence. Thirty-five years later, what were our successes and what were our miss-takes?

EXTERNAL INFLUENCES

We began to get regular funding, small amounts at first, and then enough for salaries. We lobbied for increased funding, arguing that we had "wait lists." In Montreal, those lists were often over one-hundred women long. How did we get to that point? Women were calling by the hundreds; many had been assaulted years ago, victims of incest or other sexual assaults. For many of those women, talking to us was the first time they were able to speak about what had happened to them, to someone who would listen and respect them and their choices. We ran support groups, we responded to the distress of those women by providing what we felt didn't exist anywhere else — a feminist counselling service. Social services agencies panicked when they heard the words rape and incest and were referring their cases to us. We hoped that by sharing our coping and survival strategies we were empowering the women who came to our centre. We tried to balance the direct service axis with prevention, education, and advocacy.

Then we became the victims of our own success. We got more money to continue providing the services that the state was not. Across Quebec we began hiring social workers, sexologists, criminologists, and psychologists along with feminist activists. Did we import neoliberal feminism along with the professionalization and institutionalization of our centres, something we had vowed not to do?

It crept in without our really being aware of it. There was always another emergency to respond to. After over ten years of trying to respond in this way, at best, I can say that we did make a difference in the lives of thousands of individual women over the years, but at what cost? Who was responding to the systemic discrimination that women face in the criminal justice system, in the immigrant and refugee process, in health and social services, and in public policies? If we were professional and credible in the eyes of our funders, then where did our loyalties lie? To whom did we owe allegiance?

We needed to be accountable for the public funds that we were spending. To whom did we owe this accountability: the bureaucrats, many of them feminist allies, or the women who were raped? When did the work we were doing become about helping "them" and not us?

Many centres were focused on establishing stable and recurrent funding in the early years. One strategy was to criticize the lack of available services for raped women and incest survivors. But once we got the funding, we got caught up in the idea that greater equality was being achieved through improved legislation and government recognition. For some of us who found ourselves in positions of privilege, this was perhaps true; however, many marginalized women still faced incredible barriers to justice and to better access to decision-making positions in our centres.

What was the political atmosphere in the late eighties and nineties in Quebec? Did the killing of fourteen young women at l'École Polytechnique make us more afraid to insist on a radical feminist analysis?[1] There was so much insistence at the time that this was not a brutal and systematic crime against women and against feminism but the work of a lone crazy. We worried about how to respond. Would we be exploiting those women who were killed if we used this attack as an example of how sexist violence works to affect all women and to keep all women afraid? Including those of us working to end it? This very same debate resurfaced following the release of the film *Polytechnique*.

PARTNERSHIP?

Over the years we have been part of various task forces, participated in round table discussions, and been invited to be "*partners*" with the state in developing public policies on sexual violence. We gained a certain credibility, but at what cost? We were presented with proposals and documents that were already written. We had no genuine power to change more than a few sentences. The representatives of the state would get to have our names on the policy for their political benefit.

What does it mean for a women's anti-rape centre to work in partnership with the police, Crown prosecutors, and hospital-based servi-

1 The twentieth anniversary of the Montreal Massacre at l'École Polytechnique in 2009 saw many Quebec feminists discussing the impact of this event on the feminist movement in Quebec.

ces? As one officer explained to me, seeing as we were all on the same side, our job was to explain the way the legal system worked to the victims. Any dissatisfaction or criticisms would then be buffered and filtered through us. We then had to explain that, no, that was not our job. Our job was to ensure that women's rights were respected and that we would be questioning the barriers to justice alongside the women who were raped. We would be defending women's rights, not the justice system. This did not go over well.

We worked hard to debunk some of the myths around rape — many of them were embedded in law. One of the most prominent myths was the need for corroborative evidence because, *of course*, "women lie about rape." In these days of special "rape squads," TV shows like "Lie to Me" and "The Mentalist," as well as attempts at "victim profiling,"[2] this myth, is alive and well. Racist profiling is also a part of this myth for we often hear that certain immigrant groups, cultural communities, or Aboriginal communities are more violent towards women and that is why women are reluctant to come forward. Again there is a failure of the institutional actors to recognize the existence of systemic discrimination, and a preference to locate the problems outside of themselves. This is the only crime where a woman has to prove that she is the "victim" and not the criminal. Clearly the law does not protect women from rape.

INTERNAL (NON)POLITICAL CHOICES

For all the times we stood up to the representatives of the justice system, there were the times when we lost, were too disheartened to act, when my eyes, for example, would glaze over as I sat through yet another meeting while the "partners" discussed what size speculum should be included in the rape kit. *Was no one else squirming in their seat over that*? Or how the new specialized rape squad officers can tell when women are lying — apparently *two-thirds*. Why was there silence around the table from the women's groups? What insidious form of internalized patriarchy was at play? Did we get used to the discriminatory remarks? Did other women not hear them? Did the personal relationships we developed with the people we met each month over a period of several years make us reluctant to challenge them? Were we afraid of losing the credibility we had fought so hard gain? Were we afraid that if we criticized the police they wouldn't help us with the cases of individ-

2 Les fausses allegations d'agression sexuelle chez l'adulte. Michel St-Yves psychologue judiciaire, Sureté du Québec et Éric Latour, Sergent, Profileur criminel, Sureté du Québec.

ual women who filed charges? Did we not want to listen to one more prosecutor ask us just *who* we thought we were to be questioning their strategies? Were we afraid to risk a fight because we thought we would lose?

Are we operating in solidarity with the other progressive social movements of the times? In many centres we are forgetting to make the links with anti-oppression theory and practice. In questioning our methods and their accessibility to women of diverse origins, we have noted that the type of inclusion that has happened over the past few years is more about providing services than about sharing of power. While there has been some advancement, most women's groups and coalitions are still struggling to adapt their practice and structures to make a real place at the table, particularly for immigrant and refugee women, racialized women, and Aboriginal women. The understanding of the intersections between oppressions and how they affect our choices for action and priorities is weak. Fighting systemic racism is a priority for women of colour and the issue of racial profiling is a feminist issue. Nowhere is this more evident than in current police practices of "victim profiling" in sexual assault cases, which also involves racial profiling, the labelling of immigrant and Aboriginal women as less co-operative and thus less worthy of attention, rather than identifying the problems as systemic, sexist, and racist.

In 2008 as I was sorting through the hundreds of emails in my inbox upon my return from a few weeks off, I came across an invitation to a conference on "sexual aggression" organized by a health and social services agency on the south shore of Montreal.[3] The presenters included social work professors, hospital-based professionals, criminologists, psychologists, psychoanalysts, a victims' rights group, Justice Department victims' aid services, crown prosecutors, police officers, youth protection ... the list goes on. Where were the voices of women? The feminist-run rape crisis centres? Who holds authority on the analysis of violence against women? It isn't even called violence against women anymore. An entire industry of professionals exists in a network, which involves millions of dollars and attempts to appear to offer a serious state response to sexual violence. Did we create this? Is this what we meant when we denounced the discrimination facing raped women in the criminal justice system? In the meantime, rape continues unabated.

3 « Libérez les mots » Forum Agressions sexuelles, 1 octobre 2008, Agence de la santé et des services sociaux de la Montérégie.

HAVE WE ABDICATED AUTHORITY AND OUR RESPONSIBILITY?

Over the last five-to-ten years our centre has been asking some tough questions. Are we service providers or are we watchdog organizations? Has the need to respond to the distress of individual women overtaken our focus on the effect of rape on women's equality rights? Are we prepared to occupy public space on the issues around sexual violence? What strategies are we using to engage the state in debate or to raise awareness and reach out to the women who are most marginalized?

As we worked with a refugee woman requesting asylum in Quebec due to the rape and continued death threats she experienced from armed militia in her country of origin, we began to think about a demonstration to call public attention to her situation. The first thought that came to mind as we were brainstorming possibilities was "who will come?" And I wondered, *where has all the anger gone*? What happened to our capacity to mobilize a public response? In Quebec there are over thirty rape crisis centres, eighty-three battered women's shelters,[4] and 104 women's centres.[5] In Montreal alone there are dozens of women's groups and yet I cannot count on more than a couple of dozen women at any given action.

Where do we go from here? One of the first discussions we needed to have involved deciding what the role of an anti-rape centre was in today's political climate. Are we a service provider or are we responsible for bringing greater public awareness to the continued shortcomings of the justice system and in public policy surrounding rape?

This is not a new discussion; in the late seventies, feminists were having this debate. Some of the arguments around focusing on service provision are still valid today. Many women are seeking a safe space to talk about their experiences of rape and incest. There are almost no services provided by the state for women who were raped in the past. For some women, the consequences of systematic childhood assaults have created a context where they find themselves marginalized and dealing with poverty, mental health problems, loneliness, and isolation. For recent assaults, women are still finding it difficult to be believed and respected unless they have a "textbook" case.

On the other hand, who is watching to ensure that the legal system is respecting the rights of women during rape trials? Who is raising the alarm, denouncing the discrimination, or informing the public about

4 Online: <http://www.fede.qc.ca/>; online : <http://www.maisons-femmes.qc.ca/index.html>.

5 Online: <http://www.rcentres.qc.ca/qui.html>.

the treatment the state provides in response to sexual violence? Who is reminding commissioners and lawyers for refugees that Canada recognizes rape as a war crime and as sufficient justification for being granted asylum in Canada? Who is witnessing the hearings? Who will accompany the women and stand beside them? *If we do not do this, who will?*

TURNING AND RETURNING

At Mouvement contre le viol et l'inceste (MCVI) we continue our frontline work with immigrant, refugee, and racialized women who have experienced sexual assault. At the same time, we use these hands-on experiences as a catalyst for change, both internal and external. Along with an ongoing analysis of our own internal structure, we continue to discuss, to question, and to evolve the focus of our efforts.

QUESTIONING: GENTLE STIRRINGS OR TSUNAMI?

About ten years ago, we began to ask ourselves whether the diversity of Montreal was reflected in our staff, our collective members, and the women accessing our services. We realized that we were not reaching immigrant, refugee, and racialized women and that we had no formalized imperative to do so. While there was an unwritten agreement that an urban centre like Montreal should be reaching a wide spectrum of women, this belief was not part of our structural documents or mission statement, nor was it mentioned in our annual action plans. It was understood to be included in the work that we were already doing in the field of sexual violence against women. When we brought the matter to the Quebec coalition, the *Regroupement Quebecois des centres d'aide et de lutte contre les aggressions à caratère sexuelle* (RQCALACS), we met with a similar response. "*These women were already included*" and did not need specific targeting. The problem, as defined by many member centres, was "*that they weren't coming to our centres.*"

From the perspective of our centre, this reaction put the responsibility for inclusivity outside of the centres and onto immigrant and refugee women. This notion that marginalized women who experience additional forms of oppression are already included in our work came up again and again. Colonialist responses such as this are part of an ongoing struggle where the majority group in power defines the standard and anyone else who is "other" is expected to conform to the "common" practice.[6]

6 See Simone de Beauvoir's concept of women as "other" in *The Second Sex*, translated and edited by Simone HM Parshley (New York: Vintage Books, 1989).

Until there is a critical mass of representation from racialized women, immigrant women, First Nations, lesbian, and disabled women, among others, there will be no significant paradigm shift.[7] If the changes that do occur remain at the theoretical level and do not translate into the shifting of power dynamics in the daily workings of women's groups and among coalition staff, the priorities will continue to be defined by the majority voice in power and the demands of marginalized women for structural and strategic changes in the violence against women sector will continue to be viewed as non-essential to the work.

OUR INTERNAL STRUCTURES AND STRATEGIES

Once we admitted that the problem was mostly with ourselves, we began to ask the questions that needed to be addressed in order to apply ourselves to the task of redirecting our efforts. We applied for and obtained a small grant that allowed us to hire a new staff member to assist our centre in developing and adopting the changes that would truly make us a place for women of diverse origins. We hired a feminist from an immigrant community as a first gesture of solidarity. (We already had some immigrant women on staff and as part of our collective.) We knew that it was important that this work become an integrated part of the centre and not a "special project" that ends when the funding runs out. In order to do this we knew that we *all* had to be doing some work, not just the new staff person.

We needed to make a commitment to changing the centre. Each of us had to be prepared to question individual ideas, practices, and presumptions as well as the programs that we had in place. Initially this was a painful process. Sometimes it is easier to create something new than to change the habits of a mature group with over thirty years of experience. The project for integrating racialized women became a scapegoat for other structural problems. Rather than using new proposals as an opportunity to update and create innovative ways of engaging in the work, suggestions for change were seen as "*adding to an already heavy workload*," "*not a priority*," or as "*requesting particular privilege for one group of women over another*."

Resistance was encountered both within our own centre and at the RQCALACS coalition level. Many women across Quebec had particu-

7 For a more in-depth discussion of trying to make anti-racism work central to the women's movement, see Sunera Thobani's interview, "Anti-Racism in the Women's Movement" (2007) 5 Upping the Anti: A Journal of Theory and Action, online: <http://uppingtheanti.org/node/3013>.

lar difficulty in accepting the idea that there are substantive inequalities among us. The inclusion of an anti-racist, anti-oppression commitment in our work and our language was seen to be outside of our sphere of activity. The fear was that we were spreading ourselves too thin and operating outside of an "antiviolence against women" framework.

In Quebec, many women came into feminism through the lens of Quebec nationalism and the "quiet revolution" of the 1960s.[8] This period was instrumental in freeing women from the stronghold of the Catholic Church and closely interwoven with the political battle of francophone Quebecers to have equal access to power structures and institutions. The demand for protection of French language and culture occurred simultaneously with the rise of feminism. The intersection between two oppressions, English colonization of Quebec and sexism, forms the identity of many Quebec feminists as members of a doubly oppressed group.[9] Has this experience contributed to impeding the anti-violence coalition, RQCALACS, from making a political commitment to moving forward with concrete actions to be more inclusive of racialized women? How much of the resistance is due to years of pressure from state sources to depoliticize our work, to operate in gender neutral terms, and to remove the advocacy aspect of the work in favour of a service provider model?[10]

After several years of discussions and debates, agreement was reached to include mention of disadvantaged groups in the language of some of the structural documents and yearly action plans of the coalition as well as agreement from each centre to do some inclusivity work. This commitment remains uneven and has been the cause of considerable division within the RQCALACS.

TRANSLATING THEORY INTO ACTION

The challenge was to create the change we envisioned: change in practices, change in attitudes, and change in the power structure. Initially, at the MCVI centre, we began to adapt some of our work by meeting with

8 "Révolution tranquille," a period of rapid social change during the 1960s in Quebec.

9 Diane Lamoureux, « L'Amère Patrie, Entre féminisme et nationalisme » *Le Devoir* [Montreal] (8 March 2001), online: <http://vigile.net/archives/01-3/lamoureux-patrie.html>.

10 See Mandy Bonisteel & Linda Green, "Implications of the Shrinking Space for Feminist Anti-Violence Advocacy" presented at the 2005 Canadian Social Welfare Policy Conference, *Forging Social Futures*, (Fredericton, New Brunswick), online: <http://www.crvawc.ca/documents/ShrinkingFeministSpace_ AntiViolence Advocacy_ OCT2005.pdf>.

advocacy groups working with immigrants and refugees, and creating a network and resource guide of groups and services for women from various cultural communities. We achieved a certain level of success in that immigrant and refugee women began calling us.

What we could not predict was that many of the women we spoke with were requesting asylum from Canada due to sexual violence that occurred in their country of origin. We did not expect to receive so many calls from this cohort. Realizing that there was a lack of support for women in this situation, we quickly began to educate ourselves and to seek training in order to support and accompany women to immigration board hearings. They often needed referrals to other forms of community support for housing, employment, food, and clothing. The boundaries of our interventions expanded, and our understanding of the social context that creates an atmosphere ripe for exploitation was deepened. It became clear to us that many immigrant and refugee women were raped by men who saw the status of these women as an opportunity to further abuse their sense of entitlement and power.

One example of how sexist violence against women and racism intersect surfaced repeatedly when we spoke with representatives of the police. The comments that we received amounted to racial profiling of women who report crimes of sexual assault.

What they said: "*That's just the way it is in some cultures*," or "*Are you sure she won't back out due to pressure from others in her cultural community?*"

What this meant for women: A police culture where racist stereotypes such as "*sexual assault is considered normal in some cultures*" prevails.[11] The result is systemic discrimination and reduced access to justice for immigrant, refugee, and racialized women.

Despite the horrific atrocities experienced by many of the marginalized women that we speak with, we continue to be inspired by their strong will and quiet determination to move forward with their life projects despite all the obstacles they have encountered. It has re-sparked our anger and our determination to find better ways to challenge the banalization of sexual violence endemic to the current state response to the issue. Of greater concern is finding ways to prevent these attitudes from creeping into the anti-violence women's movement.

Too many of us continue to get lost in the overwhelming task of pro-

11 Yasmin Jiwani, "Organizing Against Violence: An Anti-Racist and Anti-Sexist Perspective" (November 1997), FREDA Centre for Research on Violence Against Women and Children, online: <http://www.harbour.sfu.ca/freda/articles/violence.htm>.

viding services to help individual women cope with the distress caused by their experiences of sexual assault, without the advocacy piece. Some of us drop the advocacy piece for the funding; some of us do it for legitimacy, credibility, and recognition; some of us do it because, as women, we feel powerless to confront a system that does not allow for the reality of women's lived experiences, a system that, at its most humane, provides for a medical model response while women continue to be raped, murdered, assaulted, and exploited. We end up contributing, in spite of ourselves, to the maintenance of the status quo.

What our centre in Montreal has been trying to do over the last few years is to understand why, despite our colossal collective efforts, systemic discrimination still infects the criminal justice system and our collective experience of sexual violence. We have rewritten our mission statement and are adjusting our internal structures, our actions, and our priorities to reflect the concerns raised in this paper. I have tried to distill them here.

This paper and these questions are a challenge to all of us working in the feminist movement and an opportunity to engage in friendly discussion and dialogue about where we need to readjust our focus and strategies. They are posed with the utmost respect, admiration, and affection for all the women who have dedicated years of extremely difficult work on the front lines to improving our collective lot.

I would like to close with a quote that always me reminds of how I need to approach the work. It is by Australian Aboriginal Dreamkeeper, Lilla Watson: "If you have come here to help me, you are wasting your time.... But if you have come because your liberation is bound up with mine, then let us work together."[12]

ACKNOWLEDGEMENTS

This paper was written with the permission of, *Le Mouvement contre le viol et l'inceste* where I work and where we have courageously examined our methods, our past miss-takes, our successes. We are continually adapting our practices to reflect the current challenges facing the women's anti-violence movement.

With much appreciation to my co-workers and friends, Denise, Diane, Louise, Nora, Pilar, Rita, Roz, Sarwat, and Sonia for graciously taking the time to read this chapter and for their input and suggestions.

12 Lilla Watson, Aboriginal educator, Brisbane, Australia. As quoted on the website of "Virtual Sister of Mudgin Gal," online: <http://www.virtualsisters.org.au/VSisters-h.PDF>.

14. Vitreous Fragility: Reimagining Women Through Art

Shary Boyle[1]

This section of the book explores feminist artistry as an essential aspect of bringing feminist knowledge about sexual assault into action. Shary Boyle uses her work to express taboo subjects like trauma and shame, and so she embraced the challenge of illustrating Jane Doe's book, The Story of Jane Doe, *with drawings that used humour to subvert the official narrative of sexual assault and to celebrate women's resistance. Her current artistic practice pushes the boundaries between media, gender, animals, humans and the natural world. By refusing to work within accepted categories, Boyle creates new space for envisioning change.*

As a visual artist, I draw inspiration from a rich history of incredible women in my field who have tenaciously battled to express their personal truths. The world of historical and contemporary art has been and remains steeped in gender inequality. The art I make comes out of a long tradition of subversive, powerful female artists who have paved the way for the next generation to carry on. I would like to introduce the audience to some of the work I have created in the spirit of feminist expression and social change.

I graduated from the Ontario College of Art when I was twenty-one, and the drawings I began creating after my school experience became the foundation for my practice today. The most important thing I have ever done as an artist and a woman is to give myself permission to explore my ideas uncensored. Early on, I began developing a visual language to express the angry, painful, or taboo subjects I was just beginning to process. Sometimes these images were very difficult to look at, but as I let the feelings move through me, I discovered my own humour and capacity for mischief and joy. Creating artwork empowered me; it

1 I would like to thank Jane Doe for her ceaseless action and strength of commitment on behalf of all of our legal rights, as well as her humour, intelligence, and vision in supporting the many ways to tell a story.

2005. *Soldiers Aren't Afraid of Blood.* Ink on paper. For the Illuminations Project, with Emily Duke. Photography by Rafael Goldchain.

1998. Untitled. Ink on paper. Originally published in *Witness My Shame*, Conundrum Press, Montreal, PQ, 2005.

allowed me to define my personal voice outside of any pre-existing system. There was no right or wrong, no class or gender restrictions to my imagination. As a girl from the blue-collar suburbs, I found this experience transcendent. It was total freedom, and for the first time I felt like I could begin to tell my own story.

This early work allowed me to safely translate the self-destructive urge produced by trauma away from my body and into marks on a page. I was able to describe my anger and invent alternative worlds that better illustrated how I wanted life to be. Truth and imagination are therapeutic when forged. As my work developed, it became more balanced, in parallel to the evolution of maturity often experienced during our twenties and thirties. My young efforts planted the seeds for many important projects, one of the most profound being an invitation to make drawings in response to Jane Doe's Book *The Story of Jane Doe.*[2]

In 2000, Jane Doe contacted me after being introduced to my art through a mutual friend, Lisa Steele. Jane's vision for the book she was about to write was radical — like her activism and character it stepped outside formal expectations into a realm of charged, inspirational brio. Jane believes art is an essential partner in activating social imagination for change, and incredibly, she invited me to translate the feeling of her narrative into images. Two years later, I had her manuscript in my hands. At the time I was living for a season in Los Angeles, in the tropical-desert of an Echo Park sublet. All that summer I sat alone outside among the cactus and bougainvillea and allowed Jane's story to sink inside of me, infusing my heart with her concise intelligence and knife-sharp wit. It was easy to envision pictures from those words. I had only to channel the fierce honesty of her observations and meet it with my own. Jane Doe shows us how to rise and take a stand.

Working with Jane's beautiful, brilliant manuscript was a challenge I was deeply honoured to accept. I tried with all of my instinct and insight to create images for her text that live between the lines, lifting and whispering to parts of the mind that might be further awakened through the visual. *The Story of Jane Doe* was an incredible collective effort, and it is my hope that some of these images served as charged conduits to inspired understanding.

Themes of subversion and resistance have always compelled my imaginaton, and feel really great to explore. I have been invited to contribute to some wonderful alternative feminist publications over the years, such as *Girls Who Bite Back*[3], edited by Emily Pohl-Weary and *Scheherazade*[4], edited by Megan Kelso. These were compilations of woman artists and writers on subjects of heroism, story-telling, friendship, and

2 Jane Doe, *The Story of Jane Doe: A Book About Rape* (Toronto: Random House, 2003).

3 Emily Puhl-Weary, ed, *Girls Who Bite Back: Witches, Mutants, Slayers and Freaks* (Toronto: Sumach Press, 2004).

4 Megan Kelso, ed, *Scheherazade: Stories of Love, Treachery, Mothers and Monsters* (Berkeley, CA: Soft Skull Press, 2004).

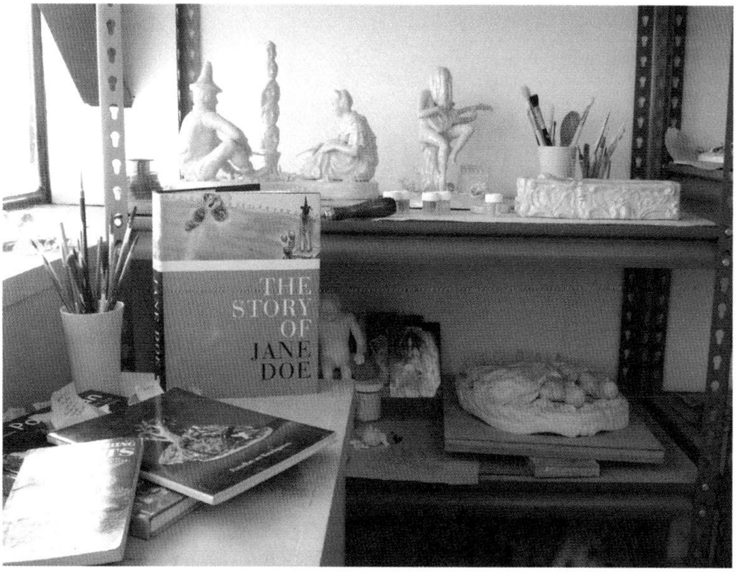

View of Shary Boyle's studio with work in progress and favourite books, Toronto, ON.

strength. I learned too from my own books, *Witness My Shame*[5] and *Otherworld Uprising*[6] that describing our own pleasure in detail is just as necessary, and even as radical, as confronting our anger.

My practice now includes performance, painting, and sculpture as well as drawing. In 2002, I discovered the medium of porcelain through a hobby-workshop I took in Seattle, Washington. This workshop was led by eighty-six-year-old Vivian Hausle and focused on creating romantic female figurines, in the Royal Doulton style. I have always been drawn towards the mystery of decorative detail. Seduced by decorative detail, I realized these dolls were a perfect foil to confront and examine societal assumptions around fragility and the feminine. Using the historically charged medium of porcelain — which is loaded with a range of female class associations from "refined good taste" to "granny's kitsch" — I set out to harness the spellbinding power of ornamental beauty to explore issues of violence, silence, restriction, and the

5 Shary Boyle, *Witness My Shame* (Montreal: Conundrum Press, 2004).

6 Shary Boyle, *Otherworld Uprising* (Montreal: Conundrum Press, 2008).

2002. *Activism.* Ink on paper. Originally published in *The Story of Jane Doe*, Random House of Canada, Toronto, ON, 2003.

sexual subjugation of women. The figurines found their own agency, by insisting on disorder and vulnerability. Porcelain is the strongest of all ceramics, and its vitreous transparency compliments difficut revelation.

The response that this series engendered caught the attention of institutions like the National Gallery, who moved to acquire my work. I

2002. *Accountability*. Ink on paper. Originally published in *The Story of Jane Doe*, Random House of Canada, Toronto, ON, 2003.

feel that the acquisition of these figurines by public collections across Canada is a victory for all women and, in particular, for female artists. It is crucial for works of art by women that give explicit voice to feminist perspectives on violence, sexuality, and identity be supported by our museums. My narrative has been included, and joins those of other women in history who have laid down their stories. I have an abiding

1999. *Camp Coochiching.* Ink on paper. Originally published in *Scheherazade*, Soft Skull Press, Brooklyn, US, 2004.

hope that tomorrow's youth, when viewing this work on public display, will feel included, curious, and most importantly, the courage to put their own voices forth into a diverse cultural dialogue.

In 2008, I was approached by the Art Gallery of Ontario with a commission to create two new porcelain sculptures in response to their collection of seventeenth-century Italian bronzes on Greek Mythology. Their invitation was to create new works that might reflect on and converse with these antiques. These works are now installed in the newly renovated Historical European section of the AGO.

I began the commission by researching the myths represented by the bronzes, in order to select which ones I would like to work with. The project was an opportunity to re-examine ancient history from an imagined perspective of the women so often subjected to rape, abduction, and the role of the victim within the stories. I selected the *Rape of Proserpine* and *Perseus Slaying Medusa*. My goal was to create a radically alternate reading of these myths, as a feminist intervention within the museum.

In the Greek telling of Proserpine's story, she is a young woman helplessly abducted by Pluto, the God of the Underworld. The omnipotence of Pluto's desire overrides any question of Proserpine's will or identity: she is no more than an object to be taken. Proserpine is abducted from the fields where she is working with her mother Ceres, the Goddess of the Harvest. In order to return to the underworld with his captive, Pluto must pass through a sacred glade tended by the water nymph Cyane. Cyane tries to rescue Proserpine, but her attempts only provoke Pluto into destroying her glade in a rage. The devastation of the nature she was steward of, and her failure to save the young woman, cause Cyane to literally dissolve into tears, replenishing the very pool that had been destroyed.

When planning *The Rejection of Pluto*, I wanted to remove the helpless quality of inevitability from the events. These women could not be inherently ineffectual. In my version, they own their strengths, express their resistance, and enforce Pluto's responsibility for his actions. Here, as Pluto emerges through Cyane's pool, three women are united to meet him. They reflect and reject his intentions, from mirrors placed on symbolic areas of their bodies.

Ceres represents the power and resilience of age, her face a mirror that shines with the flame of intelligence. Proserpine represents the emotional position of the child, the witness and subject of our adult abuses of power. She holds out her slashed arms in a calm display of the effects of trauma, forcing the viewer to consider her vulnerability.

Porcelain doll artist Vivian Hausle in her Seattle, WA studio.

Between them sits Cyane, a figure of mature sexual potency. The full strength of her fertility and erotic autonomy refracts all negative intention to harm or possess. Pluto, embodying human greed and violence against the entire natural world, and our futile need to control it, does not stand a chance.

In researching the second bronze, I discovered Medusa as a young woman had also been raped, by one of the lesser gods of the sea. It is written that the beauty of her hair "overcame him." For her "crime" of stolen virginity, her seductive locks were transformed into a nest of snakes as punishment. A classic blame-the-victim narrative, you can read the long-established contemporary rape myths throughout this entire scenario.

Ultimately, Medusa and her Gorgon sisters were reduced by circumstance to isolated monsters living on a remote island in the sea. There is a sense in the stories that they were much happier there, alone together!

Perseus, in pursuing romance, was given the impossible challenge to behead her for no other purpose than to prove his heroism. Medusa

2004. Untitled (*Pregnancy*). Porcelain, china paint, gold luster. Collection of the Art Gallery of Ontario. Photography by Rafael Goldchain.

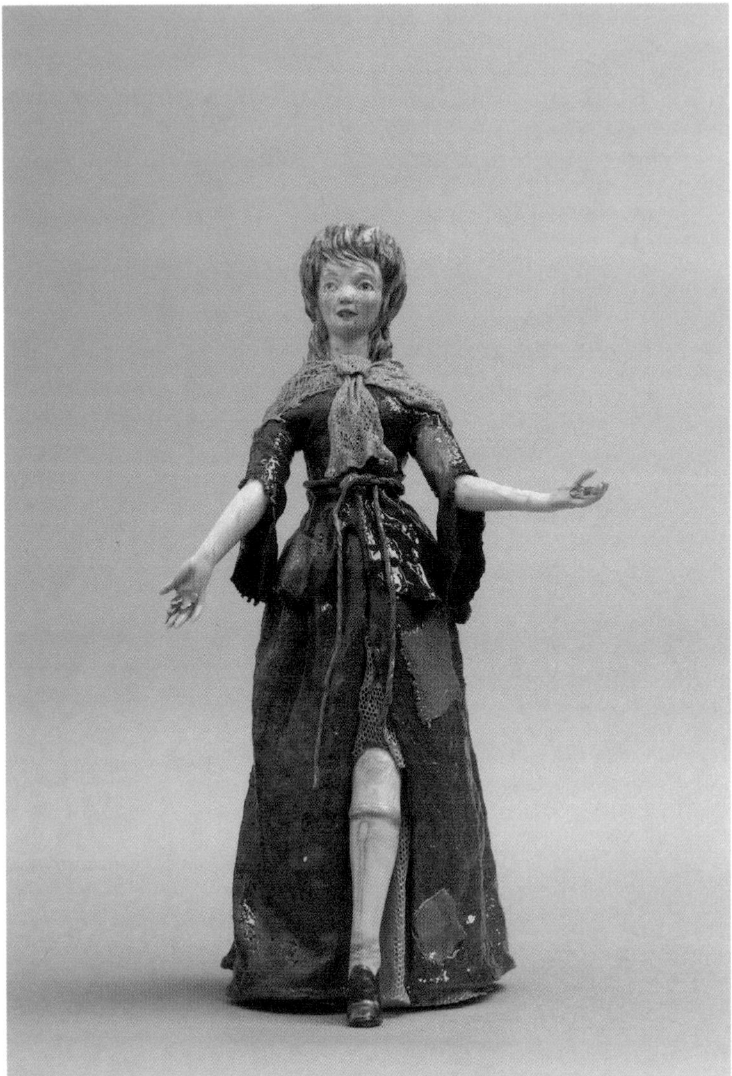

2004. *Untitled* (Poverty). Porcelain, china paint, gold and silver luster. Collection of The Rooms, Newfoundland. Photography by Rafael Goldchain.

2004. Untitled (*Flowers*). Porcelain, china paint, silver luster. Collection of The National Gallery of Canada. Photography by Rafael Goldchain.

2005. *Ouroborous*. Porcelain, china paint, gold and silver luster.
Photography by Rafael Goldchain

was a resource to be plundered, in the service of furthering his personal goals. She represents the unknown, the foreign, the marginalized — the Monster.

In *To Colonize the Moon*, I seek to draw attention to the relationship between environmental destruction and colonization. My response to the classic Medusa myth asks us to consider our fear of the unknown, and the repercussions of our need to villainize and dominate what is foreign to us. My Medusa is a woman of indeterminate race, her disembodied portrait a testimony to the repercussions of violence. Her head sits on a cairn of little brown bats and honeybees as maligned creatures facing their own destruction. Perseus as a child becomes a metaphor for the selfish compulsiveness that leads us to exploit nature, acknowledging our very human capacity for greed. The hero stands to destroy himself by the very outcome of his short-sighted victory.

Cultivating our creative powers as women adds strength to all of our lives and stories. Art can allow us to imagine change. Describing experience through acts of imagination can be a powerful way to strengthen the voice of the marginalized.

2008. *The Rejection of Pluto*. Porcelain, china paint, mirror, LED light, gold luster. Created by commission for the collection of the Art Gallery of Ontario. Photography by Rafael Goldchain.

2008. *The Rejection of Pluto* . Porcelain, china paint, mirror, LED light, gold luster. Created by commission for the collection of the Art Gallery of Ontario. Photography by Rafael Goldchain.

2008. *The Rejection of Pluto* (detail). Porcelain, china paint, mirror, LED light, gold luster. Created by commission for the collection of the Art Gallery of Ontario. Photography by Rafael Goldchain.

2008. *To Colonize the Moon*. Porcelain, china paint, diamond, mirror, gold and silver luster. Created by commission for the collection of the Art Gallery of Ontario. Photography by Rafael Goldchain.

I believe it is crucial to envision preferable realities, and to lay those ideas down like train tracks. One day this line will support a train of thought to hold the collective force of all our dreams, with the weight and momentum to carry them into the future.

2008. *To Colonize the Moon* (detail). Porcelain, china paint, diamond, mirror, gold and silver luster. Created by commission for the collection of the Art Gallery of Ontario. Photography by Rafael Goldchain.

2008. *To Colonize the Moon* (detail). Porcelain, china paint, diamond, mirror, gold and silver luster. Created by commission for the collection of the Art Gallery of Ontario. Photography by Rafael Goldchain.

15.
The Jane Doe Coffee-Table Book About Rape: Reflections on Rebellious Writing and Teaching[1]

Gillian Calder and Rebecca Johnson[2]

Gillian Calder and Rebecca Johnson return Part I full circle to focus on Jane Doe's The Story of Jane Doe, *discussed in the first chapter, as a piece of feminist law-making. By paying attention to the details of the book's layout, use of text, photographs, and news files, they show how Jane Doe made brilliant use of art — not only Shary Boyle's but her own — and of narrative to tell her story. Gillian and Rebecca challenge the notion that "law" exists separately from activism and art, arguing that Jane Doe's book is not only a book, but is also a feminist activism against sexual assault, as vividly shown by the Garneau Sisterhood's postering campaign, and is more important than the* Jane Doe *case itself for its disruptive intervention in women's struggles to end sexual assault.*

Rebecca: I hope people who wanted them got copies of Jane's book — *The Story of Jane Doe: A Book About Rape.*[3] Did you know that some of my students this year couldn't get copies? They were told it was out of print.

Gillian: Get out! I don't believe you.

Rebecca: I'm not kidding. Seems unbelievable, eh? At first, I thought maybe the students were trying to get out of doing the assignment. But then,

1 Earlier versions of this chapter were presented at the conference in honour of Jane Doe, 7 March 2009, in Ottawa, Ontario, and again at "Law, Culture and the Humanities" on 4 April 2009 in Boston, Massachusetts. We are grateful to the audiences in both places for their challenging feedback and whole-hearted responses. The images were part of a gift made to Jane Doe from the conference presenters, each of whom was asked to send a photo of him or herself with Jane Doe's book, or a picture of the book doing what they thought the book would do. We are grateful for the creativity and bravery that surrounds us, and that attaches itself to Jane Doe.

2 Both Gillian Calder and Rebecca Johnson teach law at the University of Victoria's Faculty of Law.

3 Jane Doe, *The Story of Jane Doe: A Book About Rape* (Toronto: Random House, 2003).

when I tried to find the book online at Amazon, I was faced with a page that read: "Currently unavailable. We don't know when or if this item will be back in stock."[4]

Gillian: Seriously — Amazon!? What are you doing buying books online — shame on you! You should be using our local feminist bookstore. What did they say when you asked them to order in Jane's book?

Rebecca: They didn't say anything, in fact, because my local feminist bookstore closed its doors quite some time ago now. Out of business, I am afraid.

Gillian: Out of business?! That is ridiculous. Both things are ridiculous. But let's talk about the book first. A book like this can't be "currently unavailable." This book matters. This book is *law* and law doesn't go out of print. In fact, this book is more law than the law itself. If you really want to know the law, then read the book! The book is more "the thing" than the thing we think the thing is.

Rebecca: Uh … that was a mouthful. Do you want to take another run at articulating that idea?

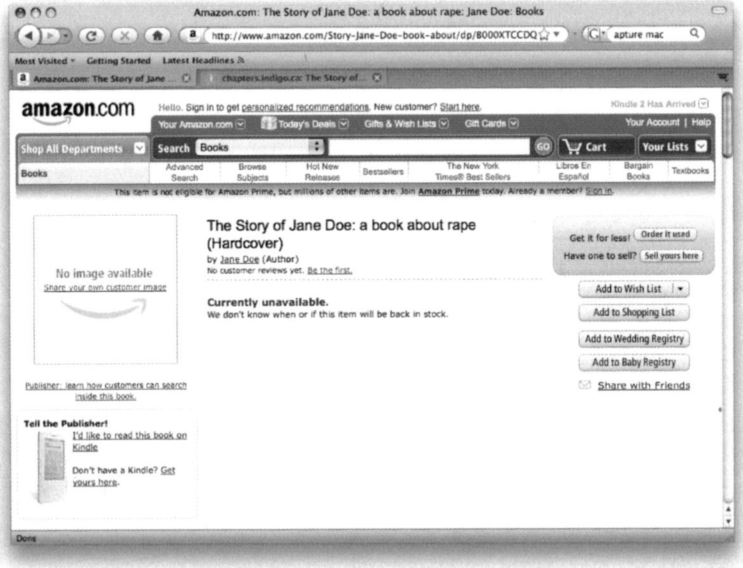

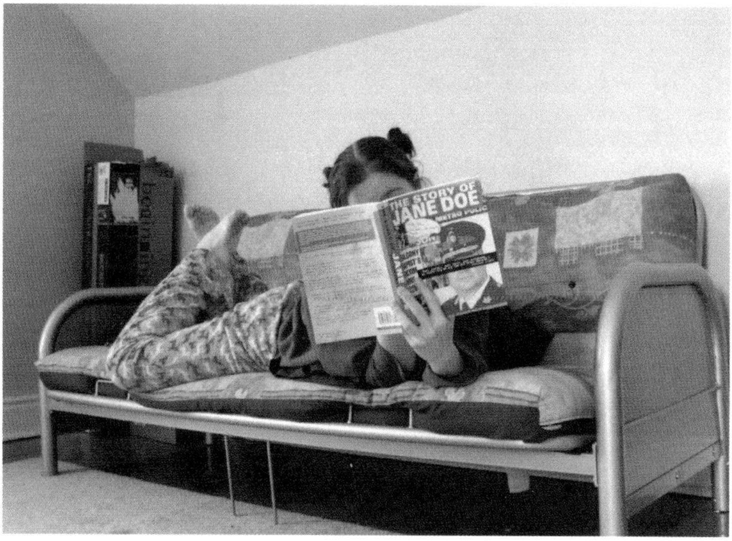

Photograph used with the permission of Katherine Mazurok.

Gillian: Yes, I do. Okay. *Jane Doe*[5] is a groundbreaking and important case. That case matters. But so does *the book*. The book is itself a paradigmatic piece of resistant and rebellious feminist activist law-making. It's irreverent, provocative, performative, and necessary. Let me make this argument: as legal text, the book is more important than the case.

Rebecca: That is a bold statement, my friend.

Gillian: I'd love to take credit for this argument — but it really is yours. It's what you told me when you said that I HAD to read the book. Actually, I think what you said was that when you first read this book it made you laugh out loud. How could that be, I thought? How could a book written by a survivor of sexual assault, who sued the Toronto Police Department and won, be funny? Feminists aren't funny.

Rebecca: Ah, so true. We feminists are not seen to be funny people. And let's push that a bit. You're not supposed to laugh when you are reading a

5 *Jane Doe v Metropolitan Toronto (Municipality) Commissioners of Police* (1998), 39 OR (3d) 487 (Ont Ct (Gen Div)).

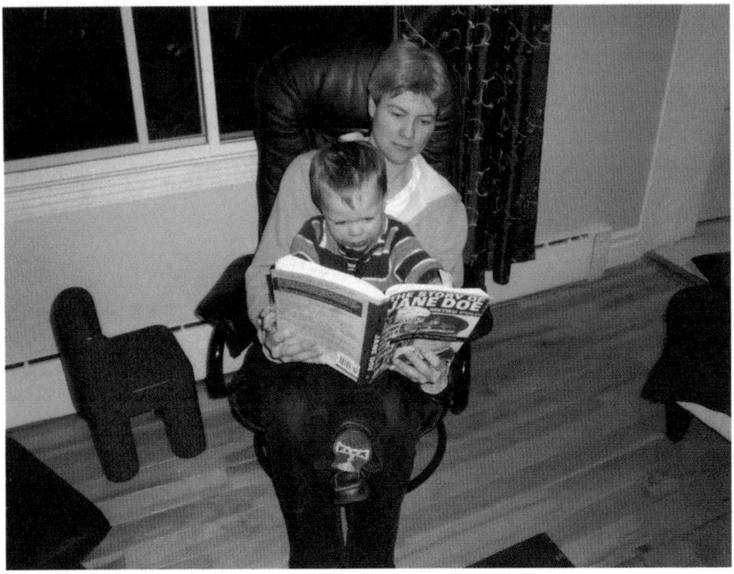

Photograph used with the permission of Kim Brooks.

book on rape. But I did. And the laughter felt like rain on the desert. It opened up a space of possibility. The experience of reading *The Story of Jane Doe* (or, as she wanted to call it, *Jane Doe's Coffee-Table Book About Rape*) provoked me in many, many ways. Though I laughed, I also felt mad, sad, culpable, empowered. And that was just me. I mean, just imagine the wider audience that reads this book. The diversity and range of experience and reaction this book can provoke is untrammeled.

Gillian: Yet everything that the book provokes, particularly the emotional response, is linked to our desires for justice. These are the kinds of responses that separate this book from other experiences of law and, at the same time, the responses keep us moving, give us the drive to keep working, challenging, struggling, pressing, dreaming, marching, and hoping. These feelings harness the power that fuels our desire for change, our hope for strategies and tactics, if not solutions. The book, we argue, is an important source of law, a treasure trove of rebellious and resistant strategies for educators, activists, academics, advocates. And because it made us mad to think that generations of students, activists, complainants, lawyers, and judges might miss out on the insights of this book, we have, in a way that draws on our strengths as teachers of the law, mapped the argument, making the simple visible, or perhaps (un)necessarily complicated.

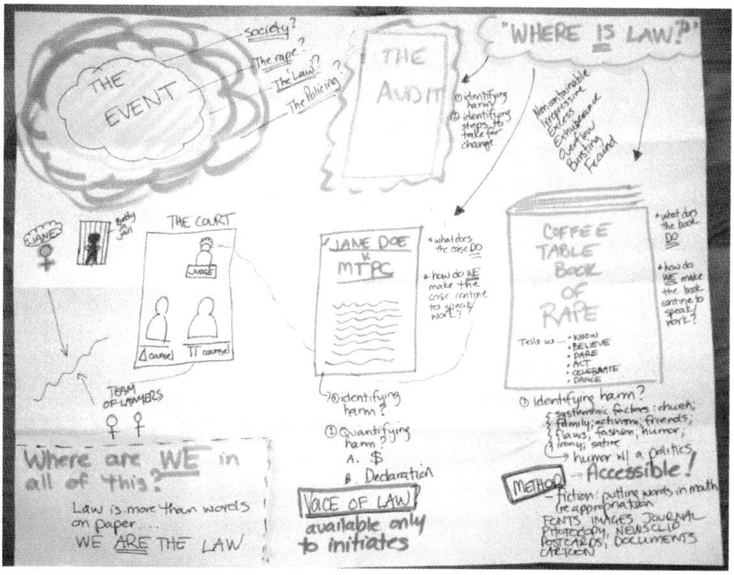

Photograph used with the permission of Rebecca Johnson.

Rebecca: Okay. So, reflecting on the structure of the book, the experience of reading the book, and the experience of teaching with the book, we argue that there are important feminist insights to see in the multiple tools of communication mobilized in the book (ie scrapbooking, journaling, art work, memoir, irony/mockery, fictionalization, doodling). These tools work together to disrupt stereotypes of both rapists and women who are raped, and unsettle received assumptions about the role of criminal law and courts in sexual violence. Indeed, without at all diminishing the importance of the legal judgment (the finding of police liability in the particular case), we argue that the book itself[6] is perhaps the more powerful and disruptive feminist intervention in ongoing struggles around violence against women.

Like the conference held in March of 2009 to honour Jane Doe's work and the ten years of activism that have passed since the decision

6 When we presented the paper this chapter is based on in Boston at the 2009 "Law, Culture and Humanities Conference" we were asked the question, did it matter that the material was presented as a book or would we still argue for the importance of the material if presented electronically instead of in print? Although accessibility to the narrative is important, we argue that the tactile experience of the book is fundamental to its power. We hope the images of the presenters from the conference and the book that you see in this paper also answer the question posed.

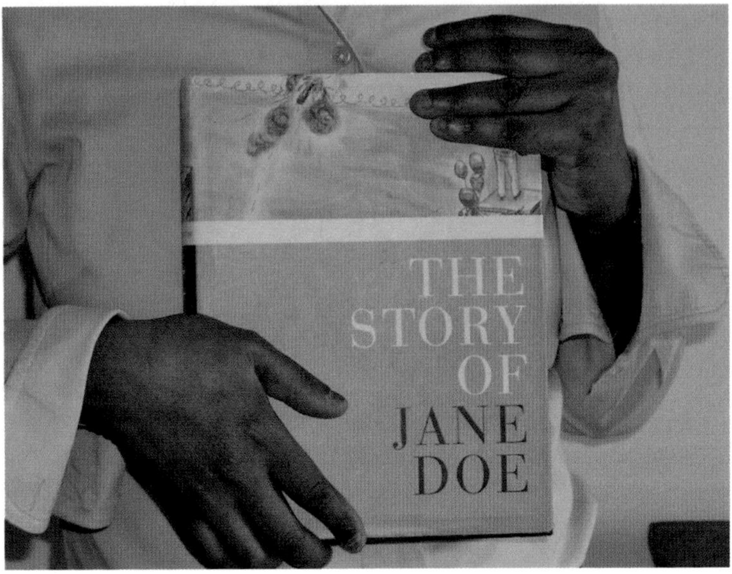

Photograph used with the permission of Beverley Bain.

was rendered,[7] the book claims the right to use law, while simultaneously refusing to allow the law to shape the terms of the debate, or to claim victory on behalf of women. The book celebrates performative storytelling, much as we saw at the conference in the presentation made by Tracey Lindberg, Priscilla Campeau, and Maria Campbell. Their paper, "Indigenous Women and Sexual Assault in Canada,"[8] told in three voices, laid bare the relationship between Canadian criminal law and the construction of Indigenous women's legal identities. The presentation, however, used an innovative methodology, challenging the audience's awareness and perception, and performing the essence of the stories being told in keeping with the significance of the subject matter.[9] Indeed, Jane's book offers innumer-

7 On 6–7 March 2009, the University of Ottawa hosted the Conference, "Sexual Assault Law, Practice and Activism in a Post-Jane Doe Era." For information on the conference, including a schedule of presenters, see online: <http://www.commonlaw.uottawa.ca/en/conference/janedoe2009/home.html>. Students at the conference also hosted a blog, see online: <http://citizen.nfb.ca/blogs/jane-doe-conference/>.

8 Chapter five in this book.

9 For a discussion of how the relationship between the form of the presentation and the substance of the presentation matters for meaning-making in law, see Elizabeth

Photograph used with the permission of Jessica Derynck. "I can't believe I read this book eight times and someone still had to point out the penis tie."

able lessons and strategies to those who consider themselves activists working in educational settings, and does so using a methodology of presentation that fits the form of the message sent. And, importantly, it continues to challenge you as a reader, no matter how many times you have opened the pages and re-read the stories told.

Gillian: These photos and images from the book are extremely important to understanding its performativity.[10] Both the cartoon drawings and the journal entries demand that stories of rape be told in certain ways, in ways that erase how colonialism, race, ableism, heterosexism, and othering shape our experience. On issues of ability, for example, Fran Odette challenged everyone present at the conference: be open to being challenged to see that the structures you work with-

Adjin-Tettey *et al*, "Postcards from the Edge (of Empire)" (2008) 17 Soc & Leg Stud 5; and Gillian Calder, "Guantanamo: Using a Play-reading to Teach Law" (2010) 142 Can Theatre Rev 44.

10 The relationship between performance, performativity, and law is best articulated in the work of Judith Butler. For a discussion of Butler's work, see Gillian Calder, "Embodied Law: Theatre of the Oppressed in the Law School Classroom" (2009) 1 Masks: The Online Journal of Law and Theatre 15–18.

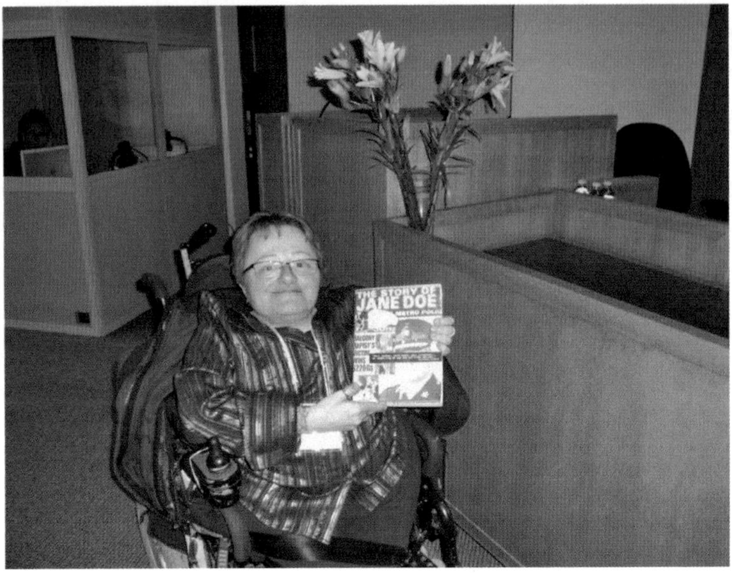

Photograph used with the permission of Fran Odette.

in fail to accommodate and include disabled persons.[11] Regardless of how you engage personally, and how the individual defines her experience, we live in a society that positions experiences as binaries — those who are different from those considered "normal" — but by whose standards? The drawing and the journaling used in the book is similarly confronting; by using different media, images, and fonts, Jane facilitates our rage. It lets us see the ridiculousness of much of what gets accepted or naturalized, and challenges us, as Fran Odette does, to continually confront the structures that surround and anchor our world.

Rebecca: I think it is fair to say that the book challenges our perceptions of normativity in numerous ways. In one example on page 146, she includes an article, but starts the article in the middle. This matches the frequency of how often we find ourselves in the middle of a story, having to wait until later to find out what happened earlier, and to figure out if what happened earlier even makes a difference. And the article that she includes has her own scribbling, scratching out the

11 Fran Odette, "Sexual Assault and Disabled Women: Ten Years After *Jane Doe*," Chapter 8 in this book.

Photo used with the permission of Random House.

name of the accused, who throughout she refers to only as "buddy." Law doesn't ordinarily let us decide who gets scribbled out and who doesn't. What we see in the performance of the act of scribbling is how we approach rationality in this context. But it also performs the agency of the author amidst the plethora of ways in which her agency to engage with the legal is denied. In this image, and within the pages of this intimate telling of her story, she gets to scribble him, not erase him, just scribble him.

Gillian: I like that the book disrupts the experience of reading by engaging us in a process of embodied reading. This is evocative of Natasha Bakht's presentation at the conference, where we as an audience were asked to think about how the law of credibility and demeanour evidence are written onto women's bodies. As in her paper,[12] in the way in which the law constructs women who wear the niqab, the law here is jarring. Jane uses the visual — in places a mere change of font — to reflect back to the reader the disjunctures embedded in the law. Her use of this form of embodied reading provokes a different means

12 Natasha Bakht, "What's in a Face? Demeanour Evidence in the Sexual Assault Context," Chapter 23 in this book.

Photograph used with the permission of Natasha Bakht.

of engaging with the words on the page, the differences between the pieces of text, and the resulting dissonances for women facing the differences those laws allow.

Jane employs a similar technique on page 92 when the page splits into two columns. In one column, the narrative continues unbroken from the previous page. In the other column is a list of "Rape Stats" adapted from a government pamphlet on rape. In neither column is there an explicit reference to the material in the other column. As a reader, you are faced with the juxtaposition of the two texts — a narrative on one side and statistics on the other — with the statistics operating in a form that is not summarized and inserted, but runs as a parallel text. You also have to choose how and when to move back and forth between the two texts, to decide the relation in which the two texts stand. The result is the conflation of text, subtext, paratext, hypertext, parallel text, in a way that is itself textual, textured, and contextual.

Rebecca: Fragments of documents (newspapers, pamphlets, checklists, legal documents, police forms, etc.) are actually sprinkled and strategically located throughout Jane's book. And although this book is not alone

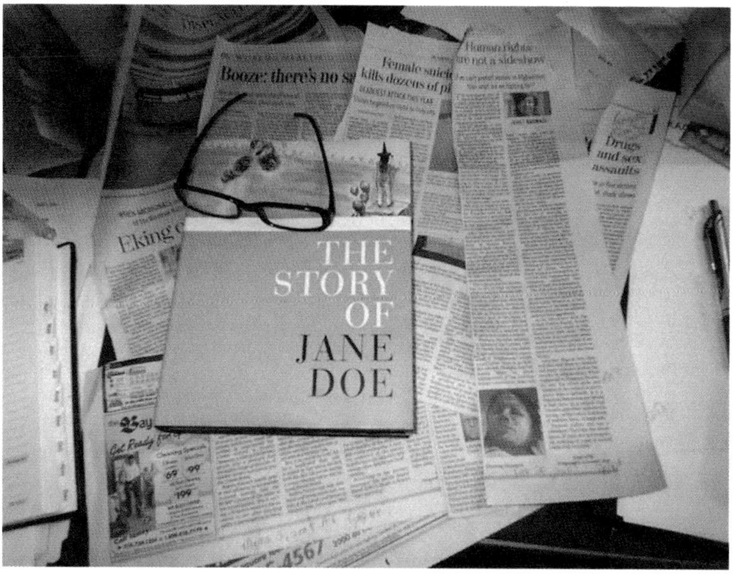

Photograph used with the permission of Yasmin Jiwani.

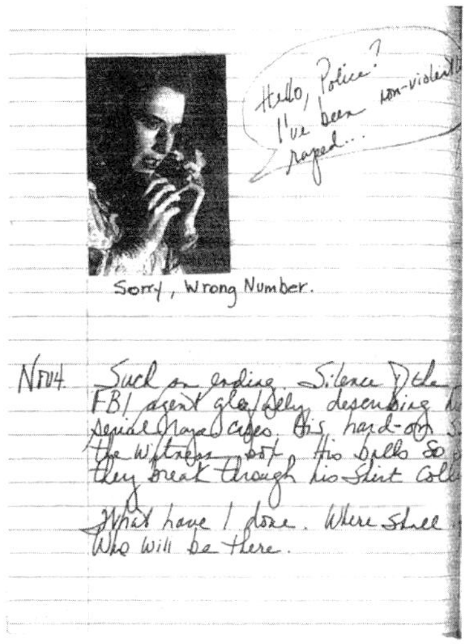

Photograph used with the permission of Random House.

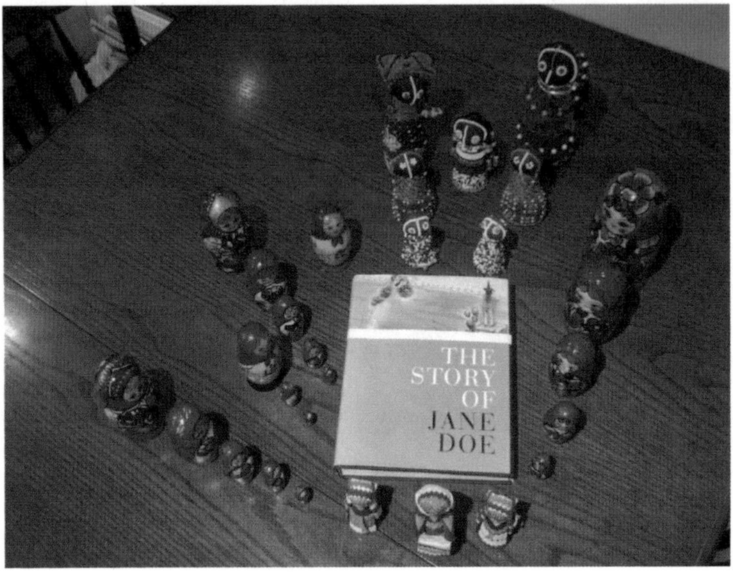

Photograph used with the permission of Susan Bazilli.

in *talking* about the processes that make the legal system so cumbersome for complainants, there is something very powerful about the way Jane *shows* it, making visible the nuts and bolts of the bureaucratic. For example, by using an image of the statement of claim on page 117, we are reminded of how much it takes to file a technical, rule-based legal document like this, how many people are knocked out of even starting an action because of what it takes to file one of these, and with this particular statement of claim, how much went into getting it filed. And so within the pages we see "law" present in its courier font, stamps, signatures, reality. And she displays one of the three victories, not to have her statement of claim struck.[13]

Gillian: And there is another example in the reproduction of the police report filled out in Alice's rape (Alice was the first woman now known to have been raped by the Balcony Rapist). The police report has one

13 Notwithstanding the "win" of damages in Jane's case, some other legal precedents were established that are recorded and given life in the book. One is not having her statement of claim struck. See Elizabeth Sheehy, "The Victories of Jane Doe," Chapter 1 in this book.

line that requires someone to enter the "reasons for crime." Typed there are the words "sexual gratification." But the words would have been nearly invisible in the busyness of the form had not someone taken a pen and circled those words, "sexual gratification," again and again, drawing our attention to them. And here, we see that the inclusion of these document fragments within the text is important not only for documenting the institutional and textual processes around rape.[14] Jane's annotation of the documents is yet another means through which the book and its story of rape are performed. The book, using documents that have passed through multiple hands, can retell and undo the very event at the heart of the story.[15] In the process, we are reminded of all that swirls around women when they are moving these issues through the courts, how law in this area remains so profoundly gendered.[16] In using the book to retell the story, Jane shows how the law of sexual assault is so ordinarily filtered into its categories and shaped by others. In the mere gesture of circling the offensive words in an ordinary court document, Jane as complainant gets to take it back. Circle in pen and take it back.

Rebecca: Jane also uses humour as a form of activism. On page 103, for example, I found myself laughing out loud, both at the intentional humour and the contradictory meanings that she uses to provoke. Look at Jane's description of feminism:

> There are many feminisms, many practices and applications. Feminism can be radical, socialist, liberal and postmodern. Well maybe it can't be postmodern ... but it can be, and is, defined differently by academics, legal practitioners, front-line workers and women who do not work directly under its umbrella.

In a text that is achingly postmodern in format, content, and effect, she tells us that feminism can't be postmodern. That's funny.

14 For a useful discussion of the ways that texts and documents structure the experiences of women in front of the legal system, see Ellen Pence, "Safety for Battered Women in a Textually Mediated Legal System" (2001) 7 Studies in Cultures, Organizations and Societies 199.

15 See *The Story of Jane Doe*, *supra* note 3 at 82.

16 It seems ironic to have to footnote that the law of rape is profoundly gendered. So we won't give you a citation for this assertion. We just make it.

Photograph used with the permission of Gillian Calder.

Gillian: The quote about feminism also points to another strength of Jane's book. It makes visible the work of activists. In amongst the narrative and the photographs and the court documents, Jane also includes the kinds of documents that many of us who have worked in Rape Crisis Centres have seen and worked with. For example, at page 88, she includes a page from a rape crisis manual, and right in the centre of the page we see a column that is dedicated to the systemic context of the issues faced. This page specifically, and the book more fundamentally, reminds us that women have been working to make visible the systemic issues in rape for a long time.

Rebecca: Again a reminder that in its "book form" the message is inherently different. That page from the manual is not all pretty formatting: it is courier font, typed on a typewriter, and it looks like the columns have been drawn in with a ruler, and the "bullet point" for each issue is coloured in with pen. It is hands-on activism. It reminds us not only how resource thin our groups are, but also about the amazing work that women have always done with whatever resources they have at hand or can cobble together. It is forward moving. We could spend nine hours figuring out how to format a document on the newest version of Windows, or we can just grab a pen and paper and

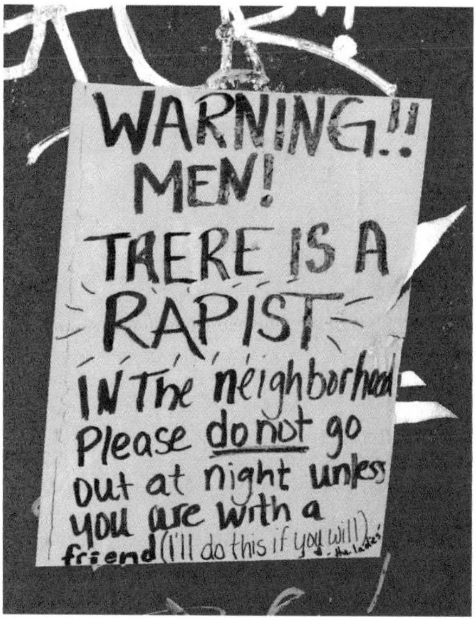

Photograph used with the permission of Lise Gotell.

do what the Garneau Sisterhood does! As Lise Gotell, Meagan Johnston, Katherine Mazurok, and Shannon Sampert showed us at their phenomenal panel on the Garneau Sisterhood, police warnings, and other media representations of myths and stereotypes, the visual is a powerful method of meaning-making.

Gillian: Juxtaposition is an important aspect of why the book tells the story in a way that the case just cannot.[17] For example, on page 75, we have the juxtaposition of the narrative text and a victim impact statement. Here we get how, amidst the irreverent storytelling, Jane still makes us feel in the moment that she is protecting the readers from what she herself has felt. It makes visible the emotional impact of this kind of bravery without wishing it upon others … helps us acknowledge why the telling of such tales is difficult and can itself cause further trauma. It helps us see why law's demand that we "tell the damage" is

17 For a good discussion of juxtaposition and how to engage with the complicated juxtaposition of history and culture, see James Clifford, *The Predicament of Culture* (Cambridge: Harvard University Press, 1988) at 11. Thank you to Hester Lessard who greatly enhanced our thought in her discussion of juxtaposition in a presentation that contextualized demands for the removal of a statute of Matthew Begbie from the lobby of the Fraser Building at the University of Victoria.

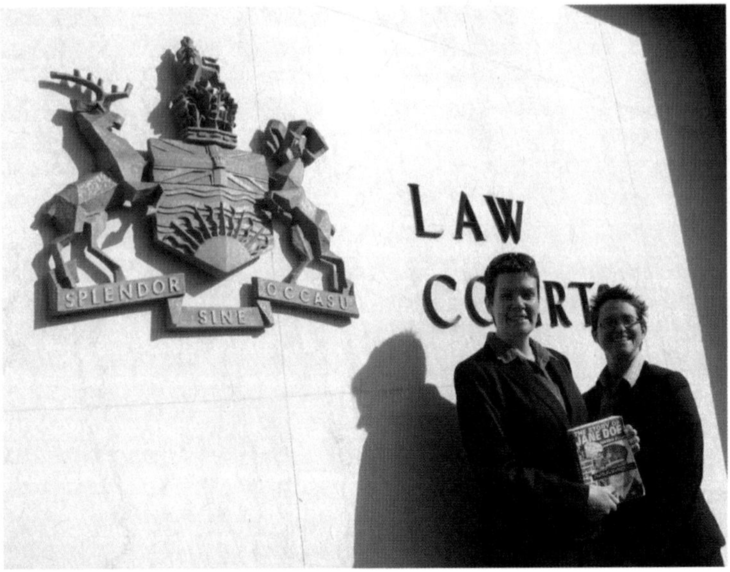

Photograph used with the permission of Jessica Derynck and Didi Dufresne.

a problem. The book reminds us of Jane's extraordinary courage and generosity, something that exists in abundance in the women's movement around sexual assault in Canada.

We saw similar courage at the Jane Doe conference when Jessica Derynck presented her paper and stood in front of an audience to recount her own story of being raped at rifle-point in Cambodia. She then complicated her story with an insightful race analysis of how and why her position of privilege on the basis of race led to differential treatment in the courts and a further "othering" of Cambodian women.[18] Similar acts of courage took place when audience members like Rosalind (whose last name we never learned) stood up and, in response to a panel on residential schools, told their own stories of sexual assault and survival.

18 Jessica Derynck's paper was entitled, "Lessons Not Learned in *Jane Doe*: Analysis of Western Involvement in a Canadian's Sexual Assault Case in Cambodia," [unpublished]. See Jessica Derynyck, "Lacking Context, Lacking Change: A Close Look at Five Recent Lower Court Sexual Assault Decisions" (2009) 14 Appeal: Rev Current L & L Ref 108.

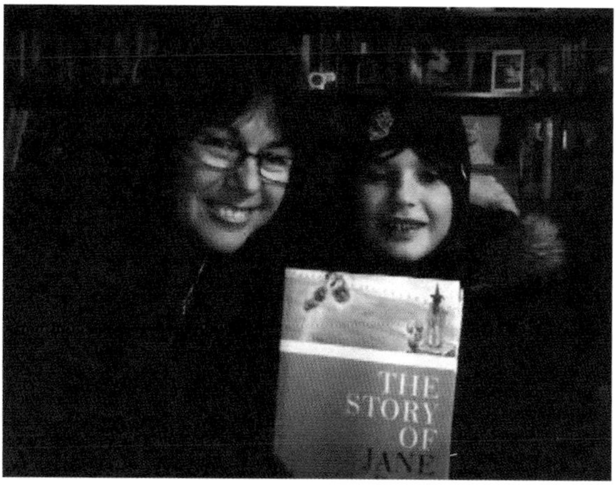

Photograph used with the permission of Kim Pate and Madison Pate.

Rebecca: And even when we pause and are moved by her bravery, Jane doesn't leave us comfortable. We see this, for example, on page 12, putting the words of semen and pubic hair on the page, letting narratives and checklists stand beside each other, or run overtop of each other. This form of jarring imagery reminds us that the private medical exam is conducted behind drawn curtains and yet is devastatingly public.[19] Again the juxtaposition demonstrates the disjuncture of what women face in the process of surviving sexual assault, showing how the deadened scientific language is so at odds with the hyper-saturation of emotions and responses that characterizes the much more textured narrative vibrating beside it.

Gillian: I see that page and it reminds me how much it annoys me when people talk about "seminal works" or "disseminating knowledge." This book makes me want to get those words out of our vocabulary!

Rebecca: The book also *is* law. On page 68, for example, Jane includes what may appear just to be a newspaper clipping, but in fact what she includes is arguably "a law report." It is the only reported version, in fact, of the decision made to enable Jane to stay in the courtroom, to hear the testimony in buddy's trial. She tells us the story of that legal

19 Jane Doe, "Who Benefits from the Sexual Assault Evidence Kit?", Chapter 16 in this book.

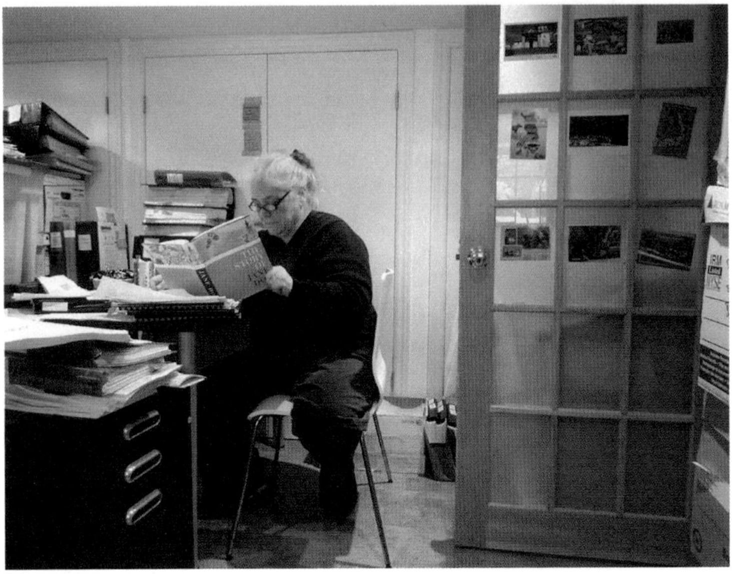

Photograph used with the permission of Mary Eberts.

action in the book. She tells us in the footnote on page 70 that the judgment is recorded in *The Globe and Mail*, yet the only place we know about that is in the book. The book IS LAW.

Gillian: There is also the use of the ironic. And it's so simply done. She shows you the images without adulteration, letting them speak, hilariously, painfully, honestly, and ironically for themselves. On page 39, we see the photograph of a bus shelter where on one side there is a poster that reads, "The Pope Sends His Best," and right next to it, as if finishing the sentence, a poster reads, "Rapist in this area." On page 274, we see the front page of the *Toronto Star* where, alongside a large headline that reads, "Balcony Rapist's Victim Wins $220 Gs," is a photograph of a woman in a bikini overjoyed at winning something quite different. Even Alanis Morissette would think that was ironic.[20]

20 A good way to discuss the proper use of the word ironic is to listen to Alanis Morissette's 1995 song, "Ironic" from *Jagged Little Pill*. Is rain on your wedding day really an example of irony?

Photograph used with the permission of Shary Boyle.

Rebecca: Pictures help us "speak" things that words just can't. Shary Boyle's paintings in the book are amazing. The paintings, commissioned specifically for the book, provide another vocabulary that calls to us, tells us to help in whatever ways we can, to celebrate ourselves, and to speak truth to power.

Gillian: Like the photos, we can read ourselves into the marchers. We get a sense of activism, of people joining together in support. People marched. They carried placards. And at the conference, as we were reminded, it is getting harder to march.[21] But not impossible. Collectively, the book challenges us to keep yelling out the slogans so integral to those marchers: "Women unite, take back the night!" "Hey mister, get off my sister!" "Whatever we wear, wherever we go, yes means yes and no means no!" and "Cut it out or cut it off!"

21 In her book, *supra* note 3, Jane discusses the ways in which "Take Back the Night Marches" are seen to be less relevant today.

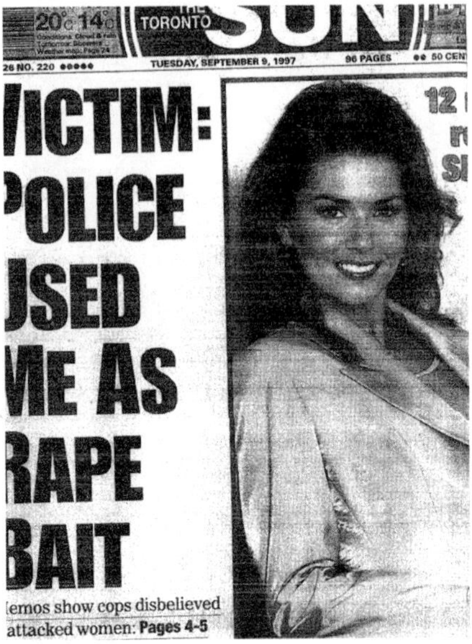
20°C 14°C
TORONTO SUN
26 NO. 220
TUESDAY, SEPTEMBER 9, 1997
96 PAGES
50 CEN

ICTIM:
OLICE
JSED
ME AS
RAPE
BAIT

emos show cops disbelieved
attacked women: **Pages 4-5**

Image of book page used with the permission of Random House.

Rebecca: The book calls us in and reminds us. And we also get glimpses of Jane. In one image near the beginning of the text (on page 5) we see her feet; in another image near the end of the text (on page 293) we see her hand.

Gillian: And, perhaps in breach of the publication, Jane actually does reveal her true identity in the book, and it turns out … she's Shania Twain.[22]

Rebecca: It's funny — but it also reminds us that good feminist work can happen in lots of places. Yes, the newspaper editors diminish the power of the headline by placing it alongside Shania. But, at the same time, it is on the first page, and the "conservative paper" is doing the better reporting. The book and the image remind us not to judge too quickly the places from which help and support can come.

Gillian: I think that finding myself in the book is part of what makes this book so compelling for me. It takes me back to when, as a young,

22 This "ironic" image can be found on page x.

Photograph used with the permission of Elizabeth Sheehy.

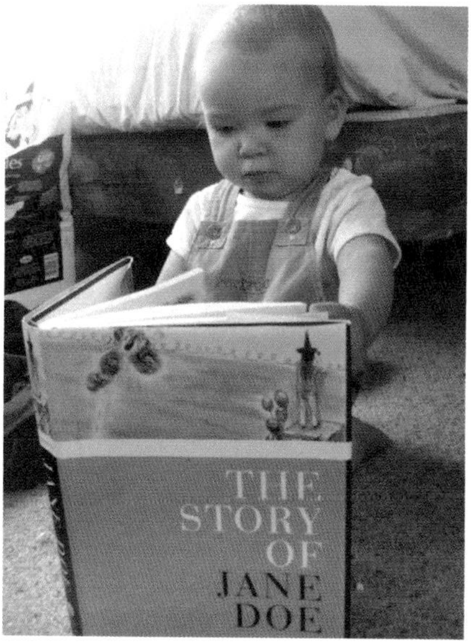

Photograph used with the permission of Julia Tolmie.

Photograph used with the permission of Teresa DuBois.

geeky reader, I found myself in the pages of Anne of Green Gables. Even though Jane is telling the narrative of a difficult and true documentary story, she still manages to harness the power of the novel in her readers. At the same time, what kept me in the text was the way that the law in this book gives power, recognition, and appreciation to all the different roles that people played; there isn't just one way to be in the story. Not everybody is Jane Doe, but so many people played a role in her case and, to my surprise, I found myself in there too. Jane's book reminds me that I am part of the solution and part of the hope.

Rebecca: And that kind of takes us back to where we started. The book is law. It may be in some places in the margins, and maybe for the written law, that is it where it belongs. But law is imbued in every page. And it seeps out, and into us, as portrayed in the images throughout this article, photographs taken and sent in by presenters at the conference, whose love of this book as a tool of political change runs deep. We can only include some of the many, many images we received, all of which showed the many and diverse ways that this book has touched, inspired, angered, moved, and given strength and support to us as a collective.

Gillian: We want to conclude our tribute to Jane and her book by urging everyone to take up the challenge of this book and, in so doing, to be part of making sure that the story of Jane Doe goes forward. Don't let books like this one go out of print. It is one of the many things we can do — keep on telling the ever-evolving story of Jane Doe.

Part II

16. Who Benefits From the Sexual Assault Evidence Kit?

Jane Doe

The first section of Part II examines the practices of evidence production, proof, and adjudication that determine whether responsibility for sexual assault will be allocated to alleged perpetrators. Jane Doe's research investigates the utility and harms caused by the Sexual Assault Evidence Kit from the perspective of women who have experienced this form of evidence gathering as well as the perspective of community-based workers who support them and those who administer the kit. This chapter bridges from Part I, which explored aspects of women's lived experience of sexual assault and the very real perils of entering the legal system, as well as the professionalization and institutionalization of rape crisis services. Here Jane Doe demands that we ask who benefits from the kit when women so consistently report it as a further assault and its legal value is so tenuous. Her persistent question, "who benefits?" from the medicalization of sexual assault upon which the kit is premised, also fuels her important challenges to feminists to make linguistic choices that do not further disempower women who have been raped and to interrogate the role of racism in sexual assault.

Examining Canadian laws and policies as they apply to women who experience sexual assault feels like a natural progression for me. It is the next step in the body of work I began when, over twenty years ago, I became the woman in the lawsuit, *Jane Doe v the Metropolitan Toronto (Municipality) Commissioners of Police.*[1]

I am interested in addressing the ways in which certain protectionist Canadian public policies in the areas of sexual assault exert control over women by limiting their choices, agency, and activities.[2] The degree to

1 *Jane Doe v Metropolitan Toronto (Municipality) Commissioners of Police* (1998), 39 OR (3d) 487 (Ont Ct (Gen Div)).

2 Jane Doe, "What's in a Name? Who Benefits From the Publication Ban in Sexual Assault Trials?" in Ian Kerr, ed, *Lessons From the Identity Trail* (New York: Oxford University Press, 2009) 265, similarly reflects on the protectionist nature of Canadian sexual assault legislation.

which the distinctively gendered and sexual nature of the violence of sexual assault elicits an exceptionally paternalistic and protectionist response on the part of the state and policy-makers cannot be dismissed.

The stigma and lack of agency afforded to women who have experienced sexual assault are powerful in constructing them/us as "victims" who are disordered or otherwise unstable, and in need of paternalistic state protections.[3] Certainly, women who have experienced sexual assault are not alone in being subjected to these myths and formulations. State policies enshrined in sexist and discriminatory stereotypes of female gender/sexuality work especially to disenfranchise women who are Aboriginal, racialized, sex workers, disabled, or women who live with poverty.[4]

In addressing the Sexual Assault Evidence Kit [SAEK] in this paper, I attempt to trace government initiatives that have relocated feminist, community-based, sexual assault, and other Violence Against Women [VAW] services into medical/hospital institutions. The negative effects of the corporatization of women's anti-violence services through the implementation of "one stop" medical and social work models of practice are observed. I identify the resultant pathologizing of rape as illness, and the loss of funding and advocacy functions within feminist, community-based rape crisis and sexual assault centres.

Questions of informed consent, and the problems regarding the gathering, efficacy, and purpose of the [SAEK] and its medico-legal functions were exposed by women I interviewed. They identify the kit and its process as unnecessary, invasive, and terrorizing.

3 In addition to many of the articles in this text, a sampling of writing on this subject includes the following: Jane Doe, *The Story of Jane Doe: A Book About Rape* (Toronto: Random House, 2003); Lise Gotell, "Rethinking Affirmative Consent in Canadian Sexual Assault Law" *(2008)* 41 Akron L Rev 865; Elizabeth Sheehy, "Causation, Common Sense and the Common Law: Replacing Unexamined Assumptions With What We Know About Male Violence Against Women or From Jane Doe to Bonnie Mooney" (2005) 17 CJWL 97 ; and Carol Smart, *Feminism and the Power of Law* (London: Routledge, 1989).

4 Rosemary Basson, "Sexual Health of Women with Disabilities" (2005) 17 CJWL 97 (1998) 159 Can Med Ass J 359; Janet Mosher, *No Cherries Grow on Our Trees: A Social Policy Research Paper for the Take Action Project to Address Women's Poverty and Violence Against Women* (Toronto: Metropolitan Action Committee on Violence Against Women and Children, 2008); Mariana Valverde, *The Age of Light, Soap, and Water: Moral Reform in English Canada, 1885–1925* (Toronto: McClelland & Stewart, 1991); Yasmin Jiwani, *Discourses of Denial: Meditations of Race, Gender and Violence* (Vancouver: UBC Press, 2006).

The legal, corroborative purpose of the kit and women's experiences of it reveal the improbability that they have given informed consent for its collection. I further observe the lack of a standard of practice in kit content and collection within and across regions, controversy amongst medical and legal institutions that administer and utilize the kit, and its insignificant effect on the legal process.[5]

THE LANGUAGE OF RAPE

Feminist activists, researchers, and scholars have been examining rape and its significance on women's equality, agency, and choice for decades.[6] Critiques of the legislation and policies that govern the crime are certainly not original to this chapter. There also exists an impressive body of Canadian research specific to the use and efficacy of the [SAEK].[7]

To my knowledge, however, there is little that situates women who have experienced the crime of sexual assault/rape as experts and analysts of their own experience. It is impossible to find research that privileges or even equates their narratives with those of other experts. There is also little that identifies sexually assaulted women's acumen, joy, or intelligence. I attempt to do some of that here.[8] In doing so, I wish to

5 This research was originally conducted through a grant received by myself and Kara Gillies from Status of Women Canada in 2006. Titled "Bound by Law: How Canada's Protectionist Public Policies in the Areas of Both Rape and Prostitution Limit Women's Choices, Agency and Activities," it treated sexually assaulted and sex-working women as distinctly separate groups who are nonetheless "sexed, classed" and similarly cast as damaged and in need of enhanced state protection. In addition to the SAEK, I researched police rape warnings while Gillies conducted separate interviews and research regarding the procuring law and how the criminalization of third-party participation in prostitution has a negative impact on sex-working women. As we prepared to enter the editing phase of our project, the Conservative government of Stephen Harper cut funding to Status of Women Canada. The work remains unpublished.

6 For example: Christine Boyle *et al*, "Tracking and Resisting Backlash Against Equality Gains in Sexual Offence Law" (2000) 20 Can Woman Stud 72; Susan Brownmiller, *Against Our Will: Men, Women And Rape* (New York: Simon and Schuster, 1975); Catharine MacKinnon, *Feminism Unmodified: Discourses on Life and Law* (Cambridge: Harvard University Press, 1987); Elizabeth Sheehy, ed, *Adding Feminism to Law: The Contributions of Justice Claire L'Heureux-Dubé* (Toronto: Irwin Law, 2004); Smart, *supra* note 3.

7 See the sources cited *infra*, note 36.

8 Janice Du Mont, Deborah White & Margaret McGregor, "Investigating the Medical Forensic Examination from the Perspectives of Sexually Assaulted Women" (2009) 68 Soc Sciences & Med 774, conducts similar research with important findings. My research, however, is differentiated from theirs on the basis that it was not influenced

address naming practices in feminist academia and research, and in the VAW movement in Canada, that designate sexually assaulted women as victims, survivors, and, recently, "thrivers." The reduction of the complexity of raped women's experience to three tiers of health status fits current medico-legal and social work bureaucracy requirements that do not work in women's best interests. It promotes a survival of the fittest rubric that marks and defines raped women through our pain and suffering only and "others" us from other (seemingly) non-raped women. The terms reduce the diversity of women's experience of sexual assault, denote passivity (victim), or infer violence (survivor), and severely limit sexually assaulted women's narrative agency.[9] I do not deny or minimize the suffering or horror raped women endure, nor am I in denial of our ability to exercise agency, choice, and control regarding our lived experience of the crime. I will use the terminology "women who have been sexually assaulted/raped" and or "sexually assaulted/raped women" throughout this paper. I encourage readers to similarly examine the very language of rape[10] — to reclaim, redefine, and expand it in order to better understand its nature and to effect meaningful change.

In keeping with this critical attention to language, I do not use the discourse of victimization or uncritically impose a victimology analysis on women's experiences.[11] I purposefully use the terms "rape" and "sexual assault" interchangeably to indicate the contested and unresolved meanings of those terms, that crime, and the understandings of sexual assault as "non-violent."

I have used the term "experiential" to denote women who have "experienced" sexual assault and "key informant" for those who advocate for and work with them.[12] The term "experiential" might be similar-

by medical institution regulations, language, or perceptions of authority from respondents; it provides a critique of the role of the hospital and the police regarding the kit; and was conducted with women whose kit had or had not been used in the criminal trial process.

9 See Tami Spry, "In the Absence of Word and Body: Hegemonic Implications of 'Victim' and 'Survivor' in Women's Narratives of Sexual Violence" (1995) 18 Women & Lang 27.

10 Susan Ehrlich, *Representing Rape: Language and Sexual Consent* (London: Routledge, 2001), examines the gendered nature of language used in sexual assault trials.

11 Certainly there are women who have experienced sexual assault/rape who choose such naming practices: I support their decisions completely.

12 I was reminded by an early reader of this paper that many women who work in community and institution-based agencies in the area of sexual assault have also experi-

ly used to refer to women who live with disabilities, poverty, or other factors that affect/define a woman's experience of life. Of late, the expression "experiential" has come to refer solely to sex-working women and in a negative or victimizing context. I propose to reclaim the word here, in solidarity with sex workers, and as phraseology that empowers women — when there is so little that does — and situates them as experts/witnesses/agents of their life histories.

I refer only to the experiences of adult women in this paper and include biological and transgendered women in that definition, although I am not informed directly by interviews with women who identify as transgendered. All names have been changed to ensure anonymity and participants were given the option to choose their own pseudonyms.

METHODOLOGY

In-depth, semi-structured interviews were conducted in four Canadian provinces with twelve women who had experienced sexual assault/rape. The crimes took place between 1999 and 2005.

Another eleven interviews were held with advocates in feminist community-based sexual assault and rape crisis centres (six), and with hospital-based social workers and health care providers (five).

Of those twenty-three women, two were Aboriginal (experiential), three were Black (one experiential, two key informants), and three were women of colour (two experiential, one key informant). Four were Quebecoise (two experiential, two key informant), and one was Acadian (experiential). Three women self-identified as Jewish, and eight (six key informant and two experiential) as lesbian. Five women disclosed that they lived at or below the poverty line (experiential), and two had previously been homeless (experiential). Ages ranged from twenty to sixty-three. The majority of key informant women were over forty years of age.

One-on-one semi-structured interviews lasted between one-and-a-half to two hours and took place between 2005 and 2006. Snowball and purposive sampling techniques[13] were enhanced by my personal

enced the crime, making the distinction less relevant. While this is undoubtedly true and of note, I am mindful of the race, class, power, and access differences that can exist between both groups of women, however minor they might be.

13 Snowball sampling consists of identifying participants who then refer researchers to other participants. Purposive sampling is used to access a particular population of respondents. In this case, I distributed an email about my proposed work to community-based rape crisis and sexual assault care centres which then assisted me in ac-

location as a woman who has experienced sexual assault and the rape kit, which allowed for greater access to a traditionally "hard to reach" group of women.

Because women with disabilities are sexually assaulted at twice the rate of the able-bodied,[14] I felt it important to ask participants about ability status. One woman identified as deaf, another as hearing impaired, and one woman lived with fibromyalgia. Six experiential women identified post-traumatic stress syndrome or disorder, bi-polar disorder, panic attacks, and other obsessive behaviours as disabilities that had been diagnosed since their rapes or were negative factors in the outcome of their investigations/trials.

Prior to the interviews, women received written information about the nature of this research. Questions were closed and open-ended and focused on their prior knowledge of the kit, their experience of it, and what they thought of it now, which also led to other perceptions and comments. Women were advised that they could choose what to answer and could stop the interview process at any time. I was in contact with counselling services in their communities should these be requested/required by the women with whom I spoke. (They were not). Experiential women were paid a small honorarium ($50) for their work and contributions.

RACE AND RAPE

It is my contention that rape and race can never be separated and certainly that is reflected in reactionary responses to the crime. There is a convenient and popular belief, for instance, that Aboriginal and racialized women are raped more and report their rapes less because their cultures promote violence against women, and they are more subject to shame, community censure, disbelief, and the fear of powerful men, than are white women.[15] While such strictures certainly exist, it is the nature and consequence of colonialism, racism, and systemic racist beliefs and stereotypes that further inhibit racialized women from re-

cessing women who were interested in being involved. See Rowland Atkinson & John Flint, "Accessing Hidden and Hard to Reach Populations: Snowball Research Strategies" (2001) 33 Soc Sciences Update 1.

14 For a recent discussion see: Statistics Canada, "Criminal Victimization and Health: A Profile of Victimization Among Persons with Activity Limitations or Other Health Problems" *Canadian Centre for Justice Statistics* (May 2009), http://www.statcan.gc.ca/pub/85f0033m/85f0033m2009021-eng.pdf.

15 Margaret Wente, "Wired for Submission" (4 November 2006) *The Globe and Mail* A 23.

porting to the police or accessing the legal system. Sherene Razack examines the degree to which we allow the term "culture" to replace words like "racism" in and outside of the courtroom, especially for Aboriginal, racialized and immigrant women:

> A knowledge of cultural difference of the Other helps those in dominant groups to classify and manage subordinate groups. The eagerness with which theories of cultural difference are taken up in the justice system, while racism, and sexism remain unnamed is a reminder that culture is a treacherous ground to travel in a white supremacist and patriarchal society.[16]

In writing about the Indian subcontinent, Ratna Kapur speaks of competing understandings between "the West and the Rest" and the essentializing of gender, culture, and victim rhetoric:

> The exclusive focus on violence against women does not reveal the complexity of women's lives, but only the different ways in which they may experience violence. Thus, culture is involved primarily to explain the different ways in which women experience violence, in the process often reinforcing essentialist understandings of culture and representing particular cultures as brutal and barbaric.[17]

In response to my research question, "Do you think that 'different' women are treated differently when they have been sexually assaulted?" there was unanimous agreement from participants that Aboriginal, racialized and immigrant women endure racism when they report their rapes. Young women, poor women, lesbians, trans-women, and sex-working women were also identified as less likely to be believed by police and the courts because of their social placement, and therefore less likely to report.

THE BIRTH OF THE KIT

The 1980s were a significant time for the women's movement in Canada. Because of the movement's frontline work in the 1970s to identify and stop the murder, beatings, and rape of women by men, and subsequent government lobbying, a network of shelters and rape crisis cen-

16 Sherene H Razack, *Looking White People in the Eye: Gender Race and Culture in Courtrooms and Classroom* (Toronto: University of Toronto Press, 1998) at 80.

17 Ratna Kapur, *Erotic Justice: Law and the New Politics of Postcolonialism* (London: Glasshouse Press, 2005) at 104.

tres was established across Canada.[18] Workers and allies used a feminist language of anti-oppression that identified gender, and intersected race, class, sexual orientation, and ability. Male violence against women was acknowledged (by some) as a systemic and gendered crime that affected women's safety of the person and their equal status.

In 1983, changes in sexual assault legislation, progressive at the time, expanded the definition of rape to include forms of sexual assault other than penetration. Bill C-127 established three levels or degrees of sexual assault, and the need for third-party corroboration or witnessing was removed as an essential element for proving the crime.

In the same period, feminists working in community-based rape crisis or sexual assault centres argued that hospital staffs were not responding adequately, or at all, to women who arrived at Emergency because of having been sexually assaulted. In addition, the evidentiary needs of the legal system to found and prosecute the crime were not being met.[19] The conception of the hospital-based Sexual Assault Care and Treatment Centre [SACTC] to provide health care, feminist advocacy, and counselling was the response. SACTCs were also mandated to regulate the collection of medical forensic evidence for use in the police investigation in a SAEK, also known as the rape kit.[20]

The kit itself is a sturdy sealed cardboard box that contains instructions, diagrams, and containers for the collection of biological specimens taken from raped women's bodies. The contents undergo forensic analysis to determine, confirm, or establish the identity of the perpetrator, whether force was used, and time of the assault as a means of independently and scientifically corroborating the raped woman's personal narrative of what occurred.[21]

18 Lee Lakeman, *Canada's Promises to Keep: The Charter and Violence Against Women* (Vancouver: Canadian Association of Sexual Assault Centres, 2003).

19 Georgina Feldberg, "Defining the Facts of Rape: The Uses of Medical Evidence in Sexual Assault Trials" (1997) 9 CJWL 89.

20 The first Sexual Assault Treatment Centres [SACTS] was established in Ontario in 1979. Known as Sexual Assault Care Centres, the "treatment" designation was added in the 1990s to better reflect their purpose. In 2004, Ontario SACTCs were restructured again to become Sexual Assault and Domestic Violence Treatment Centres. This paper focuses on sexual assault and I will use the term SACTC when referring to hospital/clinic-based sexual assault care centres in all regions. The inclusion of "domestic violence" in the SACTC mandate is also an issue of concern and debate in the VAW shelter sector.

21 Janice Du Mont & Deborah Parnis, "An Overview of the Sexual Assault Care and Treatment Centres of Ontario" [revised and expanded] (2002) *World Health Organization*, online: http://www.womensresearch.ca/ PDF/programs/whoapr2003.pdf.

The SACTC has developed to such an extent that it currently employs teams of nurses, doctors, and social workers. The evolution of the SACTC, however, is such that it now purports to serve multiple agendas in addition to the interests of the woman who has been sexually assaulted. Government ministries and interests have expanded the scope and number of SACTCs so that, consequently, they have replaced many shelters and rape crisis centres by (i) relocating them within the hospital or clinic environment; (ii) reallocating their funding within the hospital budget; and (iii) mandating corporate models of governance and operation.[22] Initially a combination of feminist politics, government agendas, and good faith, hospital-based services for women who have been sexually assaulted have transformed into a nationwide infrastructure of highly regulated medical and social work teams that provide services to women, the police, Crown and defence lawyers, and not necessarily in that order.

Andy worked in a rape crisis centre in central Canada and has this to say:

> So when the sexual assault care and treatment centres came into being, for rape crisis workers at the time, it was like: "how come our saying out loud what was important for women has turned into a whole other service that has the potential for not being really great for women?" It's kind of like antiviolence activists identifying that children witnessing violence was a problem, and then that turns into a whole terrible legislation that CAS uses to take kids away from mom.

THE INSTITUTIONALIZATION OF SEXUAL ASSAULT

Feminist writers and researchers have begun to examine what is referred to as the professionalization or corporatization of the VAW movement.[23] They refer to, among other things, the adoption and subsequent co-optation of advocacy and counselling services for adult women who experience sexual assault by institutions of medicine/health and social work. One result they document is the defunding

22 Mandy Bonisteel & Linda Green, "Implications of the Shrinking Space for Feminist Anti-Violence Advocacy" (2005), online: www.crvawc.ca/.../ShrinkingFeminist-Space_AntiviolenceAdvocay_OCT2005.pdf.

23 *Ibid*; see also Betsy A Harvie, *Regulation of Advocacy in the Voluntary Sector: Current Challenges and Some Responses* (Ottawa: Voluntary Sector Initiative, 2002) and Carol Latchford, "Gimme Shelter in 2006" (2006) 25 Can Woman Stud 6.

and devaluing of autonomous, feminist, anti-oppression apparatuses in women's anti-violence agencies. Another is the medical pathologizing of women's response to sexual assault as diagnosed in the fourth edition of the Diagnostic Statistical Manual [DSM IV], the medical psychiatric "bible" that defines and dictates forms of mental illness and competence.

This collusion of medical and legal institutions to assess a woman's claim of sexual assault has become the new standard in sexual assault investigation and prosecution. According to a conference paper delivered by Mandy Bonisteel and Linda Green:

> In the past few years, the enormous uptake of medicalized approaches to trauma treatment has overtaken investment in non-medical, alternative supports. In institutional settings, psychiatric best-practice guidelines have been developed for the treatment of post-traumatic stress disorder (PTSD), for the treatment of women diagnosed with Borderline Personality Disorder and for women who self-harm. Some studies have begun using women in shelters to test and develop psychological measures ... Differences in the power of medicine in relation to [anti-violence] sectors result in credibility differences regarding who is best suited to deal with social issues [when in] reality numerous perspectives and strategies are required to take up social issues and provide community alternatives for those who seek support.[24]

Today, the largest subspecialty of forensic nursing is the provision of care to women who have been sexually assaulted. This role is filled by the Sexual Assault Nurse Examiner [SANE], "an experienced nurse who provides comprehensive care to sexual assault victims, usually after completing a brief but extensive training programme plus clinical supervision within a local institution. Their instructors include professionals from the fields of law enforcement, criminal justice, forensic science, nursing and medicine."[25]

THE KIT AS A FORENSIC TOOL

The process of administering the full sexual assault evidence kit takes about four hours (although some women I interviewed reported seven and eight hours), and women who undergo it are required to sign a consent form, as is common for most medical procedures. Uncommonly, women must also give additional written consent to hand the

24 Bonisteel & Green, *supra* note 22..

25 Susan Kagan-Krieger & Gail Rehfeld, "The Sexual Assault Nurse Examiner" (2000) 96 Can Nurse 26.

test results over to police officers to be used as part of the investigation into their sexual assaults.

The purpose of the kit is as follows:

> Forensic evidence is collected to establish three things: that a recent assault has occurred, that force occurred during the assault and that the identity of the assailant has been confirmed (through DNA analysis). The collection of evidence is done in a systemic, controlled and consistent manner. Such an operation ensures that the highest quality of objective evidence is collected, and minimizes the potential for loss of evidence. Furthermore the evidence is more reliable and has a greater chance of admissibility in court if it is collected according to standard protocol.[26]

In examining the actual application of the kit, however, researchers have identified that there is no standard practice or protocol regarding the number, nature, or collection of the tests that compile the SAEK.[27]

The kit requires the administration of physical "tests" as well as documentation in which the woman involved answers questions about the assault and her current and past medical history. SANEs record all visible injuries on diagrams indicating their type and size and are required to document any signs or reports of physical resistance as kit components. In some regions, health professionals who administer the kit provide written assessment of the woman's emotional status, scrape under fingernails, and ask if she scratched or otherwise "fought back." Kit requirements and evidence of this sort can reinforce the myths that "real" rape involves a certain emotional response and attendant physical injury and that "good" women resist.

Some urban hospitals have modified their kits in response to the recommendations of coalitions and committees that include representatives from SACTCs, policing, law, government, and medicine in their attempt to make it more user friendly. In some cases, women who work in community-based rape crisis centres have been at those tables. On the other hand, experiential women, those who have had the kit conducted on their bodies, are not included.[28]

26 *Ibid* at 25.

27 Feldberg, *supra* note 19 and Du Mont & Parnis, *supra* note 21.

28 My repeated attempts and inquiries, over a period of years, to consult with such committees were not responded to by government and hospital-based personnel charged with overseeing the kit, its functions, and its requirements.

Esther, a community-based rape crisis counsellor who prefers that her agency not be identified in any way, sits on such a committee:

> There was endless discussion at this round table that we were a part of where you'd have police, prosecutors, and doctors talk about the slides that should be used to take samples and how they should pull hair out. Totally disembodied from the reality of what that must mean to a woman who has just been sexually assaulted. Sitting around a table for years, it was Kafkaesque, and at one point we became infuriated and left. We felt that it was a diversion of the issues that we were asking to be addressed and the problems of the criminal justice system.

For sexually assaulted women who consent to it, photographs, clothing, swabs, urine, hair, and blood samples appear to be standard requirements in all kits. Blood and urine are taken to determine women's alcohol and drug consumption levels. Health care in the form of medication for STDs, HIV, and pregnancy prevention is administered except in Catholic hospitals where the morning-after pill is not available to any women.[29] Three participants indicated that the large doses of antibiotics and the "morning-after" pill caused them to feel ill. One of them said she felt that her expressed preference to see her own doctor for the medication caused suspicion on the part of the SANE and worked to her disadvantage.

A vaginal examination or internal to detect injury and the detection of sperm or semen is a critical component of the process. The procedure is conducted without a lubricant to prevent contamination of evidence. Some centres have adopted protocols that include the use of a "harmless" blue dye (Toludine) to "stain" the external genital area (one of my research participants spoke of her shock at "peeing blue" shortly after being stained) to better detect injuries. Another is a procedure called a colposcopy, which allows for the magnifying and photographing of the vagina to identify microtrauma not visible to the naked eye. Kits must be conducted within 72 hours of the assault in order to detect evidence. All of the women I interviewed agreed that the internal (vaginal and/or anal) examination, which (if consented to) is standard when penetration has occurred, is painful, humiliating, intrusive, and/or a viola-

29 In some Catholic hospitals, strategies to include the morning-after pill in the kit have been developed.

tion — a veritable second assault.[30] As Scarlett, one of the experiential women I interviewed said

> The internal was painful, but I didn't say anything. The nurse was already talking about all the things that weren't there. While she was doing [it] she was saying there are no lacerations, no signs of rape, no bruising. I wondered if they were going to believe me and where this was going to go.

Michelle, an advocate and health care practitioner in central Canada, voices the concerns of many women:

> For the love of god, why do they have to get DNA from 80,000 different areas? I go for a Pap test myself and I have a complex about my own doctor doing it. I hate it. Vaginal tearing would be the only reason that I could actually see a need for it. Other than that, they've got nails, they've got clothing, they've got skin to skin. I don't see a need for it.

As a forensic tool, the rape kit requires that the bodies of raped women function as crime sites, much as would occur in a homicide investigation where the (deceased) body is mined for evidence, or the site of a bank robbery, where areas are closed off except for police access and inspected for clues, especially DNA. Raped women are instructed not to wash, urinate, or defecate, and their outer and undergarments are required for inspection and evidence.[31]

THE KIT AS CORROBORATIVE EVIDENCE

Neveah was sexually assaulted and says this about how the contents of her kit were used in court:

> I wore a skirt and it was leopard and velvet, not to mention that my underwear were thongs. So that was a big deal. "And your pink thong underwear!" was what they [defence lawyer] kept going on about, and they took them

30 Feldberg, *supra* note 19.

31 Women who must urinate/defecate are warned not to "wipe" for fear that sperm/semen evidence will be destroyed. In the CBC TV movie "The Many Trials of One Jane Doe" (2002), the Jane Doe character sits on her toilet, guarded by police officers as she instructs them that the urethra should never be confused with the vagina. See also *The Story of Jane Doe*, *supra* note 3 at 30.

> out in court and held them up. They even put it in the paper. I was mortified. It was terrible.

Pamela, who also underwent the kit, adds:

> They had big bags of plastic to take my clothes while they were undressing me, shaking them, it was very odd, I don't know much about the kit, I knew it was about DNA but the clothes thing was just really, really odd, you know? The semen was there, they had pieces of my hair — what else do you need? Isn't that enough?

Women I interviewed reinforced the view that their lived experience, their first-person evidence as to the crime — what they saw, knew, believed — was not sufficient evidence. It appears to be required instead that they measure up to rape mythology that qualifies "good" or "real" rape as "an act of forceful penetration committed by a stranger during a blitz attack in a public, deserted place. The victim is portrayed as a morally upright white woman who is physically injured while resisting."[32]

Anne was a key informant in this research and has a fifteen-year history of work in a community-based rape crisis centre:

> We see that the 1983 legislation removed the onus to provide third-party corroboration that a rape had occurred. The idea being that women were lying. But that myth still informs us. The third party is now the kit. The doctor is the third party or the nurse who collects forensic evidence from the woman's body, primarily through a pelvic examination to corroborate what she is saying. To prove to the courts that she is not lying. If they don't find semen, if she isn't cut or bruised, well—good luck with the investigation. If, in addition to that, she's a woman of colour or English isn't her first language or she has any prior convictions or conflict with the law, she's going to have a bad time, can be seen as bad, not virtuous enough or innocent enough.

Michelle, the central region health care worker and advocate, agrees:

> Why do we do the kit? Why do we need that validation? It's intrusive, it's demeaning, it's insulting. I think it's entirely because women aren't believed. We have such a high ability to get DNA off so many things. Why do we keep

32 Janice Du Mont, Karen Lee Miller & TL Myhr, "The Role of 'Real Rape' and 'Real Victim' Stereotypes in the Police-Reporting Practices of Sexually Assaulted Women" (2003) 9 Violence Against Women 469.

> subjecting women to this? Why do we need a doctor to validate? Someone else who was not present, a man in most cases who has eight years of school to say yes she's telling the truth!

Such accounts confirm Feldberg's claim that the laying of charges and any subsequent prosecution of sexual assault continue to rely on corroborative evidence as gathered in the rape kit.

While conducting this research, I learned that there is controversy and debate amongst SANEs, community advocates, police, and forensic scientists about kit requirements, especially hair samples, which are taken from the woman's head and/or pubic area, sometimes by the root. Increasingly, some hospital protocols do not require hair samples at all. Paradoxically, in cities with two SANEs or more, some take hair and some do not. As key informants Esther and Brenda, respectively, report

> If they don't take hair, the Crown or the defence lawyer can argue that standard procedure was not followed and that works against the woman.

> We don't do any hair samples. We already have DNA, you don't need more. Besides, many young women [I have examined] don't have pubic hair these days. They shave themselves.

There is an initiative in one province to add a test that would require additional head hair sampling to be taken one month after the assault to detect the presence of "date rape" drugs in the new hair growth follicle. Marie, a nurse examiner from western Canada, decried the worth of an additional test:

> That won't work in court. All you have to do is suggest that she ingested the drugs herself after she finished the kit and it raises what is called reasonable doubt. Plus, how do you ensure that women will return a month later?

Lillian, who works in a rape crisis centre in a central province, was clear on the matter:

> We need to look at root cause not root hair. The collection of hair or anything else in the kit does not prevent sexual assault or resolve it.

RCMP kits, as administered in regions and provinces under their law enforcement jurisdiction, absolutely require hair, skin cell and nail scrapings, and saliva samplings, as do some cities and regions with their own police forces. The ongoing debate on the gathering and use of raped women's hair is indicative of the conflict and in many cases confusion that define the kit, as well as its relevancy.

To determine the type of forensic evidence that needs to be collected, the SANE obtains a thorough sexual assault and medical history. To do so women are questioned about recent consensual sex, pregnancy (in some cases they are asked about past pregnancies, miscarriages, and abortions), any current medication including anti-depressant or other mental-health related medications, and recent intake of alcohol or recreational drugs. Five of the women I interviewed who had undergone the kit had no memory of this Q&A component.

Research questions put to experiential women, specific to the timeline in conducting the kit and its storage, elicited conflicting responses. For example, when a woman consents to undergo the sexual assault evidence kit, she is informed by some SANEs that she can do part of the kit or stop the process at any time. But this is in no way standard and the practice can differ between nurse examiners at the same hospital. Nor are sexually assaulted women always informed that they can wait 72 hours after the assault to have the kit conducted or that the completed kit can be stored for between two to six months before the woman decides to press charges. Four of the experiential women I interviewed denied that these options had been presented to them at all, and three could not remember. This must lead us to question the reality of raped women's "options" and the validity of their "consent" to undergo the kit.

WHOSE KIT IS IT, ANYWAY?

None of the experiential women interviewed for this research were aware that upon completion rape kits became the property of the police and all evidence they contain must, under law, be made available to the accused, their lawyers, and the office of the Crown Attorney. They were not informed at the time that the kit was collected that it may work to their disadvantage, rarely contributes to conviction, and is unlikely to even be used in court.[33] Women were not aware of where the kit is stored, for how long, or what happens to it after trial. Except for three participants, women had no knowledge of how the kit is compiled or its cost per unit. Key informants in western regions told me that in one

33 Feldberg, *supra*, note 19; see also Margaret McGregor & Janice Du Mont, "Sexual Assault Forensic Medical Examination: Is Evidence Related to Successful Prosecution?" (2002) 39 Annals Emerg Med 639.

city, the kit is assembled by a volunteer group of nurses and counsellors who come together regularly, and in other areas of the province, kit assembly is labour conducted by prison inmates.

There is an understanding embedded in practices and policies about the SAEK that information regarding the kit's purpose and use must be restricted in order to ensure against contamination of what is considered scientific evidence for use in a court of law. Researchers suggest that the physical evidence obtained via the kit has marginal influence on the outcome of a trial but instead can be used to discredit the woman who consented to undergo it.[34] They argue that forensic medicine is a nascent science, inaccurate, and without regulations, and they query the legal dash to enshrine it as scientific evidence in a rape trial. This scepticism is supported in a report published in November of 2006 by Statistics Canada that states that DNA and other technology-based crime-solving tools have not affected the rate of crime solving in police forces across Canada.

Women who consent to undergo the kit are treated as if the body fluids and samples it contains do not belong to them, as if the crime that has been committed against them is separate from them. And when raped women sign the required consent forms that give authority of the kit over to police investigators, that separation becomes official.

Ronnie, whose kit was not used, attempted to have it returned to her:

> The nurse gave me the written part. She was so awesome. I'm with a legal clinic to try and get a Freedom of Information to get my kit and my interview back. They [police] are appealing the Information, so it could be months.

Scarlett did not get that far:

> [When I asked to have it back] The detective laughed. My counsellor thought I was exhibiting signs of post-traumatic stress or something.

34 Feldberg, *supra* note 19; see also Janice Du Mont & Deborah Parnis, "Symbolic Power and the Institutional Response to Rape: Uncovering the Cultural Dynamics of a Forensic Technology" (2006) 20 Can Rev Soc & Anthropology 73; Margaret J McGregor & Grace Le, "Examination for Sexual Assault: Is the Documentation of Physical Injury Associated with the Laying of Charges? A Retrospective Cohort Study" (1999) 160 Can Med Ass J 1565.

THE KIT AND INFORMED CONSENT

Georgina Feldberg's groundbreaking research on the medicalizing of women's experience of sexual assault examines what she refers to as the "medico-legal" use or purpose of the SAEK: "[the kit] can obfuscate issues of consent, serve as a vehicle for introduction of information about past sexual history, and create a power imbalance between the voice of the claimant and that of the experts that contributes to the victim's negative experience of the trial."[35] She concludes that in Canada, as in the US, medical evidence obtained in the SAEK makes few positive contributions to the raped woman's case.

If Feldberg broke ground and silence in exposing the negative influence of the kit and its protectionist nature, the contributions of Janice Du Mont, Deborah Parnis, Margaret McGregor, Karen Lee Miller and others noted below, map a route to better understand the use and efficacy of forensic evidence as collected in the sexual assault evidence kit.[36] Du Mont and Lana Stermac conducted an exploratory study that scrutinizes the "consent to be contacted" forms obtained from women who attended at a Toronto SACTC. On signing, sexually assaulted women agree to be contacted for requests to participate in future related research conducted through the hospital. Du Mont and Stermac's findings were that 93.3% of the interviewed women did not recall signing a consent form at the time of contact with the Women's College Hospital Sexual Assault Care Centre. The authors conclude, "Such 'forgetfulness' may be specific to women under the stress of a recent sexual assault. If so, consent given during a crisis admission may seldom be informed."[37]

If sexually assaulted women are not remembering their signed consent to participate in research studies, what does that say about the na-

35 Feldberg, *supra* note 19 at 70.

36 See sources cited *supra* notes 21, 33, 34, 43, 44, 45. See also Janice Du Mont & Deborah Parnis, "Judging Women: The Pernicious Effects of Rape Mythology" (1999) 19 Can Woman Stud 74; Janice Du Mont *et al*, "Predicting Legal Outcomes from Medicolegal Findings: An Examination of Sexual Assault in Two Jurisdictions" (2000) 1 J Women's Health & L 219; Janice Du Mont & Deborah Parnis, "Sexual Assault and Legal Resolution: Querying the Medical Collection of Forensic Evidence" (2000) 19 Med & L 779; Janice Du Mont, Deborah Parnis & Brydon Gombay, "Co-operation or Co-optation? Assessing the Methodological Benefits and Barriers Involved in Conducting Qualitative Research Through Medical Institutional Settings" (2005) 15 Qual Health Research 686; and Janice Du Mont & Deborah Parnis, "Rape Laws and Rape Processing: The Contradictory Nature of Corroboration" (1999) 5 Can J Human Sexuality 74.

37 Janice Du Mont & Lana Stermac, "Research With Women Who Have Been Sexually Assaulted: Examining Informed Consent" (1996) 5 Can J Human Sexuality 185 at 189.

ture of their consent to the kit itself and the release of its contents to investigating police officers?

My observations are that the twelve experiential women I interviewed have one of three experiences: (i) they have no memory of giving consent; (ii) they felt coerced into agreeing; or (iii) they believed that their consent was necessary for the state to pursue criminal charges or otherwise "protect" them. Some of their comments follow:

> I didn't understand. I just did everything they asked me to. I was numb and confused and scared.
>
> — Aimee, kit used at trial

> I figured I had to do it. It was my role as a victim. I knew it [the kit] was a waste of time but saying no would have made them suspicious. I wanted to be compliant in order to be believed.
>
> — Scarlett, kit not used

> I don't think I did [sign]. I don't remember them asking. I remember thinking that everything I did was necessary.
>
> — Neveah, kit used

> I don't remember anything like that. I was out of my mind. He [her assailant] put something in my drink.
>
> — Rachelle, kit not used

> I don't remember. I think they just informed me that it was a long process and I'm either kind of in it or I'm not.
>
> — Pamela, kit not used

> I signed a release at the beginning saying I was consenting to the kit and another that I was willing to relinquish all medical records [to the police]. I did it all. I knew I wanted to lay charges and I knew about the kit and that I would have to do it. If you deleted parts of it, what's the point of doing it at all? I know that the police would say, "Why'd you stop? Well, this wasn't a real rape because you didn't even get a vaginal done or you opted not to take this [medication]. Why? What are you hiding?"
>
> — Hermione, kit not used

Participants who work in community-based rape crisis/sexual assault centres were concerned about definitions of informed consent, given that the extreme nature of the harm of sexual assault invariably results in emotional, psychological, and physical reactions and, in many cases, trauma. Following are some of their comments and analyses:

> It's considered a treatment women say yes to with an educated consent, but it's not.
>
> — Andy, key informant

> My experience is that women are not given a choice. Women I have accompanied were not told of the six-month waiting option.
>
> — Michelle, key informant

> When you're assaulted you are so vulnerable, there is total disarray and confusion, you're not thinking about court and are in no state to make decisions.
>
> — Frankie, key informant

> I'm sure that they are asked if they consent but it's not informed and is made under duress. It's the kind of consent that would get thrown out of court in another crime.
>
> — Ramat, key informant

> My experience has been that they have not been given a choice. One woman [I know of] was slipped a date rape drug and wanted [a kit] and one was not done on her.
>
> — Michelle, key informant

Esther is the community-based rape crisis worker who sits on a committee struck to examine the design and use of the SAEK in her province. Her comments regarding the issue of consent to undergo the kit are as follows:

> Why would someone who had just been raped want to have someone else in their vagina pulling out hairs? It's basically asking them to undergo torture after they have just been tortured. Theoretically the woman has the right to refuse [consent] but it is seen as questioning procedure and ruffles feathers or causes serious damage to the woman's case. Everything is presented and defended with "we're only trying to help women" so she feels that she has to consent in order to get help. This is how it's always presented. "Why wouldn't you want to do the kit? It's going to help you!" "You should tell this to women who come to see you [we are advised]." "It's going to help them; it's a good thing!"

Andy worked in a rape crisis centre in Ontario and is a trained nurse who spoke of a normalized deference to authority in the hospital or health care setting:

> When a health care worker says to the patient: "we're going to do such and such, do you give your permission?" the client, the patient, the health care user is predisposed to say yes. That's why they're there. I think patients are mostly obedient because they already know they have less power and the practitioner has lots of technique to shift lack of obedience. One way to do it is just to carry on, and say, "I'm going to put some lubricant on this or I'm going to pull some hair" which is different from saying "Now the next thing I'm going to do is get some hair samples, do you give me permission?"

Charlene works for a Sexual Assault Centre in eastern Canada:

> Women do not necessarily understand what [consent] is going to involve. And you can only inform them to a certain degree because we don't know what's going to happen either. Once the ball gets rolling, you've lost control. You have no control of how it will unfold. And it's really hard to provide that information to people so that they can make an informed decision.

Several of the community-based feminist rape crisis workers interviewed were unaware of the range of harm the kit can inflict or the fact that it is seldom used as evidence in court. Advocates seem to believe that despite its invasive and violent nature, the kit serves as critical evidence in support of a woman's rape claim. And it is true that in some cases, especially if she does not know the man who raped her, the kit can produce critical DNA evidence. Even in cases where it is not used, a "successful" kit can encourage the Crown's office to proceed to trial, the legal logic being that if the woman involved co-operated in undergoing the kit and there is forensic evidence to assist in establishing that she is telling the truth, the odds for conviction are better.[38] (Or, is it trial by ordeal — if she submits she must be telling the truth?) But what of the vast majority of women who undergo the kit, believing that it is an opportunity for them to effect justice, whose kit is not used, whose rapist is not convicted? What about the women whose cases are not "founded" because the kit was not conclusive? What of the women who are not believed? The women who do not report? The seventy-five percent

38 Feldberg, *supra* note 19.

majority of raped women who know the identity of the man who has raped them?

Gracia has worked as a counsellor in a Rape Crisis Centre and in a SACTC in a central region of the country:

> I think that in order [for women] to make an informed decision, they have to know that the kits are rarely used and that the conviction rate is negligible. If they knew that, their choices would be different. "Why am I going through this if there's a really, really slim chance that it's going to be of any benefit?" But that information is not out there. I don't think even people working within this field [community rape crisis centres] know that. Women are guilted into having a kit. "Well ... if you don't do it — what if he doesn't get caught? So the kit kind of presents itself as the only time the woman is actually involved, has any agency, and yet that agency is so limited, is so negative ... and still we cling to it.

It is problematic that the Sexual Assault Evidence Kit, which women experience in such harmful ways, can ironically be one of the few small areas where they feel they have been given agency and control. Several experiential women explained that regardless of any negative feelings about the kit, undergoing it made them feel that at least they were doing *something*, including protecting other women. Whether the administration of the kit is an intentional manipulation or not, those who advocate its use often do so without full knowledge of its purpose, harms, and consequences. We like to believe that the kit can provide health care, although it is not designed to serve that purpose (and is not called the Sexual Assault *Health Care* Kit), but we excuse ourselves from understanding the kit's larger political context and the injury it can cause. Feminist anti-violence workers and social workers must examine the degree of complicity that occurs when we do not inform ourselves and each other of the paternalistic and protectionist nature of the SAEK. We must question if the kit is dangled, almost as bait, to reinforce beliefs that limit definitions of women's sexuality to good or bad, virtuous or fallen. Is it implied that women can regain control and power by having a kit done? If so, is their consent contrived? Is it informed? If women knew that the kit can be used against them and is seldom used at all, would they consent? Why is that information being withheld?

The Sexual Assault Nurse Examiners I interviewed also had contradictory opinions and understandings of the kit. The lack of standardization accounts for a great deal of the differences of opinion, but they have much to add on the matter. An eastern community-based Sexual Assault Care Centre, for example, has pioneered an alternative to the institutional SAEK used in other regions. Their SANEs are administered and trained by them and accountable to them versus a medical/health institution. A centre employee commented:

> When the nurses are hired, the process is one whereby they are looking at the Centre's mission statement and guiding principles and what governs how we work as a woman-centred feminist organization. The nurses are asked to review this and if they have some difficulty with that they wouldn't be asked to join the team. So I think that's unique compared to many of the other similar programmes.

In practice, these SANEs receive training and education developed and delivered by the centre, are on call 24/7, and operate in pairs. They are keen on involving sexually assaulted women in the kits' administration, including the internal. They support the use of the kit but have strong constructive critiques and understand it to be "traumatizing and invasive." They have modified it considerably and actively encourage women to wait before consenting to its collection.

In an interview, one of their SANEs stated:

> The thing is, we don't push it. We encourage women to come back within the 72 hours to do the kit. Our number one concern is their medical care, if they need it.

In a western region, where SANEs are called SARTs [Sexual Assault Response Team] and kits are provided by the RCMP, some nurses who administer them and deliver training to other nurses have also significantly modified their process to reduce the number of tests, body parts probed, and secretions collected.

Like no other health institution I interviewed, these SART nurses were clear and unconflicted about their role and the actual benefits of the Sexual Assault Evidence Kit. The frankness of their approach was matched with a commitment and dedication to providing the best health care for raped women.

Regarding consent to undergo the kit, a SART member offered the following:

> It has nothing to do with whether we think the kit should be done, or if the victim thinks the kit should be done. It's the police decision.

SARTs travel to the hospital or clinic and do not offer kit storage. They do it then, or it's not done at all:

> We sit down with the victim, the client, the patient, and we say to them "tell us what happened." This is after we go through the consent and say that we do the same [physical] exam with or without the police, but the police are the ones that can decide whether the kit's done. We write their story as they tell it. We don't medically summarize it, we don't change the words.... We have a direct number for the sex crime detective who is on call. We talk to them, tell them what the history was that the patient gave us. And at that point the sex crime detective will make the decision to do a kit or not do the kit. Usually, they do the kit.

SACTCs in three of the four provinces in which I travelled employ social workers to provide counselling services to women who attend at their hospital/clinic. The counselling is short term (although it can be extended), one-on-one with group sessions, and is offered free of charge. In some provinces, SACTC social workers also assist women who have been sexually assaulted with housing, legal matters, criminal injuries compensation, and other services. They practise a clinical model of social work versus a feminist, anti-racist, anti-oppression advocacy model as is offered in most community-based rape crisis/sexual assault centres. SACTC social workers perform their jobs in tandem with psychiatric and other medical personnel who ascribe to psychiatric diagnoses as listed in DSM IV, especially post-traumatic stress disorder [PTSD], that assign disorders and syndromes to women who have experienced sexual assault. While it might sometimes be relevant to do so, the root cause of the violence against the woman does not factor into their medical findings, prescriptions, or prognosis:

> Feminist anti-oppression and anti-violence supports developed originally as a reaction to the insufficiency and ill fittingness of psychiatric and psychological responses to women's experiences of violence and social inequity. And as a corrective to the misnaming of these experiences as illnesses and disorders.[39]

The professional associations and licensing bodies to which medical and social work professionals belong require adherence to internal

39 Bonisteel & Green, *supra* note 22 at 27.

guidelines — before any responsibility to the clients/patients/consumers/victims who seek their services. Doctors, for instance, are responsible to the guidelines, regulations, and principles of the College of Physicians and Surgeons, nurses to their provincial nurse association or College of Nurses. Similarly, social workers are responsible to the institution that employs them and, in some provinces, have their own College of Social Work. The regulations, mandates and codes of behaviour of such professional affiliations supersede how members work or want to work in a smaller group that draws on its own overriding ethics or principles in determining policy, practice, and protocol.

So, as Andy, a key informant explains, while many women working in hospitals as counsellors or nurses are feminist advocates, the competition of cultures that takes place privileges the institution that employs them over feminist practice or community concerns:

> Even though you have caring, benevolent, political thinking people working in a place that's actually an institution, you can only be as flexible as the overarching institution will allow … so even if the SACTC has some core staff that have some very strong, feminist, demystifying peer-skills, when they do counselling, even if the medical oversight of that sexual assault care and treatment centre has good politics, they still have [medical] residents, they have all kinds of people coming through it. There's more purpose to it [the hospital] than just being the [SACTC] centre. In a Rape Crisis Centre, they would be in control of who they trained and who was on the crisis line. And just that — the system of the organization itself being in control of who does the work, that becomes lost in a Sexual Assault Care and Treatment Centre. Which means that no matter how well it tries to provide different service, it has its limitations. Because they don't have anyone there that *doesn't* have the professional credentials. And they are not functioning in an organization that allows for the sort of ongoing personal and professional, anti-oppression, anti-racist, anti-misogyny constant kind of work that we know feminism requires.

Hermione, who experienced a sexual assault, reported to the police, and underwent a kit, has this to say:

> This city has a very large problem with the police and sexual assault. The hospital is doing a follow up for people who report to the police, but it's like a private social work investigation. When I went for my follow-up I filled out a questionnaire so I know that they are wary of the police and I think that nurses are trying their best to be there for women and are on the

> woman's side. But they're also nurses in an institutionalized setting — and there are no feminist nursing classes.

And from Gracia, who was employed as a counsellor in a SACTC:

> A lot of them [SANEs] just do the obligatory. You know, a preliminary collection of forensics like the pulling of hair and all that. A lot of them are not aware of the dynamics, what the patients need and how they need to be supported. We hear time and time again, people say "my introduction into the system with that nurse! If that's how I was treated by the nurse, then I certainly don't want to get into counselling, you guys are supposed to know better!" It's a problem, definitely an issue, so much so that the managers asked the counsellors to do training for the nurses. But it's not happened yet.

In a central province, where hospital and health-care-centre-based SACTCs are referred to as "designated centres," they utilize two kits. One is to collect legal evidence while the other is "psycho-social." Kits have different parts or modules to facilitate requests/offers that only portions of the kit be conducted. They have a team of social work counsellors on call who manage the intervention. A doctor performs the medical exam. There is a provincial training program and each centre adapts it to their needs. Paulette, the SANE I interviewed, said that she practiced from a feminist perspective, but that "The kit is a legal tool and people are concerned about interjecting politics." Her centre is part of a group that includes police, lawyers, and representatives from the VAW community who are currently meeting to assess the kit and its process. She feels that it is important "to work within the system and to try and effect change from within, in a less political way." Paulette continued to explain how she understands her work versus that of community-based agencies:

> We don't run groups; clients aren't counsellors — that kind of stuff has happened before. People are realizing that just because we experienced the same thing [sexual assault] we can't share together. We are not offering self-help. We've never felt that there is something wrong in having an education, and professionals are not bad people.

FULL CIRCLE?

Has the privileging of the SACTC and its workers regarding sexual assault contributed to the exclusion of community-based anti-violence feminists in policy design and direction? Has funding also been affected? There is additional concern that SACTC social workers, who increasingly provide practical and critical resources for sexually assaulted women, such as housing, have better access to the institutions that can provide it. While there is no doubt that such services (versus the collection of forensic evidence) are what women need most, their provision should not be partnered with attendance at a SACTC:

> Pressure on the feminist anti-violence sector to medicalize anti-violence work has intensified in direct relationship to credentialism and funder control. The language of post-traumatic stress disorder and PTSD symptomatology is being used more frequently in the feminist anti-violence sector because of these pressures, and perhaps because alternative feminist language used to name the severe distress of women's oppression lacks medical credibility. Some organizations in the anti-violence sector have responded by promoting a mental health treatment approach (Yellow Brick House 2003; Brown, Gallant and Junaid 2002) and by adopting hiring practices that some feminists argue support the medicalization of oppression.[40]

And, according to Feldberg, "The SACTC has come to represent the standard of care for women who experience sexual assault."[41]

The medical professionals and social workers I interviewed, who work in SACTCs or their counterparts, do not believe that there is an institutional bias or pressure to encourage women to consent to undergo the kit in a speedy manner, or at all. As one central-Canadian SANE, Paulette, said

> We have a role in the kits, filling them out if you want, and giving them off to the police. It's part of a chain, a continuum. We are always trying to work that out to improve it, in the best interests of the women we see. It's working as well as can be expected. We feel that the kit is an option a possibility, whereas it's an evidence thing for the police.

The view is quite different, however, from that expressed by experiential and key informant women like Andy:

> I think that there is a lot of law and order institutional paranoia and the belief is that we are doing something like this because the police need it, and the

40 Bonisteel & Green, *supra* note 22 at 35.

41 Feldberg, *supra* note 19 at 114.

> kit's not right if you don't do it a certain way. I don't know how a client would perceive the nurse examiner administrating the kit as separate from the police. Even if the police are not in the room — which they never should be.

Barbara was sexually assaulted by a man she knew in central Canada:

> The [SANE] nurse was a good friend of the [sexual assault] detective and said she would call the detective and speak with her about me that night. She said "[Officer's name] is my good friend."

Ramat, who works in a feminist community-based centre in western Canada, says this:

> There is a perception that the nurses have your best interests at heart. The nurses are soft spoken and doing a lot of uhm-hmms which limits the woman's allowance to be angry. The women are asked if they want the police called, but there is definitely a push to have them called. The sexual assault nurses don't get any analysis [in their training] about using the police.

Gracia, a SACTC counsellor, adds:

> The police sit in the waiting room [of the SACTC] and they complain about how long this [the kit] is going to take and that we don't have good reading material. The nurses tell the women they don't have to undergo the kits, that is what they're supposed to say, but I have it on very good authority that some of the nurses are known to be more persuasive, let's just say, than others.

POLICE TRAINING AND THE KIT

During the course of conducting this research project, I had the opportunity, through related work, to observe sexual assault investigation training delivered to Toronto police officers at a police training facility in Ontario.[42] In the training module titled "Sexual Assault and For-

42 In 1999, as a result of my case, Toronto City Council ordered an audit or inquiry into how police investigate sexual assault and how they treat women who report the crime. I worked with other VAW activists to establish a committee that included us as consultants. See Jeffrey Griffiths, *Review of the Investigation of Sexual Assault—Toronto Police Service* (Toronto: Toronto Audit Services, 1999) produced 57 recommendations for change. In 2006 after seven years of additional community lobbying, Beverly Bain and I were permitted to observe the two-week Sexual Assault and Child Abuse investigative training course delivered at CO Bick Police College in Ontario. For more detailed information see, Jane Doe, Amanda Dale & Beverly Bain, "A New

ensic Biology," learners (police detectives who were training to qualify as sexual assault investigators) were given information that contradicts and even negates the mandates and policies of the province's Sexual Assault Care and Treatment Centres. For instance, the biologist who delivered the police training material stated that SANEs take samples (in the SAEK) that are not relevant, and her forensic team does not accept them. Officers were instructed to get only the relevant samples based on the case history, as the Centre of Forensic Science will only accept fifteen items. They were encouraged to collect hair samples and the option of freezer storage for later use was discouraged due to lack of proper storage space. Other presenters on the kit, including a provincial Crown Attorney, stressed the importance of conducting the kit immediately, and its use as a tool to corroborate the victim's story.[43] My observations of police training further illustrate the divergent interpretations of the use and purpose of the rape kit by legal players who utilize it in their job performance.

WHO BENEFITS?

Canadian academic and research experts on the sexual assault evidence kit have established a significant body of work on its use and efficacy. In a collaborative paper, researchers McGregor, Du Mont, and Li extrapolated data from 462 women who consented to the rape kit between 1993 and 1997. They report that: "Charges were laid in 151 (33%) cases, perpetrators were found guilty as charged in 18 (3.9%) cases, and convictions secured in 51 (11%) of the 462 cases examined." They also note that their conclusions are "similar to findings in hospital-based studies in the United States and slightly lower than those reported in the Scandinavian literature," and "that two decades of legal reforms designed to improve prosecution and legal reforms [in Canada] have not been entirely successful." The authors go on to state:

> The greater than threefold increased likelihood of charges being filed in the presence of forensic samples collected by the examiner, irrespective of the test results, suggests that a victim's willingness to submit to a forensic examination might play a role in assessing the strength of a case. Specifically the examiner's collection of biologic samples for submission to police appears

Chapter in Feminist Organizing: The Sexual Assault Audit Steering Committee" (2010) 28 Can Woman Stud 6.

43 From course material presented in 2006 at the Sexual Assault Child Abuse Course, CO Bick Police College, Toronto, Ontario.

> to provide some perceived scientific validation of a victim's allegations. The fact that most examples were run *only after charges were filed* suggests that the presence of sperm-semen plays a limited role in the police processing of sexual assault cases[44] [italics mine].

In her 2004 paper presented at the Global Forum for Health Research in Mexico City, Du Mont relied on data collected from a central and a western Canada SACTC to conclude: "Nor was the presence of a positive sperm-semen sample related to conviction."[45] In additional research, Du Mont and Parnis suggest that "medico-legal evidence may be socially constructed... Comprehensive and systemic investigation of court transcripts and first-hand experiences of women who have undergone a medico-legal exam and testified in court may be the key to determining whether the kit serves to perpetuate negative stereotypes in the rape mythology, most notably that women lie about being sexually assaulted."[46] Georgina Feldberg writes of the symbolic value of the rape kit as opposed to any evidentiary worth and that "lack of evidence [collected in the kit] seems to do more harm than its presence does good."[47]

My primary finding from my interviews is that the nature of the consent women give to undergo the kit is seldom informed legally or otherwise. It is supported by a decade of research on the subject of the SAEK and cannot be divorced from additional data in this research and in others that clearly indicate that:

- Women experience the kit as a second assault
- Consent to undergo the kit influences the filing of charges by the police
- The kit does not influence conviction
- The kit can be used to negatively influence the outcome of a trial and to discredit the woman involved

44 Margaret McGregor, Janice Du Mont & Terri L Myhr, "Sexual Assault Forensic Medical Evidence: Is Evidence Related to Successful Prosecution?" (2002) 39 Annals Emerg Med 645.

45 Janice Du Mont, "Documenting the Health Impacts of Sexual Violence: An Evaluation of Two Forensic Protocols." Paper presented at Global Forum for Health Research, Forum 8, Ministerial Summit on Health Research, Mexico City, 16–20 November 2004, at 6.

46 Janice Du Mont & Deborah Parnis, "Constructing Bodily Evidence Through Sexual Assault Evidence Kits" (2001) 10 Griffith L Rev 63. See also Margaret McGregor & Grace Le, "Examination for Sexual Assault: Is the Documentation of Physical Injury Associated with the Laying of Charges? A Retrospective Cohort Study" (1999) 160 Can Med Ass J 1565.

47 Feldberg, *supra* note 19 at 107.

- The kit's most invasive test, the internal, is not related to conviction
- There is no formal standard of practice in SAEK collection, content, or administration.

Such conclusions force the question — why are we using the Sexual Assault Evidence Kit? If it denies women agency, choice, and control and its detrimental impact so grossly outweighs any gain, who benefits from its use?

Women who have had the kit conducted on their bodies and those who support and advocate for them respond:

> The police benefit, they feel it strengthens their investigation and allows them to determine who is a real victim. The state benefits, the assailant benefits.
>
> — Esther, key informant

> They want to get it done and they want to get it over with and they're not concerned about who you are. You get lost.
>
> — Neveah, experiential

> The police benefit and the legal system. Good old justice benefits, not women.
>
> — Hermione, experiential

> It [the kit] is a "feel good." As a nurse I get to feel like I've done something good at the end of the day. But the day a [raped] woman came in and said "I don't want to do a kit. I want you to get me housing so that I won't get assaulted again," I understood that it was a waste of time.
>
> — Christine, key informant

> It [the kit] may have been groundbreaking in its time, even ahead of its time — before DNA. It's outlasted its use though, and now it's just because the police, the judiciary system refuse to change.
>
> — Michelle, key informant

> I don't remember the kit so I don't really know.
>
> — Ronnie, experiential

> It's for legal. That's all. The victim can benefit if it provides the DNA that will find a stranger assailant.
>
> — Marie, key informant

WHO BENEFITS FROM THE SEXUAL ASSAULT EVIDENCE KIT?

> It makes the police look good. It's of no use to the woman, just another traumatizing event. It was a waste of time.
>
> — Scarlett, experiential

> The Crown benefits. Rapists benefit.
>
> — Ramat, key informant

> Not me.
>
> — Barbara, experiential

This paper is dedicated to Georgina Feldberg (1956–2010) with great respect and appreciation.

17. Perpetuating — and Resisting — Rape Myths in Trial Discourse[1]

Susan Ehrlich

In this chapter, Susan Ehrlich focuses on language to track how linguistic and rhetorical devices in direct and cross-examination are deployed by lawyers in sexual assault trials to shade the narrative rendering of the event. She argues that we must pay attention to the language and everyday practices that shape how sexual assault is adjudicated. Recalling the chapters by Julia Tolmie and Laura Robinson in Part I, where acts that fully met the legal definition of sexual assault were nonetheless successfully recast in high profile trials as "just sex" or "unwanted sex," Susan's analysis shows how rape myths continue to be re-enacted through linguistic strategies despite decades of progressive law reforms. Her work echoes the spirit of the Garneau Sisterhood from Part I by laying the groundwork for women who testify as complainants and Crown attorneys to anticipate and disrupt these regressive narratives.

Feminist critiques of the law have often cited the rape trial as exemplifying much of what is problematic about the legal system for women. Carol Smart, for example, argues that the rape trial is illustrative of the law's *juridogenic* potential: that is, frequently the harms produced by the so-called remedy are as negative as the original abuse.[2] Other legal theorists have created terms for the rape trial — "judicial rape"[3] and "rape of the second kind"[4] — in order to make visible the *re*-victimization that women can undergo once their complaints of rape enter the legal system. What is perhaps surprising about these kinds of claims is the fact that they persist, in spite of widespread reform of sex-

1 This chapter is a revised version of a chapter that appeared in Malcolm Coulthard & Alison Johnson, eds, *The Routledge Handbook of Language and the Law* (London: Routledge, 2010) 265.

2 Carol Smart, *Feminism and the Power of Law* (London: Routledge, 1989) at 161.

3 Sue Lees, *Carnal Knowledge: Rape on Trial* (London: Hamish Hamilton, 1996) at 36.

4 Greg Matoesian, "Language, Law, and Society: Policy Implications of the Kennedy Smith Rape Trial" (1995) 29 Law & Soc'y Rev 676.

ual assault and rape statutes in Canada and the United States over the last four decades. For example, legislation in the 1970s through the 1990s in Canada and the United States abolished, among other things, marital exemption rules, which made it impossible for husbands to be charged with raping their wives; resistance rules, which required that complainants show evidence that they physically resisted their attackers; and recent complaint rules, which obligated complainants to make prompt complaints in order that their testimony be deemed credible. In addition, rape shield provisions were introduced, restricting the conditions under which complainants' sexual histories could be admissible as evidence.

So, given this kind of reform, why do rape trials continue to defy the law's statutory objectives? Following John Conley and William O'Barr, I suggest that the rape trial's failure to deliver justice to raped women lies *not* in the details of rape and sexual assault statutes, but rather "in the details of everyday legal practices."[5] And, because *language* plays a crucial role in everyday legal practices, this chapter demonstrates how *linguistic analysis* can reveal some of the discriminatory qualities of rape trials as well as how they have been contested.

THE ADJUDICATION OF RAPE CASES

In her book-length study of well-known American acquaintance rape trials, Peggy Sanday[6] comments on the discrepancy that often exists between "law-as-legislation" and "law-as-practice."[7] On the one hand, Sanday praises recent rape statutes in the states of New Jersey, Illinois, Washington, and Wisconsin that deem sexual aggression as illegal in the absence of what she terms the "affirmative consent" of complainants. On the other hand, Sanday points to the failure of such statutory reform in the context of sexist and androcentric cultural stereotypes: "although our rape laws define the line [between sex and rape] ... these laws are useless if juror attitudes are affected by ancient sexual stereotypes."[8] Within the Canadian context, Elizabeth Comack makes similar observations about judges' attitudes: despite the widespread re-

5 John Conley & William O'Barr, *Just Words: Law, Language, and Power* (Chicago: University of Chicago Press, 1998) at 3.

6 Peggy Reeves Sanday, *A Woman Scorned: Acquaintance Rape on Trial* (New York: Doubleday, 1996).

7 Carol Smart, "Feminism and the Law: Some Problems of Analysis and Strategy" (1986) 14 Int'l J Soc L 109.

8 *Ibid* at 285.

form to Canadian sexual assault law in the 1980s and 1990s, Comack argues that "judicial decisions continue to reflect traditional cultural mythologies about rape."[9]

Comack's claims are supported by research on the language of sexual assault trial judgments. For example, in investigating judges' decisions in Canadian sexual assault trial cases between 1986 and 1992, Linda Coates, Janet Bavelas, and James Gibson found judges to have extremely limited "interpretive repertoires" in the language they deployed in describing sexual assault. In describing "stranger rapes," judges employed a language of assault and violence; however, in describing cases where perpetrators were familiar to the women they assaulted and often trusted by them, the language judges used was often that of consensual sex. For example, the unwanted touching of a young girl's vagina was described as "fondling" in one trial judgment; in another, a judge described a defendant as "offering" his penis to his victim's mouth.[10] Thus, in spite of the fact that 1983 statutory reforms in Canada explicitly reconceptualized sexual assault as a crime of violence, many of the judges adopted a language of erotic, affectionate, and consensual sex when describing non-stranger rape.

These kinds of results give empirical substance to Sanday's and Comack's claims about the "ancient sexual stereotypes" and "traditional cultural mythologies" that inform the adjudication of rape cases. They are also illustrative of the legal system's differential treatment of stranger rape versus acquaintance rape — a phenomenon also documented within the American legal system by legal scholar, Susan Estrich. Estrich, in her book *Real Rape*,[11] makes the argument that the legal system takes the crime of rape seriously in cases where the perpetrator is a stranger and, in particular, an armed stranger "jumping from the bushes" and attacking an unsuspecting woman. By contrast, when a woman is forced to engage in sex with a date or an acquaintance, when no weapon is involved and when there is no overt evidence of physical injury, the legal system is much less likely to arrest, prosecute, and convict the perpetrator. One could argue that in these latter kinds of cases, when there is no physical evidence and/or corroboration that rape has occurred, it is much easier for judges and juries to invoke their

9 Elizabeth Comack, *Locating Law: Race/Class/Gender Connections* (Halifax: Fernwood Publishing, 1999) at 234.

10 Linda Coates, Janet Bavelas & James Gibson, "Anomalous Language in Sexual Assault Trial Judgments" (1994) 5 Discourse & Soc'y 189.

11 Susan Estrich, *Real Rape* (Cambridge, MA: Harvard University Press, 1987).

own (potentially problematic) ideas about male and female sexuality. As Peter Tiersma[12] points out, consent can be communicated indirectly (eg, through silence), with the result that, in situations where a man has not physically hurt or overtly threatened a woman, judges and juries must *infer* whether a woman has consented to sex or not. And, in line with Sanday's and Comack's comments above, Tiersma acknowledges that "these inferences may rest on questionable or offensive ... assumptions." For instance, Tiersma cites a recent US case "in which a Texas judge determined that a woman's request that a man use a condom was evidence of consent, despite the fact that he had threatened her with violence."[13] In the words of Carla da Luz and Pamela Weckerly, "caution [was] construed as consent" by this particular judge.[14]

The remainder of this chapter has two goals. First, I consider research that has investigated the discourse of rape trials and demonstrated that the kinds of questionable cultural assumptions discussed by Sanday, Comack, and Tiersma (among others) are not only evident in the attitudes of some juries and judges: they also circulate within trials. In particular, defence lawyers in criminal rape trials have been shown to draw strategically upon cultural mythologies surrounding rape as a way of impeaching the credibility of complainants. Second, I consider research that explores the possibility that the kinds of cultural mythologies drawn upon by judges, juries, and defence lawyers in rape trials can be contested. In fact, I suggest that, because of its *adversarial* nature, the rape trial provides a unique forum for investigating ways that dominant notions of sexual violence are reproduced discursively *as well as* ways they might be resisted and challenged.

QUESTIONS IN TRIAL DISCOURSE

Adversarial dispute resolution, of which trials are a notable example, requires that two parties come together formally, usually with representation (eg, lawyers), to present their (probably different) versions of the dispute to a third party (eg, judge, jury, tribunal) who hears the evidence, applies the appropriate laws or regulations, and determines the guilt or innocence of the parties. Lawyers have as their task, then, convincing the adjudicating body that their (ie, their client's) version

12 Peter Tiersma, "The Language of Consent in Rape Law" in Janet Cotterill, ed, *The Language of Sexual Crime* (Basingstoke, UK: Palgrave Macmillan, 2007) 83.

13 *Ibid* at 93.

14 Carla M da Luz & Pamela C Weckerly, "The Texas 'Condom-Rape' Case: Caution Construed as Consent" (1993) 3 UCLA Women's LJ 95.

of events is the most credible. Apart from making opening and closing arguments, however, lawyers do not themselves testify. Rather, it is through the posing of questions that lawyers elicit from witnesses testimony that will build a credible version of events in support of their own clients' interests in addition to testimony that will challenge, weaken, and/or cast doubt on the opposing parties' version of events. J Maxwell Atkinson and Paul Drew note that while trial discourse is conducted predominantly through a series of question-answer sequences, other actions are accomplished in the form of such questions and answers. For example, questions may be designed to accuse witnesses, to challenge or undermine the truth of what they are saying, or in direct examination, to presuppose the truth and adequacy of what they are saying. To the extent that witnesses recognize that these actions are being performed in questions, they may design their answers as rebuttals, denials, justifications, etc.[15]

Atkinson and Drew have called the question-answer turn-taking system characteristic of the courtroom, *turn-type pre-allocation*, to indicate that the types of turns participants can take are predetermined by their institutional roles.[16] In courtrooms, for example, lawyers have the right to initiate and allocate turns by asking questions of witnesses, but the reverse is not generally true; witnesses are obligated to answer questions or run the risk of being sanctioned by the court. An important dimension of this type of asymmetrical turn-taking, according to Drew and John Heritage, is the fact that it provides little opportunity for the answerer (typically a lay person) to initiate talk and thus allows the institutional representative "to gain a measure of control over the introduction of topics and hence of the 'agenda' for the occasion."[17] Within the context of the courtroom, researchers have argued that the interactional control of questioners (ie, lawyers) is most pronounced during cross-examination when the use of leading questions allows cross-examining lawyers to impose their version (ie, their clients') of events on the evidence.[18] As John Gibbons points out, one way that cross-examining lawyers manage to construct a version of events that

15 J Maxwell Atkinson & Paul Drew, *Order in Court* (Atlantic Highlands, NJ: Humanities Press, 1979) at 70.

16 *Ibid.*

17 Paul Drew & John Heritage, "Analyzing Talk at Work: An Introduction" in Paul Drew & John Heritage, eds, *Talk at Work: Interaction in Institutional Settings* (Cambridge: Cambridge University Press, 1992) 3 at 49.

18 See Conley & O'Barr, *supra* note 5.

serves the interests of their own clients is by "includ[ing] elements of this desired version ... in the questions."[19]

While a number of researchers have developed taxonomies of questions used in the courtroom,[20] for the purposes of this chapter I elaborate on Hanna Woodbury's taxonomy of question "control"[21] because it categorizes questions according to questioners' ability to "control" information, or in Gibbons' words above, according to questioners' ability to include "elements of the[ir] desired version of events" in questions. Indeed, for Woodbury, control refers "to the degree to which the questioner can impose his (sic) own interpretations on the evidence."[22] Thus, within Woodbury's continuum of control, broad wh- questions, such as *And then what happened?*, display little control because they do not impose the questioner's interpretation on the testimony: there is no proposition communicated to a judge and/or jury other than the notion that "something happened." By contrast, yes-no questions display more control than wh- questions within Woodbury's taxonomy. For example, the yes-no question with a tag, *You had intercourse with her, didn't you?*, contains a substantive proposition — ie, "the addressee had intercourse with some woman" — that is made available to a judge and/or jury, irrespective of the addressee's (ie, witness's) answer. Indeed, for Conley and O'Barr, controlling questions, in Woodbury's sense, have the effect of transforming cross-examination "from dialogue into self-serving monologue." That is, even if a controlling question with damaging content is answered in the negative, Conley and O'Barr argue that "the denial may be lost in the flow of the lawyer's polemic."[23]

In my own work, I have expanded Woodbury's taxonomy of "control" to include questions with presuppositions — questions that I argue are even more controlling than the kinds of yes-no questions exemplified above.[24] That is, on one analysis, a question always contains a variable

19 John Gibbons, *Forensic Linguistics: An Introduction to Language in the Justice System* (Oxford: Blackwell Publishers, 2003) at 98.

20 See, for example, Brenda Danet *et al*, "An Ethnography of Questioning" in Roger Shuy & Anna Shnukal, eds, *Language Use and the Uses of Language* (Washington, DC: Georgetown University Press, 1980) 222; Sandra Harris, "Questions as a Mode of Control in Magistrates' Courts" (1984) 49 Int'l J Soc Lang 5; Anne Graffam Walker, "Linguistic Manipulation, Power and the Legal Setting" in Leah Kedar, ed, *Power Through Discourse* (Norwood, NJ: Ablex, 1987) 57.

21 Hanna Woodbury, "The Strategic Use of Questions in Court" (1984) 48 Semiotica 197.

22 *Ibid* at 199.

23 Conley & O'Barr, *supra* note 5 at 26.

24 Susan Ehrlich, *Representing Rape: Language and Sexual Consent* (London: Routledge, 2001).

or unknown quantity, which the addressee of a question is being asked to supply.[25] For example, the addressee of the yes-no question with a tag exemplified above, *You had intercourse with her, didn't you?*, has the ability to disconfirm the proposition (ie, "the addressee had intercourse with some woman") contained within the declarative part of the question. By contrast, presuppositions cannot be denied with the same effectiveness or success. Consider, for example, the question in (1):[26]

(1) Lawyer: When you were having intercourse with her the first time, did you say anything to her then?

In uttering this question, the lawyer takes for granted (ie, assumes) that the witness has had intercourse with some woman and is asking about speech events that might have taken place during the intercourse. What is important for my purposes is that this presupposition continues to be taken for granted (ie, remains in evidence) even if the addressee answers the question in the negative. Thus, in contexts where cross-examining lawyers attempt to include elements of their own client's version of events in their questions, presuppositions are even more powerful than the declaratives of yes-no questions in controlling evidence. The contrast among the kinds of propositions made available and/or presupposed by the question -types discussed here can be seen in (2) and (3). The question -types are ordered from less "controlling" to more "controlling."

(2) Yes-No questions without presuppositions, eg, *You had intercourse with her, didn't you?*

Proposition made available (but denied if question answered in the negative): the addressee had intercourse with some woman.

(3) Yes-No questions with presuppositions, eg, *When you had intercourse with her, you said something to her, didn't you?*

Proposition made available (but denied if question answered in the negative): the addressee said something to some woman when having intercourse with her.

25 John Lyons, *Semantics* (Cambridge: Cambridge University Press, 1977).

26 This question is adapted from Atkinson & Drew, *supra* note 15 at 211.

Proposition presupposed: the addressee had intercourse with some woman.

THE POWER OF QUESTIONS TO CONTROL INFORMATION IN RAPE TRIALS

A central argument of this chapter is that the problematic cultural assumptions typically brought to bear on the adjudication of rape trials are also evident within the discourse of rape trials; in particular, defence lawyers invoke cultural mythologies surrounding rape as a way of undermining the credibility of complainants. In this section, I demonstrate how these kinds of cultural myths are encoded within the "controlling" questions of defence lawyers when cross-examining complainants, in particular, within the presuppositions and declaratives of the lawyers' yes-no questions.

The specific kinds of cultural assumptions discussed in this section involve what Sanday might call "an ancient sexual stereotype" — an outdated statutory rule within sexual assault and rape law called the "utmost resistance" standard.[27] Until the 1950s and the 1960s in the United States, the statutory requirement of utmost resistance was a necessary criterion for the crime of rape; that is, if a woman did not resist a man's sexual advances to the utmost, then rape did not occur.[28] While, as noted above, this standard is no longer encoded in rape statutes in the United States and Canada, it does circulate within the discourse of rape trials. The following examples come from a Canadian acquaintance rape trial[29] in which the accused, Matt (a pseudonym), was charged with sexually assaulting two different women, Connie and Marg (pseudonyms), in their university residences three nights apart. (Matt was convicted of sexual assault in the case involving Marg, on the basis of corroboration from witnesses, and acquitted in the case involving Connie.) Although both complainants described their experiences as sexual assault, in the examples that follow, the defence lawyer represents the women's behaviour as lacking in forceful and direct resistance. Because the complainants' actions do not seem to meet the standard of resistance deemed appropriate by the defence lawyers, I suggest

27 See for discussion Ehrlich, *Representing Rape, supra* note 24 and Susan Ehrlich, "Coercing Gender: Language in Sexual Assault Adjudication Processes" in Janet Holmes & Miriam Meyerhoff, eds, *The Handbook of Language and Gender* (Oxford: Blackwell Publishers, 2003) 645.

28 Estrich, *supra* note 11.

29 *R v Ashton* (18 April 1995) Ontario Court, General Division, Toronto Ontario [unreported trial transcript on file with he author]. This analysis comes from my 2001 book: *Representing Rape, supra* note 24.

that these types of representations have the effect of calling into question the complainants' allegations of sexual assault.

Many of the questions (shown in italics below) asked by the defence lawyer identified options that the complainants could have pursued in their attempts to resist the accused; moreover, these options were consistently presented as reasonable options for the complainants to pursue. Examples (4) and (5), for instance, show the cross-examiner suggesting that "seeking help" was a reasonable option for Connie.

(4) Q: And I take it part of your involvement then on the evening of January 27th and having Mr A come back to your residence that you felt that you were in this comfort zone because you were going to a place that you were, very familiar; correct?
CD: It was my home, yes.
Q: *And you knew you had a way out if there was any difficulty?*
CD: I didn't really take into account any difficulty. I never expected there to be any.
Q: I appreciate that. *Nonetheless, you knew that there were other people around who knew you and obviously would come to your assistance, I take it, if you had some problems, or do you know?* Maybe you can't answer that.
CD: No, I can't answer that. I can't answer that. I was inviting him to my home, not my home that I share with other people, not, you know, a communal area. I was taking him to my home and I really didn't take into account anybody else around, anybody that I lived near. It was like inviting somebody to your home.
Q: Fair enough. And I take it from what you told us in your evidence this morning that it never ever crossed your mind when this whole situation reached the point where you couldn't handle it, or were no longer in control, to *merely* go outside your door to summons someone?
CD: No.

(5) Q: What I am suggesting to you, ma'am, is that as a result of that situation with someone other than Mr A, you knew what to do in the sense that if you were in a compromising position or you were being, I won't use the word harass, but being pressured by someone you knew what to do, didn't you?
CD: No, I didn't. Somebody had suggested that, I mean, I could get this man who wasn't a student not be permitted on campus and that's what I did.

> Q: What — *but I am suggesting that you knew that there was someone or a source or a facility within the university that might be able to assist you if you were involved in a difficult situation, isn't that correct, because you went to the student security already about this other person?*
> CD: Yeah, okay. If you are asking if I knew about the existence of student security, yes, I did.

The italicized sentences in examples (4) and (5) are "controlling" questions in Woodbury's sense. That is, in producing such questions, the defence attorney communicates certain propositions to the judge and jury in the declarative portion of the yes-no questions, specifically, that Connie knew there were university resources available to women who found themselves in difficult situations. The italicized questions in (4) and (5) also contain presuppositions. The predicate, *know*, is a factive predicate, which means that it presupposes the truth of its complement. Thus, in uttering the three italicized questions above, the defence lawyer presupposes that "there was a way out," "there were other people around who knew Connie," and "there were resources at the university to help those in difficult situations." Indeed, due to the presupposed nature of these propositions, even if Connie had denied her knowledge of the availability of help, what is communicated by the lawyer's questions is the fact that help *was* available within the university. Note that the final question of example (4) not only identifies an option that Connie could have pursued, it also represents this option as an unproblematic one, given the presence of the word, *merely* — *It never ever crossed your mind ... to* merely *go outside your door to summons someone?*

So, what are the inferences that a judge and jury might draw from the information communicated by the defence lawyer's questions? If help was available, and if Connie admits at certain points in the questioning that she was aware of its availability, as we see in the last turn of example (5), then her failure to seek help suggests that she was *not* in "a difficult situation" and that she did not require assistance. Put somewhat differently, Connie's failure to seek help casts doubt on her credibility, specifically, it calls into question her allegations of sexual assault.

Examples (6) and (7) show both the judge and the cross-examining lawyer asking Connie and Marg, respectively, why they didn't utter other words in their various attempts to resist Matt's sexual aggression. Again, we see an emphasis on the seemingly reasonable options that were not pursued by the complainants.

(6) Q: And in fact just raising another issue that I would like you to help us with if you can, this business of you realizing when the line was getting blurred when you said "Look, I don't want to sleep with you," or words to that effect, yes, you remember that?
CD: Yes.
Q: Well, when you said that, what did that mean or what did you want that to mean, not to have intercourse with him?
CD: Yeah, I mean, ultimately, that's what it meant. It also, I mean –
The Court: *You didn't want to sleep with him but why not, "Don't undue (sic) my bra" and "Why don't you knock it off"?*
CD: Actually, "I don't want" — "I don't want to sleep with you" is very cryptic, and certainly as he got his hands under my shirt, as he took off my shirt, as he undid my bra, as he opened my belt and my pants and pulled them down and I said, "Please don't, please stop. Don't do that. I don't want you to do that, please don't," that's pretty direct as well.

(7) MB: And then we got back into bed and Matt immediately started again and then I said to Bob, "Bob where do you get these persistent friends?"
Q: Why did you even say that? You wanted to get Bob's attention?
MB: I assumed that Bob talked to Matt in the hallway and told him to knock it off.
Q: You assumed?
MB: He was talking to him and came back in and said everything was all right.
Q: Bob said that?
MB: Yes.
Q: But when you made that comment, you wanted someone to know, you wanted Bob to know that this was a signal that Matt was doing it again?
MB: Yes.
Q: A mixed signal, ma'am, I suggest?
MB: To whom?
Q: What would you have meant by, "Where do you get these persistent friends?"
MB: Meaning Bob is doing it again, please help me.
Q: *Why didn't you say, "Bob, he was doing it again, please help me?"*

> MB: Because I was afraid Matt would get mad.
> Q: You weren't so afraid because you told Bob, "Where do you get these persistent friends?" Did you think Matt would be pleased with that comment because it was so general?
> MB: I didn't think about it but I thought that was my way of letting Bob know what was going on.

Connie reports saying *Look, I don't want to sleep with you* at a certain point in the evening and Marg recounts one of several incidents when she attempts to elicit Bob's help (Bob is the pseudonym for a friend of the accused's) by saying *Bob where do you get these persistent friends.* Yet, in the italicized questions above, these expressions of resistance are problematized by the judge and the defence lawyer, respectively. In example (6) the judge asks Connie why she hadn't said *Don't undue (sic) my bra* and *Why don't you knock it off*, and in example (7) the defence lawyer asks Marg why she didn't say *Bob, he was doing it again, please help me.* It is significant that both of the questions that preface the words not produced by the complainants are negative interrogatives (ie, *why not* and *why didn't you say*) — interrogatives that Heritage argues are often used to "frame negative or critical propositions."[30] This means that when the judge and the defence lawyer produce questions of the form "Why didn't you say X," not only are they calling attention to utterances that were *not* produced by the complainants, they are also communicating a negative and/or critical attitude towards the fact that such utterances were not produced. Once again, then, the inferences generated by these questions serve to call into question the complainants' allegations of sexual assault: because they did not express their resistance directly and forcefully, the judge and/or jury might wonder whether they had really been threatened by the accused.

The examples above are illustrative of the way cross-examining lawyers (and, in one case, a judge) use "controlling" questions to create a version of events that supports their own clients' case and undermines the credibility of the opposing side's case. My argument is that the information contained within the declarative portions and the presuppositions of the defence lawyer's questions created a powerful ideological lens through which the events in question came to be understood. More specifically, by repeatedly posing questions that represented the complainants as *not* pursuing "obvious" and "easily-executed" strat-

30 John Heritage, "The Limits of Questioning: Negative Interrogatives and Hostile Question Content" (2002) 34 J Pragmatics 1427.

egies of resistance, the defence lawyer suggested that the complainants' behaviour did not meet the "utmost resistance" standard, thereby undermining the complainants' allegations of sexual assault. From my point of view, what is problematic about the resistance standard invoked by the defence lawyer is the fact that it downplays and obscures the unequal power dynamics that often characterize male/female sexual relations. In excerpt (6), for example, Marg reports enlisting Bob's help in order to end Matt's sexual aggression because she feared that a more direct approach would provoke Matt's anger. The defence lawyer, however, suggests that Marg should have employed more direct words in resisting Matt's violence and characterizes her strategic act of resistance as nothing more than a *mixed signal.* Thus, Marg's act of resistance, which could have been framed as an intelligent and thoughtful response to a man's escalating sexual violence, was instead characterized by the defence lawyer as an inadequate act of resistance.

RESISTING THE CULTURAL MYTHOLOGIES SURROUNDING RAPE

The Power of Answers to Control Information

A defining characteristic of institutional discourse is the differential speaking rights assigned to participants based on their institutional role. In legal contexts, as we have seen, lawyers (and judges) have the right to initiate and allocate turns by asking questions of witnesses, but the reverse is not generally true; witnesses do not typically ask questions of lawyers and, if they do, they risk being sanctioned by the court. While the claim that "asking questions amounts to interactional control"[31] is a pervasive one in the literature on courtroom discourse, it is not a claim that has gone unchallenged. Based on a study of Aboriginal witnesses in Australian courts, for example, Diana Eades argues that the syntactic form of questions has no predictable effect on the form of witness responses.[32] In a similar way, Greg Matoesian has questioned the assumption that "questions … are more powerful than answers," suggesting that such an assumption "risks the problem of reifying structure."[33]

31 Diana Eades, *Courtroom Talk and Neocolonial Control* (Berlin: Mouton de Gruyter, 2008) at 37.

32 Diana Eades, "I Don't Think it's an Answer to the Question: Silencing Aboriginal Witnesses in Court" (2000) 29 Language in Soc'y 161.

33 Greg Matoesian, "Review of *Language and Power in Court: A Linguistic Analysis of the OJ Simpson Trial* by Janet Cotterill" (2005) 9 J Sociolinguistics 621.

> Just as we assume questions do more than merely question (for instance in court they may work as accusations, etc.), why presume any less of answers (which may recalibrate the question, produce a new question and so on)? A more detailed consideration of answers and how they function in detail may demonstrate just how powerful they are.[34]

Drew provides precisely this kind of "detailed consideration of answers" in his analysis of a rape victim's cross-examination.[35] In particular, Drew shows how the complainant (ie, the rape victim) in this particular trial often produced "alternative descriptions" in her answers — descriptions that contested the cross-examining lawyer's version of events. That is, rather than providing "yes" or "no" answers to the cross-examining lawyer's yes-no questions, the complainant provided competing descriptions that transformed the lawyer's damaging characterizations into more benign ones. In (8) below, for example, the cross-examining lawyer, through the use of "controlling" questions, attempts to represent the events that preceded the alleged rape as precursors to a consensual sexual interaction.[36]

(8) 16 A: Well yuh had some uh (p) (.) uh fairly lengthy
17 conversations with the defendant uh: did'n you?
18 (0.7)
19 A: On that evening uv February fourteenth?
20 (1.0)
21 W: Well we were all talkin.
22 (0.8)
23 A: Well *you* knew, at that time that the
24 defendant was *in*terested (.) in *you* (.)
25 did'n you?
26 (1.3)
27 W: *He* asked me how I'(d) bi*n* en
28 (1.1)
29 W: J- just stuff like that

34 *Ibid.*

35 Paul Drew, "Contested Evidence in Courtroom Examination: The Case of a Trial for Rape" in Drew & Heritage, *supra* note 17 at 470.

36 This example is taken from Drew, *ibid* at 486. In the passage quoted, silences are indicated as pauses in tenths of a second and a period in parentheses indicates a micropause (less than two tenths of a second).

While the lawyer's questions in lines 16–17 and 23–25 suggest that there was a closeness or intimacy developing between the defendant and the complainant, Drew argues that the complainant's answers, although not containing any "overt correction markers," do not support this version of events.[37] Rather, the complainant provides answers that depict a lack of intimacy between the complainant and the defendant, that is, a scene in which there were a number of people who *were all talkin* and in which the defendant issued a greeting that was more friendly than intimate. What is significant about Drew's analysis for the present discussion is the fact that the answerer is shown to "control" evidence (in Woodbury's sense) by resisting and transforming the propositions contained in the declarative portions of the lawyer's yes-no questions. In fact, Drew comments explicitly on the need to be attentive to the way that competing descriptions from witnesses may influence juries: "the complainant's attempts to counter the lawyer's descriptive strategies, and hence herself control the information which is available to the jury, should not be overlooked."[38]

Direct Examination

Given the adversarial nature of the English common law system, there are always (at least) two competing versions of events put forward in the courtroom. Thus, in the same way that answers may contest the version of events put forward by the questions of cross-examining lawyers, it should also be possible for the question-answer sequences of *direct* examination to convey an alternative narrative to the one provided by cross-examining lawyers. Indeed, in what follows, I provide examples from a Canadian rape trial[39] where, I suggest, the prosecuting lawyer anticipated and attempted to challenge the kind of defence strategy seen in examples (4) through (7) above: that the complainant did not resist her perpetrator sufficiently and therefore engaged in consensual sex. This particular case involved a sexual assault that took place during a job interview; the accused interviewed the complainant for a job and subse-

37 *Ibid* at 487.

38 *Ibid* at 517.

39 *R v Ewanchuk* (7 November 1995) Alberta Court of Queen's Bench, Edmonton, Alberta [unreported trial transcript on file with the author]. For further discussion and analysis of this trial, see Susan Ehrlich, "Constraining the Boundaries of Gendered Identities: Trial Discourse and Judicial Decision-Making" in Judith Baxter, ed, *Speaking Out: The Female Voice in Public Contexts* (Basingstoke, UK: Palgrave Macmillan, 2006) 139; Susan Ehrlich, "Legal Discourse and the Cultural Intelligiblity of Gendered Meanings" (2007) 11 J Sociolinguistics 452.

quently invited her to see his work in the trailer attached to his van. According to the complainant's testimony, the accused sexually assaulted her in the trailer for a period of approximately two hours. The accused was acquitted by the trial judge and by the Alberta Court of Appeal (a provincial court). Upon appeal to the Supreme Court of Canada, the acquittal was overturned and a conviction was entered for the accused.

Atkinson and Drew, in their investigation of courtroom discourse, have noted that witnesses often display their recognition that a series of questions is leading to a "blame allocation" by producing "justification/excuse components in answers."[40] In other words, witnesses will provide defences and justifications in their answers even though the questions asked of them "do not actually contain any blame-relevant assessments of witnesses' actions."[41] Such defences and justifications will thus appear *prematurely* within the course of a trial, that is, before they are actually elicited by a cross-examining lawyer. In the same way that witnesses may provide justifications for their actions prematurely, I am suggesting that examples (10) to (15) show that lawyers may also anticipate critical assessments of their witnesses' actions from opposing lawyers and will thus design their questions to elicit premature or pre-emptive defences and justifications for such actions.

In contrast to the adversarial, combative nature of cross-examination, direct examination has been characterized by both legal practitioners and by scholars as supportive and co-operative. In particular, open-ended questions, or questions that display little "control" in Woodbury's sense, tend to be more frequent in direct examination than in cross-examination. This can be seen in the excerpts (9–14). In each of the examples, the prosecuting attorney begins her turn by asking a broad wh- question, such as *What happened then?*, to which the complainant responds by describing an event or a series of events. Immediately following such an answer, the lawyer asks a narrower wh- question — a why- question that attempts to elicit the complainant's motivation for performing a particular action that she has described. What is significant about these why- questions, for the purposes of this paper, is that they allow the complainant to represent herself as having actively pursued strategies of resistance, either strategies meant to discourage the defendant's sexual advances or strategies meant to avoid more intense and/or prolonged instances of violence from the defendant.

40 Atkinson & Drew, *supra* note 15 at 136.

41 *Ibid* at 138.

(9) Q: Was he inside the van or trailer when you first got there?
A: I believe he was inside the van, but — he might have stepped out to meet me.
Q: What happened once you got there?
A: I asked him if we could go inside the mall, have a cup of coffee and talk about whatever
Q: Why did you want to go inside the mall to talk?
A: *Because it was — it was a public place. I mean, we could go in and sit down somewhere and talk.*

(10) Q: What happened then?
A: He said, Why don't we just talk inside the van here. And he sat into his driver's seat, and I opened the door, and I left the door open of the passenger seat and I sat down there.
Q: And why did you leave the door open?
A: *Because I was still very hesitant about talking to him.*

(11) Q: What happened after you agreed to see some of his work?
A: He went around to — no, first, he said, Okay, I'd like to pull the van into the shade. It was a hot day, and there was cars that were parked under the shade ... of a tree, I believe, and he got out, and he went and he stepped inside, and he said, Come on up and look. So I stepped up inside, took about two steps in, I didn't, like, walk around in it. And then he went to the door, closed it, and locked it.
(some intervening turns)
Q: Had you expected him to lock the door?
A: Not at all. I left the door completely wide open when I walked in there for a reason.
Q: And what was that reason?
A: *Because I felt that this was a situation that I shouldn't be in, that I — with anybody to be alone in a trailer with any guy with the door closed.*

(12) Q: Did he say anything when he locked the door?
A: He didn't say anything about the door being locked, but he asked me to sit down. And he sat down cross-legged.
Q: What did you sit on?
A: Just the floor of the trailer.
Q: Now, why did you sit down when he asked you to sit down?
A: *Because I figured I was in this trailer, the door was locked, he*

was not much more than this stand is away from me here, probably only a couple of feet away from me. I felt that I was in a situation now where I just better do what I was told.

(13) Q: And what happened then?
A: He told me that he felt very tense and that he would like to have a massage, and he then leaned up against me with his back towards me and told me to rub his shoulders and I did that.
Q: And up to the time he told you he was tense and wanted a massage, had the two of you talked about you giving him a massage?
A: I believe all he had said right before that is that he liked to have them, and he was tense feeling and that was all.
Q: Had you ever offered to give him a massage?
A: No.
Q: Did you want to give him a massage?
A: No.
(some intervening turns)
Q: If you didn't want to give him a massage at that point in time, why did you touch his shoulders?
A: *I was afraid that if I put up any more of a struggle that it would only egg him on even more, and his touching would be more forced.*

(14) Q: And what happened then?
A: Then he asked me to turn around the other way to face him, and he said he would like to touch my feet or he would like to massage my feet, so I did. And he was just touching my feet.
Q: Did you want him to massage your feet?
A: No.
Q: Why did you turn around?
A: *Because I guess I was afraid. I was frozen. I just did what he told me to do.*

In the italicized portions of (9) to (11), the complainant represents herself as attempting to create circumstances that will discourage that accused's sexual aggression: she suggests going inside the mall to talk because it is a *public* place and she leaves the doors open to the van and the trailer respectively because she is hesitant about talking to the accused alone in a confined space. In the italicized portions of (12) to (14), the complainant represents herself as attempting to prevent more extreme acts of violence from the accused: she complies with all of his requests (eg, that she sit down, that she massage him, that she turn around so he can massage her feet) out of fear that not complying will *egg him on even more*. Indeed, such responses reflect strategies that many victims of sexual violence employ to prevent more prolonged and extreme instances of violence. As researchers on violence against women have asserted, submitting to coerced sex or physical abuse can be "a strategic mode of action undertaken in preservation of self."[42] That is, if physical resistance on the part of victims can escalate and intensify violence, as some research shows[43] and many women (are instructed to) believe, then submission to coerced sex is undoubtedly the best strategy for survival.

In a general way, then, what is important about the prosecuting attorney's questioning in examples (9) to (14) is the fact that her why-questions served to elicit responses that highlighted and emphasized the complainant's active deployment of strategies meant to resist the accused's escalating sexual violence. In this way, the lawyer can be viewed as anticipating, and attempting to pre-empt, a certain kind of "blame allocation" from the defence — that the complainant did not resist the accused "to the utmost" and thus engaged in consensual sex. The preceding discussion is significant because it shows that the cultural rape mythologies often invoked by defence lawyers can be challenged in courtrooms by alternative kinds of narratives. More specifically, in the direct examination of the sexual assault trial just described, the complainant's actions were contextualized within a sense-making framework that acknowledged the structural inequalities that can characterize male–female sexual relations and the effects of such inequalities in shaping women's strategies of resistance.

CONCLUSION

According to Gibbons, the primary way that cross-examining lawyers construct a version of events that supports their own clients' interests is by including "elements of this desired version" of events in their questions.[44] Drawing upon Woodbury's notion of question "control,"[45] I

42 Lora Bea Lempert, "Women's Strategies for Survival: Developing Agency in Abusive Relationships" (1996) 11 J Family Violence 269.

43 See, for example, R Emerson Dobash & Russell P Dobash, *Women, Violence and Social Change* (London: Routledge, 1992).

44 Gibbons, *supra* note 19 at 98.

45 Woodbury, *supra* note 21 at 197.

have shown how cross-examining lawyers in acquaintance rape trials can incorporate "elements" into their "controlling" questions that are strategically designed to undermine the credibility of complainants. More specifically, by encoding damaging cultural mythologies (eg, the utmost resistance standard) into the declarative portions and presuppositions of questions, I have argued that defence lawyers can cast doubt on complainants' allegations of sexual assault and rape.

I began this chapter by pointing to the cultural mythologies that often inform the adjudication of sexual assault and rape cases in Canada and the United States in spite of four decades of progressive statutory reform. What this chapter has demonstrated is the way that these same cultural mythologies can make their way into rape trial discourse, potentially reinforcing the problematic cultural assumptions held by judges and juries. As Steven Shulhofer says about the failure of rape law reform in the United States, "social attitudes are tenacious, and they can easily nullify the theories and doctrines found in the law books. The story of failed reforms is in part a story about the overriding importance of culture, about the seeming irrelevance of law."[46] If it is true that culture is of paramount importance in the legal system's treatment of rape and sexual assault, then the rape trial becomes an important site for viewing this culture "in action." Defence lawyers exploit damaging cultural narratives about rape as a way of undermining the credibility of complainants; at the same time, given the *adversarial and dynamic* nature of the trial, witnesses in their answers and prosecuting lawyers in their questions have the potential to produce competing cultural narratives about rape, as I have demonstrated. Put somewhat differently, if the rape trial provides a window onto culture "in action," then it not only provides a forum for viewing discriminatory narratives about rape but also for viewing the potential for these narratives to change.

46 Steven Schulhofer, *Unwanted Sex: The Culture of Intimidation and the Failure of the Law* (Cambridge, MA: Harvard University Press, 1998) at 17.

18. Questioning "Expert" Knowledges

Sunny Marriner[1]

In her contribution to this section, Sunny Marriner echoes Jane Doe's critique of the medicalization of women's experiences of sexual assault and acknowledges, like Diana Yaros, how much authority feminist advocates have conceded to the "professionals." Sunny argues that in spite of feminism's powerful critique of the "psy-" disciplines, "psy-" "expertise" has thoroughly permeated legal space in the courtroom in sexual assault trials and extends far beyond to control the lives of women caught in the criminal justice and child protection systems. She demonstrates that both law and the "psy-" disciplines are profoundly inexpert on sexual assault, yet feminist expertise has been decentred not only by these disciplines, but also by feminists' efforts to seek "professional" credentials to prove their own authority. Feminist expertise is grounded in political commitment to women's equality and women's experiential knowledge, as articulated by Jane Doe in this section, and must be reclaimed and reasserted by women's centres and feminist advocates.

> The collusion of perhaps the two most powerful systems we have (legal and medical) to judge rape and assess guilt, when neither is versed in the true nature of rape, has set us down a dangerous path.
>
> — *The Story of Jane Doe*[2]

1 I am foremost indebted to the many young women who have shared their knowledge with me on their paths of survival through violence, the state-care system, the legal system, criminalization, and incarceration. I am further grateful for the support and wisdom of the Sexual Assault Support Centre of Ottawa collective, past and present and, in particular, the enduring political commitment of Susan Havart. Thanks are also due to Diana Majury for assisting me in straddling the line between life and the academy, to Doris Buss, and to Linda Green (OISE) for her generous sharing and responsiveness to questions about resources.

2 Jane Doe, *The Story of Jane Doe: A Book About Rape* (Toronto: Random House, 2003) at 259.

It was a terrible trial. A victim[3] of brutal sexual violence was being forced to testify against her will, despite having repeatedly asserted she could not, and the days were not going well. Defence counsel were "whacking the complainant"[4] with everything they had and she was going in and out of flashback on the stand. That this is what was occurring was patently obvious to me, sitting in the body of the court, and yet it was not openly acknowledged or identified by anyone in the room. Instead there were many long breaks and the court's patience was wearing thin. During the breaks, the flashbacks continued, increasing in intensity, causing her to throw up, scream, and, several times, briefly lose consciousness. Eventually the Crown had to accept that they simply could not make her continue and they reluctantly requested an adjournment. Defence counsel fought tooth and nail and I was called to the stand to testify as to what I had witnessed while supporting the woman over the course of her testimony.

What I witnessed was a woman being triggered repeatedly by a non-consensual process; ruthless, repeated cross-examination; forced, descriptive repetition of the most terrifying experiences of her life while in a hostile space surrounded by entirely unsafe people; and close proximity to individuals accused of savage acts of violence against her. The result was increasing, ever-more terrifying flashbacks that left her physically, mentally, and emotionally debilitated.

This was not, however, what I testified to. Instead, I was required to describe in detail for the court what movements the woman made, whether or not her eyes were focused, what her body was doing, what words she was saying, and whether she "appeared" to lose consciousness. I could describe everything about a flashback — what I couldn't do was say the word "flashback." Despite having spent thousands of hours with women in flashback over more than a decade of support work, this, according to the defence, would amount to expert testimony I was of questionable qualification to give.

The judge, on hearing my description of what I saw, queried the Crown, "Were paramedics called?" When it was established that they were not, the judge expressed consternation, asserting that it would

3 The use of the word "victim" here is deliberate, as victimization was ongoing through this process and survival was, as yet, undetermined.

4 "... an array of strategies used by defence lawyers to undermine the character and credibility of complainants so that they are unwilling to testify against the accused." See Elizabeth Comack & Gillian Balfour, *The Power to Criminalize: Violence, Inequality and the Law* (Halifax: Fernwood, 2004) at 110.

seem that an ambulance should have been requested. Had I been asked, I would have informed the court that what transpired was not extraordinary for women experiencing severe flashbacks, and that flashbacks do not constitute a medical emergency. I was not asked.

Instead, the court expressed the opinion that this woman should be medically assessed for a possible organic cause, as the response could be indicative of a serious illness. Once an organic cause was ruled out, she should next certainly be assessed by a psychiatrist. The adjournment was granted with the judge's strong suggestion to the Crown that they use the time to seek out expert advice and require the woman to attend for diagnosis.

Ultimately, the Crown took the position that the unwilling woman had to undergo psychiatric assessment so an expert could render an opinion as to what was happening during her attempts to testify and on her capacity to go forward, before they would abandon the prosecution.

In over a decade of feminist political practice, this story is only one of many examples I've witnessed of a legal system divorced from any common sense ability to deal with survivors of sexual violence. I chose it to launch this discussion as it illustrates the legal and social fictions of "expertise" that have pervaded both the legal system and the violence against women[5] movement as a whole.[6] Here we see:

- a Crown's office substituting their "expert" opinion about a woman's ability to testify for her own;
- a judge, overwhelmed by her own lack of understanding of intense responses, believing that medical "experts" will demystify a non-medical problem;
- a courtroom full of purported "experts" in trying sexual assault cases unable to notice or recognize when a survivor is in flashback on the stand;
- a referral to "expert" psychological assessment for a "credible" opinion to prove to the Crown what the (apparently not-credible) woman herself already identified; and
- the suppression of relevant experience that could have resolved significant questions before the court and spared the survivor further unwelcome intrusion on her body and mind.

5 Also VAW.

6 Another key reason for this choice was that the events described occurred publicly.

Throughout this episode, the spectre of "expertise" was invoked and, in each instance, the consequences were borne by only one person: the sexually assaulted woman.

To locate myself, I draw these observations from a body of thirteen years of work in a frontline feminist sexual assault centre collective. The Sexual Assault Support Centre [SASC][7] is a women's equality-seeking organization with a basis of solidarity rooted in a theory of linked oppressions. As such, collective members believe feminist equality-seeking work must be, by definition, anti-oppression work and actively challenge racism, classism, ableism, heterosexism, colonialism, and other forms of oppression. We define our work with women survivors of violence as what I here term "feminist political practice," as opposed to the simple provision of services, or "service work." This feminist political practice includes providing support and advocacy to women using a survivor-based, survivor-directed model that acknowledges women as the experts in their own lives.

It might, at one time, have been unnecessary to begin this discussion with such a recitation of meanings, as they could be taken as implied in the term "frontline feminist sexual assault centre." However, today's changed landscape of sexual assault centre practice demonstrates that there is no longer a broad consensus about what role political location and engagement should play in the work of supporting survivors of violence. Instead, in a culture of increasing credentialism and professionalization, we see sexual assault centres moving ever-further from the radical challenges of feminism, the expert knowledge it developed, and its at-once hopeful and skeptical aspiration to alter the social terrain for women. Today, courtrooms and sexual assault centres have begun to bear startling resemblances since both spaces engage more and more deeply with psy-disciplines,[8] whose claims to "expert knowledge" of women survivors of violence are arguably largely self-awarded.

Critically engaging the concept of expertise is a gargantuan work in and of itself. What constitutes expertise? Who decides what is expert, and with what criteria? Do these criteria reflect women's lived experience? How do expertise discourses and claims to expert knowledge lead us nearer or further from our equality-seeking aims? The psy-disci-

7 Sexual Assault Support Centre of Ottawa, online: <http://www.sascottawa.org>.

8 Psychiatry, psychology, psychotherapy and, less so today, psychoanalysis. Many critics (early and contemporary) include social work under the psy-discipline umbrella, particularly as it increasingly professionalizes to vie for status with the aforementioned fields. Social workers are implied in this usage in most instances in this paper.

plines, the legal system, and the women's movement have each held positions on what constitutes expertise within their own fields and in others. Each has mobilized notions of expertise in different ways, and seemingly to different and shifting ends. Employing expert knowledge sometimes appears quite formalized on the surface (as in the criteria for adducing expert testimony in court); on other occasions, the term "expert" is simply thrown down like a trump card without any apparent sense of obligation to back up the truth claims it implies. All argument on the matter must now halt, as The Expert has been invoked. A concept wielding such enormous power is surely one that equality-seeking organizations cannot afford to ignore.

Under closer scrutiny it becomes clear that "expertise" is a less concrete, more contested arena than some of its vaunted claimants would have us believe. The apparent consensus on who has the right to speak, with what voice, and with what authority is actually a thin veneer at best, and often constructed for us by the very disciplines most invested in being seen as expert. This suggests that not only are we misled when we rely on psy-discipline authority in matters relating to women survivors of violence, but further that the deep, and mostly unacknowledged, permeation of this theory into legal space both exemplifies and reinforces the encroachment of expertise claims into social life and our social movements. What occurs in our legal system not only mirrors dominant discourses in society as a whole, but it also contributes to shaping those discourses, providing authority for them, and reinserting them into the populace with the newfound weight of legal validation. As the opening example demonstrates, psy-discipline expertise claims are deeply embedded in every stage of a legal process and are clearly influencing the thinking of most legal players. Despite this, critical analysis of expertise, law, and violence against women is often limited to a discussion of the role of expert witnesses or courtroom testimony. I submit that such a reductionist view paints a dangerously narrow picture of how psy-legal expert authority is employed with survivors of violence, and contributes to masking the reach of this power over them even when they are outside what is considered formal legal space. I argue instead that we must expand our understanding of how both "expertise" and legal space are considered, and begin to look much further afield than the witness chair to locate where and when psy-legal truth claims are acting upon women.

This paper first confronts the psy-disciplines' dubious claims to expertise about women survivors of violence, and next illustrates how those claims are reified rather than challenged through the power and deference they are accorded by the weight of legal authority. Through what Jane Doe called "the collusion of perhaps the two most powerful systems we have," psy-discipline theory is translated into legally mandated action in the lives of women such that both domains expand their expert claims in a process of exponential reinforcement. In this generative loop of expert power, women's anti-violence organizations play a crucial contributory role. Once critical sites in generating a body of women's own expert knowledge, today a shift away from political goals in sexual assault centres increasingly serves to buttress legal and psy-discipline fictions about women survivors. Where resisting harmful expertise claims was once a pillar of frontline feminist organizations, the final section argues that those same claims are today adopted as arguments to professionalize, credentialize, and ultimately depoliticize feminist anti-violence work. By broadening our gaze and examining psy, legal, and feminist expertise claims as three parts of a larger whole, we can reveal the intersecting impacts of expert knowledges in the lives of survivors — impacts that are easily obscured when focussing only on the component parts.

Feminism teaches us that *how* we have a conversation often communicates as much as the words we say. A conversation about racism, for example, designed by white women in accordance with an agenda they set, with the players they choose to invite and using the process they deem most effective, does as much to reinforce white women's position of power in the discourse as would choosing not to have the conversation at all. In keeping with these insights, I am mindful of who is invited to this table and acknowledge that paradoxes arise in the very act of writing this paper. There is an inescapable irony in using a largely inaccessible academic style and language to challenge the tendency of feminist equality-seekers to adopt ever-more inaccessible academic style and language. This paradox runs still deeper when we ask whether the concept of expertise can be critically engaged without invoking "the experts"? For experts there are, as the numerous scholarly works theorizing the concept demonstrate.[9] The study of expertise has become an expert discipline in its own right, which is a notion that threatens to leave our heads spinning when beginning any analysis. In lieu of get-

9 See K Anders Ericsson *et al*, *The Cambridge Handbook of Expertise and Expert Performance* (Cambridge: Cambridge University Press, 2006) for a comprehensive overview of the scholarship and Evan Selinger & Robert P Crease, *The Philosophy of Expertise* (New York: Columbia University Press, 2006) for critiques.

ting lost in ever-deepening levels of abstraction, Occam's razor[10] might shave off some layers of entanglement by suggesting the most common understandings and roles of expertise are probably also the ones holding the most sway in the lives of women.

PART I

Who Gets to be the Expert?

Most definitions of "expert" suggest that the term refers to someone "very skilled or knowledgeable" about a particular field.[11] Of note is the fact that education, while listed as a characteristic of expertise, is not generally as heavily emphasized as experience or "practice." Moreover, "knowledge" is clearly the preferred term. K Anders Ericsson, in *The Cambridge Handbook of Expertise and Expert Performance*, explains that expertise "refers to the characteristics, skills, and knowledge that distinguish experts from novices and less experienced people."[12] The same handbook, however, takes pains to point out that in many "domains" designated experts often "disagree and make inconsistent recommendations for action" and their performance may be indistinguishable from non-experts "*even on tasks that are central to the expertise*" [emphasis added].[13] Ericsson specifically mentions psychotherapy as one of those "domains." These less-identifiable "experts" must therefore rely on peer-recognition for their expert designation.[14] Some sociologists argue that this reliance on peers to accord expert status inevitably creates "closure" in domains that rely on subjective criteria to determine skill level.[15] Only those who already support and agree with the fundamental tenets of the discipline are involved in awarding cred-

10 A logical maxim attributed to William Ockham that generally states, "entities should not be multiplied unnecessarily," or, a more recognizable variant, "the simplest explanation is usually the best."

11 See definition, online: <http://dictionary.reference.com/browse/expert>; and Ericsson *et al*, *supra* note 9 at 3.

12 K Anders Ericsson, "*An Introduction to Cambridge Handbook of Expertise and Expert Performance*: Its Development, Organization and Content," in K Anders Ericsson *et al*, *supra* note 9 at 3, 3.

13 *Ibid* at 4.

14 *Ibid.*

15 Julia Evetts, Harald S Mieg & Ulrike Felt, "Professionalization, Scientific Expertise, and Elitism: A Sociological Perspective"in K Anders Ericsson *et al*, *supra* note 9 at 105, 106, 109, 118.

ibility, thereby creating a self-perpetuating expert designation that can fairly be described as self-awarded. Ericsson, in summarizing, adds this most arresting observation:

> Finally, Shanteau (1988) has suggested that "experts" may not need a proven record of performance and can adopt a particular image and project "outward signs of extreme self-confidence" (p. 211) to get clients to listen to them and continue to offer advice after negative outcomes. After all, the experts are nearly always the best qualified to evaluate their own performance and explain the reasons for any deviant outcomes.[16]

While it may be unintentional, Ericsson's overview thus suggests that individuals, and indeed whole domains, may still be considered expert even if their greatest consistency is that their expert predictions, opinions, and/or performances frequently turn out to be wrong. According to James Shanteau, as long as they are *seen* to be expert by others who already share their belief in the domain's authority, or can convincingly *present* themselves as expert despite their unreliability, then "expert" status still holds.

Questioning expertise, then, would appear a daunting and somewhat defeatist task. Closure and a lack of emphasis on outcomes mean that criticizing from anywhere other than inside the discipline itself may be dismissed as the misunderstandings of a "non-expert." The "expert" status, in and of itself, acts as protection against challenge, insulating the knowledge or opinions said "experts" generate from critique by any but those who share the same investment in the discipline.

"Historically, the demeaning of women is an essential part of psychotherapy theory"[17]

> Like all salespeople, personality "experts" can be intimidating because of their aura of mystery because they want us to think they have some special knowledge. We are often left feeling we couldn't possibly understand the subtleties of what they know, so we satisfy ourselves with relying on their expertise.[18]

16 Ericsson, *supra* note 12 at 4.

17 Dorothy Tennov, *Psychotherapy: The Hazardous Cure* (New York: Anchor Books, 1976) at 229.

18 Paula J Caplan, *The Myth of Women's Masochism* (New York: New American Library, 1985) at 28.

Consider these reflections on expertise, then, in the context of the history of psy-disciplines with women. This history offers a primary example of a domain with a consistent record of being reliably inexpert about women. The Woman of the psy-disciplines has variously suffered from hysteria, masochism, narcissism, passivity, penis envy, Castrating Woman Complex, Angry Woman Syndrome, a desire to have sex with her father which causes her to imagine having been sexually abused,[19] and on and on. Our wombs and reproductive systems have been described as the biological seat of our instability or outright insanity:[20]

> The psychoanalytic orientation, which has dominated clinical psychology, psychiatry, and social work for decades, is one in which women are viewed as biological, intellectual, social, and moral inferiors of men... In the writings of psychotherapists, especially psychoanalysts, outright hostility toward women is a recurrent theme. Entire books have been written which attempt to validate misogynist views.[21]

This history of attributing women's distress to their sex effectively allowed the patriarchal psy-disciplines to erase male culpability in abuse and ensure that men's dominant position in society did not come under fire. After all, if women's discontent was biologically determined, why would changing anything in their immediate environment or society as a whole alleviate the problem? As Dorothy Tennov comments:

> Many women with just grievances against the social order considered themselves, and were considered to be, psychologically ill and received "treatment" at the hands of practitioners who interpreted their difficulties as the outcome of internal pathology rather than as a reaction to oppressive social forces.[22]

The record of psy-disciplines' various perspectives on sexual violence is profoundly disturbing. From Freud's pronouncement that women's stories of sexual abuse were actually fantasies they wish were fulfilled,

19 Susan Brownmiller, *Against Our Will: Men, Women and Rape* (New York: Bantam Books, 1975) at 305; and Paula J Caplan, *They Say You're Crazy: How The World's Most Powerful Psychiatrists Decide Who's Normal* (Reading, MA: Perseus, 1995) at 37.

20 See Barbara Ehrenreich & Deirdre English, *For Her Own Good: 150 Years of the Experts' Advice to Women* (New York: Anchor Books, 1978).

21 Tennov, *supra* note 17 at 220–21.

22 *Ibid* at 220.

to the odious theory that sexually abused children were likely "seducers" of the abusers,[23] to the claim that women love sexual violence and male battery due to our inherently masochistic personalities,[24] the psy-disciplines have denied, condoned, excused, and perpetuated sexual violence against women and children. Further, they have placed the responsibility for women's oppression, misogyny, male violence, and sexual abuse squarely on the shoulders of females, whether they are children, partners, or mothers, in both theory and practice. Psychiatrist and biopsychiatric critic Peter Breggin writes, "Both poles of modern psychiatry, the biopsychiatric and the psychoanalytic, have led the way in covering up the victimization of women and female children and in exonerating men in general."[25]

One of the great contributions of the second-wave feminist movement was a wealth of critical writing about the psy-discipline's long history of presenting the female as pathological. Amid a rising tide of voices challenging psy-discipline truth claims,[26] this era saw an explosion of woman's resistance to the predominantly white, male psychiatrist's "expert" claim to authority in defining her and her apparent pathologies.[27] Phyllis Chesler's influential *Women and Madness* "argued convincingly that women are in double jeopardy: Women are institutionalized both for veering from their socially proscribed role and for overly conforming to it."[28] Chesler further "demonstrated ... [that] understandable emotional reactions in women are often labelled as pathological, but understandable emotional responses in men are not classified as signs of disturbance."[29] Chesler was far from alone in her skepticism of psychiatric "expertise" about women. This period saw the inherent masculine bias of the psy-disciplines beginning to be first identified, and then challenged, by a broad range of critics, some of whom were members of the very disciplines they unmasked.[30] The psy-disciplines themselves now appeared to be under the microscope. Studies began to show that "recovery" rates for people who did not seek psychotherapeutic treatment were actually higher than for those who

23 See Brownmiller, *supra* note 19 at 305–07; Tennov, *supra* note 17 at 108.

24 Caplan, *supra* note 18 at 30.

25 Peter Breggin, *Toxic Psychiatry* (New York: St Martin's Press, 1991) at 336.

26 Two notables are sociologist Erving Goffman, and psychiatrist and academic, Thomas Szasz, who remains active today.

27 Ehrenreich & English, *supra* note 20 at 316.

28 Bonnie Burstow, *Radical Feminist Therapy* (London: Sage Publications, 1992) at ix.

29 Caplan, *supra* note 18 at 140.

30 See discussion in Burstow, *supra* note 28 at ix; and Carol Gilligan, *In a Different Voice* (Cambridge, MA: Harvard University Press, 1982) at 7.

did.[31] Women, tired of being told their experiences of oppression and particularly of male violence were either imagined or their own fault, began to reject the men of the psy-disciplines' claims to expertise on women. They instead began building their own systems of support, grounded in the experiences of those who *could* be said to be "very skilled" and "knowledgeable" about their distress — other women, most particularly, other survivors of male violence. It was through this refusal to accord the "expert" credential to psy-knowledge that the first sexual assault and rape crisis centres were born, and it is clear that, for a time, many women believed the psy-disciplines had been thoroughly, and perhaps permanently, discredited.

That Was Then, This is Now

So what happened? Far from discredited, the psy-sector's claim to expert knowledge of survivors is today more entrenched than ever before. A persistent societal habit of severing today's knowledges from their roots has resulted in the all-too familiar "that was then, this is now" argument, rejecting the notion that disciplines, theories, and thinking are still strongly girded by their historical biases. Current psy-discipline discourse accordingly paints a picture of its anti-woman pedigree as being a relic of a long-distant past that is no longer relevant.[32] In reality, much of the critical scholarship has only been introduced in the last twenty-five years. *The Myth of Women's Masochism*, for example, was first published in 1985. Many of the first psy-discipline critics are still alive, kicking, and publishing today. Arguments that the psy-disciplines have somehow managed to purge their pathological-woman origins in this brief time span appear to crumble in the face of new "women's diagnoses," like Borderline Personality Disorder[33] and Self-Defeating Personality Disorder which, as Paula Caplan illustrates,[34] is arguably Masochistic Personality Disorder dressed up with a new name. The pièce de résistance was delivered with the addition of Premenstrual Dysphoric Disorder (known to the laywoman as "bad PMS") to the Diagnostic and Statistical Manual [DSM] IV in 1994.[35] Clearly the psy-

31 Tennov, *supra* note 17 at 80–86.

32 Similar arguments claim that racist and sexist oppressions no longer exist as these groups are ostensibly "equal now" under the law.

33 Clare Shaw & Gillian Proctor, "Women at the Margins: A Critique of the Diagnosis of Borderline Personality Disorder" (2005) 15 Feminism & Psychology 483–90.

34 Caplan, *supra* note 19 at 91.

35 To which Caplan engagingly asks, "Do half a million American women go crazy once a month?" (*ibid* at 122); Caplan exhaustively documents the struggle and ultimate defeat of the opposition to this addition: *ibid*.

disciplines continue to see women's basic physiology as synonymous with disorder.

A shift in language from "psychiatric problems" or "psychological problems" to "mental health issues" is equally troubling, although it is cloaked in a guise of benevolence and destigmatization. "Mental health" obviously implicates everybody at one time or another, as everybody can be said to have better or worse mental health at different times in their lives. Through the simple use of language, the potential market for psy-discipline services and pharmaceutical interventions has expanded from a relatively small, stable proportion of the population to today including infants, toddlers, and everyone who has ever struggled through a difficult period or simply felt pervasively unhappy. Far from destigmatizing, this language has instead encouraged widespread labelling, without the guilt. It was once a significant statement to claim that someone suffered from "psychiatric problems." Further, those wielding this label usually had to supply some empirical support, however faulty. Today we hear people, including those in the VAW movement, referring to "women with mental health issues" on a daily basis. Newly minted, pharmaceutically marketed "mood" and anxiety disorders are being diagnosed in women at anywhere from 1.6 to 6 times the rate of men, depending on the condition, and two-thirds of SSRI[36] prescriptions are written for women.[37] These facts cast still more doubt on the claims of many psy-practitioners that, despite their sordid history with women, "things have changed." A wholesale return to biopsychiatric truth claims has kept apace with a flood of psychiatric medications geared to treat every conceivable emotion, despite, once again, a flood of critical literature on efficacy, long-term impacts, and lack of testability. Several SSRI's have been associated with violence and suicide,[38] including some of the most popular off-label[39] prescriptions given to children.[40]

36 Selective Serotonin Reuptake Inhibitors, or anti-depressants.

37 Janet Currie, "The Marketization of Depression: The Prescribing of SSRI Antidepressants to Women" *Women and Health Protection* (May 2005), online: <http://www.whp-apsf.ca/en/documents/ssri.html>.

38 Breggin, *supra* note 25 at 164.

39 "Off-label" is the practice of prescribing drugs outside of their approved purpose and/or to groups for whom they have not been approved as safe. This is the case for nearly all psychotropic drugs given to children.

40 Shankar Vendantam, "FDA Links Anti-depressants, Youth Suicide Risk" *Washington Post* A01. (3 February 2004).

If anything, neo-liberal individualizing strategies in psy-disciplines are once again explaining women's moods, emotions, and coping through brain chemistry. Far from demonstrating that psy-disciplines have abandoned their quest to control the individual — the core purpose of a discipline that claims the ability to define "normal" and then trains people to be more like it — this emphasis on brain chemistry illustrates that the psy-disciplines have yet to accept that structural factors like racism, sexism, and poverty shape how people feel and cope. Even those psy-practitioners who do claim to recognize the impact of structural inequality tend to defend biomedicalization by arguing that the drugs assist people in "coping better" with their bad situations, potentially allowing them to escape more quickly. This stance not only suggests that it is a deficiency of the individual that they have yet to find "paths out" of societal oppression, but it is also the same argument that supported teaching abused women to cope better with abusive fathers and husbands, rather than raising an alarm about epidemic levels of violence perpetuated against women and children. This stubborn failure to learn from what they would have us dismiss as "early mistakes" only casts further doubt on the psy-discipline's modern claim that their expertise has grown.

Neither the history synthesized above, nor the fact of the psy-disciplines' collusion in violence against women, are revelatory. Rather, there is a wealth of scholarship, and innumerable personal narratives and historical accounts, all laying bare these same facts. As noted, a large number of the well-known critics of psy-discipline claims to expertise about women have themselves been psychiatrists or psychologists. If it is true that claims to expert knowledge are leveraged to ensure that psy-theorists need only be evaluated by other psy-theorists (as opposed to their patients or their efficacy), it has been of critical importance that these credentialed voices spoke, and continue to speak, out.

But to what effect? How have the psy-disciplines been held to account for this record and to what extent, if at all, has their claim to expert status been diminished? Despite a poor track record that would, in most other fields, connote a demonstrable *lack* of skill and knowledge, we see social institutions, including the law, continuing to turn to those who have proven least adept in this area and granting them top status in the expert hierarchy. The paradox emerging from the history, the evidence of survivors, critics in the same disciplines, and detailed feminist analysis is that psy-credentials may actually indicate that the holder is *inexpert*. Despite this, we legally and societally maintain and reinforce the fiction that the credentialed are the experts and consequently their voices are privileged and relied on almost exclusively in the legal domain.

Enter the Theorists

At this juncture it might be useful to take a moment and look at where some of these themes have been articulated before. To this point, I have deliberately chosen to avoid straying into abstract theory;[41] however, some legal theorists and interested feminists will have already made links between these observations and the work of Michel Foucault. While rendering a *Reader's Digest* condensed version of Foucauldian theory is done at one's own peril, his theoretical framework offers a useful lens through which to consider these questions of expertise, truth claims, power, and knowledge. Many feminist theorists have taken up Foucault's work as compatible with a feminist analysis (although not without some struggle), and I suggest that there may be some demonstrable validity to this, as we move through the next sections.

Foucault's much-discussed concept of "governmentality"[42] posits that the concentration of power has been dispersed from *government* (the state) to be located in technologies of *governance*, such as discipline, surveillance, and regulation. In what has been termed "the conduct of conduct," disciplinary technologies effect a totalizing yet subtle process of normalization, such that the subject and/or subject population becomes an active participant in their own control and regulation. The "everywhere and nowhere" nature of disciplinary mechanisms operates on physical, mental, spatial, and theoretical[43] levels to erase and/or correct deviance, thereby rendering populations more governable. These mechanisms have been intriguingly termed "the colonization of the mind": their workings are total, yet meant to remain largely invisible, leaving the individual to believe she is regulating herself on the basis of independently formed ideas. It may be helpful to think of

41 I have instead opted to remain rooted in political practice, meaning the method privileges observation and independent evaluation, supported by historical and experiential evidence. My choice of methodology is intended not only to promote accessibility while honouring feminist experiential process, but also to address the twin paradoxes raised at the outset — the paradox of employing "expert" language to critique the use of expertise to gain power, and the paradox of referring to "the experts" to speak in an authoritative voice about expertise.

42 Michel Foucault, "Governmentality" in Graham Burchell, Colin Gordon & Peter Miller, eds, *The Foucault Effect: Studies in Governmentality* (Chicago: University of Chicago Press, 1991) 87.

43 Michel Foucault, *Discipline and Punish: The Birth of the Prison* (New York: Random House, 1977) at 135, 170, 195, 73, respectively.

disciplinary mechanisms as systems of "production, domination and socialization"[44] that work in globalizing ways to generate individuals and populations with specific types of beliefs, thoughts, norms, and behaviours. In this way, discipline is not only practiced *on* us, it is built in all around us and thus, ultimately, *in* us.

The disciplinary society generates and collects knowledge about individuals and populations. Foucault presents power and knowledge as inseparable: "... at least for the study of human beings, the goals of power and the goals of knowledge cannot be separated: *in knowing we control and in controlling we know*" [emphasis added].[45] Further, Foucault links truth claims to power and knowledge, as feminist legal theorist Carol Smart discussed in *Feminism and the Power of Law*:

> Foucault uses [truth] to refer to the ensemble of rules according to which the true and the false are separated and specific effects of power attached to the 'true' (Gordon 1980: 132)... he is interested in discovering how certain discourses claim to speak the truth and thus can exercise power in a society that values this notion of truth.[46]

Here the links to what this project has been terming "expertise" are obvious. The "experts" largely self-identify their own expertise with little regard for how it may be evaluated by those outside their disciplines. They then present their conclusions as "truths," which go on to be taken up by other discourses. Foucault's focus is on analyzing *how* this is effected more than by who, and he links the "how" directly to the production of knowledge through surveillance. Documentation, bureaucracy, assessment, examination, registration, evaluation ... all of these exercises generate "knowledge" on populations and individuals that can then be deployed to control their conduct. Thus, the production and collection of knowledge about human beings is at once the acquisition and collection of power, and is deeply linked to both truth claims and who holds the power to make them.

Foucault singled out the psy-disciplines in particular as enacting a type of disciplinary power. He saw the knowledge-power-truth triad

44 David Garland, "Review: Foucault's 'Discipline and Punish' — An Exposition and Critique" (1986) 11 Am Bar Found R J 847 at 852.

45 Gary Gutting, "Michel Foucault" in Edward N Zalta, ed, *The Stanford Encyclopedia of Philosophy*, online: <http://plato.stanford.edu/archives/win2008/entries/foucault/>.

46 Carol Smart, *Feminism and the Power of Law* (New York: Routledge, 1989) at 9.

as a pervasive means of designating certain ways of being as "normal" and others as deviant.[47] He argued that this disciplinary power was colonizing not only the mind, but also traditional, state-based forms of power, such as law. By this he meant that the power is shifting from the "old" forms of control to the "new," ultimately rendering the old less relevant.[48] Smart suggested that in a contest between law (what she called "the discourse of rights") and the psy-disciplines ("the discourse of normalization"[49]), Foucault would argue the psy-disciplines will ultimately win out as the more pervasive and totalizing form of power.

Smart, however, maintained that while the rise of the psy-disciplines and other disciplinary mechanisms may signify a shift in power, the law has by no means lost its authority or special claims to "truth." She theorized instead that law retains its power by translating psy-discipline truths back into a legal framework and expressing them in the discourse of rights. In this way, the "old" power of law operates parallel with the rise of disciplinary power. Further, she contends that legal power, or legal "truths," may in fact be extending further into society rather than diminishing, as Foucault's analytics would suggest. Smart instead posits both a fluctuation where one discourse will dominate the other at differing points in time, and a symbiotic relationship between law and the psy-disciplines wherein they work in coalition.[50]

This idea of a contest of powers is interesting when considering the location and impact of psy-discipline expertise in law's dealings with women. It may well be that legal truths are succumbing to psy-discipline incursion or, conversely, as Smart suggests, that law maintains its power by re-casting psy-discipline knowledge into legal truths. True psy-legal hazards for women, however, may be less grounded in a struggle between powers than they are in Smart's "moments of coalition." In the section to follow, a picture of law emerges that does indeed appear to be "colonized" by psy-discipline truth claims. However, closer examination reveals benefits to both domains in reifying one another's expertise, such that they ultimately reinforce one another's power.

What has been termed "Foucauldian analytics" counsels us that to see the workings of disciplinary colonization or, alternately, to locate

47 Foucault dedicated an entire work to this idea, *Madness and Civilization: A History of Insanity in the Age of Reason* (New York: Random House, 1965).

48 Smart, *supra* note 46 at 8.

49 *Ibid.*

50 *Ibid* at 19.

power, one must look to "practices" — what might be seen as the minutia of daily life. He directs us to look to "the institutions, procedures, analyses and reflections, the calculations and tactics that allow the exercise of this very specific albeit complex form of power."[51] Feminist political practice also stresses the importance of practices (or what is done versus what is said) to reveal embedded patriarchal power ribboned throughout the social world. The feminist attention to process is rooted in a recognition that subtle forms of power and control can be encoded and exercised in how we do things, which has obvious parallels to Foucault's work. As we shall see in our discussion of the intersection of law and the psy-disciplines, observing practices changes the terms of the usual conversation about the location of "the expert" in matters of law and for survivors of sexual violence.

PART II

Law and the Psy-Disciplines: Mutually Reinforcing Propositions?

> That psychiatric abuses of women exceed the norm in society derives from the fact that its legal authority is excessive and that its orientation is power and control.
>
> — Peter Breggin, MD[52]

Law and the psy-disciplines are often described as being in an "uneasy relationship," but a firmly entrenched one nonetheless. While theorists argue that there is tension between these "expert" arenas, the legal record makes it clear that their disagreements have rarely extended to the "problem" of women. The law and the psy-disciplines instead have much in common in terms of the historical status they have accorded women, which would follow from their common genesis in male dominance. The briefest glance at history shows that "Woman" did not acquire her inferior status when she was deemed pathological by the psy-disciplines; instead, the domain offered new language and "expert" theory to assist in authenticating existing cultural beliefs as "scientific." The addition of "expert" psy-discourses to law generated new arguments to *explain* and *support* the already distorted legal view of women.

51 Foucault, *supra* note 40 at 102.

52 Breggin, *supra* note 25 at 324.

The words of legal expert John Wigmore give us a cogent example of the reinforcing nature of the discourses:

> Modern psychiatrists have amply studied the behaviour of errant young girls and women coming before the court in all sorts of cases. Their psychic complexes are multifarious, distorted partly by inherent defects, partly by temporary psychological or emotional conditions. One form taken by these complexes is that of contriving false charges of sexual offenses by men... The real victim, however, too often in such cases is the innocent man... [53]

Here we see that not only does law reify the expert status of psy-disciplines by referencing their theories, but it also stands to gain from the psy-disciplines' expert claim. Law no longer needed to rely on a *belief* that women are apt to lie about men in sexual assault cases; women's mendacity could now be argued as a matter of *science*:

> ... making the claim to be a science is in fact an exercise of power because, in claiming scientificity, other knowledges are accorded less status, less value. Those knowledges which are called faith, experience, biography, and so on, are ranked as lesser knowledges. They can exercise less influence, they are disqualified.[54]

Belief, as a "lesser knowledge," has a far lower threshold for challenge than does science, and is more vulnerable to critique. The solidity of legal truth is concretized through being supported by psy-discipline "scientific fact." The legal discourse of rights is maintained through wielding "fact" as protection for "the innocent man."

As noted, not only does the "expertise" of the psy-disciplines thus translate the existing legal position on women from a legal to a "scientific" one but, by invoking the study of psychiatrists as scientific support, law reciprocally reinforces the psy-disciplines as "expert" and gives them legal weight. Hence the psy-discipline claim to expertise is no longer only self-awarded; it is now made real and, importantly, expanded through its recognition in law. Thus it can be said that, far from being in contest, the psy-disciplines and law are mutually reinforcing, constitutive propositions, as the truth claims of both are benefited by invoking the other.

53 In Rosemary Tong, *Women, Sex and the Law* (Totowa, NJ: Rowman & Allanheld, 1984) at 101.

54 Smart, *supra* note 46 at 9.

While at first glance this might appear to be an example of the symbiotic relationship Smart described, I suggest that we take the analysis one step further and query whether "symbiosis" fully describes the process occurring here. The relationship is symbiotic in that it is interconnected and potentially beneficial to both domains, but it is also *generative* in that it serves to increase the influence of both exponentially. Thus, in light of these mutually constitutive-generative properties, I think it is appropriate to posit a third category of discourse, one that mobilizes the claims to expertise of both disciplines, and expands the scope of their associated power as they act in combination. This form of discursive and generative power can most easily be dubbed *psy-legal* and, as I will argue, it can be exerted through unexpected means when aimed at women survivors of violence.

Locating the Expert

It is no simple task to locate the expert in law, as the example that opened this paper demonstrates. Claims to expertise are mobilized at all different stages of the legal process, and are encoded in the very structure of law itself as a professional discipline. Police officers, Crown attorneys, medical personnel, child protection workers, social workers, probation officers, facility staff, psy-professionals, victim/witness workers — all make expertise claims within the legal system, and that is to say nothing of lawyers and judges themselves. In a discussion about expert knowledge and the law it is reasonable to ask, "Whose knowledge are we talking about? Where? When?"

A scan of the literature about expert knowledge and the legal system invariably turns up lengthy, academic articles about the role and admissibility of expert testimony and qualification of expert witnesses. While certainly not determinative, a snapshot view like this suggests some singularity of thought on the location and role of experts in law. While specific aspects of evidentiary rule in the use of "experts" are voluminously discussed, less apparent are the significant yet near-silent psy-discipline incursions into law, albeit in non-testimonial garb. The absence of an "expert" on the stand does not mean their authority may not be felt through all aspects of legal process. Instead, as was argued by Foucault and as is observable by feminist advocates, evidence of legal permeation by psy-discipline truth claims is best located in the micro, in the subtle ways legal power reinforces the authority of the "experts" on the lives of women without questioning or testing those claims. To illuminate these processes, we have to first locate the survivor. The "expert" will certainly be close by.

Hidden Survivors

When we consider that the vast majority of survivors of sexual violence will never see the inside of a courtroom in connection with their assault, it is questionable why scholars have focused so much attention on this small space of "expert impact." At least 90 percent of survivors of sexual violence never report the crime to police[55] and, of the 10 percent who do, the vast majority will not see charges laid against the perpetrator, let alone see him come to trial. Does a very generous estimate of only 5 percent of all survivors of sexual violence ever testifying in a court proceeding suggest that the other 95 percent are not subject to psy-legal expert authority? Quite the contrary: many of these women are no less impacted by psy-legal expert claims as survivors of sexual violence. Often, they are affected significantly more.

A survivor of violence can expect to be streamed toward psy-disciplines from the moment she discloses, be it to a friend, a family member, an authority figure, or a "professional." The immediate, and generally well-meaning, response from the supportive person is "you should get some counselling." It is telling that our first instinct is to refer the violence *away* from ourselves, the person to whom she chose to disclose, to someone more "expert" in handling these matters. That "someone" is generally understood to be a psy-discipline practitioner. This tendency suggests that the domain's claims that sexual violence is an issue for "experts" have been fully integrated into popular belief.

Interpersonal responses can here be extrapolated to the systemic, as this same referral process occurs throughout the myriad other spaces where women disclose male violence. Should she disclose to a doctor, she may be advised to "get some counselling," while being simultaneously handed a prescription for a psychotropic medication. Should she disclose to a parent, the parent is informed to "get some counselling" for their child and the referrals will almost always be to psy-practitioners or hospital-based programs (who employ psy-practitioners). Should she disclose to police and be believed, she may be given a contact with a victim crisis unit, a victim-witness assistance program, or a community health centre, all of which are institutionally based, apolitical, psy-grounded services. In these examples and more, the survivor will either be speaking to, or referred to, psy- or social work practitioners with varying degrees of legally bestowed authority over her.

55 Statistics Canada, Canadian Centre for Justice Statistics, *Sexual Assault in Canada* 85F0033M No 19 (Ottawa: Minister of Industry, 2008), online: <http://www.statcan.gc.ca/pub/85f0033m/2008019/findings-resultats/trends-tendances-eng.htm>.

Thus it is plain that sexual violence is still directly linked with "mental health issues," despite years of feminist work to establish that reacting to sexual violence is *reasonable*, not indicative of poor mental health. A survivor in contact with the legal system for any reason can expect to be pushed to psy-systems repeatedly and with increasing intensity. Whether she appears at law in the role of victim, apprehended ward of the court, accused person, or impugned mother, the referral (or compulsion) to psy-disciplinary expertise is never more than a half-step away.

So where is the survivor, when not testifying against a perpetrator? Based on my 15 years of work with young women in conflict with the law, I assert that the easiest place to find her is in jail.[56] Another is in a youth group home as a ward of the Children's Aid Society [CAS].[57] If she runs away from the group home before you get there, just camp out at your local courthouse, because she'll arrive there before long.[58] You can also find her over in Family Court, fighting the apprehension of her children. She may be in the Diversion Office, getting ready to participate in a program for women charged with prostitution-related offences. Or she might be in one of our newest spaces of psy-legal power, the Drug Treatment Court or the Mental Health Court. Family Court Clinic Assessments, CAS-supervised visitation rooms, outreach centres for pregnant and parenting young women, making a claim to the Criminal Injuries Compensation Board — all of these places are sites of interaction between survivors of sexual violence and "expert" psy-legal discourses. With so many opportunities for survivors to be acted upon, a full discussion of the degree of disciplinary power expert knowledges wield over them would require a project of its own. Two common ex-

56 I do not mean to suggest that the majority of survivors are incarcerated; instead, that the majority of incarcerated women are survivors. Most statistics cite rates of approximately 80 percent of incarcerated women report experiencing physical and/or sexual violence. In my own experience, a much higher percentage of young women in custodial environments describe experiences of sexual abuse and/or assault, with percentages closer to the high nineties for sexual violence alone. While anecdotal, frontline workers across service organizations report similar rates to me. First-hand survivors' accounts of their interactions with researchers suggest to me that academic methodology creates a barrier to accurate information about the true rate of sexual violence experiences among incarcerated women.

57 Children's Aid Society of Eastern Ontario.

58 Office of Child and Family Service Advocacy, *Crossover Kids: Care to Custody* (Draft Report) (Toronto: Office of the Provincial Advocate for Children and Youth, 2003), online: <http://provincialadvocate.on.ca/main/en/publications/publications.cfm> at 1.

amples may nonetheless assist in demonstrating the mechanisms of these myriad practices: (1) conditions of release for criminally charged young and adult women, and (2) child protection legislation and legal compulsion of mothers.

(1) Conditions

One of the most pervasive and simultaneously puzzling psy-incursions into law is found in a release condition — be it for bail, probation, parole, or conditional sentences — in the form of an order to "take all prescribed medications." From an advocate's perspective it is difficult to understand how this condition finds its way into probation and bail orders with such seeming regularity, as case law would appear to prohibit it.[59] Despite this, and without pretending to an explanation, advocates will tell you the condition is certainly imposed and not merely in "exceptional circumstances." How this happens is an explanation better left to lawyers, and yet counsel who have clients released under these orders every day often appear not to have considered the question when I have put it to them. This is disheartening from a rights perspective, but entirely unsurprising from the vantage point of feminist advocates.

The feminist advocate, along with the survivor, resides in a psy-legal world of "supposed to's"; as in, "that's not what's supposed to happen." and "the policy doesn't say that," "they're supposed to let her [*x*]," and "you should have been allowed to [*y*]." Our days are filled with puzzled looks from system players[60] who insist that the oppressive experience of the woman we're supporting constitutes an exception, as in, "well, that's not what's supposed to happen, so something must have gone wrong there." This suggests that the system player, while claiming to be critical of the system, ultimately does not believe it is structurally flawed. Instead, individual women have bad experiences for case-specific reasons, which are the exceptions, not the rule. Advocates, however, are familiar with the informal maxim that the only sure thing when nego-

59 *R v Rogers* (1990), 61 CCC (3d) 481 BCCA; and *R v Kieling* (1991), 64 CCC (3d) 124 (Sask CA), both overturned forced medication probation conditions, with *Rogers* finding they are a violation of the *Charter* s 7 right to life, liberty, and security of the person. *Rogers* qualifies this "where there is a finding of incompetence or an exception recognized in law."

60 System players can include Crown attorneys, defence counsel, court support workers (system-provided), probation officers, social workers, so-called "clinical" staff, diversion-program staff, police officers, mandated treatment staff, and more.

tiating psy-legal systems is "whatever is 'supposed to' happen, won't." This maxim appears to apply in the case of "take all prescribed medication" conditions.

These four words, "take all prescribed medications," stand as a damning testament to just how much expert status psy-discourses have been accorded in law. The order is not in place because the court is concerned that a woman will refuse antibiotics for an ear infection. The condition clearly refers to psychiatric medications, and it is leveraged against those who might reject medications that they believe are inappropriate, or are making them feel worse. As women are prescribed these medications at far higher rates than men, it follows that they are also disproportionately affected by the imposition of these orders.

In making the order it may appear that law has ceded authority to the medical/psy-disciplines completely. The law presumes that nothing inappropriate will be prescribed,[61] and thus it is appropriate to force ingestion as a matter of law. These orders appear wholly beneficial to the psy-disciplines in (1) guaranteeing a consumer group for psychiatric medications; (2) ensuring a client base that has been ordered to continue attending; (3) reifying the claim to expertise of the psy-disciplines; and (4) reifying the assumption that biopsychiatry is harmless, uncontroversial, and effective.

However, as noted in the above description of the psy-legal "third discourse," there is a reciprocal benefit to law in making this order that must also be considered. A released person is often presented in terms of their risk to the community; what is not discussed is their perceived risk to the good reputation of law. When judges allow people to remain in the community, whether awaiting trial or serving a sentence, there is always a risk that the individual may re-offend. This creates potential for high criticism of law as the public reacts strongly when persons under charge or sanction commit new crimes, particularly if someone is harmed. Media tend to sensationalize these instances and neo-conservative voices raise a hue and cry about "revolving door justice" and "slaps on the wrist." Here law faces a dilemma, as it cannot and, more importantly, should not impose a loss of liberty if lesser alternatives are available and appropriate in the circumstances. Nor are there resources in the system to monitor every released person around the clock, and doing so would likely (and rightly) be challenged as a significant

61 Even though *R v Rogers*, *supra* note 59, specifically mentioned this concern.

incursion into rights.[62] At this juncture, support for and alliance with psy-expertise becomes invaluable to law. By imposing the "take all prescribed medications" condition, the law effectively employs what one charged person described to me as "chemical handcuffs." The law is able to extend the reach of its surveillance and its shackles to people in the community by the act of ordering chemical alteration intended to result in greater docility and manageability. Thus, psy-disciplines offer the law the possibility of continuous control through chemical restraint that would not otherwise have been available to it. The released person has no recourse outside of argument by defence counsel at the time of the order, but I have yet to see a lawyer object to this condition, despite hearing it imposed scores of times.

Even without the legally questionable "take all prescribed medications" condition, other conditions can be used to ensure the same result by less direct means. Common to most youth orders, for example, is a condition that they "be amenable to" or "follow" the rules, routines, and discipline of any residence the young woman is released to (these are very often group homes overseen by child welfare authorities). Thus, if intake psychological assessment, meeting with a residential clinician, or seeing the psychiatrist for mental health screening is routine in the group living environment, refusal to do so will amount to a breach of the woman's release conditions. Additionally, discontinuing medications that have been prescribed can constitute a breach of the "be amenable" rule. This application is particularly problematic for adult women who are coming to residential environments from provincial detention centres, where many women are prescribed psychiatric drugs almost the instant they arrive, even for very short-term detention. The rates, the speed, and the types of medications all indicate that psy-"expertise" is being mobilized to support "institutional adjustment" by means of "managing the population through drugging." Once released, however, the women now have a prescription that must be maintained, regardless of whether they have the money or the inclination to do so.[63] A

62 This is not to say that law might not enjoy the ability to monitor people at this level — if Foucault's theories of surveillance hold true, and if crime-monitoring cameras and other technological public surveillance innovations are any indication, it is arguable that the legal sphere would extend this power as far as it were able.

63 There is a related question here about the ethics of starting women on prescriptions that radically upset brain chemistry and have strong cognitive and physical discontinuation effects, knowing (1) they will be released in a few days or weeks time with no resources to maintain the prescription; (2) they may be using other chemicals on the street that could have dangerous interactions; and (3) coming off these drugs has

worker in a downtown homeless shelter recently remarked to me that despite a 4:1 ratio of men's to women's beds, "the women's medication cupboard is twice the size of the men's." She expressed frustration that more and more women were carrying these prescriptions when coming to the shelter from a detention centre, shelter staff were being made responsible for ensuring they took them every day, and some had even been told to alert probation officers if women "fail to comply."

If these two conditions are not enough to ensure the deep embedding of psy-legal power over the survivor, the condition to "attend for such assessment, treatment or counselling as is directed by your (youth) worker" covers off the last of any loopholes that might allow her to avoid psy-streaming. By including a blanket condition giving probation officers the power to direct women into counselling and assessment, the law firmly reinforces the claims of psy-discipline expertise in working with women. The direction to seek counselling and assessment also becomes increasingly specialized; should she already have support as a survivor of violence, she is then told she needs to get specific counselling for "anger management." If she is seeing two psy-professionals for those, she'll next hear that she needs to seek an addictions counsellor to work with her on that issue, while continuing to see her family doctor to "monitor her prescriptions." Her probation officer may then tell her they'd like her to be "assessed" for any of a wide range of "disorders," and seek diagnosis-specific counselling in those. Should this woman have children, the same process will likely be occurring simultaneously through CAS involvement (frequently initiated as a result of having witnessed violence against their mother). As the mother is diagnosed and prescribed, so is the child, and the legally facilitated reach of the psy-disciplines extends still further through generations. Women caught up in this way commonly end up with tangled, multi-layered levels of "workers" in their lives, all of whom are continuously suggesting more and more possibilities for what is "wrong" with them and their children. All of these interactions are copiously documented, such that the "file" on an individual woman becomes thicker and thicker. This information becomes available to probation, the courts, and facilities and residences she is sent to, and can influence sentencing decisions, residential placements, ordered treatment schemas, and fitness to parent. The women at the centre of this concentration of disciplinary surveillance are commonly survivors of violence: their experiences of

been described by women as similar to "going crazy," yet there is no accountability to possible withdrawal consequences, including rearrest or new charges.

violence are intrinsically linked to their current connection to the legal system, and they are being medicated and otherwise acted upon at astonishing rates. Further, the power of legal authority and the threat of sanction are wielded to tell them this psy-discipline intervention and supervision is not only expert, but in their "best interests."

(2) Psy-legal Power, Light on the Legal

A second example of mobilization of psy-legal discourses over women survivors that needs interrogation occurs through the child protection system.[64] Here psy-legal claims are regularly made by extra-legal players such that women are not only subjected to exquisitely minute levels of scrutiny, they are also regularly compelled by the leverage of law without ever actually accessing a legal process. A difficulty with exposing the subtle means by which psy-legal discourses act on women lies in the fact that their most coercive power is often mobilized in extra-legal settings, delivered by collaterals who would be technically identified as non-legal system actors. As such, the very fact that these practices do occur fails to find its way into documentation, as they would not likely survive court challenges or review by competent counsel. Here, again, the view from feminist political practice can assist us, in that advocates are often witness to otherwise invisible extra-legal practices that reveal the most penetrating implications of the legal adoption of psy-discipline expertise claims, and their power to compel survivors to acquiesce to disordered identities.

Contextually, it is important to note that being a survivor of abuse, or having been a child "in care" oneself, are both considered risk factors to children in the Ontario Child Welfare Eligibility Spectrum.[65] This is a disturbing indication of how the psy-legal gaze can pathologize women survivors who dare to disclose the violence against them, as children or later in life. Those who would assert that the psy-disciplines have abandoned their victim-blaming lineage need only consider the implications of constructing survivors as "risky." Although popular mythology teaches that being sexually abused as a child increases an individual's risk of sexually abusing children as an adult, there are numerous data to suggest that this correlation for males is low, and that it has not been re-

64 In Ontario, child protection is governed by the *Child and Family Services Act*, RSO 1990, c C 11.

65 Ontario Child Welfare Eligibility Spectrum, Ontario Association of Children's Aid Societies, 2000 (revised 2006), p 10 and s 5, scales 3 and 4, online: <http://www.oacas.org/pubs/oacas/eligibility/>.

liably demonstrated for women.[66] In other words, although there may be some truth to "cycle of violence" theories, particularly for physically abused men, studies do not support the theory that women who were sexually abused as children are at higher risk to sexually abuse children as adults.[67] Despite this, child protection risk scales and individual protection workers[68] continue to consider a woman's own history of abuse when assessing her potential risk to her children. When we consider the vast numbers of women who have experienced childhood sexual abuse and gone on to become parents, one might be forgiven for thinking that it is a miracle that there are any healthy, unharmed children on the planet at all. Mothers would seem to be a very risky bunch indeed.

We see here, as elsewhere, the pervasive influence of psy-disciplines in "disordering" survivors and constituting them as mentally unstable. Child protection agencies might counter that they consider a parental history of abuse a generalized risk factor to be considered in intervention, but maintain that they are not arguing there is a specific risk of mothers being sexually abusive themselves. Even making allowances for possible explanation, it remains highly questionable that general risk to children is demonstrably higher among women survivors than for others with a wide range of negative childhood experiences that could influence parenting. Regardless, under these "expert" schemas, the sexually abused woman in particular is cast as potentially dangerous. This "risk" then supports the use of heightened surveillance, scrutiny, and directive authority over women who have disclosed.

There is irony in the fact that women who have broken silence about abuse, have sought support or assistance, or have been transparent with child protection authorities about their histories are, as a result, cast as a greater risk than women who have chosen to do none of these things. This double bind often exists for survivors in contact with psy-legal power and is startlingly reminiscent of the very message carried by the abuse itself. Should she disclose, she risks the heavy-handed interven-

66 M Glasser *et al*, "Cycle of Child Sexual Abuse: Links Between Being a Victim and Becoming a Perpetrator" (2001) 179 Brit J Psychiatry 493; US Department of Justice, Office of Justice Programs, "Victims of Childhood Sexual Abuse: Later Criminal Consequences" (NIJ Research in Brief Series) NCJ 151525 (National Criminal Justice Reference Service, 1995), online: <http://www. ncjrs.gov/>.

67 Glasser *et al*, *ibid*.

68 While the Eligibility Spectrum counsels caution in its references to abuse histories, women frequently report being directly informed by workers that they are being supervised and/or mandated to complete treatment schemas due to their own experiences of abuse.

tion of the law as compulsion; should she stay silent, she doesn't. It is hard not to see "don't tell anyone" as the end result. Feminist sexual assault centres recognized this practice of effectively punishing women for disclosing early in their inception, and this was the genesis of the very strict confidentiality policies most centres adopted. These "no records" policies were designed to create safe space for women to disclose abuse without incurring the type of stigma-based consequences we see encoded in child protection risk assessments.

Psy-legal authority, in this case wielded by child protection workers, mobilizes to act on the identified survivor by writing a prescription of what she must do in order for child protection to end supervision and close her file.[69] Each direction is backed by the threat of the legal authority to apprehend her child. Consider, for example, the young mother who is told by a child protection worker that she must take psychiatric medications or her child may be apprehended. Even if the woman does not agree with bio-psychiatric truth claims, or the specific diagnosis (which, for young, poor mothers, are frequently made by family doctors during the course of visits scheduled for other purposes), she is likely to see little option but to comply. She generally has no access to legal representation[70] and, even if she did, psy-discourses have been accorded such unchallenged expert status at law that many judges either do not question their validity, or are happy to cede the authority to a "qualified professional." Challenging this use of psy-legal power might actually have the opposite effect of enmeshing the survivor still further in disciplinary power. The predictable next step may occur, whereby she is ordered *back* to psy-disciplines for psychological testing and assessment to ensure an "appropriate diagnosis."[71] The circularity is dizzying.

In this example, we see how psy-legal power is leveraged against survivors by what are traditionally seen as non-legal players in extra-legal environments. The child protection worker does so out of what she perceives to be benevolent intentions, and with two likely justifications: (1) her own training is grounded in psy-discipline truth claims about both survivors of violence and the necessity and benefit of psy-interventions;

69 New conditions are regularly added as soon as old ones are completed; some women we have worked with having ongoing, biweekly child protection supervision in all aspects of their lives for as long as eight years. These restrictions are imposed, despite the lack of any court order, hearing, or legal finding that she has done anything wrong.

70 Legal Aid in Ontario will generally only become available *after* her child is apprehended.

71 Note that the assumption always begins with the notion that there is a diagnosis.

and (2) her mandate is to work for "the best interests of the child," not the mother. Any concerns about possible rights incursions for mothers, when weighed against the possibility that a child may be endangered, are easily forgotten or overlooked. For the targeted mother, the mere idea that her child may be removed will usually ensure compliance with psy-discipline regimes.

This use of psy-legal power is not limited to psychiatric medications. Young, poor women in contact with child protection are regularly told to attend counselling, to sign consents to allow the child protection worker to speak to counsellors and doctors, to attend programs, to enroll their children in programs, and to accept assessment and diagnosis of their children. This psy-legal authority is extended even so far as women's sexual autonomy if they have any history of abusive relationships. Young women who have been physically abused[72] are regularly told they must disclose the identities of any new men in their lives, sexual partners or otherwise, to child protection for screening. It is common in our work with pregnant and parenting young women to learn that they have been ordered not to have any men in their homes whatsoever. Thus, an entire group of women (mothers) may be subject to a level of gendered sexual policing most people believe no longer exists in Canada.[73]

These directives are grounded in the *Child and Family Services Act* definition of a "child in need of protection" as one exposed to "a risk that the child is likely to suffer emotional harm."[74] The perceived harm here is that the child may witness violence, as the woman has been in abusive relationships. Thus she is constituted as a possible risk in that she might "fail to act" to protect her child from witnessing male violence against her. Lest we make any mistake as to who is being responsibilized under this legislation, it must be pointed out that the child protection file is opened under the mother's — not the abusive male's — name. Interviews and assessments are conducted with her, and she is made to agree to a "plan of service" that often requires her to sign blanket consents for CAS access to her medical, social, legal,[75] financial, and

72 Physical abuse usually means that a young woman has also experienced sexual abuse, as she has no power to give or withdraw consent with respect to someone she is afraid of.

73 It is relevant to note that we see these practices aimed almost entirely at young, poor mothers. In our experience these same conditions are not routinely placed on white, middle-class mothers when CAS attends after a domestic violence report.

74 *Child and Family Services Act*, *supra* note 64 at s 37.2.

75 Including closed young offender and probationary records.

counselling information. She is often the parent ordered to take "programs" such as Healthy Relationships, Understanding Abuse,[76] and parenting classes. The professionals who account for 90 percent of reports in Ontario domestic violence investigations[77] are the same individuals abused women have turned to for assistance, medical attention, counselling, or social supports. Thus, the people society continuously insists are available to support the abused woman have become a policing arm of the law, such that turning to them means the woman will be constituted as a potential risk to her children.

It should be underscored again that most, if not all of the above, occurs outside of courtrooms and outside of any legal process or representation whatsoever, although all of it is carried out using the authority of law. Thus we see how psy-disciplinary power has been invested with legal authority, with no actual legal accountability for what is done with it. While it is legally questionable whether child protection has the authority to order women to take medication or to sever most contact with men under threat of child apprehension, these dictums are often issued verbally in spaces not generally considered "legal," and as such remain invisible from the very authority used to leverage them.

The law does enter, however, should a woman's children eventually be apprehended under the "failure to protect" rule, but this often only activates greater psy-discipline authority. In order to fight permanent loss of custody, the mother will likely undergo what is known as a Family Court Clinic [FCC] Assessment[78] — a process conducted by a psychiatrist and one or more social workers — in which a battery of psychological tests are conducted on the woman; her childhood history is documented (including experiences of physical or sexual abuse); reports from collaterals, including child protection opinions, are collected; her behaviour and attitude toward the interviewer are meticulously reported; and her interactions with her now-separated children

76 These are the names of two groups the YWAR Program has facilitated with pregnant and parenting teen women for the past nine years. Fully 95 percent of the young women participating are initially present due to CAS concerns that they may "fail to protect" their children as a result of their "unhealthy relationships." The bulk of child apprehensions from group members are linked to what CAS deems a "failure to protect" the child from a male whose behaviour they suspect may be abusive.

77 Trocmé Rivers *et al*, "Reporting and Beyond: Current Trends in Child Abuse and Neglect Call for Broader Reforms" (November 2002) *Voices for Children Report*, online: <http://www.voicesforchildren.ca/report-Nov2002-1.htm>.

78 Often referred to simply as "the FCC", these are court-ordered Parenting Capacity Assessments (PCA's) conducted by designated, usually institutionally based, mental health agencies.

are observed in a supervised setting. A completed FCC will usually make recommendations about whether a woman's children should be returned home or, if removed, whether she should be allowed any future access to them. These recommendations are then tendered for judicial consideration in wardship hearings. FCC opinions are difficult to challenge, as there is usually only the psychiatrist's written record as to the substance of the discussions to rely on, and his/her subjective interpretation of their meaning. Not surprisingly, these frequently differ significantly from the mother's recollection and interpretation of events. While she may be able to relate her experience as part of the hearing, it is well known to defence counsel and advocates that her interpretation will rarely win out over that of "the expert." One long-time defence counsel shared that she had never seen a judge rule against "a bad FCC," and there is little counsel can do with them, as the psy-discipline opinions are treated as neutral and unassailable.[79] While anecdotal, I can relate that in over a decade of work with young, poor women undergoing these assessments, I have yet to see one come out in a woman's favour. In the informal networks of young, impoverished single mothers fighting to parent their children, these assessments are widely identified as something to be avoided.

Summary

The notion of a third discourse posits that not only is the power of psy-disciplines expanded, but so, too, is the power of law. The child protection example demonstrates the former quite plainly, in that the implications for psy-disciplinary power are vast. But how is the power of law expanded through this alliance? Quite simply, the increasing pressures on legal systems to adjudicate what were once seen as private problems have not been embraced by law (as illustrated by either reluctance or ineptitude in prosecuting violence against women), with many lawyers openly espousing their hatred of "these kinds of cases." By entering into a partnership with psy-discipline experts, formal law has little to do but empower them to go forth and manage the messiness, with the bulk of legally extended authority taking place outside of the much more orderly courtroom. In this way, law is able to extend its regulatory power directly into the daily lives and behaviours of the citizenry, but the courts rarely have to process anything but the epilogue.

These examples demonstrate that psy-legal expertise claims about women can be encoded in legislation, mobilized through surveillance,

79 Personal communication.

and wielded both in and out of what is traditionally seen as legal space by both legal and psy-discipline collaterals. The expert stature the disciplines are accorded through law reinforces an otherwise self-awarded claim to expertise, and thus further solidifies the public perception of their knowledges as "truths." While it may appear initially that law has ceded power to psy-disciplines, instead, through the process of accepting and thus reifying their expert authority, law commensurately expands its own power. It does so first by concretizing its existing legal expertise by investing it with the "science" of psy-disciplines; next by employing them to oversee and regulate the population (and women's behaviour, in particular) in ways that law, on its own, could not; and finally, by utilizing those expert opinions to claim its own expert ability to rule on matters that it has historically preferred to avoid as the "private" domain of the family. This buttressed authority stretches even to deciding which women are permitted to mother.

PART III

The VAW Movement: The Slippery Slope of the Quest for Recognition

> One of the difficulties, I think, is that there's a large part of the movement that wants to look respectable. And if that's what you want, you tend to have a lot of trouble knowing when you're being co-opted. And the hard-core, real stuff can fall by the wayside. Social movements have always needed to say what to a lot of people would be unspeakable. When we stop being able to say those things, we're no longer at the cutting edge of anything. We've been bought and sold.
>
> — Bonnie Burstow[80]

What have been the impacts of these expert knowledges? For a beleaguered women's movement that first saw the psy-disciplines tell women they were pathological and then saw the law tell them that psy-disciplines were the experts, these discourses have wrought deep changes in once-politicized feminist practices. Not unlike the psy-discipline cycle from biological, to psychological, and back to biological explanations of women's disordered natures, the sexual assault centre, once a power-

80 Quoted in Irit Shimrat, *Call Me Crazy: Stories from the Mad Movement* (Vancouver: Press Gang, 1997) 41 at 43.

ful site in the larger field of the fight for women's equality, appears to be charting a circular path back, requiring us to relearn old lessons.

At one time, the words "women are the experts in their own lives" held deep meaning in the VAW movement. This was a call for resistance: resisting medicalization, resisting damaging expertise claims, resisting silencing survivors, and resisting allowing male "professionals" to continue to describe and define women's reality in their terms. In the preceding two sections, pictures emerged of both the psy-disciplines and the law, tracing how they have wielded, and wedded, claims to expertise to create and maintain social fictions about women survivors of sexual violence. This is not the first time that these stories have been told, as seen in the vast literature thoroughly documenting both histories far more comprehensively than can be achieved here. The critical scholarship so broadly available today grew from the voices of survivors of pathologization[81] who formed their own movements, their own organizations, their own support networks, and their own expertise in the face of totalizing claims that would have forever had them categorized and managed as disordered persons.

Feminist sexual assault centres (SACs) were spaces where survivors came together and politicized to name male violence and reject the "experts" who said they were mentally ill for having experienced it (or, more precisely, for having disclosed it). Instead, survivors began to identify women's inequality as the structural support for violence that they now knew as a manifestation of patriarchal power and control. No more did survivors want to hear "there, there, dear, go home and take a hot bath, you'll feel better," the equivalent of what they were told by credentialed "experts" when not being accused of fabricating or causing the violence. Instead, survivors built organizations that would work politically to end women's inequality in both the larger society and in the practice of supporting survivors of male violence. This work meant advocating for both individual women facing oppressive systems and expertise claims, and on a broader political level challenging government, institutions, structures, and knowledges that re-inscribed women's inequality into the fabric of daily life.

From this movement, new forms of expert knowledge were also born. Survivors taught themselves, and each other, what they needed to be supported and move forward, and identified what had caused them such serious harm in the psy-disciplines. They recognized how

81 Both in the feminist and the anti-psychiatry movements.

their own knowledge had been devalued in the face of credentials and expertise claims that knew little about their lives or experiences. An ethics of feminist support began to take shape, one that named the importance of confidentiality, survivor-direction, boundaries, non-judgmental listening, believing, validation, and social context. SACs were adamant in rejecting the psy-medical model of labelling, individualizing, and pathologizing, and instead richly valued experiential and collective expertise. Having learned from sexual violence and the abuses of the legal and psy-disciplines, a feminist support model highlighted power dynamics and paid critical attention to their equalization. Organizational structure too was therefore non-hierarchical, and consensus-based. Accountability was critical — women who had never seen any accountability taken by their abusers, or a society that refused to believe them or acknowledge structural inequality, could not be similarly denying other women's experience. Being accountable for one's own actions, oppressive behaviours, and use or misuse of power was the personal responsibility of every worker, and the larger commitment of every centre.

Feminism, as a political movement, also had expertise to build. Like every other social movement, feminism generated its own internal hierarchies of power, with the same assumed entitlements and denials. White, heterosexual, middle-class, able-bodied women who had not had to challenge their own privilege at first rebuilt the same "othering" and marginalizing structures into their movement and organizations that men had built against women in the larger social sphere. Women who were marginalized in the broader society were now doubly so as they found themselves silenced within a movement claiming, yet failing, to speak for them. Thus the feminist analytics of power had to deepen and grow, to understand the internalization, maintenance, and replication of hierarchies of privilege and domination in a system of linked oppressions ribboned through both our internal and external worlds. Feminism represented the fight for women's equality, but it matured to understand that women's oppression was inseparable from all forms of oppression: the kitchen table movement was actually a global one. All of this and more came to make up the body of expert knowledge on which feminist sexual assault centres built their foundations.

This expert knowledge, finally, looked like it might be one that could meet and demonstrate the expectations of expertise. If the core components of expertise are being very skilled and knowledgeable about a particular subject or type of work, then women's feedback certainly supported feminist political practice. While the "expertise" of the psy-disciplines does not concern itself with outcomes,[82] and thus positive "performance" is not a requirement for their expert status, the feminist sexual assault centre's emphasis on accountability has always placed the woman's experience of her support in the foreground. In studies designed to determine what women consider "most helpful" in healing from sexual violence, the support of feminist sexual assault centres and their advocates continues to be identified first by survivors.[83] These data certainly reflect what is regularly reported to SAC workers, and are consistent with internal survivor evaluations that highlight the importance of supporting women's expertise, maintaining protection from record keeping, and rejecting diagnostic or mental-health labelling.

Enter the Credentialed

However, what at first looked like it might be the undoing of the age of the experts instead took unexpected turns. As newly emboldened women began to speak out about sexual violence and, in particular, about the incest that psy-expertise had previously claimed was fantasy, the psy-disciplines took a new approach. They would no longer deny the existence of childhood sexual abuse outright; instead they simply named themselves the experts in it while simultaneously erasing the role of inequality. As Louise Armstrong, author of *Kiss Daddy Goodnight*, one of the first feminist works to expose incest, writes:

> ... they fed on us. They took ownership of our stories. They dismissed our politics. They ignored our goal. And they re-cast the entire issue in their professionalized language. For good measure, they also borrowed our language — words like empowerment, courage, change.
>
> What happened was that virtually overnight — out of the vast pool of ignorance and darkness that had existed on the issue five minutes earlier — suddenly, amazingly, knowledge appeared. Suddenly — when we started talking about holding normal men who were normal fathers accountable — there were experts. A million experts, a billion experts — it was a great miracle — an act of divine intervention. (or an infestation, depending on your view.)[84]

82 Apart from external social manageability of patients.

83 Sarah E Ullman & Stephanie M Townsend, "Barriers to Working with Sexual Assault Survivors: A Qualitative Study of Rape Crisis Centre Workers" (2007) 13 Violence Against Women 412 at 412–13; see also Rebecca Campbell, "Rape Survivors' Experiences With the Legal and Medical Systems: Do Rape Advocates Make a Difference?" (2006) 12 Violence Against Women 30 at 32, 40.

84 Louise Armstrong, "Incest: A Feminist Core Issue that Needs Repoliticizing" (Dec

Once again, psy-discipline voices geared up to bring women's experience, and now women's organizations, "under the domain of their expertise."[85] They moved to dominate the discourse, and along with them, a newly professionalized and legitimized social work jumped into the fray.[86] Against these voices, feminist sexual assault centres continued to amass women's knowledge, building a critical literature of the psy-discipline and legal system collusion in violence against women. Sexual assault centre workers went to universities and began to write theses about sexual violence and feminist politics. Some stayed and undertook the work of trying to change an academy that had also invisiblized male dominance and male violence, creating new controversy for a still-fledgling women's movement that critiqued institutionally based education.[87]

As the feminist literature grew, so did the work of psy-disciplines. Further, violence against women was "mainstreamed" as an issue. Political feminist voices found themselves more and more marginalized, as some centres began to strive for legitimacy by remaking themselves in the image of the very disciplines they formed to resist. Many long-time political workers left, or were pushed out on the issue of "credentials," to be replaced by degree holders who were more amenable to hierarchical structures and uncritical collaboration with institutions whose oppressive practices early political feminists worked to expose.[88] Feminist voices challenging the psy-disciplines began to subside, and political feminists watched, dismayed, as psy-disciplines began to gain more credibility than ever before. Troublingly, instead of the once-critical

2003) *Arte Sana*, online: < http://www.arte-sana.com/articles/incest_feminist_core.htm>. See also Louise Armstrong, *Kiss Daddy Goodnight: A Speak-Out on Incest* (New York: Pocket Books, 1978).

85 *Ibid.*

86 Jeffrey J Olson, "Social Work's Professional and Social Justice Projects" (2007) 18 J Progressive Human Services 52.

87 "The women's anti-violence movement was born from the philosophy that institutionally-based education, especially in the fields of social work, psychology and medicine, serves to encode the social, political and institutional conditions that maintain women's subordinate social and economic position. The idea that credentials are required to advocate for and provide services to women who have experienced violence is antithetical to the meaning of feminism." Anna Willats, Mandy Bonisteel & Marilyn McLean, "The Struggle to Maintain Grassroots Feminist Responses to Male Violence" (Sept/Oct 2005) 53 New Socialist Magazine 16 at 17, online: <http://www.newsocialist.org/attachments/123_NewSocialist-Issue53.pdf>.

88 Shana L Maier, "Are Rape Crisis Centers Feminist Organizations?" (2008) 3 Fem Crim 83–4.

and deeply analytical grassroots response of feminist political practice, more and more sexual assault centres were now racing to "keep up," to prove they could hold the same impugned credentials that had been used to silence and discredit women speaking out about sexual violence.

That Was Then, This Is Now (Redux)

Given that the most clear-headed critiques of psy-discipline knowledge and practices once came from the VAW movement, it is more than a little baffling that the same movement today is in a race to become more like them. In what appears to be a bid to win the contest of "experts" with psy- and institutionally based services, many of today's SACs have attached credibility to being perceived as "every bit as professional" as government-created apolitical victim-service models. This shift has had nothing to do with ethical, competent, and accountable practice. It has instead meant hiring only university-educated women, restructuring collectives to board models, and implementing management, performance, and evaluation practices originally designed to maximize capital outputs of business or industry,[89] not human needs. Many SACs have removed references to feminism or gender-based violence from their mission statements,[90] and have ceased to employ a political, equality-seeking analysis, defining themselves instead as "service providers." Perhaps most disturbing has been the overwhelming erosion of confidentiality, once the keystone of feminist political practice and the seat of its expert knowledge in supporting survivors. If Foucault's disciplinary mechanisms are the colonization of the mind, the technologies of surveillance have certainly become the colonization of a women's movement now uncritically engaging in "knowledge collection" on an unprecedented scale. Assessments, intake checklists, case noting, type-of-abuse statistics, contact-frequency tracking, demographic information, and record-keeping of all kinds have now found their way into the once sacrosanct safe-space of feminist centres. These tools of categorizing and managing survivors as opposed to perpetrators were the very ones employed by psy-disciplines that led to such peril in disclosure.

89 Mandy Bonisteel & Linda Green, "Implications of the Shrinking Space for Feminist Anti-Violence Advocacy" presented at the 2005 Canadian Social Welfare Policy Conference, *Forging Social Futures* (Fredericton, New Brunswick) at 2 [unpublished], online: www.crvawc.ca/documents/ShrinkingFeministSpace_AntiViolenceAdvocacy_OCT2005.pdf.

90 Maier, *supra* note 88 at 90.

As evidenced by the psy-legal mobilization of this documentation outlined in the last section, the dangers associated with disclosures and record-keeping are perhaps more profound now than ever before.

Numerous commentators have linked these changes to centres' charitable status, acceptance of government funding, and associated regulatory requirements and reporting mechanisms. There is some validity to this[91] as government has maintained a steady depoliticizing pressure on women's organizations,[92] and taken an active role in forcing collectives to restructure into board models. Government intervention through funding does not, however, serve as a full explanation. SACs were once adamant about taking an active and equal role in these funding agreements, revising incorrect assumptions about what activities were necessary, what reporting requirements were appropriate, and what outcomes could be expected. Centres were often proactive in critiquing contracts and grant terms, requiring that they be reworked to acknowledge the structural inequalities, the autonomy of centres, and the expert direction of survivors themselves. Thus the initial slide into depoliticization, while likely impacted by funding, cannot be fully attributed to it. Despite this, it is common today to see centres structuring their priorities and activities around funder requirements and, worse, believing they must engage in practices that feminist expert knowledge long ago identified as damaging to survivors out of fear of "getting in trouble with the funders." The extensive documenting of survivors outlined above is only one of these practices, many of which are often misleadingly shrouded in cloaks of benevolence as being for the "protection of the client."[93]

Today's SACs and advocates are moving progressively toward the adoption of a "triage" role, operating as frontline assessors and referrers for psy-disciplines. Some of this is likely attributable to resource scarcity, as centres are forced to cut ongoing support services to survivors, and to maintain long waiting lists. Also reflected, however, is the steady influence and increased acceptance of psy-discipline expertise, as is evidenced by SAC adoption of medicalized language, creation of "clinical" roles, and diagnostic stances with survivors. Increasingly, too,

91 Particularly in charitable status advocacy restrictions.

92 See Bonisteel & Green, *supra* note 89, for a comprehensive overview of the mechanisms of this pressure.

93 See Nick Totten, "The Baby and the Bathwater: 'Professionalisation' in Psychotherapy and Counselling" (1999) 27 Brit J Guidance and Counselling 320, for a refutation of the "best interests" argument.

we see centres categorizing survivors into subsets, problematizing some as "less treatable" under the rubric of "mental health" othering. Where feminist expertise once recognized that women with "extreme" presentations had often experienced severe social marginalization and abuse denial[94] and thus most needed the non-judgmental, non-pathologizing support of a SAC, today this is identified as reason for sending them elsewhere. The traditional psy-discipline framework of isolating issues to individual women rather than acknowledging the role of structural inequities and social messaging thus finds new life in depoliticized sexual assault centre practice. What should be warning signs of lack of capacity and flexibility in organizational analysis and practice instead become justification to structure policy and services to support the needs of only those best able to access them. Marginalized, criminalized, racialized, and disabled women, those with language and cultural barriers or addictions issues — all are pushed into the category of "difficult to serve" and are streamed out to psy-disciplines and psychopharmacology. In this way, the past rises to meet the present, as the similarities to the early exclusivity of "white, middle-class" feminist dominance are unmistakable.

What has the sexual assault centre's slow transformation from political organization to service deliverer meant for women survivors of violence? "Core competencies" or, more plainly put, "things you're very good at," have been some of the first things to fall in the face of a rapidly credentializing women's movement. As a movement there were core things feminists knew, things learned from the experience of watching the "expert" psy-legal discourse play out on women in therapist's offices and legal systems every day. The feminist sexual assault centre's body of expert knowledge included methods of supporting women, theoretical underpinnings to those methods, a local and global analysis of gendered violence and linked oppressions, and a political vision for change. It is ironic that the very things that set feminist sexual assault centres apart, the skills that drew most on the expert knowledge of women, have also been among the first things sexual assault centres are preparing to abandon. A disturbing picture emerging from this analysis of expert knowledge is one of a movement that has begun to devalue its own expertise. Somewhere along the line, centres began to move away from resisting the denigrating messages of the psy- and legal disciplines, and

94 Ritual abuse survivors, particularly, found themselves diagnosed and psychiatrized at every turn until SACs created space to illuminate and expose these experiences to a disbelieving public.

toward an attempt to gain their recognition. Today's landscape sees advocates taking their leadership from those same repudiated credentialed knowledges in training, the fraught arena of "best practices" and professional development, while simultaneously de-emphasizing the expertise of the survivor herself in speaking authoritatively on the subject. Most tellingly, this harkens a full-circle return to individualizing and treating the disordered survivor while abandoning a gendered power and equality analysis in the feminist frontline understanding of sexual violence.

CONCLUSION

The psy- and legal disciplines have been reinventing their narratives to reinforce pathologizing claims about women for a long time. There is no reason to believe they will stop, but nor should they be granted more purchase, especially when there is so much more critical information available today with which to interrogate their claims to expertise. This exploration of expert-knowledge truth-claims started with some misleadingly simple questions: How has our contemporary society decided which experts are "the" experts? On what basis? What have been the impacts of that acceptance, and the attendant power that comes with it, on women survivors of violence?

This project, in its glance at the historical underpinnings of these expert knowledges, demonstrates that the psy-discipline claim to expertise in matters involving violence against women simply cannot be convincingly supported. Historical psy-perspectives on women would be laughable and quaint in their antiquity, were it not so plain that they have not faded into the stuff of history. Instead, acceptance of psy-discipline authority has led to increased legal power over women in a system that already constructed them as disordered. The traditional collusion of the disciplines to discredit women is even more embedded today, such that the negative power of both in the lives of women has only deepened, even as their claims to expert status expand. This partnership between the psy-disciplines and the legal system has significant implications. As long as law acknowledges and supports psy-knowledge as expert and calls on it to provide not only expert opinion, but a long arm of community supervision and social control, the power of the psy-legal discourse over the minutia of survivors' lives will only become more deeply ingrained. It is difficult for contemporary theorists and advocates to step outside what has become generally accepted "wisdom" to interrogate something so culturally embedded as psy-knowledge. Its permeation into everyday life has been so complete as to be unnoticeable, playing itself out in courtrooms, in language, on daytime television, in our homes, and in the colonized space of our minds. Despite the difficulty, interrogating these claims is exactly what I suggest we must do to resist the pull toward biological explanation and reorientation of non-biological problems. For survivors of sexual violence, so often the targets of these interventions, raising this challenge is critical.

Without challenge, psy-disciplines are free to promote diagnosis and psychopharmacology, particularly as "treatment" for sexual violence. Law continues to be free to pathologize and disorder the survivor: on the witness stand, in the prisoner's box, and in her fight for the right to mother her children. Both domains extend their reach, while neither faces any serious challenge to their patriarchal foundations, frameworks, or practices. Thus, fundamental change cannot be expected to occur in either. Absent an active, politicized front line women's movement using its own expertise to resist and expose psy-legal practices, today's survivors are more vulnerable than ever before.

Of the three expert knowledges discussed here, only the expertise of the feminist movement was generated by women, and grounded in women's experiences. Of the three, feminist expertise is the only one to have mounted any serious resistance to the archetypal Pathological Woman of the psy-legal domains, thus having demonstrable benefits for both individual women and women as a group. This is not to say that no woman has ever benefited from the support of a psy-practitioner, or that no woman accessing the legal system has ever had a positive experience. These relieving moments, however, cannot obscure the overwhelming numbers of women who have instead experienced medical, mental health, and legal interventions as sources of "secondary victimization."[95]

Yet, despite women's positive accounting of the support and empowerment achieved through feminist political practice, this third expert knowledge of women survivors themselves is the only one steadily losing purchase. Disturbingly, the VAW movement itself appears to be relinquishing this knowledge base in favour of apolitical models mirroring many of the same problematic elements of the psy-disciplines. When over 90 percent of child protection reports in domestic violence cases are coming from the very supports women have turned to for aid, we can truly say the women's movement has been made to turn on itself. Today's feminist front line must once again examine its own premises and practices. If we are going to hold law to account for reifying

95 Ullman & Townsend, *supra* note 83 at 413.

psy-expertise and pathologizing survivors, what has to be the accountability of the women's movement in doing so?

Feminist legal advocates, activists, and academics are left with some critical questions. It is time to ask ourselves why we are not challenging an expert knowledge that legally compels survivors to take psychiatric drugs, or constructs them as threats to their children? Why do we so often fail to locate the intersecting impacts of expert knowledge where they are? What questions do we need to be asking and what are the dialogues we are not having? In order to move forward, it is critical that we begin to remember how to both locate and question "the experts," not simply on a theoretical, academic level, but on the ground, in courtrooms, in our movements. For those engaging the legal system, this is a call to examine practices, to look between the lines of policy and codification to see how the unscrutinized power lent to expert claims is wreaking havoc in the lives of mostly invisible survivors. For feminist sexual assault centres, this is a call to once again rely on and defend the expert knowledge of feminist political practice, and eschew the individualizing practices of biopsychiatry and mental health disordering. The race for institutional recognition is one that cannot be won without a loss of decades of expertise built by women who have experienced sexual violence, resisted psy-discipline pathologizing, and lived under the bright microscope of the legal system. Honouring their wisdom means a return to politicization in the violence against women movement, and a return to earlier understandings of the feminist sexual assault centre as both a site of expert knowledge and of women's resistance.

19.
Zero Tolerance Some of the Time? Doctors and Sexual Abuse in Ontario

Sanda Rodgers

Sanda Rodgers considers another form of resistance and backlash to sexual assault reforms — the disciplinary response of the College of Physicians and Surgeons to women's reports of sexual assault by doctors. While Susan Ehrlich discussed the subversion of sexual assault criminal law reforms through practices of trial discourse, Sanda's research shows how the disciplinary process, which is another avenue through which women can seek redress for sexual assault and which offers the potential to avoid the many aspects of the criminal process that complainants experience as punitive, has been captured by criminal law principles and practices. She highlights reliance on psychiatric "expertise" to pathologize women and to excuse perpetrators, echoing a theme introduced by Jane Doe and further problematized by Sunny Marriner. Sanda's analysis of "psychiatric therapy" imposed on doctors, usually as proposed by their own experts and supervised by their subordinates, illustrates the reification of psychiatric "expertise" over the safety of women patients.

> [Confirming] the College's commitment to the safety of the public by affirming the philosophy of Zero Tolerance of sexual abuse, and in accordance with that philosophy, developing policies, procedures, practices, and education programmes that support it.
>
> — College of Physicians and Surgeons of Ontario, Council Motion, 27 May 1991

> The purpose of the provisions of this Code with respect to sexual abuse of patients by members is to encourage the reporting of such abuse, to provide funding for therapy and counselling for patients who have been sexually abused by members and, ultimately, to eradicate the sexual abuse of patients by members.
>
> — *Regulated Health Professions Act,* Procedural Code 1993

In 1991, the College of Physicians and Surgeons of Ontario (CPSO) established a task force on the sexual exploitation of patients, and began a systematic review of doctors' sexual abuse.[1] CPSO records revealed that the abuse of patients was well documented, and was not occasional or anomalous. However, little had been done by the CPSO to respond to the abuse and to offer protection to patients.

The 1991 task force found that the CPSO response to patient complaints of doctors' sexual abuse amounted to re-abuse of complainants. Penalties imposed on doctors were lenient. The doctors who staffed the discipline committees hearing the individual complaints over-identified with the accused physician. Minimal penalties were imposed and these were little more than a slap on the abuser's professional wrist. In those cases where the CPSO imposed significant penalties, Ontario courts regularly overturned these penalties, substituting lesser ones, and undermining the CPSO response to sexual abuse.[2]

In 1993, the Province of Ontario with the support of the CPSO, undertook major legislative reform, introducing changes to the *Regulated Health Professions Act*,[3] implementing zero tolerance of sexual abuse, and imposing mandatory license revocation as the penalty for the most serious cases of abuse.[4]

Prior legislation had defined professional misconduct to include sexual impropriety with a patient. However, the revised legislation included specific measures defining "sexual abuse," imposing a mandatory reporting obligation on all health care professionals to report sex-

1 *The Final Report of the Task Force on Sexual Abuse of Patients* (Toronto: College of Physicians and Surgeons of Ontario, 1991).

2 *Ibid.* See also Paul Taylor, "4 Key Rulings Involving MDs Overruled Medical Body to Appeal Decision in Case Concerning Abuse of 3-year-old" *The Globe and Mail* (28 January 1991) A4.

3 *Regulated Health Professions Act*, SO 1991, C 18, as am by SO 1993, C 37 [*Act*]. Schedule 2 to this *Act* sets out the *Health Professions Procedural Code*, which is deemed by s 4 of the *Act* to be part of each health profession *Act* enacted by the province. The amendments dealing with sexual assault are found primarily in the *Procedural Code.* See Bill 100, *An Act to Amend the Regulated Health Professions Act,* SO 1991, C 18, as am. by SO 1993,C 37. They define sexual abuse and impose mandatory license revocation for a minimum period of five years for the most serious forms of sexual abuse [s 72(3)(a)].

4 For a more detailed review of the enactment of these provisions and their impact see: Sanda Rodgers, "Health Care Providers and Sexual Assault: Feminist Law Reform?" (1995) 8 CJWL 159; Sanda Rodgers, "Sexual Abuse by Health Care Professionals: The Failure of Reform in Ontario" (2004) 12 Health LJ 71. For a detailed study of the five-year assessment of the impact of the Ontario legislation and proposals for amendment, from which this article is drawn, see Sanda Rodgers, "Zero Tolerance Some of the Time? Doctors, Discipline and Sexual Abuse in Ontario" (2007) 15 Health LJ 353.

ual abuse by other health care providers,[5] introducing specific penalties and restrictive licensing reinstatement provisions, and listing specific forms of sexual misconduct punishable by mandatory license revocation.

The most important reform was the mandatory revocation penalty imposed for sexual abuse of patients. License revocation was made mandatory for sexual intercourse; genital to genital, anal or oral contact; masturbation; or encouragement to masturbate in the presence of the professional. While *mandatory* revocation applied only to the listed acts, licence revocation could be imposed for other forms of sexual abuse. Under the new provisions, where a professional's license was revoked for sexual abuse of any kind, no application for reinstatement could be made for a minimum period of five years.

Fifteen years of experience with the zero tolerance provisions provides sufficient time to assess the impact of the 1993 reforms. How have the CPSO and the disciplinary processes responded to the objectives of the legislation? What has been the impact of the new provisions on disciplinary penalties? To determine the impact of the new provisions of the *Act* on CPSO proceedings, I have examined the decisions of the CPSO complaints and discipline committees concerning sexual abuse between 1994 and 2005. I have relied on two primary sources of information. The first is information provided by CPSO to PricewaterhouseCoopers as part of a statutorily mandated five-year review. The second is my own review of those post-1993 discipline decisions involving allegations of sexual abuse available on the CPSO website, whether in summary or complete form. In some cases, decisions that appeared in summary form are only available in full from other databases. Occasionally, I specifically refer to other sources. Where this is the case, the source of the information is noted here. While the information available from these sources is not coterminous, in each case it supported the same conclusions.

Regrettably, my review of the implementation of the 1993 zero tolerance provisions by the CPSO revealed widespread resistance, failure

5 Originally, the *Act* provided the legislative framework for twenty-one, now twenty-five, health professions governed by its provisions. These include audiologists, chiropodists, chiropractors, dental hygienists, dental surgeons, dental technologists, denturists, dietitians, homeopaths, kinisiologists, massage therapists, medical laboratory technicians, medical radiation technologists, midwives, naturopaths, nurses, occupational therapists, opticians, optometrists, pharmacists, physicians and surgeons, physiotherapists, psychologists, respiratory therapists, and those practising traditional Chinese medicines.

to focus on public protection, and undermining of the zero tolerance provisions. This resistance primarily takes the form of a persistent and unacknowledged requirement that the complaint is independently corroborated, the disciplinary process gives advantage to the abusing doctor, and the defence relies on psychiatric "expertise" to pathologize the complainant and exculpate the offender. In addition, CPSO discipline decisions demonstrate narrow technical readings of the provisions of the *Act* and of CPSO guidelines, which undermine both the letter and the spirit of the legislative reforms.

Despite important legislative changes designed to ensure that sexual abuse is taken seriously and that those who transgress legislatively defined sexual boundaries are de-licensed, only 5.53 percent of cases involving allegations of sexual abuse between 1994 and 2005 ever reached the disciplinary stage. In those that did, there was an unacknowledged reliance on corroboration in the form of eye witnesses or multiple victims, replicating and reinforcing stereotypes of unreliable and retributive women complainants so often found in the response to male sexual violence.

There is an increasing criminalization of the disciplinary process and of the rules applicable to hearings. Both of these departures from the rules of civil procedure create increased and inappropriate barriers to protection of the public and undermine the objectives of zero tolerance legislation. Quasi-criminal burden of proof requirements are apparent in the decisions of the discipline committee and in attempts by counsel for accused doctors to access complainant's private and personal records. There is ample evidence of the psychiatrization of complainants for the purpose of their discreditation, while similar techniques are used to exonerate abusing physicians.

Arguably, this resistance is neither deliberate nor intentional CPSO policy. Rather, it is the result of the very nature of the regulatory self-disciplinary process and of the fragmentation that occurs where each decision is understood to stand alone, rather than be considered as a part of a possible pattern. My purpose here is to identify those patterns. The CPSO must then take steps to address these patterns in order to return to its original commitment to the implementation of the 1993 reforms and the eradication of sexual abuse of patients.

I. BARRIERS TO COMPLAINTS OF SEXUAL MISCONDUCT

The 1993 legislative reforms required that a complaint of sexual misconduct be received by the CPSO, investigated, and considered by the complaints committee and, should the complaints committee consider it warranted, be forwarded to the discipline committee for a full adversarial hearing and the imposition of an appropriate penalty. Such penalties included both discretionary and mandatory license revocation.

There are two ways in which information concerning physician sexual misconduct can come to the attention of the CPSO. The first is through a mandatory report made by another health care professional. In fact, few members of the health professions comply with the mandatory reporting provisions. Between 1994 and 1998, there were 887 complaints by health care professionals of sexual misconduct by doctors.[6] As well, the CPSO admitted that it was unlikely that a mandatory report would be the basis for an investigation of a health care professional unless the name of the abused patient was provided. They also indicated that they did not use mandatory reports to track multiple complaints against a member, nor as similar fact evidence to trigger an investigation, nor to provide support for an existing complaint.[7]

The failure by the CPSO to use information obtained from mandatory reports is not the only barrier to effective implementation of the sexual misconduct provisions. The second source of sexual miscon-

6 PricewaterhouseCoopers, *Evaluation of the Effectiveness of the Health Professional Colleges' Complaints and Discipline Procedures with Respect to Professional Misconduct of a Sexual Nature and Status of the Colleges' Patient Relation Program* (Toronto: PricewaterhouseCoopers, 1999) [*PwC Report*]. The *PwC Report* was twenty-seven volumes in length, with a specific report on the performance of each of the health disciplines governed by the legislation. These numbers must be assessed taking into account under-reporting. See Table 2: Statistical Summary: Complaints and Mandatory Reports.

7 *PwC Report*, vol 6, *ibid* at 16. It should be noted that section 75 of the *Act* allows for an investigation where a mandatory report has been received. See also s 85.11 (2)(2)(1). See the recommendations of the Health Professions Regulatory Advisory Council, with regard to obtaining the patient's consent to disclose her identity and recommending that an investigation be undertaken where the registrar has reasonable and probable grounds to believe the member has abused a patient. Health Professions Regulatory Advisory Council, *Final Report to the Minister of Health and Long-term Care: Effectiveness of Colleges Complaints and Discipline Procedures for Professional Misconduct of a Sexual Nature* (Toronto: Ministry of Health, 2000), Health Professions Regulatory Advisory Council, online: <http://www.hprac.org/en/reports/resources/ComplaintsDiscipline_1996.pdf>, [*HPRAC Report*]. Contrast this to the recommendations of the Special task force on Sexual Abuse of Patients, *What About Accountability to the Patient?: Final Report of the Special task force on Sexual Abuse of Patients*, Chair: Marilou McPhredran (Toronto: College of Physicians and Surgeons of Ontario, 2000) [*2000 Report*] that mandatory reports should trigger an investigation where there is a reasonable suspicion that there is a risk of harm to patients *or upon two reports* [emphasis added] (at 39–40).

duct complaints are members of the public.[8] Between 1994 and 2001, the CPSO received 13,000 complaints of physician misconduct of all kinds, including sexual misconduct.[9] CPSO reported that 99 percent of these complaints were dismissed or were resolved internally without proceeding to a disciplinary hearing.[10]

Many obstacles impede an individual patient from personally filing a complaint of physician sexual misconduct. These include individual feelings of denial, complicity, shame, self-doubt, trauma, and loss, as well as a concern that the institution will favour its own members. These barriers suggest that those patients who do file complaints are only a small percentage of those who have been abused. The CPSO reported that between 1993 and 1998, 448 independent individual complaints of sexual abuse were filed with the college.[11] Of these, 213 were

8 It should be noted that those most likely to be abused may be the least likely to report abuse. "Immigrants, non-English speaking persons, the physically and mentally challenged, persons with life threatening illnesses, and persons in counselling and psychotherapeutic relationships are more likely to be reluctant or challenged in their ability to make a complaint against a health professional": *HPRAC Report, ibid* at 3. See also *2000 Report, ibid* at xii. The *Act* requires a formal complaint [s 25(4)]. A few of the colleges assist complainants by travelling to their homes, directing the complainant to resources for emotional support, or offering information in more than one language. Only the College of Nurses engages in outreach to the public or to at-risk or vulnerable groups. Three complainants indicated that the College of Physicians and Surgeons failed to support their special needs so that they could participate in the disciplinary process. These included a developmentally delayed complainant and two complainants who required financial assistance in order to attend the discipline committee hearing in Toronto: *2000 Report, ibid* at 17–18.

9 There are 28,000 members of the college in total.

10 Robert Cribb, Rita Daly & Laurie Monsebraaten, "How System Helps Shield Bad Doctors: College Admits Flaws in Process" *Toronto Star* (5 May 2001), online: <http://pqasb.pqarchiver.com/thestar/search.html>. Data calculated by the *Toronto Star* indicated that 111 doctors had been found guilty of incompetence or misconduct, including sexual misconduct, with only thirty-four losing their license to practice. Of the 141 that proceeded to a hearing between 1994 and 2001, seventy-seven concerned sexual misconduct, nineteen concerned patient death, and ten concerned psychological harm. It is difficult to reconcile this data with data generated by PwC. However, the years surveyed by PwC were 1994–1998. The *Star* data includes 1994–2001. Most recent data from the CPSO indicates that, in 2005, seventy-three of the complaints received by the complaints committee, including sexual abuse complaints, resulted in no action: CPSO, *Annual Report*, (Toronto: College of Physicians and Surgeons of Ontario, 2005) at 10 [*Annual Report*].

11 These are complaints against individual doctors. There may be multiple complainants. In 2005, there were 705 complaints on all matters of professional competence and conduct, 73 percent resulted in no action. Four percent were forwarded to discipline: *Annual Report, ibid.*

never referred by CPSO staff to the complaints committee because of the withdrawal of the complaint, the resignation of the member, or a formal or informal alternative dispute resolution process.[12] Two hundred and forty-three[13] complaints were forwarded to the complaints committee. Of these, ninety-nine received no action by the committee; eighty doctors received a written caution; and fifty-one doctors received an oral caution.[14] Only sixty-one doctors, or 14 percent (61/448), were referred to the discipline committee for a disciplinary hearing.[15] Of these, twenty-three doctors, or 38 percent (23/61), were found guilty by the discipline committee.[16] Twenty-nine (29/61) were found not guilty and thirty-one cases were withdrawn.[17] Overall, only 5 percent (23/448) of defendant doctors who were the subject of complaints of sexual abuse went on to be found guilty by the discipline committee.[18] On appeal to the courts, six were abandoned, ten were upheld, and one appeal was allowed.[19]

Thus, added to the failure of professionals to meet their mandatory reporting obligations, and the failure of the CPSO to follow up on those reports when received, is a significant drop-off rate between the filing

12 There were 181 pre-complaint dispositions and 108 ratifications of a resolution otherwise achieved between the parties — the college and the doctor: *PwC Report*, vol 22, *supra* note 6 at 29.

13 These numbers are discrepant with those above. The discrepancy arises in the numbers provided by the CPSO to PwC and relied on by PwC in its report. For the first set of numbers, see *PwC Report*, *ibid* vol 6: Summary of Key Findings. For the second set of numbers, see vol. 22: Report on the College of Physicians and Surgeons of Ontario: *PwC Report*, *ibid*.

14 Four were the subject of ratification of a resolution reached through ADR; one of legal ratification; three were referred to the quality assurance committee; four were referred to the executive committee, and two are indicated as "other": PwC Report vol 22, *ibid* at 30. The complainant may appeal to the Health Professions Appeal and Review Board.

15 *Ibid* at table 2: Statistical Summary: Complaints and Mandatory Reports. There are small discrepancies in the numbers provided. Volume 6 of the *Report* lists 23 findings of guilt. Vol 22 lists 28. Additionally, not all complaints would have been resolved, even informally, during the time period being tracked by PwC.

16 *Ibid* at table 3: Statistical Summary of Referrals to Discipline. The college reported to PwC that the caseload of the discipline committee grew exponentially following the changes in the legislation and that successful prosecutions decreased by 50 percent by the end of 1996.

17 *Ibid* at 31.

18 *HPRAC Report*, *supra* note 7 at 16.

19 *PwC Report*, vol 22, *supra* note 6 at 10.

of a complaint by an individual and any resolution on the merits by the discipline committee.[20] Overall, the percentage of mandatory reports plus individual complaints of sexual abuse referred to discipline was 5.53 percent of all complaints that the CPSO received.[21]

This is a significant level of attrition.[22] It likely understates the real problem. The reluctance to file, high withdrawal rates, and the negative consequences of filing experienced by complainants, combined with the failure to pursue mandatory complaints, creates significant fall off. When combined with the informal screening and dismissal of complaints that are filed, these all combine to result in few complaints being subjected to the disciplinary process. Despite the zero tolerance legislation, this situation has not improved.

II. BARRIERS TO GETTING HEARD BY THE DISCIPLINE COMMITTEE

What accounts for the 47.5 percent (213/448) of all complaints that never make it to the complaints committee, and for the 74.9 percent (182/243) of those that never make it from the complaints committee to the discipline committee? The non-founding of these complaints is the

20 The complaints committee may refer a doctor subject to a complaint to the executive committee for incapacity, or to the discipline committee for misconduct or incompetence, or require a member to appear before it to be cautioned or to take any action that it considers appropriate and consistent with the *Act*. It may not refer a doctor to the quality assurance committee for behaviour or remarks considered sexual, but it may refer a member to attend a continuing education or remediation program (Bill 171, *Health System Improvements Act, 2007*, 2d Sess, 38th Leg, Ontario, 2007, Sch M, assented to 4 June 2007, SO 2007, C 10) [*Bill 171*]. It may also dismiss the complaint if it is "frivolous, vexatious, made in bad faith or otherwise an abuse of process" [s 26(4)]. Among Colleges with ten or more patient complaints and mandatory reports, the proportion of complaints referred to the discipline committee ranges from 3.9 percent to 29.7 percent: *HPRAC Report, supra* note 7 at 9.

21 *HPRAC Report, ibid* at 16.

22 In one case, described in the *2000 Report*, the College of Physicians and Surgeons determined not to proceed to discipline. The committee made the decision without having consulted an expert to assess the practice methodology of a young doctor who engaged in psychotherapy with a previously abused patient, then further abused her. Under the *Act*, a complainant may appeal the decision not to proceed to the Health Professions Appeal and Review Board [HPARB]. The complainant appealed, and the board ordered the college to proceed: *supra* note 7 at 43.) The task force reported that those who did appeal to the HPARB generally considered that the delays and treatment that they experienced were disrespectful and insensitive. There is also a significant backlog: *supra* note 7 at 36).

result of a number of factors, each disturbing in its own right.[23] The imposition of any screening process diverts sexual abuse cases.

The language of the *Act* indicates that it is the statutory obligation of the complaints committee to investigate any complaint formally received. In fact, a preliminary investigation usually is carried out by staff of the CPSO and not by the committee.[24] The CPSO reported that complaints regularly were "resolved" without ever having been referred to the complaints committee for investigation.[25] In addition, some of the drop-off is attributable to the use of informal dispute resolution processes to respond to complaints not forwarded to the complaints committee for investigation.[26]

Whether the investigation formally is carried out by the complaints committee as required by the legislation, or is carried out informally, the scope of the investigation is key. The CPSO admitted that investigatory standards that it had implemented specifically to assist the complainant after the 1993 amendments were abandoned in 1997. The motive for discarding complainant-friendly strategies was the percep-

23 The failure to pursue complaints is the equivalent of the non-founding of sexual assault complaints in the criminal justice system. The non-founding of complaints does not mean that they are *unfounded*, but rather that active steps have been taken to disqualify them from proceeding. In contrast, criminal law statistics indicate a non-founding rate of 6 percent of sex assaults reported to police. Of those reported, 40 percent result in charges; 66 percent result in a conviction. Ontario Women's Directorate, *Sexual Assault Reporting Issues*, Ontario Women's Directorate, online: <http://www.citizenship.gov.on.ca/owd/english/resources/publications/dispelling/reporting/>; Statistics Canada, *The Violence Against Women Survey* (Ottawa: Ministry of Industry, 1993).

24 HPRAC recommended that the investigatory role of the complaints committee be transferred to the registrar with oversight maintained by the complaints committee. This would separate the investigatory role from the adjudicative role of the complaints committee, although somewhat diminishing the public oversight role played by the public member of each complaints committee (recommendations 20, 21). PwC reports that thirteen of the colleges conducted some level of investigation prior to referral to the complaints committee. The College of Physicians and Surgeons is one of these: *supra* note 6 at 15. See also Richard A Steinecke, *A Complete Guide to the Regulated Health Professions Act* (looseleaf), (Aurora, ON: Canada Law Book, 1995).

25 The college claims that no serious complaint of a sexual nature is resolved but that "investigators may resolve issues that concern inappropriate comments or misunderstanding about proper physical examinations": *supra* note 6 at 17–18.

26 *Supra* note 6 at 17. The CPSO used Alternative Dispute Reolution [ADR] to respond to four complaints, of which only two were resolved. This occurred despite the position of Dr Bienstock, then president of the college, that ADR was inappropriate for *any* matters of sexual misbehaviour. This was recently formalized by amendments to the *Act* that now stipulate that ADR may not be recommended in cases of sexual abuse: *Bill 171*, *supra* note 20 at s 25(1).

tion that they were responsible for difficulties in concluding successful disciplinary prosecutions.[27] These supportive mechanisms included the provision by the CPSO of an investigatory team of women with experience and commitment to issues of sexual abuse. This team was dismantled. In addition, investigators were advised no longer to act as support persons for the complainant. Nor was the complainant any longer allowed significant control of the process. In addition, allegations of sexual abuse that could be re-characterized as clinical deficiencies were transferred by the CPSO for clinical investigation.[28] As well, the policy on collection of complainants' medical records changed, with those records being collected regardless of the possible prejudice to the complainant.[29] Furthermore, the CPSO determined formally that complaints could be resolved prior to referral to the complaints committee, despite the fact that the language of the *Act* contains no such authorization.

The 86 percent fall-off rate for those cases that do reach the complaints committee but do not get referred on to disciplinary adjudication is equally disturbing. The test used by the committee in deciding whether to send a complaint forward to the discipline committee is of critical importance to the profession's response to sexual misconduct. The decision to send to discipline is assessed on a number of factors: whether the alleged conduct constitutes professional misconduct, whether it warrants a discipline hearing, and whether the CPSO has clear and convincing proof of professional misconduct.[30] This is tan-

27 This change is confirmed by the remarks of Susan Vella: "Particularly in the past four to five years, the proverbial pendulum has swung back in favour of a tangible bias against patients: so much so that many lawyers, including myself, cannot recommend that patients ever go to the college": *2000 Report*, *supra* note 7 at 43.

28 For example, allegations of inappropriate sexual touching of a patient's breast might be characterized as inadequate training in performing a breast examination rather than as sexual misconduct.

29 The *2000 Report* recommended the use of a specially designated sexual abuse investigator, following the model used by the Canadian and Ontario Human Rights Commission. The *HPRAC Report* rejects the recommendation but makes alternative recommendations designed to increase the support available to the complainant: *supra* note 7 at 11–12.

30 *Matheson v College of Nurses of Ontario* (1979), 27 OR (2d) 632 at 638, 107 DLR (3d) 430 (Ont H Ct Just). The College of Nurses uses a two-pronged test: is there *prima facie* evidence of sufficient quantity and quality that would meet the burden of proof for a finding of professional misconduct or incompetence; is it a very serious matter for the college. The sufficient standard of proof is clear and cogent evidence. The *HPRAC Report* draws an analogy between the role of the complaints committee under current legislation and that of a preliminary inquiry judge. This inappropri-

tamount to a requirement for *prima facie* evidence. It sets up multiple barriers before any complaint is referred for a disciplinary hearing, including assessment of the admissibility of evidence, determination of the credibility of the complainant and other witnesses, and the appropriate burden of proof in disciplinary matters. This amounts to the making of determinations of admissibility,[31] credibility, and probity at the informal stage, even though they must again be assessed at the formal investigatory stage.

It is clear that in considering complaints of any kind, multiple levels of screening create opportunities for systemic bias to operate. They allow for stereotypical myths about the credibility of women and children in sexual abuse matters to inform the decision whether or not to send a complaint to discipline. Yet this reliance on myth will be completely undocumented and therefore not subject to scrutiny. A better and more purposive approach that balances public interest in combating sexual abuse with fairness to the accused could be achieved by presuming that the facts as claimed are capable of proof for the purposes of deciding to forward a complaint to the discipline committee. At the disciplinary stage, full procedural fairness is available and the accused's interests are fully protected. In effect, by screening out complaints at this early stage of the process, the CPSO has created a form of preliminary hearing not authorized by statute.

ate evidentiary burden was noted by the task force in 1991, and again in 2000: *supra* note 7 at 37. See also Sydney L Robins, *Protecting Our Students: A Review to Identify and Prevent Sexual Misconduct in Ontario Schools* (Toronto: Ministry of the Attorney General, 2000) at 225: "There are obvious and important distinctions between criminal and administrative proceedings. It should be remembered that, in some areas, special and more relaxed evidentiary and procedural rules apply to administrative proceedings...."

31 The test for admissibility of hearsay evidence, for example, is relevant. Arguably, the threshold test in administrative matters is governed by more flexibility than in criminal matters. The *2000 Report*, in recommendation 13.0, suggested section 49 of the *Act* be repealed and that evidentiary rules be governed by the *Statutory Powers Procedure Act*: *supra* note 7 at 40. See also Robins, *ibid* at 231–32:

It is appropriate to apply a lower threshold of reality and necessity in civil and, most particularly, in administrative proceedings. This accords with the interests at stake in those proceedings.... In the context of hearsay statements by student complainants or witnesses in sexual misconduct cases, it also accords with the position advanced throughout this chapter that, in striking the balance between competing interests, the rights of children or sexual complainants may acquire equal or greater prominence, particularly where the adverse party cannot lay claim to a right to make full answer and defence arising out of a potential deprivation of liberty.

A second barrier arises from the quasi-criminal evidentiary standards applied by the complaints committee in deciding whether to send the file on to discipline. Determinations of credibility of the complainant and the accused are properly the role of the discipline committee. The task of the complaints committee should be limited to screening out obviously frivolous complaints. Even where a case is forwarded to the discipline committee for a hearing, a full hearing may never occur. If the doctor pleads guilty, or there is an agreed statement of facts, a full hearing likely never will take place.[32] Screening out complaints so that they never reach a disciplinary hearing evades the public interest in delicensing the offender and in educating practitioners and members of the public.

III. DISCIPLINE COMMITTEE DECISIONS 1993–2005

The CPSO has published the outcomes of the disciplinary hearings against 120 doctors[33] in sex misconduct cases decided after 1993. These fall into two categories. One group involves acts of misconduct that occurred prior to the amendments, but where the hearing occurred after 1993. In these, the 1993 new definition of sexual abuse and the mandatory license revocation provisions did not apply. While revocation was not mandatory, it could be imposed for serious professional misconduct. The second group involves acts of misconduct that occurred after the 1993 amendments came into force. In these, mandatory licence revocation was required for certain categories of sexual abuse. Both the pre- and post-1993 cases include acts of sexual misconduct that fall short of requiring license revocation. Each case decided after 1993 was heard by the discipline committee in an environment in which it was clear that sexual abuse was being taken seriously by the CPSO and by the province. My review of the post-1993 decisions of the discipline committee revealed a number of striking features, and suggests that the disciplinary hearings fall short of the achievements promised by the 1993 legislation.

Requiring Corroboration

In the criminal law context, male-centred assumptions about women's sexuality and morality and about male sexual entitlement have in-

32 Jenny Manzer, "Is *Health Professions Act* All Bark and No Bite?" *Med Post* (14 May 2000) 36.

33 For the purposes of this study, multiple cases brought separately against a single doctor are counted as one.

formed the criminal law on sexual assault. This has resulted in evidentiary rules unique to sexual assault offences. These include definitions of rape that require penile penetration, non-consent demonstrated by violent resistance, and rules regarding the doctrine of recent complaint. Among these, the rules regarding the need for corroboration have been the most longstanding, pernicious, and intractable, rendering past sexual history relevant to present consent or refusal, and insisting on warnings concerning the danger of convicting on the otherwise uncorroborated evidence of a woman or child. All of these have been the subject of political, legislative, and judicial reform and of backlash to reform.[34] Legislatures and courts have found them, variously, to be irrational, discriminatory, and unconstitutional. Too often, despite explicit legislative repeal or judicial direction that such requirements are no longer valid, reliance on these legal markers of resistance resurfaces in slightly altered forms. It is not surprising, therefore, to find their resurgence in the context of physicians' sexual misconduct. This is despite the strong legislative message of the 1993 amendments that sexual abuse by professionals would not be tolerated.[35]

Extraordinary requirements with regard to corroboration have been a continuing and pernicious marker of law's resistance to the eradication of male sexual violence against women and to legal and social recognition of the full equality and personhood of women. The most striking subversion of the implementation of a policy of zero tolerance is the apparent persistence of an unwritten and unacknowledged requirement for independent corroboration of the complaint and resistance to proceeding where the only evidence of sexual abuse is the uncorroborated evidence provided by the woman herself. It should be noted that nowhere in the *Act* is there reference to any formal requirement for corroboration and that such requirements have been explicitly repealed in the criminal law context.

It is clear that many complaints never formally make it to the complaints committee and, of those that do, only a few are forwarded to the discipline committee. The most striking feature of those that *are* forwarded is the presence of independent corroboration of the complaint.

34 Sheila McIntyre *et al*, "Tracking and Resisting Backlash Against Equality Gains in Sexual Offence Law" (2000) 20 Can Woman Stud 72.

35 This was noted by the task force prior to the amendments to the legislation: "It would seem that tribunals are most likely to render a finding of not guilty (a) where a physician denies the conduct and offers evidence as to good character in the community; and (b) where there is a lack of corroboration for the complaint": *supra* note 7 at 186. It is entirely discouraging to find that this has not changed.

The corollary is, of course, that in the absence of corroboration the cases do not come forward at all — either because they never make it to the complaints committee or because the complaints committee fails to forward them to discipline committee. Furthermore, the relatively high failure rate of the few cases that do go forward without corroboration demonstrates the persistent resistance to finding sexual abuse on women's uncorroborated evidence.

In the cases heard by the discipline committee, corroboration takes a number of forms. The most decisive comes from a successful criminal conviction, or a disciplinary finding against the physician in another jurisdiction.[36] In such cases, the existence of a formal finding of criminal responsibility or disciplinary penalty constitutes the grounds for misconduct, without the need for a full investigation or full disciplinary hearing. The most striking form of corroboration is through the admission by an accused that the complaint of sexual abuse is true. This may take the form of a voluntary resignation, a guilty plea, or an admission that the abuse occurred by way of an agreed statement of facts or consent order. A second group of cases includes both the physician's guilty plea and additional independent corroboration. The third group demonstrates corroboration alone.

Even where the doctor pleads not guilty, most cases forwarded to the discipline committee include corroborative evidence of the complainant's claim. Occasionally, the abuse is actually documented in the doctor's own files concerning the patient. More frequently, there is tangible evidence, including letters of apology, cards, telephone calls, video and audio tapes, email messages, gifts, photos, hotel bills, or independent witnesses who were present when the complainant and accused were together. Multiple complainants and similar fact evidence also provide corroboration.

Forms of Corroboration

Of the 120 cases of doctors[37] disciplined for sexual misbehaviour that were decided between 1993 and 2005, thirty-seven were resolved by the guilty plea of the accused. Twenty-four of the cases involved both a

36 Previously, summaries of the tribunal decisions individually referred to below could be found on the CPSO website under the heading *Summary of discipline committee Decisions*. More recently, the CPSO revamped its website requiring that each doctor's name be searched individually. Only doctors holding current registration are indexed, online: <http://www.cpso.on.ca/docsearch/default.aspx?id=2054>. See eg *Campbell* (2007); *Singh* (1991); *Verma* (2001).

37 Some doctors were the subject of multiple complaints.

guilty plea and additional corroborative evidence. The remaining cases involved a not-guilty plea by the doctor.[38] Despite the denial of guilt, at least thirty of these cases showed clear corroborative evidence in direct contradiction with the not-guilty plea. The corroboration took the form of multiple complainants, criminal convictions, similar-fact evidence, or tangible evidence such as photos, phone calls, and hotel receipts.[39] In only sixteen of the cases that were forwarded to the discipline committee by the complaints committee between 1993 and 2005, in which a not-guilty plea was entered, was there no clear evidence of corroboration.[40] Thus of the 120 doctors whose cases were forwarded to the discipline committee, all but sixteen[41] came forward either with clear corroborative proof: a guilty plea or its equivalent with or without additional corroborative evidence, or a claim of not guilty but clear evidence belying that claim. Few cases were forwarded in the complete absence of corroborative evidence. Of those that were, almost all resulted in findings of not guilty.

It is clear that the cases forwarded to the discipline committee were those where a successful prosecution could be most assuredly predicted, confirming the admission that the CPSO tightened the evidentiary requirements at the screening stage and reduced its willingness to

38 Some cases do not fit completely into the guilty or equivalent/not-guilty dichotomy. For example, there are some cases where no one appears for the doctor. Cases that do not clearly include a guilty plea or clear equivalent have been categorized as not guilty.

39 *Abelsohn* (2004); *Bocking* (1995); *Boodoosingh* (1993); *Bradford* (1995); *Carll* (2002); *Caughell* (1999); *Clemes* (2001); *Deitl* (1996); *Deluco* (2005); *Dobrowolski* (2004); *Frelick* (1996); *Gabrielle* (1995); *Howatt* (2000); *Johnson* (1993); *Im* (2003); *Koffman* (2003); *Lambert* (2002); *Leibl* (2001); *Markman* (1999); *McRae* (1994); *Miceli* (2002); *Mussani* (2001); *Rafaj* (2000); *Ramesar* (2000); *Rosenberg* (2003); *Sidhu* (2002); *Totsoni-Flynn* (2002); *Verma* (2001); *Verma* (2003); *Williams* (1996).

40 *BVZ*, [1995] OCPSD No 4; *ERM*, [1995] OCPSD No 30; *FLS*, [1998] OCPSD No 9; *FYF*, [2002] OCPDS No 17; *Jabouin*, [1995]; *KLG*, [1998] OCPSD No 3; *LJL*, [1995] OCPSD No 33; *MYS*, [1996] OCPSD No 20; *O'Connor*, [1997]; *OKS*, [1995] OCPDS No 18; *PVM*, [1995] OCPSD No 2; *QLN*, [1996] OCPSD No 2; *RBA*, [1996] OCPSD No 27; *STO*, [1997] OCPSD No 3; *SDE*, [1995] OCPSD No 14 and *ZHJ*, [1994] OCPSD No 29.

41 *Alfred* (1994); *BVZ*, [1995] OCPSD No 4; *ERM*, [1995] OCPSD No 30; *ETM*, [1995] OCPSD No 8; *FLS*, [1998] OCPSD No 9; *FYF*, [2002] OCPDS No 17; *Henderson* (2004); *Jabouin* (1995); *Jagoo* (1998); *KIG*, [1998] OCPSD No 3; *LJL*, [1995] OCPSD No 33; *Longdon* (1995); *Lurie* (2004); *MYS*, [1996] OCPSD No 20; *O'Connor* (1997); OKS, [1995] OCPDS No 18; *Pilo* (1994); *PVM*, [1995] OCPSD No 2; *QLN*, [1996] OCPSD No 2; *RBA*, [1996] OCPSD No 27; *Ross* (2004); *SDE*, [1995] OCPSD No 14; *Sharma* (2003); *Singh* (1995); *Smith* (2003); *STO*, [1997] OCPSD No 3; *UUO*, [1996] OCPSD No 13; *Wyatt* (2001); *ZHJ*, [1994] OCPSD No 29.

bring cases forward that represented the risk of unsuccessful prosecution. The cases that were brought forward make it clear that the CPSO took few risks. This resulted in a higher rate of prosecutorial success and avoided the possible political and financial costs associated with failure for members of the CPSO.

Despite the over-representation of corroborated complaints among the cases actually heard by the discipline committee, cases of sexual abuse where corroboration is present are anomalous. Sexual abuse occurs out of the sight of others,[42] making the easy availability of corroborative evidence unlikely and the over-representation of corroboration among the cases that are sent forward that much more notable. This is perhaps particularly true of the abuse that occurs between doctor and patient. Arguably, the CPSO is avoiding cases in which only the complainant's voice speaks authoritatively of the abuse. In so doing, it replicates both the unfounding of sexual assault complaints prevalent in the criminal law context[43] and the historical resistance to women's uncorroborated claims of assault. As a result, it leaves many cases of abuse unaddressed and abusers undeterred.

Avoiding the Provisions of the Legislation

The mandatory revocation provisions apply only to the sexual abuse of "patients." The term "patient" is not defined by the legislation. In 1992, the CPSO issued guidelines with regard to doctor–patient "dating."[44] Policies also are in place that prescribe the steps to be taken when the doctor wishes to terminate the doctor–patient relationship.[45] Because these are guidelines, their content is advisory only.

The guidelines recommend that "dating" relationships be avoided during treatment and for a year following the termination of treatment. They specify that this one-year period may be extended or shortened,

42 See *1991 Report, supra* note 1 at 80: "Witnesses to such acts of sexual abuse are rare. The legal processes used to determine the veracity of complaints of sexual abuse must be responsive to the reality of this kind of abuse if abusers are to be found and stopped".

43 Scott Clark & Dorothy Hepworth, "Effects of Reform Legislation on the Processing of Sexual Assault Cases" in Julian V Roberts and Renate M Mohr, eds, *Confronting Sexual Assault: A Decade of Legal and Social Change* (Toronto: University of Toronto Press, 1994) 113.

44 See CPSO, "Physician–Patient Dating" (May 1992). See also CPSO, "Maintaining Boundaries with Patients" *Members' Dialogue* (Sept/Oct 2004).

45 See CPSO, "Ending the Physician–Patient Relationship" Policy #3–08 (Sept 2000, reviewed and updated 2008), online: <http://www.cpso.on.ca/policies/policies/default.aspx?ID=1592>.

depending on the nature of the treating relationship, taking into account the nature of the treatment, its duration, the degree of emotional dependency, and other circumstances. If the treatment has involved psychoanalysis or psychotherapy, or if this is a significant component of the treatment, "dating" relationships continue to be proscribed even after termination of treatment.

The definition of "patient" is key to the rigorous enforcement of the legislation. The failure of the *Act* to define it forms the basis on which the requirements of the *Act* are avoided in certain cases. In a number of cases, the outcome of the discipline committee decision has foundered on the abrupt termination of the doctor–patient relationship, followed immediately by the doctor engaging in acts that otherwise would be sexual abuse.

The penalties imposed by the discipline committee where the doctor terminated the treatment relationship and immediately entered into a sexual relationship with the patient have been minimal. This is true even though the dynamics of the abuse are virtually identical and would require mandatory license revocation had they occurred within the doctor–patient relationship. Abrupt termination of the doctor–patient relationship specifically to evade the legislation has been sufficient to avoid license revocation, even where the relationship was one of psychotherapy.[46] Even when hasty termination of the doctor–patient relationship is for ulterior motives and violates CPSO directives and guidelines on doctor–patient termination, the penalties imposed are modest. The doctor has artfully fragmented the abusive and exploitative relationship. The grooming of the victim of abuse is implausibly divided into notionally unrelated acts that occur prior to or after tech-

46 Most of these cases involve psychotherapy offered by general practitioners and sexual relationships that began within months of the termination of the doctor–patient relationship. Because the physician–patient relationship had been terminated, the penalties imposed in most cases were minimal. See eg *Bothwell* (2003); *Dore* (1999); *Dube* (2001). All received a one month suspension and were required to take a boundaries course. *Henderson* (2004) received a three-month suspension and was required to take a boundaries course. See also *Hurst* (1998); *Ives* (2002); *Kavouris* (2004). In *Kavouris*, see the complainant's impact statement: "I feel as if Dr Kavouris preyed on me. He knew my vulnerabilities and he took advantage of that. I trusted him for 7 years, as a 'doctor,' as OUR family doctor. He knew that he could sell me anything and I would buy it, that I believed in him more than anyone." See also *Levy* (2003) (paediatrician, psychotherapy for eating disorder); *Lurie* (2004) (GP, affair with patient's wife, also after affair began, treated her as patient); *Richardson* (2002) (GP); *Shiozaki* (2004) (GP); *Totsoni-Flynn* (2002) (GP, within one month of psychotherapy, revocation); *Wyatt* (2001) (GP, within one month of terminating psychotherapy; twenty-four months suspension, twenty suspended).

nical termination of the doctor–patient relationship. Acts that form part of a continuum of abuse are understood as separate acts. The arbitrary or manipulated timing of the acts as pre- or post-termination becomes key with regard to the imposition of the mandatory revocation penalty.

One example will suffice. Dr David Levy provided psychotherapy to patients with eating disorders. He began treating the complainant in 1993.[47] During treatment, Dr Levy disclosed information about his personal life, encouraged her to use his health club membership, conducted therapy sessions while jogging and skating with her, took her out for drinks and for meals, bought her flowers, and sent her personal cards and letters. In October of 1995, the doctor–patient relationship was terminated and Dr Levy advised her that she could contact him for further treatment if necessary. From that time on he contacted her continually, seeking a personal relationship. In March of 1996 they entered into a sexual relationship, which terminated in November of 1998. The discipline committee treated the abuse as occurring after the termination of the doctor–patient relationship and suspended Levy's license for one year. Four months of that period were lifted if he met a number of conditions, including completing a boundaries course and undergoing a psychiatric assessment. The decision of the discipline committee to treat the period prior to termination and the abuse that occurred after termination as unrelated, and the relationship as not triggering the mandatory revocation provisions because not technically occurring between a doctor and a patient, clearly circumvents the zero-tolerance spirit of the legislation.

CPSO committees stretch the provisions of the *Act* to avoid the imposition of penalties that otherwise would follow. It is impossible to be certain how many cases are deliberately diverted from the anticipated requirements of the *Act* at the inquiry stage or by the complaints committee. However, like the *Levy* case described above, there are several cases where the extent to which the discipline committee will go to avoid the imposition of mandatory penalties is visible on the face of the decision.

In particular, the discipline committee appears to have a soft spot for those (abusive) relationships with patients that are formalized by marriage or that show some measure of longevity.[48] *CPSO v Wyatt* is

47 *The College of Physicians and Surgeons of Ontario v Dr Lance David Levy*, online: <http://www.cpso.on.ca/uploadedFiles/Discipline_Decisions/K-M/LevyLD200302.pdf>.

48 See generally *AB v College of Physicians and Surgeons Prince Edward Island*, 2001

one such case.[49] Dr Wyatt treated the complainant B from 1988–1994, providing general care as well as psychotherapy. She began treating B's partner, A, in 1992. She provided A with psychotherapy as she did B, and provided them both with couple counselling. Dr Wyatt began an intimate relationship with A in July of 1994, one month after terminating the doctor–patient relationship with A and in the same month in which she terminated the doctor–patient relationship with B. In August and September of 1995, Dr Wyatt disclosed her relationship with A to three therapists, two of whom also were her patients. All three therapists notified the CPSO.

In the view of the discipline committee, the termination of the doctor–patient relationship with A and with B removed Dr Wyatt from the provisions requiring mandatory revocation. This was despite the fact that the period between doctor–patient termination and the beginning of the personal relationship was merely a month, despite the psychotherapeutic nature of the relationship, and despite CPSO guidelines on terminating the psychotherapeutic doctor–patient relationship. Referring to the guidelines on physician–patient relationships following psychotherapy, the discipline committee concluded that a "severe" penalty was called for, but declined to impose revocation.

The committee relied heavily on the evidence of the expert witness for Dr Wyatt. The expert testified that Dr Wyatt had disclosed an earlier sexual relationship with another previous patient. Nonetheless, in his view, she exhibited no signs of an "impulse control disorder" or "emotional breakdown," nor any evidence of exploitation or of "predatory" behaviour. The committee was influenced by the fact that Dr Wyatt had contacted the CPSO for advice in advance and disclosed the relationship and that, at the date of the hearing, the relationship with A had continued for a five-year period. The discipline committee imposed a twenty-four month suspension on Dr Wyatt with twenty months lifted so long as she undertook a boundaries course, continued in psychotherapy, and refrained from practising psychotherapy. The effective result was a four-month suspension from practice.

It is hard to believe that the CPSO takes sexual abuse of patients seriously when the technical and exploitative termination of a doctor–patient relationship, which included long-term psychotherapy, distin-

PESCTD 75, 205 Nfld. & PEIR 131, 204 DLR (4th) 750 (PEI S Ct); *N v College of Physicians and Surgeons British Columbia* (1997), 143 DLR (4th) 463, 86 BCAC 181 (BCCA); *Melunsky v College of Physiotherapists of Ontario* (1999), 85 ACWS (3d) 458 (Ont Ct Just (Gen Div)).

49 *CPSO v Wyatt*, [2000] OCPSD No 10.

guishes behaviour giving rise to a five-year mandatory revocation from that which results in the most minor of penalties. What is clear is that the discipline committee, despite lip service to the need for a severe penalty, fails to understand the fiduciary obligations of the doctor or the exploitative and abusive nature of physician sexual abuse, especially in a psychotherapeutic relationship.[50]

Similarly, in *CPSO v Abelsohn*[51] the committee again went to great lengths to avoid the mandatory revocation provisions. It also resisted imposing revocation as a discretionary matter. Dr Abelsohn, a general practitioner, provided psychotherapy over a two-and-a-half-year period to a "difficult" patient. In addition to inappropriate hugging and other physical behaviour during the therapy, on six occasions the patient masturbated in Dr Abelsohn's presence. Even after terminating the treatment relationship, Dr Abelsohn continued to meet his patient in public places.

The discipline committee concluded that sexual abuse as defined by the *Act* occurred on more than thirty occasions. In the view of the committee, this behaviour did not trigger mandatory revocation, although it did give rise to suspension of the doctor's license. The committee split on whether Dr Abelsohn had "encouraged the patient to masturbate in his presence," behaviour that would have required mandatory revocation.[52] Two committee members concluded that he did so. Two members concluded that he did not. It was the view of those members that because of the mandatory penalty, the "level of encouragement [required to trigger the mandatory revocation provisions] was high." In their view, mandatory revocation was required only for the worst type of predatory sexual behaviour motivated by the desire for sexual grati-

50 This pattern continues. For a very recent example, outside of the period of this study, see *Schogt* (2004), online: <http://www.cpso.on.ca/docsearch/details.aspx?view=6&ddid=397&id=%2052488> at 43. The psychotherapeutic relationship extended from 1992 to 2001, involving sessions several times a week. The doctor terminated the doctor–patient relationship and entered into a personal relationship. The CPSO withdrew the allegation of sexual abuse and the discipline committee imposed a nine-month suspension for misconduct, with three months lifted for participation in a boundaries and ethics course.

51 *CPSO v Abelsohn* (2004). This hearing was the subject of a series of newspaper columns supportive of Dr Abelsohn and highly critical of the complainant, online: <http://www/cpso.on.ca/uploadedfiles/Discipline_Decisions/A-B/AbelsohnAR200408.pdf?terms=abelsohn>.

52 This despite the fact that a fundamental tenet of the sexual abuse provisions is that the doctor is always responsible for the abuse regardless of any seductive or otherwise sexualized behaviour by the patient.

fication. Encouragement required active "inducement, incitement, inspiring with courage, emboldening or energizing." They concluded that allowing the behaviour to occur did not necessarily mean that it was encouraged. This split precluded imposition of the mandatory penalty. Instead, the committee imposed a one-year suspension and a prohibition on practising psychotherapy in the future.

Wherever mandatory revocation can be construed as not strictly required by the terms of the *Act*, the penalties imposed by the discipline committee are minimal. This is demonstrated in cases that involve facts arising before the change in the *Act*; by complaints where exploitative and abusive conduct is artificially characterized as occurring after termination of the doctor–patient relationship; in cases where narrow interpretation of the mandatory provisions appears contrary to legislative intent; or in cases where the facts are simply described as extraordinary. More particularly, the discipline committee decisions demonstrate a romanticization of doctor–patient sexual abuse in some cases. In other cases, they reveal a misunderstanding of the nature of physician sexual abuse as perpetrated by demonized individualized predators seeking sexual gratification. They fail to understand physician sexual misconduct as an abuse of power in a relationship of heightened vulnerability.

Criminalizing the Disciplinary Process: The Standard of Proof

In addition to the informal but persistent reliance on corroboration, the decisions of the Disciplinary Committee rely on an elevated standard of proof. The *Act* provides that the rules governing civil actions are applicable to the admissibility of evidence in disciplinary proceedings.[53] The burden of proof lies on the CPSO to establish that the case for professional discipline is made out. The civil standard of proof generally is described as requiring proof "on the balance of probabilities." However, because professional reputation and livelihood are at stake, the

53 Readmissibility of evidence: "Despite the *Statutory Powers Procedure Act*, nothing is admissible at a hearing that would be inadmissible in a court in a civil action and the findings of a panel shall be based exclusively on evidence admitted before it" (1991, c 18, Sched 2, s 49). However, no evidence admitted in a disciplinary proceeding before the Complaints or discipline committee is admissible in a civil proceeding. See Steinecke, *supra* note 24 at 1170. See also *Re Gillen and the College of Physicians and Surgeons of Ontario* (1989), 68 OR (2d) 278 (H Ct Just, Div Ct); *Board of Opthamalic Dispensers v Toth*, [1990] OJ No 1802 (Ont CA): "The correct standard is that applicable in civil cases, ie proof on a balance of probabilities, with the qualification that before that standard can be said to have been met one must have regard for the proposition that the more serious the allegation to be proved, the more cogent must be the evidence" (1).

language of the burden of proof to be met creeps toward the criminal, at the same time as the disciplinary tribunals regularly acknowledge that the criminal standard of "beyond a reasonable doubt" does not apply.[54]

The question of standard of proof in disciplinary matters was considered by the task force. While the preliminary report of the task force recommended a specific statutory provision confirming that the applicable standard should be the balance of probabilities,[55] the final report revealed a lack of confidence that even a specific legislative directive would be sufficient.[56] Instead, the final report abandoned its recommendation that the burden of proof be specifically identified as civil. It suggested instead that the absence of corroboration and the presence of good character evidence has the most dramatic effect on whether a guilt finding is likely. Addressing these issues specifically, the task force recommended that good character evidence expressly be countered by counsel for the CPSO in each case as having no bearing on propensity to abuse.[57] It also recommended that the legislation specifically provide that corroboration not be required in sexual abuse cases.[58] Neither of these recommendations was adopted in the 1993 revisions. Nor was clarification of the standard of proof made explicit.

IV. THE USE OF PSYCHIATRIC EVIDENCE: PATHOLOGIZING THE COMPLAINANT, EXCULPATING THE PHYSICIAN

Discipline committee decisions reveal reliance by the accused physician on psychiatric expert evidence and on the complainant's personal records to pathologize and discredit the complainant.[59] At the same time, psychiatric expertise is used by counsel to exculpate and to re-

54 Steinecke, *ibid*, argues that earlier cases holding that the standard of proof is "beyond a reasonable doubt" are probably wrongly decided. While it is clear that the criminal standard technically does not apply, the earlier jurisprudence and the persistence of an enhanced requirement for proof continue.

55 *CPSO v Boodoosingh* (1990), 73 OR (2d) 478 at 35 (H Ct Just, Div Ct).

56 *2000 Report*, *supra* note 7 at 186.

57 Recommendation 44, *ibid* at 51.

58 Recommendation 52, *ibid* at 52.

59 See eg Lise Gotell, "The Ideal Victim, the Hysterical Complainant and the Disclosure of Confidential Records: A Case Study of the Implications of the Charter for Sexual Assault Law" (2002) 40 Osgoode Hall LJ 251; Susan M Vella, "Credibility on Trial: Recovered Traumatic Memory Evidence in Sexual Abuse Cases" (1980) 32 UBC L Rev 91.

habilitate the accused physician.[60] The persistence of these arguments reiterates the continual focus on the professional's reputation and economic prospects rather than on public protection, on recognition and prohibition of abuse, and on fair and equitable consideration of the complainant's allegations.

Often it is the impact of prior abuse that brings the complainant into contact with the doctor in the first place. The patient's vulnerability — arising out of a history of abuse, addiction or alcoholism, youth, depression, disability, or family difficulties — positions her as a target of additional abuse at the hands of the physician to whom she turns for healing. A review of the disciplinary decisions reveals an over-representation of psychiatrists among those found to have abused their patients and an over-representation of women who are survivors of abuse as complainants.[61]

The accused doctor's records concerning the complainant are available to him in mounting his defence and are part of the disciplinary file. It is not possible to know how many discipline hearings specifically considered not only the complainant's records generated by the accused physician but also third-party health or counselling records. Discipline committee decisions that explicitly refer to an attempt to access the complainant's third-party records,[62] or to question the stability and credibility of the complainant without evidence of a formal request for records, reveal the accused's use of the complainant's emotional and mental health issues or prior history of abuse to undermine her credibility. In doing so, the accused re-abuses the complainant.[63]

60 McIntyre *et al*, *supra* note 34.

61 See eg *Abelsohn* (2004); *Ahmed* (2002); *Bergstrom* (2000); *Brawley* (1995); *Campbell* (2007); *Carriere* (2001); *Dobrowolski* (2004); *Dore* (1999); *Flynn* (2002); *Frith* (2002); *Ives* (2002); *Johnson* (1995); *Kambite* (2001); *Leibl* (2001); *Rafaj* (2000); *Seidman* (2003); *Totsoni-Flynn* (2002); *Umar Khitab* (2001); *Wyatt* (2001) — all involving psychotherapy.

62 See UUO, [1996] OCPSD No 13 (14 pages of psychiatric records released); MYS, [1996] OCPSD No 20 (upon motion for disclosure of the names of complainants seen at a counselling office or sexual assault centre, committee concluded probative value outweighed privacy interests); *Cameron* (1994) (psychiatric records); *Deitl* (1996); *Alfred* (1994) (committee reviewed complainants' psychiatric records); *Williams* (1996) (names and addresses of complainants); *Heath* (1995); *Bocking* (1995); *Gabrielle* (1995); *Deluco* (2005).

63 "When we listened to what patients told us, we felt that time had stood still during the nine years since we submitted our first report. Very little has improved and the kinds of difficulties that patients experience in trying to access self-regulation processes

In *Jagoo*, the complainant was described as anxious and emotional, an ex-alcoholic, who had suffered sexual abuse as a child and was vulnerable to the influence of another complainant. In *QLN*, the complainant was described as suffering from an erotic and "eroticized transference" and "erotomania" in part resulting from her early unhappy family, obesity, low self-esteem, and failing marriage. In *Williams*, two defence experts testified on so-called "recovered memories" or "pseudo memories" claiming that "memory is an area fraught with pitfalls and requiring corroboration."[64] Experts for the CPSO countered with evidence relevant to sexual abuse and by rebutting the spurious claims of those relying on "false memory syndrome" as a factor in their defence. In *Deitel*, the committee denied the accused's motion to produce the complainant's third-party psychiatric records. The discipline committee commented that there was no evidence of collusion or false accusation. In *Heath*, the committee pointed out that the complainant had "no motive to fabricate ... no history of psychiatric problems or substance abuse." In *Gabrielle*, the discipline committee again went to great lengths to counter evidence of "false memory syndrome" introduced on behalf of the accused physician, with findings that the *seven* complainants had no motive to fabricate the complaint.

The abusive and re-abusing impact of these tactics has been commented on by the discipline committee in several cases. One of the more egregious examples is found in *Deitel*, who earlier had been found guilty of professional misconduct involving sexual misconduct with a female patient. The case involved complaints by two women patients. A third patient served as a witness for the CPSO. The decision of the discipline committee revoking Deitel's license was appealed by the doctor on the issue of the admission of similar-fact evidence. Upholding the decision of the discipline committee, Mr Justice Corbett commented on the abusive conduct of counsel for the physician at the disci-

remain much the same": *2000 Report, supra* note 7 at xi; "The information indicates that, despite the efforts of Colleges in striving to meet the requirements of the Act the complaints and discipline procedures of the RHPA implemented by Colleges fail to protect the public from sexual abuse by regulated health professionals and do not adequately deal with the special dynamics of sexual abuse cases that require people to be treated with sensitivity and respect": *HPRAC Report, supra* note 7 at 1; "Individuals who were interviewed and who had been abused by a member of a Regulated College found the complaint process was an amplification of an already traumatic experience": *PwC Report*, vol 6, *supra* note 6 at 3.

64 *Williams* (1996) at para 149.

pline hearing and the impact of that conduct on the complainants and witness. He noted that "[t]he length and vigour of cross-examination was directly proportionate to the degree of psychological vulnerability of the patient" and that "the attack on the credibility of the complainants was unrelenting and, often was unnecessarily brutal."[65]

In stark contrast to the use of psychiatry to impugn, undermine, and belittle complainants, in numerous disciplinary proceedings, expert psychiatric evidence is relied on to explain, exonerate, and rehabilitate the abusing physician.[66] Thirty years of scholarship has debunked the myth that sexual abuse is committed only by deviant or disordered men. Yet the decisions of the discipline committee often reflect counsel's attempt to distinguish the accused from a mythic abuser in order to discredit the allegations against him. This takes two forms: those in which the accused is described as "normal" and thus not an abuser, and those in which he is described as "ill" and therefore not deserving of sanction. In some cases both strategies are utilized.

In the first group of cases, expert evidence is offered attesting to the fact that there is "no evidence that he is a predator,"[67] "no evidence of psychopathic traits or anti-social personality disorder,"[68] that he does not "meet the diagnostic criteria for a sexual disorder ... for any paraphylia," that the "risk of professional misconduct is low if his practice is subject to conditions" and that he is "not currently professionally impaired."[69] In *Dobrowolski*, which involved four disciplinary hearings and seventeen complainants, the expert testified that Dobrowolski "is neither predatory nor anti-social," but rather had marital and financial difficulties and "inadequate training in the understanding of transfer-

65 *Deitel v College of Physicians and Surgeons of Ontario* (1997), 99 OAC 241 at para 224, 70 ACWS (3d) 1018 (Ct Just (Gen Div)). He notes that the transcript of the examination-in-chief of one of the complainants was 17 pages; the transcript of the cross-examination extended to 250 pages (para 224).

66 In some of the disciplinary decisions, the expert witness is identified only by his or her initials. This means that there is no way to track the recurrence of the use of the same expert witness on multiple occasions on behalf of different accused physicians.

67 *Wesley* (2002): pled guilty, evidence of corroboration; see also *Comeau* (2001): "Does not suffer from a psychiatric disorder, personality disorder or physical illness that would cause him to be at risk of harming patients, not a predator."

68 *Nguyen* (2003): pled guilty, criminal conviction; *Crainford* (1998): "does not have a psychopathic mind set, not a predator, not seeking vulnerable clients, no major character flaws."

69 *Yong-Set* (2001): guilty plea.

ence and counter-transference."[70] In *Nagahara*, where the physician pled guilty to professional misconduct and had a criminal conviction arising from the same abuse, testimony was offered that there was "no evidence of anti-social behaviour, psychopathy, impulsivity, sexual disorder or deviation, no personal or professional problems, no history of substance abuse, no features predictive of recidivism and that the re-offence potential was minimal." The penalty involved an order that Nagahara undergo treatment with the testifying expert as a condition of continuing to practice.

Evidence also often is offered of biochemical, phallometric, psychological, and physiological testing to support the claim that no "major mental illness or personality disorder" is present.[71] In one case, expert evidence was offered that because the accused physician had a "partner" (wife) who was a psychiatrist, it was unlikely he would have committed the abuse.[72] In another, the fact that the physician had been in a stable relationship for the last ten years was offered as exonerating evidence.[73]

There is no consistent evidence with regard to the length of treatment or evaluation that underlies these "expert" assessments, provided at the request and expense of the accused. In at least one case, the forensic psychiatrist interviewed the physician for only four hours, before concluding that he was "unable to detect any evidence of improper ethical behaviour, impulsive behaviour or indication of mental illness associated with aberrant behaviour."[74] In *Im*, the expert was "unable to detect evidence of conscious sexual intent in [the doctor's] actions" and concluded that the "factors usually seen in recidivism are not present," that there are no "antisocial feelings, impulsive behaviour or psychopathic tendencies … no evidence of sexual deviancy or psychosis." He reached these conclusions despite Im's criminal conviction for five sexual assaults.

70 *Dobrowolski* (2001): guilty plea to some charges, evidence of corroboration.

71 *ETM* (1995); *Oosterholt* (1995); *Alfred* (1994): "No evidence of paraphilia, antisocial, narcissistic or impulsive disorder, major mental illness, alcohol or drug abuse or hostility to women. I would have expected some abnormality in testing [phalometric] if a sex offender."

72 *McRae* (1994).

73 *Irvine* (1996). But see *contra* GR Schoener *et al, Psychotherapists' Sexual Involvement with Clients: Intervention and Prevention* (Minneapolis: Walk-In Counselling Center, 1989) at 71: "disintegration in the relationship may occur at any time, even years later. Thus, one must be careful in making judgments of post-therapy relationships that appear harmonious."

74 *Fernandez* (1997).

Exculpatory psychiatric expertise is also offered to explain and excuse the physician's sexual abuse of his patient. In *Re: Markman*,[75] Markman relied on both his treating psychiatrist and an "independent" expert psychiatrist to claim that "the stresses of his job environment led to a chemical abnormality of the brain, resulting in 'toucherism.'"[76] Markman was the subject of six complaints of sexual abuse, all heard together. All of the complainants worked at the hospital in which he practised. Markman had been found guilty of criminal sexual assault with regard to four of the incidents. In the last of the six assaults, against an intern in the teaching program at the hospital, Markman threatened he would kill her if she told anyone. He warned her that, as a mere intern, she would not be believed if she complained about his attack.[77] The discipline committee found him guilty of sexual abuse.

This reliance on psychiatric expertise to exonerate the physician is misplaced. In "Psychological Evaluation in Sexual Offence Cases,"[78] WL Marshall critically reviewed the literature on the reliability of the various psychiatric tests used to identify male sexual deviance and concluded that "[t]here is no justification for using interview or test data as a basis for determining the likelihood that an accused male did or did not commit a sexual offence."[79] He argued that the various tests used in such evaluations, including phallometric testing, although identified as objective and therefore scientific or respectable, are not so. He outlined their limited ability to reliably distinguish between those accused individuals who are dissimulating and those who are truthful about their involvement in deviant sexual behaviour.[80] He concluded that neither personal interviews nor file reviews are accurate. In his view the "evidence clearly indicates little can be said which is helpful" about propen-

75 [1999] OCPSD No 6. See also *Beresford* (1994) where the sixty-eight-year-old doctor was allowed to continue practising where he identified a bipolar affective disorder as the cause of his sexual relationship with a psychiatric patient. His practice was restricted to male patients; *Bingham* (2003): committee took into consideration a psychiatric report on his physical and emotional health; *Seidman* (2003): medical issues — mood changes in high school, breakdown during fellowship and diagnosis with ADD.

76 *Ibid* at para 50.

77 See *R v Charalambous* (1997), 92 BCAC 1, 34 WCB (2d) 530 (BCCA). In *Charalambous*, the doctor arranged to have his former patient, Sian Simmonds, killed.

78 WL Marshall, "Psychological Evaluation in Sexual Offence Cases" (1995–96) 21 Queen's LJ 499 and see sources cited by Marshall.

79 *Ibid* at 500.

80 *Ibid* at 501, 505, 506.

sity to abuse[81] and that experts are more likely to "mislead than to help the court."[82]

Many discipline committee penalties impose a requirement of psychiatric therapy on the abusing physician as a condition of returning to practice.[83] The theory is that therapy will ensure that he does not return to abusing his patients.[84] Such conditions overlook that the expert who proposed the rehabilitative plan is employed by the abusing physician himself and is not an independent assessor.[85]

In fact, many abusers may be untreatable and therapy unable to ensure that the physician returns safely to practice.[86] The literature reveals that such reliance on therapy as able to ensure rehabilitation is misplaced. Schoener et al, in their leading text *Psychotherapists' Sexual Involvement with Clients: Intervention and Prevention*,[87] found the scholarly literature on therapist abuse both limited and lacking in methodology. They raised concerns both about the procedures for assessment of the physician and the lack of clear understanding of rehabilitation. They noted that in the US, a number of perpetrators are known to have reoffended.[88] They specified that in some such cases "far too much reli-

81 *Ibid* at 509.

82 *Ibid* at 514.

83 See eg *Beresford* (1994); *Bingham* (2003); *Irvine* (1996); *Nagahara* (1996); *Wesley* (2002); *Yong-Set* (1998); *Deitl* (1996); *Heath* (1995); *Johnson* (1995); *Oosterholt* (1995); *Turton* (1994); *Lazare* (1999); *Levy* (2003); *Wyatt* (2001).

84 See eg *Beresford* (1994); *Bingham* (2003); *Deitl* (1996); *Genereux* (1994); *Irvine* (1996); *Johnson* (1995); *Lazare* (1999); *Levy* (2003); *Nagahara* (1996); *Oosterholt* (1995); *Turon* (1994); *Wesley* (2002); *Wyatt* (2001); *Yong-Set* (1998).

85 In some cases these penalties are the joint submissions of the accused and the CPSO. Nonetheless, they are based on assessments arranged for by the accused.

86 Schoener: "many perpetrators may not be treatable, thus challenging the prevalent notion that a referral to long-term therapy will cure the problem and render the perpetrator a safe practitioner": *supra* note 73 at 399.

87 *Ibid*. See also Annette M Brodsky, "The Distressed Psychologist: Sexual Intimacies and Exploitation" in RR Kilburg, PE Nathan & RW Thoreson, eds, *Professionals in Distress: Syndromes and Solutions in Psychology* (Washington: American Psychological Association, 1986) 153; L Nielson *et al*, "Supervision Approaches in Cases of Boundary Violations and Sexual Victimization by Therapists" in Barbara E Snaderson, ed, *It's Never O.K.: A Handbook for Professionals on Sexual Exploitation by Counsellors and Therapists* (St Paul, MN: Minnesota Department of Corrections, 1989) 55; SM Plaut & BH Foster, "Roles of the Health Professional in Cases Involving Sexual Exploitation of Patients" in Ann W Burgess & Carol R Hartman, eds, *Sexual Exploitation of Patients by Health Professionals* (New York: Praeger, 1986) 15.

88 This is also the case in Canada, although it is impossible to be clear about the numbers who do so. In Ontario see eg *Genereux* (1994); *Deitl* (1996).

ance was placed on psychotherapy as a 'cure all' and on supervision of whatever sort as a safety net."[89]

They also noted many serious weaknesses in the imposition of supervisory structures on the doctor's practice as a condition of his returning to practice. In their view, meaningful supervision requires authority to review the physician's records, discuss cases, and have direct client contact. They noted the failure of supervisory models to prevent both continued sexual abuse and the incompetent health care that accompanies it. They pointed out that where supervisory orders are imposed, the person chosen to act as chaperone to the abusing doctor is most often a person who is in a subordinate relationship to the physician, such as a nurse or other assistant. As well, orders prohibiting the physician from seeing women patients ignore the possibility that the physician may engage in abusive behaviour with male patients and that sexually abusing seductive practices can occur in the treatment of couples. Supervisory orders of this kind are relatively common in discipline committee decisions, and all of these concerns are borne out by the reported cases.[90]

Even more prevalent than orders that require psychiatric treatment and/or supervision are those that require (re)education. Often all three conditions — therapy, third-party supervisory monitoring, and re-education — are imposed as part of the disciplinary penalty.[91] The

89 *Supra* note 73 at 419. They go so far as to say that licensing boards may be liable for the failure to obtain competent assessment and to develop sound rehabilitation plans. "It may be that the elimination of bogus rehabilitation efforts and the overly hasty granting of 'Rehabilitated' status ... will be facilitated by malpractice suits filed against those who are less than adequate, professional, careful, thorough, and knowledgeable in assessing and rehabilitation offending therapists." See also *McClelland v Stewart*, [2006] BCSC 1948, 154 ACWS (3d) 1048 (S Ct).

90 See eg *Deluco* (2004); *Deitl* (1996); *Genereux* (1994); *Im* (2003); *Johnson* (1995).

91 See *Wesley* (2002) (psychiatric treatment and chaperone); *Davis* (1993) (psychiatric treatment, chaperone, and course); *Dobrowolski* (2004) (psychiatric treatment, chaperone, and course); *Carll* (2002) (boundaries course); *Comeau* (2001) (therapy); *Bergstrom* (2000) (course); *Crainford* (1998) (therapy); *Irvine* (2006) (therapy and course); *Nagahara* (1996) (therapy and chaperone); *Deitl* (1996) (therapy and monitoring imposed on earlier offences when last offence occurred); *Johnson* (1995) (therapy and chaperone); *Oosterholt* (1995) (therapy and chaperone); *Longdon* (1995) (course); *Turton* (1994) (therapy); *Genereux* (1994) (chaperone); *Bingham* (2003) (course); *Bothwell* (2003) (course and chaperone); *Deluco* (2005) (chaperone); *Dore* (1999) (course); *Dube* (2001) (course); *Henderson* (2004) (course); *Hurst* (1998) (course); *Im* (2003) (course and chaperone); *Ives* (2002) (course); *Jabouin* (1995) (course); *Kavouris* (2004) (course); *Koffman* (2003) (therapy and course); *Lambert* (2002) (therapy and course); *Levy* (2003) (psychiatric treatment, chaperone, and course); *Lurie* (2004) (course); *Miller* (2001, 2004) (chaperone); *Noreiga* (2003)

discipline committee often understands the abuse as a failure of education or training and orders re-education as a condition of continuing to practice. Generally referred to as a requirement that the physician obtain training in "appropriate boundaries," this device is used to lift a significant part of any license suspension imposed.[92]

Schoener et al also question the usefulness of ethics courses as rehabilitative measures.[93] Kenneth Pope found that "neither education nor psychotherapy has shown any evidence in published research studies of inhibiting sexual abuse of patients, and according to some studies, they actually appear to be positively associated with tendencies to abuse."[94] Nor is there any evidence that abuse by physicians is the result of insufficient training in either ethics or boundaries. In a number of cases, the physician subsequently was disciplined for sexual abuse despite the imposition of some or all of therapy, monitoring, or re-education. The reliance on therapy or on ethical re-education to excuse or to "heal" the sexual abuser of his misconduct is misplaced. It ignores exactly that understanding of sexual abuse that the revisions to the *Act* were meant to address — that sexual abuse is abuse of power and constitutes violence against women and children.[95]

(course and chaperone); *Rosen* (2002) (course and chaperone); *Ross* (2004) (therapy and chaperone); *Sharma* (2003) (course and chaperone); *Shiozaki* (2004) (course); *Silva-Ruette* (2003) (course); *Wong* (2003) (course and chaperone); *Wyatt* (2001) (therapy and course).

92 For an idea of what is meant by boundary training see, for example, Jill Hefley, "Strategies for Preventing Sexual Abuse" (1993), online: Member's Dialogue 8; Laurel Dempsey & Janet Ecker, "Understanding the Dating Guidelines" (1994), online: Member's Dialogue 9 (1994); Federation of State Medical Boards of the United States, Ad Hoc Committee on Physician Impairment, "Report on Sexual Boundary Issues" (1996), online: <http://www.fsmb.org/pdf/1996_grpol_sexual_boundary_issues.pdf>. This is an extraordinarily prevalent order in imposed penalties.

93 Scheoner, *supra* note 73 at 415; *JL* (1995); *M* (1995).

94 Kenneth S Pope, "Therapist–Patient Sex as Sex Abuse: Six Scientific, Professional, and Practical Dilemmas in Addressing Victimization and Rehabilitation" (1990) 21 Professional Psychology Research & Practice 232; JL Bernard *et al*, "The Failure of Clinical Psychologists to Apply Understood Ethical Principles" (1987) 18 Professional Psychology Research & Practice 489.

95 See also Schroener, *supra* note 73 at 422: "If sexual exploitation of clients by therapists is to be taken seriously by mental health professions and the public, it is important to establish that certain kinds of exploitation are regarded seriously, and they warrant a serious response, regardless of the motives or psychological status of the perpetrating therapist. This is the same attitude that is taken toward other serious transgressions against society, such as rape and incest".

CONCLUSION

The College of Physicians and Surgeons of Ontario and the Province of Ontario both showed early and important leadership in seriously responding to sexual abuse of patients by doctors. This leadership was informed by an understanding of sexual abuse as an abuse of trust and of power, deserving of mandatory license revocation in the most serious cases. It is deeply disturbing that the momentum of this important initiative has been undermined in its implementation. Barriers to the continuing achievement of the zero tolerance objectives contained in the legislation exist at multiple locations in CPSO processes. Their combined impact effectively avoids the specific provisions of the *Act*.

These barriers occur at multiple locations. Physicians fail to meet their statutory obligation to report those health professionals who they know to be engaging in sexual misconduct. When mandatory reports are filed, the CPSO fails systematically to respond to those reports. Few reports from members of the public make it past the informal screening mechanisms and are seen by the complaints committee. When the complaint is forwarded to the complaints committee, few are forwarded from the complaints committee to the discipline committee.

The complaints that do make it to adjudication by the discipline committee generally are those where independent corroboration of the complainant's accusation is available, although there is no such requirement in the legislation. In those few discipline committee hearings that do go ahead despite the absence of corroboration, a guilty determination is unlikely. Furthermore, discipline committee panels often demonstrate unwillingness to apply the *Act* vigorously and appropriately, avoiding the provisions of the legislation, ignoring CPSO policies, and criminalizing the disciplinary process in ways that protect the accused doctor. Criminalization of the process occurs particularly by raising the burden of proof on the CPSO from a civil towards a criminal standard, paying undue attention to the impact of disciplinary proceedings on the doctor's reputation and economic situation, and ignoring their obligations to the public, to the profession, and to the injured complainant. Expert witnesses, acting on behalf of the accused doctor, are allowed to pathologize the complainant and to exculpate and rehabilitate the accused. Where penalties are imposed, discipline committee panels are much too eager to assume that the imposition of ethics or boundary training, of therapy, and of third-party supervision will provide the public with protection from re-abuse by the doctor, and to reduce already short license suspensions even further.

A renewed allegiance by the CPSO to their original commitment to zero tolerance of sexual misconduct is required. The CPSO must ensure that the letter and spirit of the legislative provisions are implemented by staff, by all committee members, and by all disciplinary panels. Vigorous training for staff and committee members will assist in ensuring that the provisions of the *Act* are not continuously undermined. It is hoped that the detailed documentation provided here of the many locations in which the provisions of the *Act* are being undermined will be of assistance to the CPSO in addressing these challenges. The CPSO must renew its commitment to respond forcefully to those doctors who so egregiously breech their obligation first to do no harm. The zero tolerance provisions of the 1993 *Act* were visionary. The leadership of the CPSO on issues of sexual misconduct was exemplary. A renewed commitment to the values and understandings represented in the 1993 amendments now is necessary.

20.
Judges and the Reasonable Steps Requirement: The Judicial Stance on Perpetration Against Unconscious Women

Elizabeth A Sheehy

In this section, Elizabeth A Sheehy's contribution focuses on one important feature of the 1992 feminist-inspired law reforms — the new "reasonable steps" requirement for the "mistaken belief in consent" defence. Her paper picks up on the themes of resistance to rape law reforms, evocation of rape mythologies, and the misuse of "expert" evidence. She reviews the legal interpretation of the revised "mistake of fact" defence, identifying judicial resistance to its implementation and the subtle re-emergence of rape myths in judges' willingness to accept "mistake" defences when the complainant is unconscious. Like Lucinda Vandervort in Part I, Elizabeth urges Crown prosecutors to exercise vigilance to ensure that sexual assault law is interpreted consistently with its aims. To do so, they must challenge "expert" evidence introduced by defence on the question of women's states of consciousness, remind judges of the "reasonable steps" requirement, expose rape myths embedded in defence arguments, and appeal decisions where judges mistakenly apply or fail to apply the requirement.

The prosecution of sexual assault cases where the complainant has no memory because she was unconscious at the time of the attack presents a paradox. On the one hand, these are cases which, to the lay person, might seem dead easy: of course this is criminal conduct — the woman assaulted could not possibly consent while unconscious! For activists who work with raped women, this is a familiar form of male sexual violence, as men have always preyed upon women who are drunk, drugged, or asleep.[1]

However, to police, lawyers, and judges, these cases seem extraordinarily complicated. When a woman is unconscious, she becomes a blank page on which a phallocentric script can be easily written. Did she secretly enjoy the sexual contact and is now lying to cover her shame?[2] How do we know that she did not consent before becoming

1 Tamara Gorin, "Rohypnol — How the Hype Tricks Women: A Rape Crisis Centre View," (2000) 20 Can Woman Stud 93 at 93–94.

2 See for example *R v JB* (2003), 60 WCB (2d) 132 (Sup Ct Just) at para 33 where the trial

unconscious and has no memory of that agreement?[3] Perhaps she imagined or dreamed the assault?[4] What if she ostensibly "agreed" by participating while unconscious?[5] Did she seduce the man by her bodily movements as she slept?[6]

Underneath such questions lurk judgments about fault and responsibility: Was the woman unconscious through her own drug or alcohol abuse? Did she make unwise decisions about whose company to keep or where to lay her head down to sleep? Perhaps she was the author of the "mistake," having erroneously believed that the man touching her was her husband or boyfriend?

In 1992, the provisions of the *Criminal Code* underwent substantive reform.[7] The *Criminal Code* now defines consent as "voluntary agreement," which suggests that the complainant must be capable of decision-making and have agreed to the sexual contact without threat or coercion.[8] Further, by virtue of common law developments, a man who proposes that a woman consented must now be able to specify how she communicated her consent, since acquiescence or passivity alone will not amount to consent.[9] And finally, a man who says that even if she did not actually agree, he *thought* she did, must be able to show, pursuant to *Criminal Code* s 273.2(b), that he took reasonable steps to ascertain the woman's consent in order to be exculpated for his "mistake."[10]

judge described the complainant's memory gap as "too convenient." Justice Bruce Glass acquitted the accused because he disbelieved the complainant's testimony that she blacked out and held a doubt about whether she had consented. The complainant was the girlfriend of the accused's best friend. After a night at a bar, the complainant's boyfriend had gone to bed but she and the accused had stayed up to watch television. She had overindulged in alcohol, and awoke in the morning with pain in her vagina and no memory of intercourse with anyone. She testified that she did not consent and was unconscious when intercourse was pursued by JB.

3 See the dissenting opinion of Madam Justice Conrad at paras 83–86 in *R v Ashlee*, [2006] ABCA 244, 391 AR 62 at para 27.

4 *R v TS*, [1999] OJ No 268 (Ct Just Gen Div); *R v Spence*, 2008 ONCJ 104, [2008] OJ No 987 (Ct Just Gen Div).

5 *R v Millar*, [2008] OJ No 2330 (Sup Ct Just).

6 *R v Osvath*, [1996] OAC 274.

7 *An Act to Amend the Criminal Code (sexual assault)*, SC 1992, c 38 [*Criminal Code*].

8 *Ibid* s 273.1(1).

9 *R v M (ML)*, [1994] 2 SCR 3.

10 *Criminal Code* s 2373.2(b): "It is not a defence to a charge under section 271, 272 or 273 that the accused believed that the complainant consented to the activity that forms the subject-matter of the charge, where:
(b) the accused did not take reasonable steps, in the circumstances known to the accused at the time, to ascertain that the complainant was consenting."

Seemingly, these reforms *should* make it easier to obtain a conviction in sexual assault cases where the complainant was unconscious. In an earlier publication in 2000,[11] I examined cases in which judges interpret s 273.2(b), focusing on a category of decisions where the prosecutions were failing: those cases where the woman was unconscious as a result of sleep, in/voluntary drug use, and/or alcohol, and the accused man was able to raise a doubt in the mind of the judge as to whether he mistakenly believed that the woman had consented. In this paper, I examine the case law on what reasonable steps are required of men who seek sexual contact with semi-conscious and unconscious women, to see what, if any, guidance the superior and appeal courts have provided to trial judges, prosecutors, and police.

Cases reported in the law reports represent only a fraction of the cases decided: it is chilling to contemplate the numbers of men, young and old, who sexually assault unconscious women. While we cannot know with certainty how many women are attacked in these circumstances, we do know that this is a far more prevalent form of male violence than any official statistics convey. Women raped while drunk, drugged, or asleep doubt themselves and doubt the criminal justice response: the vast majority of women do not report their rapes.[12] They are told by hospitals that it is too late to detect drugs that may have tainted their drinks; they know, if they drank too much or used drugs, that they will be blamed and disbelieved if they attempt to claim the terrain of "innocent victim." And if they are as brave as to report, they face formidable barriers to their cases being prosecuted at all, let alone successfully.[13]

A surprising number of cases involve men who are charged with having sexually assaulted several unconscious women in one night, conduct that suggests deliberate and opportunistic predation by men. These cases also reveal a cowardly practice: men who commit rape

11 Elizabeth Sheehy, "From Women's Duty to Resist to Men's Duty to Ask: How Far Have We Come?" (2000) Can Woman Stud 98 at 100–02.

12 Bonnie S Fisher *et al*, "Reporting Sexual Victimization to the Police and Others: Results From a National-Level Study of College Women" (2003) 30 Crim Just & Behav 6 at 10, 14–15. See also *R v Seaboyer*, [1991] 2 SCR 577 at para 145 per L'Heureux-Dubé J, dissenting: "Although all of the reasons for failing to report are significant and important, more relevant to the present inquiry are the numbers of victims who choose not to bring their victimization to the attention of the authorities due to their perception that the institutions, with which they would have to become involved, will view their victimization in a stereotypical and biased fashion."

13 In an overview of studies from Great Britain, Canada, and America, the unfounding rates ranged from 1%-43%: Teresa DuBois, "Police Investigation of Sexual Assault Complaints: How Far Have We Come Since *Jane Doe*?", Chapter 9 in this book.

against unconscious women engage in an attack without risk, without looking their victims in the eye, or giving them a chance to defend themselves. The notion that young men on university campuses or local bars distribute rape drugs to other men, plan together to supply alcohol to young women, or organize to isolate from her friends and assault a woman who falls asleep at a party, raises the spectre of rape as "sport,"[14] if you could call shooting fish in a barrel "sport."

These cases are particularly disturbing because even though we cannot know the race of the women, we can be sure that racialized women's rapes form a significant portion of the cases where prosecution is not even pursued or acquittals result. Canadian legal decisions often erase or fail to mention the race of the parties, submerging the role of racism in litigated conflicts.[15] In sexual assault cases, where the complainant's name and identifying information are concealed to guard her privacy, it is impossible to know the race of the women who have been raped.

We must assume, however, that many of these cases involve Aboriginal women, given the rate at which Aboriginal women experience sexual assault.[16] The early work by authors such as Teressa Nahanee[17] on

14 Karen M Kramer, "Rule By Myth: The Socio and Legal Dynamics Governing Alcohol-Related Acquaintance Rapes" (1994–1995) 47 Stan L Rev 115 at 122–23. See also Elizabeth Ehrnhardt Mustaine & Richard Tewksbury, "Sexual Assault of College Women: A Feminist Interpretation of a Routine Activities Analysis," (2002) 27 Crim Just Rev 89 at 97.

15 Constance Backhouse, "Racial Segregation in Canadian Legal History: Viola Desmond's challenge, Nova Scotia, 1946" (1994) 17 Dal LJ 299 at 349–50. See also *R v Desmond*, [1947] 4 DLR 81 (NS Sup Ct).

16 Factum of the Intervenors Aboriginal Women's Council, the Canadian Association of Sexual Assault Centres, Disabled Women's Network of Canada, and the Women's Legal Education and Action Fund in *R v O'Connor* at 6–7 cited in Jennifer Koshan, "Aboriginal Women, Justice, and the Charter: Bridging the Divide?" (1998) 32 UBC L Rev 23 at para 29. Amnesty International released a report highlighting the US Department of Justice Report which found that rates of sexual assault for Indigenous women were three times that of non-Indigenous women in the US. See *Stolen Sisters: A Human Rights Response to Discrimination and Violence Against Indigenous Women in Canada*, http://www.amnesty.ca/amnestynews/view.php?load=arcview&article=1896&c=Canada-Reports, p. 25 of the pdf. Kate Rexe, of the Native Women's Association of Canada [NWAC], stated that based on the work done by NWAC and studies done on rates of violent crime against Canadian Aboriginal women, parallels can be drawn between the sexual assault statistics for Aboriginal women in the US and for Aboriginal women in Canada even though a similar comprehensive study has not been undertaken by the Canadian government. Interview of Kate Rexe by Kate Greenberg (7 July 2009).

17 Teressa Nahanee, "Sexual Assault of Inuit Females: A Comment on 'Cultural Bias,'" in Julian V Roberts and Renate M Mohr, eds, *Confronting Sexual Assault: A Decade*

judicial sentencing practices regarding sexual assault against unconscious Inuit women suggests that police and prosecutors see sexual assaults against unconscious Aboriginal women as low in criminality. Recall, for example, the remarks made to the press by Judge Michel Bourassa in 1989 wherein he attempted to explain what he saw as the difference between sexual assault in the north, where "a woman is drunk and passed out and a man comes along and helps himself to a pair of hips" versus sexual assault in the south, where "a dainty co-ed is jumped from behind."[18] Although these words prompted an outcry and a judicial inquiry into Judge Bourassa's behaviour, he was vindicated by Madam Justice Conrad who, in a convoluted ruling, found that "Bourassa did not say that sexual assault is less violent in the North than in the South, but that rapes in southern Canada were frequently accompanied by more violence before the act of rape occurs."[19]

Jennifer Temkin and Barbara Krahé's 2008 book, *Sexual Assault and the Justice Gap: A Question of Attitude*, reports several studies that show that sexual assaults against racialized women are particularly difficult to prosecute.[20] One study suggests that when black women have been raped, their rapes are perceived as less serious than rape committed against white women;[21] another study indicates that acquaintance rape against black women is less recognizable as criminal by jurors than acquaintance rape against white women or stranger rape against either group of women.[22] A final study found that it is harder for subjects to assess perpetration by white men against black women as criminal than white male perpetration against white women or black male perpetration against either group of women.[23]

of Legal and Social Change (Toronto: University of Toronto Press, 1994) 192 at 197–99 [Roberts & Mohr].

18 Comments of Territorial Court Judge Michael Bourassa as quoted in L Sarkadi, "Sex Assaults in North are Often Less Violent, Judge Says, *The Edmonton Journal* (20 December 1989) A1 in Margo L Nightingale, "Judicial Attitudes and Differential Treatment: Native Women in Sexual Assault Cases," (1991) Ottawa L Rev 71 at 73.

19 *In the Matter of an Inquiry Pursuant to Section 13(2) of the Territorial Court Act, SNWT 1978 (2), c 16* and *In the Matter of an Inquiry into the Conduct of Judge RM Bourassa.*

20 Jennifer Temkin & Barbara Krahé, *Sexual Assault and the Justice Gap: A Question of Attitude* (Portland, OR: Hart Publishing, 2008).

21 LA Foley *et al*, "Date Rape: Effects of Race of Assailant and Victims and Gender of Subjects on Perceptions" (1995) 21 J of Black Psychol 6, cited *ibid* at 45.

22 CE Willis, "The Effect of Sex Role Stereotype, Victim and Defendant Race, and Prior Relationship on Rape Culpability Attribution" (1992) 26 Sex Roles 213, cited *ibid* at 46.

23 WH George & LJ Martinez, "Victim Blaming in Rape: Effects of Victim and Perpetra-

Other women whose victimization is rarely recognized by the criminal justice system include female partners and ex-partners — where, as Melanie Randall has described in a recent publication, men can exploit past sexual history and mistaken judicial beliefs about what reasonable steps are/not required if the woman is a wife, girlfriend, or former partner.[24] Women with disabilities are also vulnerable to having their rapes decriminalized because they may be unable to offer an account of the assault to challenge the accused's version.[25]

Similarly, where the woman is unconscious, a man's "mistake" argument can succeed if the woman cannot counter or deny a man's version of events. These men claim that women fall asleep in the middle of consensual sexual contact; or they protest that they were unaware that the women had passed out; or they ask us to believe that women "come on" to them while unconscious by rubbing their sleeping bodies against them, moaning, co-operating in allowing their clothing to be removed, and so on. These men may be complete and utter strangers to the women they assault; some of these men have been rejected by the women while awake; and others are friends of the women's boyfriends or husbands, for example, who have bided their time for the opportunity to assault their friend's female partner.

Men's stories can aspire to "reasonableness" not only because the women assaulted have been silenced by sleep, alcohol, drugs, or some combination, but also because these stories tap into phallocentric beliefs. Such beliefs condition our willingness to disregard women's accounts of rape and instead to accept that their bodies have betrayed them, and that honest men, bewildered by what Carol Smart calls the unknowability of women's sexual desires and consistent with male pornographic imagination, have been seduced by unconscious women.[26]

tor Race, Type of Rape, and Participant Racism" (2002) 26 Psychol Women Q 11, cited *ibid* at 46.

24 Melanie Randall, "Sexual Assault in Spousal Relationships, 'Continuous Consent,' and the Law: Honest but Mistaken Judicial Beliefs" (2008) 32 Man LJ 144 at paras 86, 101–02.

25 Isabel Grant & Janine Benedet, "Hearing the Sexual Assault Complaints of Women With Mental Disabilities: Evidentiary and Procedural Issues" (2007) 52 McGill LJ 515 at 524–28.

26 See Carol Smart, "Law's Truth/Women's Experiences," in Regina Graycar, ed, *Dissenting Opinions: Feminist Explorations in Law and Society* (Sydney: Allen & Unwin, 1990) 1 at 16–20. See also Carol Smart, *Feminism and the Power of Law* (London: Routledge, 1989), esp Chapter 2, "Rape: Law and the Disqualification of Women's Sexuality."

In this chapter, I situate the reformed law in its historical context and discuss its rhetorical significance as well as its proof obligations. I examine the jurisprudence of the Supreme Court of Canada, mapping the boundaries of men's criminal responsibility for their claimed "mistakes." I look at recent case law to identify the guidance provided by provincial appellate and superior courts to the lower courts.

I conclude that the "reasonable steps" reform is applied unevenly by Canadian courts and is also misinterpreted, to the detriment of the public interest and women's rights to equality and security of the person, protected by *Charter* ss 7 and 15. Although there are positive developments in some appellate decisions that set parameters around the availability of the reformed mistake defence, many other decisions ignore the larger policy and equality implications of the issues before them and have, through narrow, fact-based judgments, failed to articulate principles that would guide lower courts and educate the public. The result is that men in Canada today remain relatively free to assault unconscious women, because these "mistakes" are rarely condemned.

THE NEW "REASONABLE STEPS" REQUIREMENT

In 1992, Bill C-49[27] passed into law, marking the first time that Canadian rape law had been reformed in a truly democratic fashion, from the grassroots up, rather than from the politicians down.[28] The 1992 reforms aimed to address the overwhelmingly negative public response to the Supreme Court's decision in *R v Seaboyer*.[29] This case struck down s 276 of the *Code*, part of an earlier reform[30] aimed at preventing the cross-examination of women testifying in rape trials on their prior sexual experience. As a result of principled feminist coalition work that relied on the expertise of women who worked in crisis centres and shelters as well as Aboriginal and racialized women and women with disabilities, a wholesale reform of rape law was effected to respond to the damage to trial fairness and women's equality rights caused by the Supreme Court's decision.

A significant and radical feature of this reform is *Criminal Code* s 273.2(b), which modified the so-called "mistake of fact" defence avail-

27 *Supra* note 7.

28 Sheila McIntyre, "Redefining Reformism: The Consultations that Shaped Bill C-49," in Roberts & Mohr, *supra* note 17 at 293 at 294–95.

29 *Supra* note 12.

30 RSC, 1985, c C46, ss 276 and 277.

able to men accused of rape in Canada. Section 273.2(b) overturned the long-standing rule from 1980 in the *R v Pappajohn*[31] decision that allowed a man to be acquitted of rape if he can raise a doubt that he honestly, even if unreasonably, believed that the woman consented. It is perhaps not coincidental that the *Pappajohn* litigation arose at the same time as the women's liberation and anti-rape movement was gaining steam across Canada. In fact, this man's rape trial was followed by feminists and the Vancouver media on a daily basis. When one digs even an inch below the judicially cleansed version of the facts in this case, one finds so much evidence of George Pappajohn's moral culpability[32] for his vicious attack on his real estate agent that it is shocking to see the lengths our highest court went to use his case to pronounce a new defence for men accused of rape.

The *Pappajohn* rule took the "rapist" out of rape, so to speak. The prosecution may be able to prove that the woman did not in fact consent and therefore experienced rape, but if the man can raise a doubt that he was honestly — albeit unreasonably — mistaken as to her non-consent, then the crime was not perpetrated by a man who could be criminally condemned as a rapist. This rule functioned to release judges and jurors from the implications of their judgments in rape prosecutions. No longer required to decide between two versions of what happened, and relieved therefore from women's pressing claims to autonomy over their bodies and credibility in the public sphere, judges and juries could acquit based on the "mistaken belief in consent" defence, but without calling women liars.

Another function of the "honest mistake" defence was to sanitize and immunize from criminalization self-serving and misogynist beliefs used by men to claim their moral innocence. Lucinda Vandervort has shown how this defence of mistake of fact is really not about factual error at all.[33] These are not mistakes about what a woman said or did; these are not perceptual mistakes caused by bad vision, poor hearing, language barriers, or other conditions that impair communication. Rather, the defence involves interpretive conflict. The man claims

31 *R v Pappajohn*, [1980] 2 SCR 120 at paras 9, 20.

32 Andrea Maitland, "Accused at Rape Trial Admits Threatening to Kill Witness" *The Vancouver Sun* (17 August 1977) 1. Detailed how Pappajohn threatened to kill a Crown witness because "he only wanted her to tell the truth." See also Pappajohn's response to the Crown's question under cross-examination, which asked whether the complainant had resisted. Pappajohn replied, "not violently": *R v Pappajohn*, [1978] 5 CR (3d) 193 at 205 (BCCA).

33 Lucinda Vandervort, "Mistake of Law and Sexual Assault: Consent and Mens Rea" (1987–1988) 2 CJWL 238 at 295–300.

that her words or her bodily movement or her passivity or her sexual past meant *to him* that she consented, even if she did not. His "error," as pointed out by Lucinda Vandervort, is as to our legal norms — what predatory conduct can he get away with? The "mistake of fact" defence permitted pernicious beliefs to remain submerged under the cover of "honest mistake," and thereby operated as legal reinforcement for women's inequality by failing to condemn rape by "honest" men.

The upshot of *Pappajohn*, Anne Derrick and Elizabeth Shilton observe, is that "sexual assault is only sexual assault in the eyes of the law if the man who is doing it thinks it is."[34] If men individually, collectively, and honestly believe women "want it," regardless of what women say, or that "bad" women are outside the law's protection, then all women are endangered by this legal rule.

Canadian women were exposed to the frightening implications of the purely subjective test for "mistake" in cases like *R v Sansregret.*[35] There, a violent ex-partner was given a first "free" rape by virtue of the *Pappajohn* defence. The accused had twice broken into his former girlfriend's home and so terrorized her that she engaged in "make up sex" in order to save her own life by pretending to consent. She had reported the crime to his parole officer the first time he did it, who had in turn told Sansregret about her report. When he repeated his crime, he was charged for the second attack. The trial judge accepted that Sansregret unreasonably but honestly believed the complainant consented, based on the woman's own testimony. She acquitted him accordingly.

In overturning the acquittal and substituting a conviction, the Supreme Court held that Sansregret was morally culpable for the second rape on the narrow reasoning that he was on notice from his parole officer that the complainant considered the first attack to be rape:

> If the evidence before the Court was limited to the events of October 15 [the second rape], it would be difficult indeed to infer wilful blindness. To attribute criminal liability on the basis of this one incident would come close to applying a constructive test to the effect that he should have known she was consenting out of fear. The position, however, is changed when the evidence reveals the earlier episode and the complaint of rape which it caused, knowledge of which, as I have said, had clearly reached the accused.[36]

34 Anne S Derrick & Elizabeth Shilton, "Sex Equality? Equally and Sex Assault: In the Aftermath of *Seaboyer*" (1991) 11 Windsor YB Access Just 107 at 108, cited in Randall, *supra* note 24 at para 48.

35 *R v Sansregret*, [1985] 1 SCR 570.

36 *Ibid* at para 23.

Never mind that Sansregret broke into the woman's home, stripped her, tore the telephone out of the wall, and plunged a knife into the wall behind her head. Even a man who deployed this amount of violence was legally entitled to rely on "honest mistake," according to the Supreme Court, as long as he was not formally on notice that the woman's sexual acquiescence was not the product of his deliberate terrorizing behaviour.

R v Osolin[37] also showed Canadian women just how much male violence is immunized by the "honest mistake" doctrine. The accused in this case was convicted at trial for a violent rape. The undisputed facts included that he had torn the complainant out of the bed of another man, ripped off her underwear, driven her some distance away, tied her spread-eagled to a bed, had sexual intercourse with her, shaved her pubic area, and then dumped her, naked and hysterical, on a highway. Because she had made self-blaming statements to a therapist afterwards, Osolin was granted a new trial where he was to be permitted access to the complainant's counselling records to show an "air of reality" to his claimed mistaken belief in consent defence. As Annalise Acorn has persuasively argued, this case again shows intolerable judicial tolerance for high levels of violent coercion by men who propose that they were "mistaken" as to women's consent.[38]

Bill C-49's "reasonable steps" requirement was intended to criminalize sexual assaults committed by men who claim mistake without any effort to ascertain the woman's consent or whose belief in consent relies on self-serving misogynist beliefs. "Mistake" can only be advanced where the accused took "reasonable steps, in the circumstances known to the accused at the time, to ascertain consent."[39] The provision assesses the culpability of the accused by reference to subjective and objective standards. The accused is judged subjectively in that the steps required of him will be those emerging from "the circumstances known to the accused at the time." This aspect of the test emphasizes the accused's actual knowledge, as opposed to what he should have known. At the same time, he cannot use his own drunkenness or recklessness to excuse his

37 *R v Osolin*, [1993] 4 SCR 595.

38 Annalise Acorn, *The Defence of Mistake of Fact and the Proposed Recodification of the General Part of the Criminal Code: A Feminist Critique and Proposals for Reform* (Edmonton: Alberta Women's and Seniors' Secretariat, 1994) at 21–22.

39 *Criminal Code* s 273.2(b), *supra* note 10.

"mistake" in such circumstances.[40] The accused is also judged on the objective standard of the steps a reasonable person would have taken to ascertain consent.

The "reasonable steps" rider must be read in the larger context of the 1992 reforms, which have been interpreted by the Supreme Court of Canada. For example, the Supreme Court ruled in *R v M (ML)* that it is an error for a judge to rule that "a victim is required to offer some minimal word or gesture of objection and that lack of resistance must be equated with consent."[41] Thus in *R v Ewanchuk*,[42] it stated that a man's mistaken belief that a woman's silence, or passivity, or ambiguous conduct amounts to consent is an error of law, not one of fact, which is no defence in law.[43] *Ewanchuk* also stated that an accused must be able to identify by what words or actions the woman communicated her voluntary agreement:

> In order to cloak the accused's actions in moral innocence, the evidence must show that he believed that the complainant *communicated consent to engage in the sexual activity in question.* A belief by the accused that the complainant, in her own mind wanted him to touch her but did not express that desire, is not a defence. The accused's speculation as to what was going on in the complainant's mind provides no defence [emphasis in original].
>
> For the purposes of the *mens rea* analysis, the question is whether the accused believed that he had obtained consent. What matters is whether the accused believed that the complainant effectively said "yes" through her words and/or actions. [44]

R v Ewanchuk emphasized that the reformed law states clearly that no consent is obtained if a woman expresses by her words or conduct a lack of agreement.[45] Therefore a man must, if rejected, desist from further sexual contact unless and until the woman changes her mind. It constitutes a sexual assault to escalate sexual contact once a woman has expressed non-consent, and the accused cannot pursue more sex-

40 *Criminal Code* s 273.2(a): "It is not a defence ... where ... the accused's belief arose from the accused's ... self-induced intoxication."

41 *Supra* note 9.

42 *R v Ewanchuk*, [1999] 1 SCR 330 at para 51.

43 *Ibid.*

44 *Ibid* at paras 46, 47.

45 *Criminal Code* s 273.1(2)(d).

ual contact in an effort to secure "consent" without facing criminal consequences.[46]

The beauty of the reasonable steps requirement is that by changing the substance of the defence of "mistake," the law has placed an obligation on the accused to identify the steps he took to ascertain the woman's consent. In turn, judges must rule — and thereby take a public stance — on whether the accused has brought forward sufficient evidence to put the defence of "mistake" before the jury. More importantly, perhaps, given that most sexual assault charges are prosecuted as summary conviction offences before a judge alone without a jury,[47] judges across Canada are themselves required to rule, as a factual matter, on what steps they consider reasonable for men to take to ascertain women's consent.

Between the law's emphasis on the need to seek women's actual and active agreement and the "reasonable steps" requirement, it ought to be relatively easy to prosecute men who perpetrate against unconscious women. Yet much of the case law is disappointing. There is clear judicial avoidance of the interpretive task demanded by s 273.2(b). My review of the case law below includes decisions of the Supreme Court of Canada, the provincial courts of appeal, and the superior courts of criminal jurisdiction (the Court of Queen's Bench in the Prairies, or the Superior or Supreme Court of the other provinces), who serve both as trial courts for more serious offences and first level appeal courts for decisions of the lower courts across the country.

Virtually no guidance has been offered by the Supreme Court on s 273.2(b). In consequence, perhaps, Canadian courts have floundered in coming to grips with the reformed mistake of fact defence in cases involving unconscious complainants. As will be shown below, some courts and judges persist in ignoring the reasonable steps requirement or in misinterpreting it. Where lower court trial judges have relied upon the reasonable steps limitation to bar a mistake defence and convict an accused, many appellate courts have overturned these convictions, asserting that the judge failed to assess the evidence properly as to the complainant's non-consent before turning to the mistake defence.[48]

46 *Ewanchuk*, *supra* note 42 at para 52.

47 See Janice Du Mont, "Charging and Sentencing in Sexual Assault Cases: An Exploratory Examination" (2003) 15 CJWL 305 at 321; Julian V Roberts, "Sexual Assault in Canada: Recent Statistical Trends" (1995–96) 21 Queen's LJ 396 at 407–08.

48 For example, in *R v Butler* (1998), 107 OAC 306, the Court of Appeal for Ontario set aside a conviction of an accused who had sexual contact with his female friend, who had allowed him to stay at her apartment provided he sleep in another room. Gregg

This pattern of judicial resistance to a reformed rape law is neither new nor surprising. Prior reforms to Canada's rape law have also been undone by judicial interpretation, as painstakingly demonstrated by Justice L'Heureux-Dubé in her dissent in *R v Seaboyer*.[49] More recently,

Allen Butler entered the complainant's room while she slept: the evidence differed as to what took place before he proceeded to sexual contact. At trial the judge had ruled that the accused had failed to take sufficient steps to ascertain consent in these circumstances, but the accused successfully appealed because the judge had not first clearly ruled that the Crown had proven her non-consent beyond a reasonable doubt. In *R v Plesh* (1996), 74 BCAC 278, the accused arrived at his ex-girlfriend's home in the middle of the night, entered an unlocked door, and proceeded to have intercourse with her. The accused and complainant agreed they had spoken on the telephone that night, but he claimed a second call in which he asked if he could come over and was told "yes" by her. She testified there was no such second call, and testified that she awoke to find herself being penetrated by Gregory Wayne Plesh. The problem here, according to the appellate court, was that the judge prefaced her analysis by stating that both the accused and the complainant were credible. The court of appeal held that the judge here failed to explain how she concluded guilt beyond a reasonable doubt having earlier found the accused "credible." In *R v Baril* (1999), 182 Sask R 272 (QB), André Baril was twenty-three years old and the complainant was fifteen. He came to her babysitting job where they played a drinking game whereby the loser of the card game, manipulated by him, would drink glasses of beer. The complainant quickly became incapacitated and passed out. She awoke to find herself being kissed and responded by kissing the accused back. She passed out again and this time woke up with her pants down and the accused on top of her engaged in intercourse. The trial judge found that the accused knew the young woman was very drunk and might have passed out, and that she was substantially younger than he. Even if she responded somewhat to his kisses, the judge found the accused did not take reasonable steps to ascertain consent to intercourse. The accused succeeded on appeal because there were some minor inconsistencies in the complainant's testimony (ie she went from being "positive" she had passed out to "pretty sure") and the judge failed to analyze the whole of the evidence and to resolve the issues on a standard beyond a reasonable doubt.

49 In discussing judicial interpretation of the amended s 142 of the *Criminal Code*, RSC 1970 c C-34, Justice L'Heureux-Dubé wrote: "Though the motives of Parliament were commendable, judicial interpretation of the section thwarted any benefit that may have accrued to the complainant. In fact, the provision, as judicially interpreted, provided *less* protection to the complainant than that offered at common law, surely a surprising result considering the obvious mischief Parliament intended to cure in enacting it." She identified the impact of judicial interpretation on s 142 in *Forsythe v R*, [1980] 2 SCR 268, stating: "Not only was the complainant held to be compellable at the instance of the accused at the *in camera* hearing, but, contrary to the position at common law, this Court held that, due to the wording of s 142(1)(*b*), credibility was elevated to the status of a material issue. Thus, as regards questions about a complainant's sexual 'misconduct' with individuals other than the accused, the complainant could no longer refuse to answer these questions, and, further, the accused could lead evidence to contradict the complainant's testimony": *Seaboyer*, *supra* note 12 at paras 183–90.

an impressive study by Jennifer Temkin and Barbara Krahé documents a similar pattern in the UK after several decades of rape law reform by the legislature. Temkin and Krahé report a manifest failure of law reform, buttressed by comments from judges who frankly acknowledge that they disagree with reforms aimed at protecting women from discriminatory practices, such as those limiting the cross-examination of women on their sexual history or the disclosure of their personal records. The judges simply refuse to apply these laws.[50] And it is not just judges who resist rape law reform: even prosecutors fail to invoke reformed rules of evidence and express fundamental disagreement with the laws.[51]

I have organized my discussion of the Canadian decisions using the questions that the courts have been called upon to decide in sexual assault cases involving the mistaken belief defence as it applies to unconscious complainants. Many of these questions overlap and are logically dependent on each other. I nonetheless separate them in order to attempt clarity in this murky area of law. First, do our courts recognize that indeed the law has changed such that purely "honest mistakes" as to consent without more are no longer exculpatory? Second, does the accused have to present an evidentiary foundation to show his reasonable steps before he can ask a judge or jury to rule on his claimed "mistake"? Third, are trial judges legally obligated to address themselves to the "reasonable steps" requirement as part of providing reasons for judgment? Fourth, can the Crown prove that a complainant was incapable of consent when the woman has no memory of the sexual assault? Fifth, can an accused engage in assaultive behaviour as part of meeting his "reasonable steps" obligation when a complainant is unconscious? And sixth, what steps are required of an accused when a woman is semi-conscious or unconscious — must he wake her up?

HAS THE MISTAKEN BELIEF IN CONSENT DEFENCE BEEN SUBSTANTIVELY ALTERED BY S 273.2(B)?

The Supreme Court of Canada was urged by Crown counsel to apply the new reasonable steps requirement in *R v Esau* in 1997 and in *R v Ewanchuk* in 1999. Yet only once, in *R v Daigle*,[52] discussed below, has

50 Temkin & Krahé, "Rape, Rape Trials and the Justice Gap: Some Views from the Bench and Bar," *supra* note 20 at Chapter 6, and "Judges, Barristers and the Evidential Law in Action in Rape Cases", *supra* note 20 at Chapter 7.

51 *Ibid.*

52 *R v Daigle*, [1998] 1 SCR 1220.

our highest court ventured, albeit briefly, into the terrain on a substantive basis to refer to the "reasonable steps" requirement. In *R v Esau*, also discussed in detail in a later section, the majority decision authored by Major J simply ignored the reform. In *R v Ewanchuk*, Major J overtly refused to apply the reasonable steps requirement, stating that it was not a live issue in the case.[53]

But *Esau* and *Ewanchuk* were not merely lost opportunities for the Supreme Court to interpret s 273.2(b). In both decisions the male justices of the Supreme Court continued to describe the "mistake" defence as if nothing had happened in terms of legislative change. In *Esau* Major J stated: "The defence of honest but mistaken belief is mandated by both common law and statute."[54] Nowhere in his judgment is there any recognition that the 1992 reform changed the law. In *Ewanchuk*, Major J repeated his mistake by describing the defence as one of "honest mistake," again ignoring the significant reform represented by s 273.2(b). He stated: "we are concerned only with the facial plausibility of the defence of honest but mistaken belief...."[55]

In contrast, the women justices of the Supreme Court preferred to decide both cases on the basis of the law as it had been enacted by Parliament. In *Esau*, Justice McLachlin found that the "reasonable steps" requirement barred a potential "mistake" claim by the accused. In *Ewanchuk* L'Heureux-Dubé J again reminded the male majority that the law had changed such that the defence of mistake of fact is no longer to be tested on a purely subjective basis when the charge is sexual assault:

> Major J ... relies on this Court's decision in *Pappajohn v The Queen* to describe the nature of the defence of honest but mistaken belief. In *Pappajohn*, the majority held that this defence does not need to be based on reasonable grounds as long as it is honestly held. That approach has been modified by the enactment of s 273.2(b) which introduced the "reasonable steps" requirement. Therefore, that decision no longer states the law on the question of honest but mistaken belief in consent.[56]

53 *Ibid* at para 60: "In view of the way the trial and appeal were argued, s 273.2(*b*) did not have to be considered."

54 *Ibid* at para 21.

55 *Ibid* at para 57.

56 *Ibid* at para 100.

Equivocation on the substance of the mistaken belief defence post-reform is, not surprisingly, evident in other appellate court decisions. For example, the Ontario Court of Appeal in *R v Conn*[57] rendered an almost incomprehensible decision on the reasonable steps requirement in 1996. The trial judge had instructed the jury on consent and on the defence of mistaken belief in consent. The accused argued on appeal that the instructions conveyed "the impression that the defence of honest but mistaken belief would only be available if the jurors were otherwise satisfied that the appellant had taken reasonable steps to ascertain consent."[58]

The Court of Appeal upheld the conviction, but its reasoning left much to be desired. Instead of stating clearly that the alleged error in instructing the jury actually represents the law, the Court of Appeal said that the judge had properly instructed the jury that the accused's belief need not itself be reasonable, which is accurate and clear. Unfortunately, it went on to say that it was "open" to the jury to consider whether the accused took reasonable steps in deciding whether his belief was honestly and genuinely held. This interpretation is misleading and legally incorrect. The reasonable steps requirement is not optional, and failure to take such steps bars the defence regardless of the honesty of the claimed belief.

In 1998, in *R v Darrach*,[59] the Ontario Court of Appeal was clearer on the fact that the defence has been reformed. In this case it was called upon to adjudicate the constitutionality of several aspects of the 1992 reforms, including the new objective test and the evidentiary burden on the accused in s 273.2(b). The accused argued that by importing an objective rider into the defence of mistake of fact, the section unfairly impinged upon his constitutional rights to be judged by a purely subjective standard because the crime of sexual assault is highly stigmatized and its penalties severe.

The Ontario Court of Appeal rejected this argument, holding that sexual assault is not one of those crimes requiring proof of a pure, subjectively assessed state of mind on the part of the accused. In any event, the court said, the test for the mistaken belief defence remains mainly subjective. Section 273.2(b) assesses the reasonableness of the steps taken by reference to "the circumstances known to the accused at the time." It requires only that an accused take some reasonable steps, not

57 *R v Conn*, [1996] OJ No 58 (CA).

58 *Ibid* at para 1.

59 *R v Darrach* (1998), 38 OR (3d) 1 (CA).

all reasonable steps. And, in the end, the accused's belief is ultimately judged on a subjective standard. In other words, an accused may take reasonable steps but still arrive at an unreasonable belief in consent, which would exculpate him with respect to a subsequent sexual assault charge.[60]

The court also rejected Darrach's argument that the provision placed an obligation on him to testify in his own defence if he wishes to argue "mistake:"

> There is no testimonial compulsion ... It may be that this provision ... will ... have the effect of placing a tactical or evidential burden on an accused person to adduce some evidence capable of raising a reasonable doubt. This does not involve any constitutional infringement.[61]

This case was appealed to the Supreme Court of Canada by the accused, but not on this issue. *Darrach* therefore stands as the highest authority we have regarding the fit between the objective and subjective branches of the reformed mistaken belief in consent defence.

MUST THE ACCUSED FIRST SHOW AN AIR OF REALITY THAT HE TOOK REASONABLE STEPS BEFORE A MISTAKE DEFENCE CAN BE CONSIDERED?

Before any defence is considered by the trier of fact, whether a judge sitting alone or a jury, a judge must first make a determination as a matter of law whether the accused has presented sufficient evidence to give the defence an "air of reality." This rule is intended to keep the trier of fact focused on the real issues of a case and prevent them from straying to consider fanciful claims. In sexual assault cases, this rule is particularly important because triers of fact are highly prone to judging these cases based on myths and stereotypes about women who report rape rather than on the law or the proven facts.[62]

For the mistaken belief defence, the "air of reality" test has meant that there must be some evidence, whether in the testimony of the accused or other evidence about how the complainant communicated consent, to support the accused's claim that he honestly but mistakenly believed she voluntarily agreed to the sexual contact. Now that the

60 *Ibid* at paras 88, 89, 90.

61 *Ibid* at para 94.

62 Temkin & Krahé, *supra* note 20 at Chapter 3, "The Problem of the Jury in Sexual Assault Trials."

defence has been altered such that it is barred unless the accused took reasonable steps, the question has become whether the judge's evaluation of the "air of reality" test must include consideration of whether there is any evidence that the accused took reasonable steps to ascertain consent.

Unfortunately, the Supreme Court has not developed a jurisprudence that filters out myths and stereotypes that are detrimental to women. *R v Esau*,[63] decided in 1997, offered the Supreme Court of Canada the opportunity to interpret the reasonable steps requirement for the first time since its enactment. It was also the first time that the Court was called upon to address how the law governing sexual assault and mistaken belief in consent should be applied when the complainant has no memory of the assault. Significantly, with the exception of dissenting judgments written by the two women justices McLachlin and L'Heureux-Dubé, JJ, the Supreme Court missed the mark in terms of addressing these two opportunities.

Able Joshua Esau was convicted at trial by a jury in the Supreme Court of the Northwest Territories when the jury rejected his story (beyond a reasonable doubt) that the complainant was an active and consenting participant in sexual intercourse. She testified that she would never have agreed to sex with her second cousin, but she had no memory of what had occurred at the party she held at her own home after a certain point in the evening. She woke up with a chipped tooth and soreness indicating intercourse had occurred. Esau denied sexual contact to police, but when the DNA came back implicating him, he changed his story and claimed consent in his criminal trial. On appeal to the Northwest Territories Court of Appeal,[64] counsel for Esau argued that the trial judge erred in failing to charge the jury on the defence of mistaken belief in consent, in spite of the fact that counsel at trial had not advanced this defence. The appeal court agreed and ordered a new trial.

At the Supreme Court, the Crown argued that the accused would have been barred from this defence at trial in any event because he did not take reasonable steps to ascertain consent. Yet the majority of the Supreme Court of Canada said that the trial judge was obliged to put "honest mistake" to the jury because there was an air of reality to the defence:

63 *R v Esau*, [1997] 2 SCR 777.

64 *R v Esau*, [1996] NWTR 242 (CA) at para 13.

> The defence of honest but mistaken belief is mandated by both common law and statute. My colleague, Justice McLachlin, in her reasons in this case, narrows the defence to where it practically ceases to exist. The trial judge's role in evaluating the legal standard of "air of reality" as a question of law is a limited one. The strictures placed on the defence by my colleague would expand the role of the trial judge and deny the jury the ability to apply its wisdom to issues that arise in these cases by removing nearly all questions of fact from them.[65]

In the later *Ewanchuk* decision, Major J stated that if the judge finds an air of reality to the claim that the accused was honestly mistaken as to consent, then it would be up to the jury to determine whether he took reasonable steps as a question of fact: "Whether the accused took reasonable steps is a question of fact to be determined by the trier of fact only after the air of reality test has been met."[66] He stated that judges "should avoid the risk of turning the air of reality test into a substantive evaluation of the merits of the defence."[67]

Justice L'Heureux-Dubé took issue with this aspect of the majority decision. She said that, logically, mistaken belief as a defence should not be put before the jury in rape cases unless there is an air of reality not just to "honest belief," but also to the accused having taken "reasonable steps to ascertain consent."[68] If the substance of the defence itself has changed, then surely the legal question for the judge charged with determining whether the defence is available must be whether there is an air of reality that the accused took reasonable steps and yet was honestly mistaken as to consent.

L'Heureux-Dubé J went on to demonstrate why the defence of mistake had no air of reality on Ewanchuk's facts by reference to the law in s 273.2(b). Her effort in this regard is crucial for lower court judges seeking examples of the application of the new law:

> In this case, the accused proceeded from massaging to sexual contact without making any inquiry as to whether the complainant consented. Obviously, interpreting the fact that the complainant did not refuse the massage to mean that the accused could further his sexual intentions is not a reasonable step. The accused cannot rely on the complainant's silence or ambigu-

65 *Ibid* at para 21.

66 *Ewanchuk*, *supra* note 42 at para 60.

67 *Ibid* at para 57.

68 *Ibid* at para 100.

> ous conduct to initiate sexual contact. Moreover, where a complainant expresses non-consent, the accused has a corresponding escalating obligation to take additional steps to ascertain consent. Here, despite the complainant's repeated verbal objections, the accused did not take any step to ascertain consent, let alone reasonable ones. Instead, he increased the level of his sexual activity. Therefore, pursuant to s 273.2(*b*) Ewanchuk was barred from relying on a belief in consent.[69]

In decisions released in 2003 and 2007 respectively, the Ontario Court of Appeal and the Saskatchewan Court of Appeal have treated Major J's discussion of the evidentiary burden in *Ewanchuk* as *obiter dicta* and instead adopted the position of Justice L'Heureux-Dubé. According to these judgments, before the judge or jury should even consider the "mistake" defence, there must be an air of reality that the accused took reasonable steps to ascertain consent. In *R v Cornejo*[70] the appeal court unanimously held that the trial judge was wrong to leave the defence with the jury because there was no evidence of reasonable steps. In *R v Despins*[71] the same conclusion was reached unanimously by the three justices deciding the case. These rulings are important because they keep alleged "honest mistakes" away from the jury or judge unless there is some evidence to support the accused having taken reasonable steps. This filter should prevent the trier of fact being misled by rape myths and sex stereotypes about men's "mistakes" and instead focus their minds on the facts of what the accused did or did not do to ascertain consent. Further, because the evidentiary burden is a question of law, the position taken in *Cornejo* and *Despins* facilitates appeals and the development of legal principles in an area where discriminatory beliefs have masqueraded as "facts" for far too long.

Not all courts are following this approach. For example, in *R v Aitken*,[72] the reviewing court overturned the conviction in part because the trial judge had first found that the accused had not taken reasonable steps to ascertain consent and then concluded there was therefore no air of reality to the defence, contrary to the majority's suggested approach in *Ewanchuk*. The appeal court believed that this error resulted in the judge unfairly rejecting the mistake argument without carefully reviewing the accused's evidence in detail. The court did not order a

69 *Ibid* at para 99.

70 *R v Cornejo* (2003), 68 OR (3d) 117 (CA) at paras 2–3, 19.

71 *R v Despins*, 2007 SKCA 119, 299 Sask R 249 at paras 12, 47.

72 *R v Aitken*, 2007 BCSC 1975, BCJ No 2973 (Sup Ct).

new trial, leaving this accused without even the risk of criminal sanction for his actions.

MUST THE TRIAL JUDGE AVERT TO THE REASONABLE STEPS REQUIREMENT?

Are judges required to refer to the new requirement in s 273.2(b) when they adjudicate sexual assault cases that involve claimed "mistakes"? If not, then the reform can become a dead letter, readily ignored by police, lawyers, and judges. On the other hand, if it must be addressed, then not only will some mistake defences be barred, but the law will become more transparent as judges explicitly rule on what reasonable steps are required in given circumstances.

At the level of the Supreme Court, only the women justices have recognized the importance of requiring that judges address the new law in clear terms. In *R v Esau*, as already noted, Major J for the Supreme Court of Canada[73] said that the trial judge was obliged to put "honest mistake" to the jury because there was an air of reality to the defence where the accused testified as to consent, where the complainant had no memory of the assault and was unable to provide a counter-narrative, and where there was no evidence of force or violence.[74] He made no mention whatsoever of the new law.

Justice McLachlin dissented on the question of whether the reasonable steps requirement could be ignored by the court:

> Major J [for the majority] does not consider s 273.2. This may be because it was not argued on the appeal or in the proceedings below. With respect, I do not believe that the force of s 273.2 may be avoided on that ground. Parliament has spoken. It has set out minimum conditions for the defence of mistaken belief in consent. If those conditions are not met, the defence does not lie.[75]

Her insistence that the new *Code* provision be addressed is particularly important because some judges have taken the position that whenever an accused claims "consent," he is implicitly also raising the alternative defence of "mistaken belief in consent."[76] If this is indeed the case, then

73 *Esau*, *supra* note 64 at paras 15, 29.

74 *Ibid*.

75 *Ibid* at para 50.

76 *R v Bulmer*, [1987] 1 SCR 782 at para 24, per Lamer J: "I should, in passing, add that in my view the issue of mistaken belief in consent should also be submitted to the jury in all

judges must avert to the reasonable steps limit in every decision to ensure that any appeal court reviewing the record has the benefit of factual findings on all the issues that arise.

The majority opinion in *R v Ewanchuk* refrained from analyzing the reasonable steps requirements because it was not argued on appeal and there were no facts in evidence to support the defence of mistake.[77] Yet a court still ought to address the issue to resolve the case appropriately and to guide lower courts. As Justice L'Heureux-Dubé put it:

> [S] 273.2(b) precludes the accused from raising the defence of belief in consent if he did not take "reasonable steps" in the circumstances known to him at the time to ascertain that the complainant was consenting. This provision and the defence of honest but mistaken belief were before the trial judge and it should have been given full effect. The trial judge erred in law by not applying s 273.2(b) which was the law of the land at the time of the trial, irrespective of whether the case proceeded on that basis.... I agree entirely with Fraser CJ that, unless and until an accused first takes reasonable steps to assure that there is consent, the defence of honest but mistaken belief does not arise.[78]

In spite of the Supreme Court's rulings in *Esau* and *Ewanchuk* that seem to suggest that s 273.2(b) can be ignored, several courts have held that trial judges must avert to the reasonable steps requirement in adjudicating mistake of fact defences. *R v Malcolm*,[79] decided by the Manitoba Court of Appeal in 2000, was an appeal against acquittal where the Crown argued that the judge erred in giving the accused the benefit of the mistake of fact defence. Here Randy Malcolm returned to the complainant's home after a New Year's Eve party, when the complainant had gone to bed and her husband had left the house. Malcolm's claim was that she had kissed him and made a suggestive remark earlier

cases where the accused testifies at trial that the complainant consented. The accused's testimony that the complainant consented must be taken to mean that he believed that the complainant consented. As a result, if the jury believes the complainant and concludes that the complainant did not consent, that does not end the matter, for the accused's assertion cannot be disposed of completely unless consideration is then given to his or her being honestly mistaken in believing that the complainant consented."

77 *Ibid* at para 60: "Whether the accused took reasonable steps is a question of fact to be determined by the trier of fact only after the air of reality test has been met. In view of the way the trial and appeal were argued, s 273.2(*b*) did not have to be considered."

78 *Ibid* at paras 98, 99.

79 *R v Malcolm*, 2000 MBCA 77, 148 ManR (2d) 143 (CA).

at the party. When he returned to her home and entered her bedroom some time later, his story was that she grabbed his arm, pulled him to her bed, and fondled him. It was only later — inexplicably according to him — that she jumped up and ordered him out of the house.

The complainant denied that she had made a suggestive remark earlier at the party. She testified that she awoke to find herself "being humped." She thought it was her husband and said, "I love you Moise," before realizing that it was her husband's friend Malcolm who was penetrating her. The trial judge's decision to acquit the accused made no reference to the legal requirement that the accused take reasonable steps to ascertain consent and made no factual findings that would have allowed the appeal court to address this legal requirement imposed by Parliament. The appeal court criticized this failure:

> Parliament introduced s 273.2(b) to address those situations which may well be few in number but which may arise when the accused's conduct does not amount to recklessness or wilful blindness as to consent, but when the circumstances preceding the sexual activity cry out for the accused to take positive steps to assure himself that the complainant is knowingly consenting to that activity. The case at bar is surely such a circumstance. After a night of partying and drinking, without any invitation to do so, the accused entered the complainant's bedroom while she was sleeping, knowing that she was married to a close friend. He did not engage in any conversation with her. He states that by her conduct, he believed she wanted to have sexual intercourse with him. Surely in such a situation, the court must be satisfied that the accused took reasonable steps to ascertain that the complainant was consenting to that sexual activity.[80]

The unanimous decision of the appeal court found that it constitutes an error of law for a judge to fail to turn his or her mind to s 273.2(b) where the facts demand that the accused take reasonable steps to ascertain consent. The defence had argued that the trial judge is presumed to know the law, had referred to other parts of s 273.2, and thus must have rendered judgment consistent with the reasonable steps requirement. The appeal court rejected this submission and instead generated a principle with respect to s 273.2(b):

> Where a case depends not upon a review of the evidence … but rather upon the application of a fairly new or infrequently applied principle of law, one

80 *Ibid* at para 36.

> that is not firmly established and one which has not been subject to close analysis or comment, then it is my view that a trial judge's failure to refer to that principle may very well give rise to appellate intervention.[81]

Randy Malcolm was therefore ordered back for a new trial.

For similar reasons, the New Brunswick Court of Appeal in *R v DIA*[82] granted the Crown's appeal against acquittal and ordered a new trial for a man who was charged with sexually assaulting his wife. The accused had testified that he and his wife regularly had sexual intercourse two and three times a day. Since they had only had intercourse twice that day, he claimed to have believed his wife wanted to engage in this activity a third time, even though she was sound asleep. He stated that he stopped his sexual pursuit of his wife when she woke up and said no. In contrast, she testified that she awoke in bed with her newborn baby to find the accused on top of her attempting to penetrate her vagina. She repeatedly said no, but then he attempted to penetrate her anus with his penis. The accused only stopped when her screaming woke the baby, who also began to scream and cry.

The trial judge had acquitted on the first charge on the basis that the accused had an honest belief in consent based on reasonable steps, but did not specify what those steps were; with respect to the second charge, he simply said he found the accused not guilty. The appeal court was unable to review the decision because the judge had not made findings of credibility with respect to the contradictory evidence. The appeal court repudiated the reasoning of the judge below to the extent that he may have relied on some notion of "implied consent," which was rejected by the Supreme Court in *Ewanchuk*. Further, the appeal court stated: "the trial judge's failure to give adequate reasons as to why the defence should apply leaves this court in a quandary as to whether he understood the defence of mistaken belief as explained in *Ewanchuk*."[83] A new trial on both counts was therefore ordered because the court was unable to determine whether the accused should have been found guilty but for the judge's error of law.

The Ontario Court of Appeal has not yet ruled that a trial judge commits legal error by failing to evoke s 273.2(b), but has overturned acquittals where judges have overtly failed to account for circumstances

81 *Ibid* at para 34.

82 *R v DIA* (1999), 215 NBR (2d) 330 (CA).

83 *Ibid* at para 15.

that cry out for "reasonable steps." *R v Girouard*[84] involved a Crown appeal against acquittal where the judge at trial had a doubt as to whether the accused held a mistaken belief regarding consent in light of "the previous night's 'consensual' sexual activity" and "the complainant's failure to express her lack of consent more forcefully, either by words or gestures."[85] The reviewing court ordered a new trial because the judge had failed to consider the effect of the accused's admission that the complainant had asked in the morning, before further sexual contact occurred, whether they had had sex the night before and he had answered her, "Yeah, a couple of times." According to the court, this interchange indicated equivocal conduct from the complainant at best, suggesting that the accused had failed to take appropriate steps to ascertain consent.

In *R v DWH*[86] the Ontario Court of Appeal held that it is a question of law permitting appellate intervention whether that judge has taken into account the relevant circumstances known to the accused that bear on the reasonable steps needed to ascertain consent. The accused was convicted at trial of sexually assaulting his wife by inserting a dildo into her vagina while she was heavily medicated with sleeping drugs after an operation. The court refused to rule that a judge must marshal and review all of the evidence in this regard, but specifically rejected the argument that the judge should have considered the prior sexual activity between the accused and the complainant because "the circumstances had changed significantly": "the complainant had undergone serious surgery and was in considerable pain."[87] Importantly, the court of appeal also held that the complainant's credibility was not significant to the "crucial" issue of whether the accused took reasonable steps to ascertain consent. The appeal against conviction was therefore dismissed.

Finally, *R v Miyok*,[88] a decision of the Nunavut Court of Appeal, also supports the idea that judges must avert to s 273.2(b) in their judgments. Unfortunately, it is a weaker decision because the reviewing court did not require the judge to rule specifically on whether the accused took reasonable steps. The Crown appealed an acquittal by a judge sitting alone on the basis that the judge found an air of reality to the accused's "mistake" defence, but did not explicitly address which

84 *R v Girouard* (2003), 18 CR (6th) 135 (Ont CA).

85 *Ibid* at para 1.

86 *R v DWH* (2006), 208 OAC 109 (CA).

87 *Ibid* at para 6.

88 *R v Miyok*, [2004] Nu J No 6 (CA).

reasonable steps he had taken to ascertain consent. The accused, Jimmy Miyok, was the complainant's income support worker. During an appointment with the complainant in his office, he suggested that he would come to her home for a sexual liaison. He acknowledged that she seemed "scared and nervous," but since she did not unequivocally reject his proposition, he showed up at her home the next day, entered her home when she opened the door, and proceeded to kiss and touch her breast. At trial, the prosecutor had argued that the power imbalance between the accused and the complainant required that he take further steps or make further inquiries before showing up on her doorstep. In rebuttal, the defence suggested that the complainant had returned the kiss, making further steps unnecessary.

On appeal, the court ruled that because of the submissions of Crown counsel before the trial judge and the fact that the judge quoted from a portion of *Ewanchuk* where the Supreme Court referred to "reasonable steps" as a question of fact, it could be inferred that the judge had turned his mind to this requirement. The court concluded that he must nonetheless have had a reasonable doubt about whether the accused mistakenly believed the complainant consented. The Crown appeal was dismissed.

CAN THE CROWN PROVE THAT THE COMPLAINANT WAS INCAPABLE OF CONSENT?

Although it is undisputed law that an unconscious woman is incapable of consent, it is difficult for the Crown to prove that a complainant was incapable of consent beyond a reasonable doubt. This is because, as Janine Benedet demonstrates in her work,[89] the standard for incapacity is very high — the complainant must be virtually unconscious to be deemed "incapable of consent." It is not necessarily enough for a woman to testify that she was unconscious, that she experienced blackout, or that she has a memory gap. In these circumstances, a court may find that the complainant is truthful, such that her incapacity is established beyond a reasonable doubt. It is also open to a judge or jury to have a reasonable doubt as to whether she is honest with respect to her incapacity,[90] or indeed mistaken.

Worse, however, is that most judges are prepared to accept a third possibility, which is that the complainant was arguably incapacitated such that she has no memory, but yet she may have been sufficiently

89 Janine Benedet, "The Sexual Assault of Intoxicated Women" (2010) 22 CJWL 435.

90 See *JB*, *supra* note 2.

capable to have validly "consented." In fact, defence lawyers have found experts willing to testify as to the plausibility of this scenario. In *R v Dumais*,[91] the defence presented only one witness. The complainant's evidence was that she had five drinks, then went to sleep, only to be awakened by the accused penetrating her. Dr John Steven Richardson testified in support of two possible defence theories. One was that that the complainant was capable and did consent. The other defence theory was that the accused was honestly mistaken as to consent. The expert testified that:

> [A] person can reach a state where he or she is too drunk to remember exactly what happened, but not too drunk to participate in an activity such as sexual intercourse. He stated that the brain often "rationalizes" these events and may come to a wrong conclusion as to issues like whether or not the activity was consensual … This witness speculated that it is possible that a person would have consumed enough alcohol to feel tired but not yet being at a state where brain cells would be shutting down and amnesia would be produced.…
>
> On cross-examination, this witness confirmed that it is possible to be in an intoxicated state and appear to be giving consent without knowing it.[92]

The trial judge's finding that the complainant lacked the capacity to consent evinced the judge's rejection of this hypothesis; the conviction was upheld on appeal.

Justice McLachlin, in her dissenting opinion in *Esau*, refuted the plausibility of the scenario whereby the complainant had sufficient capacity to "consent" but insufficient capacity to have any memory whatsoever of the event. She argued that the issue remains a credibility contest between the accused and the complainant, and does not admit of some third, "mistaken belief" explanation. Either the complainant, who says she would never have consented and was unconscious when assaulted, will be believed, or the accused, who claims active and conscious agreement by the complainant, will be believed. She flatly refused to accept a third scenario, in which the complainant, though unconscious, appeared to be acting consciously and voluntarily:

> Drunkenness cannot constitute evidence of a situation in which the complainant might appear to be consenting when in fact she was not. If this

91 *R v Dumais*, [2008] Sask QB 207, 315 Sask R 268 (QB).

92 *Ibid* at paras 15, 16.

> were so, the defence would be available in every case where the complainant was drunk at the time of intercourse. If the complainant is so drunk that she is unable to communicate (the Crown's position at trial), she is incapable of giving consent, and no question of honest mistake can arise. If she is less drunk, and able to communicate (the defence's position at trial), the question is what she communicated.[93]
>
> [T]he assertion that the complainant's drunkenness and lack of memory raise the defence of honest but mistaken belief depends not on the evidence but on speculation. It depends, moreover, on dangerous speculation, based on stereotypical notions of how drunken, forgetful women are likely to behave.[94]

One judge has called upon Crowns in such cases to present expert evidence to prove the complainant's incapacity or her non-consent where she has no memory of the assault. In his judgment of the Ontario Supreme Court, *R v R(J)*,[95] Justice Todd Ducharme suggested that where the Crown seeks a ruling that the woman was incapable of consent, or seeks to rely on the woman's complete lack of memory of the sexual assault to prove non-consent, "while not required as a matter of law, for such evidence to be probative, some expert evidence will almost always be essential."[96]

However, the judge also said that evidence of blackout or memory loss can, along with other circumstantial evidence, support the inference either that the woman was incapable of consent or that she did not in fact consent. On the facts in this case, which involved a woman who was raped by three men while unconscious, the judge convicted both co-accused. Ducharme J accepted the complainant's evidence that she had undergone an abortion two days earlier and would not have consented to intercourse with anyone because she had been advised by the doctor to abstain for at least two weeks for her own health and safety. Further, she testified that she was in love with the man who had impregnated her and hoped to meet up with him at the party where she was raped.

In support of the claim that she was incapable of consent and would not have consented if conscious, the complainant testified as to her own

93 *Esau*, *supra* note 64 at para 94.

94 *Ibid* at para 95.

95 *R v R(J)* (2006), 40 CR (6th) 97 (Ont Sup Ct).

96 *Ibid* at para 20.

racism. She claimed that she was not in the least attracted to either accused. Specifically, she was not attracted to JR because he was black: "I am a person who believes in, say, being with your same race.... I have just never been attracted to a black man before."[97] She explained that "she had lost her virginity to a black man" and "it was that experience that made me against them."[98] Although the other accused, JD, was Aboriginal, she said she would not have had sexual relations with him because he was just a "good friend."

There are many ways to read the complainant's invocation of racism as evidence of her non-consent. This woman was raped by three men in one evening while unconscious, and must have experienced great suffering and anxiety about being believed. Given that she admitted that her first sexual liaison was with a black man, it seems improbable that she never experienced attraction to men of other skin colours due to her proclaimed racist views. It may be that this complainant seized upon a persuasive device that accords with our "common sense" racism.[99] It certainly worked for Justice Ducharme, who commented, "While I find these views distasteful, they are also a very powerful reason that KP would not agree to have sex with JR."[100]

While missing the opportunity to dispel racist myths and stereotypes that women do or do not consent based on the race of another, Justice Ducharme did refute another misogynist myth. In response to the defence suggestion that because the complainant was drunk she may have had consensual, unprotected intercourse with three men over a period of hours, he said: "While such a belief in the aphrodisiacal powers of alcohol might find a home in some works of pornographic fiction, it does not accord with common sense, common experience or the evidence in this case."[101] He found that the complainant was incapable of consent beyond a reasonable doubt based on toxicology evidence regarding her blood alcohol levels, the absence of injuries or sign of struggle, her many reasons for not being interested in either of the accused sexually, and her evidence that had she been willing, she would have insisted on condom use.

97 *Ibid* at para 34.

98 *Ibid.*

99 Himani Bannerji, *Thinking Through Essays on Feminism, Marxism and Anti-racism* (Toronto: Women's Press, 1995) at Chapter 3, "Introducing Racism: Notes Towards and Anti-Racist Feminism."

100 *R(J)*, *supra* note 95 at para 38.

101 *Ibid* at para 39.

The judge also considered the availability of the mistaken belief in consent defence. JD did not testify, so there was simply no evidence to give an air of reality to any claim that he believed the complainant communicated consent. And, because the judge rejected JR's evidence wholly, he too was denied the defence. The convictions were upheld against appeal.[102]

In *R v BSB*[103] the judge referred to *R(J)* above and noted that the Crown in the case before him had not introduced expert testimony to demonstrate that the complainant's memory loss was indicative of her lack of capacity to consent. This Crown had presented an expert toxicologist to testify as to the manifestations of different types of drugs used to rape women. The evidence of the other witnesses in this case described the behaviour of the complainant that night as extremely bizarre, dramatically out of character, hyper-sexual, and shockingly inappropriate. The complainant said that she began to fade in and out of consciousness soon after accepting a mixed drink prepared by the accused, and had no memory of the words and actions ascribed to her. The judge observed that the woman before him was painfully shy, and that the behaviour described by the witnesses seemed completely out of character for her.

While his reasoning is unclear, the expert apparently testified that the complainant's symptoms were consistent with a drug other than GHB, which would have been undetectable because too much time had passed from ingestion to testing. Yet the expert also said that the tests did not reveal the presence of any of these other drugs. Thus the judge was forced to conclude, "I have no evidence before me that that type of drug was consumed by the complainant...."[104]

Nonetheless, Romilly J convicted the accused for sexually assaulting the woman, whose body was covered in nineteen bruises and whose vagina showed lacerations caused by blunt trauma. He considered her absence of memory along with the evidence of two other witnesses who observed her state, and drew the inference that she was incapable of consent at the time of the attack. He went on to find non-consent, even had she been capable, based on the accused's fabricated lies to police, the complainant's injuries, and the fact that she vomited just before the assault. Finally, Romilly J rejected a claimed mistaken belief in consent

102 *R v R(J)*, 2008 ONCA 200.

103 *R v BSB*, 2008 BCSC 917, BCJ No 1319 (Sup Ct).

104 *Ibid* at para 31.

because there was no evidentiary basis to support it in light of the complainant's vomiting and the injuries that suggested her resistance.[105]

In some cases, other witnesses provide testimony that proves the complainant's incapacity.[106] For example, in *R v Jesse*,[107] the British Columbia Supreme Court relied upon non-expert evidence to find that the complainant was incapable of consent at the time the accused assaulted her. First, the court relied on similar-fact evidence that the accused had been convicted of attacking another unconscious woman. In both cases, he had inserted objects into the women's vaginas when they were passed out due to alcohol consumption. In the case at hand, the accused denied that he was the perpetrator, but he had been witnessed by two others fleeing the crime scene. The past assault persuaded the judge beyond any doubt as to his guilt. Second, counsel for the accused also attempted an alternate defence of "consent." This defence was rejected because the judge did not accept the possibility that the complainant had voluntarily agreed to have various household objects inserted in her body. Given how hard it was for the police and witnesses to rouse her when she was discovered post-assault, the judge found that the complainant was incapable of consent at the time.

Yet in some of these cases, judges' decisions on complainants' incapacity may suggest that adherence to rape mythologies is more determinative than the evidence at hand. For example, Justice McKinnon, in a perplexing decision acquitting the accused David William Millar,[108] first relied on the evidence of the complainant's friend to find that the complainant was incapable of consent, but then went on to speculate

105 *Ibid* at para 98.

106 See also *R v Bell* (2007), 223 OAC 243 and *R v Zarpa*, 2009 NLTD 145. In *Bell*, the trial judge and the Ontario Court of Appeal reviewed the evidence and found that the accused had drugged the male and female complainants with a stupefying substance and that neither was capable of consent in consequence. Although no drugs were detected in testing of the complainants two days later, the evidence of the two complainants as to their experiences of coming in and out of consciousness and other symptoms, including hallucinations, and that of a doctor who testified as to his view that they had been drugged, supported a guilty verdict. In *Zarpa*, the intoxicated complainant was asleep in her parents' bed: they were awakened by the realization that a fourth person was in the bed, on top of their daughter. Upon turning on the light they found their daughter still passed out but naked from the waist down, as was the accused. The Newfoundland and Labrador Supreme Court had no difficulty convicting Samuel Thomas Zarpa of sexual assault on the basis of the complainant's incapacity.

107 *R v Jesse*, 2007 BCSC 1355, 74 WCB (2d) 802 (Sup Ct).

108 *Supra* note 5.

on the (unconscious) complainant's motives. The witness had helped put the extremely intoxicated complainant to bed, noting that she was speaking in "baby talk," could not chew properly (when the witness encouraged her to eat something), and later vomited in a basket beside her bed. The complainant testified that she was awakened by being penetrated, but the accused testified that he had turned on the light, she had said "hey" to him, and had not objected when he switched the light back off and climbed into bed with her. McKinnon J remarked on the complainant's rejection of the accused at the point of penetration: "I find it to be quite possible that the complainant at that stage was feeling guilty because she had a boyfriend and was overcome by guilt."[109] Did the judge mean that the complainant was unconsciously participating and "enjoying" the accused's actions? It seems that the judge's indulgence in the myths that women secretly enjoy sexual assault or that they "cry rape" to hide their promiscuity overrode his own finding that she was incapable of consent.

In *R v Correa*,[110] the rape myths that posit women as ready for intercourse with any man, at any time and in any place, and as responsible for their own rapes, emerge from the judicial analysis. The complainant had consumed four drinks over the course of five hours, and shared a joint of marijuana with Keith Correa, a co-worker to whom she was not the least attracted. She testified that the joint must have been laced with some other drug because she immediately became incapacitated to the extent that she could not recall how she exited the accused's car. She was found on the ground in the parking lot with her pants around her ankles, her lower half naked and exposed, and she was unable to stand up. She threw up repeatedly and was taken to hospital in a highly distressed state. The accused had also taken photographs of her with her pants off. A toxicologist testified that the state described by the complainant was not consistent with the drugs allegedly consumed that night.

Justice Arthur M Gans concluded, relying on the toxicologist's testimony, that he had a reasonable doubt as to whether the complainant had been incapable of consent: "In my opinion, while Ms HR probably was incapacitated, or at least thought she was, I am nevertheless left with a reasonable doubt that she, in fact, was at the relevant time."[111] He went on to say: "there was a period, albeit but brief, where she may have consented, or implicitly consented, to the actions or advances of Mr

109 *Ibid at* para 34.

110 *R v Correa* (2005), 64 WCB (2d) 233 (Ont Sup Ct Just).

111 *Ibid* at para 13.

Correa and not recalled the details of such complicity on an after-the-fact basis."[112] These judicial statements reveal confusion about the law, since our courts have firmly rejected "implied consent" as a defence to sexual assault.[113] The notion that the complainant may have consented in the five to ten minutes she was in the accused's car in a parking lot behind a club where she was working, and in light of the state in which she was found, crawling half-naked in a parking lot and unable to stand, is highly implausible. The judge's reference to the complainant's "complicity" communicates both scepticism and victim-blaming.

Further, Gans J also supported the acquittal of Correa on the basis that he may have mistakenly believed the complainant consented, without regard to any "reasonable steps." It seems that the accused did not testify or lead evidence regarding "mistake." However, the trial judge said he found the air of reality in other evidence, which must have been the complainant's testimony or that of the toxicologist: "the evidence of her condition up to the moment that they shared the joint and the events immediately preceding the picture taking, sometime after they shared the joint, do not satisfy me beyond a reasonable doubt that he was reckless or wilfully blind to her sudden state of incapacity, if it existed."[114] "Nor would this same constellation of pre-occurrence circumstances put a reasonable person on notice that it would be necessary to make further inquiries or take further steps before proceeding with the relevant sexual activity."[115]

One argument advanced by the Crown in response to defence claims that the complainant consented in the twilight between consciousness and unconsciousness is that consent terminates upon unconsciousness. Sensibly, several courts have accepted this position, and have also ruled that there is no such doctrine as prior or advance consent for unconscious sex: *R v Ashlee*[116] and *R v Tookanachiak*.[117] These precedents ought to assist Crown prosecutors whose primary witness has no memory due to unconsciousness, for this strongly suggests that by the time the sexual contact occurred any possible consent had been vitiated by sleep or blackout experienced by the complainant.

112 *Ibid* at para 15.

113 *Ewanchuk*, *supra* note 42.

114 *Ibid* at para 18.

115 *Ibid* at para 19.

116 *Ashlee*, *supra* note 3. The court was not unanimous on this point: Madam Justice Conrad dissented at paras 83–86.

117 *R v Tookanachiak*, 2007 NuCA 1, 412 AR 42 (Nu CA) at para 5.

However, the Ontario Court of Appeal in *R v JA*[118] held, in a 2:1 decision, that nothing in law prevents a woman from providing "advance consent" to sexual contact while unconscious. In reaching this decision, the court drew upon the dissenting opinion of Justice Carole Conrad in *Ashlee*, where she argued that the *Code* does not prohibit advance consent and instead is aimed at respecting a woman's right to choose how and when she will be touched. The Ontario appeal court rendered its decision in a highly contentious factual context, where the complainant had first been strangled into unconsciousness before being bound and then penetrated anally with a dildo. The accused had been previously convicted three times of assaulting a female partner, two such charges having involved the complainant, and so perhaps it was not surprising that at trial she recanted her allegation of non-consent. While the trial judge followed the majority in *Ashlee* and held that the law does not recognize "advance consent" to unconscious sexual contact, the Court of Appeal disagreed, likening it to consent to surgery while unconscious and framing it as consistent with women's autonomy rights.

This decision was reversed by the Supreme Court of Canada in a 6:3 decision.[119] Justice McLachlin wrote the majority decision on behalf of herself, the three other women justices, and two of the men justices. In rejecting "advance consent," they decided that consistent with the *Criminal Code* consent must be voluntarily given by a person capable of consent and must be ongoing, subject to revocation by the complainant.

Any other result would have had a profoundly negative impact on the criminal prosecution of men who sexually assault unconscious women, who would have been placed in the difficult position of disproving "advance consent." It would have furthered the vulnerability of women with disabilities, Aboriginal women, and of course intimate partners, who are all subject to discriminatory credibility assessments and whose experience of harm from non-consensual sexual contact is often minimized.[120]

Most importantly, for the purpose of this analysis, the reasonable steps requirement would be rendered meaningless if "advance consent" were to be recognized, as the accused would then have no obligation to take reasonable steps "in the circumstances known to him at the time" of the sexual contact, but could instead rely on earlier events. The ma-

118 *R v JA*, 2010 ONCA 226.

119 2011 SCC 28.

120 See Factum of the Intervener, Women's Legal Education and Action Fund in *R v JA*, File No 33684, in the Supreme Court of Canada at paras 21, 22, 28–31.

jority decision in *JA* recognized the conflict that such an interpretation would pose to the law of consent:

> How can one take reasonable steps to ascertain whether a person is consenting to sexual activity while it is occurring if that person is unconscious? ...[B]y requiring the accused take reasonable steps to ensure that the complainant "was consenting", Parliament has indicated that the consent of the complainant must be an ongoing state of mind.[121]

Another route defence lawyers have taken when complainants are incapacitated is to argue that the accused was unaware of the woman's state. They have thus countered that even if the complainant was in fact incapacitated, the accused may be morally innocent because he may not have realized that the woman was unconscious. *Tookanachiak* demonstrates, I would argue, the brazen implausibility of such an argument.

Here the Crown proved that the accused sexually assaulted an unconscious complainant because a witness came upon the assault in progress and then woke the complainant. In spite of the fact that the accused did not testify in his own defence, the prosecution failed because the trial judge was not satisfied that the complainant had not consented *before* she fell asleep. On appeal, the Nunavut Court of Appeal followed the Alberta Court of Appeal's decision in *Ashlee* and held that even if she had consented, consent disappeared once she fell asleep. Yet it refused to disturb the acquittal because the Crown failed to prove that the accused *was aware* that the complainant was asleep: "The evidence and the findings of the trial judge allow for the possibility that the sexual activity began with consent and that the appellant continued this activity without awareness that the complainant had fallen asleep...."[122]

This appeal decision is deeply troubling. If the witness who came upon the complainant was immediately aware that she was indeed unconscious, how could the accused have failed to be aware of this fact? He cannot use his own recklessness or intoxication to explain his "mistake" regarding consent as per s 273.2(a) of the *Code*, which bars the defence where the accused's intoxication or recklessness caused his error. How then could he, consistent with these principles, be lawfully mistaken as to her capacity? It makes no sense to bar a man from a mistake defence if he was reckless as to a woman's non-consent, but give him free reign to pursue sexual contact with reckless disregard as to her

121 *Ibid* at para 42.

122 *Supra* note 117 at para 12.

unconscious state. Further, to show that the accused was not morally culpable because he was unaware that the complainant was incapable of consent, the court should be looking for evidence to provide an "air of reality" to such a mistake.

If the evidence of the witness for the Crown who came upon the accused in the act of sexual assault is not enough, then how can the Crown ever prove culpable awareness on the part of an accused who does not testify and therefore cannot be cross-examined on what he did or did not know? Such cases require a judge willing to draw the inference of guilty knowledge beyond a reasonable doubt, based on the obvious condition of the complainant. Ultimately, this willingness may well depend on unarticulated beliefs about what is "normal" sexual conduct on the part of men, or "normal" female behaviour in a sexual context. Are our judges saying that men cannot be expected to discern whether their sexual partners are conscious or not?

Tookanachiak also reinforces systemic racism in subtle ways. This case clearly involved an Inuit accused, and one might speculate that the complainant shared this background. While the identity of the complainant is speculative, one might nonetheless wonder whether the decision is partly dependent on its social context. Might the message be that this is normal behaviour, at least in Nunavut, or at least if the accused is Inuit?

CAN PHYSICAL OR SEXUAL CONTACT CONSTITUTE A REASONABLE STEP?

While it would seem to be trite that a reasonable step to ascertain consent cannot itself be an assault, especially when the woman is unconscious, only one appellate court has stated and applied this rule. In *R v Despins*, discussed in more detail below, the court sent the accused back for a new trial where he would be denied a "mistake" defence on the basis that he "attempted to base his belief in consent by seeking signs of apparent responsiveness in eye contact and bodily movement *after* initiating and engaging in sexual contact. . . ."[123]

In contrast, there are several cases in which it is apparent that even on the evidence of the accused, he engaged in initial physical contact while the complainant was semi-conscious at best. Rather than labelling this behaviour as assault or sexual assault, some judges seem willing to view touching as "reasonable steps," on the assumption perhaps that men are entitled to try and wake up sleeping women to see if they

123 *Despins*, *supra* note 71 at para 10.

will agree to engage in sexual intercourse. Some courts are even willing to accept sexual touching as "reasonable steps."

For example, the Nunavut Court of Appeal in *R v Tessier*[124] reviewed a trial judge's decision to acquit Darrell Francis Tessier of one of the two charges he faced for sexually assaulting two complainants on a certain evening. Tessier was convicted of assaulting the other complainant, JE, that same night, arguably showing a pattern of deliberate predation.

The accused testified that "the evening was charged with all types of sexual conversations," including "sexual content in terms of explicit talk."[125] He testified as to "the manner in which [MR] dressed and went jogging," "her stripping right in front of him."[126] After much alcohol consumption, both complainants had gone to bed. Some time thereafter the accused entered MR's room while she slept, took off his clothing, and shook her shoulders to wake her up. He claimed she opened her eyes briefly and moaned. He then started to touch her back, which was facing towards him, and he claimed she rolled over: "I thought well, that's very provocative, that's very, very positive feedback..." "she looked like she was enjoying it and she was conscious."[127] She must have woken up soon after and thrown him out because the appeal judgment reads, "as soon as the complainant said no, that was the end of it."[128]

The trial judge, Judge Foisy, found that the accused's actions in attempting to wake the complainant by shaking her while he was naked and touching her constituted "reasonable steps." He accepted that the accused believed the complainant had "come to" and was amenable to sexual contact. He acquitted the accused on the basis of mistaken belief regarding her consent. The Crown appealed the acquittal, but the Nunavut Court of Appeal dismissed the appeal on the basis that there was no error of law in the judge's ruling on "reasonable steps":

> The fact that [the accused] wanted to have sexual congress with her and the fact that he had prepared himself by having no clothes on for this purpose does not in my view change the nature of the question. There is nothing in s 273.2(b) ... which specifically requires that reasonable steps be taken before any *ability* to carry out sexual activity occurs [italics in original].

124 *R v Tessier*, 2007 Nu CA 5, 422 AR 84.
125 *Ibid* at para 14.
126 *Ibid* at paras 20, 23.
127 *Ibid* at paras 37, 38.
128 *Ibid* at para 49.

> [The judge] found, in effect, that the physical acts that he had done up to this point, while perhaps running up against the border of going a little too far, were not of the category or quality of conduct ... of being persistent or increasingly serious advances absent consent.
>
> Those findings ... are within the scope of a trial judge's capacity to make findings of fact about what constitutes reasonable steps in law.
>
> I am not suggesting that in another context there might not be a different trial judge who might actually disbelieve the respondent on this point or that he finds the respondent was in fact engaging in experimentation and not actually a genuine honest effort to try and wake up the person.[129]

This decision is clearly wrong in law. For a man to touch a sleeping woman while he is naked, with the intention of pursuing sexual intercourse, amounts to a sexual assault. It is a non-consensual touching in circumstances that any reasonable observer would find to be "sexual."[130] Failure to identify the so-called "reasonable steps" of the accused as in and of themselves a sexual assault should surely have qualified as an error of law justifying appellate intervention, consistent with the ruling by the Supreme Court in *Ewanchuk*.

R v Aitken, mentioned earlier for the BC Supreme Court's ruling that the trial judge must first ask whether the "mistake" has an "air of reality" and only then consider "reasonable steps," is another case that makes the error of treating sexual contact with a sleeping woman as "reasonable steps." In this case, the BC Supreme Court was critical of the trial judge for focusing on the fact that the accused had entered the room and bed of a woman he did not know after a party, and had proceeded to sexual touching while she slept: "the trial judge appears to have moved directly to the conclusion that in the absence of a conversation between them which would indicate the appellant had taken reasonable steps to ascertain she was consenting to the touching or had invited any touching, it could not possibly be said the touching was consensual."[131]

The accused had first begun stroking the complainant and tried to kiss her. He acknowledged in his testimony that she had pushed him away and told him to stop. She testified that she thought it was her roommate, and decided to tolerate his presence in her bed until

129 *Ibid* at paras 43, 44, 45, 46 respectively.

130 This is the test for what makes an assault a "sexual" assault: *R v Chase*, [1987] 2 SCR 293.

131 *Aitken*, *supra* note 72 at para 29.

the morning when she would confront him. He claimed to have fallen asleep, and woke with his arms around her, "cuddling" her. The accused then began sexual touching in earnest, waking the complainant a second time and bringing her to the realization that it was not her roommate sharing her bed. She testified that she attempted to get away, but could not escape the accused's aggressive sexual assault that continued, despite her objection, until he left to go to the bathroom. The accused claimed in contrast that he stopped immediately on the second occasion after twenty seconds of sexual touching when the complainant realized he was not "Paul."

The Crown defended the conviction, arguing that pursuant to *Ewanchuk*, once the accused was rebuffed the first time, he could not attempt further sexual touching without first ensuring that the complainant had changed her mind. The BC Supreme Court took a completely different view of the facts, suggesting that since the complainant did not force the accused to leave her bed after the first contact and since she must have tolerated some physical contact in light of the fact that the accused woke up with his arms around her, the accused may have made an honest mistake as to consent. Justice Mary-Ellen Boyd concluded:

> I am unable to find that a reasonable man in the circumstances in which the accused found himself would necessarily have taken further steps to ascertain the complainant's consent before attempting the limited sexual touching which he did following a second wakening.[132]

This decision is troubling on many levels. Although the complainant's evidence was that the sexual assault went far beyond "limited sexual touching," including penetration and the use of force to hold her in the bed, because the trial judge had elsewhere said he found the accused's version of events to be "reasonably true," the appeal judge based her decision on the accused's account of the facts.

More importantly, the court refused to apply *Ewanchuk* to these facts, suggesting that it was not clear what the complainant's "no" meant to the accused, "where he and the complainant continued to sleep together through the balance of the night."[133] This decision appears to repudiate the intent and substance of the reform effected by Bill C-49, often referred to as the "no means no" law. What else could her "no" have meant in these circumstances?

132 *Ibid* at para 43.
133 *Ibid* at para 40.

Finally, this case again supports the misapprehension that sexual touching can be a lawful reasonable step to ascertain consent. If a man who is a stranger to a complainant is entitled in law to touch her sexually while she sleeps for the purpose of ascertaining whether she might consent to a sexual activity not of her making, then the criminal law elevates male sexual prerogative over women's bodily integrity and equality to the discredit of our legal system.

In *R v Murphy*,[134] the PEI Supreme Court also failed to condemn physical contact with a sleeping woman as unreasonable steps. Here the trial judge had convicted Gerard Patrick Murphy when she disbelieved his account of how he came to engage in sexual intercourse on a living room couch with a sleeping woman after a party. The complainant hardly knew the accused, having only had a brief conversation with him that night at the party. Like many complainants, she testified that she awoke to find herself being penetrated on a couch where she had gone to sleep alone; she grabbed her clothes and fled the room. In contrast, Murphy claimed she placed herself on his couch and then began to press her bottom against his crotch fifteen minutes later. He described half an hour of increasing sexual activity that culminated in consensual intercourse. The PEI Supreme Court overturned the conviction, stating that the trial judge had made numerous errors by failing to deal with contradictions in the evidence and failing to apply the criminal standard of proof beyond a reasonable doubt.

Most worrying, the appeal judgment refuted the trial judge's ruling that Murphy was precluded from the mistake defence because he took no reasonable steps to ascertain consent. The trial judge had found that even if she accepted the accused's claim that the complainant had placed herself on the couch beside the accused, he had initiated physical contact by first rubbing her arm and leg. Only thereafter did she allegedly press her body against his crotch. The trial judge held that he failed to take reasonable steps to ascertain consent prior to intercourse given that the complainant was asleep. She stated:

> It seems that the myth here is that everyone who goes out to a party, has too much to drink and sleeps on a friend's sofa at a friend's place is looking for sexual action. No questions need be asked. Just assume that when you find someone on your sofa that consent has been given for anything or for everything, even if the person doing so is intoxicated or asleep or under the effects of one or both.[135]

134 *R v Murphy*, 2004 PEISCTD 31, 237 Nfld & PEIR 312 (Sup Ct).
135 *Ibid* at para 29.

The appeal judge ignored the findings of fact and focused instead on the accused's narrative, which described escalating sexual activity between them: "There was more than one point when the accused observed GB as being awake, and more than one point when he was satisfied that she had communicated consent."[136] Since consent can be communicated by actions, the accused was entitled to rely on the complainant's "movements, gestures and sounds" as manifesting her consent. The court said there was evidence of some reasonable steps to ascertain consent requiring the trial judge to resolve the issue on the evidence, beyond a reasonable doubt. Yet it is arguable that stroking a woman's arm and leg while she sleeps is itself a sexual assault from the perspective of a reasonable observer; it is, at the very least, an assault because this woman, to the knowledge of the accused, did not communicate consent at this point. All other so-called "reasonable steps" by Murphy were indisputably sexual touching. In the end, the appeal court ruling arguably supports the "myth" described by the trial judge as a male prerogative immune from the criminal law.

DO REASONABLE STEPS REQUIRE MEN TO WAKE WOMEN UP?

These cases bring us to the heart of what the law says when unconscious women are approached by men who seek sexual intercourse. What are reasonable steps to ascertain consent when women are asleep or unconscious for any reason? The answer seems simple: at the very least the law must require men to ensure that their partners are conscious before proceeding. Reasonable steps might require that the accused wait some period of time to ensure that the woman is truly awake and giving her unequivocal agreement, rather than embarking on sexual contact while the woman is still prone in her bed, hazy and half-conscious. To proceed without ascertaining that the woman knows who the accused is and what his intentions are — when the most an accused can say is that the sleeping woman moved her body or murmured something in her sleep — is surely predatory conduct that the criminal law should forbid. If a woman is intoxicated by alcohol and or drugs, then further steps must include waiting until the next day when she will have recovered from her incapacity. Yet the courts have been uneven in setting clear parameters for non-criminal sexual contact.

The only Supreme Court pronouncement on the reasonable steps requirement as a substantive matter came in 1998 in *R v Daigle*. Here the Court unanimously upheld the Quebec Court of Appeal, which had

136 *Ibid* at para 26.

substituted a conviction for an acquittal where the accused had admittedly used a "date rape drug," PCP, to rape and humiliate the complainant. Justice L'Heureux-Dubé added one sentence to a terse judgment dismissing the appeal: "We would simply add that the appellant could not rely on the defence of honest but mistaken belief since he had not taken reasonable steps to ascertain that the victim was consenting."[137]

To its credit, the Court was attempting to remind the courts below that s 273.2(b) now represented the law of the land and must be applied in these cases. But what on earth would reasonable steps to ascertain consent be when the accused had deliberately deprived the complainant of agency by drugging her with a substance that causes loss of inhibition, sexual acting out, and unconsciousness? Unfortunately, this cryptic statement fails to convey that nothing short of waiting thirty-six hours until a drug has passed through the complainant's system will suffice as a reasonable step to ascertain consent.

Lower courts, police, and Crown attorneys require specific guidance on "reasonable steps," for without it, they will be left with "common sense" or worse — unexamined myths and stereotypes. Indeed, the trial judge in *Daigle* described the drugged complainant as "responsible for her own actions." Both the abject criminality of deliberately drugging a woman so as to be able to prey upon her as if the accused were a star in a pornographic movie, and the misogynist victim-blaming by the presiding judge need to be resoundingly repudiated by our courts. As Justice L'Heureux-Dubé commented in *R v Ewanchuk*, "It is part of the role of this Court to denounce this kind of language, unfortunately still used today, which not only perpetuates archaic myths and stereotypes about the nature of sexual assaults but also ignores the law."[138]

Not surprisingly, perhaps, in light of the Supreme Court's failure to lead, some of the lower courts have had trouble answering what ought to be an easy question. *R v Osvath*,[139] the Ontario Court of Appeal's first take on the reasonable steps requirement, remains one of the most appalling judgments to date on the reasonable steps requirement. It also squarely raised the question of the availability of a "mistake" defence when the complainant is unconscious. At trial, the judge rejected the accused's testimony that the complainant had actually consented to sexual intercourse. The complainant had fallen asleep on a couch in the living room during a party where she had become intoxicated. The

137 *Ibid at* para 3.

138 *Ewanchuk*, *supra* note 42 at para 95.

139 *Osvath*, *supra* note 6.

complainant testified that she awoke on the couch to find a complete stranger — Csaba Osvath — penetrating her. She testified that at first she thought it must be her boyfriend who had accompanied her to the party, but was shocked when she turned around to look at who it was.

Three other witnesses all testified that they saw Osvath pursue contact with a sleeping woman. Two men testified that they saw Osvath slide down onto the couch behind her while she slept: one observed Osvath roll around until they were face to face; the other heard creaking noises come from the couch once Osvath had positioned himself there. Another man saw a male begin to touch the sleeping woman and saw her push him away before returning to sleep. In contrast, Osvath claimed that he went to sleep on the couch where the complainant slept only because there was no room elsewhere and that she woke him by rubbing her buttocks against him. He testified that he asked her if she wanted sex, she replied "yes," and then removed her own clothing.

The trial judge found the accused to be culpable on the basis that he was wilfully blind to the non-consent of the complainant and failed to take reasonable steps to ascertain consent:

> He most presumptuously lay down with the complainant without her consent. He took sexual advantage of a young woman who he had never spoken to and knew virtually nothing of. He compromised her when he knew she had been drinking and was in a very deep sleep. I find also that … [t]he accused took no steps to ascertain that the complainant was consenting to sexual intercourse with him. I find that in these circumstances known to the accused at the time, that the complainant was not acquainted with him, that it would have been reasonable to ascertain by direct conduct that the complainant wished to have sexual intercourse with a man she had never spoken to and, on the basis of the accused's own knowledge, had absolutely no interest in.[140]

Two of the three members of the court of appeal who heard Osvath's appeal against conviction decided that he deserved a new trial because the trial judge had failed to consider an alternative version that could have exculpated the accused:

> If the trier of fact believed the complainant initiated the sexual activity, or even participated in it, whether or not she realized what she was doing at the time, it would be too onerous a test of wilful blindness to require an ac-

140 *Ibid* at para 25.

> cused to stop the activity and, in effect, say, "Wait a minute; do you know who I am?" after having already obtained her consent.[141]

The majority did not address the reasonable steps requirement, leaving the impression that no further steps are required in such circumstances. Worse, this judgment also seems to suggest that the woman could have consented even though the factual findings of the trial judge were that the complainant was in a "deep sleep."

Justice Rosalie Abella dissented, pointing out that Osvath had failed to take even the most minimal of steps: "Anyone seeking sexual activity in these circumstances could hardly fail to know that he was obliged, at a minimum, to let the person from whom permission was sought for such activity, know who was seeking the consent."[142] The Supreme Court refused to hear the Crown's appeal on the basis that it did not involve a question of law alone.[143] Justice L'Heureux-Dubé and two others dissented on this refusal to give leave.

Fortunately, some appeal courts are setting limits on the use of the mistake defence when a sleeping or unconscious woman is the target of the assault through their interpretation of the reasonable steps requirement in this context. Justice Abella was in the majority the next time a case raising the issues from *Osvath* came before Ontario's highest court.

In *R v Cornejo* the complainant woke up to find Luis Cornejo attempting to penetrate her: she had no memory of even speaking to him that night, let alone of his entering her apartment while she slept. He was an acquaintance of the complainant who had attempted, in the past, to start a sexual relationship with her. She had rebuffed him. After a company golf tournament at which he and the complainant had had no contact, he made repeated phone calls to her home. He admitted in his testimony that she had told him that she wanted to free the telephone line for an incoming call from her boyfriend. During his third call to her she told him her boyfriend was not coming over and he testified that when he asked if he could come over, her response was "mm-hmm," which he took to be "yes."

Cornejo entered her unlocked door at 1:30 am and found her asleep on her couch. Although he admitted she said "what the hell are you doing here?" he did not leave. Instead he began caressing her and kissing

141 *Ibid* at para 22.

142 *Ibid* at para 29.

143 *R v Osvath*, [1997] 1 SCR 7 at para 1.

her. He also acknowledged that told him not to kiss her on the mouth. When he asked why, she responded, "because I don't love you."[144] He also admitted that she never touched him in return and remained lying on the couch with her eyes closed throughout. He removed her jeans and underwear but claimed she lifted her hips; he then proceeded to attempt to penetrate her until she woke up in great confusion and ordered him out of her home.

The trial judge had ruled that there was an air of reality to the accused's mistake of fact defence so as to send it to the jury. He found that, if believed, Cornejo's testimony that the complainant had lifted her pelvis could have led him to think he had her "unambiguous consent." In ordering Cornejo back for a new trial, Abella J ruled:

> The complainant's prior rejections of his sexual advances, his apology to her in the past for his inappropriate sexual advances, her request to him that he hang up so she could speak to her boyfriend, her ambiguous response to his third phone call, her failure to answer the door, his entering the apartment without permission and finding the complainant sleeping and shocked by his presence, all required that he take reasonable steps to clarify whether she was consenting to sexual activity. She never touched him, her eyes were closed, he knew she had been drinking that day, and every rejection by her that evening, even according to his own evidence, resulted in more aggressive sexual conduct on his part.[145]...
>
> No reasonable person ... when being told that someone was uninterested in being kissed because she did not love him, would assume that she would, in the alternative, be interested in having her clothes removed and engaging in sexual intercourse.[146]

Similarly, in *R v Despins*, the Saskatchewan Court of Appeal issued a strong ruling to the effect that an accused who makes sexual advances towards a sleeping woman must wake her up before he can access a "mistake" defence. The complainant, this time with her boyfriend lying beside her and both of them fully clothed, fell asleep after drinking at a party. She woke up to find David Despins penetrating her with his penis. At first she believed it to be her boyfriend, but when she saw her partner asleep beside her, she realized that a complete stranger was on top of her. Despins claimed active participation by the complainant —

144 *Cornejo*, *supra* note 70 at para 7.
145 *Ibid* at para 30.
146 *Ibid* at para 34.

ie, kissing, hugging, moaning — but was unable to recall how he came to be on the mattress with her, how his own clothing was removed, or how his sexual interaction with the woman began. The trial judge left the defence of mistake of fact regarding consent with the jury, and it returned an acquittal.

On appeal, two of the three judges on the panel ruled that there was no air of reality to his defence and that it should not have been put before the jury. Despins was unable to offer any evidence as to reasonable steps taken by him to ascertain consent given his complete lack of memory as to events that preceded his sexual touching of the woman. Madam Justice Jackson, for herself and Chief Justice John Klebuc, held that Despin's claimed mistake could not be divorced from the actual context: "It must be assessed in light of the fact that the accused has no recollection of what transpired that led him to remove his clothes and move to the bed of a woman he did not know — with whom he had no prior exchanges, and who is lying asleep on a single mattress next to her boyfriend — and engage in sexual relations with her."[147]

The judges relied on Supreme Court jurisprudence for the proposition that "it is simply not enough for an accused to say that he thought a complainant was consenting where the circumstances include advances from an intoxicated stranger towards a sleeping complainant."[148] A new trial was ordered because the Crown was able to persuade the majority of the judges that the verdict would not have been the same had the judge not made this error. Madam Justice Smith dissented on the basis that the jury's acquittal must have been based on a reasonable doubt as to whether the complainant had consented, since there was no rational basis for it to have found that the accused took reasonable steps to ascertain consent.[149]

In *GAL*, the Nova Scotia Court of Appeal[150] upheld a trial judge's conviction of an accused whose *modus operandi* was to attempt intercourse from behind sleeping women. The trial judge and the judges on appeal resisted the defence lawyer's efforts to invoke discriminatory practices and reasoning. This man waited outside the bedroom the complainant shared with her partner, where she had earlier retired to sleep after a party. GAL watched television with her partner until he fell asleep, and then went into the bedroom, lay down behind the woman,

147 *Ibid.*

148 *Ibid* at para 12.

149 *Ibid* at para 48.

150 *R v GAL*, 2001 NSCA 29, 191 NSR (2d) 118.

and proceeded to have intercourse with her. He claimed that she participated willingly, but she testified that she woke up to being penetrated from behind, and said, "hon don't, go to sleep, leave me alone." She only realized it was not her boyfriend afterwards, when she got up to use the washroom, saw GAL's coat on the floor, then moments later heard his truck leave and realized that her partner was fast asleep outside the bedroom. She woke her partner to tell him what happened and they phoned police.

The trial judge permitted two other women to testify that the accused had similarly attempted to penetrate them while they slept "some years previous," as relevant to the complainant's credibility and to rebut a defence of mistaken belief in consent. At the same time, the judge refused leave to the defence to introduce evidence from the accused, refuted by the complainant, that she had had sexual contact with him in the past.

On appeal, the defence lawyer argued that the judge should have admitted evidence of an alleged prior sexual contact between GAL and the complainant, in order to discredit her. Kenneth Fiske, QC, suggested that this evidence if admitted would show a "quickness in pattern" that would in turn support the proposition that "it would be impossible for [the complainant] to mistake GAL for her boyfriend RW." In turn, Fiske proposed, that evidence would suggest that she had "consented" to GAL's acts of predation.[151] He also proposed that the complainant was motivated to fabricate the allegation and hide her "consensual" participation because she had just resumed living with her partner and did not want to lose her home or her relationship.

The court of appeal upheld the judge's rulings on admissibility and agreed that the accused's prior assaults upon sleeping women were more probative than prejudicial to the accused:

> [H]is method bears unique and distinctive qualities. In each incident the woman was asleep. In each incident GAL, in varying degrees, attempted to have sexual intercourse from behind and in silence. In each incident there was no indication of any prior sexual overtures between the woman and GAL.... by any objective standard, the method GAL adopted in attempting to have sexual intercourse with each woman ... is clearly unique and, therefore, highly probative and relevant ...[152]

151 *Ibid* at para 25.
152 *Ibid* at para 23.

With respect to defence counsel's argument that the accused's alleged prior sexual history with the complainant was relevant, the appeal court found no evidence supporting his claim that somehow, his sexual "approach" would have allowed her to differentiate him from her boyfriend. In any event, the court rejected the proposed "motive to fabricate" as implausible, given that the complainant woke her boyfriend to tell him she had been raped. It noted that, in any event, she had not consented to "her boyfriend" either, given the clear rejection in her words "hon, don't….leave me alone."[153]

Yet in spite of these appellate rulings, the obligations trial judges are willing to impose on men bent on sexual contact with sleeping women are few and weak. For example, in *R v Millar*,[154] David William Millar and his friend met the complainant and her friend for the first time when they danced at a bar. The four went to the complainant's friend's home after; the complainant went upstairs to sleep because she was extremely intoxicated. She was so intoxicated that she vomited in a waste basket in the room. Downstairs, Millar expressed interest in the complainant to her friend, who informed him she had a boyfriend. Some time later, the accused went upstairs in search of the complainant. As is typical in these cases, her evidence was that she awoke to find herself being penetrated by the accused. She screamed and fled the room, seeking refuge in the kitchen where she grabbed a corkscrew, inflicted some puncture marks upon the accused and called 911, sobbing hysterically. The accused in contrast claimed that he entered the bedroom, turned on the light briefly. He said that she looked him in the face and said "hey." He turned the light off, climbed into bed with her and proceeded from "spooning" to massaging to sexual touching, which he claimed she responded to by moaning. Millar told police that he stopped when she told him to, upon penetration. He claimed she was upset because she was "feeling guilty about fooling around on her boyfriend."

In acquitting the accused, Justice MacKinnon commented negatively upon the complainant's demeanour at trial, but accepted her testimony that she did not consent in fact and that she lacked the capacity to consent. However, he acquitted the accused on the basis that he took reasonable steps to ascertain consent by turning the light on so the complainant could identify him. Further:

153 *Ibid* at para 36.

154 *Supra* note 5.

> There was no resistance made to his joining her in the bed. There was no aggressive, urgent or violent activity on the part of the accused. His approach was slow and progressive, in accordance with her reactions. No force was applied at any time. She co-operated in the removing of her jeans and underwear and accepted oral sex by shifting her pelvis and moaning.[155]

Justice McKinnon distinguished this case from *Cornejo* on the basis that Cornejo had previously been rejected by the complainant whereas here the complainant had met the accused that evening, danced with him, accepted drinks from him, and continued socializing after they left the bar: "At no time did the complainant rebuff the accused prior to the point of penetration."[156] Yet if the complainant was passed out and incapable of consent, as the judge found, how could she have been capable of demonstrating non-consent?

This case squarely raises the issue of what indeed are reasonable steps to secure consent to intercourse when a man has met a woman for the first time; she has gone to bed intoxicated; and he decides to pursue her. She did not invite him to her room; she did not sit up in bed and talk with him; she did not initiate sexual contact. She bore no obligation to "resist." Flicking on a light briefly when a woman is sound asleep does not even come close to the steps needed to ascertain consent. Common sense tells us that a momentary disturbance in one's sleep often will not result in a return to consciousness: indeed, this is what many such men seem to count on. Slipping into bed with a sleeping woman and proceeding to "spoon" or rub against her sleeping body is a sexual assault and ought to preclude any "mistake" argument.

Justice Anne Molloy in *R v Williams*[157] also accepted that the complainant did not consent, but acquitted the accused on the basis of the accused's honest belief in consent. Here the complainant was emotionally upset about problems with her boyfriend, and spent an afternoon hanging out with a male friend, drinking beer and playing video games and commiserating. At one point he was trying to distract her and grabbed her breasts. She told him immediately to stop and he did. Some time later she blacked out from the beer and awoke with the accused on top of her. She testified that she said no repeatedly, tried to push him off her, cried, begged and struggled, but that he managed to

155 *Ibid* at para 35.

156 *Ibid* at para 38.

157 [2009] OJ No 1356 (Sup Ct Just).

get her pants down and penetrate her. He testified that she remained awake on the bed but never said a word as he proceeded to remove her clothing and touch her sexually: she only protested when he started to penetrate her because she did not want to get pregnant. The judge had this to say about the complainant's evidence that she fought back:

> I believe Ms C does not clearly recall what happened between her and Mr Williams. However, I do not believe this lack of memory is attributable to alcohol impairment. She simply was not that drunk. She was vague about some key details such as whether she had passed out, whether Mr Williams performed oral sex on her and how he managed to get her pants and underwear off. Given her belief that she did not consent to sex and her vague recollection of details, it is entirely possible, that she has a genuine belief she screamed, struggled and repeatedly told Mr Williams to stop. However, I do not believe that actually happened. Whether it was because of shock, or disgust, or panic, or fear, or some other emotional reaction, Ms C did nothing overt to communicate her lack of consent to Mr Williams.[158]

Justice Molloy found the accused's version of events plausible, using the complainant's body against her: "Ms C is a very large woman, by her own estimation in excess of 300 pounds. I believe Mr.Williams when he says he would not be able to lift her or get her pants and underwear off without any injury to her or the clothing unless she provided the minimal co-operation he described."[159] The justice also concluded that the complainant was neither asleep nor incapacitated by alcohol, presumably rejecting that aspect of her testimony as well.

But the most worrisome aspect of this case is the judge's analysis of the reasonable steps requirement, where, like the courts in *Osvath* and *Correa*, the context is used to relieve the accused of any obligation to take steps to ascertain consent. Noting that the accused conceded that he had taken no steps, the justice found that the circumstances did not require that he do so:

> Within the context of two adults of equal standing who know each other very well and are good friends, the absence of any indication of unwillingness to participate is significant. When this passivity or acquiescence is accompanied by an overt act of assistance by facilitating the removal of clothing, Mr Williams' belief that Ms C was consenting is completely under-

158 *Ibid* at para 45.

159 *Ibid* at para 39.

> standable. I do not see his conduct as reckless in this regard, nor do I see any circumstances to give rise to the doctrine of wilful blindness. He believed she was consenting, based not only on her failure to object but also on her positive actions to assist him. In all of the circumstances as he knew them, his belief was reasonable and honest.[160]

As Janine Benedet comments, "Looking at it from another perspective, why should a man assume that a woman who is close friends with his girlfriend, upset about her own boyfriend's infidelity, has earlier rebuffed his attempt to grab her breasts while horsing around and is tipsy from alcohol consumption and not eating, would be interested in sexual activity with him? She might be, but arguably some sort of active agreement would be expected."[161] This decision wrongly puts the onus on the complainant to object or resist, rather than on the accused to take reasonable steps. It effectively creates a different legal standard for complainants and accused who know each other,[162] and reinforces the myth that rape is committed by men who are strangers, not those men who women know and trust.

At the superior court level, there are some cases in which a trial judge has clearly set parameters for men who approach sleeping women. Madam Justice Silja S Seppi of the Ontario Superior Court convicted Lyndale Nigel Graham of sexual assault[163] perpetrated against one of the two complainants in the case before her, ruling that nothing less than waking up a sleeping woman will suffice as "reasonable steps." She acquitted him with respect to the allegation made by a second complainant, his then girlfriend, on the basis that she had a reasonable doubt as to whether he desisted when she expressed non-consent.

The accused and another man, whom he did not know, had been called in the middle of the night to Graham's girlfriend's home. Each couple headed to separate bedrooms. The accused's attempt at intercourse with his girlfriend was halted by her objections. He claimed he stopped right away; she testified that he persisted. He then went downstairs to where the first complainant was sleeping, her partner having left the house. This complainant testified that she was awakened by pain caused by being penetrated by the accused. His statement to police ac-

160 *Ibid* at para 69.

161 Janine Benedict, "Annotation" (2009), 67 CR (7th) 363.

162 This decision resonates strongly with those discussed involving spouses, as discussed by Randall, *supra* note 24.

163 *R v Graham* (2008), 77 WCB (2d) 578 (Sup Ct Just).

knowledged that the complainant was "in and out of sleeping," but he claimed he asked her and she said "yeah, yeah." He also explained himself by claiming that the complainant had seen his penis a few days before and therefore wanted to have sex with him, and that the plan for the evening included a "threesome." The judge rejected his explanations and found beyond a reasonable doubt that the complainant was asleep, did not consent, would not have consented if awake, and that the accused knew she did not consent. Further, "[e]ven if he spoke to her and believed she was 'in and out of sleeping' ... that would not have constituted reasonable steps by him to ascertain her consent. Reasonable steps in these circumstances would have been to wake her up, speak to her and ensure she was wide awake, aware of what he wanted to do and voluntarily agreeing to have sex with him."[164]

There are several other superior court decisions where trial judges have used common sense to reject "mistake" defences where complainants have been unconscious, even if they have not explicitly delineated the reasonable steps needed in these circumstances. For example, Justice Glass in *R v PD*[165] clearly understood that the accused was engaged in deliberate, predatory conduct and convicted him accordingly. Here the twenty-one-year-old complainant testified that her forty-five-year-old uncle climbed on top of her in the night and that she pushed him away and went back to sleep. She awoke again to find him penetrating her, but passed out again, due to over-consumption of alcohol. In the morning, she found herself naked from the waist down and wet in the area of her vagina. She went to the hospital and was medically examined. The judge rejected mistake of fact by applying *Ewanchuk* to the effect that the accused did not take reasonable steps to ensure that the complainant had changed her mind after a clear rejection — "He simply continued and got what he wanted."[166] His actions thus showed recklessness or wilful blindness.

Finally, although Justice Gans in *R v Baynes*[167] did not refer to the reasonable steps requirement in convicting the accused for one of two sexual assaults alleged against the seventeen-year-old niece of his girlfriend, he did use an analysis that shows attention to the law of sexual assault as well as practical wisdom. Sean Baynes was found to have entered the young woman's room at night, intending "to engage in sex-

164 *Ibid* at para 38.
165 [2002] OJ No 3593 (Sup Ct Just).
166 *Ibid* at para 35.
167 [2007] OJ No 633 (Sup Ct Just).

ual touching from the get go," including unprotected intercourse. The judge rejected the accused's claim that he relied upon her body language as indicative of consent: "Mr. Baynes had little or no track record with Ms S by which he could read her wakeful body language let alone her motions while sleeping or while groggy from sleep ... at worst he acted recklessly or was wilfully blind."[168] The judge said that her bodily movements could at best be described as "ambiguous," not giving rise to a defence of mistaken belief in consent.

CONCLUSION

This review of the case law has shown that our higher level courts have an uneven record interpreting the "reasonable steps" limitation to the mistake of fact defence for sexual assault. These cases are also haunting because of what they tell us about our culture of masculine entitlement and our disregard for the safety and autonomy of women. To the extent that our judiciary remains wilfully blind to the systemic perpetration by men against unconscious women, we will fail to develop legal principles that serve the public interest by condemning predatory male violence against women. The Supreme Court of Canada took an important first step in rejecting the proposed doctrine of "advance consent" in *JA*. The effect of this decision is to affirm women's equal rights to security of the person and to sexual autonomy when they are unconscious.[169]

It is particularly important that judges of the superior courts demonstrate for the lower courts the application of the law in this area in light of its extraordinary complexity and the frequency of men's sexual assaults against unconscious women. The credibility of our criminal justice system is seriously undermined when such a large category of cases is so difficult to prosecute successfully.

Proof issues for sexual assaults where the complainant was unconscious remain complex. Unfortunately, expert testimony is unlikely to assist the Crown in proving that the complainant was incapable of consent because most drugs used to rape women are so rapidly metabolized that they escape detection. Further, the speculative nature of scientific evidence about the likely effects of drug or alcohol ingestion upon the complainant's capacity means that using expert evidence as proof of

168 *Ibid* at para 22.

169 However, the three justices who dissented took the opposite view, arguing that the majority decision undermined women's sexual autonomy by depriving women "of their freedom to engage by choice in sexual adventures...." *JA* (SCC), *supra* note 119 at para 73.

a complainant's incapacity beyond a reasonable doubt is problematic. In fact, it seems more likely that expert testimony will, in this context, be used by defence to generate a reasonable doubt.

Crown attorneys are thus forced to rely on the probative value of complainants' testimony that since they have no memory of the attack, they must have been unconscious and therefore legally incapable at the time. In this context, it is important for Crowns to argue that to be believed, women should not have to provide reasons, as did the complainants in *Esau* and *R(J)*, as to why they would not have consented to sexual contact with the accused had they been conscious. Women's rights to equality and autonomy require that we reject the proposition that women are presumptively consenting,[170] or that they consent based on "such extraneous circumstances as the location of the act, the race, age or profession of the alleged assaulter."[171] It would be powerful for a judge to affirm women's unqualified right to choose their sexual partners without couching their choices in racist claims to credibility.

Crown prosecutors will also need to ask judges to reject expert testimony such as that presented in *Dumais*, where the defence witness proposed that "people" who engage in sexual activity while extremely intoxicated "often insert inappropriate conclusions into their breaches of memory to help them make sense of what has happened to them."[172] The sex discriminatory assumptions buried in propositions like this must be aired and repudiated. This "scientific" opinion is simply a more polite and de-gendered restatement of the old adage that women "cry rape" in the morning, when they come to regret their poor judgment of the night before. In this regard, prosecutors may draw upon judicial statements such as that of Justice Ducharme in *R(J)*, who attributed the belief that women are more likely to consent while under the influence of alcohol to "pornographic fiction." Justice McLachlin in *Esau* also warned that giving men access to the "mistake" defence where women are unconscious "depends ... on dangerous speculation, based on stereotypical notions of how drunken, forgetful women are likely to behave."[173]

In prosecutions involving women who testify that they were unconscious, Crowns should continue to insist on a rigorous application of the law governing the "mistake" defence. This is necessary not only

170 Fraser, CJ, dissenting in *R v Ewanchuk* (1998), 57 Alta LR (3d) 235 at para 67 (CA).

171 *Seaboyer, supra* note 12 at para 209 per L'Heureux-Dubé J.

172 *Dumais, supra* note 91 at para 32.

173 *Esau, supra* note 64 at para 95.

to breathe life into the law on "reasonable steps," but also to develop a strong jurisprudence that attends to the public interest by respecting the will of Parliament and women's constitutional rights to security of the person. Thus the "reasonable steps" limit should be argued in every case where the accused claims consent or "honest mistake" as his defence. Judges who preside over sexual assault prosecutions must be aware that judicial failure to address s 273.2(b) explicitly has been held to be an error of law by appeal courts in *DIA* and *Malcolm*, making their judgments vulnerable to appeal.

Cornejo and *Despins* can be used to persuade judges that they must be able to find an "air of reality" that some reasonable steps were taken before a "mistake" defence can be considered by the jury or themselves, if it is a judge sitting alone. To hold otherwise, that an "honest mistake" defence should be entertained even though there is no evidence supporting a critical component of the defence,[174] would once more position sexual assault as an anomalous crime where special, discriminatory rules are imposed, to the detriment of women.[175] When considering this evidentiary burden, women's equality demands that the mistake defence be barred where the defence is solely based on conjecture as to "mistake" as opposed to evidence of actual reasonable steps. For example, the reasoning of the trial judge and the appeal court in *Dumais* demonstrate what it means to attend seriously to the reasonable steps requirement: "The postulations by the expert that it is possible for one to appear to consent when they do not actually have capacity are simply that. No evidence was placed before this trial judge to suggest that any steps had been taken to determine reasonable consent."[176]

In the context of adjudicating both the "air of reality" test for mistaken belief, where the accused claims reasonable steps to ascertain consent, and the factual question of whether the accused in fact took reasonable steps in the circumstances known to him, judges ought to take a strong and consistent position that men cannot "test the waters" by touching unconscious or semi-conscious women. Too many of the cases reviewed show sloppiness in attending to the facts, and disregard for women's bodily security. What social interest can possibly justify allowing men to shake, stroke, or straddle unconscious women in order

174 See for example *R v Stone*, [1999] 2 SCR 290 at paras 182–92 where the Court tailored the evidentiary burden or "air of reality" test to align with a reformed defence of automatism.

175 See generally L'Heureux-Dubé J's dissent in *Seaboyer*, *supra* note 12.

176 *Ibid.*

to pursue their own sexual desires? Women's security of the person interests should be protected while they sleep or recover from drug or alcohol ingestion. Self-serving, non-consensual touching of women by men they do not know and in whom they have no sexual or romantic interest cannot be condoned. It is imperative that we ask why we should de-criminalize non-consensual sexual touching where, for example, a man strips naked and begins touching an unconscious woman. Why should judges call this conduct "reasonable steps to ascertain consent"? What is so special about men's interest in sexual gratification that the law should not require them to wait until the woman is not in the vulnerable position of being startled awake? And if we are not prepared to insist that men wait to proposition unconscious women until they are conscious, then reasonable steps should surely require that men wake women without touching them in any way. There is a fundamental question underlying this jurisprudence: do women matter?

The position taken by the courts in *Cornejo*, *Despins*, and *Graham* that nothing short of waking an unconscious woman will suffice to constitute reasonable steps must be adopted by all appellate courts as the minimum that the law requires. Judges should also insist that men ensure that their prospective partners do indeed "know who they are," contrary to the Ontario Court of Appeal's judgment in *Osvath*. In fact, when one considers how disorienting and frightening it is to be awakened from a deep sleep, at least by one who is not an intimate partner, it would not be at all unreasonable to require men who seek intercourse with unconscious women to wait until consciousness returns.

Ewanchuk needs to be followed in cases where semi-conscious women express their non-consent. Cases like *Aitken* should be appealed on this basis. Reasonable steps after "no" has been communicated cannot include further physical or sexual contact without risking criminal responsibility. Further, men whose conduct reveals a predatory intent — such as the accused in *Daigle* who drugged the woman — should be absolutely barred from their disingenuous claim to "mistake." There are no steps that are reasonable after a woman has been deliberately rendered helpless by the accused or by others to his knowledge, or where he has waited, in a calculating manner, until she has gone to sleep to begin his assault.

The reasonable steps requirement should also be read as making necessary more onerous steps when there are additional inequalities between the accused and the woman. Some Crown attorneys have argued that differences in age, the relationship of the accused as a person who is or was in a step-parent relationship to the complainant, or in some position of authority over the complainant, such as *Miyok* where the accused was the complainant's income support worker, heighten the obligation to take reasonable steps. These features are part of the "circumstances known to him at the time," and therefore shape the kinds of steps needed to ensure lawful consent.

Should similar arguments be made where the complainant preyed upon is an Aboriginal woman or a racialized woman? Given the important role played by colonization in rendering Aboriginal women "prey"[177] and by systemic racism in emboldening perpetrators who target racialized women, should the lived experience of oppression based on racial identity be named as part of articulating the reasonable steps needed to ascertain consent? After all, perpetrators count on the shame and silence of women who have been raped, or at least they count on our disbelief of racialized women's accounts of their rapes. Would it challenge systemic racism and white privilege to articulate the race of complainant and accused in the context of the rape of unconscious women, or would it instead reinforce harmful stereotypes and the vulnerability of these women to male violence? I do not have an answer, and look for leadership from Aboriginal and racialized women's groups as to when and how we must articulate the role of racism in the criminal process. At the same time, it is deeply disturbing to read these cases knowing that many of the women must surely be Aboriginal or racialized, and yet our legal response in terms of "reasonable steps" remains oblivious to what "everybody knows."[178]

Much work lies ahead for Crown attorneys who prosecute rape every day and for judges tasked with interpreting a law that requires attention to uncomfortable truths about male sexual violence and their ability to exploit the inequalities generated by sexism, racism, colonialism, and disabilityism. I believe that the reform accomplished by s 273.2(b) holds potential for social change and disruption of men's relative immunity from criminal liability for sexually assaulting unconscious women. But it will take many more brave women prepared to come forward as complainants, the pressures exerted by a feminist movement, and prosecutors and judges able to identify and repudiate discriminatory myths

177 Mary Eberts, "Surviving Non-Citizenship" (Paper presented to the Sexual Assault Law, Practice, and Activism in a Post-Jane Doe Era Conference, University of Ottawa, 7 March 2009) [unpublished].

178 Leonard Cohen & Sharon Robinson, "Everybody Knows," in *Lyrics. The Essential Leonard Cohen* (Sony Music Canada Inc, 2002): "Everybody knows the deal is rotten / old Black Joe still picking cotton for your ribbons and bows / everybody knows."

masquerading as legal argument together to realize the potential of the "reasonable steps" requirement.

21.

An Equality-Oriented Approach to the Admissibility of Similar Fact Evidence in Sexual Assault Prosecutions

David M Tanovich[1]

The power of rape mythologies to shape criminal law doctrine drives David Tanovich's chapter, wherein he considers the rule of evidence that excludes from consideration by the judge or jury evidence of the accused's "bad character," even when it involves past sexually assaultive conduct that resulted in criminal conviction. This aspect of the criminal law governing sexual assault prosecution has not been the subject of feminist law reform in Canada, although Julia Tolmie's chapter in Part I, "New Zealand's Jane Doe," describes one of the outcomes of several high profile prosecutorial failures in New Zealand as a renewed public debate on the issue of whether an accused's criminal convictions for other sexual assaults should be withheld from judges and juries. In recognition of the role of gender bias in shaping the current law, and consistent with women's equality rights, David proposes a nuanced new rule that would presumptively admit evidence of an accused's past sexual misconduct in sexual assault prosecutions with some exceptions, including cases where systemic racism may operate against the accused person.

PART I: INTRODUCTION

There has been very little critical and feminist commentary in Canada on the admissibility of prior sexual misconduct evidence as similar fact evidence in sexual assault cases.[2] Similar fact evidence is a specific type of bad character or conduct evidence.[3] It is distinguished from more general bad character evidence because it shares similar features with

1 I wish to thank the tremendous research assistance of Jillian Rogin (Windsor Law 2008) and the generous funding of the Law Foundation of Ontario.

2 It is unclear why the issue has received such little critical attention in Canada. One of the only such pieces is Lynne Hanson, "Sexual Assault and the Similar Fact Rule" (1993) 27 UBC L Rev 51. The only other piece to look specifically at the issue is Lee Stuesser, "Similar Fact Evidence in Sexual Offence Cases" (1997) 39 Crim LQ 160.

3 Bad character or discreditable conduct evidence, as it is sometimes referred to, is any evidence that tends to place the accused or a witness in a negative light. See *R v B(L)* (1997), 116 CCC (3d) 481 (Ont CA).

the offence charged. So, for example, evidence that the accused sexually assaulted person(s) other than the complainant could be an example of similar fact evidence in sexual assault prosecutions assuming satisfaction of the threshold legal test. Similar fact evidence is a narrow exception to the general exclusionary rule that the Crown cannot lead bad character evidence in criminal trials. As the Supreme Court of Canada noted in *R v B(CR)*:

> Nineteenth century courts started from the premise that a person should not be convicted on the basis that he had committed other offences. They developed a general exclusionary rule with the following exception: evidence of previous misconduct could be admitted if it possessed special probative value … Viewed thus, the so-called similar fact rule was in reality an exception — narrowly defined — to the general rule excluding evidence of prior misconduct or propensity.[4]

The exclusionary rule, in theory, is grounded on a concern that jurors will convict because the accused is a bad person (ie, moral prejudice), or they will give it too much weight or it will distract or deflect them from rendering a true verdict based on the evidence (ie, reasoning prejudice). Because the default position for bad character evidence is exclusion, the onus is on the prosecution to establish, on a balance of probabilities, that the prior sexual misconduct evidence qualifies under the similar fact evidence exception.

The lack of critical attention to this area of evidence law is surprising given that the similar fact evidence rule, like other rules of evidence, serves as a site for gender, race, and sexual orientation bias.[5] Using the Supreme Court of Canada decision in *R v Handy*,[6] this article attempts to locate the nature of systemic gender bias in similar fact adjudication. It is argued that such bias is manifested in an expressed "suspi-

4 [1990] 1 SCR 717 at 725.The rule has evolved considerably from the approach in the nineteenth century. A principled approach to admissibility balancing probative value and prejudicial effect has replaced the categorical approach. This is discussed *infra*.

5 An example of sexual orientation bias could be seen in cases involving allegations of sexual assault of young boys where courts equated homosexuality and pedophilia. See *R v Thompson* (1918), 13 Cr App R 61 (HL) [Lord Sumner] ("homosexual offences" exception); and *R v Sims* (1946), 31 Cr App R 158 (CA) "sodomy is a crime in a special category because … persons who commit [it] … seek the habitual gratification of a particular perverted lust…"). In Canada, see *R v Guay*, [1978] 1 SCR 18 where the Supreme Court twice refers to charges of gross indecency on boys as "homosexual acts."

6 [2002] 2 SCR 908 [*Handy*].

cion" of prior sexual misconduct evidence and in a preoccupation with sex rather than violence in deciding similarity. *Handy* is the centerpiece of the discussion because it is the leading similar fact evidence case in Canada. In addition to its precedential value, it is significant because it recognizes that propensity reasoning (ie, inferring that because the accused has done a similar thing before, he committed the act in question) can be a stand-alone basis of admission.[7] As discussed in Part III, this opens the door to a presumptive approach to admissibility. The decision is also important because it reveals many of the stereotypes and fallacious reasoning associated with our understanding of sexual assault.

This article is not intended as an attack on the general bad character exclusionary rule. There is no question that bad character evidence can infect and corrupt the trial process. This article's focus is on developing an approach to admissibility that promotes equality, accuracy, and fairness in the adjudicative process in sexual assault cases. The article's thesis, set out in Part III, is that in cases that turn on the *commission* of the *actus reus* (which includes the issue of *consent*), admission rather than exclusion should be the rule for prior sexual misconduct evidence. It is an approach grounded in equality principles rather than an assessment of probative value and prejudicial effect. It is also in keeping with the common law's tradition of moving incrementally and the Supreme Court's principled approach to the law evidence.[8] The approach advocated is not absolute. For example, identification cases are excluded from the presumption. In addition, putative collusion cases and those with Aboriginal and racialized accused require additional layers of analysis because they raise reliability, probative value, and prejudicial concerns that need to be addressed by the trial judge. These special cases are discussed in Part III.

The argument is, therefore, not for an implementation of the categorical approach of Rules 413 and 414 of the *Federal Rules of Evidence* in the United States that makes admission the rule for *all* sexual misconduct cases.[9] These categorical rules came about, in part, as a result

7 Prior to *Handy*, courts, generally speaking, refused to recognize that similar fact evidence could be used for propensity reasoning. Instead, they tried to find some other basis for admission. For example, as evidence to rebut a defence of innocent association.

8 See S Casey Hill, David M Tanovich & Louise P Strezos, *McWilliams' Canadian Criminal Evidence*, 4th ed (Toronto: Canada Law Book, 2010) at Chapter 3 for a discussion of the Supreme Court's approach to the law of evidence.

9 Rule 413 states:

of high profile acquittals in sexual assault cases where prior misconduct had been excluded, the most notable being the Kennedy-Smith trial.[10] The Federal Rules have been justified on necessity grounds including the difficulty of proving sexual assault cases and a belief that sexual assault perpetrators are more likely to repeat their crimes than other offenders.[11] Others have argued that politics more than probative value led to their enactment.[12] These justifications have been thoroughly criticized.[13] Arguments centred on media attention, politics, or recidivism do not form part of the equality foundations for this article's proposed rule. Nor is the difficulty of prosecution justification relied upon. This is not to suggest that this necessity argument could not be part of an equality argument only that it is, in my view, less persuasive than the other equality arguments advanced here.[14]

(a) In a criminal case in which the defendant is accused of an offence of sexual assault, evidence of the defendant's commission of another offense or offenses of sexual assault is admissible, and may be considered for its bearing on any matter to which it is relevant.

Rule 414 states:

(b) In a criminal case in which the defendant is accused of an offense of child molestation or offenses of child molestation, evidence of the defendant's commission of another offense or offenses of child molestation is admissible, and may be considered for its bearing on any matter to which it is relevant.

These Rules were part of the *Violent Crime Control and Law Enforcement Act of 1994*, Pub L No 103–322, s 3209535(a), 108 Stat 2135 (1994). A number of commentators have written in support of these Rules. See Tamara Larsen, "Sexual Violence is Unique: Why Evidence of Other Crimes Should Be Admissible in Sexual Assault and Child Molestation Crimes" (2006) 29 Hamline L Rev 177; Joyce R Lombardi, "Because Sex Crimes are Different: Why Maryland Should (Carefully) Adopt Contested Federal Rules of Evidence 413 and 414 that Permit Propensity Evidence of a Criminal Defendant's Other Sex Offences" (2004) 34 U Balt L Rev 103; and Karen M Fingar, "And Justice for All: The Admissibility of Uncharged Sexual Misconduct Evidence Under the Recent Amendment to the Federal Rules of Evidence" (1996) 5 S Cal Rev L & Women's Stud 501.

10 See David P Bryden & Roger C Park, "'Other Crimes' Evidence in Sex Offense Cases" (1994) 78 Minn L Rev 530; and David J Karp, "Evidence of Propensity and Probability in Sex Offense Cases and Other Cases" (1994) 70 Chi-Kent L Rev 15.

11 See Bryden & Park, *supra* note 10 at 556–57; Karp, *supra* note 10 at 20. See also the discussion in Stuesser, *supra* note 2 at 161–63.

12 See Michael S Ellis, "The Politics Behind Federal Rules of Evidence 413, 414 and 415" (1998) 38 Santa Clara L Rev 961.

13 See the discussion in Benjamin R Sachs, "Beyond Sex Crimes: A Principled Approach to Admitting Evidence of Prior Bad Acts", online: <http://papers.ssrn.com/sol3/papers.cfm?abstract_id=1402950> (last accessed 16 July 2009).

14 A necessity argument is grounded in the low conviction rate for sexual assault offences as compared to other violent offences; the stereotypes and myths that nega-

In support of admissibility in *actus reus* cases, the article examines both formal and substantive equality justifications. Part IV sets out the formal equality argument grounded in the "tit for tat" principle that has emerged in the law of evidence. This general principle recognizes that the defence can sometimes open the door to a Crown response by the tactics it employs (eg suggesting that someone else committed the offence). Where the door is open, the Crown is entitled to respond, including with what would otherwise be inadmissible evidence, in order to ensure that the trier of fact is not left with a distorted picture. In sexual assault prosecutions, that door should be deemed opened by the usual "whack the complainant" defence tactics. Part V advances a substantive equality argument grounded in the need to address the inherent suspicion associated with prior sexual misconduct evidence and our courts' failure to properly give effect to the fact that sexual assault is not a crime of sex and passion but one of violence and domination. These manifestations of gender bias have had a negative impact on cases, as is evident from a survey examining post-*Handy* cases where courts frequently excluded the evidence because of a lack of so-called similarity between the prior sexual misconduct and the complainant's evidence. The survey is discussed in Part V. Finally, in Part VI, the chapter briefly identifies and responds to feminist criticisms of a presumptive rule of admissibility.

PART II: THE FACTS OF *HANDY*

As *Handy* serves as the backdrop for much of the discussion, it is necessary to provide at the outset a brief summary of the facts and results.

tively impact on credibility assessments; and the heightened vulnerability of sexual assault complainants. See the discussion of this relevant social context in *R v Find* (2001), 154 CCC (3d) 97 at 117, 130–31 (SCC); *R v Seaboyer* (1991), 66 CCC (3d) 321 (SCC) (as per L'Heureux-Dubé J); Elizabeth Sheehy & Christine Boyle, "Justice L'Heureux-Dubé and the Canadian Sexual Assault Law: Resisting the Privatization of Rape" in Elizabeth Sheehy, ed, *Adding Feminism to Law: The Contributions of Justice Claire L'Heureux-Dubé* (Toronto: Irwin Law, 2004) 247; John McInnes & Christine Boyle, "Judging Sexual Assault Law Against a Standard of Equality" (1995) 29 UBC L Rev 341; Christine Boyle, "The Judicial Construction of Sexual Assault Cases" in Julian V Roberts & Renate M Mohr, eds, *Confronting Sexual Assault: A Decade of Legal and Social Change* (Toronto: University of Toronto Press, 1994) 136; Kathy Mack, "Continuing Barriers to Women's Credibility: A Feminist Perspective on the Proof Process" (1993) 4 Crim L Forum 327; Margot Nightingale, "Judicial Attitudes and Differential Treatment: Native Women in Sexual Assault Cases" (1991) 71 Ottawa L Rev 71; Elizabeth Sheehy, "Canadian Judges and the Law of Rape: Should the *Charter* Insulate Bias?" (1989) 21 Ottawa L Rev 741; and Lynn Hecht Schafran, "Gender Bias in the Courtroom" (1989) 22 Creighton L Rev 413.

Handy was charged with sexual assault causing bodily harm. This was not the first time he had been charged with sexual assault. He had twice been convicted for sexually assaulting two other women.[15] He had also faced sexual assault charges involving his ex-wife.[16] With respect to the incident at issue on appeal, in early December of 1996, the complainant went to a bar with a friend. At the bar, she met Handy whom she had met six months earlier. He appeared intoxicated. After a night of "drinking and flirting," they went to a friend's house to smoke marijuana. They left together in a car and drove to an Econo Lodge motel. The car crashed into a ditch.[17] Once in the hotel room, they commenced what started out as consensual sex. The complainant told Handy to stop when the sex became painful. He refused and anally raped her. He punched and choked her when she tried to stop him. After the incident, he allegedly said, "What the hell am I doing here? Why does this kee[p] happening to me?"[18] A number of witnesses testified to seeing bruises on the complainant's throat, chest, and arms following the incident. There was also evidence that the complainant suffered from post-traumatic stress following the incident.[19] The trial judge ruled that seven alleged incidents of physical and sexual abuse, including allegations of anal rape, by Handy against his ex-wife were admissible as similar fact evidence.[20]

Handy's defence was that the sex was consensual and that the complainant and his ex-wife had colluded for financial gain. The two had met in the summer of 1996 during which time the ex-wife told the complainant about Handy's past and that she had received $16,500 in compensation from the Criminal Injuries Compensation Board. The conversation included the following testimony from the ex-wife:

> Q. You told her that he had been to jail?
> A. Yes, I did.
> Q. You told her that he abused you?

15 *Supra* note 6 at para 142.

16 This was referred to as an "incomplete trial" in the Supreme Court judgment. See *Handy, supra* note 6 at para 133.

17 These additional facts come from the Court of Appeal judgment reported at (2000), 145 CCC (3d) 177 (Ont CA) at paras 10–11.

18 *Handy, supra* note 6 at para 4.

19 *Ibid* at para 5.

20 These seven incidents are described in detail in paras 6–13 of *Handy, supra* note 6.

A. Yes, I did.
Q. And you told her that you collected $16,500 from the government. All you had to do was say that you were abused.
A. Yes.
Q. So, she knew all that before December of 1996?
A. Yes.[21]

Handy was convicted of sexual assault. On appeal, both the Ontario Court of Appeal and the Supreme Court of Canada held that the trial judge had erred in admitting the prior misconduct evidence involving his ex-wife. A new trial was ordered. As is often the case where sexual assault convictions are overturned on appeal, the new trial was never held.[22] The Supreme Court's reasoning on the similar fact issue is discussed throughout the article.

PART III: AN EQUALITY-ORIENTED RULE OF ADMISSIBILITY

The Supreme Court of Canada has repeatedly stated that there is no special similar fact admissibility rule for sexual assault cases. In *Handy*, for example, Justice Binnie, for the Court, held:

> The "common sense" condemnation of exclusion of what may be seen as highly relevant evidence has prompted much judicial agonizing, particularly in cases of alleged sexual abuse of children and adolescents, whose word was sometimes unfairly discounted when opposed to that of ostensibly upstanding adults. The denial of the adult, misleadingly persuasive on first impression, would melt under the history of so many prior incidents as to defy innocent explanation. That said, *there is no special rule for sexual abuse cases.*[23]

21 *Handy*, *supra* note 6 at para 15.

22 See RJ Delisle, Don Stuart & David M Tanovich, *Evidence: Principles and Problems*, 9th ed, (Toronto: Carswell, 2010) at 273. Some of the post-*Handy* commentary includes Hamish Stewart, "Rationalizing Similar Facts: A Comment on *R v Handy*" (2003) 8 Can Crim L Rev 113; Christopher Morris, "The Possibility of Collusion as a Bar to the Admissibility of Similar Fact Evidence" (2003) 11 CR (6th) 181; Ron Delisle, "Annotation" (2002) 1 CR (6th) 209; Don Stuart, "Annotation" (2002) 1 CR (6th) 209; and Andras Schreck, "*Handy*: Raising the Threshold for the Admission of Similar Fact Evidence" (2002) 1 CR (6th) 245.

23 *Handy*, *supra* note 6 at para 42 [emphasis added].

Similarly, in *R v B(CR)*,[24] Justice Sopinka (with Chief Justice Lamer concurring) stated that "[t]here is not support in the cases in our Court for the theory that the rule has special application in sexual offences."[25] The problem is that the court has simply stated its position with no justification or meaningful analysis.

While *Handy* rejected the idea of a "special rule" for sexual assault cases, it nevertheless did open the door for arguments in favour of a new approach to admissibility. For the first time, a unanimous Supreme Court recognized that similar fact evidence can be admissible where it shows a *specific* (as opposed to a general) propensity to engage a particular kind of behaviour, including sexual assault. Relying on Chief Justice McLachlin's decision in *B(CR)*,[26] Justice Binnie observed that "evidence classified as 'disposition' or 'propensity' evidence is, exceptionally, admissible."[27] Again referring to *B(CR)*, Justice Binnie identified the propensity in that case as "a situation specific propensity to abuse sexually children to whom he stood in parental relationship."[28] Finally, he noted that "Canadian case law recognizes that as the 'similar acts' become more focussed and specific to circumstances similar to the charge (ie, more situation specific), the probative value of propensity, thus circumscribed, becomes more cogent."[29]

The Court's specific propensity reasoning is not grounded in traditional character analysis but rather in the doctrine of chances, that is, the improbability of coincidence that a complainant would not be telling the truth about someone who has done the same thing before.

As Justice Binnie put it at various points in *Handy*:

> The inferences sought to be drawn must accord with common sense, intuitive notions of probability and the unlikelihood of coincidence.[30] …
>
> It was thus held in *Makin* that the accumulation of babies found dead in similar circumstances permitted, in relation to the accused, the double in-

24 [1990] 1 SCR 717 [*B(CR)*].

25 *Ibid* at 740.

26 *Ibid* at 735.

27 *Handy, supra* note 6 at para 51–52.

28 *Ibid* at para 90.

29 *Ibid* at para 48.

30 *Ibid* at para 42.

> ference of propensity mentioned above. The improbability of an innocent explanation was manifest.[31] …
>
> Probative value exceeds prejudice, because the force of similar circumstances defies coincidence or other innocent explanation.[32]

In addition to acknowledging the availability of propensity reasoning, the *Handy* Court recognized that its relevance can be proof of the *actus reus* that in many cases turns on the credibility of the complainant.[33] As Justice Laskin observed in *R v B(R)*: "the question to be decided was whether the sexual assaults occurred. The similar fact evidence was probative of the *actus reus* of the offences, which in turn depended on the credibility of the complainants' evidence about the assaults."[34]

In light of the recognition in *Handy* that similar fact evidence can be used as specific propensity evidence, the door is now open for the adoption of an approach that presumes admissibility in cases where the issue is commission of the *actus reus* (ie, did the act occur and, where the complainant is of age, whether there was consent). Although the judge would always have discretion to exclude the evidence under this presumptive approach, such an exercise, outside of the special cases discussed below, would be rare. The onus would rest with the defence. The rule should either be judicially or legislatively created. Contrary to those who see this approach as opening up the bad character floodgates, a presumption of admissibility does not open the door for similar arguments in other cases. In most non-sexual assault cases, where the Crown seeks to lead similar fact evidence, the issue is identity, which is not included in the presumption, or the accused has done something to open the bad character door. In other cases, the Crown will have available other means of impeaching credibility such as a criminal record. Finally, in other cases involving violence, we rarely see the kind of outright and vicious attack on the credibility of the complainant. And so, in other cases, there is rarely the same kind of equality argument that would justify admission of similar fact evidence.

31 *Ibid* at para 46.

32 *Ibid* at para 47.

33 *Ibid* at para 120.

34 (2005), 77 OR (3d) 171 at para 11 (CA). See also *R v B(T)* (2009), 95 OR (3d) 21 at paras 21–24 (CA); *R v T(C)* (2005), 74 OR (3d) 100 at para 56 (CA); and *R v Thomas* (2004), 72 OR (3d) 401 at paras 43, 54 (CA).

Moreover, as noted earlier, the approach advocated is narrower and less categorical than Rules 413 and 414 of the *Federal Rules of Evidence*. For example, the presumption does not apply in cases where the issue is mistaken belief in consent or other cases where the issue is knowledge or wilful blindness. And, even where the issue is *actus reus*, there is an exception for identification cases and additional layers of scrutiny or safeguards in cases involving possible collusion or where the accused is Aboriginal or racialized. These special cases are discussed below.

ID Cases

Equality arguments are not applicable in cases where the issue is one of identification because these cases turn, generally speaking, on the reliability of the identification evidence and not on the credibility of the complainant.[35] Rarely is it ever suggested that the complainant is lying in these cases. The issue is whether he or she correctly identified the assailant. In addition to traditional reliability concerns, identification cases also raise additional fairness concerns. A presumptive rule of admissibility runs the danger of encouraging the police to simply round up the usual suspects in hopes of a positive line-up identification. Justice Binnie alluded to this concern in *Handy* when he noted:

> If propensity evidence were routinely admitted, it might encourage the police simply to "round up the usual suspects" instead of making a proper unblinkered investigation of each particular case. One of the objectives of the criminal justice system is the rehabilitation of offenders. Achievement of this objective is undermined to the extent the law doubts the "usual suspects" are capable of turning the page and starting a new life.[36]

The prospect of a wrongful conviction is, therefore, real in this context. This not only serves to undermine confidence in the administration of justice but it also means that the real perpetrator remains at large. The presumption of admissibility should not apply here and instead identification cases should continue to be assessed using the "strikingly similar" standard from *R v Arp*.[37]

35 A similar argument is made in Bryden & Park, *supra* note 10.

36 *Supra* note 6 at para 38.

37 [1998] 3 SCR 339. In *Handy*, *supra* note 6 at para 77, the Supreme Court described this *Arp* standard as follows:
Thus in *Arp*, where the issue was identification, Cory J cited at para 43 *R v Scopelliti* (1981), 63 CCC (2d) 481 (Ont CA), where Martin JA observed that evidence of pro-

Putative Collusion Cases

As noted earlier, using a doctrine of chances reasoning process in cases of similar fact evidence addresses the classic "character" concerns associated with this kind of evidence. The reasoning does not require any moral evaluation of the accused but rather a detached analysis of the likelihood of coincidence that two people would independently make similar allegations unless they were true. The doctrine of chances is destroyed, however, where the similar fact evidence is tainted. Coincidence is now replaced by collusion. This concern is addressed by the *Handy* approach requiring the Crown to negative collusion on a balance of probabilities where there is an "air of reality" to the allegation. And so, under this article's approach, the presumption would not apply where the defence raises an "air of reality" to collusion.

Cases Involving Aboriginal or Racialized Accused

It is now widely accepted in Canadian courts that systemic racism exists in the criminal justice system.[38] This racism translates into negative credibility assessments and propensity reasoning for Aboriginal and racialized accused. As Chief Justice McLachlin recognized in *R v Williams*:

> In my view, there was ample evidence that this widespread prejudice included elements that could have affected the impartiality of jurors. Racism against aboriginals includes stereotypes that relate to credibility, worthiness and criminal propensity. As the Canadian Bar Association stated in *Locking up Natives in Canada: A Report of the Committee of the Canadian Bar Association on Imprisonment and Release* (1988), at p. 5:
>
> > Put at its baldest, there is an equation of being drunk, Indian and in prison. Like many stereotypes, this one has a dark underside. It reflects

pensity on the issue of identification is not admissible "unless the propensity is so highly distinctive or unique as to constitute a signature" (p. 496).

Martin JA made the propensity point again in his lecture on "Similar Fact Evidence" published in [1984] *LSUC Spec Lectures* 1, at 9–10, in speaking of the Moors Murderer case (*R v Straffen*, [1952] 2 QB 911):

> Although evidence is not admissible to show a propensity to commit crimes, or even crimes of a particular class, evidence of a propensity to commit a particular crime in a *peculiar and distinctive way* was admissible and sufficient to identify [*Straffen*] as the killer of the deceased (emphasis in original).

38 See, for example, the discussion in *R v Williams*, [1998] 1 SCR 1128 at paras 58–59 and *R v Parks* (1993), 84 CCC (3d) 353 at paras 42 to 55 (Ont CA). See also David M Tanovich, *The Colour of Justice: Policing Race in Canada* (Toronto: Irwin Law, 2006).

> a view of native people as uncivilized and without a coherent social or moral order. The stereotype prevents us from seeing native people as equals.
>
> There is evidence that this widespread racism has translated into systemic discrimination in the criminal justice system: see *Royal Commission on Aboriginal Peoples, Bridging the Cultural Divide: A Report on Aboriginal People and Criminal Justice in Canada, at* p. 33; *Royal Commission on the Donald Marshall, Jr, Prosecution: Findings and Recommendations*, vol. 1 (1989), at p. 162; *Report on the Cariboo-Chilcotin Justice Inquiry* (1993), at p. 11. Finally, as Esson CJ noted, tensions between aboriginals and non-aboriginals have increased in recent years as a result of developments in such areas as land claims and fishing rights. These tensions increase the potential of racist jurors siding with the Crown as the perceived representative of the majority's interests.[39]

Justice Doherty acknowledged this in the context of anti-black racism in *R v Parks*:

> Racism, and in particular anti-black racism, is a part of our community's psyche. A significant segment of our community holds overtly racist views. A much larger segment subconsciously operates on the basis of negative racial stereotypes. Furthermore, our institutions, including the criminal justice system, reflect and perpetuate those negative stereotypes. These elements combine to infect our society as a whole with the evil of racism. Blacks are among the primary victims of that evil.
>
> In my opinion, there can be no doubt that there existed a realistic possibility that one or more potential jurors drawn from the Metropolitan Toronto community would, consciously or subconsciously, come to court possessed of negative stereotypical attitudes toward black persons.[40]

In *R v C(D)*,[41] Justice Doherty specifically recognized the prejudice facing black accused charged with sexual assault in the context of whether to question prospective jurors for partiality based on race and the nature of the crime:

39 *R v Williams, supra* note 38 at para 58.

40 *Ibid* at paras 54–55.

41 (1999), 139 CCC (3d) 248 at paras 4–5 (Ont CA).

> If anything, the potential for partiality in a case involving the alleged sexual assault of a 16-year-old white girl by a black man is greater than in the case of alleged violence by one man against another man.

In light of this reality, courts must be cognizant of the very real danger of racial bias impacting the trier of fact in its assessment of the cogency of the similar fact evidence. Courts should be flexible in allowing the defence to rebut the presumption with arguments that the prejudicial effect outweighs its probative value. This might be the case, for example, where the prior acts involved issues relating to identification. In cases where the evidence is admitted, a strong caution to the jury should be required.[42]

PART IV: A FORMAL EQUALITY JUSTIFICATION

A common defence tactic in sexual assault cases is, as recognized by the Supreme Court in *R v Mills*, to "whack the complainant."[43] The Court was referring to a speech by a senior Ottawa defence lawyer to other defence lawyers about sexual assault prosecutions in which he said, "[g]enerally, if you destroy the complainant in a prosecution absent massive corroborating evidence or eye witnesses, you destroy the head.... [T]he defence, really now is slice-and-dice time for the complainant. You have to go in there as a defence counsel and whack the complainant hard...."[44]

This "whack the complainant" tactic is commonly manifested in:

- electing to have a preliminary inquiry where defence counsel can cross-examine the complainant before trial;
- explicit or implicit reliance on myths and stereotypes to impugn the credibility of the complainant;

42 See, more generally, the discussion of the issue of race and character evidence in Montré Denise Carodine, "'The Mis-Characterization of the Negro': A Race Critique of the Prior Conviction Impeachment Rule" (2009) 84 Indiana LJ 521; Christine Chambers Goodman, "The Color of Our Character: Confronting the Racial Character of Rule 404(b) Evidence" (2007) 25 Law & Inequality 1; Sherilyn Johnson, "Racial Imagery in Criminal Cases" (1992–93) 67 Tul L Rev 1739; and Sherilyn Johnson, "The Color of Truth: Race and the Assessment of Credibility" (1996) 1 Mich J Race & L 261.

43 [1999] 3 SCR 668 at para 90.

44 Cristin Schmitz, "Whack Sex Assault Complainant at Preliminary Inquiry" *The Lawyer's Weekly* (2 May 1988) 22.

- suggesting to the complainant, in many cases a child complainant, that she has come to court prepared to perjure herself in the absence of any legitimate motive to lie;
- reliance on a specious motive to lie such as revenge or financial profit;
- attempting to cross-examine the complainant on her prior sexual history; or, seeking to introduce the complainant's medical and counselling records.[45] One of the purposes of doing so is to "depict the sexual assault complainant as the irrational, incredible, and hysterical other of the rational legal subject";[46]
- lengthy, embarrassing, intrusive cross-examination often focusing on clothing, alcohol consumption, lifestyle, employment or lack thereof, marital status, minor inconsistencies, lifestyle, drug or alcohol use;
- aggressive, lengthy, embarrassing and confusing cross-examination of child complainants;[47] and,
- putting suggestions to the complainant concerning consent that the lawyer knows are likely false;[48] or, otherwise aggressively cross-examining a witness the lawyer knows is telling the truth.[49]

45 Even the application itself will have a detrimental impact on the dignity, privacy, and psychological well-being of the complainant.

46 See Lise Gotell, "The Ideal Victim, the Hysterical Complainant and the Disclosure of Confidential Records: A Case Study of the Implications of the Charter for Sexual Assault Law" (2002) 40 Osgoode Hall LJ 251 at 256. See further, Lise Gotell, "When Privacy is Not Enough: Sexual Assault Complainants, Sexual History Evidence and the Disclosure of Personal Records" (2006) 43 Alta L Rev 743; and Janine Benedet & Isabel Grant, "Hearing the Sexual Assault Complaints of Women with Mental Disabilities: Evidentiary and Procedural Issues" (2007) 52 McGill LJ 515.

47 See John Phillipe Schuman, Nicholas C Bala & Kang Lee, "Developmentally Appropriate Questions for Child Witnesses" (1999) 25 Queen's LJ 251 at 297–301 for illustrations of some of the tactics and questions used to intimidate and confuse a child. See also Nicholas Bala *et al*, "Judicial Assessment of the Credibility of Child Witnesses" (2005) 42 Alta L Rev 995; Child Abuse Prevention and Counselling Society of Greater Victoria, *Children as Witnesses* (Victoria, BC, 1999); *R v F(CC)*, [1997] 3 SCR 1183 at 1205; Christine J Eastwood, Sally M Kift & Rachel Grace, "Attrition in Child Sexual Assault Cases: Why Lord Chief Justice Hale Got it Wrong" (2006) 16:2 J Judicial Admin 81; C Eastwood, W Patton & H Stacey, "Child Sexual Abuse and the Criminal Justice System" *Trends and Issues in Crime and Criminal Justice* (Australian Institute of Criminology, 1998).

48 See the discussion of the Kevin Barlow case in David M Tanovich, "Law's Ambition and the Reconstruction of Role Morality in Canada" (2005) 28 Dal LJ 267 at 294–96.

49 See David Layton, "The Criminal Defence Lawyer's Role" (2004) 27 Dal LJ 379.

It is now trite law that the conduct of the defence can impact on the admissibility of bad character evidence. So, for example, applying traditional principles, prior sexual misconduct evidence is admissible to rebut a defence of accident or innocent association;[50] or mistaken belief in consent.[51] In other contexts, allowing the Crown to lead bad character evidence to respond to defence tactics is commonly referred to as the "tit for tat" principle. The issue is not strictly one of assessing probative value and prejudicial effect but rather admission grounded in policy and fairness much like the underpinnings of the approach advanced in this article. Under the "tit for tat" principle, the Crown is able to lead bad character evidence where, for example: (i) the accused cross-examines Crown witnesses about their criminal record;[52] (ii) the accused suggests that another person committed the offence;[53] (iii) the accused impugns the character of the victim;[54] or (iv) the defence impugns the police investigation and failure to focus on other suspects.[55] The purpose of the "tit for tat" principle is one of fairness including ensuring that the trier of fact has a balanced picture.[56] As the Ontario Court of Appeal held in *R v Parsons*:

> ... if the appellant chose to throw sticks at [a third party], the Crown should be able to counter this evidence with any similar evidence relating to the propensity [of the appellant] ... To rule otherwise would leave the jury with a highly misleading impression... [57]

Despite the fact that the "tit for tat" argument does not appear to be argued by Crowns in sexual assault cases, the principle does apply given the nature of the defence tactics in these cases.[58] Indeed, there are

50 See, for example, *R v B(FF)*, [1993] 1 SCR 697.

51 See, for example, *R v Clermont*, [1986] 2 SCR 131.

52 See *R v Corbett*, [1988] 1 SCR 670 at 690.

53 See *R v Parsons* (1993), 84 CCC (3d) 226 at 237–38 (Ont CA) [*Parsons*]; *R v Vanezis* (2006), 213 CCC (3d) 449 (Ont CA); and *R v Woodcock* (2003), 177 CCC (3d) 346 at paras 136–137 (Ont CA).

54 See *R v Truscott* (2006), 213 CCC (3d) 183 at para 36 (Ont CA); and *R v Scopelliti* (1981), 63 CCC (2d) 481 at 497–98 (Ont CA).

55 See *R v Mallory* (2007), 217 CCC (3d) 266 at paras 85–87 (Ont CA); and *R v Dhillon* (2002), 166 CCC (3d) 262 at para 51 (Ont CA). See further the discussion in *R v Van*, 2009 SCC 22 at paras 25, 46.

56 See *R v Williams* (2008), 233 CCC (3d) 40 at paras 58–60 (Ont CA).

57 *Supra* note 53 at para 25.

58 A similar argument is made in Mary Childs, "The Character of the Accused" in Mary

far more fairness concerns in sexual assault cases than in cases involving self-defence or third-party attribution.[59] In addition to "whack the complainant" tactics, the defence is impugning the character of sexual assault complainants when they make the suggestion in cross-examination that the complainant is committing perjury and lying about the assault. As noted earlier, it is rare for a complainant in other crimes involving violence to be challenged as a liar. The usual defence is that they are mistaken in their identification of the accused, not that they are lying about being harmed. Interestingly, this "tit for tat" justification was relied upon by Justice L'Heureux-Dubé in her dissenting opinion in the similar fact case of *R v D(LE)*[60] wherein she observed:

> In the present case, defence counsel launched an attack on the credibility of the complainant....
>
> When children are sexually assaulted there are generally no witnesses. When such matters become the subject of criminal prosecution it is usually the victim's word against the accused's. Under such circumstances, the credibility of the victim is of crucial importance to the determination of guilt or innocence. When, as in this case, the credibility of the victim is attacked by defence counsel, the victim should not be denied recourse to evidence which effectively rebuts the negative aspersions cast upon her testimony, her character or her motives.... [61]

PART V: THE SUBSTANTIVE EQUALITY JUSTIFICATION

Prosecutors have traditionally faced an uphill battle in trying to introduce pattern evidence in sexual assault cases. Part of the reason is what Justice McLachlin referred to in *R v B(CR)* as the common law having taken a "strict view of similar fact evidence, regarding it with suspicion."[62] She does not elaborate on the etiology of the "suspicion" other than to trace the common law's concern about the prejudicial effect of bad character evidence on the deliberative process. However, since the majority of the modern era similar fact cases heard in the Supreme Court of Canada (and almost all of the leading cases) involve

Childs & Louise Ellison, eds, *Feminists Perspectives on Evidence* (London: Cavendish Publishing, 2000) 211 at 231–35.

59 See the discussion *infra* and the necessity discussion at note 11.

60 [1989] 2 SCR 111.

61 *Ibid* at 133–34.

62 [1990] 1 SCR 717 at 723 [*B(CR)*].

sexual assault,[63] the "suspicion" would appear to have more to do with the nature of the case than concerns about prejudice.[64] Indeed, as Professor Winter has observed, "it may be that it is not fear of forbidden reasoning which has prohibited inclusion of evidence of past rapes, but a more elusive judicial belief system in rape cases."[65] Moreover, as Professor Hanson stated:

> Much of the case law on the rules of similar fact evidence has related to incidents of rape, incest and child sexual assault. The argument put forward in this article is that the predominance of such offences in the case law is not coincidental. Rather, their over-representation can be seen to flow from

63 In Canada, fourteen of the twenty-two Supreme Court of Canada modern-day similar fact evidence (SFE) *admissibility* cases have involved sexual assault. Cases where the issue was the adequacy of the charge to the jury or application of the curative proviso have not been included. Pre-1970 cases have not been included because they largely date back to the early part of the century and contain very little analysis. See, for example, *R v Brunet*, [1918] 57 SCR 83; and, *R v Koufis*, [1941] SCR 481. It was only in the last twenty-five years that the Supreme Court really began to develop its own approach to similar fact admissibility.

Sexual Assault SFE Cases Post-1970 [14]	**Non-Sexual Assault SFE Cases Post-1970 [8]**
R v Guay, [1979] 1 SCR 18	*R v LeBlanc*, [1977] 1 SCR 339 (crim neg cause death)
R v Sweitzer, [1982] 1 SCR 949	*R v Boulet*, [1978] 1 SCR 332 (murder)
R v Bell, [1985] 1 SCR 594	*R v Alward*, [1978] 1 SCR 559 (robbery/murder)
R v Clermont, [1986] 2 SCR 131	*R v Hewson*, [1979] 2 SCR 82 (theft)
R v Robertson, [1987] 1 SCR 918	*R v LePage*, [1995] 1 SCR 654 (drugs)
R v Green, [1988] 1 SCR 228	*R v Arp*, [1998] 3 SCR 339 (murder/sexual assault)
R v D(LE), [1989] 2 SCR 111	*R v Perrier*, [2004] 3 SCR 228/
R v B(CR), [1990] 1 SCR 717	*R v Chan*, [2004] 3 SCR 245 (home invasion)
R v C(MH), [1991] 1 SCR 763	*R v Trochym*, [2007] 1 SCR 239 (murder)
R v B(FF), [1993] 1 SCR 697	
R v Handy, [2002] 2 SCR 908	
R v Shearing, [2002] 3 SCR 33	
R v Harvey, [2002] 4 SCR 311	
R v Blake, [2004] 3 SCR 503	

In six of the fourteen sexual assault cases, the Supreme Court held that the evidence was not admissible. More troubling is the fact that since 2000 (ie, the post-*Handy* propensity era), the Supreme Court has held that the evidence was not admissible in three of the four cases it has heard. These include *R v Handy*, [2002] 2 SCR 908; *R v Harvey*, [2002] 4 SCR 311; and *R v Blake*, [2004] 3 SCR 503. The one exception is *R v Shearing*, [2002] 3 SCR 33.

64 The same can be said of the leading similar fact evidence cases in other common law jurisdictions. See, for example, *DPP v Boardman*, [1975] AC 421 (HL); and *R v H*, [1995] 2 AC 596 (HL).

65 Jo Winter, "The Role of Gender in Judicial Decision-Making: Similar Fact Evidence, the Rose West Trial and Beyond" (2004) 8 Int'l J Evidence & Proof 31 at 35.

> a number of factors: the historical tendency of the courts to doubt sexual complainants; the law's tendency to confine analysis to a restricted set of facts and to view incidents as discrete events in isolation from their context; and, finally, a reluctance to acknowledge the situatedness of decision-makers and potential bias in determinations of what might be probative or prejudicial.[66]

In other words, it is reasonable to assume that the myths and stereotypes that manifest themselves in sexual assault cases have and continue to impact on similar fact adjudication. Some of the myths relevant to this context include that "women lie about being raped; that women are not reliable reporters of events; that women are prone to exaggerate; and, that women falsely report having been raped to get attention."[67] The depths of this inherent "suspicion" can be seen in *Handy* itself. Notwithstanding that Handy was a sexual predator who had been twice previously convicted of sexual assault of different women,[68] and was now alleged to have raped both the complainant and the similar fact witness, the Supreme Court of Canada and Ontario Court of Appeal expressed concerns about the reliability of the similar fact evidence including suggesting that it was "dicey"[69] and possibly tainted by the prospects of financial profit.[70] For example, in summarizing the Court of Appeal's decision, the Supreme Court noted:

66 Hanson, *supra* note 2 at 51.

67 See *Jane Doe v Metropolitan Toronto (Municipality) Commissioners of Police* (1998), 39 OR (3d) 487 (Ont Ct (Gen Div)). (MacFarland J) at para 13 [*Jane Doe*].

68 *Handy*, *supra* note 6 at para 142. It is interesting to point out that, in a previous decision, the Supreme Court recognized that delayed disclosure is irrelevant in the assessment of a complainant's credibility. As Justice Major, for the majority, held in *R v D(D)*, [2000] 2 SCR 275 at para 65:

> A trial judge should recognize and so instruct a jury that there is no inviolable rule on how people who are the victims of trauma like a sexual assault will behave. Some will make an immediate complaint, some will delay in disclosing the abuse, while some will never disclose the abuse. Reasons for delay are many and at least include embarrassment, fear, guilt, or a lack of understanding and knowledge. In assessing the credibility of a complainant, the timing of the complaint is simply one circumstance to consider in the factual mosaic of a particular case. A delay in disclosure, standing alone, will never give rise to an adverse inference against the credibility of the complainant.

> Moreover, it was entirely reasonable for Handy's ex-wife to wait until he was no longer able to harm her before filing a complaint.

69 *Ibid* at para 113.

70 *Ibid* at paras 23, 111, 133.

> The credibility of the ex-wife was problematic. She had considerably delayed reporting any of the incidents. The eventual timing of her complaints raised issues with respect to her motives. The complaint with respect to four incidents had first been made in support of an uncontested application for compensation before the Criminal Injuries Compensation Board when the respondent was in prison. The rest of the complaints had been made after her final separation from the respondent shortly after she had learned of the charges laid in this case.[71]

What makes this "suspicion" in *Handy* even more troubling is that there was corroborating evidence to support the complainant's allegation that arguably bolstered the reliability of the similar fact evidence. This included witnesses who saw bruises on the complainant's chest, arms, and throat in the days following the attack, and a statement attributed to the accused, "why does this keep happening to me."[72]

The fueling of this "inherent suspicion" by myths and stereotypes associated with sexual assault cases can also be seen in a court's willingness to view similar fact evidence as possibly tainted by collusion. In *B(CR)*, the accused was charged with sexually assaulting his daughter. The Crown wanted to lead evidence of sexual activity between the accused and his step daughter. The defence did not argue collusion and there was no evidence of it. Nevertheless, in his dissenting opinion, Justice Sopinka (with Justice Lamer concurring) raised the possibility of collaboration on his own motion:

> In considering the admissibility of the evidence in this case, I observe that no attempt appears to have been made to negative the possibility of collaboration. No questions were directed to Crown witnesses to determine whether this possibility existed.[73]

In *Handy*, the Crown wanted to lead evidence of the accused's alleged sexual and physical abuse of his ex-wife. The Crown sought to lead seven incidents between March of 1990 and October of 1996 to establish the accused's "propensity to inflict painful sex and when aroused will not take no for an answer."[74] In assessing the admissibility of the seven incidents, Justice Binnie, for the Court, was concerned that the

71 *Ibid* at para 23.

72 *Ibid* at paras 4–5.

73 *Supra* note 62 at 734.

74 *Handy*, *supra* note 68 at para 6.

evidence may have been tainted by the "potential collusion" between the ex-wife and the complainant. As noted earlier, prior to the alleged rape, the complainant and Handy's ex-wife had met and discussed Handy's conduct including a criminal injuries compensation claim that the ex-wife had earlier made and the settlement she had received. The court thus identified the root of collusion as the "whiff of profit":

> The ex-wife acknowledged that she had told the complainant of the $16,500 she received from the Criminal Injuries Compensation Board on the basis, she agreed, that "[a]ll you had to do was say that you were abused." A few days later the complainant, armed with this information, meets the respondent and goes off with him to have sex in a motel room.[75]

The depth of the Court's concern here is clearly manifested in its mistake on the facts. Justice Binnie suggests that "*a few days later*" and "armed with this information," the complainant potentially set the stage for a false complaint. In fact, the meeting between the complainant and Handy's ex-wife took place in the summer of 1996 and the alleged rape on the evening of 6 December 1996.[76] It is also manifested again in its decision in *R v Shearing*[77] where the Court characterized the summer meeting in *Handy* as a "*consultation* between the complainant and the similar fact witness prior to the alleged offence about the prospect of financial profit."[78]

The Court's theory of collusion makes little sense. The concern with collusion is the reliability of the similar fact evidence and whether it is the product of collusion, not the reliability of the complainant's evidence. Whether or not the complainant's evidence is somehow tainted is an issue for the trial, not the similar fact application. In *Handy*, the ex-wife's testimony was, in no way, impacted by this meeting as the compensation claim had been previously filed. Although the Court did not come to a final conclusion on the issue of collusion, it is clear that they were heavily influenced by this issue and were satisfied that there was "some evidence of actual collusion …. "[79] The Court's discussion

75 *Ibid* at paras 99, 111.

76 *Ibid* at paras 4, 15.

77 [2002] 3 SCR 33 [emphasis added]. *Shearing* is important on the issue of collusion because it at least recognizes that communication between complainants is not on its own to raise an "air of reality": *ibid* at paras 43–44.

78 *Ibid* at para 44.

79 *Handy, supra* note 68 at para 112.

of collusion further reveals the heavy burden placed on the Crown and sexual assault complainants. All nine justices appeared to have been satisfied that there was at least the possibility that the complainant lied about the rape because of the "whiff of profit." The clear implication that the complainant put herself in this position for money is demeaning and offensive. Again, it caters to the stereotype that women are prone to lie and sometimes motivated by money to do so. It is not clear how the Court factored her bruises into their theory, although presumably they would have concluded that she allowed Handy to hit her to further her false claim.

Ensuring that Sexual Assault is Treated as a Crime of Violence Not Sex

Similar fact adjudication in sexual assault cases is marked by a troubling failure to understand the nature of sexual assault. Courts appear to be focused on the issue of sex rather than on the domination and violence aspect of the encounter. As Justice McFarland recognized in *Jane Doe v Metropolitan Toronto (Municipality) Commissioners of Police*, sexual assault is a crime of violence, not sex:

> [S]exual violence is a form of violence; it is an act of power and control rather than a sexual act. It has to do with the perpetrator's desire to terrorize, to dominate, to control, to humiliate; it is an act of hostility and aggression. Rape has nothing to do with sex and everything to do with anger and power.[80]

This failure to properly understand the nature of the offence and, therefore, the propensity of those who commit it, has had a dramatic impact on the admissibility of similar fact evidence as exemplified by both the *B(CR)* and *Handy* cases.

In *B(CR)*, a majority of the Supreme Court (5–2) upheld the trial judge's decision to admit the similar fact evidence of the accused's step daughter in a case where he was charged with sexually assaulting his other daughter. Justice McLachlin for the majority, held that if she were the trial judge she may have found this to be a "borderline case."[81] Why? What troubled her were the dissimilarities in relation to the two complainants and the underlying conduct. She pointed out that the ages of the complainants were different (one was 15 years old, the other 11–13

80 *Jane Doe, supra* note 67 at para 8.

81 *Supra* note 62 at 739.

years old); one complainant was sexually mature, the other only a child when the abuse started; one complainant was a blood relation, the other was not; and the sexual abuse of one child involved urination, the other did not.[82] None of these dissimilarities would appear relevant when the focus is on domination and aggression rather than the sexual aspects of the conduct. Justice Sopinka, in dissent, would have excluded the similar fact evidence, in part, because of the dissimilarities in the evidence.

A similar focus on the sexual nature of the conduct is evident in *Handy*. In assessing the similarity of the ex-wife's allegations to the allegation of the complainant, the Court pointed out the following dissimilarities:

> Incident five involved choking, did not demonstrate sexual misconduct and was not remotely connected to the factual allegations in the charge.[83]
>
> ...
>
> None of the incidents described by the ex-wife began as consensual, then allegedly became non-consensual ...
>
> ...
>
> The dynamic of these situations is not the same as the motel scene ... [84]
>
> ...
>
> Perhaps the most important dissimilarity ... lies not in the acts themselves but in the broader context. The 'similar fact' evidence occurred in the course of a long-term dysfunctional marriage where the charge relates to a one-night stand following a chance meeting of casual acquaintances in a bar.[85]
>
> ...
>
> The jury would likely be more appalled by the pattern of domestic sexual abuse than by the alleged misconduct of an inebriated lout in a motel room on an isolated occasion.[86]

Again, it is submitted that when the focus is placed on the true nature of sexual offences, these dissimilarities become irrelevant to the issue of propensity. Moreover, such an analysis can only serve to demean and diminish the gravity of the harm caused. For example, in order to make their point in *Handy*, the Court had to characterize Handy as an "inebriated lout" and the encounter as a "one-night stand" or the

82 *Ibid.*

83 *Handy*, *supra* note 68 at para 124.

84 *Ibid* at para 125.

85 *Ibid* at para 129.

86 *Ibid* at para 140.

"motel scene." These comments are eerily reminiscent of Justice McClung's characterization of Ewanchuk's conduct as "clumsy passes" in *R v Ewanchuk*,[87] the case where a majority of the Alberta Court of Appeal upheld the acquittal of Ewanchuk of sexual assault despite the factual finding that the complainant had repeatedly said "no."

The heightened scrutiny by courts of the dissimilarities in the sexual nature of the incidents can be seen in the high number of exclusions post-*Handy*, particularly in cases involving female complainants under the age of nineteen. To identify this trend, a survey of reported post-*Handy* appellate and trial court decisions was conducted. Cases where the issue was identification or where there was an issue of collusion were excluded from the survey so that it could focus on assessing admissibility in cases that turned on credibility. Between 2003–06, similar fact evidence was excluded in 44 percent of the cases involving female complainants under the age of nineteen.[88] The most common reason was the perceived dissimilarities between the proposed evidence and the evidence of the complainant.[89] Consider the following cases.

87 See the discussion in the Supreme Court decision where the Court set aside the conviction and entered an acquittal and, in particular, Justice L'Heureux-Dubé's concurring opinion: [1999] 1 SCR 330 at para 91.

88 It is beyond the scope of this paper but worth noting the extent to which courts have little difficulty admitting evidence in cases involving male complainants under the age of nineteen and female complainants over the age of eighteen. There would appear to be far less concern with the degree of similarity in these cases. For example, the evidence was admitted in all nine reported cases involving males under the age of nineteen. See *R v Creswell*, [2009] OJ No 363 (CA); *R v Brown*, [2006] OJ No 5276 (CA); *R v C(T)* (2005), 27 CR (6th) 94 (Ont CA); *R v B(R)*, [2005] OJ No 3575 (CA); *R v Morin*, [2005] OJ No 4402 (CA); *R v Titmus* (2004), 191 CCC (3d) 468 (BCCA); *R v C(V)*, [2004] NJ No 311 (CA); *R v Wells* (2003), 174 CCC (3d) 301 (BCCA); *R v Gelesz*, [2002] OJ No 3883 (CA). Similarly, in cases involving female complainants over the age of eighteen, the similar fact evidence was admitted in nine of the ten reported cases in the survey. See — **Admitted** — *R v Chen*, [2008] BCJ No 2573 (CA); *R v McNight*, [2006] OJ No 1849 (CA); *R v Whitehead*, [2004] OJ No 4030 (CA); *R v D(TJ)*, [2004] OJ No 1444 (CA); *R v Stewart* (2004), 183 CCC (3d) 421 (BCCA); *R v L(D)*, [2004] OJ No 4692 (CA); *R v S(JGE)*, [2005] BCJ No 3161 (SC); *R v D(M)*, [2005] OJ No 5629 (SCJ); *R v Byer*, [2004] OJ No 5887 (SCJ) — **Excluded** — *R v W(WJ)*, [2003] NSJ No 328 (PC).

89

Admitted	**Excluded**
R v D(D), [2006] OJ No 3934 (CA)	*R v H(J)* (2006), 215 CCC (3d) 233 (Ont CA)
R v Camacho, [2005] OJ No 4417 (CA)	*R v Candale* (2006), 205 CCC (3d) 167 (Ont CA)
R v P(CJ), [2004] OJ No 1531 (CA)	*R v T(L)*, [2005] OJ No 139 (CA)
R v S(W), [2004] OJ No 4164 (CA)	*R v Blake*, [2004] 3 SCR 503
R v W(J), [2004] OJ No 3591 (CA)	*R v P(C)*, [2004] OJ No 4732 (CA)
R v Thomas (2004), 190 CCC (3d) 31 (Ont CA)	*R v K(A)*, [2006] BCJ No 823 (PC)

In *R v Blake*,[90] for example, the accused was charged with sexual assault and interference on an eight-year-old complainant. She alleged that after swimming, she was alone with the accused in his bedroom and that he blew on and kissed her vagina. The alleged incident occurred in the summer of 1996. The Crown was permitted at trial to lead two previous convictions as similar fact evidence. One of the convictions from 1986 involved touching the vagina of a ten-year-old girl while she was fully clothed. The other conviction from 1987 involved inviting an eight-year-old boy into his van. While inside the van, he put his hand down the boy's pants and touched his penis.[91]

On appeal, the Ontario Court of Appeal held that the trial judge had erred in admitting the evidence and ordered a new trial. On further appeal, the Supreme Court of Canada adopted the reasons of the majority of the Ontario Court of Appeal, which included the following statements:

> … In describing the similarities as generic, I mean that the identified similarities describe general, rather than specific, aspects of the conduct and contain limited detail, with the result that the identified similarities are likely to be present in most incidents of sexual touching involving children.…
>
> In my view, these descriptions relate to non-specific conduct and lack detail. Moreover, the fact that none of the incidents involved more intrusive conduct does not change the generic quality of the identified similarities.…
>
> I conclude that apart from generic similarities, there are no distinctive unifying features of the discreditable conduct evidence and the complainant's evidence. Moreover, particularly when considered in conjunction with the distinguishing features of the evidence (including remoteness in time), the identified similarities fail to establish a persuasive degree of connection.[92]

R v Shearing, [2003] 3 SCR 33
R v S(E), [2006] OJ No 1750 (SCJ)
R v D(RW), [2004] OJ No 3091 (SCJ)
R v Adams, [2005] BCJ No 1499 (PC)
R v Sauriol, [2004] OJ No 5876 (SCJ)
R v L(D), [2005] OJ No 4914 (SCJ)
R v C(R), [2003] OJ No 3919 (SCJ)
R v Collier, [2006] NJ No 283 (PC)
R v B(TJ), [2004] NJ No 71 (PC)
R v H(JM), [2003] OJ No 5511 (SCJ)
R v M(C), [2003] OJ No 529 (SCJ)
R v W(J), [2006] OJ No 3328 (SCJ)

90 [2004] 3 SCR 503.

91 These facts are summarized in the Ontario Court of Appeal judgment reported as *R v B(R)* (2003), 68 OR (3d) 75 at paras 2–4, 9–10.

92 *Ibid* at paras 61, 63, 69.

In the Court of Appeal, Justice Abella dissented. In her opinion, there were sufficient similarities to warrant admission:

> Most notable, perhaps, is the extent to which the evidence of the prior acts of sexual abuse is similar to the offence charged. The two prior acts were committed on children who, like the complainant in this case, were ten years old or younger. The incidents involved brief touching of the children's genitalia ... As well, the two prior assaults, as well as the alleged assault, were followed by the appellate either apologizing to the child, or telling them not to disclose what had happened....
>
> Where, as here, the probative value of similar fact evidence lies in its similarity with the charged offence, its admissibility turns on whether the similarities disclose a propensity with the requisite degree of specificity to justify reception of the evidence despite the unfair prejudice to the accused. The similar fact evidence in this case falls at the admissible end of the spectrum as it discloses a type of circumstance in which the appellant is disposed to sexually abuse children in a particular way. The issue in question is not the appellant's general disposition to sexually abuse children but rather whether the evidence is probative of repeated conduct of a similar type in a specific type of situation.[93]

In *R v T(L)*,[94] the Ontario Court of Appeal overturned a trial judge's admission of similar fact evidence because of the dissimilarities between the acts. Here is how the Court of Appeal described them:

> ... the connection between KR's allegations and the other counts and the connection between counts was weak. As between counts, the nature of the allegations made by the complainants varied considerably and the allegations were disparate in time. In regard to KT, the counts involved incestuous touching with a pre-pubescent child, progressing to masturbation and oral sex as she grew older. The count relating to JL alleged that the appellant raped his wife's 15-year-old sister. The counts in relation to the appellant's sister-in-law, AB, and the similar fact evidence of KR involved sexual touching of the girls during and after puberty.[95]

93 *Ibid* at para 25.

94 [2005] OJ No 139 (CA).

95 *Ibid* at para 15.

Similarly, in *R v W(J)*,[96] a trial judge excluded the similar fact evidence because of the lack of so-called non-generic similarities:

> Moreover, many factors distinguish the proposed evidence from the case before me:
>
> - PB was 18 years old at the time of the assault, whereas RH was 10
> - JW had no previous relationship with PB and came into contact with her on a single occasion, when she visited the home, whereas he stood in a position of trust toward RH, who lived in the home, and had a longstanding relationship with her
> - The assault against RH involved full sexual intercourse, whereas the incident with PB involved digital penetration
> - PB testified she was screaming and struggling to run away during the assault, and that JW's father witnessed the attack, whereas RH never suggested she called out or that anyone was aware of the assaults.
>
> In sum, a comparison of the proposed evidence to the case before me reveals significant differences in the ages of the complainants, their relationship to JW and the type of assaults committed. Therefore, although generic similarities exist (all the conduct was sexual and took place in the home), the lack of distinctive unifying features combined with the distinguishing features between the former incident and this case fails to establish a persuasive degree of connection. Having so concluded, I need go no further to consider the potential prejudice to JW.[97]

And, in *R v K(A)*,[98] a trial judge was compelled to exclude similar fact evidence because of the lack of similarities including the fact that the similar fact witness was not allegedly assaulted while she was lying in her bed as was the case with the two complainants.[99]

PART VI: THE FEMINIST CRITIQUE OF A PRESUMPTIVE RULE

A number of feminist evidence scholars are critical of relaxing the similar fact rule in sexual assault cases. Although their focus is on the categorical rule of admission of Federal Rules 413–414, they have ex-

96 [2006] OJ No 3328 (SCJ).

97 *Ibid* at paras 21–22.

98 [2006] BCJ No 823 (PC).

99 *Ibid* at para 29.

tended their criticisms to cases where the basis of admission is more circumscribed and so it is important to attempt to identify and respond to their arguments.[100] The first concern expressed is that a presumptive rule will reinforce the stereotype that sexual assault complainants require corroboration. This is a valid concern but not a convincing argument in favour of exclusion. The logical extension of the argument would be that no corroborative evidence should be called in sexual assault cases for fear of reinforcing the stereotype. Moreover, no one has ever suggested that pointing out corroborative evidence in a Crown's closing address in a sexual assault case serves to perpetuate the stereotype. Finally, there is always the risk that ameliorative action will reinforce stereotypes but that the good usually outweighs the harm. It is not likely, as Professor Orenstein posits, that cases without similar fact evidence will not be prosecuted with a relaxation of the strict exclusionary rule.[101]

A second concern is that a presumptive rule will reinforce the stereotype that men who commit sexual assaults are "deviants." Professor Orenstein describes this concern as follows:

> Rather than seeing rape as an aberration and rapists as a small group of sick individuals, feminists examine the factors in our society that make us tolerant of rape.... Feminists believe, and there is abundant empirical evidence for this belief, that many otherwise normal seeming, socially acceptable men are potential rapists, and that rape may be as much a crime of opportunity as a test of character. Rape, and acquaintance rape in particular, is wide-spread, occurring throughout all strata of society.[102]

Again, while a legitimate concern in sexual assault prosecutions, it is not a convincing argument. It is present with or without reliance on similar fact evidence. In order to be valid, it assumes that the trier of fact will consciously or unconsciously draw a negative inference from the absence of evidence of previous sexual misconduct. One solution, proposed by Orenstein as an alternative to a presumptive rule of admissibility, would be to develop jury instructions to educate jurors about

100 Aviva Orenstein, "No Bad Men!: A Feminist Analysis of Character Evidence in Rape Trials" (1998) 49 Hastings LJ 663; Childs, *supra* note 58 at 220–27; and Katherine K Baker, "Once a Rapist? Motivational Evidence and Relevancy in Rape Law" (1996) 110 Harv L Rev 563.

101 Orenstein, *supra* note 100 at 694.

102 *Ibid* at 692. See also the discussion at 691–93.

the prevalence of sexual assault in society and how rape is not an aberration or committed only by a "sick" individual. This could be done in conjunction with the approach set out in this article.

Other concerns advanced include general mistrust of character evidence based on the law's historical reliance on prior sexual history evidence in sexual assault cases, further marginalization of racialized groups, and opening the door to a defence response. I have tried to address these issues in the formulation of the proposed rule. While there is good reason to be suspicious of character evidence, the reasoning here is grounded in probabilities more so than disposition. The evidence is relevant because the law of probabilities makes it unlikely that a person would be falsely accusing an individual who has done the very thing before. To the extent that this might be a motive to lie where the complainant is aware of the prior misconduct, one would expect that the defence would want the evidence as part of the record in order to put forward this theory. In addition, the proposed rule recognizes that there should be additional safeguards put in place in cases involving racialized accused because of the very real danger that systemic racism will lead to additional prejudice in the assessment of the evidence. Finally, the rule is largely grounded in a response to defence tactics (ie, the "tit for tat" principle), which would then foreclose any attempt by the defence to respond to the Crown's response.

PART VII: CONCLUSION

The similar fact evidence exception to the bad character exclusionary rule has undergone a considerable transformation in Canada over the last two decades. We have moved from a categorical approach to admissibility to a more principled approach balancing probative value and prejudicial effect. More recently in *Handy*, the Supreme Court recognized that probative value can include a situation-specific propensity to engage in a particular kind of behaviour. It is now time to recognize that the admissibility of prior sexual misconduct in sexual assault cases requires special attention. This article has advanced both formal and substantive equality arguments to argue that similar fact evidence should be presumptively admissible in cases where the issue is one of commission of the *actus reus*.

22.

Raising the Age of Sexual Consent: Renewing Legal Moralism?

Julie Desrosiers

In contrast to the 1992 sexual assault reforms analyzed by Elizabeth A Sheehy earlier in this section, the law reform discussed in this chapter was neither initiated nor shaped by feminist intervention. Instead, Julie Desrosiers argues that the 2008 reform that raised the age of consent is based in deeply conservative moralism. Although she acknowledges that feminists worry about the ability of young women to freely "consent" to sexual contact with adult men, particularly in the context of a society that teaches young females that their value lies in their attractiveness to males, she suggests that feminist process requires that we engage with young women to ascertain their experiences and their input on the issue. Like Alison Symington, who writes in Chapter Twenty-Five about the risks of criminalizing failure to disclose one's HIV status, Julie cautions that using the repressive force of the criminal law will further disempower young women's claims to autonomy and will discourage them from seeking services and information when they need it most.

Toward the end of the eighteenth century, Blackstone stated that any use of force, however minimal, could constitute an assault.[1] This principle acquires its full meaning within the context of sexual aggression where either a caress or a beating can sustain charges of sexual assault.[2] Charges of sexual assault do not depend on the extent of violence employed, but rather on the absence of consent in so far as a person — female or male — does not consent to being touched and is entitled to the protection of their physical integrity.[3] Obviously, women have had to fight to challenge sexist prejudice that undermines the legal protection

1 William Blackstone, *Commentaries on the Law of England: Book the Third: Of Wrongs and Their Remedies, Respecting the Rights of Persons* (London: Clarendon Press, 1765–69), online: <http://avalon.law.yale.edu>.

2 *R v Cuerrier*, [1998] 2 SCR 371 at para 11, per L'Heureux-Dubé J.

3 *R v Park*, [1995] 2 SCR 836 at paras 41–42.

of their physical integrity,[4] yet the fact remains that on formal grounds, the criminal law has always prohibited sexual touching in violation of the person's will to be touched.

Canadian criminal law has also prohibited sexual contact with children, be they consensual or not. This prohibition is based upon two serious concerns. First, a child's body is in no way prepared for coitus, and penetration of any kind may result in injury or laceration. And second, children do not have the capacity to give free and enlightened consent because their self-autonomy still requires time to evolve. They are vulnerable to all forms of depredation and duress. They have no means of defending themselves when facing threats or physical constraints. In a word, they are simply not equal sexual partners. The criminal sanctioning of sexual contacts between children and adults carries the day with universal agreement and approval.[5]

How are these two rules —sexual contact without consent is prohibited and sexual contact with children is prohibited— applied to adolescents? While an adolescent cannot be forced into sexual contact, may the adolescent consent to such contact? If such be the case, then at what age can they consent in law? Moreover, must any prohibition be total, or only apply under certain circumstances?

Western democracies have all ruled on an age of sexual consent that varies between twelve and eighteen years of age.[6] Yet the age of consent says very little about how adolescents are to be governed because this is but one factor amongst a rather complex set of rules intended to protect children while ensuring the sexual freedom of adolescents.[7]

4 Up until its repeal in 1984, proof of rape required evidence of vaginal penetration by a man of a woman not his wife. Violent oral or anal assaults were not classified as rape. The law was thus mainly concerned with protecting men's property rights in their wives and daughters, and particularly women's reproductive capacity: Lorenne MG Clark & Debra J Lewis, *Rape: The Price of Coercive Sexuality* (Toronto: Women's Press, 1977). The rules of evidence under the *common law* constituted further obstacles: namely the need for corroboration, evidence of recent complaint, and admissibility of evidence of the sexual reputation of the woman. See, in particular, Josée Néron, *L'agression sexuelle et le droit criminel canadien: l'influence de la tradition* (Cowansville: Yvon Blais, 1997).

5 See *R v L (JJ)*, [1998] RJQ 971 (CA).

6 Helmut Graupner, "Sexual Consent: The Criminal Law in Europe and Outside of Europe" in Helmut Graupner & Vern L Bullough, eds, *Adolescence, Sexuality and the Criminal Law: Multidisciplinary Perspectives* (Binghamton, NY: Harworth Press, 2004) 111.

7 *Ibid.* It would be normal to set a high level of age of consent in a country where this would be the sole means of protecting minors, since such an age of consent would allow the continuance of relations between adolescents and persons in a position of

To clearly understand the Canadian regime, the spectrum of analysis must be enlarged. As such, the age of consent has for many years been set at fourteen years of age, but it coexisted with various "other" threshold ages: age eighteen for consenting to anal penetration as well as for consenting to sexual contacts within a framework of authority, trust, or exploitation.

In 2008, the age of consent was raised to age sixteen for purposes of better protecting adolescents from sexual abuse and exploitation.[8] A cross analysis of relevant criminal provisions indicates, however, that increasing the age of consent produces legal effects in only one scenario: namely that of sexual contacts consented between an adolescent (age fourteen to sixteen) and an adult (with an age difference of five years) in a social setting of relative equality. Bearing in mind that the average moment of adolescents' first sexual relationship takes place at about age fourteen, and that data on the impact of sexual relations between adolescents and adults are piecemeal and non-conclusive, what will the raising of the age of consent accomplish? The application of liberal, conservative, and feminist analytical grids shed light on the values underlying this new prohibition. All in all, a measure of skepticism is in order. For underlying the crusade against sexual predators, there is clearly a renewal of legalistic moralism.

1. The Ups and Downs of the Age of Sexual Consent

In Canada, the age of consent was set at age fourteen in 1890.[9] It was strictly prohibited to engage in sexual relations with a young woman of less than age fourteen, save where she was the legitimate spouse of the accused. The consent of an adolescent over age fourteen was deemed to be valid except in instances of seduction of a person under age eighteen who was of *previously chaste character*.[10]

authority (Belgium and Luxembourg, where the age limit is set at sixteen). Likewise, a higher age of consent presents fewer risks of criminalization if implemented with a process for filtering complaints (Finland and Norway, where the age of consent is set at age sixteen, but where two-thirds of cases do not go to trial). Lastly, a relatively low age of consent is appropriate if other measures of protection are in place (setting the age of consent at fourteen, but at eighteen for those in positions of trust or authority).

8 *Tackling Violent Crime Act*, SC 2008, c 6.

9 *An Act to Amend the New Criminal Act*, SC 1890, c 37 ss 3, 7, quoted in Committee on Sexual Offences against Children and Youth, *Sexual Offences Against Children: Report of the Committee on Sexual Offences Against Children and Youth* [*Badgley Report*], vol 1 (Ottawa: Department of Supply and Services Canada, 1984) at 337.

10 *Ibid* at 342–49.

In 1984, the Badgley Report concluded that offences by seduction did not sufficiently protect young women age fourteen to eighteen, especially because proof of such offences depended on the victim's sexual reputation and on evidence of vaginal penetration.[11] Then, in 1988, new offences pertaining to sexual contact with adolescents and exploitation were drafted in order to remedy these deficiencies, yet the age of consent would remain the same. At the time of their adoption, sections 151 and 152 of the *Criminal Code* prohibited any form of sexual contact with a person under age fourteen, whether or not there had been consent, while s 153 prohibited any form of sexual contact between an adolescent age fourteen to eighteen and an adult in a position of trust or authority, regardless of consent. As such, an adolescent over age fourteen could consent to sexual contact with a person of any age insofar as the person was not in a position of trust or authority. However, s 159, consent to anal intercourse, required that the adolescent had attained eighteen years of age.

Section 150 was also added at this time to permit a lower age of consent, between twelve and fourteen years, if the age difference between the two persons was not more than two years. This section was added to recognize important realities. Pursuant to the reforms in 1984[12] and 1988,[13] sexual assault covers a vast array of behaviours — from an unwanted kiss to intercourse. By setting the age of consent at fourteen, the legislator would have criminalized kisses and caresses freely consented to between, for instance, thirteen-year-old adolescents. Hence the adoption of a two-year proximity of age clause that opened a small escape-provision in the otherwise impenetrable prohibition whereby an adolescent between twelve and fourteen years may consent to sexual activities with another adolescent insofar as an age difference of less than two years separates one from the other.[14]

11 *Ibid* at 437–41.

12 *An Act to amend the Criminal Code in relation to sexual offences and other offences against the person and to amend certain other acts in relation thereto or in consequence thereof*, SC 1980-81-82-83, c 125, in force on 4 January 1983. This statute repeals the crimes of rape and indecent assault and replaces them with the crimes of sexual assault (*Criminal Code*, RSC 1985, c C-46 ss 271ff).

13 *An Act to Amend the Criminal Code and the Canada Evidence Act*, SC 1987, c 24, in force on 1 January 1988. This statute specifically puts into effect the crimes of sexual abuse and exploitation of minors (ss 151–53).

14 *Ibid* at s 150.1 (2).

In 2008, the conservative government raised the age of consent to sixteen,[15] without modifying the structure of the regime set in place in 1988. Consensual sexual activity between adolescents and adults in a position of trust, authority, or exploitation remains prohibited until the legal age of majority. The same applies to consensual anal intercourse. But the reform has important consequences for consensual sexual contacts between young adults and adolescents by criminalizing otherwise formally lawful sexual relations. A fourteen- to sixteen-year-old adolescent no longer has the option of freely choosing a partner; she or he may consent to sexual contacts (kisses, caresses, or other sexual acts), but only with a partner who is not much older than he or she is. The new provisions prohibit consensual sexual relations between adolescents age fourteen to sixteen and persons more than five years older than they are. As for adolescents age twelve to fourteen years, their liberty to engage in sexual relations remains subject to a proximity age clause of two years. The sexual autonomy of adolescents is therefore quite relative: they may indulge in sexual relations, but only amongst themselves. The ensuing synthesis — presented in Table 1 — should facilitate the understanding of the law and the 2008 amendments.

Thus, in practical terms, the raising of the age of consent goes further in restricting the sexual autonomy of fourteen- to sixteen-year-old adolescents who may no longer consent to having sexual contacts with persons who are "too old." It is noteworthy that prior to the reform, their autonomy was already quite relative since they could not consent to sexual contacts with adults in position of authority, trust, or exploitation. It is also noteworthy that the legislator had already stipulated in an amendment in 2005 that the age difference had to be taken into account at the time of deciding if the relation constituted exploitation.[16] Adolescents were, however, already protected from unscrupulous sexual predators many years their senior. The nature of the relationship has become irrelevant; sexual assault is now only a function of age difference.

Nonetheless, a small legislative work-around makes it possible to avoid the criminal law proscription. Redemption comes from marriage. Any person age fourteen to sixteen years of age may consent to sexual contacts with any adult — no matter how many years his or her senior — provided the adult is his or her legally wedded spouse.[17] To ensure total legality, the betrothed couple must abstain from kissing,

15 *Supra* note 8.

16 Section 153(1.2).

17 Section 150.1(2.1)(b).

Table 1: Age of Consent Law, 1988 versus 2008

	1988	2008
Sexual contacts adult/child	Prohibited (s 150.1(1))	Idem
Sexual Contacts adolescent/adult or adolescent/adolescent in a position of trust, authority or exploitation	Prohibited until majority (s 153)	Idem
Other sexual contacts among adolescents	Permitted between a youth of age twelve to fourteen and another youth who is less than two years older than he or she (s 150.1(2)) 12 ↔ less than age 14 13 ↔ less than age 15 14 -1 day ↔ less than age 16 Unrestricted permission as of age fourteen, with the exception of anal intercourse.	Idem Idem (the reform has no impact upon adolescent couples)
Other sexual contacts adolescent/adult	Unrestricted permission as of age fourteen (s 150.1(1)), with the exception of anal intercourse (s 159(2))	Permitted between a youth of age fourteen to sixteen and a person who is less than five years older than the youth (s 150.1(2.1)) 14 ↔ less than age 19 15 ↔ less than age 20 16 -1 day ↔ less than age 21 Unrestricted permission as of age sixteen (s 150.1(1)), with the exception of anal intercourse (s 159)

touching one another, or having sexual relations prior to consecrating their union legally. Lastly, it is noteworthy that matrimony also makes legal consensual anal intercourse — little does the age of the participants matter.[18]

2. Youth and Their Sexuality

In Canada, *The Canadian Youth, Sexual Health and HIV/AIDS Study*, published in 2003, remains the last landmark study investigating adolescent sexuality. The vast canvassing of samples upon which it is based ensured result reliability: 11,082 students in seventh, ninth, and eleventh grades, or in first, third, and fifth years of secondary school, participated in the study — namely adolescents generally twelve, fourteen, and sixteen years old.[19] Upon analysis of their answers, it was noted that the adolescent sexual experimentation proceeded progressively and that they indulged in a variety of sexual acts (kisses, caresses, oral sex) prior to having fully completed sexual intercourse.[20] The study established that a large number of adolescents had already had sexual contact at age twelve (prolonged kissing and caresses), which is the case for a decisive majority of adolescents at age sixteen. Oral sex is practiced by 30 percent of fourteen-year-old adolescents and by 52.5 percent of sixteen-year-old adolescents. Sexual intercourse with penetration, has been experienced by at least 2 percent of twelve-year-old students, by 21 percent of fourteen-year-old-students, and by 43 percent of sixteen-year-old students.[21] Finally, the average age of the first fully-completed sexual intercourse within the age-sixteen group claiming to be sexually active was 14.3 years of age.[22]

18 Section 159(2).

19 Council of Ministers of Education, *The Canadian Youth, Sexual Health and HIV/AIDS Study: Factors Influencing Knowledge, Attitudes and Behaviours* (Ottawa: Council of Ministers of Education, 2003) at 9–11.

20 Studies on adolescent sexuality are generally undertaken from the perspective of focusing on sexual health; they hence evidence a specific interest in preventing pregnancies and sexually transmitted diseases. As such, the focus tends to enquire into sexual intercourse with penetration. Yet, in order to grasp adolescent sexuality as a whole, the analysis spectrum must be enlarged. Thus, the drop in the rate of sexual intercourse with penetration, for example, cannot be considered in isolation, but must also take into account the correlative increase in oral sexual relations. See David Weiss & Vern L Bullough, "Adolescent American Sex" in Graupner & Bullough, *supra* note 6 at 43 at 44–45.

21 All these figures were culled from *The Canadian Youth, Sexual Health and HIV/AIDS Study*, *supra* note 19 at 83–92.

22 *Ibid* at 93.

Table 2: Results from The Canadian Youth, Sexual Health and HIV/AIDS Study

	Seventh grade & secondary 1 (generally age 12)	Ninth grade & secondary 3 (generally age 14)	Eleventh grade & secondary 5 (generally age 16)
Prolonged kissing and caresses	42%	66%	81%
Oral sex	At least 1%[1]	30%	52.5%
Sexual intercourse (penetration)	At least 2%	21%	43% (average age: 14.3)

1 The authors of the report explain that there were no questions specifically addressing oral sex or sexual intercourse with penetration for the twelve-year-old group; nonetheless, some students made mention of this under the heading "other." See The Canadian Youth, Sexual Health and HIV/AIDS Study at 84.

Data compiled in Quebec in 2002 within the framework of promoting "sexual health" are comparable with the Canadian profile: about one-half of thirteen-year-olds had already had an intimate relationship (which implies kissing and caresses) and 4.2 percent of them had experienced sexual intercourse with penetration. Among sixteen-year-old students, these figures rise to 80 percent (intimate relationship) and 40 percent (sexual intercourse with penetration).[23] The average age for the first sexual relationship amongst sixteen-year-olds claiming to be sexually active was 14.5 years old.[24]

The first observation that must be made is that adolescents twelve to sixteen years old often do have sex lives. This information should come as no surprise since adolescence is a period of intense physical transformation that results in the sexual maturity of the body, ie, the prerequisite necessary for ensuring the reproduction of the human species. Each individual is biologically programmed to have sexual contacts as

23 Institut de la statistique du Québec, *Enquête sociale et de santé auprès des enfants et des adolescents québécois* (Québec: Publications du Québec, 2002) at 277–78. This survey was performed on 3,700 girls and boys aged nine, thirteen, and sixteen. The survey claims to be representative of all Quebeckers in these age groups.

24 *Ibid* at 285.

puberty runs its course.[25] The second observation regarding sexuality is that normality is an elastic concept. Adolescents do not conform to one standard behavioural profile. Some have already had sexual relations at age thirteen (roughly 4 percent), others have never kissed anyone at age sixteen (19 percent). Sexual maturing is an ongoing process amongst all adolescents. Young people reach various stages of readiness for sexual experimentation at widely different ages, all within the range of "normal." When the legislators set a minimum age of consent without taking those realities into account, they risk criminalizing the normal sexual behaviour of a significant proportion of adolescents.

Turning now to the issue of sexual contacts between adults and adolescents, what can be said? First of all, there is a dearth of data concerning this phenomenon.[26] Canadian researchers observe that female adolescents undergo precocious physiological maturing when compared to young males, and they usually choose partners somewhat older than themselves.[27] Extrapolating the extent of this phenomenon is difficult. A few studies in the United States have sought to document the prevalency of adolescent female/male adult relations — the most frequently observed sexual combination — where age difference is an issue.[28] While data findings are insufficient for drawing well-founded conclusions, and many methodological problems hamper their interpretation, it appears that this type of relationship is relatively frequent: depending on the studies, 3.5 percent to 13 percent of female adolescents reported these sexual experiences.[29] If such relations may have negative effects upon female adolescents, they may also have positive effects. As such, generalizations are far too speculative to be made.[30] It is also noteworthy that we do not have any information on the prevalency and potential effects of female adolescents/adult women couples.

25 Traditionally, the age of consent was simply the age of puberty. See Vern L Bullough, "Age of Consent: An Historical Overview" in Graupner & Bullough, *supra* note 6 at 23 at 25.

26 But see the recent study of Bonnie B Miller, David N Cox & Elizabeth M Saweyc, "Age of Sexual Consent Law in Canada: Population-Based Evidence for Law and Policy" (2010) 19 Can J Human Sexuality 105.

27 *Enquête sociale et de santé auprès des enfants et des adolescents québécois*, *supra* note 253 at 278; *The Canadian Youth, Sexual Health and HIV/AIDS Study*, *supra* note 19 at 115.

28 Denise A Hines & David Finkelhor, "Statutory Sex Crime Relationships Between Juveniles and Adults: A Review of Social Scientific Research" (May 2007) 12 Aggression and Violent Behaviour 300 at 302.

29 *Ibid* at 302–04.

30 *Ibid.*

With respect to male adolescents/adult women couples, they seem to comprise about 5 percent of male adolescents and, on the whole, seem to be overall beneficial for both parties to the relationship.[31] The same may be applied to young gays, who tend to react positively to sexual interactions with more mature adult men.[32] In the preceding case, adolescent males state that their relationship with an adult male has assisted them in coming to terms with their sexual orientation and having a more positive outlook on life. Therefore, available data strongly refutes a presumption of trauma caused by sexual relations with adult men, at least for gay youths. Nonetheless, with knowledge in this area at its current state, additional research is needed, especially with regard to relationships between adults and female adolescents.

3. The Conceptual Foundations for Raising the Age of Sexual Consent

Adolescents are sexual beings who, on occasion, share sexual intimacy with adults. Should this be prohibited? Criminalizing behaviour is a serious undertaking: it transforms a citizen into a criminal.[33] The assertion that the criminal law should be a last resort has become a commonplace statement. Contemporary Canadian authors generally restate the moderation principle set forth by the Law Reform Commission in past times:[34] the implementation of criminal law must only be directed towards the repression of conduct that infringes upon some fundamental social value and that is in addition deemed harmful.[35] Are consensual sexual contacts between adolescents and adults in circumstances of relative equality to be considered criminal conduct? The answer depends on the theoretical perspective that informs it.

31 *Ibid* at 305. See also Bruce Rind, "An Empirical Examination of Sexual Relations Between Adolescents and Adults: They Differ from Those Between Children and Adults and Should be Treated Separately" in Graupner & Bullough, *supra* note 6 at 55.

32 Hines & Finklehor, *supra* note 28 at 304; Rind, *ibid.*

33 Herein the author draws inspiration from Elizabeth Comack & Gillian Balfour, *The Power to Criminalize: Violence, Inequality and the Law* (Halifax: Fernwood Publishing, 2004) at 9: "To criminalize, according to the standard dictionary definition, means to turn a person into a criminal."

34 Law Reform Commission, *Our Penal Law* (Ottawa: Law Reform Commission of Canada, 1976).

35 Gisèle Côté-Harper, Pierre Rainville & Jean Turgeon, *Traité de droit pénal canadien* (Cowansville: Yvon Blais, 1998) at 61; See also Don Stuart, *Canadian Criminal Law*, 4d ed (Toronto: Carswell, 2001) at 62.

3.1 Liberal Perspectives

The emblematic figure of liberalism, John Stuart Mill, advocated the broadest liberty of individual action possible with the conviction that the sum of individual liberties benefits all humanity by ushering in new fields of knowledge and new ways of doing, knowing, living.[36] Government must therefore restrain its resort to repressive actions in order not to impose an oppressive norm. The principle is clear: the only prohibitions ought to be those of behaviours that cause harm to another. Since the concept of harm is notoriously difficult to determine, liberals have outlined various criteria to determine if a specific behaviour should be singled out for criminal sanction.[37] For that matter, the criminalization of consensual relations between adults and sixteen- to eighteen-year-old adolescents is quite problematic in light of several of these criteria: the criminalization of a consensual relationship, the random application of the prohibition depending on arbitrary age cut-offs, and an inappropriate legal response to an issue more social than criminal in nature. Some illustrations are in order.

Liberals have a marked hesitancy to brand a purely consensual relationship as a criminal offence. A fifteen-year-old adolescent who voluntarily, enthusiastically, and even with love and passion pursues a relationship with a young adult certainly does not consider him or herself to be a victim. From a liberal perspective, there can be no crime without a victim and it is highly problematical for the state to force its citizens to respect its views in matters of morality.

Furthermore, the criminalization of consensual relations between adults and adolescents between ages fourteen and sixteen raises genuine problems regarding consistent and fair application of the prohibition. The number of these relationships is unknown, but sexual relationships between adults and adolescents are likely to be relatively widespread. Although there are no Canadian data on this subject, it is

36 John Stuart Mill, *On Liberty*, 2d ed (London: John W Parker and Son, 1859). See also its first French language translation: John Stuart Mill, *La liberté*, translated by Charles Brook Dupont-White (Paris: Guillaumin, 1860), online: <http://books.google.fr>.

37 See Herbert Packer, *The Limits of the Criminal Sanction* (Stanford: Stanford University Press, 1968), who raises six issues: (1) Generally speaking, does the prohibited conduct constitute an important social threat? (2) Does criminalization of the conduct produce deterrent effects? (3) Does criminalization of the conduct hamper the pursuit of lawful and socially beneficial activities? (4) Is it possible to repress the prohibited conduct in a non-discriminatory manner (which is not the case when such conduct is widespread and measures taken against it are selective and sporadic?) (5) Is the prohibited conduct a consensual activity in which no one is a victim? (6) And last of all, besides criminalization, are there other efficient ways to solve the problem?

a known fact in the United States that the majority of investigations are instigated by complaints to authorities from worried or disapproving parents.[38] Yet, while some parents deem such a relationship to be criminal, others disapprove but refrain from alerting authorities, while still others simply decide to have confidence in their adolescents and their sexual choices. Hence, the law is enforced sporatically, and potentially unfairly, for purposes of controlling adolescent sexuality.

Finally, and just supposing — which has not yet been documented — that the consensual relations between adults and fourteen- to sixteen-year-old adolescents are prejudicial for the latter, criminalization does not appear to be the best of solutions. Sexual education programs would likely be far more appropriate in order to equip adolescents with the knowledge and skills needed for developing and exercising their capacity to exercise good judgment about their sexual relationships.

Objections expressed before the parliamentary committee entrusted with reviewing the legislative bill spoke to the risks inherent in criminalizing adolescent sexuality, namely youth abandonment of sexual education services and programs intended for adolescents. It is feared that adolescents would be disinclined to exhibit their intimacy if it meant risking criminal repression.

At a time of constitutionalizing human rights and freedoms in Canada, liberal perspectives occupy a preponderant place in legal analyses. Of course, our Supreme Court refused to recognize the *"harm principle," the idea that the government can only criminalize those acts that cause demonstrable harm to others,* as a constitutional principle of fundamental justice, such that the state may criminalize conduct without having to demonstrate that the conduct causes serious harm.[39]

Nonetheless, the *harm principle* vigourously reappeared in the *Labaye* case when the Supreme Court ruled that "conduct" only acquired the character of criminal indecency when it caused or risked causing some serious harm, such as physical or psychological injury to anyone participating in the activities.[40] There can be no doubt that in a *Charter* challenge to the new prohibitions based on the violation occasioned to fundamental rights, the liberal assumption would be cen-

38 Todd Melby, "When Teens Get Arrested for Voluntary Sex" (2006) 40 Contemporary Sexuality 1 at 5: "A 1997 American Bar Association study, written by Sharon G Elstein and Noy Davis, observes that nearly two-thirds of reports to prosecutors about underage sex came from parents."

39 *R v Malmo-Levine*; *R v Caine*, [2003] 3 SCR 571.

40 *R v Labaye*, [2005] 3 SCR 728 at para 62.

tre stage since the state would be required to demonstrate that the infringement caused to sexual freedom is justified under s 1 of the *Canadian Charter of Rights and Freedoms.*

Does the debate lend itself to being framed in terms of constitutional rights? Sexual freedom is not overtly recognized in the *Charter* as a right and its legal status remains ambiguous, somewhat akin to "the political history of sex in the Western World."[41] Taboos associated with Christianity have meant that human sexuality has only recently entered public and legal debates, painfully and slowly. In principle, sexual freedom involves two aspects, both of equal importance: the right to indulge in sexual relations and the corresponding right to refuse such contact. Without evoking all the legal subtleties that an exhaustive legal analysis would require,[42] it may be asserted that in its positive version, sexual freedom is an aspect of the right to privacy. As such, individuals claim the right to live their sexuality as they see fit, to say "yes" to whomever they please and in whatever manner pleases them, insofar as no harm is done to third parties. In its negative form, sexual freedom is also an aspect of the right to physical integrity,[43] whereby consent must be to specific sexual acts and can be withdrawn at any time. The two facets of sexual autonomy are expressed in two distinct and opposing expressions: the right to say "yes" (privacy) and the right to say "no" (protection of physical integrity). As such, if the state has the duty to act to protect the physical integrity of its citizens, it must also respect their privacy:

> Sexuality and sexual life is at the core of private life (privacy) and its protection. State regulation of sexual behaviour interferes with this right, and such interference can only be justified, if demonstrably necessary for the prevention of harm to others. Whereby "necessity" in this context is linked to a democratic society, whose hallmarks are "tolerance, pluralism, broadmindedness," those hallmarks require that there is a pressing social need for the measure and that the measure is proportionate to the aim sought to achieve. Attitudes of the majority can not serve as valid ground for justification. It is the core task of human rights to protect the individual and minorities against unjustified interference by the majority... Interferences solely based

41 Daniel Borrillo, "Liberté érotique et exception sexuelle" in Daniel Borrillo & Danièle Lochak, eds, *La liberté sexuelle* (Paris: Presses universitaires de France, 2005) 38 at 41.

42 For a European starting point, see Danièle Lochak, "La liberté sexuelle, une liberté (pas) comme les autres?" in Borrillo & Lochak, eds, *ibid* at 7.

43 *Supra* note 3 at para 41.

> on the views of the majority Mill called a "betrayal of the most fundamental values of the political theory of democracy."[44]

Thus, the raising of the age of consent would not be a means of protecting young people, but rather a means of controlling them. To borrow the expression of another author, we are witnessing the creation of offences against sexual autonomy.[45]

3.2 Conservative Perspectives

From a conservative perspective, it is legitimate to use penal law to protect majority values. Traces of the concepts of "good" and "evil" are found throughout the *Criminal Code*, solidifying the very foundations of society. It is both impossible and inadvisable to ignore them because law that is not grounded in morality would lead purely and simply to social disintegration.[46] Thus, insofar as most of the population considers sexual relations between adolescents and adults to be unacceptable, they may be criminalized. Liberals and conservatives may very well agree on the immorality of a given sexual behaviour, yet the former would refuse to criminalize such behaviour without there being tangible evidence of harm occasioned by the behaviour.

Conservatives and liberals have torn one another apart over different understandings of "morality." For example, the legal status of homosexuality served as the departure point for fundamental doctrinal debates. On the one hand, conservatives called for the criminalization of a sexual practice contrary to family values. On the other, liberals opposed the prohibition of an inoffensive sexual practice.[47] Conservatives are deeply attached to traditional family values and value the sacred institution of marriage, while remaining wary of "social progress" that undermines the institution. In following this line of thinking, legitimate sexual fulfilment resides in procreation within the institution of marriage.

In the debate on the raising of the age of consent, several conservative arguments were presented. Those most favourable to the bill issued

44 Helmut Graupner & Vern L Bullough, "Introduction" in Graupner & Bullough, *supra* note 6 at 1 at 2–3.

45 Michael C Baurmann, "Sexuality, Adolescence and the Criminal Law: The Perspective of Criminology" in Graupner & Bullough, *supra* note 6 at 84: "offences against sexual self-determination."

46 Patrick Devlin, *The Enforcement of Morals* (London: Oxford University Press, 1965).

47 Patrick Devlin, *ibid*, and Herbert LA Hart, *Law, Liberty and Morality* (Stanford: Stanford University Press, 1963).

from police and religious organizations. The Director of Public Policy of the Evangelical Fellowship of Canada spoke out strongly against the precocious sexualization of children and adolescents, stating that he was firmly convinced "that the best and most enriching expression of sexuality is to be found within a lifelong conjugal relationship."[48] From his standpoint, parents and spiritual communities must promote "the teaching of values that educate young people, and include an understanding of their sexual identity from a Christian point of view."[49] Sexual relationships between adults and adolescents were presented as deviant relationships. For example, many of the presentations used a sexual exploitation schema, referring to the adults involved as "sexual predators" and the adolescents as "children" and "victims." They issued a plea for enhanced penal severity so as to dissuade "pedophiles" here and elsewhere.

Protection of children and protection of the institution of marriage are two settings that come together in the new legislation. Because, if it is necessary to dissuade sexual predators, one must also permit marriage, independent of age differences. From which issues a new form of marital immunity, independent of age differences. Hence, this new form of marital immunity, codified under s 150.1(2.1)(b) states that the consent of a person age fourteen to sixteen is valid if it is given to his or her spouse. A young woman age fifteen may therefore have lawful sexual relations with her forty-year-old husband, but she may not have a twenty-one-year-old lover.

Yet it is perhaps the silence in the law that best reveals its conservative influences. The change in the age of consent would have been the natural opportunity for correcting the discriminatory treatment afforded to gay youth, who cannot consent to anal intercourse prior to eighteen years of age. It would have been simple to state that the age of consent would be sixteen years of age without reference to anybody's sexual orientation, all the more so since certain appellate courts have ruled that the different age limit in s 159 discriminates on the basis of sexual orientation, contrary to s 15 of the *Charter*.[50] Partisans for this

48 Before the Standing Committee on Justice and Human Rights: Canada, *Témoignages de comités*, 39th Parl, 1st Sess, No 56, (22 March 2007), Doug Cryer, Director of Public Policy of the Evangelical Fellowship of Canada, online: <http://www.parl.gc.ca/HousePublications/Publication.aspx?DocId=2791741&Language=E&Mode=1&Parl=39&Ses=1#Int-1969620>.

49 *Ibid.*

50 *R v M(C)* (1995), 41 CR (4th) 134, 98 CCC (3d) 481 (Ont CA); *R v Roy*, [1998] RJQ 1043, 125 CCC (3d) 442 (CA); *R v Talbot* (2002), 161 CCC (3d) 256 (Ont CA).

course of action made representations before the Committee; however, the legislator ignored their efforts. The age of sexual consent is therefore fourteen years for heterosexual adolescents who have partners of about the same age, sixteen years for heterosexual adolescents who have adult partners,[51] and eighteen years for gay adolescents, regardless of the age of their partners.

Conservatism, it would seem, currently expresses itself in a more convoluted manner than during the twentieth century. In a society as pluralistic as ours, it is a difficult undertaking to identify moral values that are supported by the majority. Furthermore, conservative claims are difficult to reconcile with fundamental rights because they carry the potential for oppressing minorities. Conservative rhetoric reappears forcefully in legislative initiatives purported to respond to "populist" demands by vocal lobby groups who claim to represent the views of "ordinary" citizens.

Raising the age of consent is a long-standing legislative project that made unsuccessful appearances in the House of Commons in 1997,[52] 2001,[53] and 2005[54] before making a forceful comeback in 2008 bearing a new name: the age of "protection." In the end, it was the fear of sexual predators that made it possible to restrict adolescents' zone of sexual liberty. Yet the reality of sexual exploitation runs little risk of being affected by this measure since most sexual crimes perpetrated against adolescents are committed on a non-consensual basis by those in their immediate circle of family and friends. Thus raising the age of consent permitted the Canadian government to claim that it took action taken against "crime," while soothing the more conservative fringe of their electorate by reasserting the paramountcy of marriage and maintaining the degraded status of gay sexual relationships.

51 It remains understood that in accordance with s 153, adolescents age sixteen to eighteen are legally incapable of consenting to sexual contacts with adults when that consent is vitiated by a position of authority, trust, or exploitation.

52 Bill C-255, *An Act to Amend the Criminal Code (prohibited sexual acts)*, 1st Sess, 36th Parl, 1997, was introduced by Art Hanger (Calgary North-East, Canadian Alliance).

53 Bill C-278, *An Act to Amend the Criminal Code (prohibited sexual acts)*, 1st Sess, 37th Parl, 2001, was also introduced by Art Hanger (Calgary North-East, Canadian Alliance).

54 The raising of the age of consent was once more debated within the framework of Bill C-2, but unsuccessfully: Bill C-2, *An Act to Amend the Criminal Code (protection of children and other vulnerable persons and the Canada Evidence Act)*, 1st Sess, 38th Parl, 2005 (1st reading).

3.3 Feminist Perspectives

The feminist vision of the law is neither that of the liberals nor the conservatives. The feminist concept is that the law must be used as a tool permitting access to greater social justice. While legislative action makes possible the destabilizing of power relations between males and females, it may also act in favour of other historically discriminated groups, such as persons with disabilities, racial or cultural minorities, and gays or lesbians.

Feminist perspectives are not necessarily opposed to the raising of the age of consent. To begin with, women were the first to publicly focus attention on the phenomenon of men's sexual aggression against women and then to transform it into an important political issue. During the 1970s and 1980s, they exposed and critiqued sexism in the criminal law of rape by drawing attention to the discriminatory and unfounded beliefs on which these laws were premised. Feminists also branded rape as an act of violence and a form of domination perpetrated against the bodies of women.[55] They lobbied for and achieved substantive law reform both with respect to the definition of the crime—now sexual assault—and the rules of evidence that govern its proof.

With the momentum thus generated, feminists also drew the attention of the media and politicians to the hidden crime of incest. In Canada, the Badgley Committee, entrusted with shedding light on sexual assaults perpetrated on infants and children, assumed its mandate with a near military outlook: it recommended enhanced protection of children against sexual abuse and of adolescents against sexual exploitation. The model that guided their investigation was that of a young child, suffering from repeated sexual abuse and hence in desperate need of protection.

The Badgley Committee was not charged with considering the case of the enthusiastic adolescent seeking sexual contacts with some young adult within an egalitarian relationship. While the committee clearly recognized that its recommendations would affect the equilibrium between the protection of children from sexual aggression and exploitation on the one hand, and, on the other, the possibility for adolescents to express themselves sexually in their evolution from early adoles-

55 There exists substantial critical literature in this respect. See, among others: Christine Boyle, *Sexual Assault* (Toronto: Carswell, 1985); Susan Estrich, *Real Rape* (Cambridge: Harvard University Press, 1987); and Catharine MacKinnon, *Feminism Unmodified* (Cambridge: Harvard University Press, 1987) at Chapters 6 & 7.

cence into adulthood,[56] it did not address the balance it should strike. Instead, it instantly dove straight to an assertion of the need to protect young victims. Thus, it was that a body of argumentative reasoning was formed, extracted directly from the feminist grid, in order to better protect an extremely vulnerable group.

Throughout history, and in all cultures, female sexuality has been dominated by male control. Rape, forced marriages, wives' marital duties, and on-the-job sexual harassment are practiced on a widespread scale. The feminist movement has insisted on women's autonomy rights—their right to control their own bodies and their sexuality. Feminist have advocated for women's right to say "no" to sexual contact and for "no" to have legal effect, principles that our criminal law now reflects. They have also established that consent cannot be inferred from the fact that a woman is submissive or passive;[57] consent must be active in order to be understood as "voluntary agreement" according to the *Criminal Code.*[58] Women's sexual autonomy has both a negative and a positive aspect, however. Women's sexual freedom — the right to choose when, how and with whom they engage in sexual relations — is supported by these same criminal law principles and is also of undeniable importance to the feminist agenda.

Nor should one ignore feminist distrust of liberal discourse, especially when dealing with the issue of consent. For the liberal, consent is a glorified act that symbolizes individual self-determination. Not so among feminists for whom the expression of true consent depends upon an egalitarian relationship. In our culture — one that excessively extolls feminine beauty and youth to such an extent that young women are commonly represented in television, film, and music as only existing through the desire of a man — should one not question the sexual consent of an adolescent? Is an egalitarian relationship possible between an adolescent female and a considerably older man? Is the risk of domination too important to be neglected? The fact of the matter is that feminists conceive the notion of harm from a standpoint far wider than the liberals' perception thereof. Should one not fear the instrumentation of young bodies in the service of adult sexual pleasure? Is there not a risk of degradation or, even worse, dehumanization of adolescent women's sexuality?

56 *Badgley Report, supra* note 9 at 294.

57 *R v M(L)*, [1994] 2 SCR 3.

58 Section 273.1(1).

Feminists also maintain a high level of distrust — perhaps even greater — with regard to conservative ideology. It was in the name of majoritarian values that women were for ages confined to their homes, without any source of income, far from the seats of religious and political power. Ironically, in the current discourse on policy, where raising the age of consent is claimed to further protect victims of sexual predators, there is some confusion, even a blending of feminist and conservative claims. We see emerging a more popular "nouveau genre" in which criminal law is raised to the level of an "answer to social problems," without undertaking any more fundamental changes.

From my standpoint — namely a feminist perspective — the "urge" to further protect young people through raising the age of consent must be resisted for two reasons. My first point is that the raising of the age of consent does not afford better protection from adult sexual predators: non-consensual sexual relations have always been criminalized. As for consensual sexual contacts with adults, they are already prohibited in the case of relationships with adults in positions of authority, trust, or exploitation. If the current legislation is intended to protect youth, it just does not do the job.

My second point is that raising the age of consent was pursued in a closed circuit, without any fieldwork for collecting data about the lives and experiences of adolescent women, in violation of feminist methology. Feminist demands are grounded in real-life experiences. The approach seeks to shed light on the dim, hidden side of reality, namely that of one-half the population. Before prohibiting sexual contact between adolescents age fourteen to sixteen years old, it is necessary to consult with the subjects of such proposed laws, to ask for their opinions. Adolescents' right to participate is not only recognized internationally;[59] it is also the starting point for anyone seeking to protect them. It is one thing to seek to protect victims of sexual assault who have made public demands for improved legal treatment; it is yet another to proceed to law reform in the absence of the victims. When this step is taken in the name of feminism, feminism shifts to moralism. In the current state of affairs, the raising of the age of consent is illegitimate because nothing has been done to explore or document the consequences of sexual relations between adolescents and adults, nor has anything been done to record what these adolescents have to say about

59 *Convention on the Rights of the Child*, 20 November 1989, 1577 UNTS 3 at 12 (entered into force 2 September 1990).

the potential benefits and harms that they experience through criminalization of their chosen sexual partners.

CONCLUSION

For many reasons, the raising of the age of consent is open to criticism. In fact, the recent increase in the age of consent, rebaptized the "age of protection," constitutes a hijacking of the initial objective (the protection of adolescents from sexual abuse and exploitation) in order to refurbish legalistic moralism. The actual effect of the new law is to prohibit sexual contact between the age fourteen-to-sixteen group of adolescents and adults, even if such sexual contact takes place in an egalitarian context. Henceforth, little does the nature of the relationship matter.

We have limited knowledge regarding the extent of intimate relationships between adolescents and adults, and limited knowledge of their consequences. The law was enacted in a vacuum, in response to the fear of sexual predators, without being solidly positioned in the social environment. Adolescents age fourteen and older often are sexually active. What do they think of this amendment to the law? Can they find their way through the muddle of rules that just add to the complexity of laws in force? Here then is a genuine risk of alienating young people further from the law. When we purport to govern young people's sexuality through laws that bear no relation to their realities, law loses its legitimacy and its relevance.

Obviously, one may question the ethics or morality of intimate relations between adolescents and adults. But to prohibit such relationships under pain of criminal sanction is one step that should never have been taken, all the more so when a prison sentence awaits "offenders."[60] The implementation of repressive measures always entails negative consequences — first for the accused, who must then serve a prison sentence and thereafter must live with the stigma of being a sexual offender. And the consequences for the adolescent? Will they avail themselves of services and information specially prepared for them if they run the risk of criminal intervention? Moreover, control over adolescent sexuality by

60 Crimes of sexual interference (section 151), invitation to sexual touching (section 152), and sexual exploitation (section 153) are all sanctioned by a minimum term of 45 days (indictable offence) or 14 days (summary conviction) of imprisonment. Bill C-10, *Safe Streets and Communities Act*, 1st Sess, 41st Parl, 2011. (Royal Accent 13 March 2012), c/s 11, 12, and 13, augments this term to a minimum of one year (indictable offense) or 90 days (summary conviction) of imprisonment. The same applies to sexual assault if the complainant is under the age of 16 years (cl 25).

means of criminal law runs the risk of pitting parents and adolescents against with one another, thereby entailing a sporadic and unpredictable application of the law. All in all, except in cases where an adult pursues sexual relations with an adolescent from a position of authority, trust, or exploitation, criminal law is just not the forum for debating issues of consensual sexual relations between adolescents and adults.

23.

What's in a Face? Demeanour Evidence in the Sexual Assault Context

Natasha Bakht

Natasha Bakht's chapter examines another manifestation of law's understanding of sexual assault — the need to test the credibility of complainants — this time expressed by a claim that Muslim women must remove their niqabs so that their "demeanour" can be scrutinized. Many authors in this collection have explored this constant in sexual assault: from the moment of reporting to police through to the criminal trial, women's accounts are disbelieved and filtered by police "unfounding" rates that are simply not comparable for other crimes, as explained by Teresa DuBois in Chapter Nine, and by other forms of "credibility-testing," such as the Sexual Assault Evidence Kit discussed by Jane Doe in Chapter Sixteen. Natasha's analysis joins with that pursued by Maria Campbell, Tracey Lindberg, and Priscilla Campeau in Chapter Five by exploring the role of racism and colonialism in marginalizing and stigmatizing complainants. She argues here that the demand that Muslim women "take off their clothes" in order to testify to their experience of sexual assault amounts to cultural and religious discrimination and to yet another form of "whacking the complainant" by defence lawyers.

Women's bodies are too often the sites of cultural conflicts. In the context of sexual violence, the criminal law has forced women to fit into rigid characterizations of the ideal rape victim. This ideal rape victim has been described not only as morally and sexually virtuous (read white), but also as cautious, unprovocative, and consistent.[1] Classist and sexist stereotypes pervade the law's understanding of victims of sexual violence.[2] Racialized women and Aboriginal women are similarly caught between a rock and a hard place[3] as they negotiate their pos-

1 Wendy Larcombe, "The 'Ideal' Victim v Successful Rape Complainants: Not What You Might Expect" (2002) 10 Fem Legal Stud 131 at 131.

2 Jane Doe, *The Story of Jane Doe: A Book About Rape* (Toronto: Random House, 2003).

3 Sherene Razack, *Looking White People in the Eye: Gender, Race and Culture in Courtrooms and Classrooms* (Toronto: University of Toronto Press, 1999) at 62.

itions in a world that conveniently erases colonial and racial aggression in its attempt to combat sexual violence.[4] More recently, the body of a religious woman, a Muslim complainant in a sexual assault trial, has become the site of cultural conflict. This time the conflict is between the legal and judicial culture that upholds the necessity of relying on demeanour evidence in a courtroom versus the religious and cultural beliefs of a devout Muslim woman who wears a niqab.[5] Underlying this more obvious conflict is the repugnance many people, including feminists, feel when they encounter a Muslim woman who covers her face.[6]

Sexual assault is an area of law that has been fraught with misogyny and racism. While efforts to reverse this trend have been enormous,[7] real, practical, on the ground change has been slow. My interest is in ensuring that women's equality is furthered, that women from minority groups in particular are not in the unhelpful position of having to choose between their cultural or religious beliefs and other fundamental rights.[8] I hope to contribute to the literature on gender-justice in the sexual assault context by relying on an intersectional analysis that examines religion and culture.[9] In doing so, I discuss the needs of a small minority of women. Though the numbers of niqab-wearing women may be few in Canada, adequately addressing their plight in this context is just and will ameliorate the workings of the judicial system for all women.

Objections to women who wear the niqab publicly are not uncommon in Canada or other parts of the Western world. In another work,

4 Margo L Nightingale, "Judicial Attitudes and Differential Treatment: Native Women in Sexual Assault Cases" (1991) 23 Ottawa L Rev 71.

5 The niqab is the full-face veil worn by some Muslim women through which only the eyes are visible. A variety of reasons have been given by women for why they wear the niqab. A common theological motivation is that Islam requires modesty, in dress particularly as between women and men who are able to marry.

6 Natasha Bakht, "Veiled Objections: Facing Public Opposition to the Niqab" in Lori Beaman, ed, *Defining Reasonable Accommodation* (Vancouver: UBC Press, in press).

7 The success of the 2009 conference, "Sexual Assault Law, Practice and Activism in a Post-*Jane Doe* Era" held at the University of Ottawa and the numerous participants who submitted abstracts, presented papers, and attended the various sessions is an example of the tremendous feminist work being done in this area.

8 Ayelet Shachar has referred to this dilemma faced by minority women as the ultimatum of having to choose between your rights or your culture. Ayelet Shachar, "The Puzzle of Interlocking Power Hierarchies: Sharing the Pieces of Jurisdictional Authority" (2000) 35 Harv CR-CLL Rev 385 at 388.

9 Culture is typically used by a racialized or Aboriginal accused in combination with a traditional criminal law defence. The use of culture in the service of victims of sexual violence is less common but perhaps even more important in its intersectional dimension.

I have canvassed a variety of these objections, including that the niqab is a security threat, it prevents Muslim integration, it causes problems with identification, and it oppresses women.[10] These and other justifications for banning the niqab rarely consider the views or lived realities of Muslim women, often distort the public interest element of the controversy, evade legal obligations to accommodate minority communities, further marginalize an already targeted and besieged religious group, and reveal more about the ignorance and biases of the objectors than the "otherness" of Muslim women.

There have been several highly publicized instances of niqab-wearing women finding themselves in a courtroom, whether as advocate,[11] plaintiff,[12] witness[13] or most recently a complainant in a sexual assault trial.[14] In Toronto, a Muslim woman complainant made a request to wear her niqab while giving testimony in a preliminary inquiry in which she alleged that two accuseds sexually assaulted her over a period of several years.[15] The accuseds' lawyers objected to the complainant wearing her niqab on the basis that it interfered with their clients'

10 For a critical examination of these and other objections that people hold of the niqab, see Bakht, "Veiled Objections" *supra* note 6.

11 Nick Britten, "Lawyer in a Veil is Taken Off Case" *The Telegraph* (15 November 2006), online: <http://www. telegraph.co.uk/news/main.jhtml?xml=/news/2006/11/14/nmuslim114.xml>.

12 *Muhammad v Enterprise Rent-a-Car*, No 06-41896-GC (Mich 31st Dist Ct, 11 October 2006).

13 *Police v Razamjoo*, [2005] DCR 408 (DCNZ) at para 99. For a critical analysis of opposition to the niqab in courtroom settings as well as an examination of accommodations that ought to be available to niqab-wearing women in their potentially multiple roles as lawyer, witness, jury member, judge, or accused, see Natasha Bakht, "Objection, Your Honour! Accommodating the Niqab in Courtrooms" in Ralph Grillo *et al*, eds, *Legal Practice and Cultural Diversity* (Surrey: Ashgate Publishing, 2009) 115.

14 *R v MS and MS* (16 October 2008), Toronto (Ont Ct J) [*MS*].

15 *R v NS*, [2009] OJ No 1766 (Ont Sup Ct J). In this case, at least one of the accused is related to the complainant whose desire not to remove her niqab while testifying is to avoid showing her face to men whom she could potentially marry. NS's relation to the accused is not significant to her plea to wear the niqab in court because she would also wish to avoid showing her face to the male judge, male lawyers, and the men seated in the public courtroom. The Court of Appeal for Ontario recently rendered its decision in *NS* stating that where an accused's right to a fair trial and a witness's right to exercise her religious beliefs are both raised, reconciling these competing interests must be determined factually on a case-by-case basis (*R v NS*, 2010 ONCA 670 at para 97). The court recognized the unreliability of demeanour evidence generally as well as in the specific context of sexual assault, noting that "[a]djusting the [court] process to ameliorate the hardships faced by a complainant like NS promotes gender equality": *ibid* at para 80.

right to make full answer and defence,[16] including the right to disclosure upon a preliminary inquiry. They argued that in order to cross-examine the complainant effectively, they needed to be able to see her face to gage her reactions to their questions.

Disagreeing with this premise, this paper will argue that the prosecution and adjudication of sexual assault must be more inclusive of the needs of Muslim women who cover their faces. It will be argued that reliance on demeanour evidence in a sexual assault trial must be limited. Just as other feminist reforms have demonstrated the importance of taking into account more than simply the accused's rights in a sexual assault trial, I will argue that a Muslim woman's equality rights and religious freedom are equally deserving of serious consideration in this context.

WOMEN'S EXPERIENCES WITH THE JUDICIAL SYSTEM IN THE CONTEXT OF SEXUAL ASSAULT

It has already been amply documented that sexual assault is most often perpetrated by men on women.[17] Sexual assault for the most part goes unreported and the prosecution and conviction rates for sexual assault are among the lowest for all violent crimes. As noted by Justice L'Heureux-Dubé in her dissent in *R v Seaboyer*:

> There are a number of reasons why women may not report their victimization: fear of reprisal, fear of a continuation of their trauma at the hands of the police and the criminal justice system, fear of a perceived loss of status and a lack of desire to report due to the typical effects of sexual assault such as depression, self-blame or loss of self-esteem.[18]

Courtrooms have not been safe spaces for women who have told their stories of sexual violence. Prior to 1981, women who were raped by their husbands had no legal recourse since marital rape was not an offence in

16 The accused has a traditional right to face his/her accuser, though *R v Levogiannis* (1990), 1 OR 3d 351 (CA) stands for the proposition that this is not a basic tenet of the legal system. While normally the accused has the right to be in the sight of witnesses who testify against him, an order under s 486(2.1) of the *Criminal Code*, permitting the twelve-year-old complainant to testify behind a screen so that he would not have to see the accused, was held to be constitutional.

17 See, for example, *R v Seaboyer*, [1991] 2 SCR 577 at para 137, L'Heureux-Dubé J dissenting in part.

18 *Ibid* at para 139.

the *Criminal Code*.[19] The adversarial nature of our criminal justice system has often made women complainants feel as though they were on trial for their non-criminal behaviour. Overtly sexist and racist remarks by police,[20] judges,[21] and over-zealous defence lawyers who use questionable tactics[22] to embarrass, violate, and denigrate the complainant's character, as well as the regular use of irrelevant information to prejudice the jury were, and many would argue still are, commonplace in our judicial system. Justice L'Heureux-Dubé has referred to the biases at play when women are sexually assaulted as rape mythologies.[23] In other words, women's descriptions of their rapes are measured against false typecasts of who she should be, who her attacker should be, and how injured she must be in order for it to be believed that she was, in fact, raped.[24]

Historically, the legal system as a whole has not served sexual assault complainants well. However, feminist legal scholars and activists have insisted upon statutory and court-interpreted reforms to rules of evidence and procedures to accord with complainants' privacy and equality rights. These reforms include the abolition of the doctrine of recent complaint,[25] and the corroboration rules,[26] both of which perpetuated

19 Section 278 of the *Criminal Code* now states that: "A husband or wife may be charged with an offence under section 271, 272 or 273 [sexual assault, sexual assault with a weapon, or aggravated sexual assault] in respect of his or her spouse, whether or not the spouses were living together at the time the activity that forms the subject-matter of the charge occurred" (*Criminal Code,* RSC 1985, c C-46, s 278).

20 Jan Jordan, "Beyond Belief: Police, Rape and Women's Credibility" (2004) 44:1 Crim Just 29.

21 Elizabeth Sheehy, "Canadian Judges and the Law of Rape: Should the *Charter* Insulate Bias?" (1989) 21 Ottawa L Rev 741.

22 Certain defence lawyers have promoted the following tactic in defending those charged with sexual assault: "You have to go in there as defence counsel and whack the complainant hard at the preliminary. You have to do your research; do your preparation; put together your contradictions; get all the medical evidence; get the Children's Aid Society Records ... and you've got to attack the complainant with all you've got so that he or she will say I'm not coming back in front of 12 good citizens to repeat this bullshit story that I've just told the judge." Cristin Schmitz, "'Whack' Sex Assault Complainant at Preliminary Inquiry" *Lawyers Weekly* (29 May 1988) 22.

23 *Seaboyer, supra* note 17 at para 140.

24 *Ibid.*

25 Section 275 of the *Criminal Code* abrogates the rules relating to evidence of recent complaint (*Code, supra* note 19 at s 275).

26 Section 274 of the *Criminal Code* states that in sexual assault offences "no corroboration is required for a conviction and the judge shall not instruct the jury that it is unsafe to find the accused guilty in the absence of corroboration": *ibid* at s 274.

distrust of women's veracity in sexual assault cases. The reforms extend to limitations on questions about the complainants' prior sexual conduct[27] and strict restrictions around access to complainants' therapeutic records.[28] This fairer and more sensitive approach to the prosecution of sexual assault has also resulted in accommodations in the form of giving independent status to a complainant to apply for an order directing that her identity and any information that could disclose her identity not be published.[29] Moreover, closed circuit television testimony and testimonial screens for complainants who are minors,[30] for whom testifying before the accused is overly traumatic, have been implemented.

Ongoing reforms to the criminal justice system such as those aforementioned are necessary to make the harrowing experiences of reporting sexual assault and testifying against accuseds in such trials more bearable and just. The increasing diversity of Canadian society means that such reforms must be tailored to meet the specific needs, interests, and characteristics of varying complainants. Religious women, for example, who are sometimes identified by outward symbols of their faith, must feel that the Canadian justice system is inclusive of their concerns. For niqab-wearing Muslim women, an accommodation of their rights will involve a re-evaluation of the use of demeanour evidence in courtrooms.

27 *Code, supra* note 19 at ss 276(1), 276(2)(c). These sections were upheld by the Supreme Court of Canada in *R v Darrach*, [2000] 2 SCR 443.

28 *Code, supra* note 19 at ss 278.1–278.91. These provisions were constitutionally upheld in *R v Mills*, [1999] 3 SCR 668. Lise Gotell has argued that despite the *Code* reforms, women's access to privacy rights as it pertains to confidential records and the "the systemic nature and complexities of sexual violence have been actively resisted in legal decision-making" in "The Ideal Victim, the Hysterical Complainant, and the Disclosure of Confidential Records: The Implications of the *Charter* for Sexual Assault Law" (2002) 40 Osgoode Hall LJ 251 at 292–93.

29 *Code, supra* note 19 at ss 486.4–486.5. Jane Doe investigates publication bans and their complicated consequences including whether they actually protect the privacy of sexually assaulted women. Jane Doe, "What's in a Name? Who Benefits from the Publication Ban in Sexual Assault Trials?" in Ian Kerr, Valerie Steeves & Carole Lucock, eds, *Lessons From the Identity Trail: Anonymity, Privacy and Identity in a Networked Society* (New York: Oxford University Press, 2009) 265.

30 Section 715.1(1) of the *Criminal Code* permits a video recording of victims or witnesses under the age of eighteen at the time of the offence as admissible evidence if certain conditions are met. Section 486.2(1) permits a witness under eighteen or a witness who has a mental or physical disability to testify outside the courtroom or behind a screen or other device that would allow the witness not to see the accused: *Code, supra* note 19 at ss 715.1(1) and 486.2(1).

THE USE AND MISUSE OF DEMEANOUR EVIDENCE

The reliance on demeanour evidence in courtrooms generally is increasingly discredited in the legal literature. However, judges and juries are nonetheless still permitted in law to assess the credibility of witnesses and the accused based on demeanour evidence.[31] Triers of fact are permitted to evaluate the trustworthiness of a person in court based on his/her appearance, attitude, behaviour, and/or disposition. Although much case law exists to support this contention in Canada, there is also a growing body of case law[32] and social science literature[33] that warns against excessive use of demeanour evidence because of its inherent unreliability.

I have argued elsewhere that the use of demeanour evidence to assess the credibility of witnesses in a courtroom is dangerous because "no one can do better than chance at spotting liars simply by demeanour."[34] The fact of the matter is that it is nearly impossible to know whether perspiration on a witness's brow is the nervous result of telling a falsehood, the anxiety of being on the stand for the first time, or any combination of other factors. Judging demeanour is particularly challenging for judges and juries who are not familiar with the witnesses. They may not have had the opportunity to observe the witness for a very long period of time; they must assess a witness in a fairly artificial environment without having a sense of how she/he normally reacts to stress.

Some social science research suggests that the facial expressions of people who are attempting to deceive differ from those exhibited when the person is telling the truth. Elizabeth Levan reports that: "A series of studies by Albert Mehrabian indicated that the facial expressions of individuals attempting to deceive were more pleasant and often ac-

31 See, for example, *R v White*, [1947] SCR 268. See also Bakht, "Objection Your Honour," *supra* note 13 at 118.

32 Justice O'Halloran noted in *Faryna v Chorny*: "[t]he law does not clothe the trial judge with a divine insight into the hearts and minds of witnesses," [1952] 2 DLR 354 at 357 (BCCA). See also *R v Levert* (2001), 159 CCC (3d) 71 at 81 (Ont CA), and *R v Norman* (1993), 26 CR (4th) 256 at para 47 (Ont CA).

33 See, for example, Gerald TG Seniuk, "Liars, Scoundrels and the Search for Truth" (2000) 30 CR 5th 244; Mark J Sandler, "Lessons for Trial Courts from the Morin Inquiry" (2005) at 38 [unpublished, on file with author]; Gilles Renaud, "Credibility and Demeanour: An Examination Based on the World of Literature" (2001) Ontario Court of Justice, online: <http://www.trussel.com/maig/credibil.htm>.

34 Bakht, "Objection, Your Honour," *supra* note 13 at 120, quoting Paul Ekman, *Telling Lies* (New York: WW Norton, 1992) at 285.

companied by smiles more often than truthful communicators."[35] This data has been both corroborated and contradicted in other studies.[36] Even if one were to start from the premise that facial expressions indicate dishonesty, research shows that little confidence should be placed in people's ability to perceive these expressions, whether they are police officers, college students, customs officials, or judges.[37]

For most people, the ability to perceive or decipher the truth of a statement from the demeanour of the communicating person is questionable. Yet there appears to be a disconnect between what one thinks one is able to perceive and what one actually does. It is very common for individuals to believe that they can determine when they are being lied to.[38] This overconfidence was expressed by one lawyer who argued:

> My cross-examination is determined by my assessment of the demeanour of the witness. I may be pursuing a certain line of questioning for the witness. Having an opportunity to see their demeanour I might conclude I believe the witness is being sincere on this point and am I really going to get anywhere with this line of questioning. No, I do not think so. I am going to move on to somewhere else. On the other hand observing the witness's demeanour I might conclude the witness is prevaricating, the witness is not being forthright and I might want to explore that area further.[39]

Judges and lawyers are not taught how to read facial expressions for truth or deceit. This is not a recognized area of their legal training. Lawyers — such as the one previously mentioned who claim to have extraordinary powers of observation — simply use and trust their gut instincts. The data on lie detection suggests that these lawyers, though they may believe otherwise, are no better than the average person in detecting accurately and consistently the "micro-expressions" exhib-

35 Elizabeth A LeVan, "Nonverbal Communication in the Courtroom: Attorney Beware"(1984) 8 Law & Psychol Rev 83 at 89, cited in Aaron J Williams, "The Veiled Truth: Can the Credibility of Testimony Given by a Niqab-Wearing Witness be Judged Without the Assistance of Facial Expressions?" (2008) 85 U Det Mercy L Rev 273 at 283.

36 *Ibid.*

37 Paul Ekman & Maureen O'Sullivan, "Who Can Catch a Liar?"(1991) 46 Am Psychologist 913, cited in Williams, *ibid* at 284–85. See also *Telling Lies*, *supra* note 34; *R v Nelles*, [1982] OJ No 3654 at para 62 (Prov Ct Crim Div).

38 *Ibid* at 283.

39 *NS*, *supra* note 15 at para 110.

ited by individuals when lying.[40] Aaron Williams notes that "[i]f a fact finder's ability to ascertain deceit through non-verbal communication is slightly greater than fifty percent, how compelling is the court's interest in requiring a witness to remove her veil, especially when the only non-verbal cues inhibited by the niqab are facial expressions?"[41]

Although the legal system presumes that judges and juries are knowledgeable about human nature, Justice Wilson in *R v Lavallee*[42] reminds us that this is not always the case. In *Lavallee*, the Supreme Court of Canada held that the use of expert evidence to assist in explaining the psychological impact of battering on wives and common law partners was relevant and necessary in a case where a battered woman killed her partner one night by shooting him in the back of the head as he left the room. A psychiatrist's assessment was used in support of Lavallee's defence of self-defence.[43] As Justice Wilson explained, the average person may think they are experts on human nature, but by virtue of popular mythology embedded in our society and unassisted by expert evidence, they may be lead to erroneous conclusions about battered women.[44] Thus, what may appear "obvious," that if a battered woman does not leave her batterer, then she must enjoy the violence, is in fact demonstrably untrue.

Similarly, it has been documented that in racial profiling cases, perfectly innocuous behaviour is often interpreted as suspicious simply because it was viewed through stereotypical lenses.[45] Observations of people, whether they appear guilty or innocent, necessarily depend on highly subjective impressions.[46] On the question of race, some social

40 Ekman in Williams, *supra* note 35 at 285.

41 Williams, *supra* note 35 at 288. Feminist activist Jane Doe of the infamous case, *Jane Doe v Toronto (Metropolitan) Commissioners of Police*, [1998] OJ No 2681 (Ct J (Gen Div)), sarcastically retorted in response to the insistence that demeanour is a useful tool in prosecuting sexual assault that what one needs in order to truly assess the credibility of women complainants is to have them testify naked. How else, she asked, can we ensure that they are not lying?

42 *R v Lavallee*, [1990] 1 SCR 852.

43 The psychiatrist explained Lavallee's ongoing terror and her inability to escape the relationship despite the violence and the continuing pattern of abuse that put her life in danger, and he testified that, in his opinion, the shooting was a final desperate act of a woman who sincerely believed that she would be killed that night (*Lavallee*, *ibid* at para 9).

44 *Ibid* at paras 31–34.

45 David M Tanovich, "The Further Erasure of Race in *Charter* Cases" (2006) 38 CR (6th) 84.

46 *R v Levert* (2001), 159 CCC (3d) 71 at 81 (Ont CA).

science research has suggested that jurors may be less capable of reading the demeanour of witnesses of a different race.[47] Given that our society struggles with systemic racism and sexism, among other oppressions, the fact that certain people appear less trustworthy than others should make us cautious in our reliance on demeanour evidence.

The concern with an overconfident use of demeanour evidence in the sexual assault context is that people will depend on what Justice L'Heureux-Dubé has called "myths and stereotypes"[48] about the appropriate way in which women ought to react to sexual assault, penalizing those who do not fit into such rigid characterizations. For example, women who appear nervous may create the impression of untruthfulness; if a woman fails to show emotion, this may be read as a lack of sincerity; if she is extremely upset, she may be seen as exaggerating. Reliance on demeanour evidence will disadvantage complainants whose attitude and disposition does not accord with fixed conceptions of the appropriate reactions to sexual violence. The use of demeanour evidence in sexual assault cases is essentially a license to use (sometimes unarticulated) racist and sexist notions about women as a way to defeat their narratives and dismiss their allegations as untrue. The legitimate fear is that lawyers and judges may perpetuate the standard of the "ideal rape victim" that few victims of sexual assault will be able to achieve.

Although judges may not state the reasons for their findings of credibility based on demeanour, this simply makes their power less accountable and more dangerous. Just as women are likely to be disadvantaged by demeanour evidence, the quiet hegemony of white supremacy and patriarchy will protect some men's accounts such that his appearance, attitude, and disposition work in his favour: "He doesn't look like a rapist; he's too well dressed, well mannered or intelligent."[49] What then is in a face? I would suggest that an undue focus on women's demeanour risks reliance on tremendously misleading evidence.

Judicial education and academic research on the unreliability of demeanour evidence has prompted judges to caution themselves about the effects of demeanour evidence and to "strenuously resist allowing demeanour to factor into an assessment of credibility."[50] Similarly, the

47 Joseph W Rand, "The Demeanor Gap: Race, Lie Detection, and the Jury" (2000) 33 Conn L Rev 1 at 4.

48 *Seaboyer, supra* note 17 at paras 125, 141, 157.

49 Online: <http://www.barrettandfarahany.com/sub/sexual-assault-bias.jsp>.

50 Gloria Epstein, "What Factors Affect the Credibility of a Witness" (2002) 21 Advocates' Soc J 10 at 12. See also *R v AW*, [2004] OJ No 5506 at paras 44 (Sup Ct), 68 where

Canadian Judicial Council's approved model jury instruction on demeanour is permeated with cautions about the unreliability of demeanour evidence:

> What is the witness's manner when he or she testifies? Do not jump to conclusions, however, based entirely on how a witness testifies. Looks can be deceiving. Giving evidence in a trial is not a common experience. People react and appear differently. Witnesses come from different backgrounds. They have different abilities, values and life experiences. There are simply too many variables to make the manner in which a witness testifies the only or even the most important factor in your decision.[51]

It is possible, of course, that demeanour evidence can be used in favour of sexual assault complainants. Indeed, several such instances can be found in the case law.[52] The scope of this paper does not allow a comprehensive analysis of whether demeanour evidence has been used favourably for the complainant and, if so, what the characteristics of these complainants are. Despite a preliminary search of sexual assault cases

the judge stated: "In the videotaped statement the Complainant spoke in a soft monotone voice without any indication of emotion. In giving her evidence in Court her demeanour was much the same … I think it goes too far to suggest in this case that, because the Complainant did not exhibit a stereotypical emotional response, it is incumbent on the Crown to adduce expert evidence. *Common sense and experience demonstrate that individuals respond differently to traumatic events and that is why demeanour evidence must be carefully and cautiously considered …*" [emphasis added].

51 Canadian Judicial Council, Model Jury Instructions in Criminal Matters, Instruction 4.11, Assessing Evidence, online: <http://www.courts.ns.ca/General/resource_docs/jury_instr_model_april04.pdf> at 46, para 10.

52 See, for example, *R v AI*, [2003] OJ No 3347 at paras 44, 52 (QL) (Sup Ct) where the judge stated: "I was impressed with both Ms KD and Ms JD. I find that they have tried to be truthful and fair in their testimony. Both appear to have been profoundly affected by adverse incidents of a sexual nature in their youth. They cried often in giving their testimony. They were each under obvious stress. They did not exaggerate in their claims and did their best to recollect as best they could. They are honest and credible witnesses who sincerely believe the allegations they make against Mr AI They have no apparent motive to make false charges against Mr AI They certainly believe in what they testified happened to them in their contact as young girls with Mr AI … As I have said already, I find both complainants and Mrs LD to be very straightforward and credible witnesses. The demeanour of each complainant was convincing. In my view, each did her best to answer questions truthfully and to relate events as best she could remember. I believe each is trying to be truthful and fair in respect of her allegations in her testimony against Mr AI It is understandable that each complainant is emotional about the situation. The complainants cried often in the course of their testimony." The accused in this case was nonetheless acquitted.

in Ontario that indicates that judges may use demeanour evidence favourably as it pertains to complainants,[53] I remain unconvinced that demeanour evidence is a reliable source of probative information. In particular, I worry that the most marginalized women — those who experience intersecting inequalities by virtue of race, Aboriginality, physical or mental disability, age, or socio-economic status — may not appear sufficiently credible.

Some research has indicated that non-verbal communication, such as body language and, specifically, "self-touching" and hand gestures, are better indicators of untruthfulness than facial expressions.[54] Because the face is the main focus of attention during conversation, the deceiver will be more aware of the face as a source of deception cues and thus more likely to disguise their facial expressions, leaving other bodily activity uncontrolled.[55] Evaluating body movements and more prolonged gestures may prove easier to decipher than the rapid micro-expressions of a face. Yet, one's ability to dependably recognize these bodily cues without any sort of training is still doubtful.[56] However, the implication for niqab-wearing women is important because other forms of non-verbal communication like gestures, body movement, and variations in voice remain perceivable despite the niqab.

THE IMPACT OF A NIQAB PROHIBITION ON MUSLIM WOMEN

In 2006, a niqab-wearing Muslim woman found herself in court. Ginnah Muhammad brought suit in Michigan against Enterprise Rent-A-

53 A preliminary search of the Quick Law Criminal Law Case database with Ontario as the jurisdiction and using the search string "("sexual assault" or rape) and ((complainant or victim) /s facial)" yielded 332 cases. Of these, there were eighty-eight examples of the use of demeanour evidence. In sixty-seven cases, the judges' assessment of demeanour was favourable to the complainant (even if a reasonable doubt was found and the accused was acquitted). In sixteen cases, the judges' assessment of demeanour was not favourable to the complainant. In the remainder of the cases, the use of demeanour evidence was unclear or equivocal.

54 Williams, *supra* note 35 at 288.

55 *Ibid.*

56 In determining credibility, judges and juries are on firmer ground if they go beyond demeanour and seek support for their findings of credibility from the entire trial record such as an examination of all of the elements and probabilities existing in the case. Opportunities for knowledge, powers of observation, judgment and memory, ability to describe clearly what has been seen and heard, as well as other factors, combine to produce what is called credibility. See Egya N Sangmuah, "After B(RH): Continuing Need to Give Adequate Reasons for Findings of Credibility" (1994) 29 CR (4th) 135.

Car. She was seeking relief for $2,750 in assessed damages to a rental car that she claimed was caused by thieves.[57] Rather than discussing her claim, Judge Paul Paruk gave her the stark choice of removing the niqab or having her case dismissed. Judge Paruk reasoned: "I can't see your face and I can't tell whether you're telling me the truth and I can't see certain things about your demeanor and temperament that I need to see in a court of law."[58] Setting aside the problematic overconfidence that Judge Paruk displayed in his ability to "see the truth,"[59] of particular note is the striking language with which Ginnah Muhammad couched her refusal to remove the niqab.[60] She said: "I wish to respect my religion and so I will not take off my clothes."[61]

Most women would agree that one should not have to remove one's clothing in order to testify in court. Claire McCusker has argued: "The dissonance was definitional: those who drafted the rules governing Paruk's courtroom would never have thought to consider a face-covering 'clothes' in the same sense that a skirt and blouse are 'clothes,' while to Muhammad this was a natural use of the word and the concept."[62]

Ginnah Muhammad's small claims dispute was eventually dismissed because she refused to remove her clothes. As I have argued elsewhere, there are very few instances that would make it necessary to see a woman's face in the courtroom. Opposition to the niqab in a courtroom, no matter the type of case at issue, must be able to definitely respond to the question, "What is the significance of seeing this woman's face to the judicial/legal task at hand?"[63] In a sexual assault trial, more than per-

57 *Muhammad*, *supra* note 12.

58 Transcript of Record at 4, *Muhammad*, *ibid.* "Rejecting an American Civil Liberties Union Argument that the Revised Michigan Rule of Evidence 611 Should Contain an Exception for Religious Dress, the court voted 5–2 to approve a standard that gives the courtroom judge the power to require witnesses to remove head or facial coverings." See Martha Neil, "Courtroom Judge Has Power to Ban Muslim Veil, Top Michigan Court Decides" (17 June 2009) ABA J, online: <http://abajournal.com/news/courtroom_judge_has_power_to_ban_muslim_veil_top._mich._court_decides/>.

59 Clearly, Judge Paruk would have disagreed with Justice O'Halloran who noted in *Faryna* that "[t]he law does not clothe the trial judge with a divine insight into the hearts and minds of witnesses" (*Faryna*, *supra* note 32 at 357).

60 Claire McCusker, "When Church and State Collide: Averting Democratic Disaffection in a Post-*Smith* World" (2007) 25 Yale L & Pol'y Rev 391 at 391.

61 *Muhammad*, transcript, *supra* note 58 at 6.

62 McCusker, *supra* note 60 at 396.

63 Bakht, "Objection, Your Honour," *supra* note 13 at 118. In situations where the identity of the niqab-wearing woman must be verified, women court staff can simply validate a woman's identity by asking her to remove the veil privately for the purposes of com-

haps in any other courtroom situation, the effect of forcing a woman to remove her niqab will be to literally strip her publicly and in front of her alleged perpetrators. Courtrooms already require women to relive their horrifying experiences of rape and sexual abuse, reproducing the powerlessness they experienced during the rape. Having to confront this situation without one's usual clothing is both perverse and grossly insensitive.

Muhammad's pronouncement, "I will not take off my clothes," rings clearly and signals the severe consequences of courts not permitting victims of sexual assault to testify with a niqab. Niqab-wearing Muslim women, who already have limited visibility in courtrooms, will be unlikely to utilize the justice system when they have been sexually assaulted. They will feel marginalized and excluded from public institutions and they would be right to conclude that justice will not be done for them. The impact of being excluded from the justice system should not be underestimated. When asked how she felt after her case had been dismissed, Ginnah Muhammad said: "When I walked out, I just really felt empty, like the courts didn't care about me."[64] It is not difficult to imagine that a woman will feel disillusioned if her sexual assault case is dismissed for lack of evidence simply because she refused to remove what she considers to be her everyday attire.

Many of the feminist reforms surrounding the prosecution of sexual assault have been for the purpose of increasing the reporting of such violent crimes. The impact of not reporting sexual assault is ongoing victimization. As put by Justice L'Heureux-Dubé in *Seaboyer*:

> Whether or not a particular woman has been sexually assaulted, the high rate of assault works to shape the daily life of all women. The fact is that many, if not most women, live in fear of victimization. The fear can become

paring a piece of photo identification with her face (*ibid* at 129). Moreover, it should be noted that it is not uncommon for judges to take evidence without being able to see the witness's face; for example, this happens when evidence is taken over the telephone or when the judge is visually impaired (*ibid* at 129–30).

64 Paul Egan, "Muslim Woman Told to Remove Veil in Court Files Lawsuit" *The Detroit News* (28 March 2007), online: <http://www.muslimnews.co.uk/news/news.php?article=12521>. In a New Zealand case that considered whether two witnesses could give their testimony in a criminal trial while wearing the burqa, one witness said that she would rather kill herself than reveal her face while giving evidence. See Rex J Ahdar, "Reflections on the Path of Religion–State Relations in New Zealand" [2006] BYUL Rev 619 at 654. Clearly, the removal of the niqab in courtrooms will have intensely disorienting effects that can lead to serious vulnerability.

> such a constant companion that its effect remains largely unnoticed and sadly, unremarkable.[65]

Some studies have demonstrated that women who have been sexually assaulted withdraw in some form from social life in order to prevent being further harmed.[66] Even where such restrictions of their behaviour are moderate, it can negatively affect the individual's sense of personal autonomy and diminish the quality of her life.[67]

In *R v NS*, the complainant testified that the niqab is "a part of me."[68] Muslim women who are asked to choose between being faithful to their religious beliefs or "opting out" of providing testimony in a sexual assault trial may well make the choice in favour of religion. The result of that supposed "choice" will be severe and negative damage to her sense of self-worth and acceptance in Canadian society. Muslims are already a globally targeted community since the events of September 11th, 2001.[69] In addition to the general concern that Muslims will avoid participation in democratic processes where they consistently feel marginalized by the state, the cultural insensitivity of not recognizing religious practices that offer comfort, security, and stability to women will send the specific message that niqab-wearing women should not report their sexual assaults as justice will not be done for them.

LEGAL ARGUMENTS TO ACCOMMODATE THE INTERSECTIONAL RIGHTS OF NIQAB-WEARING COMPLAINANTS

There are several legal approaches that can be taken to ensure that niqab-wearing complainants are permitted to testify in court while wearing their niqabs. I will address these various legal avenues; however, the crux of the issue is that the integrity of the criminal justice process lies in recognizing that a fair trial protected under the *Canadian Charter of Rights and Freedoms*[70] is a right enjoyed not only by the accused, but

65 *Seaboyer, supra* note 17 at para 150.

66 *Ibid.*

67 *Ibid* at paras 150–52.

68 *NS, supra* note 15 at para 29.

69 Sherene Razack, *Casting Out: The Eviction of Muslims from Western Law and Politics* (Toronto: University of Toronto Press, 2008). See also Bakht, *supra* note 6.

70 *Canadian Charter of Rights and Freedoms*, Part I of the *Constitution Act, 1982*, being Schedule B to the *Canada Act 1982* (UK) 1982, c 11.

also the complainant and the public, who have a right to the proper administration of justice. The proper administration of justice requires consideration of the competing interests at stake in the criminal justice process, such as the intersecting equality rights and religious freedom of the complainant and the public's interest in the effective prosecution of criminal charges through criminal processes that are sensitive to the needs of victims and witnesses.

Such a contextual argument is by no means novel. In 1999, the Women's Legal Education and Action Fund [LEAF][71] successfully argued in *R v Mills*,[72] a case about the constitutionality of provisions in the *Criminal Code* that limited the production of women's personal records for the defence in sexual offence proceedings, that "[i]t is not only the accused but also the complainant and the public at large who are entitled to the equal benefit of a fair and just trial process."[73] The Supreme Court of Canada held in *Mills* that a complainant's rights to privacy, security of the person, and equality are to be analyzed as equal to the rights of an accused person.[74] LEAF argued that courts must be precluded from drawing inferences about what is relevant in a criminal trial on the basis of discriminatory or stereotypical reasoning. Thus, assessments of relevance must be made through an equality prism wherein the *Charter* value of equality informs how relevance is determined.[75] Respecting women's rights to equality during a sexual assault trial would encourage victims to report sexual offences and to testify in sexual offence trials; it would centrally engage the public interest in the pursuit of justice on behalf of all members of society.[76]

The defence argument in a sexual assault case is that the right to a fair trial as protected by ss 7 and 11(d) of the *Charter* includes the right to make full answer and defence. In other words, in order to be fully prepared to meet the charges against the accused, the defence would argue that they must be able to see the complainant's face in order to follow her expressions as she answers questions under cross-examination.

71 LEAF is a national charitable organization that works toward ensuring that the law guarantees substantive equality for all women in Canada. Since its inception in 1985, LEAF has intervened in over 150 cases and assisted in establishing landmark legal victories for women on a wide range of issues. In 1999, LEAF intervened at the Supreme Court of Canada in *Mills*, online: <http://www.leaf.ca/>.

72 *Supra* note 28.

73 *Mills*, *ibid* (Factum of the Intervener LEAF at para 45).

74 *Mills*, *supra* note 28 at paras 21, 61, 90.

75 LEAF Factum, *supra* note 73 at paras 35, 38.

76 *Ibid* at paras 50, 51.

Counsel for the accused in *NS* argued that they could not adequately represent their clients because being unable to follow the complainant's expressions hampered their ability to gauge in which direction to take their line of questioning. They felt that their right to full answer and defence would be circumscribed by an inability to cross-examine the complainant without her veil.[77] As LEAF argued in *Mills*:

> An accused's right to a fair trial is not a right to perfect justice according to his determination of what this would involve, but fundamentally fair justice taking into account the rights of others involved in the process ... The right to a fair trial does not mean that an accused person is entitled to everything that might *possibly* be helpful to his defence.[78] (emphasis added)

Indeed, the fair trial rights of the accused do not "trump" the rights of the complainant. As the Supreme Court of Canada held in *Dagenais v Canadian Broadcasting Corporation*, "When the protected rights of two individuals come into conflict ... *Charter* principles require a balance to be achieved that fully respects the importance of both sets of rights."[79] Just as the court held in *Mills* that a complainant's rights to privacy, security of the person, and equality are to be analyzed as equal to the rights of an accused person, a complainant's rights to sex equality and religious freedom must likewise be accorded equal status with the accused's right to make full answer and defence.

A niqab-wearing complainant's interests in a sexual assault trial will engage the intersecting rights of equality and freedom of religion. The religious aspect of such a claim is perhaps obvious. The niqab-wearing complainant would argue that her desire to wear the niqab while testifying is a practice that has a nexus with religion, Islam in particular, and that she sincerely believes that she must wear the niqab publicly in

77 *R v MS and MS*, *supra* note 14 (Factum of the Applicant at para 12).

78 LEAF Factum, *supra* note 73 at paras 46–47. Given the unsubstantiated value in the need to see a witness's face in order to properly assess credibility, the interference with the right to make full answer and defence may, in fact, be minimal. Consequently, there may be no need for the court to engage in a reconciliation of two rights. "In *Amselem* ... the Court refused to pit freedom of religion against the right to peaceful enjoyment and free disposition of property, because the impact on the latter was considered 'at best, minimal.' Logically, where there is not an apparent infringement of more than one fundamental right, no reconciliation is necessary at the initial stage": *Multani v Commission Scolaire Marguerite-Bourgeoys*, [2006] 1 SCR 256 at para 28.

79 [1994] 3 SCR 835 at para 72.

order to conduct herself according to her faith.[80] Most *Charter* claims of freedom of religion that are sincere are successful at the s 2(a) stage because the test articulated by the Supreme Court of Canada is fairly broad and subjective:

> [F]reedom of religion consists of the freedom to undertake practices and harbour beliefs having a nexus with religion, in which an individual demonstrates he or she sincerely believes or is sincerely undertaking in order to connect with the divine or as a function of his or her spiritual faith, irrespective of whether a particular practice or belief is required by official religious dogma or is in conformity with the position of religious officials.[81]

The balancing of freedom of religion against other public interests is typically done at the stage of s 1 of the *Charter*, the justificatory analysis.

However, to understand the niqab-wearing complainant's issue as merely one of religious freedom is to misinterpret what is at stake in such a case. The gendered aspect of this issue lies in the fact that this is a case of sexual assault allegedly committed by two men upon a woman.[82] The context of this offence cannot be forgotten: a majority of the sexual assaults in Canada are committed by men on women.[83] Moreover, the religious requirement of wearing the niqab is a specific article of faith exclusive to women.[84] While the Islamic requirement of modesty is interpreted differently by Muslims globally, no interpretation requires men to cover their faces by wearing a niqab.

80 An individual advancing an issue premised upon freedom of religion must show that (1) he or she has a practice or belief, having a nexus with religion, which calls for particular conduct; (2) he or she is sincere in his or her belief (*Syndicat Northcrest v Amselem*, [2004] 2 SCR 551 at para 56).

81 *Ibid* at para 46.

82 *NS*, *supra* note 15 at paras 3–6.

83 *Seaboyer*, *supra* note 17.

84 Three recent religious accommodation cases to have reached the Supreme Court of Canada have all involved male applicants and religious practices uniformly shared by men and women of the particular faith. See *Amselem*, *supra* note 80 where Orthodox Jewish residents of a Montreal condominium sincerely believed it was necessary to build a succah or religious hut on their balconies during the festival of Succot. In *Multani*, *supra* note 78, a Sikh youth sincerely believed he was required by his faith to carry a kirpan or religious dagger at all times, including to school. In *Alberta v Hutterian Brethren of Wilson Colony*, [2009] 2 SCR 567, members of a Christian religious group sincerely believed that voluntarily having their photograph taken for a driver's license violated the Bible's second commandment against idolatry.

The case in question involves the religious and gendered practice of wearing a niqab in court. Thus, the denial of the right to testify in a sexual assault trial while wearing the niqab will not only impact the complainant's religious beliefs, but will also significantly hamper her sex equality rights under the *Charter*. Testifying in a sexual assault trial is a stressful experience that provokes much anxiety for complainants. The public and adversarial process makes for an extremely difficult place to answer questions about sensitive and highly traumatic incidents. Prohibitions on wearing the niqab while giving testimony will only discourage Muslim women, who regularly dress in such a fashion, from reporting sexual assaults. Thus the historic under-reporting of the crime of sexual assault that Parliament has attempted to combat through other legislation[85] will simply be undermined for this group of women.

An intersectional analysis offers a more nuanced approach to rights litigation and is more likely to reflect the multiple and complex affiliations of people's lives. The concept of intersectionality, first coined by theorist Kimberlé Crenshaw, emphasizes that subordination may manifest itself in multiple ways in the lives of some people.[86] Racialized women, for example, frequently experience racism and sexism in the same course of events. Intersectionality insists that the multiple identities and corresponding consequences for such people are not ignored. For religious women, such an approach is particularly significant since their plight is often the result of multiple forms of oppression. In *NS*, the complainant referred to the niqab as "a part of me."[87] Indeed, religious women should be able to use legal instruments such as the *Charter* to reflect both their religious and gender identities.

It is possible that a niqab-wearing complainant could make an intersecting claim of discrimination on the bases of sex and religion using s 15 of the *Charter*. Although in *Law v Canada (Minister of Employment and Immigration)*, it was held that it "is open to a s 15(1) claimant to articulate a discrimination claim on the basis of more than one ground,"[88] few courts have recognized intersectionality in their section 15(1) jurisprudence.[89] Alternatively, an intersectional argument can be made us-

85 *Seaboyer, supra* note 17 at para 253.

86 Kimberlé Crenshaw, "Mapping the Margins: Intersectionality, Identity Politics, and Violence Against Women of Color" (1991) 43 Stan L Rev 1241 at 1252.

87 *NS, supra* note 15 at para 29.

88 *Law v Canada (Minister of Employment and Immigration)*, [1999] 1 SCR 497 at para 37.

89 Beverley Baines notes that two provincial appellate courts have tried to reconcile

ing s 2(a) of the *Charter* combined with s 28.[90] Kerri Froc has argued that section 28 of the *Charter* may provide a conceptual tool that recognizes and redresses an integrative approach to *Charter* litigation. She states that the aim of section 28 should be to ensure that the multidimensional oppression experienced by women as whole persons is given due recognition with respect to all applicable *Charter* rights.[91] Finally, section 27[92] of the *Charter* may offer something new in the way of an intersectional approach.[93] Combined with another *Charter* right, s 27 is a reminder to interpret a law of general application in such a way as to enhance the cultural diversity and pluralism of Canadian society. Ideally, a truly multicultural interpretation of section 27 would take into account women's understanding of their cultures.[94] Thus, women could articulate an infringement of rights that occurs simultaneously and that together are distinctive from each alone. Such an analysis will acknowledge the significance of wearing the niqab to the identity of the complainant, as well as the subjective experience of its forced removal as a form of public nakedness and violation, which is particularly problematic in a sexual assault trial.

CONCLUSION

In this paper, I have argued that actors in the criminal justice system must consider the intersecting needs of niqab-wearing complainants in sexual assault trials. Women who cover their faces for religious reasons

section 15(1) with the litigants' real life experiences of intersectional discrimination. Beverley Baines, "Section 28 and the *Canadian Charter of Rights and Freedoms*: A Purposive Interpretation" (2005) 17 CJWL 45 at 65. See *Dartmouth/Halifax County Regional Housing Authority v Sparks*, [1993] NSJ No 97 (CA); and *Falkiner v Ontario (Ministry of Community and Social Services, Income Maintenance Branch)*, [2002] OJ No 1771 (CA).

90 Section 28 provides that: "Notwithstanding anything in this Charter, the rights and freedoms referred to in it are guaranteed equally to male and female persons": *Charter, supra* note 70.

91 Kerri Froc, "Will 'Watertight Compartments' Sink Women's *Charter* Rights? The Need for a New Theoretical Approach to Women's Multiple Rights Claims Under the Canadian Charter of Rights and Freedoms" in Beverley Baines, Daphne Barack-Evez & Tsui Kahana, eds, *Feminist Constitutionalism*, (Cambridge University Press, 2012) 132.

92 Section 27 of the *Charter* reads: "This *Charter* shall be interpreted in a manner consistent with the preservation and enhancement of the multicultural heritage of Canadians": *Charter, supra* note 70.

93 Natasha Bakht, "Reinvigorating Section 27: An Intersectional Approach" (2009) 6 J L & Equality 135.

94 For a more fulsome discussion of how section 27 can be interpreted intersectionally, see *ibid.*

in everyday life should not have to remove their veils in courtrooms regardless of the type of case at issue. But in the context of a sexual assault trial, it is particularly crucial to accommodate niqab-wearing women because the experience of testifying in court about such sensitive and distressing matters puts women in a highly vulnerable situation. Over the years, court processes and rules of evidence in criminal law have changed to recognize the law's discriminating impact on complainants of sexual assault. Knowing that court processes are receptive to all women's circumstances will encourage more women, including niqab-wearing women, to report sexual violence. The accommodation of religious women in such a context is necessary because it is just — not because Canadian law makers are doing a favour to certain Muslim women. Indeed, the majority of evidence indicates that the use of demeanour evidence, such as the expression on a witness's face to evaluate credibility, is dangerous and unreliable. Niqab-wearing women should not have to remove their clothing in court in order to perpetuate the misapprehension that this will further the fair trial rights of the accused. An intersectional approach to rights litigation that acknowledges both the sex equality and religious freedom dimensions of this issue is most likely to reveal the full nature of the claims at stake. As LEAF argued in *O'Connor*, court processes must be "subjected to continuous critical scrutiny to ensure that they evolve congruently with advancing knowledge and insight into the unique plight of complainants."[95]

95 *R v MS and MS*, Applicant's Factum, *supra* note 77 at para 34.

24. Limits of a Criminal Justice Response: Trends in Police and Court Processing of Sexual Assault

Holly Johnson

In this final section of Part II, Holly Johnson's paper puts in perspective the criminal law response to sexual assault. She examines the filtering effect of the criminal justice process, with the end result that only .3 percent of perpetrators are convicted whereas fully 99.7 percent are never held accountable for their crimes. Holly reviews current trends in the legal processing of sexual assault, revisiting the issue of the police response to sexual assault reports explored in Part I and raising questions about a seeming downturn in women's reporting rates — possibly in response to the continuing barriers erected by police and defence counsel. In light of the overwhelming trend by police to charge sexual assault at the lowest level of seriousness, the declining rate of conviction, and the use of conditional sentences (house arrest) for sex offenders, her chapter forces us to ask what possible role the criminal law can play when it condemns only a tiny fraction of this pervasive crime.

Sexual assault is the most gendered of crimes. Only 3 percent of those charged by police with sexual assault offences in Canada in 2007 were women, yet 86 percent of those victimized were women and girls.[1] It is no coincidence that the most gendered crime is also the most underreported. According to Statistics Canada's crime victimization survey, which interviews women anonymously, an estimated 460,000 Canadian women were victims of sexual assault in 2004 and just 8 percent reported the crime to the police.[2]

1 Data for this article were retrieved from Statistics Canada's Uniform Crime Reporting Survey (UCR), which incorporates data provided by all police departments across the country on an annual basis since 1962. Aggregate trends on sexual assault are available back to 1983, and data on rape and indecent assault back to 1977. The more detailed Revised UCR Survey (UCR II) contains complete information about victims, accused persons, and incidents for 2007 only.

2 Maire Gannon & Karen Mihorean, "Criminal Victimization in Canada, 2004" 25 Juristat 85-002-XPE (Ottawa: Statistics Canada, 2005) 7 at 23.

Rape laws underwent major reform in Canada in 1983, in part to improve the dismal rate of reporting and the high rates of attrition throughout the criminal justice processing of these offences, by reducing prejudicial attitudes toward women in the investigation, rules of evidence, and instructions to the jury.[3] Twenty-five years after law reform, there is evidence that simply eliminating the formal expression of bias in the law has not made a real difference in the treatment of sexually assaulted women throughout the justice system. The purpose of this article is to present a critical analysis of the criminal justice response to sexual assault in Canada by drawing on available statistical evidence from the perspective of women, police, prosecution, conviction, and sentencing. This paper argues that widespread discriminatory attitudes toward sexual violence and the way these attitudes play out for women and for criminal justice processing of these cases continue to minimize women's experiences, exonerate violent men, and distort public understanding of this crime.

TRENDS IN SEXUAL ASSAULT

The true incidence of sexual violence in women's lives will likely never be known. The stigma, shame, and blame associated with sexual violence have cast a shroud of silence over women's experiences and affect their willingness to report to police or to disclose to other public agencies.

The most reliable information available to chart the prevalence of sexual assault among women in the population is obtained when researchers bypass police and other agencies and interview random samples of women directly. These victimization surveys are based on a methodology developed in the 1970s to interview samples of the population about their experiences and perceptions of crime without having to rely on victims or witnesses reporting to police. However, these early surveys skirted around the issue of sexual violence based on an assumption that it was inappropriate to ask women about such private experiences. Early versions of the National Crime Victimization Survey [NCVS][4] conducted annually by the US Bureau of Justice Statis-

3 Sheila McIntyre *et al*, "Tracking and Resisting Backlash Against Equality Gains in Sexual Offence Law" (2000) 20 Can Woman Stud 72 at 75. The objective of law reform was broader than this and included de-genderizing the law (in order to comply with the gender equality provisions of the newly created *Charter of Rights and Freedoms*) and shifting the focus from the sexual to the violent nature of the assault.

4 The original name of the survey was the National Crime Survey [NCS].

tics did not ask respondents directly about rape or attempted rape but screened them into questions about rape only if they said they were attacked or threatened. The first such large-scale survey in Canada, the 1982 Canadian Urban Victimization Survey, was somewhat more direct and included a screening question that specified that an attack included rape and molesting.[5] Precise definitions were not provided leaving it up to respondents to determine whether their experiences fit within these categories. In the 1980s, feminist researchers began to conduct independent surveys of rape and intimate partner violence, the results of which raised questions about the reliability and validity of estimates of rape produced by government surveys. One of the most influential was the Sexual Experiences Survey developed by US researcher Mary Koss,[6] which incorporates detailed questions about rape and attempted rape as well as unwanted sexual experiences. When applied to college women, more than one-quarter disclosed experiences of rape or attempted rape, which was significantly higher than the rate of 0.12 percent estimated by the NCVS.[7] Later replicated with Canadian colleges and universities, the Sexual Experiences Survey produced similar results.[8] Canadian researchers Michael Smith[9] and Melanie Randall and Lori Haskell[10] were among the first in this country to develop innovative methods of interviewing women about partner violence and sexual violence. This work led to doubts about the validity of estimates produced by Canadian government victimization surveys.[11]

5 Holly Johnson & Myrna Dawson, *Violence Against Women in Canada: Research and Policy Perspectives* (Toronto: Oxford University Press, 2011) at 41.

6 Mary Koss, Christine Gidycz & Nadine Wisniewski, "The Scope of Rape: Incidence and Prevalence of Sexual Aggression and Victimization in a National Sample of Higher Education Students" (1987) 55 J Consulting and Clinical Psych 162.

7 Mary Koss, "The Underdetection of Rape: Methodological Choices Influence Incidence Estimates" (1992) 48 J Social Issues 64.

8 Walter Dekeseredy & Katherine Kelly, "The Incidence and Prevalence of Woman Abuse in Canadian University and College Dating Relationships" (1993) 18 Can J Soc 137.

9 Michael D Smith, "Sociodemographic Risk Factors in Wife Abuse: Results from a Survey of Toronto Women" (1990) 15 Can J Soc 39.

10 Melanie Randall & Lori Haskell, "Sexual Violence in Women's Lives: Findings from the Women's Safety Project, a Community-based Survey" (1995) 1 Violence Against Women 6.

11 The first victimization survey conducted by Statistics Canada in 1982 produced an estimate of 0.6 percent for sexual assault while admitting that "this survey was not designed specifically to measure sexual assault" (1985) 2 Bulletin 11, Solicitor General of Canada, Female Victims of Crime, Canadian Urban Victimization Survey.

The work of Koss, Diana Russell,[12] and others was influential in persuading the Bureau of Justice Statistics to rethink their method of measuring sexual violence and intimate partner violence on the NCVS. In 1992, this survey underwent a significant redesign. Questions about sexual violence were expanded and question wording improved to ask more directly about experiences of rape, attempted rape, and other unwanted sexual experiences involving threats or harm. Rates produced by this expanded method jumped three to four times what they had been in previous years.[13] Influenced by these events, Statistics Canada determined that a survey dedicated entirely to women's experiences of violence would yield the most comprehensive information.[14] The agency fielded the national Violence Against Women Survey in 1993, funded by the federal department of health and welfare and developed through extensive consultation with community groups, advocates, service providers, and researchers. Its unique methodology took account of safety concerns and incorporated a broad range of questions on sexual harassment, sexual assault, and intimate partner violence in recognition of the interconnections among these acts. Similar surveys followed in several other countries, and aspects of this approach have been incorporated into Statistics Canada's ongoing crime victimization survey. However, the breadth of questions on sexual violence is much more limited in scope compared to the specialized survey.

Victimization surveys produce more reliable estimates of the prevalence of sexual assault compared to police statistics;[15] however, they are conducted only periodically and thus are an imperfect measure of trends over time. Victimization surveys have been conducted in Cana-

12 Diana Russell, "The Prevalence and Incidence of Forcible Rape and Attempted Rape of Females" (1982) 7 Victimology: Int J 81.

13 Ronet Bachman & Linda Saltzman, "Violence Against Women: Estimates from the Redesigned Survey" (1995) in Washington, Bureau of Justice Statistics, NCJ-154348; Ronet Bachman & Bruce Taylor, "The Measurement of Rape and Family Violence by the Redesigned National Crime Victimization Survey" (1994) 11 Just Q 499.

14 Johnson & Dawson, *supra* note 5 at 52.

15 While far superior to police statistics for researching women's experiences of male violence, victimization surveys are not without important limitations. Surveys conducted by telephone effectively exclude marginalized populations living in shelters, unstable housing, or on the street; those without landlines; those who cannot respond in English or French; and cultural and linguistic minorities for whom telephone surveys are not a familiar medium for disclosing personal or sensitive experiences. The extent to which they can be used to explore intersections of violence and other forms of oppression based on race, ethnicity, sexual orientation, and disability is also limited.

da in 1993, 1999, and 2004 and all estimate that the incidence of sexual assault has affected about 3 percent of women in the previous twelve-month period.[16] By contrast, police recorded a drop in the rate of sexual assault since 1993. Over the longer term, police recorded a small but steady rise in rates of rape and indecent assault on females prior to law reform in 1983, followed by a sharp increase following implementation of the new law of sexual assault (Figure 1). In 1993, the rate of sexual assault reached a peak of 121 per 100,000 of the population and by 2007 had dropped to 65 per 100,000.

It is not clear whether this trend reflects a real rise and fall in the occurrence of sexual assault in the population, changes in the way police respond to the assaults reported to them, or a rise and fall in women's confidence in the criminal justice system reflected by their reporting behaviour. Some researchers attribute the rise prior to 1993 to an increased willingness of sexually assaulted women to report to the police as a result of law reform[17] and other social changes that occurred simultaneously, such as an expansion of services, growth in specialized sexual assault units and training for police, and development of Sexual Assault Nurse Examiner programs in hospital-based sexual assault care centres.[18] It is difficult to test this claim empirically since so few women report to the police and victimization surveys are conducted too infrequently to establish with certainty whether reporting behaviour has influenced this trend. Yet, in all three victimization surveys between 1993 and 2004, fewer than 10 percent of sexual assaults were reported to police. If improvements to the justice system response to sexual assault were indeed associated with the rise in reported sexual assaults prior to 1993, it is feasible that negative experiences with the legal process since that time may have reduced women's confidence that they will be treated with dignity, fairness, and compassion, resulting in a decline in willingness to engage with the criminal justice system.

16 Gannon & Mihorean, *supra* note 2; Rebecca Kong *et al*, "Sexual Offences in Canada" (2003) 23 Juristat 85-002-XPE 6 at 19; Sandra Besserer & Cathy Trainor, "Criminal Victimization in Canada, 1999" (2000) 20 Juristat 85-002-XIE 10 at 19.

17 Julian Roberts & Michelle Grossman, "Changing Definitions of Sexual Assault: An Analysis of Police Statistics" in Julian Roberts & Renate Mohr, eds, *Confronting Sexual Assault: A Decade of Legal and Social Change* (Toronto: University of Toronto Press, 1994) 57.

18 Scott Clark & Dorothy Hepworth, "Effects of Reform Legislation on the Processing of Sexual Assault Cases" in Roberts & Mohr, *ibid* at 113.

Figure 1: Police-Recorded Rates of Rape, Indecent Assault, Total Sexual Assault, and Level I Sexual Assault

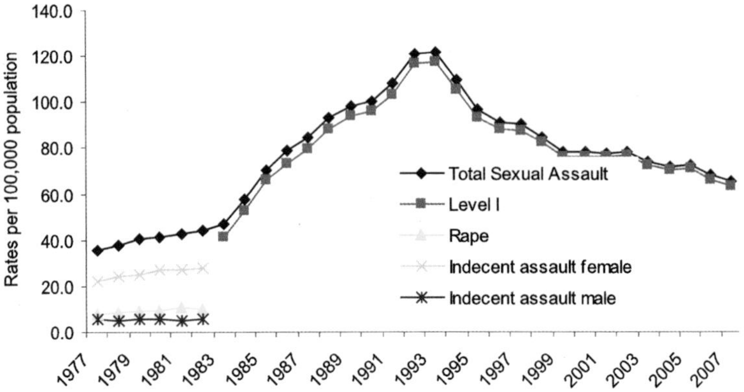

Source: Uniform Crime Reporting Survey, Statistics Canada.

POLICE RECORDING PRACTICES

Rape reform in 1983 abolished the offences of rape, attempted rape, indecent assault on a male, and indecent assault on a female and replaced them with a gender-neutral gradation of three levels of sexual assault. The most serious, level III, contained in section 273 of the *Canadian Criminal Code*, includes aggravated sexual assaults that result in wounding, maiming, disfiguring, or endangering the life of the victim. Level II, contained in section 272, is defined as sexual assaults that occur with a weapon present, that cause bodily harm, that involve threats of bodily harm to a person other than the victim, or that are committed with another person. Level I, contained in section 271, is undefined and is presumably any sexual assault that does not include elements of levels II or III. A man who commits forced penetration, formerly legally known as rape, can be charged and prosecuted under any of these sections, including 271 if it is determined that the attack did not involve a weapon, bodily harm, or multiple assailants.

Tracking trends in police-recorded sexual assaults over time reveals some troubling patterns in the way police have classified these crimes. Since the inception of the sexual assault law in 1983, police have recorded the vast majority of these crimes as level I. This proportion has grown to the point that sexual assaults are recorded almost exclusively in the least serious category. In 2007, 98 percent of all sexual assaults were recorded as level I, up from 88 percent in 1983. The percentage re-

Figure 2: Police-Recorded Rates of Levels II and III Sexual Assault

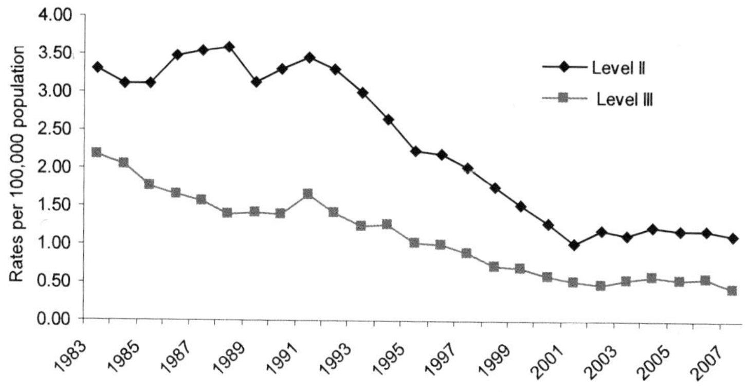

Source: Uniform Crime Reporting Survey, Statistics Canada.

corded as levels II and III have always been relatively small, but have dropped dramatically from 7 percent to 2 percent in the case of level II, and from 5 percent to 1 percent in the case of level III (see Figure 2 for trends in rates of level II and III sexual assaults recorded by police. Because of the much different scale, level I is shown in Figure 1). The law is supposed to account for different degrees of severity yet, unless the nature and severity of the sexual assaults reported to the police have changed dramatically (and there is no evidence that this is the case), these figures suggest that some incidents that previously would have been classified as level III are now being classified as level II or level I and many previously classified as level II are now treated as level I offences.

In an independent research study of hospital, police, and prosecution records, Janice Du Mont[19] found support for the claim that police under-classify large numbers of sexual assaults. The purpose of this study was to examine the congruency between the seriousness of sexual assault offences as indicated by the *Criminal Code* and the seriousness of charges at three points in the criminal justice processing of sexual assault cases: charges laid by police, offences for which offenders were convicted, and the sentences imposed. She concludes that the

19 Janice Du Mont, "Charging and Sentencing in Sexual Assault Cases: An Exploratory Examination" (2003) 15 CJWL 305.

expected charge corresponded to the charges laid by police in only 40 percent of cases, and in only 20 percent of cases resulting in conviction. Many cases charged under sexual assault level I involved rape, the use of force, and injury to the victim. In just half of cases where the charges laid matched the severity of the crime were offenders convicted of the same offences without charges being reduced.

Further evidence of misclassification emerges from statistics submitted by police across Canada to Statistics Canada's Revised Uniform Crime Reporting (UCR II) Survey. Out of a total of 17,374 level I sexual assaults recorded in the UCR II Survey in 2007, 386 involved some type of weapon. Twenty-eight of these weapons were firearms, seventy-four were knives, and thirty-nine were blunt instruments. Furthermore, 17 percent of level I sexual assaults resulted in physical injury and this likely undercounts the true percentage since many injuries, such as bruising and internal injuries, are not immediately evident to police investigators. Classifying these incidents as level I sexual assault is contrary to the *Criminal Code*, which clearly specifies that any sexual assault involving a weapon or resulting in bodily harm warrants categorization at least as a level II offence.

The view of sexual assault from the perspective of women on the receiving end adds another dimension to this discussion. Statistics Canada's victimization surveys ask women about their experiences of sexual assault in two categories as follows:

1. Has anyone forced you or attempted to force you into any unwanted sexual activity, by threatening you, holding you down or hurting you in some way?
2. Has anyone ever touched you against your will in any sexual way? By this I mean anything from unwanted touching or grabbing, to kissing or fondling.

Together, these questions are intended to capture the range of assaults included under the sexual assault sections of the *Criminal Code*. When women are directly interviewed about their experiences, 19 percent are classified as sexual attacks involving force or the threat of force and the remaining 81 percent are classified as unwanted sexual touching.[20] What is more, sexual attacks involving force or threats are more likely than unwanted sexual touching to be reported to the police, which

20 Shannon Brennan & Andrea Taylor-Butts, *Sexual Assault in Canada, 2004* (2008) Statistics Canada 85F0033M No 19 at 11.

logically would suggest that a higher proportion of assaults recorded in police statistics should be level II or III assaults.[21]

Under-classification of sexual assaults has obvious implications for the treatment of these cases in court and for the sentences imposed.[22] Under-classification of sexual assaults by police also has implications for the way this crime is understood by police officers as professionals who respond to sexual assault complainants, and by members of the general public. Statistics legitimated by official government sources can negatively influence public perceptions when levels II and III sexual assaults are described as very low and dropping and the vast majority are described as not serious, whether or not there may have been weapons, force, injuries, or long-lasting emotional trauma. Feminists point out that one result of law reform has been to downgrade the offence substantially since rape and unwanted sexual touching technically can now occupy the same offence category, and both can be dealt with under section 271 as summary conviction offences punishable by a maximum of eighteen months imprisonment.[23] Prior to law reform, rape made up almost one-quarter of police-recorded sexual offences, many of which are now coded and portrayed as "non-violent" or "less serious" level I offences. While the shift from rape to sexual assault was intended to reduce the stigma associated with being a victim of rape, as Elizabeth Sheehy points out, in de-gendering the law and replacing rape with a gradation of sexual assault offences, an important shared social understanding of the meaning and impact of rape for women has been lost.[24]

In a research experiment designed to assess public perceptions of rape law reform, Roberts and his colleagues[25] found empirical support for the concern that a change in name has served to downgrade the offence. When presented with scenarios depicting the same acts but labelled either rape or sexual assault, study participants attributed

21 According to the 1993 Violence Against Women Survey, 11 percent of cases of forced sexual activity were reported to police compared to 4 percent of cases of unwanted sexual touching.

22 Julian Roberts & Robert Gebotys, "Reforming Rape Laws: Effects of Legislative Change in Canada" (1992) 16 Law & Hum Behav 555.

23 Jennifer Temkin, *Rape and the Legal Process* (New York: Oxford University Press, 2002) at 162.

24 Elizabeth Sheehy, "Legal Responses to Violence Against Women in Canada" in Katherine McKenna & June Larkin, eds, *Violence Against Women: New Canadian Perspectives* (Toronto: Inanna Publications, 2002) 480.

25 Julian Roberts, Michelle Grossman & Robert Gebotys, "Rape Reform in Canada: Public Knowledge and Opinion" (1996) 11 J Family Violence 146.

less punitive responses to scenarios described as sexual assault than the same acts defined as rape. This suggests that the general public interprets sexual assault according to understandings of rape and that the crime of sexual assault is seen as less severe. The unforeseen consequences of law reform may have been to minimize the crime of sexual assault in public consciousness, legal discourse, and the legal response.

BARRIERS TO JUSTICE

Defining and talking about experiences of sexual violence is a difficult process for women and is undertaken with considerable risk. When women disclose to others that they have been sexually assaulted, they are often confronted with skepticism, doubt, and outright blame for provoking or at least not resisting the attack strenuously enough. Reactions from others in the woman's social world contain both explicit and implicit messages about how to make sense of what happened. These reactions have a direct impact on her ability to interpret the experience as a violent act for which she is not responsible.[26]

A rich literature documents the widespread acceptance of negative stereotypes about women who complain of rape held by the police, defence counsel, prosecutors, judges, juries, and the general public.[27] The widely held belief that "real rape" happens when a previously chaste woman is assaulted by a stranger, suffers serious injury, and immediately reports the attack to the police also affects the way women perceive their own experiences of sexual violence. At this very first step, when a decision is made to engage with the justice system, to seek support elsewhere, or to remain silent, this decision is affected by deeply engrained societal attitudes that hold women responsible for sexual assault and absolve men of wrongdoing. Research has documented the widespread acceptance of prejudicial attitudes and belief in myths and negative stereotypes about rape victims among the general public.[28] For

26 Rebecca Campbell, Emily Dworkin & Giannina Cabral, "An Ecological Model of the Impact of Sexual Assault on Women's Health" (2009) 10 Trauma, Violence & Abuse 225; Denise Lievore, *No Longer Silent: A Study of Women's Help-seeking Decisions and Service Responses to Sexual Assault* (Canberra: Australian Institute of Criminology and Office for Women, 2005).

27 See Jennifer Temkin & Barbara Krahé, *Sexual Assault and the Justice Gap: A Question of Attitude* (Oxford: Hart Publishing, 2008) 31–51 for a review.

28 Michael Flood & Bob Pease, "Factors Influencing Attitudes to Violence Against Women" (2009) 10 Trauma, Violence & Abuse 125; Temkin & Krahé, *ibid* at 31; Colleen Ward, *Attitudes Toward Rape: Feminist and Social Psychological Perspectives* (London: Sage, 1995).

instance, in a representative survey of Australian adults, 23 percent disagreed with the statement that "women rarely make false claims of being raped" and 11 percent were unsure.[29] In other words, one-third of Australians are fairly certain or suspect that women "cry rape" falsely. Almost one-quarter agreed or were unsure that women often say "no" when they mean "yes" (15 percent and 8 percent respectively), and over 40 percent agreed or were unsure that rape results from men not being able to control their need for sex (38 percent and 5 percent respectively). In a representative sample of adults in the United Kingdom, substantial proportions believed a woman is partially or totally responsible for being raped if she behaved in a flirtatious manner (34 percent), was drunk (30 percent), was wearing sexy or revealing clothing (26 percent), or has had many sex partners (22 percent).[30]

Rape myth adherence has been the subject of extensive study by social psychologists. It has been established that belief in rape myths and negative stereotypes are correlated with gender (men are more likely than women to adhere to rape myths), culture and religion, hostile attitudes toward women, and beliefs about adversarial gender roles.[31] Although attitudes and beliefs do not always predict behaviour, there is evidence that bystanders who hold prejudicial beliefs are less likely to be empathetic or to report the incident to police, and are more likely to attribute blame to victims and recommend lenient penalties;[32] men who score higher on rape-supportive beliefs and negative attitudes toward women are more likely to say that they would be sexually violent or coercive;[33] and women who hold stereotypical beliefs about rape and rape victims are less likely to define their own experiences as sexual as-

29 Natalie Taylor & Jenny Mouzos, *Community Attitudes to Violence Against Women Survey: A Full Technical Report* (Canberra: Australian Institute of Criminology, 2006) at 67.

30 Amnesty International UK, *Sexual Assault Research Summary Report* (2005) at 5, online: <http://www.amnesty.org.uk/uploads/documents/doc_16619.doc> (retrieved 29 May 2009).

31 Flood & Pease, *supra* note 28; Kimberly Lonsway & Louise Fitzgerald, "Attitudinal Antecedents of Rape Myth Acceptance: A Theoretical and Empirical Re-examination" (1995) 68 J Per & Soc Psych 704.

32 Flood & Pease, *supra* note 28 at 127.

33 Veanne Anderson, Dorothy Simpson-Taylor & Douglas Hermann, "Gender, Age, and Rape-supportive Rules" (2004) 50 Sex Roles 77; Sarah Murnen, Carrie Wright & Gretchen Kaluzny, "If 'Boys Will Be Boys,' then Girls Will Be Victims? A Meta-Analytic Review of the Research that Relates Masculine Ideology to Sexual Aggression" (2002) 46 Sex Roles 359.

sault or to seek help.[34] Consequently, sexual assaults reported to the police are more likely to be those that conform to "real rape" stereotypes.[35]

Biases and myths about women, men, and rape have also been formally and informally entrenched in the administration of the law. Research provides evidence that negative attitudes and beliefs about sexual assault complainants often overshadow the facts of the case in police charging, prosecutorial decision making, and jurors' deliberations.[36] Far from being impartial, gender-neutral, and objective as the "official version of law"[37] would have us believe, much of the decision making around sexual assault — from initial decisions by the woman to tell anyone about the assault, to the decisions of police, courts, prosecutors, juries, and judges — are influenced by long-standing, deeply entrenched biases. Claire L'Heureux-Dubé, former justice of the Supreme Court of Canada, has identified myths and stereotypes entrenched in the Supreme Court that have skewed the law's treatment of sexual assault claimants:[38]

34 Zoe Peterson & Charlene Muelenhard, "Was It Rape? The Function of Women's Rape Myth Acceptance and Definitions of Sex in Labelling their Own Experiences" (2004) 51:3/4 Sex Roles 129.

35 Ronet Bachman, "The Factors Related to Rape Reporting Behaviour and Arrest: New Evidence from the National Crime Victimization Survey" (1998) 25 Crim Just Beh 8; Janice Du Mont, Karen-Lee Miller & Terri Myhr, "The Role of 'Real Rape' and 'Real Victim' Stereotypes in the Police Reporting Practices of Sexually Assaulted Women" (2003) 9 Violence Against Women 466; Rosemary Gartner & Ross Macmillan, "The Effect of Victim-offender Relationship on Reporting Crimes of Violence Against Women" (1995) 37 Can J Crim 393.

36 Janice Du Mont a& Terri Myhr, "So Few Convictions: The Role of Client-related Characteristics in the Legal Processing of Sexual Assaults" (2000) 6 Violence Against Women 1109; Bonnie Fisher *et al*, "Reporting Sexual Victimization to the Police and Others" (2003) 30 Crim Just Beh 6; Jan Jordan, "Beyond Belief?: Police, Rape and Women's Credibility" (2004) 4 Crim Just 29; Denise Lievore, "Victim Credibility in Adult Sexual Assault Cases" in *Trends and Issues in Crime and Criminal Justice* (Canberra: Australian Institute of Criminology, 2004) 288; Natalie Taylor, "Juror Attitudes and Biases in Sexual Assault Cases" in *Trends and Issues in Crime and Criminal Justice* (Canberra: Australian Institute of Criminology, 2007) 344; Elizabeth Comack & Gillian Balfour, *The Power to Criminalize: Violence, Inequality and the Law* (Halifax: Fernwood, 2004); Jeffrey Spears & Cassia Spohn, "The Genuine Victim and Prosecutors' Charging Decisions in Sexual Assault Cases" (1996) 20 Am J Crim Just 183; Emily Finch & Vanessa Munro, "The Demon Drink and the Demonized Woman: Socio-sexual Stereotypes and Responsibility Attribution in Rape Trials Involving Intoxicants" (2007) 16 Soc & Leg Stud 591; Tempkin & Krahé (2008) *supra* note 27 at 84.

37 Ngaire Naffine, *Law and the Sexes: Explorations in Feminist Jurisprudence* (Sydney: Allen & Unwin, 1990).

38 Claire L'Heureux-Dubé, "Beyond the Myths: Equality, Impartiality, and Justice" (2001) 10 J Social Distress & Homeless 89.

- The rapist is a stranger
- Women are less reliable and credible as witnesses if they have had prior sexual relations
- Women are more likely to have consented to sexual advances if they have had prior sexual relations
- Women will always struggle to defend their honour
- Women are "more emotional" than men so unless they become "hysterical," nothing must have happened
- Women mean "yes" even when they say "no"
- Women who are raped deserve it because of their conduct, dress, and demeanour
- Woman fantasize about rape and therefore fabricate reports of sexual activity even though nothing happened

According to McIntyre et al, rape myths serve an important purpose:

> … these "myths" help men individually and as a class to rationalize their sexual abuses or to distinguish their own "natural" sexual aggression or ordinary sexual opportunism from the really culpable and injurious kind practiced by those aberrant, truly violent, genuinely scary men the criminal law is meant to isolate and jail.[39]

Acceptance of rape myths is linked to minimization of harm and attribution of blame to victims, and reduction of responsibility attributed to perpetrators.[40] The widely held belief that "real rape" happens when a previously chaste women is assaulted by a stranger, suffers serious injury, and immediately reports the attack to the police affects decisions women make to engage with the justice system, to seek support elsewhere, or to remain silent.[41] They also influence decisions made by police to treat the complaint as false, prosecutors' decisions not to proceed with a prosecution, jurors' decisions that complainants' claims of non-consent are not credible, and judges' decisions about sentencing in the rare event that a perpetrator is convicted. Decisions based on these biases obviously disadvantage certain women more than others — including those who are poorly educated; those who are inarticulate or poorly spoken in the dominant language; those who are ethnic minority or Aboriginal; those who have chosen certain occupations; those who have mental health problems or a history of abuse; and those

39 McIntyre *et al, supra* note 3 at 74.

40 Temkin & Krahé, *supra* note 27 at 38.

41 *Ibid* at 32.

who generally transgress stereotypes of the "good" woman.[42] According to Liz Kelly, "rape law defines the mental element ... in terms of the social meaning of the woman's conduct, rather than the legal meaning of a man's."[43] These biases demonstrate a lack of understanding of the contexts in which most sexual assault occurs, typically by men known and trusted by women engaging in normal activities such as accepting a lift home or socializing, and the complex range of responses victims adopt — such as failing to resist strenuously in order to avoid further injury, and taking time to make the difficult decision of making the attack public.

ATTRITION THROUGH THE CRIMINAL JUSTICE SYSTEM

One objective of reform of the sexual assault law was to reduce the attrition of these cases through the criminal justice system, from reporting to police to conviction in court. Attrition refers to the gradual dropping off or discontinuation of cases due to decisions by women who have been raped and justice officials as cases proceed through the system. While it is true that all criminal incidents are subjected to multi-layered decision-making processes, none are forced to endure the level of skepticism and outright bias that greet women who report sexual assault.

Unless the attack occurs in a public place in full view of witnesses who make the decision for her, a woman who is sexually assaulted must first weigh the benefits and costs of sharing this with others in her social network, asking for medical assistance, emotional support, or help from police. She must first consider whether others in her social network will support her decision — whether they will support her perception of events or see her as somehow complicit or responsible for the attack.[44] If significant proportions of a woman's social and familial network believe that women falsely complain about rape, that they do not know their own minds when it comes to agreeing to sex, or that the uncontrollable male sex drive renders men blameless for their actions, she is unlikely to bring a complaint forward.[45] Her decision to report to

42 Denise Lievore, "Prosecutorial Decisions in Adult Sexual Assault Cases" in *Trends & Issues in Crime and Criminal Justice* (Canberra: Australian Institute of Criminology, 2005) 291; McIntyre *et al*, *supra* note 3 at 74; Constance Backhouse, *Carnal Crimes: Sexual Assault Law in Canada, 1900–1975* (Toronto: Irwin Law, 2008).

43 Liz Kelly, *Routes to (In)justice: A Research Review on the Reporting, Investigation and Prosecution of Rape Cases* (London: Child and Woman Abuse Studies Unit, University of North London, 2001).

44 Lievore, *supra* note 26.

45 A common reason for not reporting the crime to the police given by women who

the police is also affected by shame and embarrassment, a desire to protect others, especially family members, and concern about whether the police will take her complaint seriously, treat her with respect, and not subject her to ill treatment.[46]

Once an assault is reported to the police, they make a decision how to respond and whether to make an official record of the crime. They make decisions about how much effort they will dedicate to investigating the crime and whether charges will be laid against a suspect. Each call to police is subject to an initial investigation at which time they can decide if a crime did not occur and will code the complaint as "unfounded." Police statistics show that sexual assaults are subjected to "unfounding" to a far greater extent than any other crime. According to coding rules for Statistics Canada's Uniform Crime Reporting Survey, incidents are to be coded as unfounded when an investigation determines that a crime did not take place.[47] Statistics Canada no longer publishes unfounding rates for any crime due to concerns that police are inconsistent in their use of this category in the absence of other coding options, and that it has become a catch-all for complaints that do not go forward. In 2000, the last year this information was made public, police across the country declared 16 percent of sexual assaults to be unfounded compared with 9 percent of other assaults.[48] In a study of four police jurisdictions in British Columbia, unfounding rates for sexual assault ranged from 7 percent to 28 percent, which suggests to the authors that there are variations in police beliefs and attitudes and investigative procedures surrounding sexual assault.[49] Unfounding was more common in cases involving non-strangers who raped women

have been sexually assaulted is that the incident was not important enough. How should this be interpreted when a large proportion of people to whom women turn for support minimize the severity of the assault or suspect her of complicity?

46 Denise Lievore, *Non-reporting and Hidden Recording of Sexual Assault: An International Literature Review* (Canberra: Commonwealth Office of the Status of Women, 2003).

47 Statistics Canada. *Uniform Crime Reporting, Version 1.0, Reporting Manual*, online: <http://www.statcan.gc.ca/ imdb-bmdi/document/3302_D7_T1_V1-eng.pdf> (retrieved 9 August 2009).

48 Julian Roberts, Holly Johnson & Michelle Grossman, "Trends in Crimes of Sexual Aggression in Canada: An Analysis of Police-Reported and Victimization Statistics" (2003) 2 Int J Comp Crim 18.

49 Tina Hattem, "Highlights from a Preliminary Study of Police Classification of Sexual Assault Cases as Unfounded" 14 Just Research (Ottawa: Department of Justice), online: <http://canada.justice.gc.ca/eng/pi/rs/rep-rap/jr/jr14/p9.html> (retrieved 15 January 2009).

without using force; in cases where women with mental health problems did not clearly say "no"; and in cases where women were not emotionally upset.

In a study for the British Home Office, 25 percent of sexual assaults were "no-crimed" (the equivalent of unfounding), ranging from 14 percent to 41 percent among individual police departments.[50] Reasons given for no-criming included a belief that the complaint was false or malicious, but also included complainants who were unwilling to testify, as well as cases with insufficient evidence, even though police are directed that no-criming is appropriate only when the complainant retracts completely and admits to fabrication. A second analysis of police data in the United Kingdom found a no-crime rate of 22 percent.[51] Included were cases where women withdrew the complaint, cases that were dropped because the woman was ill or especially vulnerable, and cases where there was insufficient evidence or no suspect was identified. Reasons behind the classification of cases as false allegations included mental health problems, previous allegation of sexual assault, and alcohol and drug use.[52] Upon closer inspection of case files, the authors determined that only 3 percent of no-crimed cases had a high probability of being falsely reported. Very little empirical research has been conducted to investigate reasons behind false reports, but a New Zealand study found that about half of all allegations of sexual assault that were later retracted were cases where someone else initially called the police or pressured the woman to make a report, which she later stated to be false.[53] Thus, recantations typically arose from misinterpretations by third parties and not vengeful or malicious complaints of rape.

Once a complaint of sexual assault is declared "founded," police may or may not follow up with an investigation. Some women opt not to proceed but to have forensic evidence taken to retain the option to pursue the case at a later time. In other cases, police determine there is insufficient evidence to establish "reasonable grounds" required to lay a charge, the circumstances of the case do not fit the officer's personal bias of what constitutes a "real" or "legitimate" victim,[54] or they consid-

50 Jessica Harris & Sharon Grace, *A Question of Evidence? Investigating and Prosecuting Rape in the 1990's* (London: Home Office, 1999) at 14.

51 Liz Kelly, Jo Lovett & Linda Reagan, *A Gap or a Chasm? Attrition in Reported Rape Cases* (London: Home Office, 2005) at 38.

52 *Ibid* at 49.

53 Jordan, *supra* note 36 at 29.

54 Tempkin & Krahé, *supra* note 27 at 36–41.

Figure 3: Percent of Founded Sexual Assaults that Resulted in Charges Laid Against A Suspect

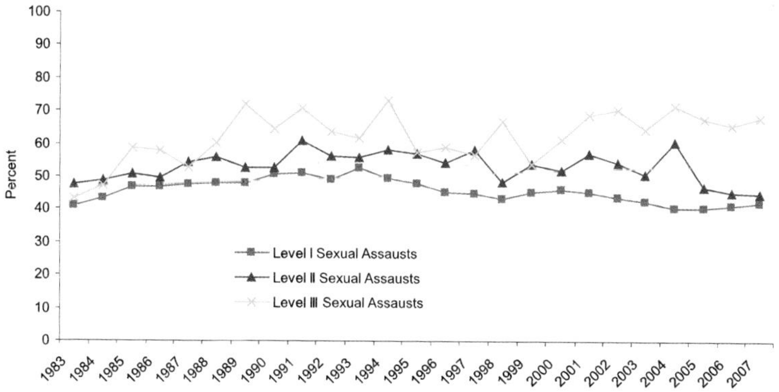

Source: Uniform Crime Reporting Survey, Statistics Canada.

er the evidence too weak to withstand typical defence counsel tactics to attack the woman's credibility. Whatever the reasons for not proceeding, the result is a charging rate of less than one-half of all founded cases. The percentage of cases in 2007 that led to a suspect being charged was less than half for those categorized as level I or level II assault (42 percent and 45 percent respectively); even those that reached the very high threshold of classification at level III sexual assaults resulted in criminal charges in only two-thirds of cases (68 percent) (Figure 3). The higher charging rate for level III offences may be a reflection of a narrowing down of cases classified as level III assaults to the top few in terms of injury and trauma, and greater resources and specialist investigators assigned to solving high profile sexual assaults. Nonetheless, this is a charging rate of just two-thirds for the most severe of all sexual assaults.

Attrition takes the shape of a pyramid where the actual number of sexual assaults forms the base and the levels of the pyramid in decreasing width are formed by the number of assaults reported to police, the number recorded by police as "founded," the number with a suspect being charged, and the number prosecuted, up to the peak, which contains a considerably reduced number of criminal convictions (shown in Figure 4). These data sources — all from Statistics Canada — are the best available to estimate the flow of sexual assault cases from occurrence to conviction, but each has important methodological shortcomings. In the first place, we will likely never know the actual incidence of sexual violence. Victimization surveys are far more comprehensive and produce more reliable estimates than any other source, but it cannot be assumed that all women will divulge such intimate and potentially stigmatizing experiences to a stranger in the context of an anonymous interview. Police may not record all incidents reported to them (even "founded" cases), and they may record a sexual assault as some other type of crime.[55] Some cases reported to the police as sexual assault may result in a suspect being charged but with a different offence. The number of charges laid does not equate to the number of persons charged since more than one person can be charged in one incident and one person can be charged with many incidents. "Charges laid" here refers to the number of sexual assault incidents that were officially cleared by the laying of a charge, not the number of offenders charged. Criminal justice datasets are not linked and use different units of count: police statistics count "incidents," which is based on the number of victims of sexual assault, while court-based statistics related to prosecutions and convictions count the number of "cases," which is based on the number of accused persons.[56] A person who is prosecuted for sexual assault may have many sexual assaults against many different victims dealt with in one court case and, at the top of the pyramid, he may be convicted of many counts of sexual assault or sexual assault in combination with other crimes. Those convicted of other crimes and not sexual assault do not appear in these calculations.

With these limitations in mind, it is possible to make general statements about attrition of sexual assault through the criminal justice system. At the base of the attrition pyramid (I) are an undetermined number of actual sexual assaults; the next level (II) are the 460,000 incidents of sexual assault reported in Statistics Canada's 2004 victimization survey. The estimated number of "founded" cases (IV) involving women and girls twelve years of age and older was 13,200; since "unfounded" figures are no longer published, 15,200 is an estimate (III) derived from the total number recorded by police as founded on the basis

55 In addition, UCR scoring rules require that if an incident contains more than one offence type, it is recorded according to the most serious, which is determined by the maximum sentence under the *Criminal Code*. Level I sexual assaults that occur in the context of an offence that carries a maximum sentence of more than 10 years imprisonment will be recorded as the other offence and will not appear in this analysis.

56 The definition of a "case" is all charges against the same person having overlapping court dates. Michael Marth, "Adult Criminal Court Statistics, 2006/2007" (2008) 28 Juristat 85-002-XPE (Ottawa: Statistics Canada) at 10.

Figure 4: The Attrition Pyramid

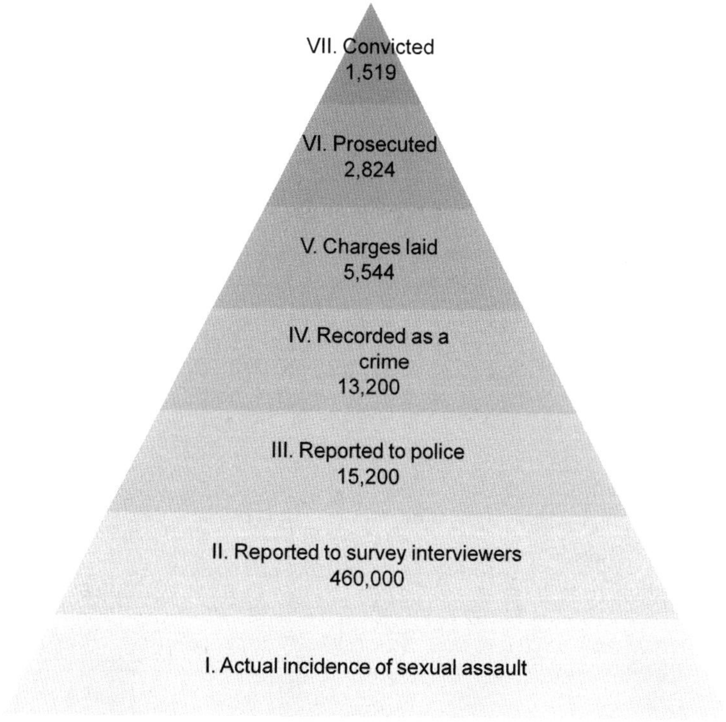

Source: Adapted from Lievore, *supra* note 46 at41.

(I) Likely will never be known; (II) 2004 General Social Survey on Victimization; (III) The number recorded by police adjusted for 15 percent declared unfounded; (IV) The number of sexual assaults against women twelve years of age and older recorded on the Revised Uniform Crime Reporting Survey in 2007. This represents 82 percent of cases involving female victims and 70 percent of all cases of sexual assault recorded by police as founded. Original data retrieval; (V) Calculated based on the number of sexual assaults in IV and the 42 percent cleared by charge in the Uniform Crime Reporting Survey; (VI) The number of males prosecuted in criminal courts in fiscal year 2006/07 on the Adult Criminal Court Survey. Original data retrieval; (VII) The number of males who were found guilty of sexual assault (following a plea of guilty or were found guilty after trial) in fiscal year 2006/07 on the Adult Criminal Court Survey. Original data retrieval.

Sources: Statistics Canada.

Figure 5: Number of Sexual Assaults Recorded by Police as "Founded"Compared to the Number of Convictions

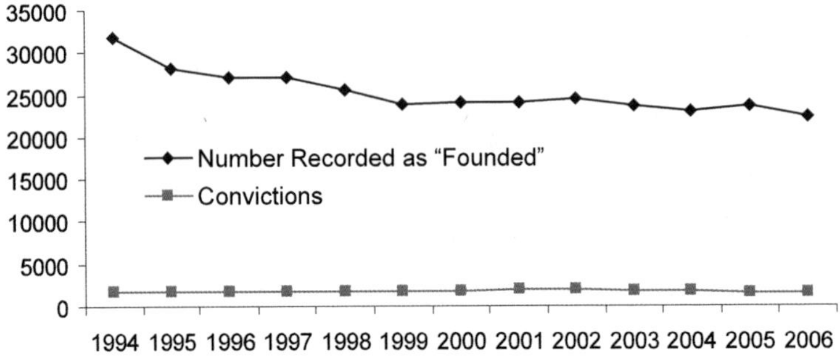

Sources: Uniform Crime Reporting Survey and Adult Criminal Court Survey, Statistics Canada.

that 15 percent are declared unfounded.[57] Less than half of these (5,544) led to a suspect being charged (V). About half of suspects (2,848) were prosecuted (VI), and half of those cases prosecuted resulted in a conviction for sexual assault (VII).[58] As a result, just 25 percent of suspects initially charged with sexual assault were convicted of sexual assault, possibly at a reduced level. If attrition is calculated from the estimated 460,000 sexual assaults that occurred in one year and follows through to the 1,406 offenders convicted in criminal court (VII), the result is that 0.3 percent of perpetrators of sexual assault were held accountable and 99.7 percent were not.[59] It would take dramatic changes in women's

57 This is a conservative estimate. If this figure were calculated on the basis of the 8 percent of 460,000 victims in the victimization survey who reported to the police, the figure would be 43,760.

58 It is not possible to identify the age and sex of victims in court statistics; therefore, these figures include some cases involving child victims and male victims. If these calculations had been possible, the final conviction rate would for sexual assault against women have been even lower.

59 Bill C-9, enacted in 2007, abolished the use of conditional sentences for serious personal injury offences, including sexual assault. In 2012, Bill C-10 revised section 742.1 of the *Criminal Code* to eliminate the reference to serious personal injury offences; now conditional sentences are unavailable in cases of level I sexual assault only where the Crown proceeds by indictment, where the accused faces a maximum sentence of ten years or more. Given that 98 percent of all sexual assaults are level I offences, a great many once again become eligble for conditional sentencing.

Figure 6: Type of Sentence for Sexual Assault Convictions

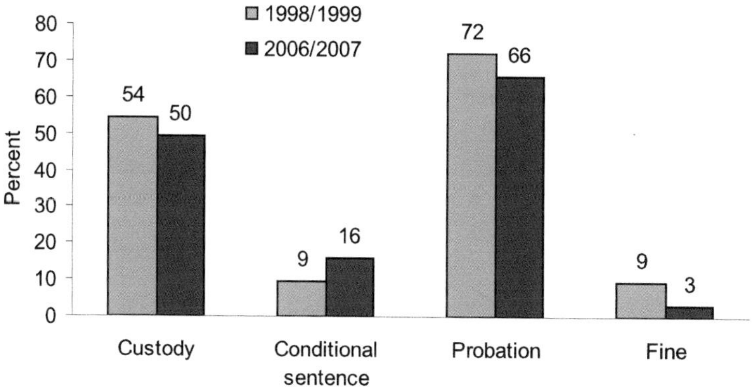

Source: Adult Criminal Court Survey, Statistics Canada.

willingness to report these assaults to the police, or a concerted effort to alter current police and prosecutor policies, to improve this dismal rate of attrition and address what amounts to impunity for sexually violent men in Canada.

The most significant point of attrition after police become involved in sexual assault cases occurs when they record the incident as a crime and fail to lay a charge. Only 42 percent of all "founded" cases result in a suspect being charged and no more than 11 percent have led to a conviction since Statistics Canada began providing court data in 1994. Figure 5 shows the declining number of sexual assaults recorded by the police as "founded" since 1994 and the consistently low number of convictions. The number of men convicted of sexual assault in the last two years recorded on the table is the lowest in this entire time period.

Furthermore, patterns in sentencing for sexual assault convictions show a decline in severity, which is consistent with the decline in the proportion of sexual assaults charged under sections 273 and 272 (levels II and III). Just half of convicted offenders were sentenced to a term of imprisonment in 2006/07, down slightly from 1998/99; the percentage sentenced to probation also declined (Figure 6). Conditional sentences were introduced in 1996 as an alternative to incarceration for offenders deemed not to pose a threat to the community and were to be considered for offences punishable by less than two years imprisonment. Section 271 (level I) sexual assaults are hybrid offences, which prosecutors can choose to proceed with summarily or by indictment; as an indictable offence, section 271 assaults are punishable by a maximum term of ten years imprisonment, and as a summary offence they are punishable to a prison term not exceeding eighteen months. While it is not possible from the available data to determine what proportion are proceeded with summarily, based on the fact that 98 percent of all sexual assaults are recorded under section 271, it can be assumed that a large portion must be considered for conditional sentences. Over this time period, conditional sentences almost doubled for convicted sexual offenders. Some of these convictions involve rape and attempted rape and others involve unwanted sexual touching, but it is not possible to discern from the adult court database the severity of cases that result in different sentencing outcomes.[60]

CONCLUSION

Twenty-five years ago, law makers and equality-seeking groups were optimistic that, by reforming sexual assault laws that were prejudicial toward women, rape myths and biases could be eliminated, women would be encouraged to come forward, and rates of attrition would be reduced. It is clear that rape law reform and the efforts of grassroots feminist organizations to raise awareness and challenge widespread discriminatory stereotypes have not resulted in improvements to women's willingness to come forward, or in the response of the criminal justice system toward women who report. This analysis suggests that while law reform can eliminate the formal expression of rape myths, on its own it cannot alter the harmful attitudes and behaviour that continue to influence the reactions of women, perpetrators, and bystanders, police screening practices, court processes, jurors' decisions, conviction rates, and sentencing practices. Far from emphasizing the assaultive nature of the crime, police practices unfound large numbers of complaints and classify almost all remaining cases as level I. The effect has been to portray sexual assault complaints as vexatious and frivolous. Until a commitment is made to address the prejudices in the response to sexual violence, women's experiences will continue to be trivialized, male-centred definitions of women's sexuality will be reinforced, violent men will not be held accountable, and women's rights to sexual integrity, equality, and justice will continue to be denied.

60 *An Act to amend the Criminal Code (Ending Conditional Sentences for Property and Other Serious Crimes Act)*, SC 2007, C 12, s 1, abolished the use of conditional sentences for serious personal injury offences, including sexual assault levels I, II and III.

25.

HIV Exposure as Assault: Progressive Development or Misplaced Focus?

Alison Symington[1]

Alison Symington's contribution to this section raises a fundamental question: should those who fail to disclose their HIV status to their sexual partners be placed in the ranks of perpetrators of sex crimes? Her concerns about whether the criminalization strategy will in fact protect women or enhance their equality and autonomy interests as equal partners in sexual matters echoes those expressed by Julie Desrosiers with respect to the new age of consent. Alison uses the available data regarding successful prosecutions for aggravated assault and aggravated sexual assault based on non-disclosure to draw a sharp contrast with the abysmal prosecution of most other sexual assaults, as previously reviewed by Holly Johnson. She suggests that these prosecutions may be fuelled by AIDS panic rather than women's safety concerns, and she demonstrates many problems in these prosecutions, including the reinforcement of racist ideologies regarding African men. Her analysis points away from a criminal law solution and towards other strategies based in health education.

In 1998, the development of the law of assault in Canada took an intriguing turn. In this year, the Supreme Court of Canada ruled that disclosure of HIV-positive status is required by the criminal law before a person living with HIV/AIDS (hereinafter "PHA") engages in sexual activity that poses a "significant risk" of transmitting HIV.[2] With this decision, *otherwise consensual* sexual encounters between PHAs and those who were not aware of the person's HIV-positive status became *criminal assaults*.

While every HIV infection is regrettable, and it is always desirable to avoid exposing others to the risk of HIV infection if possible, wheth-

1 Special thanks to Celeste Shankland for her research assistance, to Glenn Betteridge, Sandra Ka Hon Chu, and Patricia Allard for their comments on an earlier draft of this paper, and to Richard Elliott for sharing his many insights and extensive experience on this issue. All errors are the responsibility of the author alone.

2 *R v Cuerrier*, [1998] 2 SCR 371.

er the criminal law of assault (including both aggravated assault and aggravated sexual assault) can appropriately be applied to the issue of HIV exposure is a live question. Many aspects of this challenging and complex (both legally and emotionally) issue merit further consideration. Is it helpful to categorize otherwise consensual sexual activities as assaults when disclosure does not take place? How is this area of law being employed and further elaborated? Moreover, what impact does the criminalization of HIV exposure have on PHAs and on HIV prevention, treatment, care, and support? How does the criminalization of HIV non-disclosure potentially impact on sexual assault jurisprudence and on police and prosecutorial practice? Does the criminalization of HIV exposure protect women from harm? Is the trend to criminalize HIV exposure an appropriate response or an extreme manifestation of "AIDS panic"?

This paper provides an overview of the use of criminal assault law with respect to HIV exposure in Canada since 1998 and raises a number of concerns and considerations with respect to this development in the interpretation and application of sexual assault law. Many of my conclusions are necessarily preliminary given the novelty of the developments and the lack of comprehensive social science evidence on the impacts. However, I believe that reflection on the criminalization of HIV non-disclosure has much to contribute to our understanding of both how the criminal justice system responds to sexual assault within our society, and how our responses to the HIV epidemic are too often ineffective and misdirected. In addition, as this area of law continues to develop, reflection on the broader impacts is critical to devising appropriate responses and recommendations.

THE STARTING POINT: *R V CUERRIER*

In its 1998 judgment in the case of *R v Cuerrier*, the Supreme Court of Canada unanimously decided that a PHA may be guilty of a crime of assault if they do not disclose their HIV-positive status before engaging in unprotected sexual activity. *Cuerrier* was the first time that any country's highest court had addressed the issue of criminal prosecutions for HIV exposure and the first decision in Canada that recognized that a PHA could be convicted of *aggravated assault* for not disclosing his or her HIV-positive status.[3] At trial, the defence had successfully moved

3 Richard Elliott, *After Cuerrier: Canadian Criminal Law and the Non-Disclosure of HIV-Positive Status* (Toronto: Canadian HIV/AIDS Legal Network, 1999) at 6. Trial and appellate level courts in several countries (including Canada, the US, the UK,

for a directed verdict of acquittal, on the ground that the Crown had not made out the offence of assault because the complainants had consented to the sexual activity. The British Columbia Court of Appeal unanimously upheld this ruling.[4] The justices of the Supreme Court, however, saw the issue in a different light.

The case arose because two women were exposed to the risk of HIV infection through sexual relations with Cuerrier, a man diagnosed as HIV-positive in August of 1992. He had been counselled by a public health nurse to use condoms for sex and tell his sexual partners about his HIV-positive status; he rejected this advice. Shortly after his diagnosis, he met KM and began an eighteen-month relationship that included unprotected intercourse. Near the beginning of the relationship, they discussed sexually transmitted infections and Cuerrier told her he had tested negative for HIV eight or nine months earlier; he did not mention his recent positive test result. Both KM and the respondent were tested in January of 1993. KM was informed that her test was negative, but that his was positive for HIV. Cuerrier and KM continued having unprotected sex for several months. Their relationship ended in May of 1994. KM testified that had she known at the outset that Cuerrier was HIV-positive she would never have engaged in unprotected sex with him.[5]

Shortly thereafter Cuerrier began a sexual relationship with another woman, BH They had sex about ten times, mostly without the use of condoms. He did not inform her that he was HIV-positive. In late June, she discovered that he had HIV and confronted him. She also testified that she would never have engaged in unprotected sexual intercourse with him had she known that he was HIV-positive.[6] He was charged with two counts of aggravated assault. Neither complainant tested positive for HIV.[7]

Mr Justice Cory wrote the majority judgment (for Justices Cory, Major, Bastarache, and Binnie). As defined in the *Criminal Code*, to make out a charge of assault, the Crown needed to prove that the accused in-

Australia, Switzerland, Finland, and France) had previously heard cases in which HIV-positive persons faced charges under various public health or criminal laws for engaging in activities that transmitted or risked transmitting HIV.

4 *Ibid* at 11.

5 *Cuerrier*, *supra* note 2 at para 78–81.

6 *Ibid* at para 82.

7 *Ibid* at para 83.

tentionally applied force without the consent of the complainant.[8] For the charge of aggravated assault, the Crown also needed to demonstrate that the assault endangered the life of the complainant.[9] Cory J readily concluded that the second element was satisfied:

> There can be no doubt the respondent endangered the lives of the complainants by exposing them to the risk of HIV infection through unprotected sexual intercourse. The potentially lethal consequences of infection permit no other conclusion. Further, it is not necessary to establish that the complainants were in fact infected with the virus. There is no prerequisite that any harm must actually have resulted. The first requirement of s 268(1) is satisfied by the significant risk to the lives of the complainants occasioned by the act of unprotected intercourse.[10]

The issue of whether the accused applied force without the consent of the complainants was not so easily resolved. The Crown contended that the complainants' consent was not legally effective because it was obtained by fraud. Section 265(3)(c) states that no consent is obtained where the complainant submits or does not resist by reason of "fraud." Up until 1983, the indecent assault provisions of the *Criminal Code* had provided that consent was vitiated where it was obtained "by false and fraudulent representations as to the nature and quality of the act," reflecting the approach to consent in sexual assault cases that had existed at common law.[11] The key question therefore was whether the 1983 re-

8 *Criminal Code*, RSC 1985, c C-46, s 265(1)(a).

9 *Ibid* at s 268(1).

10 *Cuerrier*, *supra* note 2 at para 95. Note that in a recent decision, Steel JA of the Manitoba Court of Appeal questions in *obiter* whether it necessarily follows that there is endangerment of life because there is a finding of risk of serious bodily harm. She notes that the advent of HIV treatment has changed the course of HIV disease progression considerably since the *Cuerrier* decision such that death from AIDS is no longer inevitable: *R v Mabior*, 2010 MBCA 93 at paras 138–46. The Supreme Court of Canada heard the appeal of this case on February 8, 2012. At the time of this writing, a decision had not yet been issued.

11 An example of the type of fraud captured under this definition is a person who falsely held him or herself out as a doctor and purported to conduct a gynaecological examination. See, for example, *R v Marantonio*, [1968] 1 OR 145 (CA). The 1983 amendments to the indecent assault provisions of the *Criminal Code* were aimed at protecting women by improving the deterrent effect of the criminal law with respect to sexual violence and redefining sexual offences in order to focus on violations of the integrity of the person rather than the sexual element of the crime. See Duncan Chappell, *Law Reform, Social Policy, and Criminal Sexual Violence: Current Canadian Responses* (Annals New York Academy of Science, 1988) at 379–87.

visions to the indecent assault provisions changed the definition of "fraud" such that HIV non-disclosure in cases of otherwise consensual sex would be captured.

Cory J concluded that yes, the legislative history and the plain language of the new provision suggested that "Parliament intended to move away from the rigidity of the common law requirement that fraud must relate to the nature and quality of the act."[12] He concluded that Parliament intended a more flexible concept of fraud in assault and sexual assault cases.[13]

He further explained that the concept of criminal fraud, which should be applied to consent in sexual assault cases as well, has two constituent elements: dishonesty, which can include non-disclosure of important facts, and deprivation or risk of deprivation.[14] He concluded that PHAs who engage in sexual intercourse without advising their partner of their infection may be found to fulfil these traditional requirements of fraud. This conclusion forms the basis for the criminalization of HIV non-disclosure related to sexual HIV exposure in Canada.[15] Notably, the cases he referred to in relation to the concept of fraud are commercial cases, looking at economic losses or risk — not at physical risks to people.[16]

Applying the fraud elements to HIV non-disclosure, he noted that the dishonest action or behaviour must be related to obtaining consent to engage in the alleged sexual intercourse and can take the form of either deliberate deceit respecting HIV status or non-disclosure (silence) as to that status. A key paragraph of the judgment is as follows:

> Without disclosure of HIV status there cannot be a true consent. The consent cannot simply be to have sexual intercourse. Rather it must be to have intercourse with a partner who is HIV-positive. True consent cannot be

12 *Cuerrier*, *supra* note 2 at para 105.

13 *Ibid.*

14 "Deprivation" in this context refers to a harm or injury.

15 Hereinafter, the terminology of "HIV non-disclosure" will be used to refer to having sexual contact without disclosing HIV-positive status to the sexual partner(s). It should be noted that there is no general obligation to disclose HIV-positive status in Canada and the discussion in this paper is limited to the sexual context.

16 Eg, *R v Olan*, [1978] 2 SCR 1175, *R v Théroux*, [1993] 2 SCR 5, and *R v Zlatic*, [1993] 2 SCR 29. See *Cuerrier*, *supra* note 2 at para 117: "The principles which have been developed to address the problem of fraud in the commercial context can, with appropriate modifications, serve as a useful starting point in the search for the type of fraud which will vitiate consent to sexual intercourse in a prosecution for aggravated assault."

> given if there has not been a disclosure by the accused of his HIV-positive status. A consent that is not based upon knowledge of the significant relevant factors is not a valid consent. The extent of the duty to disclose will increase with the risks attendant upon the act of intercourse. To put it in the context of fraud the greater the risk of deprivation the higher the duty of disclosure. The failure to disclose HIV-positive status can lead to a devastating illness with fatal consequences. In those circumstances, there exists a positive duty to disclose. The nature and extent of the duty to disclose, if any, will always have to be considered in the context of the particular facts presented.[17]

With respect to the second requirement of fraud — that the dishonesty result in some form of deprivation — he noted that:

> [I]t cannot be any trivial harm or risk of harm that will satisfy this requirement in sexual assault cases where the activity would have been consensual if the consent had not been obtained by fraud. For example, the risk of minor scratches or of catching cold would not suffice to establish deprivation. What then should be required? In my view, the Crown will have to establish that the dishonest act (either falsehood or failure to disclosure) had the effect of exposing the person consenting to a significant risk of serious bodily harm. The risk of contracting AIDS as a result of engaging in unprotected intercourse would clearly meet that test. In this case the complainants were exposed to a significant risk of serious harm to their health. Indeed their very survival was placed in jeopardy. It is difficult to imagine a more significant risk or a more grievous bodily harm.[18]

And with that, arguably, the interpretation and application of sexual assault law in Canada was significantly transformed. "Significant risk of serious bodily harm" became a new standard, extending the law that criminalizes a rape or brutal beating to the otherwise consensual act of sex where there was no disclosure of HIV-positive status. HIV non-disclosure could now result in up to fourteen years imprisonment for an HIV-positive person if convicted of aggravated assault, or to a maximum of life imprisonment if convicted of aggravated sexual assault.[19]

There were two minority judgments in the case. Madame Justice L'Heureux-Dubé agreed with Cory J that the 1983 amendment to the

17 *Cuerrier, supra* note 2 at para 127.

18 *Ibid* at para 128.

19 *Criminal Code, supra* note 8 at ss 268(2) and 273(2)(b).

Criminal Code indicated Parliament's intention to move away from the strict common law approach to the vitiation of consent by fraud. She noted that the assault scheme laid out in the *Criminal Code* is very broadly constructed, aimed not only at protecting people from serious physical harm, but also at protecting and promoting people's physical integrity by recognizing their power to consent or to withhold consent to any touching.[20] Therefore, only consent obtained without negating the voluntary agency of the person being touched is legally valid, according to L'Heureux-Dubé J.[21]

In response to Cory J's "significant risk of serious bodily harm" test, she states that:

> my colleague's test has the effect of creating a different interpretation of "fraud" depending on the sexual nature of the particular offense with which an accused has been charged. In my view, my colleague's interpretation has the effect of undoing what Parliament accomplished with its 1983 amendment of the *Criminal Code*: it reintroduces, in the sexual assault context, artificial limitations as to when fraud will negate consent to physical contact.[22]

She argued that in the context of the assault scheme in the *Criminal Code*, the issue is whether the dishonest act induced another person to consent to the ensuing physical act, irrespective of the risk or danger associated with that act.[23] Furthermore, the dishonesty of the consent-inducing act would be assessed based on the objective standard of the reasonable person. The Crown would also be required to prove that the accused was aware that his or her dishonest actions would induce the complainant to submit to the particular activity.[24] Her formulation is inherently broader than that put forth by Cory J, not requiring that the complainant be exposed to any significant physical harm, consistent with her focus on protecting the complainant's autonomous will.

Madame Justice McLachlin also wrote a dissenting opinion (on behalf of herself and Gonthier J). In contrast to L'Heureux-Dubé J's broader formulation of what would constitute fraud, McLachlin J proposed a more modest reconsideration. She explained that:

20 *Cuerrier, supra* note 2 at paras 11–12.

21 *Ibid* at para 12.

22 *Ibid* at para 14.

23 *Ibid* at para 16.

24 *Ibid.*

> I agree with the courts below (indeed all courts that have hitherto considered the issue since the adoption of the new definition of fraud), that the submission that Parliament intended to radically broaden the crime of assault by the 1983 amendments must be rejected. I approach the matter from the conviction that the criminalization of conduct is a serious matter. Clear language is required to create crimes. Crimes can be created by defining a new crime, or by redefining the elements of an old crime. … It is permissible for courts to interpret old provisions in ways that reflect social changes, in order to ensure that Parliament's intent is carried out in the modern era. It is not permissible for courts to overrule the common law and create new crimes that Parliament never intended.[25]

She concluded that the 1983 amendments did not oust the common law governing fraud in relation to sexual assault. She further concluded that it would be inappropriate for the courts to make broad extensions to the law of sexual assault, such as those proposed by Justices Cory and L'Heureux-Dubé. Recognizing that the proposed rules had the potential to criminalize a vast array of sexual conduct, she remarked that:

> Deceptions, small and sometimes large, have from time immemorial been the by-product of romance and sexual encounters. They often carry the risk of harm to the deceived party. Thus far in the history of civilization, these deceptions, however sad, have been left to the domain of song, verse and social censure. Now, if the Crown's theory is accepted, they become crimes.[26]

In terms of Cory J's introduction of the qualifier — that there must be a significant risk of serious bodily harm before consent is vitiated — McLachlin J pointed out that it introduces uncertainty into the law and that consequences as serious as criminal prosecutions should not turn on the interpretation of vague terms like "significant" and "serious."[27] Moreover, she recognized that the equation of non-disclosure with lack of consent oversimplifies the complex and diverse nature of consent in sexual situations.[28]

Finally, she noted that criminal liability is generally imposed only for conduct that causes injury to others or puts them at risk of injury. She argued that Cory and L'Heureux-Dubé J's theories of criminal lia-

25 *Ibid* at para 34.
26 *Ibid* at para 47.
27 *Ibid* at para 48.
28 *Ibid* at para 49.

bility for sex without disclosure would impose liability for conduct that is causally unrelated to harm or risk of harm, creating problems with *mens rea* and raising the possibility of *Charter* violations.[29] Based on these concerns, amongst others, she concluded that the theoretical and practical difficulties involved in extending the law around non-disclosure of HIV-positive status as proposed preclude such an action on the part of the court.[30]

McLachlin J did, however, agree that non-disclosure of HIV-positive status to sexual partners should attract criminal liability. In her words:

> Consent to unprotected sexual intercourse is consent to sexual congress with a certain person and to the transmission of bodily fluids from that person. Where the person represents that he or she is disease-free, and consent is given on that basis, deception on that matter goes to the very act of assault. The complainant does not consent to the transmission of diseased fluid into his or her body. The deception in a very real sense goes to the nature of the sexual act, changing it from an act that has certain natural consequences (whether pleasure, pain or pregnancy), to a potential sentence of disease or death. It differs fundamentally from deception as to the consideration that will be given for consent, like marriage, money or a fur coat, in that it relates to the physical act itself. It differs moreover, in a profoundly serious way that merits criminal sanction.[31]

As such, McLachlin J's analysis also leads to the conclusion that deceit about sexually transmitted disease that induces consent to unprotected sex should be treated as fraud vitiating consent under s 265 of the *Criminal Code*, but without redefining consent as Cory J's judgment dictated.

THE SUBSEQUENT APPLICATION OF *CUERRIER*

In the little more than a decade since the Supreme Court issued its judgment in the *Cuerrier* case, at least 140 persons in Canada have been charged in relation to non-disclosure of HIV-positive status with respect to sexual activities.[32] Of these charges, the vast majority were

29 *Ibid* at paras 50, 53.

30 *Ibid* at para 57.

31 *Ibid* at para 72.

32 This estimate is based on tracking of the cases conducted by the Canadian HIV/AIDS Legal Network. The tracking is based on reported cases, media reports, and personal communications from lawyers, community-based organizations, and those individu-

laid against men having sex with women.[33] The majority of the cases involved *Cuerrier*-like situations — unprotected vaginal or anal intercourse without disclosure — but some cases have included charges in relation to non-disclosure and oral sex and/or protected intercourse.[34] In some of the cases, the sexual relationships went on for many months, while in others the allegations relate to brief encounters.[35]

From the mid-2000s onwards, there has been a marked escalation in the use of criminal law with respect to HIV non-disclosure. For example, of those charged to date, more than 70 were charged from 2006 through 2011.[36] In addition, several high-profile cases involving multiple complainants and violent or exploitative circumstances have gone to trial (and received prolific media coverage) since 2007.

Furthermore, an increasing number of accused are facing charges of *aggravated sexual assault* as opposed to the lesser charges of aggravated assault or criminal negligence causing bodily harm.[37] There are no

als facing prosecution. As of February 2012, the Legal Network was aware of 148 cases of HIV exposure without disclosure (with several individuals having been charged more than once). Of course, there may be others of which the Legal Network is not aware. See also, Eric Mykhalovskiy, Glenn Betteridge & David McLay, "HIV Non-Disclosure and the Criminal Law: Establishing Policy Options for Ontario," a report funded by a grant from the Ontario HIV Treatment Network (Toronto, 2010) at 8. Mykhalovskiy *et al* identified a total of 104 cases in which ninety-eight individuals had been charged with criminal offences related to HIV non-disclosure from 1989 to 2009.

33 According to the Legal Network's tracking, only 13 women have faced charges in Canada (one of them was charged on two separate occasions), and approximately 22 of the prosecutions have involved men having sex with men. For some of the cases, however, the sex of the complainant(s) is not known; therefore, it is possible that there may be a few more men charged in relation to sexual activities with other men.

34 *Ibid.* In Canada, aggravated assault charges have also been laid in cases of spitting, biting, and scratching, and one woman has been charged in relation to vertical HIV transmission (that is, from a mother to her infant). These cases are not discussed in this paper, which focuses on the sexual exposure cases.

35 *Ibid.*

36 *Ibid.* Mykhalovskiy *et al*, *supra* note 32 at 9 found that approximately 65 percent of cases for which the year of charge is known have occurred in the five-year period between 2004–09.

37 It should also be noted that Johnson Aziga was found guilty of two counts of first degree murder and eleven counts of aggravated sexual assault in 2009 in relation to HIV exposure without disclosure. Two of the female complainants died of AIDS-related cancers: *R v Aziga*, 4 April 2009, Court File No CR-08-1735. Subsequent to the *Aziga* verdict, three men in Ontario have been charged with attempted murder in relation to HIV non-disclosure allegations. It is assumed that the escalation from charges of aggravated sexual assault to attempted murder was solely in reaction to the

clear factual differences in terms of who is charged with aggravated assault and who is charged with aggravated sexual assault, and no judicial decision indicating that aggravated sexual assault is more appropriate in certain circumstances. The trend towards aggravated sexual assault charges seems to be based solely on police and prosecutorial discretion. The implications of being charged with aggravated sexual assault, rather than aggravated assault, however, are quite significant. In addition to longer potential jail terms, those convicted of aggravated sexual assault are considered sex offenders, which means that their names will be included in the sex offender registries and that, with this label, they might receive harsher treatment in prison and from their communities. In addition, classifying these crimes as serious sexual offences may contribute to the construction of PHA offenders as sexually deviant and invite myths and stereotypes about rape and sexuality into the public understanding of HIV transmission.

In the cases since *Cuerrier*, few courts have interrogated the legal reasoning or test established in that case. Often, the trials primarily focus on the factual determination of whether or not disclosure took place before the sexual relations and other related factual questions. These factual determinations, however, can at times be quite problematic.

To take one example, a woman originally from Thailand was found guilty of criminal negligence causing bodily harm and aggravated assault in January of 2007 for not disclosing her HIV-positive status to her then husband who became infected with HIV.[38] The woman admitted that she did not reveal her HIV-positive status to her husband, but explained that she did not do so because she did not believe she was HIV-positive. While she had previously tested positive to HIV at a clinic in Hong Kong, she believed that she had subsequently tested HIV-negative through her immigration medical exam when she came to Canada and therefore believed herself to be HIV-negative. The judge found that her "simple story does not correspond with common sense."[39] Basing his conclusions on his own expectations of an ordinary person, he stated that he would have expected her to seek out a second test as soon as she arrived in Canada, especially given her doubts about

precedent set by the *Aziga* verdict. There appear to be no factual or legal distinctions that would result in different charges.

38 *R v Iamkhong* (16 January 2007), Toronto, Ontario (Ont Sup Ct J) (unreported).

39 *Ibid* at 15.

the reliability of the Hong Kong clinic and its testing. He also rejected her assertion that she genuinely thought the medical test required by Citizenship and Immigration Canada included an HIV test, and found that even if she thought that a second test indicated that she was HIV-negative, he would have expected her to make greater efforts to clarify the conflicting result rather than relying on incomplete information provided by her employer.[40] Because the judge decided that the woman knew she was HIV-positive, a guilty verdict easily followed because she admitted that she had not told her husband that she was HIV-positive.

Consider that this woman grew up in a small village in Thailand, has only a fourth-grade education, and speaks limited English. She had undergone her first HIV test at a small clinic in Hong Kong in 1994 (presumably without adequate pre- and post-test counselling or understanding about the illness, at a time when treatment was not yet available). She immigrated to Canada to work as an exotic dancer. In these circumstances, is it so unreasonable that she would have been misinformed regarding the content of the immigration medical exam? Is it so unreasonable that she would have accepted that she could be HIV-negative despite the previous positive test result? Is it so unreasonable that she would not have told her new Canadian husband or Canadian health care providers about the previous test result, believing that the result was incorrect? Surely when an intersectional gender, race, and class analysis is applied, recognizing her dependant, vulnerable position in Canada, the judge's factual determination is open to challenge.[41]

With most of the cases turning on questions of fact, many of the questions emanating from the majority reasoning in *Cuerrier* have remained unresolved and significant uncertainty remains regarding the precise scope of the legal obligation on PHAs. The current state of the criminal law with respect to HIV disclosure in Canada, as laid out by a national HIV/AIDS legal organization, is as follows:

- A person has a legal duty to disclose his or her HIV-positive status to sexual partners before having sex that poses a "significant risk" of HIV transmission.
- A person can be convicted of a crime for not disclosing his or her HIV-positive status before having sex that poses a significant risk of transmission even if the other person does not actually become infected. The crime is exposure without disclosure.

40 *Ibid* at 15–17.

41 The decision was unsuccessfully appealed: *R v Iamkhong*, 2009 ONCA 478.

- A person may have a legal duty to disclose his or her HIV-positive status before having sex that poses a significant risk of transmission even if he or she knows that a sexual partner also has HIV.
- A person who knows there is a risk that he or she has HIV (but has not received an actual HIV-positive diagnosis) may have a legal duty to tell sexual partners about this risk before having unprotected sex.[42]

A central concern to the HIV community[43] is whether the legal obligation to disclose applies with respect to protected sex and lower risk sexual activities (ie, when condoms or latex barriers are used, performing oral sex), or only to unprotected intercourse. The *Cuerrier* decision is only explicit with respect to unprotected intercourse, suggesting that "the careful use of condoms might be found to so reduce the risk of harm that it could no longer be considered significant so that there might not be either deprivation or risk of deprivation," leaving a clear ruling on this issue for another day.[44]

This uncertainty around a so-called "condom defence" has caused considerable anxiety amongst PHAs and the HIV community. Every person taking responsibility for his or her own sexual health and always practising safer sex is central to public health messaging about prevention of sexually transmitted infections. A legal rule that penalizes PHAs even if they are responsibly practising safer sex seems unjust, disproportionate, and unwarranted. At the same time, most people would want to know that their partner is HIV-positive (or of other possible risks related to intercourse with that partner) and respect for bodily integrity might favour a legal standard that requires disclosure in order that each partner is entitled to decide which risks they will undertake.

In several cases, trial courts have considered whether a "significant risk" of HIV transmission existed in circumstances where condoms were used. In at least four of these cases, it is suggested that there is no legal duty to disclose HIV-positive status when a condom is used during sexual intercourse.[45] A recent decision of the Manitoba Court of

42 Canadian HIV/AIDS Legal Network, "Criminal Law and HIV – Info Sheet 1: Criminalization of HIV Non-Disclosure: Current Canadian Law" (2011), online: <http://www.aidslaw.ca/criminallaw>.

43 The term "HIV community" is being used in this paper to refer to the community-based organizations, health care providers, HIV-focused advocacy organizations, and PHAs who are involved in such organizations or related advocacy activities.

44 *Supra* note 2 at para 129.

45 *R v Nduwayo*, 2006 BCSC 1972 at paras 7–8; *R v Smith*, [2007] SJ No 166 (Sask PC) at

Appeal is the first decision from a court at the appeal level on this issue. After considering the scientific evidence on the efficacy of condoms in reducing HIV transmission, Steel JA held that the "consistent and careful use of condoms can reduce the risk of transmission, not to zero, but below the level of significance."[46] By this reasoning, there would be no legal obligation to disclose HIV status when using condoms carefully and consistently. Whether this decision will be appealed and/or the reasoning adopted in other jurisdictions remains to be seen.

Related concerns about uncertainty in the law arise in respect to lower risk sexual activities (such as oral sex) where we know the risk of transmission to be lower than that associated with unprotected vaginal or anal intercourse. A recent decision of the Supreme Court of British Columbia grappled directly with these tricky questions of transmission risk levels and what is a legally "significant risk." Taking into consideration various factors, the medical expert put the risk of transmission to the complainant in the case at four in 10,000 per incident of intercourse.[47] As there were three occurrences, the judge took the risk to be twelve in 10,000 and found that "a risk of transmission of HIV of 0.12 percent is not material enough to establish deprivation invalidating the consent of the complainant."[48] She further stated:

> In reaching this conclusion, I should not be taken to condone the behaviour of the accused. He had a moral obligation to disclose his HIV-positive status to his partner and to give the complainant the opportunity to assume or reject the risk involved in sexual activity with the accused, no matter how small. But not every immoral or reprehensible act engages the heavy hand of the law. Aggravated sexual assault is a most serious offence — a person convicted of this charge is liable to imprisonment for life, the harshest penalty provided for in law. Only behaviour that puts a complainant at significant risk of serious bodily harm will suffice to turn what would otherwise be a consensual activity into an aggravated sexual assault. In my view, a risk of transmission of HIV of 0.12% falls short of that standard.[49]

Whether other courts will follow this approach remains to be seen.

para 59; *R v Charron*, [2008] Longueuil 765-01-010423-024 (CQ) at para 40; *R v Imona-Russel*, [2009] Toronto (Ont Sup Ct J) at paras 28, 50, 68.

46 *Mabior*, *supra* note 10 at para 87.

47 *R v JAT*, [2010] BCSC 766 at para 29.

48 *Ibid* at para 88.

49 *Ibid* at para 89.

Another area of uncertainty and concern relates to issues of viral load and treatment.[50] In the years that have passed since *Cuerrier*, our understanding of HIV disease and transmission has advanced considerably. Moreover, the advent of highly-active antiretroviral treatment (HAART) has transformed HIV and AIDS from a fatal illness to a manageable, episodic disability for most people living with HIV.[51] Newer research also demonstrates that successful treatment with HAART not only improves the health of people living with HIV, but considerably reduces the infectivity of PHAs.[52] Given these developments, can we continue to accept that, as a result of the *Cuerrier* decision, unprotected vaginal or anal intercourse *always* poses a "significant risk of serious bodily harm" for the purposes of the criminal law? The above mentioned Manitoba Court of Appeal decision also addressed this issue and was the first Canadian court to acquit an accused based on his low viral load at the time of the sexual encounters.[53] With respect to the testimony of the accused's doctor that there was a high probability that he was not infectious during the period of time under consideration, Steel JA remarked:

> I do not see how that evidence can support a finding with respect to these complainants that the Crown has proven beyond a reasonable doubt the lack of consent arising from the presence of a significant risk of serious bodily harm. "Significant" means something other than an ordinary risk. It means an important, serious, substantial risk. It is the opposite of evidence of a "high probability" of no infectiousness, especially given the statistical percentages referred to earlier.[54]

IS CRIMINALIZATION OF HIV EXPOSURE A PROGRESSIVE DEVELOPMENT IN CANADIAN LAW?

The majority decision in *Cuerrier*, as discussed above, posits criminal liability for HIV non-disclosure as an appropriate HIV prevention tool

50 Viral load refers to the amount of HIV virus in a PHA's blood. The best viral load test result is "undetectable." This does not mean that there is no virus present, but that there is so little that the test can not register it. The HIV viral load is used as a measurement of how active the HIV disease is and also indicates whether the medication regimen is working.

51 HAART was developed in the mid-1990s and is now widely available in developed countries.

52 See Susana Attia, "Sexual transmission of HIV according to viral load and antiretroviral therapy: systematic review and meta-analysis" (2009) 23 AIDS 1.

53 *Mabior*, *supra* note 10 at paras 130, 133, 137.

54 *Ibid* at para 127.

as well as a proper application of Canada's assault laws in line with the 1983 amendments. Arguably, however, the criminalization of HIV exposure is failing on both fronts.

Criminalization of HIV Non-Disclosure as an HIV Prevention Tool

With respect to HIV, my starting point is that any use of coercive legal powers by the state (whether within the criminal justice or public health systems) must be evaluated on its ability to prevent further HIV infections and/or promote care, treatment, and support for PHAs, in line with the best available evidence and human rights standards. In fact, the majority decision in *Cuerrier* addressed some of the public policy concerns commonly raised with respect to the criminalization of HIV non-disclosure, which were raised by *amicus curiae* at the time.[55] Cory J stated:

> [T]he criminal law does have a role to play both in deterring those infected with HIV from putting the lives of others at risk and in protecting the public from irresponsible individuals who refuse to comply with public health orders to abstain from high-risk activities. ...[56]
>
> ...The risks of infection are so devastating that there is a real and urgent need to provide a measure of protection for this in the position of the complainants. If ever there was a place for the deterrence provided by criminal sanctions it is present in these circumstances. It may well have the desired effect of ensuring that there is disclosure of the risk and that appropriate precautions are taken.[57]

55 The British Columbia Civil Liberties Association, the Canadian AIDS Society, Persons with AIDS Society of British Columbia, and the Canadian HIV/AIDS Legal Network intervened in *R v Cuerrier* at the Supreme Court. On the public policy arguments against the criminalization of HIV non-disclosure see: Canadian HIV/AIDS Legal Network, "Criminal Law and HIV — Info Sheet 3: Does Criminalizing HIV Exposure Make Sense?" (2008), online: <http://www.aidslaw.ca/criminallaw>; Scott Burris & Edwin Cameron, "The Case Against Criminalization of HIV Transmission" (2008) 300 JAMA 578; and Ralf Jürgen *et al*, "10 Reasons to Oppose Criminalization of HIV Exposure or Transmission" (2008) Open Society Institute, online: <http://www.soros.org/initiatives/health/focus/law/articles_publications/publications/10reasons_20080918>.

56 *Supra* note 2 at para 141.

57 *Ibid* at para 142.

Fourteen years on from *Cuerrier*, however, there remains little, if any, evidence to support the proposition that criminal charges for HIV non-disclosure contribute to HIV prevention aims by deterring PHAs from not disclosing their status or practicing unprotected sex.[58]

Any preventative effect that a criminal prosecution can have is minimal. Charges are brought after exposure has taken place and often after the relationship has ended. Therefore, with respect to the particular accused, retribution, not prevention, may be the motivation for criminal charges. The only realistic possibility of some prevention benefit from criminal prosecutions — and one of the primary arguments put forth in favour of criminalization — is through *deterrence*. That is, the fact that non-disclosure is criminal where there is a significant risk of transmission will cause PHAs, who otherwise might have had sex without disclosing, to instead disclose their HIV-positive status (or in the absence of disclosure, take steps to ensure they do not put their partners at a significant risk of HIV infection). But embedded is an assumption that disclosure of HIV status will lead sexual partners to change their sexual practices and either engage only in lower risk sexual activities, consistently use protection, or refrain from sexual activity altogether.

What little evidence exists suggests that people are guided in their decision making about sexual or other risks more by their sense of what is right and wrong than by what the law actually says.[59] It is questionable whether legal provisions could ever be a significant factor in decision making about safer sex "in the heat of the moment," particularly if alcohol, drugs, or domestic violence are involved. Moreover, a review of the empirical literature on HIV disclosure and subsequent sexual risk taking found that significant barriers and disincentives to revealing one's HIV diagnosis persist, including fears of abandonment, discrimination in housing and employment, violence, and other forms of abuse. They found that criminal charges against PHAs who are sexually active are another impetus to remain silent about one's HIV-positive status, concluding that "[t]hese psychological, practical and legal barriers may contribute to the refusal of many individuals with

58 Note that Cory J specifically mentions encouraging safer sex as a probable outcome of the decision: "Yet the Criminal Code does have a role to play. Through deterrence it will protect and serve to encourage honesty, frankness and safer sexual practices" (*supra* note 2 at para 147).

59 See, for example, Scott Burris *et al*, "Do Criminal Laws Influence HIV Risk Behaviour? An Empirical Trial" (2007) 39 Ariz St LJ 467. It is important to note that Cory J's reasoning about deterrence and behaviour changes are directed only at PHAs, in keeping with the fact that the legal duty rests solely with PHAs.

HIV to divulge their serostatus to sexual partners."[60] The deterrence aim of the criminalization of HIV non-disclosure therefore merits reconsideration.

Another important limitation to the deterrence objective is the fact that approximately one-quarter of the people in Canada who are infected with HIV are unaware of this fact.[61] If people are unaware of their infection, then they have nothing to disclose and therefore the disclosure requirement can have no prevention benefit. At the same time, scientific studies reveal that those in the early stages of HIV infection, who are least likely to be aware that they are HIV-positive, are the most infectious and are responsible for a high percentage of onward HIV transmission.[62]

Thus, emphasizing disclosure, as the Canadian criminal law currently does, is not necessarily associated with higher rates of protected sex or lower rates of HIV infection.[63] Even if disclosure can be effective as an HIV prevention tool in certain circumstances, uniformly requiring disclosure does not take into consideration the realities of dis-

60 Jane M Simoni & David W Pantalone, "Secrets and Safety in the Age of AIDS: Does HIV Disclosure Lead to Safer Sex?" (2004) 12:4 Topics in HIV Medicine 110.

61 Public Health Agency of Canada, *HIV/AIDS Epi Updates — July 2010* (Ottawa: PHAC, 2010). Note that according to the judgment in *R v Williams*, a person who has reason to believe that they may be infected (for example, they have been contacted by public health as a contact of a PHA and advised to be tested) may have a duty to disclose that risk (*R v Williams*, [2003] 2 SCR 134).

62 See, for example, Maria Wawer *et al*, "Rates of HIV-1 Transmission per Coital Act, by Stage of HIV-1 Infection, in Rakai, Uganda" (2005) 191 J Infectious Diseases 1403, demonstrating that the rate of sexual infection is more than tenfold higher during acute infection. See also Bluma G Brenner *et al*, "High Rates of Forward Transmission Events After Acute/Early HIV-1 Infection" (2007) 195 J Infectious Diseases 951, estimating that approximately half of all new HIV infections could be attributed to those who are only recently infected themselves and likely in the period of early, acute infection where they have not yet been diagnosed with HIV but their viral load is very high during the process of seroconversion.

63 Barry Adam, "What Effect is the Criminal Justice System Having in HIV Prevention?" presented at: From Evidence and Principle to Policy and Practice, Symposium on HIV, Law and Human Rights (Toronto, 12–13 June 2009) [unpublished]. Adam reported that studies looking at sexual practices of gay and bisexual men found that the consistent practice of safer sex usually proceeds without discussion, and it is those who decide from encounter to encounter whether to disclose or not who have higher rates of unprotected sex. See Benny Henriksson & Sven Axel Månsson, "Sexual Negotiations" in Han ten Brummelhuis & Gilbert Herdt, eds, *Culture and Sexual Risk* (London: Routledge, 1995) at 170. Trevor Hart *et al*, "Partner Awareness of the Serostatus of HIV-Seropositive Men Who Have Sex with Men" (2005) 9 AIDS and Behaviour 163; Limin Mao *et al*, "'Serosorting' in Casual Anal Sex of HIV-Negative Gay Men is Noteworthy and is Increasing in Sydney, Australia" (2006) 20 AIDS 1204.

closure, which is a difficult and often complex act frequently associated with deep trust and intimacy. For example, many women experience great difficulty in disclosing to men on whom they are dependent, and disclosure can be particularly challenging for those who feel disadvantaged by their age, attractiveness, or ethnocultural background.[64] HIV disclosure can also be a prelude to violence. HIV prevention initiatives that promote safer sex and empower individuals to take control of their sexuality and sexual health are therefore more effective than focusing on disclosure.[65]

Not only is criminalizing HIV non-disclosure likely to have limited prevention benefits at best, but a number of legitimate concerns have been raised about its potential to be *counterproductive* to this aim. First, people may hesitate to seek HIV testing and related counselling and support if they fear that providing information to service providers could lead to breaches of confidentiality, condemnation, and possible criminal charges. As a result, people may engage in further risk activities without the benefit of harm reduction materials and counselling, or miss out on available treatment and support services.[66] Second, expansive use of criminal law can contribute to the already substantial public misunderstanding of transmission risk. In Canada, criminal charges have been laid against PHAs in relation to biting, scratching, and spitting, despite the extremely low or non-existent risk of HIV transmission in these circumstances. Media coverage of these cases — together with coverage of sexual exposure cases in which the risks of transmission, the "window period" during which infection may not yet show up on standard lab tests, and the negative impacts of living with HIV are misstated or exaggerated — undermine efforts to educate the public about HIV and PHAs.[67] Third, criminal prosecutions for HIV exposure, and the sensational media coverage they often generate, can contribute to stigma and discrimination against people living with HIV. Such cases place the responsibility for preventing HIV transmission entirely on PHAs and they risk portraying all PHAs as vectors of

64 Karolynn Siegel, Helen-Maria Lekas & Eric Schrimshaw, "Serostatus Disclosure to Sexual Partners by HIV-Infected Women Before and After the Advent of HAART" (2005) 41 Women and Health 63.

65 See, for example, the Centres for Disease Control and Prevention's *2008 Compendium of Evidence-based HIV Prevention Interventions* for examples of what sorts of interventions work and why, online: <http://www.cdc.gov/hiv/topics/research/prs/evidence-based-interventions.htm>.

66 Info Sheet 3, *supra* note 55.

67 *Ibid.*

disease and potential criminals. Increasing stigma and discrimination is counterproductive to HIV prevention efforts and to the well-being of PHAs.[68]

Criminalization of HIV Non-Disclosure as Sexual Assault Law

While increasing numbers within the HIV community are now paying attention to the criminalization of HIV non-disclosure — seeking information about their rights and responsibilities as PHAs or service providers, researching the impacts of HIV non-disclosure charges on PHAs and HIV prevention efforts, or advocating for changes in applicable laws and practices — the issue has received less attention from the academics, service providers, and activists focused on violence against women. It is therefore worth exploring the question: are prosecutions for non-disclosure a misuse of (sexual) assault laws?

A preliminary question to consider may be, "when is HIV non-disclosure properly understood as an assault, and in particular an aggravated sexual assault?" In one sense, HIV non-disclosure can be characterized as a "crime of knowledge." The offence is not one of using force against someone or physically harming them.[69] The essence of the crime is knowingly exposing your sexual partner to a risk, when the partner does not specifically know that they are accepting that risk (although most sexually active adults in our society today have some degree of knowledge of the general risks of engaging in unprotected sex, including pregnancy and sexually transmitted infections). Is it consistent with the underlying motivation for criminalizing sexual assault (and classifying some assaults as "aggravated") to apply those sanctions to this "crime of knowledge"?

In some ways, the question begs an exploration of the crime of fraudulent sexual assault. Traditionally, the definition of "fraud" in such cases was narrow, relating only to the nature and quality of the act. The classic example is someone misrepresenting themselves as a doctor in order to secure consent to do a gynaecological examination. The majority judgement in *Cuerrier* developed a specialized rule for sexual assault cases that centres around a risk assessment, creating the situation where courts today are having to grapple with medical and scientific evidence about HIV transmission risks rather than focus on what the complainant's assessment of the risk would have been, an inquiry more consistent with sexual autonomy and the court's understanding of con-

68 *Ibid.*

69 Recall that the essence of the crime is HIV exposure without disclosure. Charges can (and have) been laid where no transmission takes place.

sent as a subjective matter in *Ewanchuk*.[70] On the other hand, if the definition of fraud vitiating consent was opened up, people could find themselves facing long terms of imprisonment for objectively inconsequential omissions or deceptions. In the case of HIV non-disclosure, it could be seen as state-sponsored AIDS-panic to find someone guilty of the serious crime of aggravated assault or aggravated sexual assault because the complainant would not have consented in circumstances where he or she had an exaggerated sense of the risk of HIV transmission. Perhaps it is because of the immense stigma and discrimination surrounding HIV, the abundant misinformation about HIV that exists in our society, and the inherent complexity of sexual risk taking that this issue is particularly challenging. It does not fit easily within the rubric of sexual assault law and determining where to draw the line between criminal and non-criminal deceptions is a fraught exercise.

Another element of these offences to consider is that both partners to the sexual acts are active participants, and both partners may exchange bodily fluids in the course of the sexual acts. In otherwise consensual sex (ie, consensual other than the HIV non-disclosure), there is no reason to assume an active (male PHA) actor and a passive (female) recipient. Is this active interaction and mutual consent to have sex consistent with the crime of assault, which is defined as one person applying force to another person?[71]

The 1983 revisions to the sexual violence provisions in the *Criminal Code* move the focus away from the sexual element of the crime to concentrate on the violations of the integrity of the person that result from an assault. Exposing someone to HIV without disclosure — either by remaining silent about the risk he or she is accepting by engaging in unprotected sex, dropping some hints about HIV status but falling short of unambiguously disclosing, or by explicitly concealing one's HIV status — surely is experienced by many as a violation of their integrity, an affront to their sexual agency, and exposure to a risk that is quite terrifying to them. In terms of how the complainant understands and experiences the event(s), is "sexual assault" the appropriate name for a sexual encounter with a PHA who does not disclose?

70 Elizabeth Sheehy & Christine Boyle, "Justice L'Heureux-Dubé and Canadian Sexual Assault Law: Resisting the Privatization of Rape" in Elizabeth Sheehy, ed, *Adding Feminism to Law: The Contributions of Justice Claire L'Heureux-Dubé* (Toronto: Irwin Law, 2004) 247 at 265.

71 To be clear, this paper is not addressing cases of rape or sexual exploitation. The focus is on cases of otherwise consensual sex between adults, where non-disclosure of HIV-positive status is the only criminal element.

One objection raised to the criminalization of HIV disclosure is that it places the exclusive responsibility for HIV prevention on PHAs, as opposed to the mutual responsibility messages that are more common from sexual and public health promotion agencies. While problematic from a prevention perspective, perhaps from a criminal law perspective this assignment of responsibility is appropriate. In sexual assault prosecutions, the focus should not be on the behaviour of the complainant — her sexual history, her actions, whether she resisted (or inquired) — but on the behaviour of the accused and whether he was certain that his partner was fully consenting.

But does such a characterization oversimplify the complexity, ambiguity, fluidity, and uncertainties inherent in sexual interactions and disclosure of personal information, such as HIV status? Denying agency to women is powerful in constructing them as damaged "victims" — in the media and in the courtroom — but does it reflect reality, or lead towards equality and the eradication of violence? In "real-life" sexual encounters, arguably facts are not quite as definitive as criminal courts would make things seem. Whether purposely or inadvertently, sexual encounters often involve certain assumptions, "leaps of faith," and elements of mystery.[72] If we want to recognize women's full rights and agency as active sexual partners, is it logically coherent to assign full responsibility for disclosure and prevention to only one partner? Is it appropriate to only consider the actions and motivations of one partner in determining possible criminality?[73] Surely, the criminal law can

72 As noted by two leading commentators on criminal law and HIV Burns & Cameron, *supra* note 55 at 579:

> Risk assessments are heavily influenced by psychological and social biases. The riskiness (and blameworthiness) of sexual behaviour depends on the observer's perceptions of the value of sex, the responsibilities of the sex partner for self-protection, and the applicable norms of sexual behaviour. Every day, millions of individuals have unprotected sex with partners they must assume might be infected. They evidently rate the risks and benefits of sex differently than people who retrospectively judge sexual behaviour in legal proceedings. Thus conduct that seems normal to many — ie, sex without protection despite the presence of risk — exposes those who have HIV to severe criminal penalties, including life imprisonment.

73 Note that the complainant does have to testify that he or she would not have had sex with the accused if he or she was aware of the accused's HIV-positive status. This requirement does not seem to figure prominently into many of the cases, however, and thus is hardly addressed in the literature and activism on the criminalization of HIV exposure. This requirement could also be seen as playing into a characterization of the complainant as "good" and the accused as "bad" (ie, she would not have been exposed but for his deceit) at trial, more so than contributing to a rational assignment of mutual responsibility around sexual health.

be a useful component in society's arsenal against sexual violence and exploitation, but perhaps this one-sided responsibility and exclusive focus on whether disclosure took place does not fit well with furthering women's empowerment and eradicating gender-based violence.

I ask these questions with full awareness that being exposed to HIV, and potentially becoming infected with this very serious medical condition, is a devastating and life-altering occurrence for most people. To know that your sexual partner had the knowledge and ability to prevent this occurrence, and that you were denied that opportunity, is without doubt shocking and unconscionable to many who have been exposed to HIV. Nonetheless, I would argue that the appropriateness of assault charges, and in particular aggravated sexual assault charges, based on one-sided responsibility, is not necessarily empowering or respectful to consenting adults, at least not in the full breadth of circumstances in which criminal charges are being laid (including where protection is used and therefore the risk of HIV transmission is negligible).

To improve upon these laws, we need to talk to women who have been infected through sex to understand their experiences and how non-disclosure is or is not experienced as a form of violence. As these women are now themselves part of the PHA community, including being subject to legal obligations to disclose their status and also to all of the stigma and discrimination that can come with an HIV-positive diagnosis, what do they see as the appropriate role for the law?[74]

If we really want to protect and empower women, we should honestly reflect on whether prosecuting PHAs for aggravated assault or aggravated sexual assault when they allegedly do not disclose their HIV-positive status contributes to our objectives. While it may provide some sense of justice to women who legitimately feel that they have been deceived and wronged by malicious men, what message does it send to women and the public generally about their role in sexual relationships, about sexual assault and violence against women, about dependency and agency and the root causes of women's vulnerability to both

74 I know of no studies that have been published to date about women PHAs or the female complaints in these cases. Some research studies have looked at HIV disclosure and gay men and further research is ongoing with PHAs in Ontario. See, for example, Barry Adam *et al*, "Effects of the Criminalization of HIV Transmission in *Cuerrier* on Men Reporting Unprotected Sex with Men" (2008) 23 CJLS 137; and Barry Adam, "Drawing the Line: Views of HIV-Positive People on the Criminalization of HIV Transmission in Canada" presented at: "From Evidence and Principle to Policy and Practice: Symposium on HIV, Law and Human Rights" (Toronto, 11 June 2010) [unpublished].

violence and HIV, including poverty, discrimination, and myths about women's sexuality?

In considering whether these prosecutions offer any protection to women, examining the different circumstances in which prosecutions have taken place provides fodder for thought. For example, a Montreal woman was found guilty of aggravated assault for non-disclosure to her partner with respect to sexual encounters at the onset of their relationship. Both admitted that she had disclosed her status to him once the relationship became more serious; they continued in a sexual relationship for several years following her disclosure. In her case, the partner allegedly became violent towards her and her son. He reportedly received an absolute discharge while she was convicted of aggravated assault.[75] The case has attracted a significant amount of attention from people who feel it is patently unjust for her to have been convicted of such a serious crime, considering that the partner ultimately accepted the risk by continuing in a sexual relationship with her for several years knowing that she was HIV-positive, and he did not become infected. In contrast to his treatment at the hands of the justice system — an absolute discharge for committing physical violence against a woman and child — justice does not appear to have been done. This woman did not receive any protection from the law.

In a very different case, a Winnipeg man was found guilty of six aggravated sexual assault charges in relation to HIV non-disclosure (plus additional charges of invitation to sexual touching and sexual interference); on appeal, four of the aggravated assault charges were overturned because the presence of a significant risk of HIV transmission had not been proven beyond a reasonable doubt.[76] One of the complainants was only twelve years old at the time of their sexual encounters, and media accounts report that he offered alcohol and drugs to teenagers in vulnerable situations to lure them into sexual relationships.[77] As these two examples demonstrate, the range of situations covered by these cases makes a simple "yes" or "no" answer to the question of whether and how these prosecutions may protect women impossible.

75 *R c DC*, [2008] Montreal 505-01-058007-051 (CQ), [2008] JQ 994. The woman was acquitted on appeal on the basis that a significant risk of serious bodily harm had not been proven: *R c DC*, 2010 QCCA 2289. The Supreme Court of Canada heard the appeal of this case on February 8, 2012, together with the appeal of *R v Mabior*. At the time of this writing, a decision had not yet been issued.

76 *R v Mabior*, [2008] MBQB 201; *Mabior*, *supra* note 10.

77 Mike McIntyre, "HIV Positive Man Convicted" *Winnipeg Free Press* (16 July 2008) A4; Dean Pritchard, "Tainted Sex on Trial; Teenager Testifies Against HIV Carrier" *Winnipeg Sun* (13 May 2008) 4.

Advocacy work on the criminalization of HIV at the international level, and with particular reference to African countries, has drawn attention to the tenuous claims of "protecting women" that are often behind pushes to prosecute those who are unwilling or unable to disclose. For example, one article notes that:

> Criminalization [of HIV transmission] is also not an effective way of protecting vulnerable populations from coercive or violent behaviour, such as rape, that can transmit HIV. Sexual violence is already criminalized. Criminal laws [on HIV transmission] do nothing to address women's subordinate socioeconomic position, which makes it more difficult for women to insist upon safer sex with nonmonogamous partners, particularly husbands, and may make it dangerous for them to disclose their own infection. Criminalization [of HIV transmission] is a poor substitute for improving women's status and offering serious protection of women's rights to sexual decision making and physical safety. Indeed, criminalization [of HIV transmission] may fall unfairly and disproportionately on women.[78]

Within Canada, however, the argument that criminalizing HIV exposure protects women has yet to be interrogated in any depth. Beyond the question of whether prosecuting an individual protects other "potential victims," there are important questions about the broader implications of classifying non-disclosure as aggravated sexual assault. If non-disclosure is an aggravated sexual assault, what is it to rape and sexually torture a woman? Should these two very distinct actions be prosecuted under the same provisions? If our definitions of sexual assault are to truly capture affronts to women's sexuality and autonomy, perhaps aggravated sexual assault is the correct label for HIV non-disclosure. Or perhaps they are too distinct and the label of aggravated sexual assault is not appropriate.

Moreover, what does it mean for the investigation and prosecution of rape if the sexual assault squad's resources are directed towards HIV non-disclosure cases? And likewise, are other key issues for women living with HIV being adequately addressed when HIV/AIDS designated resources are being directed to dealing with criminal law and disclosure issues? How are people controlled and manipulated when police issue warnings that a "non-discloser" (as opposed to a rapist) is on the loose in one's community? How is a subclass of sexual beings being cre-

78 Burns & Cameron, *supra* note 55 at 580. See also Jürgens *et al*, *supra* at note 55 at 12–14. Reason #5 is: "Instead of providing justice to women, applying criminal law to HIV exposure or transmission endangers and further oppresses them."

ated through the application of sexual assault laws to behaviours that relate exclusively to HIV-status? In other words, in practice, does this legal development protect women, or does it limit their options, activities, and agency? Does it protect women, or undermine programs, relationships, and understanding that could support true gender and sexual equality? Are these policies empowering, just, and fair, or paternalistic and protectionist?

In considering these questions, it is revealing to consider *who* is being prosecuted for non-disclosure of HIV status. As mentioned above, the vast majority of the accused are men and the majority of the complainants are women. Given that women represent an increasing proportion of those living with HIV in Canada (approximately 22 percent at the end of 2008), and men who have sex with men continue to have the highest HIV prevalence in Canada (48 percent of PHAs at the end of 2008), one must question why the trend in prosecutions is as it is.[79] Possible factors may include those who look to the police and criminal justice system for protection in a complaints-driven process (more likely to be women than men) and gendered sexual ethics and practices. For example, while much of the gay community holds that everyone is responsible to protect themselves because anyone could be infected, this ethic may not apply equally in heterosexual communities.

Moreover, while it is impossible to know the precise racial breakdown of those charged, based on media coverage, public warnings issued by the police, and other available information on the cases, it would seem that at least 35 people who have faced charges are men of colour, including numerous immigrants from Africa (and in many of the cases the race of the accused is not publicly known and therefore the number of people of colour prosecuted could potentially be considerably higher).[80] Furthermore, much of the sensational media coverage about these trials has centred on cases against immigrants from Africa.[81] We know that systemic racism is a problem in the Canadian crim-

79 *HIV/AIDS Epi Updates, July 2010*, *supra* note 61 at 28, 60.

80 This estimate is derived from the tracking of cases by the Canadian HIV/AIDS Legal Network. Mykhalovskiy *et al*, *supra* note 32 at 10–11, further note that when attention is focused on heterosexual men who have been charged since 2004 (that is, on the group most represented in criminal cases during the most intensive period of criminal law application), black men account for a full 50 percent of all cases, a higher proportion than white heterosexual men. Official statistical data on the race of those charged and complainants is not kept. As explained by Professor Scott Wortley, there is little data available in Canada on the relationship between race and crime in the criminal justice system. See "A Northern Taboo: Research on Race, Crime and Criminal Justice in Canada" (July 2003) 41 Can J Crim Just 263.

81 E Mykhalovskiy & C Sanders, "Racialization, HIV and Crime: An Analysis of the

inal justice system, and that racial and sexual stereotypes have long played a role in sexual assault law.[82] To what extent do racism, myths about black sexuality, and barriers that limit access to appropriate, culturally sensitive support and health services and information play into this trend? To what extent do these cases (and the media coverage about them) feed myths that HIV is an "African disease," and black men are sexually aggressive, dishonest, and dangerous (particularly to white Canadian women)? Anything that fuels stigma and discrimination is likely to have a negative impact on HIV prevention, make disclosure more difficult for people living with HIV, and impact negatively on the well-being of PHAs. Therefore, the criminalization of HIV exposure is necessarily becoming an issue of increasing concern to black communities in Canada.

While the same provisions of the *Criminal Code* are used to prosecute reported rapes and HIV non-disclosure cases, there are some glaring differences between the two types of cases. For example, the conviction rate in rape cases is extremely low (5 percent according to the Ontario Women's Directorate and Ontario Women's Justice Network), yet in the HIV non-disclosure cases well over half of those accused plead guilty or are found guilty at trial.[83] And while women who have experienced rape report not being believed unless there is sufficient independent evidence of an attack, forceful penetration by a stranger, or physical injury to a victim who is seen as morally upright,[84] a review of judgments in the non-disclosure cases demonstrates a much higher level of belief of complainants — without the need for independent evidence, penetration, physical injury, or even that the complainant made attempts to use protection or determine the partner's health status. In terms of sentencing, while just over 40 percent of those convicted of sexual assault are sentenced to a prison term, almost all

Representation of HIV Non-Disclosure Criminal Cases in Canadian Print Media" (MS in progress) [on file with the author].

82 See, for example, Toni Williams, "Sentencing Black Offenders in the Ontario Criminal Justice System" in Julian V Roberts & David P Cole, eds, *Making Sense of Sentencing* (Toronto: University of Toronto Press, 1999) 200; Commission on Systemic Racism in the Ontario Justice System, *Report of the Commission on Systemic Racism in the Ontario Criminal Justice System* (Queen's Printer for Ontario, 1995); Jeane Gregory & Sue Lees, *Policing Sexual Assault* (New York: Routledge, 1999).

83 Based on the tracking of cases conducted by the Canadian HIV/AIDS Legal Network.

84 Nora Currie & Kara Gillies, "Bound by Law: How Canada's Protectionist Public Policies in the Areas of Both Rape and Prostitution Limit Women's Choices, Agency and Activities" at 88 [unpublished manuscript on file with the author].

of those convicted in relation to non-disclosure serve time in prison.[85] Clearly, while rape and HIV non-disclosure are both considered sexual assaults, there are some very different dynamics at play in these cases. It is worthy of pause to consider why HIV non-disclosure is seemingly considered more grave, and whether so-called "AIDS-panic" is a factor.

It is also important to note that police warnings, as used to warn women about stranger rapists, are now commonly used in HIV non-disclosure cases. Typical public safety alerts include identifying information about the accused (ie, name, age, hometown, and photograph), the charges, and the circumstances, which will include the accused's HIV-positive status and the sex of his or her sexual partners. It will then encourage anyone who has had sexual contact with the accused to seek medical advice and contact police. Given the sensationalism surrounding these cases, the media tend to report on all such warnings and publish the photographs.

Members of the HIV community have expressed concern about these warnings because they publicly reveal the accused's identity and HIV status, often based only on an allegation. The warnings may also reinforce the myths that PHAs are deceitful, that sex with them is dangerous, and that disclosure is simple and to be expected. Warnings may also contribute to misinformation and panic about HIV, advising people to seek medical advice with no regard for the actual risks of HIV transmission in different circumstances. In analyzing the interconnections between police practice with respect to cases of HIV non-disclosure and sexual violence, the role of public safety alerts is an important component. There are no policies governing how and when such warnings are used.[86] There is also little communication between the two communities with respect to advocacy concerning how and when they should appropriately be used. Developments with respect to one set of crimes may potentially influence practice with respect to the other. More coordinated analysis and action is clearly warranted.

Finally, it is worth considering how legal developments with respect to assault charges for HIV non-disclosure may influence the use of criminal law to address rape and sexual violence in Canada. For ex-

85 For example, a man in Ontario was sentenced in 2008 to a twelve-month conditional sentence to be served in the community for failure to disclose to his then girlfriend (who did not seroconvert). On appeal, a one-year prison term was substituted for the conditional sentence because the appeal judge deemed the conditional sentence unfit with respect to deterrence and denunciation objectives, and not proportionate to the gravity of the offence: *R v McGregor* (2008), 94 OR (3d) 500 (CA)).

86 *Supra* note 84 at 8–9.

ample, how might the redefinition of fraud in the *Cuerrier* decision be applied to situations other than HIV non-disclosure? A first glimpse at the possibilities here is provided by the *Hutchinson* case. In this case, a man poked holes in his girlfriend's condoms resulting in her pregnancy and an abortion. The Crown argued that the complainant was not consenting to *unprotected* sex, and if there was consent it was vitiated by the fraud committed by Mr Hutchinson when he sabotaged the condoms.

Applying the *Cuerrier* test of "significant risk of serious bodily harm," the trial judge acquitted with a directed verdict.[87] On appeal, a new trial was ordered.[88] Two of the three judges concurred that a properly instructed jury could conclude that there was no voluntary agreement to take part in unprotected sexual intercourse, and therefore no consent to the sexual intercourse. Alternatively, in line with *R v Cuerrier*, a properly instructed jury could find that there was consent but that it was vitiated by fraud, there was evidence of actual serious bodily harm as a result of the accused's deceit, and there was evidence of endangerment of life as required for a conviction of aggravated sexual assault. A challenging question in the reasoning is whether pregnancy can be considered a "serious bodily harm." This decision is exemplary of the sort of convoluted reasoning that may result from trying to apply the *Cuerrier* test to the multitude of different frauds and harms that occur in relation to sex. What the focus on consent with respect to full disclosure of relevant information may mean in the longer term for the development of sexual assault law and practice remains to be seen. These issues have yet to be analyzed in either the literature or in court decisions, but following the *Hutchinson* example, further tests to the limits of sexual assault jurisprudence may be just around the corner.

CONCLUSION

With each charge that is laid, this area of criminal law continues to develop and escalate. Where it will go next, and the implications for sexual assault law and practice, remain to be seen. The need for further research, informed policy dialogue, and strategic advocacy work on this issue are, however, patently clear.

Addressing the questions of when criminal charges are appropriate with respect to HIV non-disclosure and what charges should be applied is central to the work that needs to be done. If the current application of the criminal law with respect to HIV non-disclosure is overly broad,

87 *R v Hutchinson*, 2009 NSSC 51.

88 *R v Hutchinson*, [2010] NSJ No 16 (CCA).

where should the lines be drawn between criminal and non-criminal conduct? Most would accept that there may be isolated circumstances in which a PHA's conduct is so egregious that criminal charges are appropriate, but what are those circumstances?

Many within the global HIV community, including international bodies such as UNAIDS, advocate for a restricted use of criminal law with respect to HIV such that charges would only be laid where the accused is aware of his or her own HIV-positive status, intends to transmit HIV, and is successful in doing so.[89] Many Canadian advocates actively working on the issue of criminal law and HIV non-disclosure accept that criminal charges are appropriate in the rare circumstances where there is an intention to transmit HIV (so-called "wilful transmission") and perhaps in some situations of reckless behaviour. A campaign to develop prosecutorial guidelines on HIV non-disclosure is underway in Ontario, aimed at providing guidelines as to when charges are appropriate in order to ensure the law is applied fairly, consistently, and in compliance with broader scientific, medical, public health, and community efforts to prevent the spread of HIV and to provide care, treatment, and support to people living with HIV.[90] Simultaneously, numerous cases remain before the court with the potential to shift the trajectory of this jurisprudence.

As poignantly stated by the dissenting judge in the *Hutchinson* appeal, "The described conduct by the respondent would amount to a gross violation of trust. While morally reprehensible, it does not amount to the offence of sexual assault. Not all morally repugnant behaviour amounts to an offence."[91] Defining and redefining what does amount to the offence of sexual assault may continually be an unfolding process, and HIV has certainly added another complicating factor to this exercise. As we look to future developments, forging strategic linkages between the analysis and advocacy work on HIV and on violence against women may be a critical next step in advancing the criminal law in a more logical and effective direction.

89 See UNAIDS, Policy Brief: Criminalization of HIV Transmission (Geneva: UNAIDS, 2008).

90 See Ontario Working Group on Criminal Law and HIV Exposure, "Sign the Call," online: <http://www.ontarioaidsnetwork.on.ca/clhe/>.

91 *Supra* note 87 at para 161.

26.
All That Glitters Is Not Gold: The False Promise of Victim Impact Statements

*Rakhi Ruparelia**

This chapter interrogates whether or not the criminal justice system holds potential for fairly representing women's experiences of harm while affirming their dignity, equality, and autonomy. Specifically, Rakhi Ruparelia questions the opportunity to present a "victim impact statement" (VIS) to the judge who is sentencing a sex offender. While not opposing a criminalization strategy, as do Alison Symington and Julie Desrosiers in the specific contexts discussed in their respective chapters, Rakhi expresses similar skepticism that the law permitting the filing of a VIS is actually premised on deeply conservative ideologies regarding who are "real victims" and what their proper role in the criminal justice system is. Like the Sexual Assault Evidence Kit originally touted as a positive development for women, the VIS is more likely to be used to discredit women's claims than to validate them when it comes to sexual assault. Rakhi explores systemic racism in sentencing and argues persuasively that Aboriginal and racialized men will bear the brunt of VIS use and that Aboriginal and racialized women have little if anything to gain from the VIS. The VIS, she argues, is really about appeasing "victims" and maintaining the individualized focus of the criminal justice system.

> The woman who comes to the attention of the authorities has her victimization measured against the current rape mythologies, ie who she should be in order to be recognized as having been, in the eyes of the law, raped; who her attacker must be in order to be recognized, in the eyes of the law, as a potential rapist; and how injured she must be in order to be believed.[1]

* I am deeply indebted to Liz Sheehy for encouraging me to pursue this project and for offering me invaluable support and feedback throughout the process. I also would like to thank Ruth Sullivan for her kindness and expert editorial assistance, and an anonymous reviewer for insightful comments.

1 L'Heureux-Dubé J in *R v Seaboyer*, [1991] 2 SCR 577 at para 140 [*Seaboyer*] (dissenting in part).

> If government policy is shaped by the unacknowledged racial categorizations inculcated and acted on in daily life, the risk is substantial that government policy reflecting racialist preferences will, in the end, prove racially oppressive.[2]

The last few decades have brought increasing attention to the experiences of victims in the Canadian criminal justice system. Such experiences have been commonly referred to as a "second victimization" given the insensitive treatment often suffered by victims of crime. Growing awareness of secondary victimization and the backlash against what is perceived as an expansion of the rights of the accused have catalyzed political momentum for the victims' rights movement.

The "plight" of the victim has become a popular cause for interests across the political spectrum. It appeals as equally to the liberal call for increased sensitivity to the needs of victims as it does to the conservative law and order approach, which seeks harsher penalties for accused persons. Indeed, politically, victims' rights are often pitted directly against those of the accused.[3] Policies to get tough on criminals have neatly coincided with an apparent concern for the victim.

In response to lobbying efforts by victims' rights groups over the years, the *Criminal Code of Canada* now offers victims of crime the opportunity to submit a written victim impact statement and to present it orally at the sentencing hearing.[4] Victim impact statements are intended to relate to the sentencing judge the harm inflicted upon the victim by providing an assessment of the physical, financial, and psychological effects of the crime. Judges "shall consider" such statements "for the purpose of determining the sentence to be imposed on an offender."[5] This right has been heralded as one of the most significant victories of the victims' rights movement.

2 Stephen L Carter, "When Victims Happen to be Black" (1988) 97 Yale LJ 420 at 436.

3 For example, see comments offered by various Members of Parliament during debate on the motion to create a victims' rights bill. As Mr Grant Hill of the Reform party stated: "Reformers, every one of us, stand here today saying that if the rights of the victim collide with the rights of the perpetrator, the rights of the victim shall take precedence." *House of Commons Debates (Hansard)*, No 35 (29 April 1996) at 1350. Similarly, Mr Leon E Benoit, also of the Reform party, described the justice system as giving "too high a priority to the rights of the accused and the criminal. Their rights are put higher than the rights of citizens and victims to feel safe and be safe." *House of Commons Debates (Hansard)*, No 141 (10 March 1997) at 1254.

4 *Criminal Code*, RSC 1985, c C-46, s 722.

5 *Ibid* at s 722(1).

In my view, the use of victim impact statements as a response to secondary victimization is misguided and problematic, particularly for women who have been raped. It is a token and flawed attempt to meaningfully include victims of crime in the process: it does little to address the true needs of complainants. Rather, it tackles the issue of victim involvement only insofar as is necessary to appease political pressures. It fails to challenge the status quo in any significant way by leaving the sources of crime unaddressed. Victim impact statements are the product of the victims' rights movement, not feminist advocacy;[6] they do not reflect anti-racist, feminist objectives. Sexual assault complainants and other marginalized victims, who are not reflected in the victims' rights agenda, have little to gain from the availability of victim impact statements.

In this paper, I will argue that victim impact statements are not useful for women who have been raped and they risk causing further harm to racialized and other marginalized women. This is because they inevitably play into and potentially reinforce the sexist and racist stereotypes entrenched in the criminal justice system that apply to both victim and accused. Any potential benefit of victim impact statements is available only to a narrow category of "ideal" victims, who are defined in terms of their identity, the type of offence committed against them, and the identity of the offender.

Victims of gendered violence, especially those from racialized communities, including Aboriginal ones, have the least to gain from the availability of victim impact statements, and racialized offenders have the most to lose. Even for the narrow category of "ideal" victims, the usefulness of victim impact statements is questionable. The main beneficiary of victim impact statements appears to be the criminal justice system itself, which secures the co-operation of victims who choose to exercise their "rights" as victims and silences those who "choose" not to exercise their rights.

6 Edna Erez notes that "[v]ictim input rights have been particularly criticized for their presumed alliance with, or exploitation by, 'law and order' campaigns." Edna Erez, "Integrating a Victim Perspective Through Victim Impact Statements" in Adam Crawford & Jo Goodey, eds, *Integrating a Victim Perspective within Criminal Justice: International Debates* (Burlington, VT: Ashgate Publishing, 2000) 165 at 168. For a general discussion on why feminists oppose law and order agendas, see also Lynne Henderson, "Co-Opting Compassion: The Federal Victim's Rights Amendment" (1998) 10 St Thomas L Rev 579; Laureen Snider, "Feminism, Punishment and the Potential of Empowerment" (1994) 9 CJLS 75.

In the first section, I examine social notions of victimhood, both as a status and a label, and certain barriers to achieving "victim" status. Specifically, I consider the construction of the ideal victim through a critical race feminist lens and reflect on what this means for sexual assault complainants. I also look at legal constructions of victim hierarchy, using US data on sentencing that shows the role of victim and offender race in death penalty and rape cases. In the second section, I examine the alleged benefits of victim impact statements and their potential impact on sentencing. I question the likelihood of victims of rape, particularly marginalized women, reaping any such benefit. I also discuss the ways in which victim impact statements may be improperly considered by judges, drawing from both American and Canadian examples. I conclude that given the invidiousness of discrimination and its permeation into every aspect of our criminal justice system, we have no reason to believe that the use of victim impact statements can be immune from racial, class, and gender biases. The appropriateness of victim impact statements at sentencing is questionable for any crime; however, victim impact statements are particularly dangerous for sexual assault.

WHO IS A VICTIM?

In ordinary language use, a victim is a person who has suffered loss or injury as a result of something outside his or her control. We speak of victims of crime, victims of war, and victims of circumstance. In different contexts, the word carries different denotations and associations. In some, it is a status to be aspired to; in others a label to be shunned.

Victim as Status

In the context of the victims' rights movement, being a victim is a status to be aspired to in that it confers rights and it is something for which one must qualify. Robert Elias points out that in this context the state is prepared to recognize someone as victim only if their injury or loss can be acknowledged without challenging the status quo.[7] As a result, the emphasis of victims' rights movements and the corresponding services and programs offered to victims is on individuals who can demonstrate immediately perceptible harm resulting from a recognized crime.[8] In these circumstances, the harm can be directly attributed to

7 Robert Elias, "Community Control, Criminal Justice and Victim Services" in Ezzat A Fatteh, ed, *From Crime Policy to Victim Policy: Reorienting the Justice System* (Basingstoke: MacMillan Press, 1986) 290 at 301.

8 Inkeri Anttila, "From Crime Policy to Victim Policy" in Fattah, *ibid*, 237 at 244.

the actions of the individual offender; other (more systemic) factors are not implicated.

This analysis is borne out by section 722 of the *Criminal Code of Canada*, which entitles a person to prepare a victim impact statement only if the person is the victim of an offence. Within this context, as defined in subsection 722(4), "victim"

> (a) means a person to whom harm was done or who suffered physical or emotional loss as a result of the commission of the offence; and
>
> (b) where the person described in paragraph *(a)* is dead, ill or otherwise incapable of making a statement referred to in subsection (1) [victim impact statement], includes the spouse or common-law partner or any relative of that person, anyone who has in law or fact the custody of that person or is responsible for the care or support of that person or any dependant of that person.

According to this definition, a victim is the person or the family of a person who was the target of a crime that has been the subject of a criminal conviction. These are persons who have suffered harm through no fault of their own and entirely because of the wrongful act of the offender. To the extent the victim is innocent and undeserving of the harm she has suffered, the criminal is deserving of condemnation and the crime and its impact is deserving of attention.

A regime of this sort serves a number of purposes. First, it ties the concept of victim to the concept of crime — a concept that is carefully controlled by the existing power structure.[9] Second, it deflects attention away from state action or inaction that results in injury or loss to marginalized groups.[10] As a result, people are not officially recognized as being harmed by state violence, war, patriarchy, racism, colonialism, inequality, or poverty since these wrongs incriminate the state. Narrowing the definition in such a way allows state actors such as the military, the police, or other criminal justice officials to avoid being identified as sources of injury and loss. Focusing on individual "deviant" offenders is a safe way to address the issue of victims' rights without challenging an important source of criminality. In the context of sexual as-

9 Elias, *supra* note 7 at 301.

10 *Ibid.*

sault, this diversion of blame absolves the state of responsibility for its role in condoning sexual assault through its creation and perpetuation of gender and racial inequality.

Thus, one reason that feminist interests do not converge with those of the victims' rights movement is because of the latter's refusal to recognize systems of domination, such as patriarchy, white supremacy, and capitalism, as root causes of violence against women. As Sandra Walklate notes, the term victim is "sterile," specifically in its inability to capture the processes of victimization.[11] Universalizing causes and experiences of victimization through a single label obscures the important distinctions that exist between various types of crime. All victims are not the same. And more importantly for the purposes of this paper, "[s]exual assault is not like any other crime."[12] Unlike other violent crimes, as Madame Justice L'Heureux-Dubé noted in *Seaboyer*, sexual assault is perpetrated largely by men against women, is mostly unreported, and is subject to extremely low prosecution and conviction rates.[13] Furthermore, "[p]erhaps more than any other crime, the fear and constant reality of sexual assault affects how women conduct their lives and how they define their relationship with the larger society."[14] Sexual assault "is an assault upon human dignity and constitutes a denial of any concept of equality for women."[15]

Focusing on the "victim" also takes attention away from the abuser, thus facilitating victim-blaming attitudes. For example, society frequently questions why a woman remains in an abusive relationship, but rarely asks why a man abuses his intimate partner. Similarly, women who have been sexually assaulted are scrutinized for their own role in the assault. This narrow focus ignores the larger social structures that enable marginalized groups, including women, to be victimized in the first place.

Victim as Label

While achieving the status of victim may entitle a person to benefits, it may also expose the person to negative stereotyping and a negative self-image. It is not surprising that some participants in a Canadian focus

11 Sandra Walklate, *Imagining the Victim of Crime* (Maidenhead, UK: Open University Press, 2007) at 27.

12 *Seaboyer, supra* note 1 at para 137 (L'Heureux-Dubé J, dissenting in part).

13 *Ibid.*

14 *Ibid.*

15 *R v Osolin*, [1993] 4 SCR 595 at para 165 [per Cory J].

group on victim impact statements resisted the term "victim" and instead suggested the statements be called "crime impact statements."[16]

Identifying oneself as a victim can be disempowering. David Weisstub notes that we consider victims to be in some way subhuman, in need of our care and assistance.[17] As a result, victimization not only violates the moral autonomy of another person; it also makes that person an "ineffectual and submissive object of our benevolence."[18] For women in particular, "the passivity and powerlessness associated with being a victim are also associated with being female."[19] Yet at the same time, "rejecting victim talk may lead to blaming powerless people for their powerlessness."[20] While a preference for the term "survivor" has emerged within the feminist movement in an attempt "to capture women's resistance to their structural powerlessness and consequent potential victimization,"[21] as Martha Minow notes, "[v]ictimhood remains central, despite the use of survivor language."[22]

The politics of victim terminology are complicated, and the label of "victim" can be troubling. While the victims' rights movement has embraced the term, it undoubtedly deters some from submitting a victim impact statement. While I share concerns about the term victim, it is the language used in the *Criminal Code* and thus will be language that is referenced throughout this paper.

Social Understandings of "Victim" Status: The Ideal Victim

It is necessary to be the victim of a crime in order to be assisted by the criminal justice system. However, all victims are not created equal. As Walklate observes, "becoming a victim is neither simple nor straightforward."[23] Rather, achieving victim status involves a process

16 Department of Justice, *Summary Report on Victim Impact Statement Focus Group* by Colin Meredith & Chantal Paquette (Ottawa: Department of Justice, August 2001) at 23.

17 David N Weisstub, "Victims of Crime in the Criminal Justice System" in Fattah, *supra* note 7, 191 at 195–96.

18 *Ibid* at 196.

19 Walklate, *supra* note 11 at 27.

20 Martha Minow, "Surviving Victim Talk" (1993) 40 UCLA L Rev 1411 at 1420.

21 Walklate, *supra* note 11 at 27.

22 Minow, *supra* note 20 at 1426. Jane Doe also takes issue with the label "survivor." She explains that she "was already surviving the normal pain and hardships of life" before she was raped. Jane Doe, *The Story of Jane Doe: A Book About Rape* (Toronto: Random House, 2003) at 120.

23 Walklate, *supra* note 11 at 28.

that requires not only recognition of one's own victimization but also social acknowledgement of that victimization.[24] This begs the question: what makes a "good" victim or someone worthy of assistance?

As Lynne Henderson remarks, "the image of the victim has become a blameless, pure stereotype, with whom all can identify."[25] Some victims are viewed as more sympathetic than others, a reality that Eamonn Carrabine refers to as a "hierarchy of victimization."[26] As Walklate explains: "At the bottom of this hierarchy would be the homeless, the drug addict, the street prostitute — all those groups of people for whom it is presumed that victimization is endemic to their lifestyle, thus rendering any claim to victim status a highly problematic one."[27]

Nils Christie describes the "ideal" victim as a person or category of individuals who is given "complete and legitimate status" of victim when affected by crime.[28] He offers the example of the "little old lady" who is attacked by an unknown assailant in broad daylight while walking home from caring for her sick sister.[29] In this example, the victim is weak (she is old), she is engaged in a respectable task (that of caring for a sick relative), and cannot be blamed for being where she is (on the street in the middle of the day). Importantly, Christie points out the crucial role that the offender plays in slotting a given victim into the hierarchy of victimization. For a woman to be the ideal victim, she also needs to be violated by the ideal offender, who in this case is "big and bad," and unknown to her.[30] It is crucial that the offender be characterized as different from the victim, seemingly dangerous and bordering on non-human.[31]

The Non-Ideal Victim

Christie's paradigm is useful for considering the role of race in the construction of the ideal victim and ideal offender. In terms of the weakness requirement, the general threat that dominant society feels from marginalized groups makes racialized people unsympathetic and a

24 *Ibid.*

25 Lynne Henderson, "The Wrongs of Victims' Rights" (1985) 37 Stan L Rev 937 at 951.

26 Eamonn Carrabine, *Criminology: A Sociological Introduction* (Florence, KY: Routledge, 2004) at 115.

27 Walklate, *supra* note 11 at 28.

28 Nils Christie, "The Ideal Victim," in Fattah, ed, *supra* note 7, 17 at 18.

29 *Ibid* at 18–19.

30 *Ibid* at 19.

31 *Ibid* at 26.

group to be feared rather than protected. The element of victim weakness must also be understood as culturally defined and reflective of a hegemonic expectation of appropriate victim behaviour. For individuals who do not react in a manner consistent with weakness, the genuineness of their victimization and its impact may be challenged.

Similarly, the situational requirement that the victim be carrying out a respectable task in a location where she cannot be blamed for being has serious implications for a racialized person and particularly a racialized or Aboriginal woman who has been sexually assaulted. What is considered respectable and blameworthy is determined from dominant raced, gendered, and classed perspectives. The luxury of being able to protect oneself from dangerous conditions is not available to everyone, whether one is working in the sex trade or simply taking the bus at night. Victims will be blamed for being the target of crime if they are perceived to have engaged in behaviour that deviates from the culturally dominant norm.

A poignant example of the construction of the unsympathetic victim is offered by Sherene Razack in her insightful analysis of the brutal murder of Pamela George, an Aboriginal woman working as a prostitute, by two young middle-class white men.[32] One of the men hid in the trunk while the other lured Pamela George into the car.[33] The men then drove Pamela George to an isolated area, and following oral sex, took turns beating her, after which they left her to die on the ground with her face in the mud. As Razack demonstrates, race "overdetermined" what brought Pamela George and her killers to this violent encounter, and race "overdetermined" how the men's culpability was minimized.[34] Pamela George's occasional work as a prostitute was viewed as inviting violence, while the white men's participation in violent domination of an Aboriginal woman was viewed as natural. As Razack notes, both the Crown and the defence suggested the fact that Pamela George was engaged in prostitution was relevant. The judge instructed the jurors to keep this in mind during their deliberations, a direction that the Court of Appeal found did not degrade Pamela George.[35]

32 Sherene H Razack, "Gendered Racial Violence and Spatialized Justice: The Murder of Pamela George" (2000) 15 CJLS 91.

33 *R v Kummerfield*, [1998] 163 Sask R 257 at para 12. See also discussion in Razack, *ibid* at 125.

34 Razack, *supra* note 32 at 126.

35 *Kummerfield*, *supra* note 33 at para 64.

As demonstrated in Pamela George's case, and consistent with Christie's model of ideal victimization, the racial identity of the offender is important in determining victim status. The ideal victim needs to be harmed by a "bad man" in order to be sympathetic. Assumptions that racialized people, especially black and Aboriginal men, are inherently dangerous and violent, are deeply ingrained in our society. White men and women benefit from these constructions of racialized criminality that render them "innocent" in comparison. Our criminal justice system not only fails to challenge these notions, but is complicit in perpetuating white supremacy through its criminalization of racialized peoples and its differential treatment of racialized offenders.

In Pamela George's case, the brutality of her two white killers was minimized by the lawyers and the judge given the raced, gendered, and classed access to respectability the defendants enjoyed as young, economically privileged white men. In other words, Pamela George, a quintessentially "bad" victim as a racialized prostituted woman, was made an even worse victim by the "innocence" of her offenders, precluding her access to legitimate victim status. As Razack notes, "because Pamela George was considered to belong to a space of prostitution and Aboriginality, in which violence routinely occurs, while her killers were presumed to be far removed from this zone, the enormity of what was done to her and her family remained largely unacknowledged."[36] "The 'naturalness' of white innocence and Aboriginal degeneracy"[37] was left undisturbed. This understanding of innocence and degeneracy has also made it possible to ignore the hundreds of Aboriginal girls and women, many of whom were prostituted women, who have gone missing over the past three decades.[38]

The Victim of Sexual Assault

The importance of the features in Christie's paradigm is amplified when the crime in question is a sexual assault. The victim of rape must effect-

36 Razack, *supra* note 32 at 125–26.

37 *Ibid* at 127–28.

38 See Yasmin Jiwani & Mary Lynn Young, "Missing and Murdered Women: Reproducing Marginality in News Discourse" (2006) 31 Can J Comm 895, for an interesting examination of the Vancouver news media's treatment of missing women from the Downtown Eastside. The authors argue "that prevailing and historically entrenched stereotypes about women, Aboriginality, and sex-trade work continue to demarcate the boundaries of 'respectability' and degeneracy, interlocking in ways that situate these women's lives, even after death, in the margins" (at 895).

ively establish her weakness and her respectability and must show that her assailant is big, bad, dangerous and unknown to her.

Women who allege sexual assault are presumed to be lying. As Madame Justice L'Heureux-Dubé remarked: "The common law has always viewed victims of sexual assault with suspicion and distrust."[39] The myth that women often lie about sexual assault forms the basis of all other rape myths ingrained in our criminal justice system.[40] In this sense, women are presumed to be guilty of manufacturing their rape unless they can prove themselves "innocent." While a defendant is presumed innocent, "there is no presumption that the complainant is telling the truth."[41] Thus, as Karen Busby observes: "One is not a victim until a conviction is entered."[42] To describe someone as a victim before conviction would be contrary to the presumption of the accused's innocence.

While all complainants are considered "alleged" victims according to the *Criminal Code*,[43] sexual assault complainants are nonetheless distinguished from "real" victims, whether or not a conviction has been entered. This distinction was sharply exemplified during the parliamentary debates on the victims' rights bill that ultimately was enacted in 1999. Art Hanger, a Reform Party MP from Calgary, agreed with the general thrust of the proposed bill, but indicated his concern that "victims" in this context included sexual assault complainants. He stated: "One must admit that when it comes to some of the sexual abuse charges which have been laid not all complainants are true victims."[44] From his experience as a police officer, he suggested that "people" sometimes come forward with false accusations.

Women's victimization in the context of sexual assault is challenged in other ways as well. For example, women who know their rapists are

39 *Seaboyer, supra* note 1 at para 165.

40 Karen Busby, "'Not a Victim Until a Conviction is Entered': Sexual Violence Prosecutions and Legal 'Truth'" in Elizabeth Comack, ed, *Locating Law: Race/ Class/ Gender Connections* (Halifax: Fernwood, 1999) 260 at 261.

41 *Ibid* at 262.

42 *Ibid.*

43 The *Criminal Code* defines "complainant" as "the victim of an alleged offence" (s 2). Madame Justice L'Heureux-Dubé rejected the term "alleged victim" in her opinion in *Seaboyer*, finding it problematic in its "presumption that the woman has nothing to complain of" (*Seaboyer, supra* note 1 at para 135, L'Heureux-Dubé J, dissenting in part).

44 *House of Commons Debates (Hansard)*, No 150 (7 April 1997) at 1555 (Art Hanger).

viewed as less credible, despite the fact that women are far more likely to be sexually assaulted by someone they know than by a stranger.[45] The racial categorization of the woman who has been raped also plays a role in attributing blame in cases of acquaintance rape. One study found that white perceivers viewed black victims raped by a dating partner as more responsible than black victims of stranger rape. However, no distinction was made between white victims in parallel contexts.[46]

Moreover, women are hyperscrutinized for any "risk-taking" behaviour that is perceived to have contributed to their assault, such as the consumption of drugs or alcohol. For Aboriginal women, as Margo Nightingale notes, being intoxicated at the time of the assault suggests they are "'looser' and less worthy of protection."[47] Similarly, prostituted women, like Pamela George, are seen as blameworthy, inviting the violence they encounter. As Yasmin Jiwani explains, "[i]deologically, such stereotypes reinforce middle-class notions of propriety and hegemonic femininity,"[48] thus affirming the genuineness of some victimization but not others. Focusing on the characteristics and actions of individual sexual assault victims leaves women vulnerable to being labelled as either "innocent" or "blameworthy" victims,[49] a determination that will be affected by racism and other systems of oppression that make some women more sympathetic than others.

In a recent example of blaming the victim, Carleton University focused on what precautions a female student should have taken to prevent her sexual assault on campus. In its Statement of Defence against

45 Canadian Centre for Justice Statistics, *Canadian Centre for Justice Statistics Profile Series: Sexual Assault in Canada 2004 and 2007* by Shannon Brennan & Andrea Taylor-Butts (Ottawa: Minister of Industry, 2008) at 13 ("in cases where the relationship could be determined, police-reported data for 2007 show that the victim and accused were known to each other in 82% of sexual assault incidents"); Melanie Randall & Lori Haskell, "Sexual Violence in Women's Lives: Findings from the Women's Safety Project, a Community Based Survey" (1995) 1:1 Violence Against Women 19 ("Women are twice as likely to be sexually assaulted by a man known to them, than by a stranger"); *Changing the Landscape: Ending Violence — Achieving Equality: Final Report of the Canadian Panel on Violence Against Women* (Ottawa: Minister of Supply and Services, 1993) at 30 (31 percent of sexual assaults occur in a dating or acquaintance context).

46 Cynthia E Willis, "The Effect of Sex Role Stereotype, Victim and Defendant Race, and Prior Relationship on Rape Culpability Attributions" (1992) 26 Sex Roles 213 at 219.

47 Margo L Nightingale, "Judicial Attitudes and Differential Treatment: Native Women in Sexual Assault Cases" (1991) 23 Ottawa L Rev 71 at 98, 87–90.

48 Jiwani & Young, *supra* note 38 at 901.

49 Carrabine, *supra* note 26 at 116. See also Wendy Larcombe, "The 'Ideal' Victim v Successful Rape Complainants: Not What You Might Expect" (2002) 10:2 Fem Legal Stud 131.

an action in negligence, the university argued that the student, after choosing to remain on the premises alone, failed to keep a "proper lookout" for her own safety, and suggested, among other things, that she should have locked the door to the laboratory in which she was working late at night.[50] Similarly, a woman who was raped at gunpoint in front of her children in the parking garage of a Marriott hotel in Connecticut "failed to exercise due care for her own safety and the safety of her children and proper use of her sense and faculties," according to the defence to the negligence action brought forth by the woman.[51] There is no shortage of examples of women blamed for their own sexual assaults.

For women who have been sexually assaulted, the ideal victim requirement, and in particular the expectation that she be weak, poses a "curious paradox."[52] Whereas any deviation from scripts of powerlessness dictated by dominant norms of femininity is viewed as suspect, women still are expected to forcefully resist their attack in cases of rape. A lack of physical resistance, corroborated by bodily injuries, is typically equated with consent[53] and responsibility for the rape.[54] Consequently, it should not be surprising that women who suffer physical injuries are more likely to report their rape to the police than women who do not have physical corroboration of their assault.[55] Yet, women who do physically resist may be seen as less sympathetic for deviating

50 Andrew Seymour, "Sex-assault victim sues Carleton; Woman claims security was inadequate; university says she didn't do enough to protect herself" *The Ottawa Citizen* (7 August 2009) A1.

51 Thomas Heath, "Marriott Disowns One Hotel's Defense in Rape Case" *The Washington Post* (19 August 2009) A16. The "victim-blaming" defence was eventually dropped.

52 Jan Jordon, *Serial Survivors: Women's Narratives of Surviving Rape* (Sydney, Australia: Federation Press, 2008) at 14.

53 *Ibid.*

54 Jennifer Temkin & Barbara Krahé, *Sexual Assault and the Justice Gap: A Question of Attitude* (Portland: Hart Publishing, 2008) at 46. One study cited by Temkin also found that women seen as less physically attractive were viewed more negatively when they resisted their sexual assault (*Ibid*).

55 See eg Janice Du Mont, Karen-Lee Miller & Terri L Myhr, "The Role of 'Real Rape' and 'Real Victim' Stereotypes in the Police Reporting Practices of Sexually Assaulted Women" (2003) 9 Violence Against Women 466 at 478 (finding in their study of a large urban centre in Ontario that "[w]omen who sustained bruises, lacerations, abrasions, bumps, internal injuries, and/or fractures were approximately three and one half times more likely to contact the police than those who were not clinically injured"; Margaret J McGregor *et al*, "Why don't more women report sexual assault to the police?" (2000) 162 Can Med Assoc J 659.

from appropriate gender roles.[56] Ultimately, women who are raped are judged harshly no matter what they do or do not do.

The same systems of oppression that deem some victims more blameworthy also render the same women more vulnerable. As Razack indicates, racialized women are viewed as "inherently less innocent and less worthy than white women, and the classic rape in legal discourse is the rape of a white woman."[57] Similarly, Kimberlé Crenshaw argues:

> [S]exualized images of race intersect with norms of women's sexuality, norms that are used to distinguish good women from bad, the madonnas from the whores. Thus Black women are essentially prepackaged as bad women within cultural narratives about good women who can be raped and bad women who cannot.[58]

White women benefit from these dehumanizing constructions of racialized women, which make them "worthy" by comparison; white women's experiences of victimization are thus privileged. The result is that only an exceptionally narrow class of "ideal" sexual assault complainants will ever have access to victim status. As Walklate notes, "[t]he power of such 'ideal' images results in some people being viewed as deserving and other people being viewed as undeserving victims who may never be labelled as victims."[59]

LEGAL UNDERSTANDINGS OF "VICTIM" STATUS: RACE AND VICTIM WORTH

The criminal justice system makes clear which victims are worth protecting by the way it treats them. In this section, I focus on how the courts value harm caused to white victims differently from victims who are racialized.

The most obvious examples emerge from the United States, where empirical research on race and criminal law is more extensive and

56 Temkin & Krahé, *supra* note 54 at 46.

57 Sherene H Razack, *Looking White People in the Eye: Gender, Race, and Culture in Courtrooms and Classrooms* (Toronto: University of Toronto Press, 2001) at 68. See also Vernetta D Young, "Gender Expectations and their Impact on Black Female Offenders and Victims" (1986) 3 Just Q 305 at 323, for a discussion on how black women are characterized as "seductress," and "loose, immoral and sexually depraved," and therefore, incapable of being a legitimate rape victim.

58 Kimberlé W Crenshaw, "Mapping the Margins: Intersectionality, Identity Politics, and Violence Against Women of Color" (1991) 43 Stan L Rev 1241 at 1271.

59 Walklate, *supra* note 11 at 27.

available than in Canada. The Baldus study, reviewed by the US Supreme Court in *McCleskey v Kemp*,[60] is one of the most comprehensive and well-known studies on race in the criminal justice system. David Baldus, Charles Pulaski and George Woodworth examined over 2,000 capital murder cases to determine the role of race in the imposition of the death penalty. They found that juries imposed the death penalty in 22 percent of cases involving black defendants and white victims; 8 percent of cases involving white defendants and white victims; 3 percent of cases involving white defendants and black victims; and only 1 percent of cases involving black defendants and black victims.[61] Even after controlling for thirty-nine non-racial variables, the study found that capital defendants convicted of killing a white victim were more than 4.3 times likely to be sentenced to death than those convicted of killing a black victim.[62] The authors concluded that race of the victim, more than any other factor, influenced prosecutors to seek the death penalty[63] and juries to impose it.[64] These findings were replicated in another study that considered persons executed between 1976 and 1997. Of the 403 persons executed during that period, 228 were white (56.6 percent), 147 were black (36.5 percent) and 23 were Latino (5.7 percent). However, the composition of the victims of those executed was more telling, with the 455 white victims constituting the vast majority at 83.2 percent.[65]

60 The study, David C Baldus, Charles A Pulaski & George Woodworth, *Equal Justice and the Death Penalty* (Boston: Northeastern University Press, 1990) was reviewed in *McCleskey v Kemp*, where the defendant's lawyer argued that his client's death sentence should be invalidated given there was a constitutionally impermissible risk that the race of both the defendant and the victim played a role in the decision to impose the death sentence. McCleskey, a black man, was convicted of killing a white police officer. Ultimately, the US Supreme Court rejected the challenge but did not question the validity of the study: 481 US 279 (1986).

61 *Ibid* at 286.

62 *Ibid* at 287.

63 *Ibid.* In the study, prosecutors sought the death penalty in 70 percent of cases involving black defendants and white victims; 32 percent of cases involving white defendants and white victims; 19 percent of cases involving white defendants and black victims; and 15 percent of cases involving black defendants and black victims.

64 For an interesting analysis of *McCleskey* from the perspective of its failure to recognize the harm done to black victims, see Randall L Kennedy, "*McCleskey v Kemp*: Race, Capital Punishment, and the Supreme Court" (1988) 101 Harv L Rev 1388.

65 NAACP Legal Defense and Education Fund, *Death Row USA. Reporter 1040* (1997), cited in Jeffrey J Pokorak, "Probing the Capital Prosecutor's Perspective: Race of the Discretionary Actors" (1998) 83 Cornell L Rev 1811 at 1812. Of the remaining victims, sixty-six were blacks (12.1 percent) and nineteen were Latinos (3.5 percent).

Discrimination in the capital sentencing outcomes for defendants in rape cases was no less startling. Of the 455 men executed between 1930 and 1967 on the basis of rape convictions,[66] 405 of them were black.[67] Between 1908 and 1949, no white man had been executed for rape, although forty-five black men had suffered that fate.[68] Again, the race of the victim appears to have been an important variable. Similarly, Marvin Wolfgang and Mark Riedel in an extensive study that looked at 1,265 rape cases between 1945 and 1965, found that black defendants convicted of raping white women were approximately eighteen times more likely to be sentenced to death than any other racial combination.[69] Indeed, as the studies indicate, the death penalty for rape cases appears to have been specifically used to target black men who raped white women.[70]

Historically in the United States, as Angela Davis notes, "the fraudulent rape charge stands out as one of the most formidable artifices invented by racism."[71] Black rapist mythology "has been methodically conjured up whenever recurrent waves of violence and terror against the Black community have required convincing justifications."[72] All

66 The US Supreme Court in *Coker v Georgia*, 433 US 584 (1977) struck down the death penalty for the rape of an adult woman as "cruel and unusual" punishment, thus ending an expanding campaign to reform racially discriminatory sentencing practices for rape. See discussion in Randall Kennedy, *Race, Crime, and the Law* (New York: Vintage Books, 1997) at 323–26.

67 These Justice Department statistics were cited by Justice Marshall in *Furman v Georgia*, 408 US 238 at 364 (1972).

68 Kennedy, *supra* note 66 at 312.

69 Marvin E Wolfgang & Mark Riedel, "Rape, Racial Discrimination, and the Death Penalty" in Hugo Adam Bedau & Chester M Pierce, eds, *Capital Punishment in the United States* (New York: AMS Press, 1976) at 111–12.

70 Both innocent and guilty black men were captured under strict and discriminatory rape laws. Moreover, in some cases where there was sexual contact, it was consensual. Given the social prohibition against interracial relationships, white women would have been reluctant to admit willingly participating in sexual relations with a black man. Moreover, as Kennedy notes, lawyers for black defendants accused of raping white women might have been reluctant to raise consent as an issue for fear of alienating the judge or jury who would have found the suggestion offensive. Kennedy, *supra* note 66 at 320. See also Jennifer Wriggins, "Rape, Racism, and the Law" (1983) 6 Harv Women's LJ 103 at 111, for further discussion on how, in some cases, jurors were permitted to infer that a black man intended to rape a white woman based on race alone, given the assumption that a white woman would never consent to sex with a black man.

71 Angela Y Davis, *Women, Race & Class* (New York: Vintage Books, 1983) at 173.

chivalrous measures to protect white women from the fabricated sexual threat posed by black men were deemed appropriate, thus justifying the lynching of black men.[73] In the aftermath of the civil war, lynching, combined with the continued rape of black women, ensured the political domination of black people as a whole.[74]

In addition to punishing black men, the "myth of the Black rapist" has been promulgated to legitimize the rape of black women, or as Davis bluntly explains, "the mythical rapist implies the mythical whore."[75] She observes:

> The fictional image of the Black man as rapist has always strengthened its inseparable companion: the image of the Black woman as chronically promiscuous. For once the notion is accepted that Black men harbor irresistible and animal-like sexual urges, the entire race is invested with bestiality.... Viewed as "loose women" and whores, Black women's cries of rape would necessarily lack legitimacy.[76]

As Davis notes, "[o]ne of racism's salient historical features has always been the assumption that white men — especially those who wield economic power — possess an incontestable right of access to Black women's bodies."[77] During slavery, black women could be raped with relative impunity. Sexual coercion was a defining feature of the slaveowner's relationship with his female slaves, a tool, Davis notes, used not only to expand property by white slaveowners but also to exercise domination over black people.[78] Until the Civil War, many states overtly differentiated between sexual assaults committed by and against blacks and whites. For example, Georgia law provided that the rape of a white woman by a black man "shall be" punishable by death, while the rape of a white woman by anyone else was punishable by imprisonment for two to twenty years.[79] For the rape of a black woman, punishment was

72 *Ibid.*

73 *Ibid* at 189–90; Wriggins, *supra* note 70 at 107–09.

74 Davis, *ibid* at 185.

75 *Ibid* at 191.

76 *Ibid* at 182.

77 *Ibid* at 175.

78 *Ibid.*

79 Stephen B Bright, "Discrimination, Death and Denial: The Tolerance of Racial Discrimination in Infliction of the Death Penalty" (1994–1995) 35 Santa Clara L Rev 433 at 439.

"by fine and imprisonment, at the discretion of the court."[80] The implementation of more facially neutral laws after the Civil War made little practical difference, as the studies above indicate.

This enduring racist legacy haunts the differential treatment raped women receive in the criminal justice system. Several important studies have found that black men who rape white women continue to receive more severe punishments than black men convicted of raping black women or white men convicted of raping white women. Gary LaFree found that the racial composition of the victim–defendant dyad, and not the individual race of the defendant or victim, was the most important racial consideration in processing decisions, predicting charge seriousness, felony screening, sentence type, place of incarceration, and sentence length.[81] White on white rape was considered less serious than black on white rape, but more serious than black on black rape. Anthony Walsh conducted a similar study, but also considered the effect of the relationship between the defendant and the victim.[82] He found that black men who had sexually assaulted white women, regardless of whether the victim was a stranger or an acquaintance, received significantly harsher penalties than blacks who had sexually assaulted blacks, or whites who had sexually assaulted whites.[83] Moreover, in cases of intraracial rape, black defendants received more lenient sentences when they were acquainted with their victim.

80 *Ibid*. For examples in other states, see Wriggins, *supra* note 70 at 105, n 8.

81 Gary D LaFree, "The Effect of Sexual Stratification by Race on Official Reactions to Rape" (1980) 45 Am Sociological Rev 842 at 852. His study examined 881 suspects charged with "forcible sexual offenses" in the US between 1970 and 1975.

82 Anthony Walsh, "The Sexual Stratification Hypothesis and Sexual Assault in Light of the Changing Conceptions of Race" (1987) 25 Criminol 153. He examined more than 400 cases of sexual assault in Ohio between 1978 and 1983.

83 Walsh, *ibid* at 161. Walsh found that blacks who sexually assaulted whites were over four times more likely to be imprisoned than blacks who sexually assaulted blacks, and twice as likely to be sentenced to prison as whites who had sexually assaulted whites.

These studies, the results of which have been replicated elsewhere,[84] should alarm us for many reasons, including the harsher penalties imposed on racialized men. But we should also be disturbed by the devaluation of racialized women as victims of rape. As Crenshaw has noted:

> Black women are not discriminated against simply because white men can rape them with little sanction and be punished less than Black men who rape white women, or because white men who rape them are not punished the same as white men who rape white women. Black women are also discriminated against because intraracial rape of white women is treated more seriously than intraracial rape of Black women.[85]

Research has confirmed this devaluation. One study involving a hypothetical date rape scenario found that rape was considered less serious when the victim was a black woman than when the victim was white. If the woman was black, respondents were less likely to define the incident as a crime and less likely to suggest that the perpetrator be held legally accountable for his actions.[86]

While the United States has a distinct history of racism that differs in significant ways from that of Canada,[87] we should not fool ourselves

84 See eg Cassia Spohn & Jeffrey Spears, "The Effect of Offender and Victim Characteristics on Sexual Assault Case Processing Decisions" (1996) 13 Just Q 649. They found in their study of 1,152 sexual assault cases in Detroit that blacks who sexually assaulted white women received considerably longer sentences than in cases of intraracial rape. They also found that the impact of race was complicated by evidence that challenged victim behaviour and credibility, which tended to result in more lenient outcomes. See also: Cassia Spohn, "Crime and the Social Control of Blacks: Offender/Victim Race and the Sentencing of Violent Offenders" in George S Bridges & Martha A Myers, eds, *Inequality, Crime, and Social Control* (Boulder, CO: Westview Press, 1994) 249 (finding black men who sexually assaulted white women faced a greater risk of incarceration than in cases of black or white intraracial rape, particularly where the offender and victim were acquainted); Robert W Hymes *et al*, "Acquaintance Rape: The Effect of Race of Defendant and Race of Victim on White Juror Decisions" (1993) 133 J Soc Psychol 627 at 628, for a useful overview of research done in this area.

85 Crenshaw, *supra* note 58 at 1277.

86 Linda A Foley *et al*, "Date Rape: Effects of Race of Assailant and Victim and Gender of Subjects on Perceptions" (1995) 21 J Black Psychol 6.

87 Although our histories of racial discrimination are distinct, there is some overlap in our legacies of slavery and racial segregation, a part of the Canadian story that is often glossed over. For brief but useful overviews of the legal history of racism in Canada, see: Ontario Human Rights Commission, *Policy and Guidelines on Racism and Racial Discrimination* (Toronto: Ontario Human Rights Commission, June 2005) at 5–8, online: <http://www.ohrc.on.ca/en/resources/Policies/RacismPolicy>; Beverley McLachlin, "Racism and the Law: The Canadian Experience" (2002) 1 JL & Equality 7 at

into thinking that our own situation is any less problematic. Until the death penalty was abolished in 1976, it was implemented in discriminatory ways in Canada as well. Carolyn Strange notes that racist paternalism in clemency decisions sometimes spared the lives of Aboriginal convicted persons who were considered "savage" and intellectually and morally inferior to whites. However, executions were rarely commuted if the victims were white.[88] Kenneth Avio, who studied executive clemency decisions between 1926 and 1957, found that an Aboriginal person convicted of killing another Aboriginal person faced a 62 percent risk of execution. If the victim was white, this risk jumped to 96 percent. In contrast, an Anglo-Canadian convicted of killing an Aboriginal person faced an execution risk of only 21 percent.[89] As Strange remarks: "Capital punishment could be an instrument of racist terror, yet selective mercy toward Aboriginal capital offenders was no less racially informed or politically hued."[90]

Our situation resembles the American one in other compelling ways as well. Historically, sexual violence against Aboriginal women was a strategy of domination by settlers in the process of colonization,[91] not unlike the tactics used against black communities in the United States. Additionally, racism continues to be a salient feature of our criminal justice system, both in its targeting and punishment of racialized individuals as offenders, and in its callous disregard for the harm racialized people suffer as victims of crime, particularly racialized women who have been sexually assaulted. This is a reality at every stage of the criminal justice process, including policing. As Yasmin Jiwani remarks, "[w]hile over-policing contributes to a greater scrutiny and criminalization of racialized peoples, under-protection renders the victims of crime within racialized groups more vulnerable."[92] In the courtroom, racialized victims face a similar fate.

10–14. For a more extensive overview, see Clayton James Mosher, *Discrimination and Denial: Systemic Racism in Ontario's Legal and Criminal Justice Systems, 1892–1961* (Toronto: University of Toronto Press, 1998) for a historical account of discrimination within Ontario's criminal justice system. No historical (or contemporary) picture of racism in Canada is complete without recognition of the role of colonialism.

88 Carolyn Strange, "The Lottery of Death: Capital Punishment, 1867–1976" (1995) 23 Man LJ 594 at 603–05.

89 Kenneth L Avio, "The Quality of Mercy: Exercise of the Royal Prerogative in Canada" (1987) 13 Can Pub Pol'y 366 at 372.

90 Strange, *supra* note 88 at 604.

91 Razack, *supra* note 32 at 130.

92 Yasmin Jiwani, "The Criminalization of 'Race'/The Racialization of Crime" in Wendy Chan & Kiran Mirchandani, eds, *Crimes of Colour: Racialization and the Criminal Justice System in Canada* (Scarborough: Broadview Press, 2002) 45 at 73.

As suggested above, the gendered counterpart to the violent black or Aboriginal male stereotype is the racialized female body upon which violence may be perpetrated without sanction.[93] The harm suffered by racialized women as victims of sexual assault is perceived to be less serious by the white mainstream. Emma Larocque described violence against Aboriginal girls and women to the Aboriginal Justice Inquiry of Manitoba in the following way:

> the portrayal of the squaw is one of the most degraded, most despised and most dehumanized anywhere in the world. The "squaw" is the female counterpart to the Indian male "savage" and as such she has no human face; she is lustful, immoral, unfeeling and dirty. Such grotesque dehumanization has rendered all Native women and girls vulnerable to gross physical, psychological and sexual violence.[94]

In the courtroom, this dehumanization is manifested in the way that male judges continue to minimize the harm suffered by Aboriginal women.[95] A well-publicized example of this diminishment of injury was evident in the comments of Judge Michel Bourassa following a particularly lenient sentencing order for the sexual assault of a young Aboriginal girl by a former politician. Judge Bourassa suggested that rapes in the (predominantly Aboriginal) North were less violent than in southern Canada because "[t]he majority of rapes in the Northwest Territories occur when the woman is drunk and passed out. A man comes along, sees a pair of hips and helps himself."[96] He further stated: "That contrasts sharply to the cases I dealt with before (in southern Canada) of the dainty co-ed who gets jumped from behind."[97] His remarks support Razack's contention that Aboriginal women are viewed as "inherently rapeable."[98] Moreover, courts fail to recognize that Aboriginal and

93 Razack, *supra* note 57 at 69.

94 Cited in Razack, *ibid.*

95 Nightingale, *supra* note 47 at 84–91.

96 Laurie Sarkadi, "Rape in North different, judge says" *Edmonton Journal* (20 December 1989) A1.

97 *Ibid.* His comments were not found to constitute judicial "misbehaviour" when later investigated. For a discussion of these comments as well as an overview of other cases involving the sexual assault of Inuit women, see Teressa Nahanee, "Sexual Assault of Inuit Females: A Comment on 'Cultural Bias'" in Julian V Roberts & Renate M Mohr, eds, *Confronting Sexual Assault: A Decade of Legal and Social Change* (Toronto: University of Toronto Press, 1994) 192.

98 Razack, *supra* note 57 at 69.

other racialized women may experience unique forms of harm.[99] Judicial reliance on degrading stereotypes allows both Aboriginal and white men to be absolved of responsibility for the rape of Aboriginal women.

Nothing in this discussion should suggest that harsher punishments are necessarily the solution to discrimination against racialized victims.[100] To the contrary, feminists have warned against adopting the law and order strategy of seeking more severe penalties for offenders. Tougher penalties disproportionately impact racialized offenders, who already suffer racist treatment at the hands of the criminal justice system. Racialized offenders are victims too, both inside and outside of the criminal justice system,[101] although their victimization remains unacknowledged in victims' rights campaigns.

Moreover, as critics of the law and order agenda have cautioned, the line between victim and offender in the criminal justice system is a blurry one, particularly for women and members of racialized communities. The Native Women's Association of Canada notes, "The law rather than protecting women vilifies, criminalizes and imprisons them,"[102] subjecting poor and racialized women to "hyper-responsibilization" for their lived realities of marginalization and victimization.[103] Criminalization has been the reality for women who act violently in self-defence against an abuser. As Donna Edwards of the National Network to End Domestic Violence remarked at a Senate hearing on a pro-

99 Nightingale notes that Aboriginal women may be ostracized from their families or communities after being sexually assaulted or after reporting it to the police. Moreover, in isolated communities, women who have been sexually assaulted may not be able to access support or counselling services (*supra* note 47 at 86). Immigrant women often face similar threats of ostracism from their communities, as well as difficulty accessing culturally and linguistically appropriate services. Further, some immigrant women may fear deportation if they report abusive partners or family members.

100 Randall Kennedy in his discussion of *McCleskey* reflects on the challenge of remedying the devaluation of black victims when equal treatment would result in harsher penalties for black offenders (*supra* note 64 at 1392–93).

101 See Fran Sugar & Lana Fox, "Survey of Federally Sentenced Aboriginal Women in the Community" (Ottawa: Native Women's Association of Canada, 1990), online: <http://www.csc-scc.gc. ca/text/prgrm/fsw/nativesurvey/surveye03-eng.shtml>; Patricia Monture-Angus, *Thunder in my Soul: A Mohawk Woman Speaks* (Halifax: Fernwood Publishing, 1995) at 173; Commission on Systemic Racism in the Ontario Criminal Justice System, *Report of the Commission on Systemic Racism in the Ontario Criminal Justice System* (Toronto: Queen's Printer, 1995) at 211.

102 Native Women's Association of Canada, "Aboriginal Women in the Canadian Justice System: A Policy Paper" (2008) at 5, online: <http://www.nwac-hq.org/en/documents/AboriginalWomenintheCanadian JusticeSystem.pdf> [NWAC].

103 *Ibid.*

posed constitutional amendment to protect victims of crime in the US, "There could be but a day's difference between the battered woman 'victim' and the battered woman 'defendant.'"[104] Given the reality that women engage with criminal justice as both offenders and victims, often simultaneously, we must, as Elizabeth Sheehy argues, employ an equality analysis when evaluating criminal law reforms. She reminds us that "women's experience of criminal law is mediated through social class, racism, lesbophobia, and disabilityism,"[105] and that "calls for law and order or victim's rights initiatives undermine democratic values and institutions, reinforce state power and relations of dominance, and divide us further along those lines."[106]

In the next section, I will explore how the context described above should inform our analysis of victim impact statements.

VICTIM IMPACT STATEMENTS: WHAT ARE THE BENEFITS AND WHO REAPS THEM?

Victim impact statements allow victims of crime to participate in the criminal justice system. It remains to be seen whether this participation is beneficial to the victim or useful to the system, or whether it does or should have an impact on sentencing.

Impact on the Victim

In delivering a victim impact statement, a victim of crime assumes a public role in the sentencing process. She tells her story in her own words, describes her experience of the crime and the loss or harm she has suffered at the hands of the offender. In principle, by telling her story at this point in the trial, after conviction, the victim's claim to victimization is vindicated. The wrong done to her is publicly acknowledged and she receives the attention and sympathy she deserves. Her own innocence is confirmed. A public vindication of this sort is likely to be gratifying and may even be therapeutic for the victim. Despite this potential benefit, participation rates in Canada appear to be very low.[107] There are a number of possible explanations for this.

104 Cited in Henderson, *supra* note 6 at 586.

105 Elizabeth Sheehy, "Equality Without Democratic Values? Why Feminists Oppose the Criminal Procedure Reforms" (1999) 19 Can Woman Stud 6 at 14.

106 *Ibid.*

107 Julian V Roberts & Allen Edgar, "Victim Impact Statements at Sentencing: Perceptions of the Judiciary in Canada" (2003) 1:4 Int'l J of Victimology 111 at 118.

First, there is the matter of prosecutorial discretion. Generally, studies have indicated that few victims exercise their right to submit a victim impact statement unless specifically informed of this opportunity and invited to participate by the prosecutor.[108] That prosecutors are to a great extent the guardians of the victim impact statement regime gives rise to concerns about the scope of discretion in this context. Prosecutorial discretion has been identified as a critical site for racially discriminatory practices.[109] One can expect that some victims are deemed more worthy than others and thus given more encouragement to participate.[110] More generally, prosecutors may find white victims more credible than racialized victims, or "their troubles more worthy of full prosecution."[111]

Second, there are cultural reasons why some women may decline to participate. The notion that describing the harm one has suffered in a public way is therapeutic turns on a particular conceptualization of healing that is not shared across (or within) cultures. For some, to express victimization in a public forum may be seen as improper, stigmatizing, and, in some cases, downright dangerous. This is especially so for women who have been abused.[112]

108 Dina R Hellerstein, "The Victim Impact Statements: Reform or Reprisal?" (1989) 27 Am Crim L Rev 391 at 399.

109 See eg Angela J Davis, "Prosecution and Race: The Power and Privilege of Discretion" (1998) 67 Fordham L Rev 13; Sheri Lynn Johnson, "Unconscious Racism and the Criminal Law" (1988) 73 Cornell L Rev 1016; Pokorak, *supra* note 65; Raymond Paternoster, "Race of Victim and Location of Crime: The Decision to Seek the Death Penalty in South Carolina" (1983) 74 J Crim L & Criminology 754.

110 Some studies have found that prosecutors selectively use victim impact statements depending on how helpful the statement will be to their case. See eg Madeline Henley, Robert C Davis & Barbara E Smith, "The Reactions of Prosecutors and Judges to Victim Impact Statements" (1994) 3 Int'l Rev of Victimology 83 at 88–89. See also Department of Justice, *Assessment of the Victim Impact Statement in British Columbia* by Tim Roberts (Ottawa: Department of Justice, 1992), cited in Kent Roach, *Due Process and Victims' Rights: The New Law and Politics of Criminal Justice* (Toronto: University of Toronto Press, 1999) at 291. In his study in British Columbia, Roberts found that victim impact statements were obtained in only 2–6 percent of cases and filed in court in only 1–2 percent of cases. The statements were most likely to be used when the prosecutor found them to be important.

111 Martha A Myers & John Hagan, "Private and Public Trouble: Prosecutors and the Allocation of Court Resources" (1979) 26 Social Problems 439 at 447.

112 As one American judge noted in a study on victim impact statements: "If she is really the victim of on-going abuse, I think that standing up in the courtroom puts her in harm's way" in Mary Lay Schuster & Amy Propen, *2006 WATCH Victim Impact Study* (1 August 2006) at 10, online: <http://www. watchmn.org/reports.html>.

There is also the important issue of trust. To ask someone to indicate how she has been harmed by an offender is to ask her not only to identify herself as a "victim" but to expose her vulnerability publicly: to the court, to her family and friends, and to the offender. To disclose this intimate harm to the court requires trust, a trust that many racialized people, women who have been sexually assaulted, and others who have had negative experiences with the justice system simply do not enjoy. Women will avail themselves of this opportunity to participate in the sentencing process only if they feel confident that their voices will be heard and their experiences validated.

Given the widespread discrimination in criminal justice administration and the negative encounters that racialized individuals have with the system both as offenders and victims, it should come as no surprise that few racialized women feel safe in the system. It would be shocking if they did. As the Commission on Systemic Racism in the Ontario Criminal Justice System stated:

> Many racialized women do not see the criminal justice system as an ally, but as an overly intrusive and destructive force ... They want in particular to limit their subsequent involvement in the criminal justice system, which they may perceive as alien, overwhelming, and a source of yet more problems.[113]

While the Commission focused primarily on the experiences of black communities, the picture is no more optimistic for Aboriginal peoples. Despite the fact that Aboriginal women are five times more likely to be sexually assaulted than non-Aboriginal women, under-reporting is particularly pronounced within this community, due in part to a lack of confidence in the system.[114] This lack of confidence stems not only from discriminatory treatment within the system, but also from an incongruence between Canadian criminal justice and Aboriginal values.[115] As Patricia Monture-Angus notes, the failure to take responsibility for the ongoing perpetuation of colonialism "magnifies the con-

113 Commission, *supra* note 101 at 211.

114 Department of Justice, *A Review of Research on Criminal Victimization and First Nations, Métis and Inuit Peoples 1990 to 2001* by Larry Chartrand & Celeste McKay (Ottawa: Department of Justice Policy Centre for Victim Issues, 2006) cited in NWAC, *supra* note 102 at 2.

115 Monture-Angus, *supra* note 101 at 173.

tempt that Aboriginal peoples have for a system that is neither fair and just nor responsible."[116] Aboriginal peoples have little reason to trust a justice system that sustains colonial relations.

Closely related to lack of trust is the fear that instead of achieving vindication, the victim will be revictimized by the very process that is supposed to help her heal. Because victims of crime may be questioned by the defence on the content of their statements, those who participate must "expose their suffering to adversarial challenge."[117] Women who have been raped also face the possibility that their statements will be greeted by sneers or smirks or other defence counsel tactics intended to undermine their credibility and minimize the harm they suffered.[118]

Women who are racialized or otherwise marginalized are also deterred by the very real possibility that no matter what they say, they will not be heard by the judge; they will not be allowed victim status. Victims will be more sympathetic when the sentencing judge can relate to them, a depressing consideration for racialized women who face a predominantly white male and upper-middle-class judiciary. Can the psychological harm of racist violence or colonialism ever be heard in this forum? If the harm they describe is not acknowledged or, worse yet, denied, the victim impact statement will be a source of additional harm.

Even sympathetic victims may find it difficult to persuasively communicate the harm they have suffered. Where the ability to express oneself effectively is hindered by language barriers, educational disadvantage, or other factors that make the person less eloquent (factors that are borne disproportionately by racialized individuals), the statement will be less compelling. Moreover, to succeed victims must not only be articulate but must also be *perceived* as articulate, a status that is selectively accessible given racist and classist stereotypes.

Given prosecutorial discretion, lack of trust, and a well-warranted fear of not being heard, those likely to benefit from a victim impact statement are few. Those who do not fit the ideal victim paradigm are more likely to experience revictimization than vindication. The case

116 Patricia A Monture-Angus, "Lessons in Decolonization: Aboriginal Overrepresentation in Canadian Criminal Justice" in David Long & Olive Patricia Dickason, eds, *Visions of the Heart: Canadian Aboriginal Issues*, 2d ed (Toronto: Harcourt Brace, 1996) 361 at 362.

117 Roach, *supra* note 110 at 291.

118 Jane Doe, *supra* note 22 at 75.

of *R v Labbe*[119] offers a helpful illustration. In this case, an Aboriginal woman, described as an alcoholic and "street" person by the judge, was viciously killed by an intoxicated man with whom she was acquainted, though it is not clear from the statement of facts whether they were in an intimate relationship. Former Justice John Bouck remarked that the victim often invited the defendant to join her in her drinking binges and mocked the defendant's efforts to abstain from alcohol.[120] Victim impact statements were filed by both her mother and brother, who were described by Bouck J in the following way:

> Mrs. Martin [the mother] admits to being an alcoholic. She is aboriginal and lives on a reserve near Duncan, BC She is angry with Mr Labbe for taking her daughter's life. She is trying to rebuild her life but finds it difficult to do so because of her tragic loss.
>
> A Mr and Mrs. Fraser adopted Ms Martin's brother shortly after his birth on 23 April 1971. He states he was brought up in a good home and learned right from wrong. Around 1989 he sought out his natural mother and moved to Duncan from New Westminster. He did not know his sister Krista very well as she lived in Victoria. Nonetheless, her death caused him much sadness. He is angry because Mr Labbe's actions deprived him of a lifetime of getting to know his sister. He hopes his surviving sisters will not suffer the same fate.[121]

That the victim's mother is an alcoholic or that her brother has good moral values has no obvious relevance to any issue in the proceedings, particularly without further elaboration by the judge. On its face, the decision puts into question not only the deceased's character and contribution to her victimization , but also the character of the family left to mourn her death. The decision to include these details about the victim and her family was likely subconscious, although it is impossible to fully evaluate this choice without the benefit of the full victim impact statements. Regardless of whether subconscious bias ultimately played a role in this particular sentencing determination, its potential to influence decisions should make us wary. The risk of subconscious bias is heightened by its typical invisibility, making it practically impossible to

119 *R v Labbe*, [2001] BCJ No 184 (SC).
120 *Ibid* at para 15.
121 *Ibid* at paras 11–12.

assess with any accuracy its impact on decision making or to challenge that impact.

For the reasons described above, I have grave concerns about relying on victim impact statements as a panacea for the ills that plague victims in the criminal justice system. They have the potential to legitimize the experiences of some victims while further harming others. As Jane Doe notes, victim impact statements were not designed to benefit women who have been raped; rather, they were intended to assist the family members of homicide victims.[122] And even that assistance may be limited to families of victims who resemble the ideal victim prototype.

Input into Sentencing

The argument most often raised in opposition to victim impact statements is the risk they pose to a defendant's fair trial rights. This fear stems from the assumption that most victims, fuelled by a need for vengeance, will campaign for a severe penalty to be imposed against the perpetrator. In Justice Casey Hill's view, personal revenge on the part of the victim should not be fostered through the victim impact statement regime, which he acknowledges is "a very real danger" if the regime is not carefully structured.[123]

Certainly, many victims assume their victim impact statement will directly influence the sentence, a misunderstanding arguably facilitated by the victims' rights movement, and they are disappointed when their input has no discernable effect. One Canadian study found that influencing sentencing was the most frequently cited reason for filing a victim impact statement.[124] However, victim impact statements, according to judicial interpretation of the relevant statutory provisions, are not supposed to include sentencing recommendations, nor are they supposed to include criticisms of the offender.[125] In some cases, judges or prosecutors must edit victim impact statements to ensure compliance with these requirements or, in more extreme cases, reject them altogether.[126]

122 Jane Doe, *supra* note 22 at 75.

123 *R v Gabriel* (1999), 137 CCC (3d) 1 at 13 (Ont Sup Ct) [*Gabriel*].

124 Department of Justice, *Victim Impact Statements in Canada: Evaluation of the North Battleford Project* by Campbell Research Associates, vol 3 (Ottawa: Department of Justice Canada, 1990) at 34, cited in Julian V Roberts, "Victim Impact Statements and the Sentencing Process: Recent Developments and Research Findings" (2002–03) 47 Crim LQ 365 at 380.

125 *Gabriel*, *supra* note 123 at 15.

126 See eg *R v Unger*, [2007] Sask R 191 at para 37 (Prov Ct) (court excised portions of the

Concerned about how victim "worthiness" may affect an offender's sentence, the United States Supreme Court in *Booth v. Maryland*[127] in 1987 held that the introduction of a victim impact statement at the sentencing phase of a capital murder trial violated the 8th Amendment prohibiting cruel and unusual punishment. The court found that the admission of a victim impact statement created "a constitutionally unacceptable risk that the jury may impose the death penalty in an arbitrary and capricious manner."[128] According to Justice Powell, the focus of a victim impact statement is "on the character and reputation of the victim and the effect on his family," factors that may be entirely unrelated to the defendant's blameworthiness,[129] and that could lead to a "mini-trial" on the victim's character.[130] Moreover, the court cautioned that while the victim's family members in the case before them were "articulate and persuasive in expressing their grief," this would not always be the case and should not determine whether a defendant lives or dies.[131] Nor should a decision "turn on the perception that the victim was a sterling member of the community rather than someone of questionable character."[132] The court cited a passage from its decision in *Furman v Georgia* to support this point:

> We are troubled by the implication that defendants whose victims were assets to their community are more deserving of punishment than those whose victims are perceived to be less worthy. Of course, our system of justice does not tolerate such distinctions.[133]

A study conducted on mock jurors in the United States following *Booth* found that the concerns raised in that judgment were valid, and

statement that contained facts of the offence, and inflammatory and vengeful comments about the defendant's character that were prejudicial); *R v Sparks* (2007), 251 NSR (2d) 181 at para 18 (Prov Ct) (court edited "suggestions as to severity of the sentence, statements that sought to achieve personal retaliation, assertions as to the facts of the offence and criticisms of the offenders"); *R v MacDonough* (2006), 209 CCC (3d) 547 at para 23 (Ont Sup Ct) (prosecutor "blacked out" sections that were inappropriate before submitting victim impact statement to the court).

127 482 US 496 (1987).

128 *Ibid* at 503.

129 *Ibid* at 504.

130 *Ibid* at 507.

131 *Ibid* at 505.

132 *Ibid* at 506.

133 *Ibid* at n 8, citing *Furman*, *supra* note 67, Douglas J, concurring.

that victim evidence impacted juries in different ways depending on the respectability of the victim.[134] It may be the case that any potentially inflammatory effect of victim impact statements will not cost a defendant his life in Canada; however, the loss of liberty remains a serious risk. Similarly, the possibility that a defendant's punishment will turn on the worthiness of his victim or on her ability to articulate grief effectively is not one that should be taken lightly. The risk is too grave in a criminal justice system saturated with racial, gender, and class bias.

Although *Booth* was concerned with the effect of victim impact evidence on juries, there is no reason to believe that judges are immune to the emotional pleas of victims during sentencing. Indeed, some judges in the United States have suggested that no distinction is warranted between judges and juries in this context.[135] Concern that the sentencing hearing could turn into a "mini-trial" for extraneous considerations has been raised by Canadian judges as well.[136] Even when the good character of the victim is not openly refuted, there remains a risk that inappropriate factors will influence the sentencing judge, even subconsciously.

Astonishingly, the US Supreme Court overturned its decision in *Booth* in 1991 in *Payne v Tennessee*,[137] finding that victim testimony introduced at the penalty phase of a capital trial did not violate the 8th Amendment. Sadly, yet perhaps predictably, the case that incited the court to overrule itself involved a black defendant and two white victims, a mother and her two-year-old daughter whom the defendant killed. A third victim, the three-year-old son of the woman, survived. According to the court, the defendant passed the day of the crime in-

134 Edith Greene, Heather Koehring & Melinda Quiat, "Victim Impact Evidence in Capital Cases: Does the Victim's Character Matter?" (1998) 28:2 J App Soc Psychol 145.

135 For example, Justice Marshall, in his dissent, wrote the following in *Post v Ohio*, 484 US 1079 at 1082 (1988):

> the presumption that judges know and apply the rules of evidence should not be converted into license to conclude that judges are inhuman, incapable of being moved by passion as well as by reason. It would be unrealistic and unwise to presume that no judge could be moved, in both heart and deed, by the anguish and rage expressed by a murder victim's family. The potentially inflammatory effect of such evidence convinced this court in *Booth* that its admission endangered the reasoned decisionmaking required in capital cases ... there is no reason to denigrate that danger simply because the recipients of the evidence wore judicial robes.

See also *People v Simms*, 121 Ill. 2d 259 at 274 (1988), where Justice Simon noted: "The sentencer is given such wide discretion to dispense mercy that it is risky to presume to know how great an influence, conscious or subconscious, a victim impact statement admitted in evidence had on the sentencer."

136 *Gabriel*, *supra* note 123 at 13.

137 501 US 808 (1991).

jecting cocaine, drinking beer, and browsing through pornographic magazines, before making sexual advances towards the adult victim. Apparently, he became violent when he was resisted.[138] Justice Rehnquist, who delivered the opinion of the court, quoted a police officer who had described the defendant following the murders as having "a wild look about him," as "foaming at the mouth."[139] As Jennifer Wood argues, "Rehnquist's crime narrative, which depends upon representation of the Christophers's innocent victimization, also carefully offers a characterization of Payne as a drug-crazed animal," [140] thus justifying the violence of his death sentence.[141]

It is difficult to assess the extent to which victim impact statements influence sentencing in practice. Studies on this issue have been mixed, but most have concluded that sentencing practices have not changed with the introduction of victim impact statements.[142] However, these studies generally fail to take into account possible outcome variations due to the nature of the crime or the identity of the victims and offenders. A notable exception to this is a study that specifically examined the relevance of an offender's sex on the influence of the victim impact statement. A study using mock jurors in Australia found that victim impact statements resulted in more severe sentences for female offenders, seemingly the result of an increase in perceived deviancy as measured by volition and future dangerousness.[143] As the study revolved around the commission of a violent offence, it appears that female offenders were punished for not conforming to accepted female roles.

Given that victim impact statements are only one of a number of factors that a judge is mandated to consider in the sentencing decision,

138 *Ibid* at 812.

139 *Ibid* at 813.

140 Jennifer K Wood, "Refined Raw: The Symbolic Violence of Victims' Rights Reforms" (Winter 1999) 26 College Literature 150 at 157.

141 *Ibid* at 158.

142 Julian V Roberts, "Listening to the Crime Victim: Evaluating Victim Input at Sentencing and Parole" in Michael Tonry, ed, *Crime and Justice*, vol 38 (Chicago: University of Chicago Press, 2009) at 373. For a helpful overview of studies on this issue, see Roberts, "VIS and the Sentencing Process," *supra* note 124 at 381–83; see also Edna Erez & Pamela Tontodonato, "The Effect of Victim Participation in Sentencing on Sentencing Outcome" (1990) 28 Criminol 451; Robert C Davis & Barbara E Smith, "Effects of Victim Impact Statements on Sentencing Decisions: A Test in an Urban Setting" (1994) 11 Just Q 453.

143 Lynne Forsterlee *et al*, "The effects of a victim impact statement and gender on juror information processing in a criminal trial: Does the punishment fit the crime?" (2004) 39 Australian Psychologist 57.

it is difficult to assess how and to what extent the statement plays a role. A recent survey of the Canadian judiciary suggested that judges found victim impact statements to be useful sources of information,[144] but it was not clear specifically how this information was used in determining an appropriate sentence. The Ontario Court of Appeal has described the role of victim impact statements in the following way:

> Parliament has provided in s 722 of the *Criminal Code*, however, that the court "shall consider" such statements "for the purpose of determining the sentence to be imposed on an offender." The court must therefore take them into account; otherwise there is no point in having them. Whether victim impact statements may be used by the sentencing judge, in themselves, to increase or decrease the fitness of the sentence, is an issue I leave for determination on another day. What they do at least, in my opinion, is help the judge to understand the circumstances and consequences of the crime more fully, and to apply the purposes and principles of sentencing in a more textured context.[145]

Justice Bouck was similarly uncertain about the intent of Parliament:

> It is not clear whether Parliament meant that judges must impose a more severe sentence than is usual for a particular crime if there is a victim impact statement, or a less severe sentence if there is not. Nor is it clear whether the more grievous the loss suffered by the victim, or the surviving family of the victim, the more severe the sentence should be.[146]

Ultimately, Bouck J found that victim impact statements offered important information to the judge, without suggesting how this information should be incorporated into the complicated sentencing determination.

If the effectiveness of victim impact statements is measured by their influence on sentencing, it then would be impossible to say at this point whether they are in fact "effective." However, defining effectiveness in this way would be problematic. A sentence should reflect a defendant's

144 Department of Justice, *Victim Impact Statements at Sentencing: Judicial Experiences and Perceptions — A Survey of Three Jurisdictions* by Julian V Roberts and Allen Edgar (Ottawa: Canada Department of Justice, 2007).

145 *R v Taylor*, [2004] OJ No 3439 at para 42 (CA).

146 *Labbe*, *supra* note 119 at para 47.

culpability, not the relative worth of the victim. As judges have often remarked, "the criminal law does not value one life over another."[147] If victim impact statements were evaluated by their ability to elicit more severe sentences, then having "effective" victim impact statements would be undesirable for the reasons discussed earlier. In conceptualizing what victim input into sentencing should look like, we need to be cognizant of its potential to perpetuate racial, gender, class, and other forms of discrimination that are presently rampant in the criminal justice system. From this perspective, victim impact statements should have no impact on sentencing.

Victim Satisfaction with Criminal Justice System

Yet another possible effect of victim impact statements is improved satisfaction with the criminal justice system. It is assumed that victims will be more satisfied with their involvement in the criminal justice process if they are given an opportunity to voice the harm they have suffered.[148] This satisfaction in turn is expected to renew confidence in the administration of justice. For the few victims who take advantage of the opportunity to submit a victim impact statement, the preponderance of studies suggest that the process is perceived as unsatisfactory, particularly when the victims have raised expectations about their ability to influence a sentence.[149] Some victims are frustrated when their statements are edited by prosecutors for inappropriate content, including sentencing recommendations.[150] On the other hand, some research has indicated that the therapeutic value of having an opportunity to participate is more critical to victim satisfaction than how se-

147 *R v M (E)*, (1992), 10 OR (3d) 481 at 486 (CA), Finlayson JA, dissenting. Similarly, Southin JA remarked: "To my mind, it matters not if the deceased is young, promising and much-loved, or old, deranged and despised by all who knew him. The law ought not to measure the value of the life taken, for to do so would be to diminish every person's essential right to live out his or her appointed span": *R v Eneas*, [1994] BCJ No 262 at para 53 (CA).

148 Dean G Kilpatrick & Randy K Otto, "Constitutionally Guaranteed Participation in Criminal Proceedings for Victims: Potential Effects on Psychological Functioning" (1987) 34 Wayne L Rev 7.

149 See eg Erez, "Integrating a Victim Perspective," *supra* note 6 at 166; Edna Erez, Leigh Roeger & Frank Morgan, "Victim Harm, Impact Statements and Victim Satisfaction with Justice: An Australian Experience" (1997) 5 Int'l Rev of Victimology 37; Robert C Davis & Barbara E Smith, "Victim Impact Statements and Victim Satisfaction: An Unfulfilled Promise?" (1994) 22 J Crim Just 1.

150 Roberts, "Listening to the Crime Victim," *supra* note 142 at 378.

verely defendants are punished.[151] At best, research can be said to be inconclusive.[152]

This begs the question: if there is no consistent evidence that victim impact statements improve victim satisfaction with the system, and they are vulnerable to discriminatory application, why do we use them? One important reason is that they clearly offer some benefit to the functioning of the criminal justice system. Victims are easier to manage when they feel they have a role, despite the fact that many feel disappointed after the proceedings. Anthony Walsh argues that victim impact statements may be useful for their "placebo value," in that they give the impression that something is being done for victims.[153] Victim impact statements facilitate the co-operation of victims while also appeasing political pressures to involve victims in the process without challenging why they were victimized in the first place. The statements have the potential to divert attention away from systemic issues by focusing on individuals, both as victims and offenders. As Julie Stubbs and Julia Tolmie note, the individualized focus of criminal law "too often translates structural disadvantage into individual deficit or pathology and obscures gender and race inequalities."[154]

CONCLUSION

Martha Minow notes that "The stories of victims are attractive because they arouse attractive emotions. Possessing some aspect of victims' lives can engender a sense of one's capacity to respond, whether or not that

151 Deborah P Kelly, "Victims' Perceptions of Criminal Justice" (1984) 11 Pepp L Rev 15.

152 While an exhaustive overview of the potential benefits of victim impact statements to victims is beyond the scope of this paper, interested readers may wish to consult Roberts, *supra* note 124 at 371–72. Professor Roberts emphasizes the importance of giving victims an opportunity to communicate with the offender through victim impact statements (375–78). Further, in one qualitative study, sexual assault complainants "explained that they had been primarily motivated in the expressive purpose of the VIS" to communicate to judges and offenders the harm they suffered. See Karen Miller, *Empowering Victims: The Use of the Victim Impact Statement in the Case of Sexual Assault in Nova Scotia; The Perspective of Victims and Victim Services Staff* (Toronto: Centre of Criminology, University of Toronto, 2008) at 33, cited in Roberts, "Listening to the Crime Victim," *supra* note 142 at 364).

153 Anthony Walsh, "Placebo Justice: Victim Recommendations and Offender Sentences in Sexual Assault Cases" (1986) 77 J Crim L & Criminology 1126 at 1139.

154 Julie Stubbs & Julia Tolmie, "Battered Women Charged with Homicide: Advancing the Interests of Indigenous Women" (2008) 41 Aust Crim & NZ J 138 at 139.

capacity is exercised in any practical way."[155] Moreover, victimhood is appealing because "it secures attention in an attention-taxed world,"[156] a "precondition for any response, including sympathy or help."[157] This is the power of "genuine" victim status in the criminal justice system; without access to this status, those impacted by crime will be given no attention and no assistance. While sexual assault complainants and other marginalized victims of crime want the criminal justice system to be attentive to their needs, they have advocated for meaningful involvement at *all* stages of the criminal justice process, not token inclusion after the most critical issues have already been resolved.

As currently structured, the use of victim impact statements is left to the discretion of the judge. Julian Roberts, who has written extensively on the subject of victim impact statements, cautions that without adequate direction, judges will exercise their discretion in inconsistent ways.[158] The studies canvassed above suggest that they will also exercise their discretion in ways that are discriminatory.

If victim impact statements carry the risk of further subordinating already vulnerable groups, then they should be abandoned altogether, particularly if adequate safeguards cannot be put into place to protect these groups from discriminatory treatment. One commentator suggests that the rights of both victims and defendants could be better protected if victim impact statements were presented *after* the sentencing determination,[159] an option that warrants further consideration in my view. In any event, victim impact statements should not be relied upon as the primary response to the innumerable problems faced by victims of crime in the justice system. In addition to risking further marginalization of particular victims, this approach carries with it the danger that the state, believing its duty to victims discharged, will fail to pursue more meaningful action to remedy the systemic problems that persist.

Even assuming that victim impact statements have a role to play in sentencing, the daunting question remains: what *should* a court do with the information presented? We need to ask ourselves, in an ideal world, what we hope to achieve through victim impact statements? Do

155 Minow, *supra* note 20 at 1414.

156 *Ibid.*

157 *Ibid* at 1415.

158 Roberts, *supra* note 124 at 370.

159 Carrie L Mulholland, "Sentencing Criminals: The Constitutionality of Victim Impact Statements" (1995) 60 Mo L Rev 731 at 747.

we want to "potentially create a situation in which sentencing length may be determined by the eloquence and social standing of the victim rather than the severity of the offense and the specific underlying facts of the crime"?[160] How would an assessment of the victim's loss in determining sentences privilege certain victims according to race, gender, class, ability, and sexuality, thereby making some lives or harms more worthy than others? How do we ensure that women are not silenced "in the name of giving victims a voice"?[161] And finally, can the focus on individual victims and individual offenders ever address larger systemic harms, including gendered and racialized violence, and the roots of such crime? There is no question that our criminal justice system is failing women who have been sexually assaulted and other vulnerable groups harmed by crime. However, token responses, such as victim impact statements, will not remedy this failure.

160 Abraham Abramovsky, "Victim Impact Statements: Adversely Impacting Upon Judicial Fairness" (1992–93) 8 St John's J Legal Comment 21 at 21–22.

161 Henderson, *supra* note 6 at 585.

27. Confronting Restorative Justice in Neo-Liberal Times: Legal and Rape Narratives in Conditional Sentencing

Gillian Balfour and Janice Du Mont

Gillian Balfour and Janice Du Mont investigate one criminal justice response to perpetrators of sexual assault already problematized by Holly Johnson: the use of conditional imprisonment — or house arrest — for those few men who become convicted offenders. The authors are careful to disavow any claim that prison works or that such restorative measures should be eschewed entirely, but they argue that these decisions ordering house arrest reproduce the rape narratives discussed by Susan Ehrlich earlier in this volume. Gillian and Janice show how women are rendered invisible in these cases, even when they have submitted victim impact statements, and how they are assigned blame for their own rapes through the rationalization of the sentence. Their analysis of the decisions reveals how, through house arrest, the state reallocates the responsibility for policing and protection to individuals, much like the deployment of "police warnings" that assign women the impossible task of protecting themselves from rape, as discussed in the chapters by Lise Gotell and Meagan Johnston in Part I.

In the sentencing decision of *R v Tulk*,[1] a sixty-year-old white male was convicted of a serious sexual assault of a female acquaintance who was in a comatose state due to diabetic shock. He received a conditional sentence of two years less a day as part of a restorative justice sentencing practice that allows offenders to serve their prison sentences in the community subject to various conditions. Although we glean little from this sentencing decision as to the impact of the "highly intrusive assault"[2] upon the victim, we are told that the perpetrator was divorced, had four children, lived with his mother, and had a good employment record, no debts, and no problems with drugs or alcohol. However, the

1 *R v Tulk*, [2000] OJ No 4315 (Ct Just).

2 *Ibid* at para 13.

perpetrator also showed no remorse or guilt over his conduct, asserting that the victim consented to sex despite her medical condition. In the sentencing transcript, Paris J of the Ontario Court of Justice stated:

> The conduct of the accused was more opportunistic than calculated; he did not plan the meeting, he did not stalk the victim, he did not contribute to her incapacity … this event took place because of an unfortunate coincidence and a terrible lack of judgment. The accused used a condom probably to protect himself, but it also protected the victim from the risk of pregnancy and disease.[3]

Through a feminist lens, the legal and rape narratives in this case reveal how rape myths continue to be enabled through the practice of law. Despite decades of feminist inspired criminal law reforms intended to denounce sexual assault as a serious crime, rape myths remain ubiquitous in the strategies of lawyers. The legal narrative in this sentencing decision decries the perpetrator's lack of remorse as "the result of poor insight as opposed to moral turpitude … His testimony confirms his lack of sophistication."[4] The rape narrative too casts the perpetrator as a reasonable man: he did not stalk and overpower his victim. Rather, he was chivalrous in his use of a condom to protect her from disease and pregnancy.

While much feminist engagement with law as both legislation and practice has focused on the rape trial,[5] in 2006, Statistics Canada released "Measuring Violence Against Women" as part of their annual Statistical Trends series. The report shows "conditional sentences were

3 *Ibid* at para 14.

4 *Ibid* at para 15.

5 Karen Busby, "Third Party Record Cases since R v O'Connor" (2000) 27 Man LJ 355; Karen Busby, "'Not a victim until a conviction is entered': Sexual violence prosecutions and legal truth" in Elizabeth Comack, ed, *Locating Law: Race/Class/Gender Connections*, 2d ed (Halifax: Fernwood Books, 2006) 258; Elizabeth Comack & Gillian Balfour, *The Power to Criminalize* (Halifax: Fernwood Books, 2004); Lise Gotell, "Colonization Through Disclosure: Confidential Records, Sexual Assault Complainants and Canadian Law" (2001) 10:3 Soc & Leg Stud 315; Lise Gotell, "The Discursive Disappearance of Sexual Violence: Feminist Law Reform, Judicial Resistance, and Neo-Liberal Sexual Citizenship" in Dorothy E Chunn, Susan B Boyd & Hester Lessard, eds, *Reaction and Resistance: Feminism, Law, and Social Change* (Vancouver: University of British Columbia Press, 2007) 127; Lise Gotell, "Tracking Decisions on Access to Sexual Assault Complainant's Confidential Records: The Continued Permeability of Subsections 278.1–278.9 of the Criminal Code" (2008) 20 CJWL 111; Carol Smart, *Feminism and the Power of Law* (London: Routledge, 1989).

used in sexual assault cases more often than in cases of other violent crimes." Therefore, we would argue that the ways in which conditional sentences are justified in sexual assault cases should be of concern to feminist socio-legal scholars and anti-violence activists. Reasons given for conditional sentences in rape cases cast light on a new frontier of feminist engagement with the criminal justice system: do rape myths operate in the legal narratives of restorative justice sentencing practices? Does restorative justice signal the retrenchment of mythologies of the woman who has been raped, the rapist, and the act of rape? The implications of conditional sentencing as a restorative justice practice should be of particular importance to feminists.

The sentencing decision in *Tulk* was part of a larger quantitative sentencing study of 221 men convicted of sexually assaulting adult women between 1993 and 2001.[6] It was reported in this study that almost half of the perpetrators received a sentence of two years less a day. Researchers found that longer sentences were imposed on those sexual assaults that conformed to the conventional notion of rape (stranger perpetrated, weapons, vaginal, or anal penetration). Their findings echoed earlier sexual assault sentencing studies.[7] They also uncovered a small subsample of thirteen sentencing decisions in which perpetrators received a prison sentence to be served in the community, despite the seriousness of the offence and multiple aggravating factors, including the perpetrator's lack of remorse.

The present study seeks to unravel the legal and rape narratives of those thirteen judgments. Although a small sample, we suggest that these decisions signify the need for feminist engagement with sentencing law reforms that appear to be progressive in their constraint of the state's use of imprisonment, yet may be regressive when addressing gendered violence. In this regard, restorative justice sentencing practices may be the thin edge of a wedge that undermines, in part, the legacy of feminist inspired legal reforms aimed at denouncing sexual violence and securing the safety of women. Our concern lies in the possibility that rape myths have become enmeshed with the restorative justice ethos. In what follows, we first outline the contested terrain of Canadian sexual assault law reforms (Bills C-127, C-49, C-46) and the

6 Janice Du Mont, Tania Forte & Robin F Badgley, "Does the Punishment Fit the Crime?" (2008) 27 Med & L 477.

7 Adrianna McCutheon-Ciccone, "Adult Criminal Court Statistics 2002/03" (2003) 23:10 Juristat; Janice Du Mont, "Charging and Sentencing in Sexual Assault Cases: An Exploratory Examination" (2003) 15 CJWL 477.

emergence in 1996 of restorative justice sentencing principles designed to limit the use of imprisonment. Finally, we present and discuss the findings of our analysis of the legal and rape narratives in these thirteen conditional sentencing decisions and suggest directions for future feminist research.

RAPE LAW REFORM IN CANADA 1983–1992: KEY MOMENTS OF FEMINIST INSURGENCY AND ANTI-FEMINIST BACKLASH

Second wave feminisms throughout most Western democracies focused on, among other things, expanding the state's social and penal responses to sexual violence. In Canada, initiatives included provision of core funding for rape crisis centres, commissioning the largest-ever national telephone survey on violence against women,[8] and the creation of the Canadian Panel on Violence Against Women (1993).[9] In the legal context, feminist lawyers, scholars, and activists argued that institutional responses by the state to sexual violence had been framed by rape mythologies drawn from a wider patriarchal culture. Defined as "prejudicial, stereotyped, or false beliefs about rape, rape victims, and rapists,"[10] rape myths and their effects upon the rape trial and wider public attitudes towards women who have been raped have been well documented by feminist anti-violence researchers and activists.[11] Criminal trials, it has been argued, can become "pornographic vignettes" and a "celebration of phallocentrism"[12] through the deployment of rape myths such as "yes to one then yes to all"; "no means maybe"; "a woman who resists cannot be raped"; "women enjoy rough sex"; "rape is a sexual act that results from a woman arousing a man"; and "rape doesn't hurt anyone."[13]

8 Holly Johnson & Vincent F Sacco, "Researching Violence Against Women: Statistics Canada's National Survey" (1995) 37 Can J Crim 281.

9 Canadian Panel on Violence Against Women, *Changing the Landscape: Ending Violence — Achieving Equality* (Ottawa: Ministry of Supply and Services Canada, 1993).

10 Martha R Burt, "Cultural Myths and Supports for Rape" (1980) 38 J Personality & Soc Psychol 217.

11 Martha R Burt & Rochelle Semmel Albin, "Rape Myths, Rape Definitions, and Probability of Conviction" (1981) 11(3) J Applied Soc Psychol 212; Janice Du Mont & Deborah Parnis, "Judging Women: The Pernicious Effects of Rape Mythology" (1999) 19:2 Can Woman Stud 102.

12 Smart, *supra* note 5 at 35

13 Comack & Balfour, *supra* note 5 at 111.

In Canada, one of the first sites of feminist engagement with criminal law to constrain the influence of rape myths was the passing of Bill C-127 in 1983. The outcome was the repeal of the *Criminal Code* category of rape and the creation of three new categories for the offence of assault, the formal repeal of the corroboration requirement (physical evidence or third-party testimony) and the doctrine of recent complaint, and the addition of limits on the ability of defence lawyers to ask questions about the sexual history of the complainant, which became referred to as the "rape shield provision."

In 1992, the Supreme Court of Canada ruled that the rape shield provision violated constitutional legal rights of the accused, and was thus unconstitutional.[14] In response, Parliament passed Bill C-49, which codified rape shield provisions that met the Court's demand for judicial discretion with regards to consideration of evidence of the complainant's sexual history.[15] In addition, Bill C-49 codified a legal definition of consent along with the reasonable steps to be taken to ascertain consent to sex. Subsequently, defence lawyers continued to challenge the constitutionality of the revised rape shield statute, oftentimes doing an "end run" around restrictions on sexual history evidence by using third-party and confidential records of therapists or counsellors.[16] In *R v O'Connor*,[17] the Supreme Court of Canada held that the accused's inviolable right to a fair trial enabled defence counsel to request access to a wide swath of personal and confidential documents about the complainant. In the wake of the Court's decision in *R v O'Connor*, in 1997, the Canadian government enacted Bill C-46 to further constrain disclosure requests and to ensure closer scrutiny of documents sought by the defence for the purposes of discrediting the Crown's case against the accused.[18] In 1999, the constitutionality of the limits on defence

14 *R v Seaboyer*, [1991] 2 SCR 577.

15 Bill C-49, *An Act to Amend the Criminal Code (prohibiting the admission of sexual history evidence)*, SC 1992, c 38, s 276, 276.1, 276.2.

16 Gotell, *supra* note 5.

17 *R v O'Connor*, [1995] 4 SCR 411. The majority of the Court ruled that sections 7 and 11(d) of the *Charter* required that the Crown obtain all documents, including privileged communication records on the complainant, and make them available to the defence for the purposes of discovery: Comack & Balfour, *supra* note 5. As Lise Gotell explains, the Court prioritized accused's rights over complainants' "even though … no one has been able to cite even one Canadian case of an innocent man wrongly convicted by a fraudulent or deluded complainant": Gotell, "Colonization through Disclosure," *supra* note 5 at 320.

18 Bill C-46, *An Act to amend the Criminal Code (production of records in sexual offence proceedings)*, SC 1997, c 30, ss 278.1–278.9. Bill C-46 requires the accused to submit to

access to third-party records was again challenged in *R v Mills*.[19] The Supreme Court of Canada upheld the constitutionality of the process set out in Bill C-46 with regards to determining the probative value of third-party records.

While these legislative reforms marked the formal recognition of certain feminist organizations as legitimate authorities and "authorized knowers,"[20] Lise Gotell[21] has argued in her study of third-party records disclosure in sexual assault decisions that, defence lawyers use such evidence for its "non-sexual features," such as inconsistent testimony or a pattern of fabrication by the complainant, thus retrenching rape myths of raped women as liars, mentally unstable, or hysterical.

Also in 1999, anti-feminist backlash in the form of regressive judicial activism reappeared with a vengeance in *R v Ewanchuk*[22] where the Alberta Court of Appeal held that the perpetrator was entitled to the defence of implied consent — although no such defence existed in law — because of the young complainant's dress and conduct during a job interview. The Supreme Court of Canada overturned the acquittal of the accused, and threw out the defence of implied consent. Justices L'Heureux-Dubé and Gonthier also articulated in the decision a feminist analysis of "[v]iolence against women," characterized as much as a matter of equality as it is an offence against human dignity and violation of human rights."[23]

As this discussion has shown, the feminist challenge to the use of rape myths in the practice of law and judicial decision-making has

the same two-stage procedure for production of applicable to records held by third parties: disclosure to the trial judge and production to the accused. The first stage obliges the accused to establish that the record in the Crown's possession is "likely relevant to an issue at trial or to the competence of a witness to testify" (ss 278.3(3)(*b*) and 278.5(1)(*b*)). The trial judge must also decide whether disclosure to the court is "necessary in the interests of justice" and consider the salutary and deleterious effects of production on the accused's right to make full answer and defence, and on the complainant's or witness's right to privacy and equality (s. 278.5(1)(*c*) and 278.5(2)). If the first step is satisfied, the second stage involves judicial inspection of the documents to determine whether and to what extent they should be produced to the accused (ss 278.6 to 278.91).

19 *R v Mills*, [1999] 3 SCR 688.

20 Laureen Snider, "Making Change in Neo-Liberal Times" in Gillian Balfour & Elizabeth Comack, eds, *Criminalizing Women: Gender and (In)Justice in Neo-Liberal Times* (Halifax: Fernwood Press, 2006) 323.

21 Gotell, "Tracking Decisions on Access to Sexual Assault Complainants' Confidential Records," *supra* note 5.

22 *R v Ewanchuk*, [1999] 1 SCR 330, reversing (1998) 57 AR 235.

23 *Ibid* at para 69.

been a hard fought battle, with both successes and setbacks. But little is known however, of the role of rape myths in the sentencing of men convicted of sexual assault, especially in the context of emerging non-custodial practices, such as conditional sentences. We are concerned with how insidious rape myths intersect with ostensibly progressive sentencing reforms. We suggest that conditional sentences represent a new sphere of contestation for feminists to challenge the retrenchment of rape myths in the practice of law. This anti-feminist juridical space has opened up in part because of the socio-political context of neo-liberal social policy and law reforms that reflect a prudent approach to risk management generated from actuarial logics rather than an ethic of care and social responsibility.[24]

As neo-liberalism has dismantled the state's responsibility for the well-being of its citizens,[25] including federal policy advisory committees and publicly funded national women's organizations, feminist advocacy resources are under siege by neo-liberalism, and violence against women is receding from the political landscape. Some feminist socio-legal scholars have begun to map neo-liberal rape mythologies in law wherein women are held responsible for managing their own risk when the state chooses not to prosecute,[26] and when judges refuse to protect a complainant's right to equality.[27] Does this "neo-liberal sexual citizenship" identified by Lise Gotell[28] resonate within restorative justice sentencing practices? In what follows, we examine the principles behind the sweeping sentencing reforms introduced in Canada 1996, and query their impact on reasons for conditional sentences in sexual assault cases.

24 Wendy Brown, *Edgework: Critical Essays on Knowledge and Politics* (Princeton: Princeton University Press, 2005) at 37.

25 Dorothy Chunn & Shelley Gavigan, "Welfare Law, Welfare Fraud, and the Moral Regulation of the Never Deserving Poor" (2004) 13 Soc & Leg Stud 219.

26 Elizabeth Comack and Tracey Peter, "How the Criminal Justice System Responds to Sexual Assault Survivors: The Slippage Between Responsibilization and Blaming the Victim" (2005) 17 CJWL 282.

27 Karen Busby, "Discriminatory Uses of Personal Records in Sexual Violence Cases" (1997) 9 CJWL 258.

28 Gotell, "The Discursive Disappearance of Sexual Violence," *supra* note 5.

SENTENCING REFORMS: AT THE NEXUS OF RETRIBUTIVE AND RESTORATIVE JUSTICE

> [T]his is one of these rare occasions in cases of this nature where restorative objectives and objectives of denunciation, and deterrence can be achieved by a conditional sentence.[29]

The purpose of punishment remains a highly contested juridical and public issue.[30] Anthony Doob has stated, "Canada does not have a sensible and defensible sentencing policy."[31] In fact, public opinion survey data shows that most Canadians expect sentencing to accomplish everything from incapacitation and offender reintegration to denunciation, rehabilitation, and deterrence.[32] Since 1969, the Canadian government has issued reports and convened sentencing commissions to advise Parliament on sentencing principles.[33] In 1987, the Canadian Sentencing Commission called for a sentencing framework based on a series of principles that sought proportionality and restraint in the use of imprisonment. In 1988, the Daubney Committee authored a report calling for sentencing principles that reflected *restorative* objectives explicitly to acknowledge harm done to victims and the community, facilitate victim/offender reconciliation, provide offenders with opportunities for rehabilitation and, if necessary, denounce and incapacitate the offender.[34]

In 1996, the government of Canada enacted a statement of purpose and principles as part of Bill C-41.[35] A stated key objective in the pass-

29 *R v Tulk, supra* note 1 at para 17.

30 Michael Tonry, *Sentencing Matters* (New York: Oxford University Press, 1996); Andrew Ashworth, Andrew Von Hirsch & Julian Roberts, eds, *Principled Sentencing: Readings on Theory and Policy*, 3d ed (Oxford: Hart Publishing, 1998).

31 Anthony Doob, "Transforming the Punishment Environment: Understanding Public Views of What Should be Accomplished at Sentencing" (2000) 39 Can J Crim 323.

32 Anthony Doob & Jane Sprott, "Fear, Victimization, and Attitudes to Sentencing, the Courts, and the Police" (1997) 39 Can J Crim 275.

33 Canadian Committee on Corrections, *Towards Unity: Criminal Justice and Corrections* (Ottawa: Queen's Printer, 1969); Law Reform Commission of Canada, *Our Criminal Law* (Ottawa: Law Reform Commission of Canada, 1977); Government of Canada, *The Criminal Law in Canadian Society* (Ottawa: Government of Canada, 1982); Government of Canada, *Sentencing* (Ottawa: Government of Canada, 1984).

34 David Daubney, *Taking Responsibility: Report of the Standing Committee on Justice and Solicitor General on its Review of Sentencing, Conditional Release and Related Aspects of Corrections* (Ottawa: Ministry of Supply and Services Committee, 1988).

35 Bill C-41, *An Act to amend the Criminal Code (sentencing) and other Acts in consequence thereof*, SC 1995, c 22.

ing of Bill C-41 was to introduce a restorative justice paradigm to the practice of sentencing that balances objectives of denunciation with reparation to victims and communities.[36] To this end, section 718.2 of the bill also set out sentencing principles to ensure that:

> (d) an offender should not be deprived of liberty, if less restrictive sanctions may be appropriate in the circumstances; and
> (e) all available sanctions other than imprisonment that are reasonable in the circumstances should be considered for all offenders, with particular attention to the circumstances of aboriginal offenders.

Bill C-41 also contained a new sentencing provision permitting "conditional sentences of imprisonment,"[37] a term of imprisonment to be served in the community for those offenders who would otherwise be sentenced to a term of custody of less than two years. In order to render a conditional sentence, judges must be satisfied that a term of imprisonment of less than two years is warranted, based on the seriousness of the offence and the moral blameworthiness of the offender. Judges then have the discretion to rule that the prison sentence is to be served in the community under conditions such as house arrest, curfews, treatment orders, and/or community service orders.

Subsequent to the passing of Bill C-41, provincial courts grappled with how to interpret the new legislation. Some of the perplexing issues include whether sentencing emphasizes retributive or restorative justice. What is the difference between a conditional sentence and probation? Should serious personal injury offences be considered for a conditional sentence? Are judges compelled to hand down a conditional sentence in all cases where the sentence is less than two years? The Supreme Court of Canada was asked to interpret section 742.1 of the *Criminal Code* to clarify these matters raised in the lower courts. Broadly speaking, the Court held that conditional sentences can be considered in any case where a prison sentence of less than two years is appropriate.[38] Thus serious personal injury offences were not necessarily excluded from section 742.1. For example, in *R v Wells*, an Aboriginal man convicted of sexual assault received a sentence of twenty

36 David Daubney & Gordon Perry, "An Overview of Bill C-41 (The Sentencing Reform Act)" in Julian V Roberts and David P Cole, eds, *Making Sense of Sentencing* (Toronto: University of Toronto, 1999) 31.

37 Bill C-41; *An Act to Amend the Criminal Code (Sentencing)*, SC 1995, c 22.

38 *R v Gladue*, [1999] 1 SCR 443; *R v Wells*, [2000] SCR 780.

months to be served in the community because, as an Aboriginal offender, he is entitled to judicial notice of systemic or background factors that contributed to the difficulties faced by Aboriginal people.[39] As well, pre-sentence reports indicated community support and resources for the offender in the community.

Data suggest an increased use of conditional sentences in cases of sexual assault. Statistics Canada reported that for the year 2003–04, conditional sentences were handed down in 17 percent of all sexual assault convictions; most received a sentence of probation.[40] However, in a later study, conditional sentences were more likely to be handed down in sexual assault cases amongst all violent crime categories.[41]

We set out to interrogate the legal and rape narratives of conditional sentencing decisions to discern whether section 742.1 is the thin edge of a wedge that threatens to undermine feminist inspired law reforms. Decades of feminist legal activism successfully challenged pernicious lawyering strategies that exploit women's sexual histories and their confidential counselling records. As we have outlined above, such backlash against feminist legal victories revealed the sexism embedded in Canadian jurisprudence. In this study, we consider whether restorative justice in the context of neoliberalism is another possible site of anti-feminist backlash.

THE STUDY AND METHODOLOGY

The purpose of the current study was to examine whether conditional sentencing — as a practice of restorative justice — is enabled by rape myths, specifically in terms of the law's treatment of the raped woman, the context and impact of the rape, and the conduct of the rapist. The thirteen cases we discuss were taken from a larger data set of 136 reported sentencing decisions in sexual assault cases involving female adolescents and adults (fourteen years and older) heard in Ontario, between 1 January 1996 (following the enactment of Bill C-41) and 31 December 2001. These decisions were retrieved from Quicklaw, Canada's online legal research service that provided access to 2,500 searchable databases of full-text reported sentencing judgments for all provinces and territories. Quicklaw has been used by many social scientists in

39 *Wells, ibid.*

40 Marie Gannon & Jodi-Anne Brzozowski, "Sentencing in cases of family violence" in Jodi-Anne Brzozowski, ed, *Family Violence in Canada: A Statistical Profile 2004* (Ottawa: Statistics Canada 2004) 53.

41 Statistics Canada, *Measuring Violence Against Women: Statistical Trends* (Ottawa: Canadian Centre for Justice Statistics, 2006) at 53.

their studies of law's treatment of gendered violence,[42] including sexual assault against children[43] and domestic violence;[44] the role of expert witnesses in historical sexual assaults;[45] and the study of the impact of key court decisions upon sexual assault trials.[46]

The thirteen conditional sentencing decisions were analyzed quantitatively to discern offence, offender, and legal characteristics of each case. Following this, open coding was used to thematically analyze the text of each decision in order to explore both the legal and rape narratives in the context of restorative justice sentencing. With respect to observations made by other feminist scholars concerning the ways that rape myths have shifted in accordance with the expansion of neoliberalism,[47] it was our aim to determine whether these erroneous beliefs appeared to play a role in framing the strategies of lawyers and judges in sentencing processes. If so, what particular rape narratives are told in the context of restorative justice? To this end, we extracted legal narratives (reasons for the conditional sentence that refer to sentencing principles of denunciation, deterrence, retribution, and reparation for harm caused) and rape narratives (reasons for the conditional sentence that refer to cultural scripts about the raped woman, the convicted rapist, and the crime of rape). Narratives that contradicted our assertion about the place of rape myths in conditional sentencing practices were also identified and are discussed.

FINDINGS

Case Characteristics

In all thirteen cases, the perpetrator was known to the woman. Of these, five were an intimate partner or ex-partner. Four of the perpe-

42 Gotell, "The Discursive Disappearance of Sexual Violence" and Tracking Decisions on Access to Sexual Assault Complainant's Confidential Records," *supra* note 5.

43 Linda Coates, "Causal Attributions in Sexual Assault Trial Judgments" (1997) 16 J Lang & Soc Psychol 278; Linda Coates & Allan Wade, "Telling it Like it is: Obscuring Perpetrator Responsibility for Violent Crime" (2004) 15 Discourse and Society 499; Clare MacMartin, "Unreasonable Doubt? The Invocation of Children's Consent in Sexual Abuse Trial Judgments" (2002) 13 Discourse and Society 9.

44 Dianne Crocker, "Regulating Intimacy: Judicial Discourses in Cases of Wife Assault (1970–2000)" (2005) 11:2 Violence Against Women 197.

45 Clare Connelly, "Prosecution of Rape and Sexual Assault" (2002) 28:15 J Family Planning & Reproductive Health Care 17.

46 Susan MacDonald & Andrea Wobick, "Bill C-46: Records Applications Post-Mills, A Caselaw Review" (2004) JustResearch 14.

47 Gotell, "The Discursive Disappearance of Sexual Violence," *supra* note 5; Comack & Peter, *supra* note 26.

trators had a history of substance abuse, and a previous criminal record. Five of the offenders were noted to have a history of mental illness. Women were penetrated in eleven cases, and forced or coerced in twelve of the assaults. A weapon was used or threatened in two assaults, and the woman was injured in three. With respect to aggravating factors, helplessness of the woman was cited in six cases, seriousness of the offence in five of cases, abuse of position of trust/authority in four, lack of remorse in four, and abuse of a spouse or child in three of the cases. In almost half of the offences, there were three or more aggravating factors cited by the sentencing judge.

Emergent Legal and Rape Narratives

In what follows we discuss four themes that appear to support our contention that conventional rape myths that render women as liars or temptresses[48] seeking vengeance intersect with neoliberal sensibilities of rape. We explore the representation of women's experiences in legal narratives and how, through these representations, raped women are "responsibilized" for the traumatic impact of the assault. We also suggest legal narratives portray men convicted of rape as easily governed in the community through therapeutic management because their conduct is understood as the result of diagnosed sexual deviance disorders or poor cognitive capacity.

(i) Locating the Woman

Throughout most of the cases, we were struck by the invisibility of the raped woman in the legal narrative. Under section 718.1 of the *Criminal Code*, judges are expected to take into account several — often contradictory — sentencing objectives such as reparation for and acknowledgement of harm to the victim and community, as well as rehabilitation, denunciation, and deterrence through incapacitation of the offender when necessary, and rehabilitation. In this regard, judges may take into account victim impact statements and pre-sentence reports, if these are available. Yet, while we expected to find narratives of women's experiences of harm in our data, we found instead that, as noted by Rakhi Ruparelia,[49] victim impact statements have a limited and sometimes troubling place in sexual assault sentencing decisions. Victim impact statements are subject to judicial review and may be

48 Busby, *supra* note 5.

49 "All That Glitters is Not Gold: The False Promise of Victim Impact Statements," Chapter 26 in this book.

edited or disregarded if the content is deemed to be "fueled by a need for vengeance,"[50] portrays the accused in a negative way, or demands a specific sentence be handed down.

In this study, we found that judges frequently explicitly rejected the woman's statement, despite the seriousness of the assaults. In *R v SR*[51] (case 55), the perpetrator was convicted of multiple offences against his ex-girlfriend, including sexual assault with a weapon and forcible confinement (punishable up to a maximum of fourteen years in prison). Referring to the facts of this case, the presiding judge declared them to be "[r]epulsive, and terrifying ... the degree of violence, actual and threatened [could not] be dismissed out of hand."[52] At the same time, the judge's insistence that "the court is not bound by the wishes of the complainant"[53] reveals the judicial disregard for the victim's experience and fear of the perpetrator. This judge went on to cite case law, asserting that "the courts should exercise restraint in placing undue influence on the victim impact statement."[54] Ultimately, the seriousness of the assault in *R v SR* was overshadowed by the perpetrator's remorse and his willingness to seek therapy, through which, the judge explained, "[he] must be given full credit for his efforts to address his difficulties."[55]

In another case of intimate partner violence, *R v TS*[56] (case 78) we see a contradictory legal narrative with regards to the victim impact statement. In this case, the perpetrator was convicted of aggravated sexual assault against his wife of thirty years. When confronted by his daughters who tried to stop the assault of their mother, the offender also threatened to kill them and the rest of the family with a butcher knife. Despite the principles of sentencing that recognize breach of trust by the perpetrator as an aggravating factor, and the judge's assertion that "this was a rape, and a rape which occurred within a breach of trust, [which] is very, very serious,"[57] the offender was sentenced to a six-month conditional sentence. The rationale given by the judge in this case was that the victim (the offender's wife) stated in her victim impact statement that she did not want her husband incarcerated. The

50 Ruparelia, *ibid.*

51 *R v SR*, [1998] OJ No 1439 at para 14 (Ct Just Prov Div).

52 *Ibid* at para 14.

53 *Ibid* at para 25.

54 *Ibid* at para 26.

55 *Ibid* at para 35.

56 *R v TS*, [1996] OJ No 3761 (Ct Just Prov Div).

57 *Ibid* at para 28.

judge in this case reconstituted the victim's statement as meaning she did not fear her husband's reprisal in the community. In a bizarre twist, the judge asserted that the victim in this case was responsible for her own safety as she was instructed to contact her husband's probation officer if the perpetrator appeared drunk or was threatening towards her:

> In light of the position taken by his wife in the Victim Impact Statement, she can always go to the probation officer or the conditional sentence supervisor, and ask that a variation be sought.[58]

The sentencing judge expressed concern for the well-being of the perpetrator, as well as his perceived vulnerability to possible revenge by his wife:

> If the revocation of the conditional sentence is in the hands of the family, then we wind up in a situation where *he suffers the anxiety that for any reason they may choose to send him back to jail, should they revoke without good reason*. [emphasis added][59]

While the judge in this case appeared to be respecting the wishes of the victim by not incarcerating the perpetrator and handing down a conditional sentence, he did so reticently, worrying that the woman would seek vengeance by falsely or unfairly turning him in. We suspect that if a victim of a robbery asked that the offender not be imprisoned, the judge would reject that request and call for denunciation and public safety through incapacitation.

In contrast, in cases involving Aboriginal offenders, the narrative of the woman holds a decidedly different place in the sentencing process. It is true that only two of the thirteen cases we examined involved Aboriginal men convicted of sexual assault. Even so, the legal narratives were much different than those found in the sentencing of non-Aboriginal offenders. In *R v Kakepetum*[60] (case 4), the offender was from an isolated reserve community in Northern Ontario and had sexually assaulted two young girls as they slept. While on bail awaiting trial, he completed a treatment program, secured a full time job, abstained from drugs and alcohol, and expressed profound remorse for his actions. What is remarkable about this case is that the girls and community

58 *Ibid* at para 17.

59 *Ibid* at para 21.

60 *R v Kakepetum*, [2001] OJ No 1511 (Ct Just).

were consulted in the sentencing process in accordance with the principles of restorative justice. The Elders of the community requested that the offender reside in a different community out of respect for the girls and to denounce his behaviour. In this context, the restorative justice model appeared to be linked to the needs of the young women.

The decision of the sentencing judge contrasted with those other decisions we examined with respect to the way he challenged the use of imprisonment in sexual assault cases. In his judgment he stated:

> A substantial jail sentence would provide a powerful disincentive for men to come forward to acknowledge their sexual offending behaviour. Considering how widespread a problem that is in so many of our northern communities, it is my view that it is far more important to create an environment where men are encouraged to come forward and take responsibility for what they have done.... It would be bad public policy to be zealous about imposing a harsh sentence on this man if the net result is that we bury so many other cases.[61]

In another case involving an Aboriginal man, *R v BK*,[62] the perpetrator pled guilty to sexually assaulting his former girlfriend. As in the previous case, the offender, the woman, and their families participated in a "community accountability conference." This restorative circle process required that he publicly acknowledge his responsibility as well as meet certain conditions agreed upon by the community. These included a six-month conditional sentence with extensive conditions and two years on probation:

> The process resulted in agreement on the part of BK to complete ... a series of undertakings which address his rehabilitation and which include attempts to raise awareness within the community of the spectre of sexual abuse and to enhance the respect for the safety and integrity of women in the community.[63]

Thus, the legal narratives in sexual assault cases of these two Aboriginal offenders and the women or girls they assaulted countered the invisibility of victims in the sentencing of non-Aboriginal men. In contrast, the legal narratives of cases involving non-Aboriginal offenders seem

61 *Ibid* at para 9.

62 *R v BK*, [2000] OJ No 2708 (Sup Ct Just).

63 *Ibid* at para 6.

to reflect a neoliberal sensibility of the responsibilized "victim" who must manage her own endangerment. It is this narrative that we examine next.

(ii) Damaged but Responsible

In *R v Corcoran*[64] (case 151), the judge handed down a conditional sentence in a case of sexual assault involving good friends attending a party with college students. The judge noted that the woman had been very drunk the night of the attack, and had flirted with the perpetrator and another male friend throughout the evening. The offender in this case pled not guilty and refused to express any remorse for what had happened. Moreover, the woman underwent a withering cross-examination over her conduct on the night she was raped. Despite the perpetrator's lack of remorse, the judge stated in his decision that both the offender and the woman were blameworthy:

> [the offender] and KH themselves [were] to blame, that what took place that night would not have taken place if they had not been drinking and had not used marijuana in the early hours of the morning. It [was a] disastrous circumstance for [the perpetrator]. [He was] tainted for life having been found guilty of sexual assault. Ms KH [had] been emotionally damaged as a result.[65]

While the devastating impact of rape was noted by the judge, the woman was clearly responsibilized for the rape as she did not exercise proper restraint or caution while attending a social gathering with friends. Women have been long cast as responsible for their victimization because of their conduct and dress, and as lustful liars who deceive the courts as to their consent to sex.[66] But these conventional rape mythologies rest upon an explicitly gendered and sexist subjectivity, whereas in a neoliberal context, raped women are "victims" without gender or social location. Rather, they are responsibilized individuals who failed to practice appropriate self-restraint. In this way, we see the spectre of a neoliberal subjectivity in legal narratives.

Similar legal and rape narratives of the woman's responsibility appear in *R v Pecoskie*[67] (case 182). Here, a business owner sexually as-

64 *R v Corcoran*, [1999] OJ No 5165 (Sup Ct Just).

65 *Ibid* at para 28.

66 Busby, *supra* note 27.

67 *R v Pecoskie*, [2000] OJ No 1421 (Sup Ct Just).

saulted a younger staff person who was comatose from alcohol intoxication after a company dinner party. The perpetrator steadfastly asserted that the woman had consented to sex, and was simply "giddy and light headed." In this case, the woman comes clearly into view. Her victim impact statement had outlined significant personal trauma as a result of the rape, and the Crown called for a three-year term of incarceration, primarily because the offender was in a position of trust in relation to the complainant. The sentencing judge, however, disagreed with the Crown and instead evoked mythical notions of the perpetrator as gentlemanly and courteous, thereby diminishing the seriousness of the rape:

> [The offender] did not abuse a position of authority in relation to the victim ... [He] did not extol his conquest to others after the assault ... [He] did not brag about [having sex with the victim] and he did not speak disrespectfully of the victim.[68]

While the woman was profoundly traumatized by a violent rape, she was nonetheless viewed as less deserving of the court's sympathy:

> Through the victim impact statement, the complainant stated the event has had a traumatic effect on her life. She has suffered a loss of confidence, low self-esteem, a sense of shame, anger and distrust towards men, impatience with others, and less interest in sex than previously. She has suffered financially, including the loss of her automobile although her evidence at trial indicated a prior existing precarious financial situation. She had missed several car payments before the offence.[69]

In this way we glimpse the intersection of rape myths and neoliberalism; we are shown a rapist narrative of a perpetrator who is deemed undeserving of incarceration through the evocation of class and gender subjectivities of the breadwinner husband and father. Meanwhile, she is irresponsible and blameworthy.

(iii) Minimizing and Managing the Risk

Legal narratives in several cases invoked therapy as a condition of sentencing. Therapy functions as a key means of discipline by reframing the purpose of sentencing from denunciation and reparation to manag-

68 *Ibid* at para 12.

69 *Ibid* at para 4.

erialism. It is a neoliberal strategy that draws upon actuarial techniques of quantifying and assessing the "risk" offenders pose to the community.[70] In this way, "crime is a calculable, avoidable, and governable risk; and criminals are characterized as a risky population to be efficiently and prudently managed."[71] Thus, any threats to public safety posed by the conditional sentencing of a sex offender can be managed through the use of various rationalities, such as curfews, house arrest, and therapy. However, as Kelly Hannah-Moffat suggests, managerialism is not only steeped in objective categories of measurable risk: it is also gendered and class-based.[72]

For example, in *R v Markham*[73] (case 43), a medical doctor, with earlier convictions for sexual assault charges against nurses at other hospitals, was convicted of sexual assault and unlawful confinement against an intern under his supervision in the hospital in which he worked at the time. In this case, the sentencing judge asserted:

> In my view the offences of which [the perpetrator] is convicted are sufficiently serious and sufficiently aggravated by his violence and blatant abuse of his position of trust and authority .... [H]is conduct in the circumstances of this case was a betrayal of his responsibilities as a man and as a physician.[74]

Nonetheless, the offender in this case was handed an eighteen-month conditional sentence. This, despite his refusal to take responsibility for the charges in this case. The judge accepted the offender to be a manageable risk to society for several reasons. First, the perpetrator had sought out therapeutic help and was under psychiatric care for various mental health problems, such as "frotteurisme or touching without consent for sexual purpose";[75] second, he subsequently secured further professional employment as a physician (despite this being the context

70 Kelly Hannah-Moffat, "Criminality, Need, and the Transformative Risk Subject: Hybridization of Risk/Need in Penality" (2004) 7 Punishment and Society 29; Kelly Hannah-Moffat, "Moral Agent or Actuarial Risk Subject: Risk and Canadian Women's Imprisonment" (1999) 3:1 Theoretical Criminology 71.

71 Kelly Hannah-Moffat, "Criminality, Need, and the Transformative Risk Subject," *ibid* at 30.

72 Kelly Hannah-Moffat, "Moral Agent or Actuarial Risk Subject," *supra* note 66.

73 *R v Markham*, [1998] OJ No 5957 (Ct Just Gen Div).

74 *Ibid* at para 23.

75 *Ibid* at para 31.

of all of his assaults); and third, he was making child support payments to his ex-wife.

The legal narratives presented in *R v Markham* accomplish a reframing of sexual violence that erases the woman's experience of rape in her workplace and the abuse of authority as an aggravating factor. Rather than taking up the sentencing objectives of reparation of harm to the woman and denunciation that realizes the impact of sexual violence, this case reveals how the gender sensibilities of hetero-masculinity and professional breadwinner are engaged to reposition rape as a psychiatric condition that can be properly managed through treatment.

In *R v Pecoskie*, discussed above, the neoliberal qualities of the successful citizen (eg, business owner, breadwinner husband) were similarly used to justify the use of a conditional sentence with house arrest. The status of the perpetrator as the woman's employer was negated, or apparently irrelevant, to the determination of the seriousness of the offence and the appropriate sentence. Yet, his status as a business owner was brought back into view as a mitigating factor when the sentencing judge deemed him to be deserving of a conditional sentence. The judge stated that:

> [H]e and his wife run their business out of their home. They employ two or three administrative people and up to fifteen part-time help in a packaging and shipping warehouse. Although the business has supported the family adequately in the past, [he] said it is on the verge of doing much better in the near future.[76]

In another case, *R v Guthrie*[77] (case 149), a man was convicted of sexually assaulting his girlfriend. Throughout the rape narrative invoked in this case, judicial notice was taken of the past sexual relationship between the perpetrator and the woman, as well as the drunkenness of the perpetrator. Despite this, Guthrie is described throughout the legal narrative as man who has "made a number of changes to [his] life, for the good ... he is a new man; he has a new lady. She is here today to support him and she is pregnant."[78] The perpetrator received an eighteen-month conditional sentence subject to mandatory conditions of abstinence and alcohol treatment. While the legal narrative in this case re-

76 *Pecoskie*, *supra* note 67 at para 6.

77 *R v Guthrie*, [1999] OJ No 4566 (Ct Just Gen Div).

78 *Ibid* at para 28.

veals the resiliency of conventional rape myths of the rapist being "too drunk to know better," we also see how these myths are enmeshed with the responsibilization of the perpetrator to transform and reconstruct his practice of self-reliance.

In a similar fashion, in *R v CG*,[79] the perpetrator pled guilty to five counts of videotaping and sexually assaulting his wife while she was passed out. In his reasons for sentence, the judge highlighted the woman's voluntary consumption of alcohol and their previous consensual sexual relationship. Here conventional rape myths (eg her drinking alcohol and their past sexual relationship) were invoked. Although the perpetrator only pled guilty after his wife was forced to testify, his moral blameworthiness was decentred and, instead, the assessment of risk eclipsed the aggravating factor of the spousal relationship between the offender and his victim. His risk to reoffend was assessed through a psychiatric discourse of the typical sexual deviant:

> [the doctor] stated that Mr CG was clinically immature and lacking assertiveness with others, especially women. [The doctor] opined that Mr CG did not appear to be a typical sex offender against adult women in that he did not show the anti-social history, substance abuse, or sexual disorder commonly seen in chronic sexually aggressive men.[80]

Clearly, the prudent management of risk and the classification of a typical sexual offender had supplanted recognition of harm done to the woman and the community as the purpose of sentencing in this case.

(iv) "Embarrassment as Denunciation Enough" (*R v KRG*)

Another dimension of conditional sentencing is legal narratives of incarceration as excessively punitive, but only for those perpetrators with middle-class standing. As in *R v Markham*, we found in two other cases that hetero-masculine social capital (credentialism and professional occupational status) seemed to frame the legal narrative, where the embarrassment of being convicted was assumed to be denunciation enough. In *R v Khalid*[81] (case 133), for example, "[the offender] was a contributing member of society with a history of public service."[82] Sim-

79 *R v CG*, [2001] OJ No 1243 (Sup Ct Just).

80 *Ibid* at para 7.

81 *R v Khalid*, [1997] OJ No 3056 (Ct Just Prov Div).

82 *Ibid* at para 59.

ilarly, in *R v KRG*[83] (case 81), the perpetrator was convicted of repeatedly sexually assaulting his stepdaughter over an extended period of time. He denied committing the assaults, expressed no remorse, and yet received a conditional sentence of nine months. The perpetrator's conduct was described as an "aberration" and his character above reproach as he had demonstrated "an enduring work ethic":

> [H]e has otherwise responsibly discharged parental duties, most recently as a single parent for and the sole support of his teenage son and daughter by his first marriage. With a special interest in coaching and in organizing bone marrow donors, he has actively participated in community volunteer work. There is no reason to question the multitude of references attesting to his otherwise good character as an active member of society.[84]

Puzzlingly, when deliberating on a term of imprisonment in this case, the judge asserted "that the fallout may be more impactive if the offender has made substantial progress on a career path for which status may be lost."[85]

In an earlier study of the practice of law in sexual assault cases, Elizabeth Comack and Gillian Balfour found that professional men were often treated with leniency because of "devastating financial and psychological impacts of conviction."[86] Michael Mandel makes an important observation in this regard:

> The courts recognize it as a legitimate part of the sentencing function to determine the severity of the sentence on the basis not only of the nature of the offence, but also of the nature of the offender, not as an offender but as a social being. Part of this has to do with the criminal record but a good part of it has as well to do with the extent to which the offender fulfils his or her role in the productive apparatus.[87]

Critical criminologists have long stated that affluent white professionals are less likely to go to prison than racialized or poor people.[88] Thus,

83 *R v KRG*, [1996] OJ No 3867 (Ct Just Gen Div).

84 *Ibid* at para 15.

85 *Ibid* at para 28.

86 Comack & Balfour, *supra* note 5 at 142.

87 *Ibid* at 143.

88 Jeffrey H Reiman, *The Rich Get Richer and the Poor Get Prison*, 5d ed (Boston: Allyn & Bacon, 1998).

it is not surprising that conditional sentences in sexual assault cases are justified through the cultural representation of the bourgeois capitalist or white collar professional as unsuited for imprisonment.

We were surprised to find that men of little sophistication also received conditional sentences, but for very different reasons. Poorly educated and unsophisticated men also needed to be protected from the dangers of imprisonment. For example, sentencing judges in *R v Tulk* and *R v Ridings* accepted that the offenders were not predators, but instead men of limited intellect and low self-esteem. In fact, in *R v Tulk*, the lack of remorse demonstrated by the perpetrator was explained by the sentencing judge in this way:

> [He] does not seem to understand that there is an obligation to obtain informed consent. His testimony and statement to the police confirm his lack of sophistication.[89]

As well, in *R v Ridings*, which involved a fifteen-year-old victim and a forty-three-year-old perpetrator, the sexual assault was described by the judge as:

> … an isolated incident not in keeping with his general character. His inferior personality does not lend itself to manipulation. He did not use violence or the threat of violence to control the victim. He is not a threat to the community to re-offend. *On the contrary there is a greater threat that the perpetrator with his limited intellect would be in danger in a custodial situation.* [emphasis added][90]

CONCLUSIONS

From a feminist legal standpoint, conditional sentencing may undermine key feminist reforms that have called for sentencing courts to denounce rape as a gendered, violent crime. In this respect, even seemingly progressive legal narratives may signal a pivotal intertwining of neoliberalism and rape mythologies. Our data suggests that conditional sentencing decisions ultimately reflect both gendered rape myths and neoliberal discursive tendencies towards governance at a distance and self-disciplinary techniques, as these may be imposed on sexual assault offenders.

Although conditional sentences in sexual assault cases are exceptional, we observed disturbing patterns in these thirteen cases that sug-

89 *Tulk, supra* note 1 at para 15.

90 *R v Ridings*, [1998] OJ No 183 at para 13 (Ct Just Prov Div).

gest that conditional sentencing in this context may represent a new site of contestation and struggle for feminist activism. We acknowledge that these questions seem to presuppose imprisonment as the criminal justice response to sexual violence that feminists demand, and that alternatives to imprisonment cannot be denunciatory or coercive. While it is certainly not our intention to contribute to a neo-conservative ethos that "prisons work," and while we recognize the detrimental effects of imprisonment that can and do contribute to furthering the problem of violence against women,[91] at the same time, we challenge the criminal justice response to the harms of sexual violence as manifest in the practices of conditional sentencing examined in this study.

Since completing this study of conditional sentencing in sexual assault cases in Ontario, a series of sentencing law reforms have been enacted by successive minority Conservative federal governments that campaigned vigorously on a "law and order" platform, promising to enact regressive omnibus legislation that focussed on truth in sentencing. In 2007, conditional sentences became unavailable for sexual assault;[92] however, in March 2012 new legislation was enacted in Bill C-10 that jettisons the 2007 law and instead makes conditional imprisonment unavailable only for sexual assault prosecuted by way of indictment where the maximum sentence is 10 years imprisonment.[93] As Holly Johnson points out in her chapter,[94] 90% of sexual assault cases are tried summarily (level 1 sexual assault), and rarely as a serious personal injury offence.

At first glance such reforms appear to be a partial feminist victory in step with demands for denunciation and protection of women from sexual violence through the incapacitation of men who rape. Yet, most rapes are processed as level one sex assaults due to the complexities of police charging practices (see Holly Johnson's chapter), thus conditional sentencing is likely to continue, and indeed increase as prison overcrowding inevitably generates pressures on sentencing courts to utilize alteratives to incarceration. In short, sentencing reforms that call for greater use of incarceration do not address the substantive causes of sexual violence: gendered and racialized inequality and misogyny that

91 Laureen Snider, "Feminism, Punishment and the Potential for Empowerment" (1994) 9 CJLS 75; Laureen Snider, "Towards Safer Societies: Punishment, Masculinities and Violence Against Women" (1998) 38 Brit J Crim 1.

92 SC 2007, c 12 s 1.

93 Bill C-10, *The Safe Street and Communities Act* (assented to 13 March 2012).

94 Holly Johnson, "Limits of a Criminal Justice Response: Trends in Police and Court Processing of Sexual Assault," Chapter 24 in this book.

lie outside of criminal law. It is these gendered conditions of endangerment (feminization of poverty, deep cuts to funding for rape crisis centres, and lack of access to justice), that are the preconditions of sexual violence. Feminists find themselves at the cross-roads of how to engage with law so as to denounce sexual violence without being a part of the law and order regime.

Thus we believe that future feminist research should continue specialized sentencing studies of sexual assault cases to document and theorize the tactics of lawyers and how the form and fit of rape mythologies are woven into the legal narrative of punishment and harm. Feminist socio-legal scholars have had little voice in the discussions surrounding sentencing in sexual assault cases. Perhaps we should seize this opportunity to define a feminist understanding of harm and reparation.

28. A Feminist Remedy for Sexual Assault: A Quest for Answers

Constance Backhouse[1]

In this final chapter, Constance Backhouse returns us full circle to the very questions posed by Jane Doe's activism and the Garneau Sisters who followed her: what is a feminist response to sexual assault? As a historian, Constance looks back at harsh sentencing laws for convicted rapists, revealing how embedded they were and remain in racial fear of and hatred directed at Africans and African-Canadians. Looking forward, she argues that feminists should not support prisons and should continue to explore restorative justice options, advocating more, not less, delegation of self-governance to offenders, in contrast, perhaps, to the directions identified by Gillian Balfour and Janice Du Mont. Constance points to a 1974 Ontario decision that awarded compensation to the complainant as a criminal remedy as an example of how to ensure restitution for women. She urges us to divest from criminal law responses and instead invest in the creative possibilities for recognizing and reimagining the harm of rape that feminist artists and authors can offer.

"Imprisonment would be of no assistance to the accused." The sentence leaped out at me as I waded through the 1,202 reported and unreported sexual assault judgments I had assembled for research I was doing into Canadian legal history.[2] It was a statement from a judgment in the case of *Angione v R*, issued by the Hon Justice Edson Livingston Haines

1 I am indebted to Carly Stringer and Sabina Mok for their research assistance. Financial support from the Social Sciences and Humanities Research Council of Canada, the Law Foundation of Ontario, the Trudeau Foundation, the Killam Trust, and the University of Ottawa is gratefully acknowledged. A preliminary version of this paper was presented at the conference on "Sexual Assault Law, Practice and Activism in a Post-*Jane Doe* Era" held at the University of Ottawa on 6 May 2009. I have benefited greatly from the input of the audience at that conference. I also want to thank Diana Majury and Marilyn Poitras for sharing their ideas with me.

2 For a fuller description of the larger research project that culminated in a book, see Constance Backhouse, *Carnal Crimes: Sexual Assault Law in Canada, 1900–1975* (Toronto: Irwin Law, 2008).

and delivered in a courthouse in Windsor, Ontario, in 1974.[3] It was pronounced in an era when feminists, including myself, were likely to be demanding more and longer prison sentences for rapists. However, by the first decade of the twenty-first century, I had learned some harrowing things about how our prisons operate and the irreparable damage they can reap. By the time I first came across Haines's judgment in 2004, I had developed a growing respect for those who identify themselves as "prison abolitionists." Haines's earlier comment struck me as surprisingly prescient, and far and away ahead of most feminist sentiment of the time. It made me want to learn more about the case.[4]

The woman involved (whose understandable desire for anonymity will leave me to refer to her as the "complainant") was a twenty-three-year-old immigrant, who had come to Canada with her husband five years earlier from Eastern Europe. She worked as a hairdresser for Francesco Angione, a forty-year-old Italian-Canadian, who had opened a beauty salon in Windsor nine years earlier. Angione began to make unwelcome sexual overtures to the complainant on New Year's Eve 1972, and his behaviour escalated that spring until, on 4 June 1973, he forced himself on his employee as they were closing up the salon at the end of the day. He locked the front door and grabbed her by the waist. At the preliminary inquiry, speaking English with some difficulty, the complainant testified: "He told me to make sex with him, I said no, because I'm married, I don't want." She fought back, and in the struggle both were bruised, scratched, and bloodied. Angione was unable to perpetrate full intercourse, and ejaculated on the complainant's leg. She fled for home, and filed charges of attempted rape at the police station the next morning.

The matter never came to trial. The result can be laid, in part, at the feet of Angione's lawyer Frank Montello, an Italian-Canadian known as "the Dean of Windsor's criminal defence bar." He counselled his client against trial as soon as he discovered that the case had been scheduled before Haines, a judge renowned for his notorious anti-offender sentiments. Montello advised Angione to plead guilty to the lesser offence of "indecent assault." In fact, he told his client, "You didn't win the lottery, you got the worst judge to try you … a reasonable doubt never factors

3 *R v Angione* (1976), 26 CCC (2d) 474 (Ont H Ct); *R v Angione*, Archives of Ontario, RG22-1890, May-Sept 1974.

4 For a detailed description of the decision, see Backhouse, *supra* note 2 at Chapter 10. The facts and quotations that follow are all drawn from the sources listed above.

into his decisions." He cautioned Angione that if he went to trial before Haines, Angione "would do penitentiary time."

As part of a plea bargain arrangement, Montello convinced his client to offer to make restitution instead of jail. Other judges might have balked at the idea, but Judge Haines was reputed to be a "maverick." A Hamilton-born judge with working-class German and Scottish roots, Haines was also an "innovator" who loved to settle cases. He accepted the plea bargain deal and ordered Angione to forfeit $1,000 in cash, payable to the complainant. Judge Haines then wrote a decision in which he asserted that the criminal law could play an important new role in the "indemnification of the victim as an alternative to imprisonment."[5]

Legislation had been on the books since 1921 authorizing courts to order a convicted offender to make "restitution" to any person "injured" by the offence for the "actual damage or loss" they had suffered.[6] Haines took this a step further and claimed that criminal courts could also quantify damages for "pain and suffering." He noted that a restitution order made compensation of the victim part of the process of rehabilitation, and was much more useful than a fine to the government treasury.[7] Haines's novel efforts were short-lived. Before the decade was out, courts in Ontario, Manitoba, and Alberta all ruled that criminal courts had no authority to make financial awards to victims for pain and suffering. Other judges refused to follow the lead of the maverick judge, and the innovation was consigned to a mere blip on the radar.[8]

Reading this unusual decision decades later, one could admittedly identify cautionary flags. Judge Haines noted that Angione could pay this sum because he was a businessman of "modest means" unlike many criminals who were usually "without funds." He also noted that he was reluctant to order a prison sentence because it would ruin Angione's "one-man business."[9] Both class and male privilege were at work here. A lighter penalty was bestowed on a man of financial means, who could claim a respectable family background and steady skilled employment. There was no indication that the principle of restitution was one that should be applied beyond this limited group. Yet despite that, Haines's

5 *Angione*, *supra* note 3.

6 SC 1921, c 25, s 19. For more details, see Backhouse, *Carnal Crimes* at 278–79, 424.

7 *Angione*, *supra* note 3.

8 For details, see Backhouse, *supra* note 2 at 282, 424–25.

9 *Angione*, *supra* note 3.

decision stood in stark contrast to the advocacy that I, and many other feminists, were invoking in the 1970s and 1980s, demanding more jail penalties for rapists. Judge Haines's decision to opt for restitution was a step in an interesting new direction.

As I pondered the creativity of a lone male trial judge in Windsor in the mid-1970s, I began to ask myself whether I and other feminists had yet caught up. I queried whether we had taken up the task of properly interrogating the penalties attached to sexual assault, of searching for better, more effective, alternatives. As we struggle to eliminate sexual assault, one of the matters we most often neglect is the remedy. All of our efforts to bring more cases into the justice system, to eradicate the sexist underbelly and misogynist trappings of our laws as we process these cases, and to hold more rapists accountable in law, are only valuable insofar as we come up with a feminist remedy. Which takes us to the all-important question: *what is a feminist remedy for sexual assault?*

This preliminary paper poses more questions than answers, and represents only one feminist's sense of a starting-off point. The debate needs to be engaged much more fully throughout our diverse feminist constituencies before we come close to identifying solid answers. This article is a *cri de coeur* to urge us all to grapple with an issue that I believe we continue to ignore at our peril.

CRIMINAL PENALTIES: AN HISTORICAL REVIEW

It may be useful to begin with a brief summary of the long-term historical framework of criminal sentences for sexual assault.[10] It is worth remembering that the first criminal penalty attached to rape in Canada was capital punishment — death.[11] Despite its draconian nature, it was rarely exacted. I have not been able to determine when the last execution for rape took place in Canada, but it appears at least that no one was executed after the 1841 union of Upper and Lower Canada.[12] In 1873, Parliament added imprisonment from seven years to life as an

10 For a more detailed analysis of the sentences prior to 1975, see Backhouse, *supra* note 2 at 278–82, 424–35.

11 See, for example, *An Act for Consolidating and Amending the Statutes in this Province Relative to Offences Against the Person*, 4 & 5 Vict. (1841), c 27 (Province of Canada): "Every person convicted of the crime of rape shall suffer death as a felon."

12 Macdonald Papers, National Archives of Canada, MG 26A, Letterbook 11, no 854, 8 June 1868 letter from John A Macdonald to William Johnston Ritchie, Chief Justice, Nova Scotia. All convicted rapists were offered royal clemency to commute their sentences.

alternate penalty, but refused to remove the capital penalty from the statute books.[13] The thinking that lay behind this was deeply racist. Canada's first Prime Minister, Sir John A Macdonald explained, "We have thought it well ... to continue [the death penalty for rape] on account of the frequency of rape committed by negroes of whom we have too many in Upper Canada. They are very prone to felonious assaults on white women: if the sentence and imprisonment were not very severe there would be a great dread of the people taking the law into their own hands."[14]

The two options — capital punishment and a maximum of life imprisonment — found their way into Canada's first *Criminal Code* in 1892.[15] Preliminary research suggests that during the twentieth century neither penalty was popular in practice.[16] No one was hanged, and life terms were imposed exceedingly rarely.[17] Most judges tended to order terms of five to ten years' imprisonment, although occasionally they dispensed terms as high as twenty-five years, and as low as eighteen months.[18]

The absence of capital sentences in practice provoked no discernible push for a legislative repeal of the death penalty. Instead, Parliament moved to compensate for a perceived lenience on the bench by adding the penalty of whipping. Corporal punishment, specifically whipping, had been available for male offenders convicted of sexual crimes such as incest, gross indecency, indecent assault on a female, indecent assault on a male, and carnal knowledge of a girl under fourteen, since the cre-

13 *An Act to Amend the Act Respecting Offences Against the Person*, 38 & 39 Vict. (1873), c 94 (Dominion of Canada).

14 Macdonald Papers, 8 June 1868.

15 *Criminal Code, 1892*, SC 1892, c 29, s 267: "Every one who commits rape is guilty of an indictable offence and liable to suffer death, or imprisonment for life." Attempts were punishable by a maximum of seven years' imprisonment under s 268. See also RSC 1906, c 146, ss 299 and 300.

16 For a more detailed discussion of the research findings drawn from a research sample of 1,202 reported and archival sexual assault cases from across Canada for the years 1900 to 1975, see Backhouse, *supra* note 2 at 6–8, 281, 425–28.

17 In *R v DeYoung, Liddiard and Darling* (1927), 60 OLR 155 (CA), the court noted that the death penalty was no longer imposed "in practice." For a rare example of a trial judge pronouncing the death sentence in a rape case, see *R v McCathern* (1927), 60 OLR 334 (CA); the appellate court reduced the sentence to twenty years and twenty lashes. For details on some of the unusual cases where life imprisonment was ordered, see Backhouse, *supra* note 2 at 426.

18 For examples, see Backhouse, *ibid* at 426–28.

ation of the first *Criminal Code*.[19] Rape had apparently been excluded in deference to its already severe capital penalty. In 1921, the decision was taken to add whipping as a new penalty for the crime of rape in recognition that courts never, in practice, imposed capital punishment.[20]

Unlike capital punishment, which was not enforced, and life imprisonment, which was rarely enforced, whipping was imposed. The *Criminal Code* stipulated that whipping was to be administered with a "cat o' nine tails" in the number of lashes stipulated by the sentencing judge.[21] Judges ordered as few as five, and as many as thirty, lashes along with imprisonment, in some cases.[22] However, the propriety of corporal punishment was hotly contested, and such penalties became much rarer over time.[23] A Joint Committee of the Senate and the House of Commons on Capital and Corporal Punishment and Lotteries noted in 1956 that the courts rarely ordered whipping anymore, and recommended its complete abolition.[24] Parliament did not heed the call.

Other major changes, however, swept in at the mid-century mark. A harsh new approach to sentencing rapists was introduced in 1948. That year Parliament provided that individuals convicted of specific sexual offences, who were also found to be "criminal sexual psychopaths," could be sentenced to *indeterminate* periods in a penitentiary.[25] The sentence had to be based upon psychiatric evidence that the offender's "course of misconduct in sexual matters" indicated "a lack of power to control his sexual impulses," and that he was "likely to attack or other-

19 *Criminal Code, 1892*, SC 1892, c 29, s 957. See also RSC 1906, c 146, s 1060. Gross indecency was removed from the list by SC 1953–54, c 51, and incest by SC 1972, c 13, s 10.

20 *An Act to Amend the Criminal Code*, SC 1921, c 25, s 4 amended s 299 to read: "Every one who commits rape is guilty of an indictable offence and liable to suffer death or to imprisonment for life and to be whipped." See also *An Act to Amend the Criminal Code*, SC 1920, c 43, s 7, applying whipping to the offence of attempted rape. These penalties were continued in RSC 1927, c 36, s 1060; SC 1938, c 44, s 52.

21 SC 1900, c 46, s 957 provided that a "cat o' nine tails" should be used unless some other instrument was specified in the sentence.

22 For a more detailed discussion of the cases where whipping was ordered, see Backhouse, *supra* note 2 at 281, 428–29.

23 *Ibid.*

24 *Senate Debates*, 27 June 1956 at 873.

25 *Criminal Code*, SC 1948, c 39, s 43, amending s 1054A. The accused first had to be convicted of indecent assault on a female, indecent assault on a male, rape, attempted rape, carnal knowledge of a girl under fourteen or between fourteen and sixteen, or attempted carnal knowledge of a girl under fourteen. See also SC 1953–54, c 51, ss 659, 661–67, which added buggery, bestiality, and gross indecency to the list of offences. See also SC 1959, c 41, s 30.

wise inflict injury, loss, pain or other evil" on others.[26] In subsequent years, the term was changed to "dangerous sexual offender" and then to "dangerous offender." Reflecting the contentiousness of the concept, the criteria for designation also went through a series of tortured alterations.[27] The shocking thing was that the federal government never offered treatment programs for dangerous sexual offenders until 1971, and thereafter the treatment that was provided was largely ineffective and inhumane.[28]

Another major change occurred in 1954 when, as part of a sweeping general overhaul of the *Criminal Code*, Parliament finally repealed the death penalty for rape.[29] The twin remaining penalties of maximum life imprisonment and whipping remained in force until 1982, when they too fell victim to the waves of rape law revision inspired by feminist demands for reform.[30] That year, Parliament eliminated the term "rape," and restructured a range of sexual crimes into a "three-tiered" offence of "sexual assault."[31] Whipping was abolished, and significantly

26 The psychiatric evidence had to come from at least two psychiatrists, one of them nominated by the minister of justice. The minister had to review the case every three years to determine if altered conditions warranted release.

27 SC 1960–61, c 43, ss 32–40 expanded the definition of "dangerous sexual offender" to "a person who, by his conduct in any sexual matter, has shown a failure to control his sexual impulses, and who is likely to cause injury, pain or other evil to any person, through failure in the future to control his sexual impulses or is likely to commit a further sexual offence." It required annual detention reviews by the minister of justice. SC 1968–69, c 38, ss 76–80 changed the definition of "dangerous sexual offender" to remove the phrase "or is likely to commit a further sexual offence." See also RSC 1970, c C-34, ss 687, 689–95. The name was changed to "dangerous offender" in SC 1976–77, c 53, s 14. See also RSC 1985, c C-46, ss 752–61.

28 See Elise Chenier, "The Criminal Sexual Psychopath in Canada: Sex, Psychiatry and the Law at Mid-Century" (2003) 20 Can Bulletin Med Hist 75; Elise Chenier, "Stranger in Our Midst: Male Sexual 'Deviancy' in Postwar Ontario" (PhD Thesis, Queen's University, 2001); now published as *Strangers in Our Midst: Sexual Deviancy in Postwar Ontario* (Toronto: University of Toronto Press, 2008); Backhouse, *supra* note 2 at 430, 433–34.

29 *Criminal Code*, SC 1953–54, c 51, s 136: "Every one who commits rape is guilty of an indictable offence and is liable to imprisonment for life and to be whipped." Attempted rape saw an increase in the maximum penalty to ten years' imprisonment, with whipping: s 137.

30 RSC 1970, c C-34, ss 144, 145 continued the penalties found in the 1954 *Code*. The next rounds of legislative revision to rape law, commencing in 1975, and continuing through 1982, 1987, 1992, and 1997 were responsive to feminist lobbying that demanded the removal of some of the sexist elements in the law. For further details, see Backhouse, *supra note* 2 at 294–97.

31 *An Act to Amend the Criminal Code in Relation to Sexual Offences and Other Offences Against the Person*, SC 1980-81-82, c 125, s 19.

lower penalties were established for forms of sexual assault deemed less serious. The remaining historical penalty — maximum life imprisonment — was retained only for the top tier of "aggravated sexual assault," which was defined as sexual assault in which the offender wounded, maimed, disfigured, or endangered the life of the complainant.[32] The mid-level tier, which encompassed sexual assaults with a weapon, threats to a third party, multiple assailants, or causing bodily harm, was allocated a maximum penalty of fourteen years.[33] The lowest tier of sexual assault drew a maximum penalty of five years.[34]

Feminists have rarely taken a consistent position in the debates about the evolving criminal penalties for sexual assault. In the early twentieth century, the National Council of Women of Canada both refused to endorse, and then advocated, castration of some sex offenders, at the same time that it opposed whipping as a debasement of both the rapist and the jailer.[35] The Royal Commission on the Status of Women critiqued whipping in 1970 as "cruel and degrading."[36] Some feminists argued — successfully — that judges should be imposing *higher* sentences for sexual assault because harsher penalties might more fully signify society's repugnance for rape.[37] Others have argued — also successfully, ironically — that the maximum prison terms should be *reduced* in the *Criminal Code* because lower penalties might result in an increase in

32 *Ibid* at s 246.3.

33 *Ibid* at s 246.2. This tier included sexual assaults where the offender (a) carries, uses, or threatens to use a weapon or an imitation thereof; (b) threatens to cause bodily harm to a person other than the complainant; (c) causes bodily harm to the complainant; or (d) is a party to the offence with any other person.

34 *Ibid* at s 246.1. This tier was undefined, and included all forms of sexual assault not described in the middle and top tier offences.

35 Henrietta Edwards, "Report of the Committee on Laws for the Better Protection of Women and Children" (1917) National Council of Women of Canada Yearbook 107; Grace Ritchie England, "Special Committee on the Revision of the Criminal Code" (1917) National Council of Women of Canada Yearbook 150–54, as quoted in Veronica Strong-Boag, *The Parliament of Women: The National Council of Women of Canada 1893–1929* (Ottawa: National Museums of Canada, 1976) at 321, 379.

36 *Report of the Royal Commission on the Status of Women in Canada* (Ottawa: Queen's Printer, 1970) at 373.

37 Much of the anti-rape activism of the second-wave Canadian women's movement still remains undocumented, but I was one of a number of feminists who personally advocated more and lengthier prison sentences, in my public lectures to women's organizations and clubs, media interviews, and in high school, college, and university classrooms. See also Dianne Kinnon, *Report on Sexual Assault in Canada* (Ottawa: Canadian Advisory Council on the Status of Women, 1981), who argued that "sentencing often does not reflect the seriousness of the crime" (at 34), and recommended that "penalties must be brought in line" (at 79).

convictions.[38] A very few dissenting feminists have argued for reduced penalties in their own right, rather than as an instrumental tool to put more men behind bars.[39] At the Jane Doe conference, some speakers (including Madam Justice Claire L'Heureux-Dubé) critiqued courts of appeal for reducing prison sentences for rapists, while others (including Jane Doe) described themselves as prison-abolitionists. What is largely missing from these conflicting positions is an attempt to identify a remedy that we could confidently classify as *feminist.*

A FEMINIST REMEDY FOR SEXUAL ASSAULT: WHAT WOULD IT LOOK LIKE?

As we struggle with this complicated question, it may be less difficult at the outset to consider what a feminist remedy *is not.* With the greatest of respect to those who continue to believe that long prison sentences are useful, I would like to pose some cautionary questions. Have we considered the dangers of locking up large numbers of violent sex offenders in institutions that are steeped in cultures of masculinist excess? In prisons that are dehumanizing, racist, homophobic, and inherently violent themselves? If prisons disproportionately house the poor, the mentally ill, and members of racially subordinated communities, can we in good conscience continue to accept such institutions as part of a feminist strategy to eliminate rape? Shouldn't we insist that a feminist penalty must not have a disparate impact on the basis of race, ethnicity, class, disability, or sexual identity?

At the time the *Angione* case was decided, it was already quite clear that prisons neither deterred would-be criminals nor rehabilitated convicted offenders.[40] Criminologists then and now have insisted that there is no demonstrable connection between harsh prison penalties

38 Lorenne MG Clark & Debra J Lewis, *Rape: The Price of Coercive Sexuality* (Toronto: Women's Press, 1977), attempted to redefine rape as a crime of violence against women, rather than sexuality, and to argue for a range of penalties with some less severe options as a way of inclining more judges and jurors to convict.

39 See, for example, a public lecture by Christine Boyle, "Women and Criminal Law Reform" delivered in October of 1987 at the University of Western Ontario, critiquing feminists' failure to scrutinize the inhumanity of prisons. See also the race-based critique of Dianne L Martin, "Casualties of the Criminal Justice System: Women and Justice under the War on Drugs" (1993) 6 CJWL 305; Dianne L Martin, "Retribution Revisited: A Reconsideration of Feminist Criminal Law Reform Strategies" (1998) 36 Osgoode Hall LJ 151. See also Laureen Snider, "The Potential of the Criminal Justice System to Promote Feminist Concerns" (1990) 10 Stud L Pol'y & Soc 143; "Feminism, Punishment, and the Potential for Empowerment" (1994) 9 Can J L & Soc 75.

40 For more details on the literature and the jurisprudence recognizing this, see Backhouse, *supra note* 2 at 281–82, 433–34.

and deterrence.[41] Instead, prisons are breeding grounds for cruelty, hatred, disease, self-mutilation, and suicide. Prisons are institutions that are filled with fear, illness, and caustic brutality themselves.[42] If prisons are designed to make our society safer, they fail abysmally since they turn out offenders who are more dysfunctional, more prone to criminal activity, than before. Furthermore, do we know what is being administered to sex offenders in the way of therapy and counselling? Have we interrogated the so-called "treatment" provided to rapists in prison, to ask if it dismantles coercive male sexuality in ways that are respectful of feminist ideals?

Prisoners testifying in Canadian courts have offered terrifying documentation about the grim consequences of solitary confinement — the torture that it inflicts upon the human mind and spirit, and the appalling insanity and psychopathic rage that can result. Buried in small concrete vaults, beaten and tear-gassed by guards, segregated prisoners experience hallucinations and psychotic disorders that provoke unremitting loathing and hatred.[43] Yet we know that rapists often serve long stretches of solitary confinement because the guards cannot guarantee their safety within prisons that are, to all practical purposes, ungovernable.

We have known ever since Susan Brownmiller published *Against Our Will: Men, Women and Rape,* that sexual assault runs rampant in prison. Inmates consistently target rapists, youth, and individuals perceived as "feminine" or "homosexual" for brutal sexual abuse.[44] How can it be a feminist remedy to consign rapists to institutions where they are at grave risk of rape themselves? If we are against rape, we are against all rape. If we are against violence, can we advocate sending offenders to prisons that are steeped in brutality, where lawlessness

41 For reference to the expert testimony of Dr Anthony Doob, one of Canada's leading criminologists, on the inefficacy of prison sentences, see *Regina v Hamilton* (2003), 172 CCC (3d) 114 (Ont Sup Ct).

42 See, for example, Angela Y Davis, *Are Prisons Obsolete?* (New York: Seven Stories Press, 2003).

43 See, for example, the vivid testimony given by Jack McCann and fellow inmates at the trial of *McCann et al v R* (1975), 29 CCC (2d) 337, 68 DLR (3d) 661 (Fed Ct (TD)), where the penal conditions surrounding solitary confinement were found to constitute "cruel and unusual punishment" under the *Canadian Bill of Rights.* For more details, see Michael Jackson, *Prisoners of Isolation* (Toronto: University of Toronto Press, 1983) at 42–80. See also Claire Culhane, *No Longer Barred from Prison: Social Injustice in Canada* (Montreal: Black Rose Books, 1991).

44 Susan Brownmiller, *Against Our Will: Men, Women and Rape* (New York: Bantam, 1975) at 285–97.

reigns supreme?[45] Justice Haines concluded in *Angione* that "Imprisonment would be of no benefit to the accused." As feminists, we need to reflect on the accuracy of that diagnosis. Indeed, we need to ask ourselves whether imprisonment of rapists "would be of no benefit" to the rest of us too.

I suspect that, at its core, much of our historic commitment to prisons has been based on what penologists describe as the principle of "retribution" or "vengeance." This is what we hear endlessly from media interviews with family and friends of victims of crime, who criticize what they perceive to be lenient prison sentences. "An eye for an eye," and so forth. The legitimacy of vengeance is rarely contested, but should feminists be so confident of its value? It may have historic origins that run centuries deep, but is it truly an "innate" and "immutable" need? Can we imagine a world in which feminists critique the social construction of this emotion called "vengeance"? Is vengeance something feminists should work to reduce? Conversely, are "compassion" and "hope" human feelings feminists should prefer? Do victims' rights and offenders' needs always have to be lined up on opposite sides?

Another long-standing principle of penology has been labelled "denunciation" — in this case, a desire to have society recognize sexual assault as a heinous crime, and to create a sentence that publicly marks the full harm done. This seems less contestable as a fundamental feature of what we might come to identify as a feminist remedy. It is important to signal symbolically that sexual assault is grievously wrong, and has enormous consequences. More complicated is the question of how we can best communicate our collective denunciation of sexual assault. Is it possible to separate denunciation and retribution? Can we accomplish the legitimate goal of denunciation while not inflicting disproportionate harm in the process of symbolic public shaming? What, apart from long prison sentences, might feminists imagine instead? What if we were to take some of the money now used for building and maintaining segregation prison cells, and use it to retain the services of talented feminist artists and writers? Could their concerted efforts produce a more fulsome and effective public commemoration of the harm of sexual assault?

45 For a discussion of the absence of due process and rule of law within prisons, see Debra Parkes, "A Prisoners' Charter? Reflections on Prisoner Litigation under the *Canadian Charter of Rights and Freedoms*" (2007) 40 UBC L Rev 629; Debra Parkes, "Ballot Boxes Behind Bars: Toward the Repeal of Prisoner Disenfranchisement Laws" (2004) 13 Temp Political & Civil Rights L Rev 71.

Is "restitution," like denunciation, another principle that feminists can support? Those who have been sexual assaulted often have physical and psychological injuries and costs that should not fall on their shoulders. The legal system has traditionally forced wrong-doers to pay those they harm an award of quantified pecuniary damages. Many of us agree that sexual assault perpetrators should pay for their crimes. We have rightly critiqued the civil justice system for the sexist thinking that diminishes the calculation of damages owed to female (and male) survivors of sexual assault. However, we also need to ask whether compensatory remedies must always be paid by the perpetrator of the crime individually. If so, there are inherent class biases built into this remedy, for only those who are assaulted by offenders with assets can obtain compensation. Is it preferable to have those who have suffered injury from sexual assault be compensated by the wider society?

Criminal injuries compensation boards have been set up in most provinces in recognition that victims of crime should be aided financially from public revenues. These systems are deeply flawed in design and execution, but the concept itself may hold great promise. Feminists should ask ourselves whether we might profitably focus increased energy toward substantial improvement in this direction. We should also look more closely at some of the "alternate dispute resolution" (ADR) processes that have been created to compensate victims of institutional sexual abuse. Is there a way to restructure future ADR processes so that they become explicitly feminist?[46] What would that mean? How might we construct feminist applications for redress, create feminist rules of evidence and procedure, select feminist adjudicators, and develop feminist forms of ADR decision making?

Female victims of sexual crime often complain that money is not an appropriate tool, and that the commercialization of this harm can be deeply insulting. Still others insist that money is the coin of the realm, that it offers the fullest recognition one can have of the harm based on our society's most deeply held principles. Is money a feminist remedy, or an insult to feminist thinking? Are there other ways of achieving "restitution" that are not monetary? Survivors of sexual assault continue to suffer untold pain from the stigma that so unfairly results in

46 For a discussion of one example of an attempt to create a feminist ADR process for the compensation of female adult survivors of emotional, physical, and sexual abuse in an Ontario juvenile delinquency facility, see Reg Graycar & Jane Wangmann, *Redress Packages for Institutional Child Abuse: Exploring the Grandview Agreement as a Case Study in 'Alternative' Dispute Resolution* (2007) Sydney Law School, Legal Studies Research Paper No 07/50, 1–43.

self-blame and societal condemnation. Are there restitution projects that would help to eradicate this undeserved stigma?

And what can we learn from those who have begun to experiment with "restorative justice" alternatives to the current criminal system? Influenced by Aboriginal perspectives in part, these programs have occasionally offered useful options, and have other times been critiqued by feminists for their inability to surmount male sexual privilege. Is this a promising direction? Could we imagine restorative justice remedies in which offenders were required to take responsibility for setting the terms of their own penalties, rather than having all the terms imposed by external agencies? Recognizing that we must guard against manipulation and shamming that often can mar offender participation, can we explore options that would encourage perpetrators to take more responsibility for the harms they have caused?

Penalties are assessed case by case under our current legal system, and imposed individual by individual on people who are scrutinized by lawyers, court officials, and judges seeking to measure criminal responsibility. Yet rarely do we inquire fully into the life experiences that bring offenders to these deplorable situations. We know full well from the backgrounds of criminalized women that agonizing histories of abuse precede most of their acts. Is it so different for male offenders? If we find out that it is not, can feminists fairly ignore the emotional, physical, and sexual violence during childhood and adolescence that goes into creating the men who commit sexual assault? We speak of the offender's debt to the sexually assaulted woman and to society at large, but shouldn't we also make the penalty reflect society's debt to the criminal? And if sexual assault originates within a deeply rooted culture of misogyny, can individualized penalties ever hope to address systemic problems? How can we develop a penalty that goes to the root of the act, attacking the causes of sexual assault rather than the symptoms? Can we conceive of a penalty that will contribute to a reduction in misogyny and sexism, one that will also avoid any reinforcement of masculinist cultures and behaviours?

Why have feminists for so long failed to interrogate the issue of remedies for sexual assault deeply? Have we been overwhelmed with the efforts of trying to address the needs of women and children who have been sexually abused, an immense and compelling project saddled with too few resources and too little societal support? Have we not had the stomach to turn to offenders and ask what feminists should do with them? Have we simply been bewildered as to how to construct feminist answers to this difficult question? We need to consider what barriers impede us in this task, and how we can dismantle them. It is not acceptable to say — this can wait. We have waited too long already.

I am conscious that I have demanded much, while offering little in the way of clear-cut direction. So I would like to close with an imaginary tale.

> *In the year 2010, in celebration of the "50th anniversary" of the second wave feminist movements in Canada and Quebec,*[47] *the newly elected government of the Feminist Party of Canada chose to release immediately from prison all of the inmates who could be designated as non-violent. The millions of dollars freed up from the budget for corrections — over $110,000 per inmate released per year*[48] *— were turned over to the newly established "Feminist Action-Research Institute* [FARI]."
>
> *Jane Doe, the first president if the FARI, appointed a shockingly diverse cast of characters to serve as a board of directors, and opened store-front offices stretching across Canada, from urban centres like Vancouver, Montreal, and St. John's, to smaller, rural communities like Lumsden, Leamington, and Pincher Creek.*
>
> *FARI hired hundreds of grass-roots activists and counsellors from the anti-violence-against-women movement, and paired them with feminists from a cross-section of disciplines: sociologists, criminologists, psychologists, psychiatrists, social workers, physicians, lawyers, and historians. Some observers expressed amazement that so many feminists had infiltrated these traditionally male-stream fields. Feminists just smiled. Feminist artists, authors, playwrights, film-makers, dancers, and musicians were added to the group to ensure that no one would think that FARI intended business as usual.*
>
> *The FARI mission? To eliminate sexual assault from the culture, to provide redress to survivors, and to find treatments* that would fully rehabilitate rapists.

47 Canadian feminists selected 2010 to celebrate the "50th birthday" for second-wave feminism because historians trace the origins of this wave to 1960, with the founding of the Voice of Women in both Anglophone and Francophone Canadian communities. Building upon this, the decade of the 1960s witnessed the appointment of the Royal Commission on the Status of Women, the establishment of the Fédération des Femmes du Québec, and the Association féminine d'éducation et action sociale, and the creation of a large number of "women's liberation" groups across the country. (The second wave is described as "second" because there was a "first wave" that ran from the late nineteenth to the early twentieth century.)

48 In 2006, it cost Corrections Canada $110,223 to keep a male inmate in a maximum-security institution for a year ($150,867 for a woman). Medium- and minimum-security inmates cost more than $70,000 a year. See Ira Basem, "Doing the Crime and Doing the Time" CBC.ca Reality Check Team, 5 January 2006, online: <http://www.cbc.ca/canadavotes2006/realitycheck/crimetime.html> (accessed 9 April 2009).

Inspired by the freshness of the task, bolstered by full funding for the first time in their lives, and energized by the collective decision to put aside old schisms within the movement, the feminists seized upon the ambitious mandate with glee. Interviewed by a feminist journalist from the National Feminist Post, *who inquired why more of the staff were not daunted by the scope of the project, Jane Doe scoffed: "How could we fail? Look around you. Can feminists possibly do worse?"*

Afterword

Jane Doe

This book represents a transformation. A conscious, lovingly-crafted collection of thought, theory, and research, born of a feminist conference in 2009. There, for the first time any of us could remember, women who are experts on rape came together to dialogue proactively — and not in response to a current legal atrocity or funding cut, or in competition or crisis. It was as if by magic.

Okay, not magic at all, but hard work, and then, something thrilling that captured us on those two winter days, warmed us, reminded us of community, its power and comfort, the exhilaration it can produce. Presentations from around the globe — about sexual assault of all things! — filled us up, made us giddy with possibility, validated our work and what we knew, introduced us to new thought and concepts. We were revitalized, renewed, transformed. And then we all went home, back to our agencies, institutions, and bureaucracies, back to our homes, reserves, and shelters. But transformation is an ongoing process and, like any good process, has multiple stages to connect, layers to mix and mash, fears to be defined and understood. This book is a layer, a piece we did not have before, a building block.

Formal comments about the conference were glorious and called overwhelmingly for more. Since then women have been raped and murdered at unprecedented rates: raped for war, for sport(s), for marriage, in pursuit of university degrees, because of poverty, disability, race, and immigration. Raped for all manner of reasons and institutions and lack of cause; raped because they are women. Funds have been cut and legal atrocities abound in Canada and globally. As it ever was.

But here is the difference, the magic. Here in these pages, this art, the very thing you hold, is the prospect to transform, to stimulate, and to inform yourself and others about one of our most grievous and systemic of crimes. Now, if all of this is sounding a bit too grand or esoteric, let me put it another way. This is the textbook you want in your law classes, as well as in journalism, medicine, social work, and the humanities — in all of the disciplines that impact and influence our responses to sexual assault and the women who experience it. Tell your professors and administrators. *Sexual Assault in Canada: Law, Legal Practice and Women's Activism* will assist all of us in beginning to understand rape. And, when we do, we can craft meaningful solutions and resolutions.

Let's get started.

Contributors

CONSTANCE BACKHOUSE is a Professor of Law at the University of Ottawa. She has published a number of books, including *Petticoats and Prejudice: Women and Law in Nineteenth-Century Canada* (1991); *Challenging Times: The Women's Movement in Canada and the United States* (1992); *Colour-Coded: A Legal History of Racism in Canada, 1900–1950* (1999); *The Heiress vs the Establishment: Mrs. Campbell's Campaign for Legal Justice* (2004); and *Carnal Crimes: Sexual Assault Law in Canada 1900–1975* (2008). She served as an adjudicator for the compensation claims arising from the physical, sexual, and psychological abuse of the former inmates of the Grandview Training School for Girls (1995–98), and for the former students of Aboriginal residential schools across Canada. She is a member of the board of directors for the Claire L'Heureux-Dubé Fund for Social Justice, and for the Women's Education and Research Foundation. She is the co-author, with Leah Cohen, of the first book on sexual harassment published in Canada, *The Secret Oppression: Sexual Harassment of Working Women* (Toronto: Macmillan, 1979).

NATASHA BAKHT (BA, MA, LLB, LLM) is an Associate Professor in the University of Ottawa's Faculty of Law. She teaches criminal law, family law, and multicultural rights in liberal democracies. She was called to the bar of Ontario in 2003 and then served as a law clerk to Justice Louise Arbour at the Supreme Court of Canada. Her research interests are focused generally in the area of law, culture, and minority rights, and specifically in the intersecting area of religious freedom and women's equality. She has written extensively on the issue of religious arbitration in family law and has edited a collection of essays, entitled *Belonging and Banishment: Being Muslim in Canada*, published by TSAR Publications. Her most recent work examines opposition to women who wear the niqab in the courtroom context and she urges that accommodations should be available for such a religious practice. She was a member of the Law Program Committee of the Women's Legal Education and Action Fund LEAF from 2005–2009 and the *R v NS* subcommittee. She also tours internationally as a dancer and choreographer.

GILLIAN BALFOUR is an Associate Professor of Sociology at Trent University in Peterborough, Ontario, where she teaches in the areas of critical criminology and socio-legal theories. Her research interests include neoliberal reframing of institutional responses to sexual violence, such as sentencing in rape cases that focuses on therapeutic control of risk rather than reparation for harm and denunciation, and how the criminal justice system organizes the relationship between women's victimization, criminalization, and incarceration. She has published, with Elizabeth Comack, two edited books: *The Power to Criminalize: Violence, Inequality and the Law*, and *Criminalizing Women: Gender and (In)Justice in Neo-Liberal Times*. She has also published in the *International Review of Victimology and Feminist Criminology*, where she examines how restorative justice sentencing in Canada has become a site of backlash against feminist inspired law reforms.

SHARY BOYLE is a Toronto-based artist whose practice includes drawing, painting, sculpture, and performance. In 2003, she created a series of illustrations to accompany the text of *The Story of Jane Doe*. Her work is exhibited and collected internationally, with pieces in the National Gallery of Canada; le Musée Des Beaux Arts in Montreal; the Paisley Museum in Scotland; and la Maison Rouge in Paris. *Flesh and Blood*, Boyle's first solo national touring exhibition, was presented at the Art Gallery of Ontario, le galerie de l'UQAM in Montreal, and the Contemporary Art Gallery in Vancouver in 2010–2011. Shary Boyle is the 2009 recipient of the Art Gallery of Ontario's Iskowitz Award and the 2010 Hynatyshyn Award for her outstanding contribution to the visual arts in Canada.

GILLIAN CALDER is an Associate Professor in the University of Victoria's Faculty of Law. Since her appointment in July 2004, she has taught constitutional law, family law, civil liberties, and advanced family law. Her current research interests include law's regulation of women, work, and family; the provision of social benefits through Canadian law; feminist, constitutional, and equality theories; and the relationship between performance and law.

MARIA CAMPBELL is a Métis storyteller from Saskatchewan. She was the eldest daughter of seven children born to parents of Scottish, Indian, and French descent. She is best known for her autobiography, *Half-breed*, which relates her struggles as a Métis woman in Canadian society. She has received many awards for her writing, including honorary doctorates in letters from both York University and Athabasca University, and honorary doctorates in laws from the University of Regina and the University of Ottawa. The Métis Nation also honoured her for her community work, especially with women and children, with the Gabriel Dumont Medal for Merit. Through 2000–2001, she was the Stanley Knowles Distinguished Visiting Professor at Brandon University. She currently serves as an Elder-in-residence at Athabasca University, as a mentor for the Trudeau Foundation and as the writer-in-residence at the University of Winnipeg. She received the Order of Canada for her contribution to Canadian literature and society.

PRISCILLA CAMPEAU is Cree and Métis from Saskatchewan. An advocate for Aboriginal women's rights and Indigenous education, she has worked for Athabasca University for ten years and is the acting director of the Centre for World Indigenous Knowledge and Research. She has published in *Cultural Survival Quarterly* and *Canadian Woman Studies*, and has published an online article on violence against Aboriginal women. Along with Maria Campbell and Tracey Lindberg, she is working with Purich Publishing to complete a book on colonial violence, colonial law, and the impact on Indigenous women.

BLAIR CREW, BA, LLB, LLM, is review counsel for the criminal division at the University of Ottawa Community Legal Clinic and an associate at Greenspon, Brown and Associates, Ottawa, where his practice includes a focus on representing women in actions for sexual battery and in actions against public authorities, including the police. He teaches an introductory course in criminal law in the University of Ottawa's Faculty of Law, and is particularly thrilled to have had the humbling opportunity to introduce, in collaboration with Professors Elizabeth Sheehy and Daphne Gilbert, the new course *Sexual Assault Law* in the fall of 2008.

JULIE DESROSIERS is an Associate Professor at the Faculty of Law at Université Laval. Her research interests include criminal law, human rights and child and youths' rights and protection. She is the author of *L'agression sexuelle en droit canadien* (Éditions Yvon Blais, 2009); *Isolement et mesures disciplinaires dans les centres de réadaptation pour jeunes* (Éditions Wilson et Lafleur, 2005); and co-author with Hughes Parent of I – Tome III : La Peine (Thémis, 2012). She is a Member of the «Commission de protection des droits de la personne et des droits de la jeunesse» of Quebec.

SEAN DEWART is a partner with Dewart Gleason LLP, a litigation boutique slightly off the beaten path in downtown Toronto. Sean received a Bachelor of Laws degree from Osgoode Hall Law School in 1983 and a Master of Laws degree from the London School of Economics in 1985. He began practicing law in 1986 and formed his present firm in 2010. Sean's practice focuses on complex commercial litigation with expertise in professional liability and prosecutorial misconduct cases. Sean is a regular speaker on a wide variety of subjects relating to trial practice and substantive law, including labour relations in bankruptcy and insolvency proceedings, and suing police agencies. As counsel in the *Jane Doe* litigation, he had the time of his life.

JANE DOE is the woman who, after a twelve-year legal battle, successfully sued the Toronto Police for negligence and gender discrimination in the investigation of her rape. Her case, *Jane Doe v Board of Commissioners of Police,* set a Canadian legal precedent and is taught in law schools across Canada. She is also a teacher, community activist, and author. Her book *The Story of Jane Doe* (Random House, 2003) was nominated for numerous awards and is on the curriculum of several university and college courses. Her article, "What's in a Name? Who Benefits from the Publication Ban in Sexual Assault Trials" (in *Lessons From the Identity Trail,* 2009) sheds further light on legal response to the crime. Jane Doe was a founding member of the Sexual Assault Audit Steering Committee, which was formed to implement change in police investigations of sexual assault and in response to the Auditor General's Review of Sexual Assault for the Toronto Police Service. A report on that process, "A New Chapter in Feminist Organizing," was published in 2010 in *Canadian Woman Studies.*

TERESA DUBOIS graduated from the University of Ottawa Faculty of Law in 2009, having completed her law degree in French. Throughout her studies, she was a crisis-line counsellor for the Ottawa Rape Crisis Centre. She was also an active member of the University of Ottawa Community Legal Clinic, both as a caseworker and a member of the Steering Committee, a member of the Editorial Board of the *Ottawa Law Review*, and a research assistant to her constitutional law professor.

Teresa received the Greenspon Brown Award for outstanding contributions to the University of Ottawa Community Legal Clinic, the Gilbert Ngième Social Justice Award, and an award from the Société franco-ontarienne de l'autisme. Teresa completed her articles by serving as a judicial law clerk at the Ontario Superior Court of Justice in Ottawa and was called to the bar in 2010. Her practice is currently concentrated in the area of family law.

DR JANICE DU MONT is a Scientist at Women's College Research Institute and an Associate Professor in the Dalla Lana School of Public Health at the University of Toronto. Dr Du Mont was holder of a 2002–2004 and 2006–2009 New Investigator Award at the Canadian Institutes of Health Research. Her research looks at gender-based violence and women's health with a particular focus on the medical and legal responses to sexual assault. She has served as an advisor to the World Health Organization initiative to document the criminalization of sexual violence across regions and evaluate the health sector response to sexual assault in low resourced settings.

SUSAN EHRLICH is Professor of Linguistics and Women's Studies at York University. She has published widely on the linguistic and discursive aspects of sexual assault trials in Canada and the United States. Recent books include *"Why Do You Ask": The Function of Questions in Institutional Discourse* (co-edited with Alice Freed, Oxford, 2010); *Language and Gender: Major Themes in English Studies* (Routledge, 2008); and *Representing Rape: Language and Sexual Consent* (Routledge, 2001).

LISE GOTELL is an Associate Professor of Women's Studies at the University of Alberta. Her research expertise is in the area of feminism, law, and sexuality and she has published on such topics as feminist litigation, constitutional equality, pornography and obscenity law, gay and lesbian rights, and sexual assault. She is a co-author of *Bad Attitude/s on Trial: Feminism, Pornography and the Butler Decision* (1997), and a co-editor, with Barbara Crow, of *Open Boundaries: A Canadian Women's Studies Reader* (2009). For the past several years, her work has focused on the implications of 1990's sexual assault reforms, including interrogating the post-*Ewanchuk* legal standard for consent and evaluating the effectiveness of legislative restrictions on sexual history evidence and confidential records. She teaches a unique Women's Studies course entitled "Feminism and Sexual Assault" in which students focus on rethinking resistance through working with Edmonton community agencies and activist groups.

HOLLY JOHNSON is Associate Professor of Criminology at the University of Ottawa. Her interest and involvement in research on violence against women spans two decades. She was principal investigator of Statistics Canada's first national survey on violence against women, which pioneered a methodology for interviewing women about their experiences of sexual assault and intimate partner violence. This methodology has served as a model for the development of similar surveys in many countries, including the International Violence Against Women Survey on which she is a collaborator. Holly served as expert advisor to the Secretary-General's report on violence against women, and is a member of the UNECE task force on Violence Against Women Surveys, the UN Expert Group on Indicators on Violence Against Women, and the World Health Organization expert panel on primary prevention of sexual violence and intimate partner violence. Her current research interests include criminal justice and societal responses to sexual violence and intimate partner violence and she is co-author of the 2011 text *Violence Against Women in Canada: Research and Policy Perspectives* (Oxford University Press—nominated for the Canadian Sociological Association John Porter Book Prize) with Myrna Dawson of the University of Guelph.

REBECCA JOHNSON studied music in her life before law. But she was seduced by the siren song of law, and began her legal studies at the University of Alberta. She was called to the bar in Calgary before spending a year at the Supreme Court as a law clerk to Madame Justice L'Heureux-Dubé. She completed her Master's and Doctorate of Law at the University of Michigan, where she was able to explore her interest in US and Canadian approaches to constitutional equality issues. She spent five years teaching in the Faculty of Law at the University of New Brunswick before moving to the University of Victoria in 2001. She has taught in the areas of constitutional law, criminal law, legal method, feminist advocacy, legal theory, and business associations. Her current favourite course is one that uses film (mostly films about murderous women) as a way of getting at issues of gender, justice, and judgment in law and in popular culture.

MEAGAN JOHNSTON is from Edmonton. While completing her undergraduate degree in Political Science, she helped re-start the University of Alberta Women's Centre. As a law student in McGill University's BCL/LLB programme she led a student seminar in Sexuality, Gender and the Law and served on the Board of Directors of QPIRG-McGill. She has worked at the Environmental Law Centre in Edmonton, Pivot Legal Society in Vancouver, and Project Genesis, a Montreal legal clinic. She is now articling at Parkdale Community Legal Services in Toronto.

THE HONOURABLE CLAIRE L'HEUREUX-DUBÉ was appointed to the Supreme Court of Canada in 1987 by Prime Minister Brian Mulroney after having served as a trial and appellate court judge for fourteen years. Her fifty-year career in law is one marked by many achievements in family law and human rights issues and as an advocate for equality. She was chair of the Canadian section of the International Commission of Jurists (1981–1983), and international president of the International Commission of Jurists (1998–2002), based in Geneva. In 1998, she received the Margaret Brent Women Lawyers of Achievement Award from the American Bar Association Commission on Women in the Profession. In 2003, she was named Companion of the Order of Canada; in 2004, she was named Grand Officer of the National Order of Quebec. She is currently active as chair of the steering committee of the Maison de Justice de Québec, a pilot project in improving access to justice in Quebec City. Upon her retirement from the Supreme Court in 2002, her many contributions to women's equality were celebrated in two publications: in *Adding Feminism to Law: The Contributions of Justice Claire L'Heureux-Dubé*, edited by Elizabeth Sheehy (Toronto: Irwin Law, 2004), and in a special issue of the *Canadian Journal of Women and the Law*, edited by Michelle Boivin and Elizabeth Sheehy (volume 15:1 2003).

TRACEY LINDBERG is Cree and Métis from Treaty 8 territory. Currently a Professor of Law at the University of Ottawa, Tracey is thought to be the first Indigenous woman to have received a Doctor of Laws from a Canadian university (the University of Ottawa). Tracey is also the recipient of numerous awards and scholarships for her academic work including a Social Sciences and Humanities Research Council doctoral award, a Governor General's medal for her doctoral work (critical Indigenous legal theory) and the 2008 Canadian Associate of Graduate Studies award for most distinguished Canadian dissertation in the social sciences and humanities. Dr Lindberg is currently the Canada Research Chair in Indigenous Knowledge, Legal Orders and Laws and an Associate Professor at the Centre for World Indigenous Knowledge and Research, Athabasca University. She has upcoming books with Guernica Press and the Oxford University Press. A well-loved blues singer and published creative fiction author, her first novel came out with Harper-Collins in 2010.

SUNNY MARRINER has been a member of the Sexual Assault Support Centre of Ottawa Collective since 1997, and is the founder and full-time coordinator of the Young Women at Risk (YWAR) Program, a support, outreach, and advocacy program for marginalized and criminalized young women. She provides over 1000 hours of direct support to young women survivors of violence and state intervention annually, and provides organizational training and education to regional agencies and to those working with youth in conflict with the law. She is a regular guest lecturer on questions of access to justice, sexual violence, and women's incarceration, and she writes on issues of criminalization and psychiatrization of women and girl survivors. She has served on regional, provincial, and national advisory committees for service, research, and political/legal policy reform in matters of violence against women.

SHEILA MCINTYRE taught constitutional law and equality law and theory at the Faculty of Law at the University of Ottawa until her retirement in June 2010. For nearly thirty years, she has been a feminist legal activist involved in test-case equality litigation, in law reform initiatives designed to reduce systemic bias in sexual offence laws, and in national coalitions formed to advance the equality of disempowered groups through law. Her research has focussed on unpacking the dynamics of systemic inequality in law, and on analyzing the poverty of the Supreme Court of Canada's understanding of and commitment to substantive equality.

FRAN ODETTE has been an advocate and educator on disability and gender for more than eighteen years. She became interested in working with women with disabilities, and with those who provide services to women who have experienced abuse, as a result of her own search for services that could support her during her own healing from an emotionally abusive relationship. Her own experience in seeking support from agencies, which had little exposure to diverse groups of women with disabilities, motivated her to ensure that disabled women and deaf women had equal and equitable access to services, including information and relevant resources on parenting, housing, sexuality, health, income security, and violence prevention.

LAURA ROBINSON is an award-winning writer and former member of Canada's national cycling team. Her work on the cyclical nature of sexual abuse in hockey resulted in a CBC documentary, and her book, *Crossing the Line: Violence and Sexual Assault in Canada's National Sport*, changed how Canadians looked at hockey. In 2002, she won the top award from Play the Game, an international journalists' advocacy group located in Europe; in 1992, she became the first journalist in Canada to write about sexual abuse in sport; and in 2002, she questioned the objectification and commoditization of women athletes in her book *Black Tights: Women, Sport and Sexuality*. Her play, *FrontRunners*, about First Nation long-distance runners, has toured Canada and Scandinavia, while the film version was broadcast on APTN and is available through the NFB. Robinson has covered six Olympics, and was an accredited journalist for the Vancouver Games. She has written critically about VANOC's lack of commitment to First Nations youth and to women athletes. She is a volunteer XC ski and mountain bike coach at Cape Croker First Nation Elementary School on the shores of Georgian Bay and she continues to compete as a master XC skier.

SANDA RODGERS is Professor Emeritus and former Dean of the Faculty of Law, University of Ottawa. She was a bencher of the Law Society of Upper Canada and commissioner of the Ontario Law Reform Commission, and is a recipient of the Women Lawyers Association President's Award for "Outstanding Contribution to the Legal Profession" and of the Business and Professional Women's Association Award for "Outstanding Contribution to Gender Equity." Her primary area of research was health law, with particular emphasis on women's reproductive rights.

RAKHI RUPARELIA is an Assistant Professor in the Faculty of Law at the University of Ottawa. After clerking at the Ontario Court of Appeal, she completed her graduate studies in law at Harvard University. She then joined the Prison Reform Advocacy Center in Cincinnati, Ohio, where she established and directed a community legal clinic to assist ex-prisoners with legal issues impeding their transition back to society. Through her involvement with the National Judicial Institute, she has conducted judicial training sessions on sexual assault law, intimate violence, and anti-racism. In her previous work as a social worker, she co-facilitated support groups for survivors of sexual violence. Her research focuses on critical race and feminist perspectives on tort and criminal law.

ELIZABETH A SHEEHY, LLB (Osgoode), LLM (Columbia), LLD (Honoris causa LSUC), has been a very happy member of the feminist community in the Faculty of Law at the University of Ottawa since 1984. She has always taught criminal law and procedure as well as "women's law" courses, such as Women and the Law, Women and the Legal Profession, Sexual Assault Law, and Defending Battered Women on Trial. She has edited several books, including *Adding Feminism to Law: The Contributions of Justice Claire L'Heuerux-Dubé* and *Calling for Change: Women, Law and the Legal Profession* (with Sheila McIntyre). She has researched and published in the area of sexual assault law and counts as proud moments her involvement in Jane Doe's successful suit against the Toronto Police and being cited by Justice Claire L'Heureux-Dubé in her exquisite dissent in the *Seaboyer* case. She credits her students in the Faculty of Law, as well as Jane Doe, with supplying the heart and soul needed to launch the March 2009 conference on sexual assault law, practice, and activism. This book is the third collection of essays arising from the conference that Elizabeth has edited. The first two were *Ten Years After Jane Doe: Reflections on the State of Rape* (2010) 22:2 CJWL 301–568 and *Women Resisting Rape: Feminist Law, Practice, Activism* (2010) 28:1 Can Woman Stud 3–161.

ALISON SYMINGTON is the senior policy analyst for the Canadian HIV/AIDS Legal Network, which she joined in September 2007. Previously, she was manager of research with the Toronto-based Association for Women's Rights in Development (AWID), where she worked on issues of human rights accountability, international trade and aid policy, and poverty eradication. She has also collaborated with international human rights and gender equality advocates, has served as a consultant for Amnesty International's global Stop Violence Against Women campaign, and has worked as an intern for the United Kingdom-based International Centre for the Legal Protection of Human Rights INTERIGHTS. She holds an Hon BA (with a major in international development studies) from the University of Guelph, an LLB from the University of Toronto, and an LLM in international legal studies from New York University.

JULIA TOLMIE is an Associate Professor in Law at the University of Auckland, where she has taught for the last ten years. Prior to that, she spent ten years as a legal academic at the University of Sydney. She teaches criminal law and women and the law. Her research specialities have included the following topics: battered woman's syndrome and defences to murder, fathers' rights groups in the context of family law, negotiating contact and care arrangements for children with the perpetrator of domestic violence, suing the police in negligence for their failure to respond adequately to domestic violence, corporate social responsibility, and alcoholism and the criminal defences. Prior to having her two children, she also had a personal life, which included a long-standing interest in the arts (particularly painting and sculpture) and the environment.

DAVID M TANOVICH, MA (Toronto), LLB (Queens), LLM (NYU) is a Full Professor at the Faculty of Law, University of Windsor where he teaches and writes in the areas of criminal law, evidence, legal ethics, and racial profiling. He is also Academic Director of the newly formed Law Enforcement Accountability Project (LEAP) at Windsor Law. Professor Tanovich has written over 40 books. His most recent book is *The Colour of Justice: Policing Race in Canada* (Toronto: Irwin Law, 2006). Professor Tanovich has been invited to present at numerous conferences and other fora, including endowed lectures at Dalhousie Law School and the College of Law, University of Saskatchewan. His research has been frequently cited by the Supreme Court of Canada and other appellate courts, law reform and human rights commissions. It has also been recognized in various awards such as the 2005 University of Windsor Award for Excellence in Scholarship, Research and Creative Activity and 2006 Canadian Association of Law Teachers' Scholarly Paper Award.

LUCINDA VANDERVORT BA Hon (Bryn Mawr) MA, PhD (McGill), JD (Queen's) LLM (Yale), is a professor of Law at the University of Saskatchewan and a member of the Ontario bar. She has done legal work with the Women's Legal Education and Action Fund (LEAF) strategic litigation program in connection with a number of Supreme Court of Canada cases and is a proponent of collaborative research and theorizing. Her legal and philosophical writings are cited by academics and law reformers in Canada and internationally; her analyses of sexual assault law, consent, theory of criminal responsibility, and mistake of law are cited, quoted, and applied in judgments by the Supreme Court of Canada and other levels of court in various provinces. Currently her research and law teaching deals with the interaction of theories of criminal responsibility, consent, sexual assault, the law of evidence, administration of justice, the design of legal institutions and legal theory. Her paper emerges from that intersection to focus on prosecutorial discretion, the rule of law, and the need for institutional changes to improve the handling of sexual assault cases by the Canadian legal system.

DIANA YAROS is a feminist activist who has been engaged in Violence Against Women work for more than thirty years. She was active in organizing some of the first Take Back the Night marches in the early 1980s and has worked to defend the individual and collective rights of sexually assaulted women in public policy, the justice systems, and other Kafkaesque situations that women face in dealing with public institutions. More recently, she is involved in developing a training program to help anti-violence, community, and healthcare workers better understand intersecting oppressions and to give them the tools to defend the rights of immigrant and refugee women.

Index

B

the possibility that physician may engage in abusive behaviour with male patients, 479
psychiatric tests used to identify male sexual deviance are not scientific or respectable, 477
psychiatrization of complainants to discredit them and exonerate the abusing physicians, 454, 475
"Psychological Evaluation in Sexual Offence Cases" (Marshall), 477
Psychotherapists' Sexual Involvement with Clients: Intervention and Prevention (Schoener et al.), 478, 480
Regulated Health Professions Act (1993) implemented zero tolerance of sexual abuse, and imposed mandatory license revocation as the penalty for the most serious cases of abuse, 452–54
sexual abuse is abuse of power and constitutes violence against women and children, 480
sexual abuse of patients is not inhibited by either education nor psychotherapy, 480
supervisory models to prevent continued sexual abuse and the incompetent health care fail, 479
task force on the sexual exploitation of patients and sexual abuse by doctors, 451–52
third-party supervisory monitoring, and re-education as a means of lifting license suspension, 479–80
Williams case, 474
medicalization
of rape as "illness," 16
of sexual assault, 357, 409
medicalized regimes for "treating victims," 252
medical records. *See also* Sexual Assault Evidence Kit
CPSO use contrary to the *Act*, 460
forced production of complainants', 3
Sexual Assault Evidence Kit and, 375
Medusa myth, 326
Mehrabian, Albert, 597–98
men. *See also* male
convicted of sexual assault of Aboriginals, 714–16
legal narratives portray men convicted of rape as easily governed by therapeutic management of their diagnosed sexual deviance disorders or poor cognitive capacity, 712
prey upon women who are drunk, drugged, or asleep, 483
who are breadwinner husbands and fathers are deemed undeserving of incarceration through the evocation of class and gender subjectivities, 717
who are poorly educated and unsophisticated men also needed to be protected from the dangers of imprisonment, 722
who are professionals are often treated with leniency because of "devastating financial and psychological impacts of conviction," 721
"mental disabilities," 177
mental health issues, 306, 420
Metro Toronto Hockey League (Greater Toronto Hockey League), 75
Middlesex-London Health Unit (London, Ontario), 83–84
Mill, John Stuart, 579
Miller, Karen Lee, 374
Minow, Martha, 671, 698–99
misogynist
beliefs used by men to claim their moral innocence, 490
bias related to sexual assault, 130
Bill C-49's "reasonable steps" requirement *vs.* belief in consent based on self-serving misogynist beliefs, 492
community beliefs and assumptions about sexual assault, 143
conflict invoked by counsel and judges using racist and sexist stereotypes, 138
"honest mistake" defence, men claim their moral innocence using self-serving and misogynist beliefs in, 490
police officers, 34, 200, 234
police sexual assault investigators trained using materials with misogynistic assumptions and stereotypes, 222
psy-disciplines erase male culpability in abuse and ensure that men's

that lack of resistance must be equated with consent," 493
systemic racism involving Inuit, 518
trial judge and reasonable steps requirement, 503–8, 520
victimization of female partners and ex-partners is rarely recognized by the criminal justice system, 488
violent ex-partner was given a first "free" rape by virtue of the *Pappajohn* defence, but morally culpable for the second rape, 491
women justices of the Supreme Court preferred to decide cases on the basis of the law as it had been enacted by Parliament, 497
women raped while drunk, drugged, or asleep doubt themselves and doubt the criminal justice response and rarely report their rapes, 485
women's bodily security, disregard for, 537
women's entitlement to dignity, equality, and security of the person should easily outweigh men's interest in sexual contact with women who neither know nor desire them, 18
women's equality demands that "mistake" defence be barred where the defence is solely based on conjecture as to "mistake" as opposed to evidence of actual reasonable steps, 537
women's equal rights to security of the person and to sexual autonomy when they are unconscious, 535
women's rights to equality and autonomy *vs.* proposition that women are presumptively consenting, 536
women's security of the person interests should be protected while they sleep or recover from drug or alcohol ingestion *vs.* men pursuing their own sexual desires, 538
women with disabilities are vulnerable to having their rapes decriminalized if unable to offer an account of the assault to challenge the accused's version, 488

refugee women, 301–2, 305, 307, 310, 754
Regroupement Quebecois des centres d'aide et de lutte contre les aggressions à caratère sexuelle (RQCALACS), 307–9
Regulated Health Professions Act (1993), 17, 452–53
Report of the Royal Commission on Aboriginal People (RCAP Report), 155–56, 163
residential school survivors. *See also EB v Oblates of Mary Immaculate in the Province of BC;* Supreme Court of Canada
- *Bazley v Curry,* 151, 157, 160–62, 165, 170–71
- *HL v Canada,* 151n1, 152n5, 157
- *Jacobi v Griffiths,* 151, 162
- *Plint* case, 157, 159
- *Report of the Royal Commission on Aboriginal People* (RCAP Report), 155–56, 163
- *Restoring Dignity: Responding to Child Abuse in Canadian Institutions,* 155–57

"restorative justice" alternatives, 737
Restoring Dignity: Responding to Child Abuse in Canadian Institutions (Restoring Dignity), 155–57
Review of the Investigation of Sexual Assaults (1999), 200–201
Review of the Investigation of Sexual Assaults: A Decade Later (2010), 201
Richards, Amy, 264
Rickards, Clint (N. Z. police officer), 56–60, 63
right of accused, 281
rights of women during rape trials, 25, 27, 306
right to a fair trial within a reasonable delay, 281
right to counsel, 281
right to remain silent, 281
risk management technologies applied to rape, 258
Roberts, Julian, 699
Robinson, Laura
- *Crossing the Line: Violence and Sexual Assault in Canada's National Sport,* 83

Ropati, Tea (rugby league star), 61–63, 70
Royal Canadian Mounted Police (RCMP), 50
Royal Commission on the Status of Women, 732

MARQUIS
Marquis Book Printing Inc.
Québec, Canada
2012